NOVO
Dicionário de Expressões Idiomáticas Americanas

Dados Internacionais de Catalogação na Publicação (CIP)
(Câmara Brasileria do Livro, SP, Brasil)

Gomes, Luiz L.
 Novo dicionário de expressões idiomáticas americanas / Luiz Lugani Gomes. -- São Paulo: Pioneira Thomson Learning, 2003.

 Bibliografia.
 ISBN   85-221-0290-2

 1. Americanismos 2. Inglês - Dicionários 3. Inglês - Expressões idiomáticas I. Título.

02-5511   CDD-423.1

Índices para catálogo sistemático:

1. Expressões idiomáticas: Dicionários: Inglês
 423.1

NOVO
Dicionário
de Expressões
Idiomáticas
Americanas

Luiz Lugani Gomes

THOMSON

Austrália   Brasil   Canadá   Cingapura   Espanha   Estados Unidos   México   Reino Unido

THOMSON

Gerente Editorial: Adilson Pereira	**Copidesque:** Andrea Filatro	**Composição:** Marco 0/Denise Chiara
Editora de Desenvolvimento: Eugênia Pessotti	**Revisão:** Ada Santos Seles e Ornilo Alves da Costa Júnior	**Capa:** Mar, GD Design
Produtora Gráfica: Patricia La Rosa		**Ilustrações de 3ª e 4ª capas (guarda):** Heitor Henrique Chabu Gomes

COPYRIGHT © 2003 de Pioneira Thomson Learning Ltda., uma divisão da Thomson Learning, Inc. Thomson Learning™ é uma marca registrada aqui utilizada sob licença.

Impresso no Brasil.
Printed in Brazil.
1 2 3 4 05 04 03

Rua Traipu, 114 – 3º andar
Perdizes – CEP 01235-000
São Paulo – SP
Tel.: (11) 3665-9900
Fax.: (11) 3665-9901
sac@thomsonlearning.com.br
www.thomsonlearning.com.br

Todos os direitos reservados. Nenhuma parte deste livro poderá ser reproduzida, sejam quais forem os meios empregados, sem a permissão, por escrito, da Editora. Aos infratores aplicam-se as sanções previstas nos artigos 102, 104, 106 e 107 da Lei nº 9.610, de 19 de fevereiro de 1998.

Dados Internacionais de Catalogação na Publicação (CIP) (Câmara Brasileira do Livro, SP, Brasil)

Gomes, Luiz L.
Novo dicionário de expressões idiomáticas americanas / Luiz Lugani Gomes. -- São Paulo: Pioneira Thomson Learning, 2003.
Bibliografia.
ISBN 85-221-0290-2

1. Americanismos 2. Inglês - Dicionários 3. Inglês - Expressões idiomáticas I. Título.

02-5511   CDD-423.1

Índices para catálogo sistemático:

1. Expressões idiomáticas: Dicionários: Inglês   423.1

*A Zilah Flora, por tudo, e, especialmente,
por sua inesgotável paciência.*

*A Antonio, Flora, Sérgio e Solange
e, naturalmente, à novíssima geração:
Heitor, Victor, Paulo e Otávio.*

Sumário

Apresentação VIII
Conteúdo VIII
Das Abonações XI
Ordenação dos Verbetes XI
Abreviaturas e Convenções XII
Dicionário 1
Bibliografia de Abonações 481
Bibliografia de Referências 501

APRESENTAÇÃO

A primeira edição do *Dicionário de Expressões Idiomáticas Americanas* foi lançada em 1964 e teve 11 reimpressões. Em meados da década de 1970, os autores iniciaram a revisão e ampliação da obra, mas a morte prematura de Donald E. Collins pôs fim ao projeto.

Resolvido a reformular o livro e a introduzir abonações, cônscio da autoridade e do valor desses recursos para uma obra de referência, Gomes coligiu um grande acervo de expressões a partir de um número expressivo de fontes: 332 obras de autores norte-americanos – ficcionistas, especialmente – publicadas durante a segunda metade do século XX, e centenas de números da *TIME Magazine* do período 1960-1992. A essas abonações foram acrescidos um bom número de exemplos elaborados pelo autor e uma porcentagem de exemplos da edição original do dicionário. De tudo isso resultou um volume com cerca de 8.200 verbetes.

O objetivo deste trabalho, que tanto esforço e tanto tempo exigiu, continua sendo o mesmo a que se propuseram os dois autores da obra original: um dicionário prático, atual e bastante abrangente, utilíssimo a estudantes de estágio intermediário e avançado, professores, tradutores e estudiosos do inglês.

CONTEÚDO

Este livro não é um estudo das expressões idiomáticas – frases, construções ou peculiaridades cujo significado real difere do significado literal de seus elementos constituintes –, mas sim uma obra de referência que registra, define e mostra as expressões em uma ou mais frases (abonações ou exemplos). Assim, sob a designação genérica de expressões idiomáticas, destacam-se aqui, especialmente:

Verbos frasais (*two-word verbs* ou *phrasal verbs*), isto é, verbos seguidos de uma partícula adverbial que altera ou modifica o sentido destes: *back up, break down, catch on, come across, fall through, get over, give off, make out, pick up, run down, set off, take in, turn out*. Há uma seleção bastante extensa desses verbos e registro de sua polissemia: *come through* e *get along*, por exemplo, mostram 5 acepções; *take in* registra 9, *set up* tem 13 e *pick up*, 20. Além disso, muitos deles combinam-se em formas nominais, como, por exemplo: *backup, breakdown, breakthrough, letdown, makeup, pickup, rundown, setup, turnout*.

Expressões verbo + substantivo: *blow one's top, burn the candle at both ends, bury the hatchet, catch someone's eye, have a good time, have someone's ear, hit the ceiling, keep an ear to the ground, kick the bucket, let the cat out of the bag, make up one's mind, miss the bus, pull someone's leg, rain pitchforks, rock the boat.*

Frases feitas – expressões fixas consagradas pelo uso: *don't give me that, give up the ship, it takes two to tango, like a cat on a hot tin roof, never say die, now you're talking, (just) one of those things, that'll be the day, that's a horse of a different color, that's all I needed, that's the way it goes, you can say that again, you said a mouthful.*

Expressões com função de adjetivos: *age-old, all-around, back-breaking, big-mouthed, big-time, bone-dry, bullheaded, chicken-hearted, cold-blooded, dark-haired, deep-rooted, devil-may-care, dog-tired, double-edged, down-to-earth, easygoing, far-fetched, fast-paced, first-rate, full-fledged, good-for-nothing, gun-shy, hangdog, happy-go-lucky, hard-and-fast, hard-boiled, hard-hearted, heavy-handed, high-minded, holier-than-thou, honest-to-goodness, hot-tempered, king-size(d), law-abiding, lighthearted, like-minded, long-winded, loudmouthed, low-keye(d), old-fashioned, one-horse, out-and-out, panic-stricken, poker-faced, razor-sharp, rough-and-ready, self-conscious, shorthanded, stagestruck, starry-eyed, straight-faced, thick-skinned, thoroughgoing, trigger-happy, two-fisted, up-and-coming, well-timed.*

Expressões com função de preposições: *according to, along with, as regards, as to, (in) back of, by way of, due to, in addition to, in order to, in spite of, in that, in the teeth of, in the way of, in with, next to, on account of, on the strength of, over and above, owing to, short of, thanks to, together with, up against, with a view to.*

Expressões com função de advérbios: *all along, as far as, as usual, back and forth, by and large, every so often, far and wide, for keeps, for sure, hammer and tongs, high and low, in a flash, in a huff, in the long run, in the shake of a lamb's tail, like a bat out of hell, now and then, offhand, (right) off the bat, off the cuff, on the other hand, once in a while, over and over, right and left, right away, sky-high, through and through, to and fro, well-nigh.*

Expressões com função de conjunções: *according as, as if, as long as, as though, in case, in order to, in so far as, so that.*

Interjeições: *cheer up!, damn it!, for Christ's/God's/heaven's/Pete's sake!, for crying out loud!, God forbid!, goddamn it!, good gracious!, good heavens!, Great Scott!, holy cow/Moses/smoke!, I'll be damned!, I'll be doggone!, my goodness!, that's a laugh!, that's rich!, what do you know!, you don't say so!, you're telling me!*

Compostos substantivo + substantivo (uso atributivo dos substantivos): *baby sitter, butterfingers, Capitol Hill, charley horse, dog days, egghead, eyewitness, fall guy, girlfriend, goose flesh, housekeeper, kid gloves, lady-killer, monkey business, movie star, paperback, pin money, pipe dream, poker face, potluck, press conference, prize fighter, rat race, salad days, sob story, spark plug, stage fright, standing room, troublemaker.*

Símiles: *(as) brown as a berry, (as) clean as a whistle, (as) cool as a cucumber, (as) dead as a doornail, (as) dry as a bone, (as) fit as a fiddle, (as) hard as nails, (as) like as two peas (in a pod), (as) plain as the nose on one's face, (as) snug as a bug in a rug, (as) thick as thieves.*

Provérbios e ditos populares: *a burnt child dreads the fire, a miss is as good as a mile, a stitch in time saves nine, birds of a feather flock together, cross a bridge when you come to it, curiosity killed the cat, don't count your chickens before they are hatched, don't put all your eggs in one basket, give a dog a bad name and hang him, it never rains but it pours, let sleeping dogs lie, love me, love my dog, never look a gift horse in the mouth, once bitten, twice shy, the early bird catches the worm, the grass is always greener on the other side of the fence, there but for the grace of God (go I), two wrongs don't make a right.*

Neologismos – contribuições das últimas décadas: *all systems go, boat people, born-again, catch-22, come out of the closet, cult movie, cutting edge, do one's (own) thing, downsize, educated guess, fast food, fat farm, hang tough, high-tech, in the ballpark, launder money, laundry list, let it all hang out, liftoff, loose cannon, mind-blowing, nuke, off-the-wall, Saturday night special, silent majority, Silicon Valley, smoking gun, soul music, spaced out, theme park, the bottom line, think tank, workaholic, yuppie.*

Coloquialismos – expressões características da conversação e da linguagem escrita informal – e gírias – expressões próprias de linguagem muito informal que não podem ser aceitas em termos do padrão convencional, da norma culta – vêm sempre indicados.

8.200 verbetes
10.200 acepções
5.900 abonações recolhidas de *TIME Magazine*
e de obras de autores norte-americanos
7.200 frases-exemplos

DAS ABONAÇÕES

Cada abonação recolhida de *TIME Magazine* é seguida da letra T e de um número que indica o ano da publicação. Por exemplo: T/87 significa que a abonação foi retirada de um número de 1987 dessa revista. Consignamos aqui nossos agradecimentos ao Departamento Editorial Rights de *TIME Magazine* por permitir a utilização desse material.

As abonações retiradas de livros são seguidas de uma sigla e de um número que identificam autor, obra, página e ano de publicação da edição citada na bibliografia de abonações ao final do volume. Por exemplo: RR,610 indica abonação colhida em *America Moves West*, de Robert E. Riegel e Robert G. Athearn, página 610.

ORDENAÇÃO DOS VERBETES

Procurou-se sistematizar a ordenação dos verbetes, de maneira clara e funcional, sob palavras-chave – aberturas em **NEGRITO** que sobressaem à margem esquerda – de acordo com o seguinte critério:

1. Pelo substantivo – ou primeiro substantivo onde houver mais de um: *at the* **head** *of, by all* **accounts***, go back on one's* **word***; get up on the wrong* **side** *of the bed, have one's* **back** *to the wall,* **press** *conference,* **waiting** *game, look a* **gift** *horse on the mouth, on the* **horns** *of a dilemma.*
2. Pelo verbo (na ausência de substantivo) – ou pelo primeiro verbo onde houver mais de um: **fall** *flat,* **make** *it hard for,* **steer** *clear of,* **talk** *big;* **can** *'t help,* **come** *to think of it,* **look** *before one jumps,* **pick** *and choose.*
3. Pela primeira palavra da expressão quando esta não contiver substantivo nem verbo: **all** *along,* **in** *for,* **out** *of it,* **right** *away.* Não se incluem como primeira palavra *a, an* e *the*.
4. Pela palavra que nos pareceu pesar mais na expressão, forma um tanto subjetiva mas inevitável em face das muitas dificuldades: *terminally* **ill,** **just** *as, not* **above**.
5. Palavras compostas ligadas por hífen são ordenadas pelo primeiro elemento: **first**-*rate,* **latter**-*day,* **good**-*for-nothing,* **one**-*sided,* **two**-*bit*. Entretanto, em casos como, por exemplo, *broken-hearted, cold-blooded, inner-city* etc., uma seta (→) remete respectivamente a *with a broken* **heart**, *in cold* **blood**, *inner* **city** etc., pois derivam destas últimas e estão exemplificadas sob elas. Tais ocorrências são sempre indicadas.

6. Palavras entre parênteses empregam-se facultativamente nas expressões e são nulas na ordenação alfabética dos verbetes: (*all*) *by oneself, lay oneself (wide) open, the* (*wild*) *blue yonder*.

ABREVIATURAS E CONVENÇÕES

[col] coloquial

[gir] gíria

[i.e.] isto é

[neg] em contextos negativos

[pas] passiva

[pej] pejorativo

[sic] textualmente

v. veja

/ Indica duas ou mais formas possíveis: **burn one's boats/bridges; have/know all the answers; get/grab/have a bite to eat**.

// Separa contrários: **bad//good mixer; so much the better//worse**.

( ) Nos verbetes, encerra termos facultativos: **(just) around the corner; scare the (living) daylights out of**.

[ ] Encerra matéria explanatória nas abonações para completar o exemplo ou tornar mais claro o contexto: *Watching [her husband] out of the corner of her eyes, Gladys went hesitantly from the room to prepare breakfast.* ♦ *Perhaps the decade's [the 1970's] most spectacular comeback was that of Marlon Brando [in Last Tango in Paris].*

= Indica significado idêntico a: **a burnt child dreads the fire** = **once bitten, twice shy**.

→ Remete à palavra-chave sob a qual se encontra a expressão: **brokenhearted** → **with a broken HEART; stick in one's CROP** → **stick in one's CRAW**. O símbolo → remete o consulente à palavra-chave **HEART**, no primeiro caso, e **CRAW**, no segundo.

... Indica supressão na citação: muitas das abonações são retiradas de contextos complexos ou longos, o que tornou inevitável o recurso à elipse e/ou a inserções elucidativas dentro de colchetes. *[An accident on the freeway] ... had traffic backed up as far as he could see.* ♦ *... the wing [of the U-2 plane]* *came off and he [the pilot] bailed out.* ♦ *... the central government's efforts ... have been halfhearted at best ...*

⇒ Indica derivação: **in cold blood** *He shot his victims in cold blood.* ⇒ **cold-blooded** *He was a cold-blooded killer*; **break out** 2 *... [he] broke out of another [penitentiary] under a hail of bullets.* ⇒ **breakout** [*The Great Escape*, a movie, is] *... a wholesale breakout from a Nazi P. W. [prisoner of war] camp ...*; **with a high hand** Mr. Fuller ran his business with a high hand. ⇒ **high-handed** a high-handed decision.

♦ Separa abonações e/ou exemplos.

ABIDE abide by ater-se a, submeter-se a, manter-se fiel a, agir de acordo com, cumprir a palavra, a promessa etc. *When you make a deal, you must abide by it.* ♦ *... he will abide by the court's decision ...* -T/73.

ABLE be able to ser capaz de, poder, estar em condições de *I hope to be able to settle all my debts in due time.* ♦ *... unless the Baron approved of his choice, he wouldn't be able to get married at all.* -YF,1.

ABLE-BODIED fisicamente forte e saudável *Able-bodied people of working age ...* T/87. ♦ *... Khomeini called all able-bodied male Iranians to combat ...* -T/87.

ABOUT (that's) (just) about it [col] (isso é) quase tudo, (isso descreve muito bem) as coisas, a verdadeira situação *... every time you sight [a sexually atractive woman] ... you've got to prove ... to yourself that you're ... [a man]. Isn't that about it?* -SEB,163. ♦ *Yes, that's just about it. There's no more to be told.*

be about 1. empenhado em, ocupado com, fazendo *If you can get a copy of* The Short Stories of Ernest Hemingway, *be sure you read "The Snows of Kilimanjaro" and while you're about it, read also "The Killers" and "My Old Man".* ♦ *A real grown-up woman, who knew what she was about and how to enjoy herself.* -BW,5. 2. referente a, concernente a *"What is his new book about?" "It's about the influence of George Orwell on modern political literature."*

be about to estar a ponto de, no ato de, prestes a *I was about to leave when he arrived.*

be not about to estar firmemente decidido a (não fazer algo ou agir de determinada maneira) *[He] ... was always determined to get where he wanted to go, and he wasn't about to let anybody stop him.* -CL,189.

what is it/this all about? de que se trata? que significa isso? *When the children began to shout all at once, he said: "What's this all about?".*

what it/something is all about o cerne (da questão), o âmago, a essência, o que significa, o que quer dizer *Love, learning – and life – are what education is all about ...* -T/66. ♦ *... the present young generation is learning what sex is really all about.* -T/69.

ABOUT-FACE 1. meia-volta [voz de comando] *[Lieutenant] Bascom came up with a stiff salute, a smart about-face and marched towards his men.* -CHT,25. 2. mudança de direção, atitude, opinião ou ação *The Federal Government has executed a crisp about-face on birth control.* -T/66. 3. fazer meia-volta *The soldier saluted, about-faced and left the major's office.*

ABOVE above and beyond além de (aquilo que se espera) ... *[the judge] commended the jurors for service "above and beyond the call of duty".* -T/71.
not above não-avesso a, não-infenso a, capaz de, inclinado a *[He was] ... a family man, and yet not above taking a peep with the other men into the windows across the street from his office.* -LA,76. ♦ *He is not above doing manual labor when he needs money.*

ABOVEBOARD (open and) aboveboard 1. honesto, sincero, claro *We all liked him because he was always open and aboveboard with us.* 2. abertamente, às claras, sem truques *Everything had been legal and aboveboard.*

ABREAST abreast of 1. lado a lado com, ombro a ombro com *He ran abreast of the other runners.* 2. a par de, ao corrente de, atualizado com, informado a respeito de *He was kept abreast of the latest political developments in Washington.* ♦ *... keep abreast of advances in biotechnology.* -T/87.

ABSENT-MINDED desatento, distraído, desligado *The absent-minded professor gave his lecture to the wrong class.*

ABSTRACT in the abstract em teoria, não na prática *It is curious that his idea has been accepted in the abstract but has remained largely ignored in practice.*

ACCIDENT accidents will happen acidentes não podem ser evitados, não há como prevenir acidentes, pois sempre acontecerão *When she spilled her drink on my new Arrow shirt I tried to cheer her up. "Don't worry. Accidents will happen."*
by accident por acaso, acidentalmente *Fleming discovered penicilin by accident.*

ACCORD of one accord concorde, da mesma opinião *We were all of one accord on the civil rights issue.*

of one's/its own accord por sua livre vontade, voluntariamente, espontaneamente *The protesters eventually left of their own accord.* -T/87.
out of accord with em desacordo com, inconsistente com, incompatível com ... *the current sex laws are unenforced and unenforceable because they are too completely out of accord with the realities of human behavior ...* -KAC,20.
with one accord sem dissensões, de comum acordo, unanimemente *With one accord the group of men gave an affirmative answer.*

ACCORDANCE in accordance with de conformidade com, de acordo com *In accordance with the plans, they left at four a.m.*

ACCORDING according as 1. dependendo de, segundo a maneira que *You may write the letter to the ambassador in English or in French, according as you decide.* 2. conforme, à medida que, à proporção que *According as a man grows older he begins to lose interest in many activities.*
according to 1. em conformidade com, de maneira compatível com *According to his promise, he paid all his debts.* 2. em proporção a, dependendo de *The workers ... are paid according to how many trucks they can build.* -T/91. 3. segundo (alguém afirma ou está declarado ou registrado em algum lugar, alguma fonte etc.), de acordo com *According to most sociologists, as freedom increases, so does crime.* -T/75. ♦ *According to Heraclitus, the Greek philosopher, "man's character is his fate".*

ACCOUNT account for 1. responder por, ser responsável por, prestar contas de *Natalie's husband was so stingy that he made her account for every penny she spent.* ♦ *... oil accounts for 80% of Lybia's national income.* -T/69. 2. dar uma explicação razoável, justificar satisfatoriamente, dar a razão de *How do you account for the rapid rise in the price of milk?* 3. matar, alvejar, destruir *Big John accounted for*

three of the dead Apache Indians and his son had shot the other two.
by all/most accounts segundo dizem todos (ou a maioria), ao que dizem *By all accounts, the bond between the President and his advisers is still strong.* -T/80. ♦ *By most accounts, the government was genuinely shocked by the defeat.* -T/87.
by one's own account segundo diz (fulano) *By his own account he was a refugee from the revolutionary government of ... Khomeini ...* -T/87.
call to account 1. chamar às contas, pedir explicações *He was called to account when he refused to follow the rules.* 2. repreender, censurar *Ruth's mother called her to account for having missed school yesterday.*
checking account conta-corrente bancária *[They have been] ... overdrawing their checking accounts ...* -T/84.
give a good account of oneself sair-se bem, causar boa impressão *He gave such a good account of himself in the game that we were all proud of him.*
have (an) account(s) to settle ter contas a acertar, vingar-se *I still have an account to settle with that guy.*
hold to account responsabilizar *Governments will be held to account for the preservation of their countries' ecosystems.*
of no account sem importância, sem valor, insignificante *What he says is of no account. Pay no attention to him.* ⇒
no-account [col] 1. pessoa inútil, sem importância *He's just a no-account who shifts from place to place.* 2. sem importância, insignificante, incapaz, imprestável *... a no-account white man.* -T/66.
on account 1. a prazo, a crédito, a prestação *He always buys things on account.* 2. Por conta (de pagamento para amortização de dívida) *Of the $500 he owed me he has only paid $200 on account.*
on account of por causa de, devido a *Many gas stations will close on account of the lack of gasoline.*

on no account de modo algum *The children were told that on no account were they to go near the yellow house near the river.*
on one's account por causa de (alguém), em consideração a, no interesse de (alguém) *Don't trouble yourself on my account.*
on one's own account por si só, independentemente, sem auxílio *Timmy was very young and unable to solve the problem on his own account.*
settle/square accounts/the account 1. pagar uma conta, acertar uma dívida *How much will it take to square all my outstanding accounts?* 2. ir à forra, vingar-se *... if we want to settle the account with Gaddafi we will have to do it ourselves.* -T/86.
take account of 1. levar em consideração *In his report to the President, he took no account of many important details.* 2. notar, atentar, reparar em, dar atenção a *At last [she] took account of me.* -CTT,74.
take into account levar em conta, considerar *... the works of the artist cannot be understood without taking into account the character of the man.* -T/87.
turn to account fazer uso de, empregar, tirar proveito ou vantagem de *Turn to account your knowledge of Portuguese when studying English for many of the words have the same Latin base.*

ACE ace in the hole [gir] trunfo de reserva, carta na manga, vantagem para ser usada quando necessário *He always keeps an ace in the hole when he starts a new venture.*
ace out [gir] sobrepujar, levar a melhor sobre *He aced out the other candidates for the job.*
ace/card up one's sleeve [gir] = **ACE in the hole** *They thought they had defeated him but he still had an ace up his sleeve.* ♦ *Just when I thought I had him in my power, he had another card up his sleeve.*
have/hold all the aces/cards/trumps [gir] ter o domínio da situação, estar em posição vantajosa *When it comes to doing*

business with small companies, the multinationals hold all the cards. ♦ *He was holding all the aces, so there was nothing I could do against him.*
within an ace/inch of por um triz, muito perto de *He came within an ace of breaking his leg when he slipped on a banana peel.* ♦ *France ... came within an inch of violent collapse last month ... -T/68.*
ACHE ache for [col] ansiar por, desejar ardentemente *As I listened to the old Tommy Dorsey and Glenn Miller songs, they made me ache for times long past.*
ACID acid test prova decisiva *The acid test for the vaccine, of course, would be for [Dr. Daniel] Zagury to inject himself with live AIDS virus to see if he is truly protected. -T/87.* ♦ *... have put this attitude to an acid test ... -T/87.*
ACQUAINT acquaint oneself with familiarizar-se com *You will have to acquaint yourself with all the facts before you take any action.*
be/get acquainted with travar conhecimento com (pessoa, fato etc.), familiarizar-se com *Anyone who wishes to get acquainted with the period of the American Revolution ought to read the novels of Kenneth Roberts.*
ACQUAINTANCE bowing/nodding acquaintance 1. conhecimento de vista, superficial *Among these particles [of electricity in the atom] is the negatively charged electron with which we already have better than a bowing acquaintance. -UM,20.* ♦ *... Johnny Friendly had a better than nodding acquaintance with Tom McGovern ... -SBW,4.* 2. pessoa a quem se conhece apenas de vista, a quem apenas cumprimentamos *I really don't know him very well. He's just one of my nodding acquaintances.*
make one's acquaintance travar conhecimento com, conhecer (pessoa) *I'm pleased to make your acquaintance, Mr. Roberts.*

ACQUIT acquit oneself desempenhar-se, portar-se, sair-se (bem, mal etc.) *We hope that he acquits himself well in his new job.*
ACROSS across from (situado) do outro lado de, do lado oposto de *He was eating breakfast in the restaurant across from the hotel when someone paused beside his table ... -HJ,55.*
ACROSS-THE-BOARD → **across the BOARD**
ACT act like imitar, comportar-se como *He's been acting like a fool lately.*
act of God ocorrência natural e imprevisível, acontecimento inevitável *She said that it was an act of God that the crops had been destroyed.*
act on/upon 1. ter efeito sobre *It was a poignant play and it acted on the emotions of the audience.* 2. agir de acordo com, seguir (sugestão, conselho etc.) *She acted on the recommendation of the committee.*
act out 1. representar, interpretar; levar a efeito, à prática, pôr em ação *Even though they moved to the cities, the descendants of the senhores de engenho continued to act out their roles as aristocrats and patriarchs. -WC,32.* ♦ *My imagination worked overtime as I dreamed up endless romances, then acted them out. -FLF,27.* 2. comportar-se de maneira inadequada, anti-social etc., sem estar consciente de que tal comportamento expressa sentimentos reprimidos *... few of us in polite society have fully acted out our rebellious impulses ... -KS,130.*
act up [col] 1. comportar-se de maneira rude, indisciplinada, rebelde, obstinada; teimar em portar-se mal; praticar travessuras, pintar o sete *[He] ... was acting up in a way I'd never seen before. -GF,294.* ♦ *If people know they are likely to get clobbered if they act up, they are likely to think twice about it ... -T/86.* 2. funcionar irregularmente, apresentar defeito *Our TV set has been acting up again and I haven't*

been able to watch my favorite shows. 3. voltar a incomodar, tornar-se novamente agudo, dolorido, inflamado etc. *My old bursitis has been acting up again and I couldn't sleep a wink last night.*

catch (someone) in the act apanhar (alguém) com a boca na botija *We have to catch this bastard in the act ...* -CGU,174.

get in on/into the act [col] participar de uma atividade (geralmente por motivos interesseiros) *... the small investor decides that he too should get in on the act and put his dollars into the market.* -T/82.

get/have one's act together [gir] organizar(se), realizar (algo) a contento; começar a atuar, agir ou funcionar de maneira competente, eficaz etc. *A bunch of American workers have shown that they can get their act together.* -T/87. ♦ *Ten years after the first launch of the space shuttle was supposed to initiate an era of routine space flight, NASA still doesn't have its act together.* -T/91.

put on an act [col] fingir, representar uma farsa, hastear bandeira falsa *He was disturbed but he wasn't putting on an act.*

ACTION bring action processar *She has brought action against her husband.*

out of action fora de combate, parado, desativado *Five cars were out of action before the race was over.*

put into//out of action ativar, executar// desativar *When his plan was put into action it worked wonderfully.* ♦ *All the lights went out when the electric system was put out of action.*

see action/combat tomar parte de batalha, lutar, participar de combate *You have seen a lot of action, and you were seriously wounded.* -FH,3. ♦ *As a young officer he saw combat in Korea and Viet Nam ...* -T/86.

take action agir, tomar medidas *[He] ... may take some action on the basis of the facts presented.* -SN,4.

where the action is a atividade mais excitante, interessante, agradável, proveitosa etc. em um determinado local, área de ação ou grupo *California, its citizens feel, is where the action is.* -T/66 ♦ *They want desperately to be "where the action is".* -TA,44.

ADAM Adam's apple pomo-de-adão *[She] ... had a ribbon around her neck that crossed her Adam's apple.* -GA,54.

not know someone from Adam [col] nunca ter visto mais gordo, desconhecer totalmente *I don't know her brother from Adam.*

the old Adam a suposta tendência humana para o pecado, instintos primitivos *Flannery O'Connor, a Catholic whose brilliant short stories lacerated characters to get at their souls, once said flatly, "I'm interested in the old Adam".* -T/76.

ADD add in incluir *They made up a list of the disliked people in our office and added her in.*

add to aumentar, incrementar *His refusal to cooperate added to our difficulties.*

add up 1. achar a soma (de), somar *Add up the two columns of figures on the left.* 2. dar o total esperado *The figures the accounting department gave him didn't add up.* 3. [col] fazer sentido, parecer razoável *The story she told me just doesn't add up.*

add up to 1. alcançar o total de, chegar à soma de *Her expenses added up to $759.* 2. [col] significar, equivaler a, indicar, resultar em *[Alfred Hitchcock's thriller, Psycho] adds up to an expertly Gothic nightmare.* -T/60. ♦ *The increase in fires in houses and industry in that area add up to an increase in delinquency.*

ADDICTED addicted to 1. inclinado a, dado a, chegado a *Carlos is addicted to western movies.* ♦ *In Brazil, [television] viewers have long been addicted to novelas, or nighttime serials.* -T/91. 2. viciado em *She is addicted to alcohol.* ♦ *[He] ... became addicted to drink and drugs.* -T/78.

ADDITION in addition (to) além disso, além (de) *In addition to broken fragments of decomposing rock, soil consists of decayed plant material.* -PR,28.

ADDRESS forwarding address novo endereço [para o qual deve ser enviada a correspondência entregue no endereço anterior] *Mr. Arbogast moved to another town but left no forwarding address.*

AD-LIB 1. falar de improviso, intercalar palavras ou frases em meio a um discurso, interpretação, encontro etc. *We ad-libbed it [a scene for the movie* Going My Way*] right on the set under Leo's [Leo McCarey's] direction.* -CBC,5. ♦ *... if I work for an hour in a night club, out of that hour I will ad-lib perhaps four minutes.* -BL,197. 2. fala improvisada *... he is still a quick man with the ad-lib.* -T/66.

ADMISSION by one's own admission confessadamente, segundo a própria pessoa diz *She is, by her own admission, too impatient with others.* -T/72.

ADVANCE in advance de antemão, antecipadamente, previamente *... he knew of the invasion in advance ...* -T/78.

in advance of antes de, à frente de, na vanguarda de *This will have to be done in advance of the meeting.*

ADVANTAGE take advantage of 1. aproveitar a oportunidade que se oferece, utilizar-se de *He took advantage of the heavy fog that blanketed the city at night and eluded the police.* 2. enganar, explorar, tratar deslealmente (alguém) visando benefício próprio *He took advantage of the situation and siphoned off all of his client's money.*

to advantage de maneira a produzir uma impressão favorável, a realçar ou aproveitar as boas qualidades de; favoravelmente, com bom efeito *The furniture in his new apartment has been arranged to advantage.*

to someone's advantage para proveito de, com bons resultados para *... I found myself ... suggesting that it might be to his advantage to talk with me.* -CCT,13.

turn to one's advantage tirar proveito, beneficiar-se *... Khomeini is adept at turning the fears and jealousies of rival nations to his own advantage.* -T/87.

AFFAIR have an affair ter uma relação amorosa, um caso *She had had an affair with a French lieutenant.*

AFOOT = on FOOT 2 *[He] ... began to suspect that something was afoot.* -T/76.

AFRAID I'm afraid... acho que..., receio que..., lamento que... *I'm afraid you'll have to come back later. Dr. Smith is not in at the moment.* ♦ *When I asked her if she had to leave, she replied: "I'm afraid so".*

AFTER be after estar no encalço de, à procura de, estar perseguindo *The gangsters are after him.* ♦ *... the army was after him.* -T/63.

AFTER-HOURS → after HOURS

AGAIN again and again freqüentemente, repetidas vezes *We have discussed this subject again and again but you keep coming back to it.*

AGE act/be one's age comportar-se como adulto, não ser infantil *The old man was told to act his age.* ♦ *Be your age! Stop behaving like a boy!*

awkward age período da adolescência *She was at the awkward age and having great difficulty preparing herself for adult life.* ♦ *... Tatum [O'Neal] says she has reached the awkward age ...* -T/79.

come of age atingir a maioridade; chegar à maturidade, à proeminência, ao reconhecimento (social, político, profissional etc.) *Girls come of age long before boys in most countries.* ♦ *John Kennedy came of age with the New Deal and World War II.* -T/87. ♦ *Many underdeveloped countries have come of age in this century.* ♦ *[French actress Catherine Deneuve] ... has clearly come of age as an actress.* -T/68.

for/in ages [col] durante um "tempão", há muito tempo, há séculos *She kept us waiting outside her office for ages.* ♦ *I haven't seen her in ages.*

middle age idade madura *He has reached middle age but still can swim very fast.*

middle-aged maduro, de meia-idade *He is short, balding and middle-aged.* -T/63.
Middle Ages Idade Média *The Middle Ages traditionally began in 476 and ended in 1450.*
of age maior de idade *She is of age now and she can do as she pleases.*
AGE-OLD antigo, que existe há muito tempo ... *"patriarchal culture," the age-old male suppression of women.* -T/81. ♦ ... *the age-old debate of free will* v. *predestination.* -T/77.
AGOG all agog ansioso, ávido, impaciente *He was all agog about the trip to Africa.* ♦ *Joe Almeida was flying to Los Angeles. He was all agog to see his grandson who had just been born there.*
AGREE agree to disagree decidir-se por um rompimento, concluir pela impossibilidade de se chegar a um entendimento *Their basic positions evolved separately and are in conflict. Frankly, I wish they would just agree to disagree.* -T/81.
agree with fazer bem (à saúde, digestão etc. de), condizer com (o caráter, temperamento etc. de) *The food she ate at lunch didn't agree with her.* ♦ *This cold climate does not agree with him.* v. **DISAGREE with**.
AHEAD ahead of à frente de, na dianteira de, em posição de vantagem *Do you think Russia is ahead of the U.S. in military power?*
AID first aid primeiros socorros *She gave first aid to the boy that had been injured in the automobile accident.* ♦ *She opened the glove compartment and got the first aid kit.*
hearing aid aparelho de surdez *[He] ... now wears a hearing aid in public.* -T/76.
AIM aim at visar a, ter em vista, ter o propósito de, procurar, pretender *Artists aim at perfection in their work.* ♦ ... *various forms and degrees of mental and physical discipline aimed at spiritual advancement ...* -RN,25.

aim for aspirar a, pretender alcançar, dirigir esforços na direção de ... *aiming for national unity ...* -T/82.
aim to aspirar a, pretender, esforçar-se por (conseguir algo) *We aim to keep our customers well served and happy.*
take aim apontar, fazer pontaria *The soldier leaned against the tree, took aim, and fired three shots.*
AIR 1. tornar público, divulgar, manifestar ... *airing his own views in the paper's columns.* -T/67. ♦ *They [President Carter and Yugoslav leaders] aired their differences on the Middle East.* -T/80. 2. transmitir (por rádio ou TV) ... *a TV movie to be aired next fall.* -T/80.
Air Force One o avião do presidente dos EUA ... *[President Ronald] Reagan boarded Air Force One and headed west* ... -T/87.
air out arejar, ventilar *Hang your sneakers outside so they can air out.*
air pocket corrente de ar descendente que faz um avião perder altitude subitamente, bolsa de ar *An air pocket caused the plane to make a sudden drop.*
air shuttle ponte aérea *The São Paulo-Rio air shuttle is one of the busiest in the world.*
by air por avião, por via aérea *go/travel by air* ♦ *transportation by air*
clear the air aliviar a situação, eliminar a tensão, afastar temores, dúvidas etc. *Bud wanted to make complete disclosure. He wanted to clear the air.* -T/87.
come up for air fazer uma interrupção temporária, tomar fôlego, dar pausa *I had just finished reading [a book] – about four times, without coming up for air –* ... -AJ,19.
disappear/vanish into thin air desaparecer, sumir *The police looked everywhere for the thief, but he seemed to have disappeared into thin air.* ♦ *When the New York Stock Exchange collapsed in 1929, many fortunes vanished into thin air overnight.*

fill the air cortar os ares, estrugir os ares, soar com força *Chants of "Death to America!" and "Death to the fascist Saudi police!" filled the air.* -T/87.

get the air [gir] levar um fora, ser rejeitado *She got the air from her boyfriend last night.*

give oneself airs bancar o importante *She gives herself airs whenever she sees us.*

give the air [gir] dar um fora, rejeitar *She gave her boyfriend the air when she found out he was dating other girls.*

hot air [gir] conversa fiada, bobagens *Everything she told you was just hot air.*

in the air 1. em circulação, no ar *There is a rumor in the air that he is going to run for President.* 2. indeciso, incerto, vago, sem fundamento *Our plans for the party are still in the air.*

off//on the air fora do ar//no ar, irradiando *Troops have occupied the town and the radio station has been off the air since last night.* ♦ *... I had seen virtually every episode [of the television series* Star Trek*] that had been on the air.* -WS,11.

open air ar livre, espaço aberto *Let's go out in the open air where we can breathe.* ⇒ **open-air** ao ar livre *open-air exercise* ♦ *an open-air prayer meeting*

put on airs = **give oneself AIRS** *Social climbers are always putting on airs.*

take the air [gir] ir-se, dar o fora *They were told to take the air.*

up in the air 1. em estado de confusão ou incerteza, ainda não decidido *... deals that are up in the air ...* -T/87. ♦ 2. [col] zangado, irado *He was up in the air because they had called him a liar.*

vanish into thin air → **disappear into thin AIR**

walk on air estar felicíssimo *Carol was walking on air after Phil asked her to marry him.*

AIR-MINDED que se interessa pela aviação ou viagens aéreas *She is one of those modern, air-minded travelers.* ♦ *Mary Jane ... [was going] to marry an aviation cadet ... a lean, air-minded boy ...* -SJD, 20.

ALARM alarm clock relógio despertador *I usually set my alarm clock to go off at seven.*

ALECK smart aleck [col] indivíduo convencido, pretensioso, sabichão *He's a smart aleck and we don't like him.* ⇒ **smart-alecky** sabichão, convencido *... she is at once sophisticated and ingenuous, smart-alecky and enraptured.* -T/65.

ALERT on the alert em estado de alerta, vigilante *We'll all be on the alert here ...* -FV,21.

red alert alerta vermelho *Attempting to deal with a crisis that was only dimly understood, the White House ... "went into a state of absolute red alert".* -T/79. ♦ *All systems were on red alert.*

ALIVE alive and kicking [col] bem vivo, gozando boa saúde, ativo *I just came from West Berlin and let me say that the city is definitely alive and kicking.* -T/76. ♦ *Tell them I'm still alive and kicking.*

alive to totalmente cônscio de, atento para *They are alive to their new business opportunities in East Europe.*

alive with cheio de, repleto de, fervilhando de *The streets were alive with people.* ♦ *... the surface waters of the ocean at night ... are alive with myriads of strange creatures never seen by day.* -CR,20.

ALL above all principalmente, acima de tudo *Above all you must consider that your duty to your family comes first.* ♦ *... Zen is above all an experience, nonverbal in character, which is simply inaccessible to the purely literary and scholarly approach.* -WAW,x.

after all afinal de contas *This must not happen again. After all, you're not a child any more.*

all aboard todos para bordo! passageiros, embarquem! (o trem, ônibus etc. vai partir) *The conductor's voice echoed along the platform. "All aboard." ... and the train began to move.* -HJ,60.

all along desde o princípio, o tempo todo ... *he had been right all along.* -T/60.

all and sundry [col] todos em geral, toda a gente, todos os tipos de pessoas ... *he had a knack of getting on well with all and sundry.* -SHE,19.

all around/round por toda a parte, por todos os lados, em todas as direções; em todos os sentidos, sob todos os aspectos *The committee began the week with optimism all around* ... -T/87. ♦ ... *maybe if I explain what has happened ... you'll feel better all around.* -GE,168. ⇒ **all-around**; **all-round** versátil, não-limitado, de muitas habilidades, talentos ou qualidades; abrangente, amplo, de grande alcance, geral ... *Mildred ("Babe") Didrikson Zaharias, the top all-round woman athlete in the world...* -T/84. ♦ *[He] ... is an effective, able all-round banker* ... -T/62. ♦ *Sammy Davis, Jr. was the all-around showman.*

all but 1. quase *A crimeless world is an ideal all but impossible to achieve.* -DJ,vii. 2. todos/tudo, com exceção de *All but [Britain's Prime Minister] Thatcher stated their support for the stronger package of sanctions [against South Africa]* ... -T/86.

all for inteiramente favorável a *He has serious qualms about accepting the new government job but his wife is all for it.*

all in cansadíssimo, exausto *He was all in after the long walk.*

all in all de modo geral *[She was] ... also a good mother and efficient housekeeper – all in all very nice, a very good wife* ... -WC,164.

all of não menos de, pelo menos [aquilo que é especificado] *Steven Spielberg was all of 26 when he was hired [to direct Jaws].* -T/75. ♦ *Rick tried to grab the little boy who had fallen into the water but the boat had floated all of twenty feet away and he was unable to reach the sinking child.*

all one = **all the SAME**

all right 1. satisfatório, correto; satisfatoriamente, corretamente *I'll pick you up at seven o'clock if it's all right with you.* 2. são, ileso, incólume, bem, seguro *He slipped and fell to the ground, but he said he was all right.* 3. [gir] bom, agradável, legal, decente *You can depend on him because he's all right. He's an all-right guy.* 4. [col] sim, muito bem, está bem *"All right", she said. "You may go with us but you'll have to obey the rules."* 5. [col] sem dúvida, de fato, com certeza *He's the same man who came here two days ago, all right.*

all round → **ALL around**

all set preparado, pronto *Our team was all set for the beginning of the game.*

all that à extensão ou ao grau sugerido, a esse ponto, tanto assim *Things can't be all that bad.*

all the more/better/worse/harder/easier etc. muito mais, ainda mais; bem melhor/pior/mais fácil etc. ... *crimes are becoming more brutal, more irrational, more random – and therefore, all the more frightening.* -T/81. ♦ *The world is all the poorer without people like Gandhi, Mother Teresa, Albert Schweitzer and others.*

all told ao todo, no total *All told, 26 died in the explosion.* -T/82.

all too demais, muito *Rachel's waistline showed all too plainly that she was expecting.* ♦ ... *he showed himself to be but all too human.* -KRI,574.

and all/everything [col] e não sei mais que, e as demais coisas (pertinentes mas não especificadas), e tudo mais, e o resto ... *I realize you're a cop and all, but I realize you're no square* ... -WJT,152. ♦ ... *if he knew Walt was – you know. Killed and everything.* -SJD, 32.

as/like all get out [col] extremamente, superlativamente *[They were] ... sincere as all get out.* -T/87.

as all that à extensão ou ao grau sugerido

ou indicado, tanto assim ... *many Americans began to wonder whether Nixon had ever really been as bad as all that.* -T/91.
at all 1. de modo algum, absolutamente, nem um pouco, nada, coisa nenhuma *In The Wizard of Oz, when Dorothy was asked whether she was a good witch or a bad witch, she replied quickly: "I'm not a witch at all."* ♦ *I'm not at all satisfied with your answer.* 2. sob quaisquer circunstâncias, na realidade, de fato, realmente *Mart realized now that a man can be free as a wolf, yet unable to do what he wants at all.* -LM, 67. 3. algum, qualquer, um tanto, um pouco, sequer, ao menos *Do you have any money at all?* ♦ *Are you worried at all about what she may tell the police?*
give one's all entregar-se inteiramente, dar tudo o que se tem, empregar toda sua energia ... *newspapers writing how you gave your all to your country.* -MAT,67.
in all ao todo *Their team wound up with 12 medals in all.*
not at all → **at ALL**
of all (people/things/places etc.) (dentre todas as possibilidades), a pessoa, coisa, lugar etc. em questão é a mais surpreendente, improvável etc. ... *a stagecoach was departing for – of all places – the new and raw Republic of Texas* ... -WPI,31. ♦ *You, of all people, shouldn't criticize the plan.*
ALL-AMERICAN 1. característico, típico ou representativo dos EUA como um todo; constituído inteiramente de elementos americanos *Becoming a movie star still seems to be the all-American dream of most girls.* ♦ ... *a boyishly all-American face* ... -T/87. 2. que representa o melhor em qualquer categoria esportiva dos EUA *[He was] An Annapolis graduate and former all-American end [football player stationed at the extremity of a line] at Ohio State [University]* ... -UL,4. ♦ *Jim Thorpe, all-American athlete who rose to worlwide fame, was an Indian.*

ALLEY blind alley beco sem saída, embaraço, dificuldade *Preliminary investigations got the police into a blind alley.*
down/up one's alley/street [gir] apropriado ao gosto, habilidade, talento, inclinação ou especialidade de uma pessoa; dentro da esfera do conhecimento ou compreensão de, fácil para ... *I had better talk about something more properly down my alley.* -TR,32. ♦ *This new job is right up his alley.*
ALL-FIRED [gir] completo, extremo, total *Why are you so all-fired anxious to get out of here?* -HJ,45.
ALL-NIGHT 1. que funciona durante a noite (atividade comercial) *They went to an all-night drugstore.* 2. que dura a noite toda ... *an all-night poker game.* -QE,57.
ALL-OUT completo, inteiro, total extremo *Most Americans aren't aware of the sober truth of the Atomic Age or of what all-out war means.* -WPT,315. v. **GO all out**
ALLOW allow for levar em conta, tomar em consideração *When you order a book by mail you have to allow for postal delays among other things.*
ALLOWANCE make allowance for considerar, levar em conta *We must make allowance for his being so young and inexperienced.*
ALL-PURPOSE que pode ser utilizado para muitas finalidades, versátil ... *a $30 million, all-purpose [air]plane* ... -T/81.
ALL-ROUND ⇒ **ALL around**
ALL-TIME de todos os tempos, que supera todos os outros ... *World Bank loans to Latin American countries are expected to reach an all-time high of $4.5 billion* ... -T/86.
ALONG along with juntamente com, na companhia de *Put that book back on the shelf, along with the others.*
be along chegar, aparecer *Mr. Winningham's secretary assured me that her boss would be along any minute.*
right along [col] sempre, continuamente, sem cessar *He had interviewed several*

candidates for the job but Reynolds had been first on his list right along.
ALSO-RAN cavalo que não conseguiu ser classificado numa corrida *I always bet on the also-rans.* 2. pessoa derrotada em qualquer tipo de competição; indivíduo sem importância, que não demonstra competitividade *My candidate was an also-ran.*
AMENDS **make amends** compensar (por alguma coisa), ressarcir, dar reparação *Perhaps his conscience is bothering him and he may want to make amends ...* -CT,15.
AMENDMENT **Fifth Amendment** Quinta Emenda à Constituição dos EUA *The Fifth Amendment to the Constitution of the United States says, among other things, that "no person shall be compelled in any criminal case to be a witness against himself ..."* v. **take the FIFTH**
AMOUNT **amount to** 1. totalizar, montar a, importar em *Her debts amount to $10,000.* 2. significar, equivaler a *His statement amounts to treason.*
amount to something valer muito, ser significativo, valioso, importante etc. *You give him some responsibility and he is going to amount to something.* -T/73. ♦ *He will never amount to anything in the political world.*
no amount of quantidade nenhuma de, volume nenhum de, nenhuma dose de *No amount of advice could persuade Danny to change his ways.*
ANCHOR **at anchor** ancorado, fundeado *... tankers flying the Greek flag lie at anchor in a harbor near Eleusis.* -T/81.
weigh anchor levantar âncora, preparar-se para zarpar *The ship weighed anchor in the morning of September 27.*
ANCHORMAN 1. coordenador de programa de telejornalismo ou de radiojornalismo *With his [Walter Cronkite's] retirement this week as anchorman from the CBS Evening News goes the man who* more than anyone else has shaped and given stature to the role. -T/81. 2. o atleta que participa da etapa final de uma corrida de revezamento *He was anchorman on our team.*
AND **and so forth/on** e assim por diante, e coisas semelhantes, e coisas assim etc. *Mr. Green raises chickens, ducks, geese, turkeys, and so forth on his farm.* ♦ *In his speech, the President touched on pollution, poverty, problems of the aged and so on.*
ANGEL **where angels fear to tread** onde os cautelosos temem pôr os pés *It was Alexander Pope who said that "fools rush in where angels fear to tread", meaning that fools are both irreverent and presumptuous.*
ANGLE FOR [col] procurar conseguir (algo) por meios ardilosos *... Iran is rumored to be angling for the nuclear know-how and materials of ex-Soviet bombmakers ...* -T/92.
ANSWER **answer back** → **TALK back**
answer for responsabilizar-se por, responder por *Be careful of what you say and do because you will have to answer for it later.*
answer to corresponder a *McCoy answered to the description of the escaped convict and the police arrested him.*
have/know all the answers [col] ser conhecedor das coisas, entender de tudo (freqüentemente dito com sarcasmo) *In time of crisis we must be extremely careful in accepting the leadership of those who claim to have all the answers.* -T/79.
ANTE UP [gír] pagar, contribuir com *... 108 million workers and their employers will ante up $112 billion to the Social Security system next year ...* -T/77.
ANY **hardly/scarcely any** quase nenhum, pouquíssimo *There was hardly any beer left after the party.* ♦ *I have scarcely any money right now.*
not any longer → **no LONGER**
not any more/anymore já não, não mais *Susan doesn't live here anymore.*

ANYTHING anything but de modo algum, absolutamente não, nada disso *She was anything but a great novelist.* -T/73 ♦ *... if there is one thing that entrepreneurs demand of their suppliers, it is reliability. And so far, NASA has offered anything but.* -T/84.

anything like nem de longe, nem ao menos perto (de algo que se pareça com) [em orações interrogativas, negativas e condicionais] *She isn't anything like they told me she was.*

for anything de modo algum, por nada, por nenhuma razão *... I fled from the Midwest and its urban decay ... and I would not return for anything.* -T/91.

if anything se há ou se houver alguma diferença; se algo mais preciso pode ser dito; mais precisamente (o que se pode dizer é isto) *The water was, if anything, lukewarm, as it often was at this hour of morning.* -SEB,116. ♦ *[The FBI's] ... files on some 6,000,000 Americans are, if anything, too complete ...* -T/73.

ANYWHERE anywhere near = **ANYTHING like** *I never made anywhere near four eighty-nine [489 dollars] a month before, sir.* -WJT,17.

APART apart from 1. separadamente de *The boy was placed apart from the other children.* 2. além de *Apart from his work he really has no other interests.* 3. independentemente de, exceto por *They got lost in the mountains and, apart from a loaf of bread, they had no other food.*

APARTMENT apartment house edifício de apartamentos *This is the apartment house in which they live.*

APE go ape [gír] entusiasmar-se muito por, ficar frenético, excitar-se, sair fora de si, inflamar-se *He went ape when he saw the girls passing by.*

APPEAR as to appear → **as to BE**

APPEARANCE keep up appearances manter as aparências (principalmente de prosperidade, apesar de dificuldades financeiras) *Even though they had lost all their money, the proud Joneses tried to keep up appearances.*

put in/make an appearance chegar, vir, aparecer, comparecer, apresentar-se *[Fidel] Castro put in one appearance during the visit of the Indianapolis delegation.* -T/87.

APPLE the apple of someone's eyes motivo de grande estima, menina dos olhos *That kid is the apple of her father's eye.*

the Big Apple Nova York *[She has been] ... a lifelong resident of the Big Apple ...* -T/81.

APPLECART upset the applecart fazer fracassar (plano, negócio etc.), frustrar as intenções (de) *Now, keep your mouth shut and don't upset the applecart.*

APPLE-PIE [col] relativo a ou caracterizado por valores tradicionais americanos *... apple-pie virtues.* -T/76.

in apple-pie order [col] em perfeita ordem *The beds were neatly made, everything was in apple-pie order ...* -CGT,99.

APPLE-POLISH [gír] adular, bajular *He apple-polished until he reached a key position in the company.* ⇒ **apple-polisher** pessoa bajuladora *I can't stand apple-polishers.*

APPLY apply for solicitar, pedir, requerer, candidatar-se a *She applied for a transfer to another department in the same company.*

APPROVAL on approval sob condição, (mercadoria) sujeita à devolução se não for satisfatória *I asked the bookstore clerk to send me some books on approval.*

APRON tied to one's mother's/wife's apron strings muito influenciado pela mãe ou esposa, agarrado à saia de *Willie is still tied to his mother's apron strings.*

ARGUMENT have an argument discutir, desavir-se, desentender-se *It looked as though the two men were about to have an argument.*

ARM an arm and a leg [gír] um preço ou custo excessivamente alto, os olhos da cara

That German automobile cost me an arm and a leg. ♦ *Most of the guys around here would give an arm and a leg to do some original research on this subject.* -SJSN,15.
arm in arm de braços dados *They came down the Official Palace steps together, arm in arm ...* -BRT,163.
the (long) arm of the law o poder da lei, a força da autoridade *You can be sure that the long arm of the law will always reach you if you commit a crime.*
as long as one's arm muito longo, extremamente extenso *... Linus Pauling's list of scientific honors is as long as his arm ...* -T/60.
fold one's arms cruzar os braços, permanecer inativo *He folded his arms and his assistant had to do all the work himself.*
give one's right arm dar algo que muito se estima em troca de alguma coisa, sacrificar(-se) *I'd give my right arm to be in his place.*
hold/keep someone at arm's length manter alguém a distância, tratar inamistosamente *She tried to hold Malcolm at arm's length.* ♦ *The President must be powerful enough to keep the military at arm's length.*
put the (strong) arm on [gír] coagir, exercer pressão ou força física contra *You will have to put the strong arm on him to get him to act on that matter.* ⇒ **strong-arm** 1. usar violência contra, tentar persuadir por meio de intimidação *Many Japanese ... are worried that Washington will try to use its greater geopolitical clout to strong-arm Tokyo in economic disputes.* -T/91. 2. violento, que emprega a força *He gets things done by his strong-arm tactics.*
twist arms [col] forçar (alguém a fazer algo), pressionar fortemente com ameaças *He will get the results that he wants even if he has to twist arms a bit.*
ARMS bear arms possuir ou portar armas; servir nas forças armadas *Opponents of gun control argue that Americans have a basic constitutional right to bear arms.* -T/81. ♦ *In early 1914 Adolf [Hitler] ... was rejected by the Austrian army ... Unable to bear arms.* -T/89.
call to arms 1. chamar às armas, convocar para o serviço militar *When war broke out, most men aged between 20 and 30 were called to arms.* 2. brado para pegar em armas, convocação para uma batalha ou luta *A call to arms brings the "students" charging from the campus to storm a palace or stone an embassy ...* -T/62.
in arms em armas, pronto para lutar *The country has many men in arms.*
lay down one's arms depor as armas, capitular, render-se *The rebels realized they had been defeated and laid down their arms.*
take up arms empunhar armas, armar-se, começar a lutar contra *[He] ... left to take up arms against his country's occupiers.* -CL,104. ♦ *... take up arms and defend yourself ...* -T/80.
under arms em armas, pronto para a guerra *At the moment, the government has about 15,000 men under arms ...* -T/80.
up in arms 1. pronto para a luta, em armas *The country was up in arms against the invaders.* 2. irado, furioso *The residents of that area were up in arms when the government revealed that a nuclear power plant would be set up nearby.*
ARMCHAIR teórico, de gabinete, sem experiência prática *When he led the attack personally he proved he was no armchair general.* ♦ *... certain armchair philosophers ...* -T/60. *... armchair therapists ...* -T/87.
AROUND-THE-CLOCK → **around the CLOCK**
ARREARS in arrears em dívida, em atraso *Your account is in arrears.* ♦ *... North Korea has fallen into arrears on its foreign debt of some $2 billion.* -T/86.
ARREST be/place under arrest deter,

prender, dar voz de prisão *The police officers told him that he was under arrest.* ♦ *He was placed under arrest.*
ARROW straight arrow [gir] pessoa honesta, decente, íntegra *[He] ... is a self-effacing straight arrow who seems like a Latin version of a 1950s all-American boy.* -T/84. ⇒ **straight-arrow** honesto, decente, íntegro *We are a straight-arrow company.* -T/87.
AS as against em face de, comparado com, em contraste com *We've had a $200,000 profit this year as against $120,000 last year.*
as ... as tanto ... quanto, tão ... como *Madge is as lovely as her sister.*
as for com referência a, no que diz respeito a *Carl is a nice guy. As for Roy, I really don't know.*
as if/though como se *He spoke as if he knew where the stolen jewels had been hidden.* ♦ *It seemed as though the boys had been afraid that no one would believe their story.* -MMA,53.
as of a partir de *You're relieved of your duties as of today.*
as one unanimemente, de comum acordo *We must act as one when dealing with this matter.*
as though → **AS if**
as to quanto a, com relação a *Archaeologists differ as to how types of pottery may be related in time and origin.* -CEO, 23. ♦ *... we can make no prediction at the present time as to the behavior of [a certain group of people] ...* -KAC,23. v. **as to BE/appear/look/seem etc.**
as usual como de costume, comumente, como sempre *The boy was teasing his little sister, as usual.*
as yet por enquanto, até agora *No fully satisfactory theory to account for the extinction of dinosaurs has been formulated as yet.*
ASIDE aside from exceto por, com exceção de, além de *Aside from what Mr. Martin has disclosed, there is little else I can tell you.*

ASK ask after perguntar por, pedir informações a respeito de *Did they ask after me when I didn't go to class today?* ♦ *They asked after Mrs. Talbot's health.*
ask for 1. pedir *He will walk up to any pretty girl and ask for her phone number.* 2. procurar por *When you go there, ask for Louis.* 3. [col] procurar (complicações, encrenca etc.) *If he gets hurt, he has been asking for it.*
ask someone in convidar para entrar *Ask him in and offer him a drink.*
ask someone over convidar para vir à sua casa *Ask him over to have dinner with us tomorrow.*
if you ask me [col] se você quiser saber a minha opinião *He was never a reliable assistant, if you ask me.*
ASKING for the asking grátis, gratuitamente, bastando pedir para conseguir *The best things in life are free and can be yours for the asking.*
ASLEEP fast/sound asleep profundamente adormecido *My wife was in bed and fast asleep when I got home.*
ASPHALT asphalt jungle a cidade grande e desumana, selva de pedra *[The Broadway musical] West Side Story [is] Romeo and Juliet in the asphalt jungle.* -T/60.
ASS make an ass (out) of oneself fazer papel de bobo *Your lawyer is going to make an ass out of himself ...* -T/81.
AT at it ocupado com (determinada atividade), ativo, fazendo algo *Honey bees are hard at it among the new blossoms.* -T/81.
ATTACH be attached to gostar muito de, ter grande afeição por *In his younger years he was much attached to his sister Dora.*
ATTEND attend to 1. tratar de, encarregar-se de *I attend to the financial part of our business.* ♦ *Please attend to this matter at once.* 2. cuidar de, dedicar-se a, aplicar-se a *There are a few things to attend to in town ...* -CT,10.
ATTENDANCE dance attendance on estar à inteira disposição de, atender alguém

em seus mínimos desejos *Those who danced attendance on Nixon suddenly disappeared after Watergate.*
in attendance presente (a fim de prestar serviço, atender alguém etc.) *... there are two doctors and a nurse in attendance.* -WI,41.
ATTENTION catch someone's attention = catch someone's EYE
pay attention prestar atenção, ouvir cuidadosamente *She never paid any attention to my words.* ♦ *... this is a fundamental scientific discovery! But nobody pays any attention!* -LMO,29.
AUCTION auction off vender em leilão, leiloar *... the jewels of the Duke and Duchess of Windsor were auctioned off last April in Geneva.* -T/87.
put up for auction pôr em leilão *The old mansion has been put up for auction.*
AULD LANG SYNE os bons tempos de outrora, os velhos tempos (que nos parecem felizes e cheios de doces lembranças) *They drank to auld lang syne.*
AVAIL avail oneself of aproveitar, valer-se de (oportunidade etc.) *She availed herself of the chance of learning a new trade.*
of/to no avail inútil, em vão, inutilmente, debalde *... their efforts have been to no avail.* -T/63. ♦ *Authorities tried to censor news of the message, but to no avail.* -T/87.
AVENUE explore every avenue examinar cuidadosamente todas as possibilidades, averiguar tudo em seus mínimos detalhes *We must explore every avenue to get at the facts.*
AVERAGE average out atingir a média (de) *The life span of an ancient Greek or Roman averaged out to 33.* -T/66.
batting average [gír] o nível médio de sucesso ou competência que alguém alcança em sua atividade *He's a competent lawyer with a fairly good batting average.*
on (an/the) average em média *... Americans today, on average, sleep one and a half hours less than they did 60 years ago.* -T/78.

AWE in awe of (sentindo) um misto de temor e respeito em relação a *... he was strong enough to attack the System and its institutions while the world at large stood in awe of them.* -JRE,48. ♦ *[He] ... admits to feeling "always considerably in awe in the presence of a President".* -T/79.
AWFUL [col] 1. desagradável, objetável, condenável, horrível, ruim, feio *He has awful manners.* ♦ *You've made an awful mistake.* 2. muito grande, enorme *There's an awful lot to be said in his favor.* 3. muitíssimo, extremamente *She's awful nice.* ♦ *I felt awful tired last night.*
AWFULLY [col] 1. de maneira desagradável, repreensível *She behaved awfully at the party.* 2. extremamente, muitíssimo *I'm awfully sorry!* ♦ *... I felt awfully good that day.* -RQ,65.
AWOL [absent without leave] ausente (do quartel, tropa etc.) sem permissão oficial *Robert E. Lee Prewitt, the main character in* From Here to Eternity, *kills Sergeant Judson in a knife duel and goes AWOL.*
AX an ax to grind [col] motivo oculto, razão pessoal, propósito egoísta, interesseiro, ressentimento *... a plain girl with no axes to grind ...* -SEB, 36 ♦ *... [magazine] articles with an ideological ax to grind.* -T/66.
get//give the ax [gír] 1. ser despedido, receber a conta// despedir, mandar embora *A few more men got the ax at the factory today.* ♦ *... more than 50 editorial employees and some 100 business staffers have been given the ax ...* -T/79. 2. levar o fora, terminar um relacionamento// dar o fora, romper relações com, livrar-se de *He got the ax from his sweetheart.* ♦ *She gave him the ax.*
AYE the ayes have it os votos a favor são maioria *When the matter was put to the vote at the board of directors, the ayes had it.*

B B movie filme cinematográfico produzido com orçamento restrito e geralmente de baixa qualidade *[Audie] Murphy ... had a surprisingly long career, especially in "B" movie westerns.* -SS,293.

BABE babe in the woods pessoa inocente, ingênua, sem experiência, facilmente enganada *... you'll be a babe in the woods, you're only nineteen ...* -WH,156. ♦ *In the television production area, I was a babe in the woods.* -WS,12.

BABY baby boom explosão demográfica (principalmente a que ocorreu nos EUA após a Segunda Guerra Mundial) *... the children of the postwar baby boom ...* -T/80. ⇒ **baby-boom** relativo ou referente à explosão demográfica *The baby-boom generation – the 76 million Americans born between 1946 and 1964 ...* -T/87. ⇒ **baby boomer** aquele que nasceu em época de explosão demográfica *... the baby boomers, a generation who grew up in the decades of economic expansion after World War II.* -BJ,148.

one's baby [col] qualquer coisa que requeira a atenção especial de alguém; objeto de orgulho, interesse, responsabilidade ou ocupação de uma pessoa *Education's my baby, actually – that's what I teach.* -SJD,195. ♦ *The captain placed the prisoners under the sergeant's care and told him: "From now on they're your babies. But be careful. They're very dangerous.".*

throw the baby out with the bathwater rejeitar algo essencial, valioso etc. ao tentar livrar-se de uma coisa indesejável *We cannot reject his proposal outright simply because it presents certain disadvantages. That would be throwing the baby out with the bathwater.*

BABY-SIT pajear, tomar conta de (bebê, criança) *When I was in the University I would often baby-sit for neighbors to get some extra money.* ⇒ **baby-sitter** pajem, ama-seca *Mr. Lynn Belvedere was hired as a baby-sitter and took over the whole house.*

BACK at/in the back of one's mind no pensamento, mas quase esquecido; no fundo da mente, existindo como uma vaga lembrança *I had in the back of my mind an interesting comment made to me only a week before by an official at the Vatican.* -NJ,58.

back and forth para diante e para trás, para cá e para lá, de um lado para o outro *For the past five minutes he had paced back and forth across the room.* -SHE,7.

♦ *If one could travel back and forth not only in space but in time ...* -SWLM,14.
back away recuar, afastar-se *She backed away from him because she was suddenly afraid of him.*
back down [col] abandonar uma posição, desistir de uma reivindicação, recuar, abrir mão de, renunciar, ceder *You never back down from a fight.* -T/87. ♦ *Not until 1912 did Washington back down and admit New Mexico and Arizona as separate states.* -BR,722.
back into envolver-se (acidentalmente) com *I backed into the feud between [the two men] ... inadvertently.* -T/78.
(in) back of por trás de, atrás de ... *back of the speculative boom were the forces – economic, cultural, psychological, and political – which made Americans susceptible.* -GJKT,xii. ♦ *Mrs. Sullivan's house is located directly in back of my father's house.*
back off = **BACK down** *Slim was a man who didn't back off from work when there was work to be done ...* -LLN,19. ♦ *The gang backed off when they saw that we were ready and well armed.*
back out desistir, retirar-se (de compromisso, empreendimento etc.) *I have accepted the invitation to speak at the YMCA and can't back out now.*
back up 1. recuar, ir para trás; fazer recuar *The Senator expects the Senate to back up his plan with the necessary funds.* ♦ *The car backed up a little and we had a full view of the street.* ♦ *Back up the car.* 2. apoiar, defender, auxiliar, secundar, coadjuvar *[He] ... was simply backing up a political friend.* -T/69. ♦ *He backed up his promises by sending troops into the troubled area.* ⇒ a. **backup** apoio, auxílio *Psychiatric backup is available twenty-four hours a day ...* -LRW,221. b. de apoio, auxiliar ... *backup musicians.* -T/77. ♦ ... *emergency backup systems ...* -T/87. 3. congestionar, entupir *[An accident on the freeway] ... had traffic backed up as far as he could see.* -WJT,45. ♦ ... *autos were backed up for hundreds of yards ...* -T/78. ♦ *his kitchen sink was always backing up when there was a lot of rain.* ⇒ **backup** congestionamento, entupimento *A shortage of landing strips at major airports can cause delays and backups at other airports from coast to coast.* -T/78.
be back voltar, regressar, estar de volta *He'll be back to work by next Monday.*
behind one's back às escondidas de, em segredo, furtivamente *I think you're all unkind to talk about Dolek behind his back.* -HJT,33.
break one's back trabalhar com afã, mourejar, suar ... *a sweatshop where I broke my back sixteen hours a day and made three dollars a week ...* -WH,156. ⇒ **backbreaking** laborioso, penoso, fatigante *backbreaking work* ♦ *backbreaking labor* ♦ *a backbreaking task*
break the back debelar, submeter, tirar a força a *There may be no way to break the back of inflation without recession.* -T/78.
get off someone's back [gir] deixar de importunar (alguém), largar do pé de *Get off my back, will you?* ♦ *Why doesn't the Government just get off our backs?* -T/87.
get someone's back up [col] deixar alguém zangado ... *I don't want to jump in and start opposing this thing and get Cindy's back up.* -HJD,9.
know like the back of one's hand conhecer como a palma da mão *[He] ... knew every judge and most of the prosecuting attorneys like the back of his hand.* -T/60. ♦ *[He] ... knows Devonshire like the back of his hand ...* -T/79.
on someone's back [gir] importunando, amolando, assediando; no pé de *The cops are on my back.* -CGT,105.
pat someone on the back animar, encorajar, estimular (alguém) *The teacher patted him on the back.* v. **PAT on the back**

put one's back to it empregar toda a energia, dar o melhor de si *If we put our backs to it, we'll be able to have this job done in no time at all.*
stab in the back [col] atraiçoar, trair ... *he could be scheming to stab the U.S. in the back ...* -T/73.
turn one's back on dar as costas a, abandonar, rejeitar *[He] ... turned his back on a promising Madison Avenue [i.e., advertising] career to work for the U.S. Post Office in Clinton ...* -BCMT,34. ♦ *He turned his back on the people who had helped him.*
with one's back to the wall encurralado, em situação difícil *They had no food and no ammunition and with the enemy moving in they were really with their back to the wall.*
you scratch my back and I'll scratch yours [col] é dando que se recebe, uma mão lava a outra ... *individuals that exchange favors – are in effect saying, "You scratch my back; I'll scratch yours".* -T/77.
BACKBREAKING → break one's BACK
BACKGROUND in the background em segundo plano, despercebido *As an F.B.I. agent, he wants to keep his family in the background as much as possible.*
BACKHANDED → left-handed COMPLIMENT
BACKSEAT backseat driver [col] passageiro que insiste em dizer ao motorista como dirigir o veículo *His wife is a backseat driver.*
take a backseat/back seat [col] ocupar posição secundária ou inferior *In many Latin American universities, education often takes a back seat to politics.* -T/62. ♦ *The era of blacks' taking a back seat and automaticaly supporting white politicians is over.* -T/84.
BACKTRACK recuar, voltar; voltar atrás, mudar de opinião *They felt that ... [he] had backtracked on campaign promises and doublecrossed them.* -T/77.

BACKTRAIL = backtrack *Let's backtrail and see if we can find where we took the wrong turn.*
BACKWARD(S) backward(s) and forward(s) [col] de cor e salteado, detalhadamente, totalmente *You can't fool him. He knows the rules of the game backward and forward.*
BACKWATER localidade atrasada ou estagnada ... *Mexico's Ciudad Juárez was little more than a depressed backwater of El Paso, Texas.* -T/87.
BACKYARD in one's own backyard em seu próprio local, território, área de ação, organização etc. *He should try to solve the problems in his own backyard before he goes abroad to solve foreign problems.*
BACON bring home the bacon [col] 1. ganhar o sustento, a vida, sustentar a família *Let Charles worry about that. He's the one who brings home the bacon.* 2. ganhar (prêmio, jogo etc.), vencer, ser bem-sucedido *Our team brought home the bacon.*
save one's bacon [col] safar-se de uma situação embaraçosa, salvar a pele *In spite of all the uproar over charges of corruption, the President managed to save his bacon.*
BAD go to the bad [col] decair moralmente, corromper-se *Despite his father's efforts, he went to the bad.*
in bad [col] em má situação, em dificuldades *He's in bad with the law.*
not (so) bad nada mau, melhor do que se espera *His new novel is not bad, but it lacks something.* ♦ *He's not so bad as a soccer player.*
too bad lamentável, uma pena *Too bad she had to leave so early.* ♦ *It's too bad that you weren't here last night.*
BAD-MOUTH [gir] falar mal de, difamar, caluniar, pichar ... *his mother bad-mouths me to him all the time ...* -JEP,241. ♦ *bad-mouthing the American worker ...* -T/92.
BAG bag and baggage [col] de mala e cuia ... *she was moving in with bag and baggage ...* -JEP,355.

hold the bag [col] sofrer as conseqüências, levar a culpa, pagar o pato *She left him holding the bag.* ♦ *... American taxpayers are holding the bag for $1.5 billion in bad loans [to Iraq].* -T/92.

in the bag [gir] garantido, concretizado, no papo *He told me to bet on number seven because the race was in the bag.*

mixed bag [col] grupo heterogêneo de pessoas, elementos, coisas, objetos etc.; um todo composto de partes nitidamente distintas, colcha de retalhos ... *a mixed bag of aristocrats, plebeians and Far-Eastern visitors at an English seaside resort.* -T/60. ♦ *... a mixed bag of songs ...* -T/67.

one's bag [col] a coisa que uma pessoa mais gosta de fazer; sua vocação, hobby etc., "a sua" *When he proposed, she said: "I'm not sure marriage is my bag".* ♦ *No matter what your bag is, he'll have it for you.* -CG,38.

overnight bag/case maleta para pequenas viagens *Did you happen to notice, Tony, that I have an overnight bag with me?* -AIM,156. ♦ *[Her handbag was] ... obviously very expensive and the size of a small overnight case.* -SEB,44.

BAIL   bail out 1. baldear (a água de um bote) *Let's start bailing out the boat or it will sink.* 2. soltar da cadeia sob fiança *He was arrested but his lawyer bailed him out next morning.* ♦ *Friends bailed her out of jail ...* -DDT,441. 3. [col] ajudar (em uma dificuldade, principalmente econômica), socorrer ... *the Bush Administration intends to help the Soviet Union ... bail out its economy.* -T/91. ⇒ **bailout** auxílio, socorro (principalmente em uma dificuldade econômica) ... *a $270 million bailout ... finally saved the day ...* -T/87. 4. saltar de pára-quedas ... *the wing [of the U-2 plane] came off and he [the pilot] bailed out.* -T/63. 5. abandonar uma situação ou posição incerta ou arriscada; safar-se, dar o fora *"If any of us had any sense", he said, "we'd all bail out now."* -T/75.

go bail pagar fiança *He had been arrested and had no one to go bail for him.*

jump bail fugir (o prisioneiro) ao se encontrar em liberdade sob fiança *He jumped bail and fled to Europe by way of Canada.*

(out) on bail (em liberdade) sob fiança *Searched and fingerprinted as a common criminal, [he was] then released on bail ...* -KRI,589. ♦ *He was out on bail in no time.*

put up bail = **go BAIL** *If she agrees to put up bail for you, you'll be out of jail immediately.*

BAKER   baker's dozen 1. dúzia de treze, treze unidades *She gave me a baker's dozen of eggs.* 2. um número pequeno, uns poucos, alguns, um punhado ... *a baker's dozen of crimes ranging from murder to rape ...* -T/69.

BALANCE   (be/hang) in the balance (estar/encontrar-se) em situação de incerteza ... *the life of ... [the] President-elect has hung in the balance.* -T/85.

keep//lose one's balance manter//perder o equilíbrio *The child couldn't keep his balance on the fence and fell to the ground.* ♦ *It's difficult not to lose your balance when you try to walk up an ice-covered hill.*

off balance 1. instável, sem equilíbrio, desestabilizado *Her method was to keep him continually off balance.* -SJE, 83. 2. despreparado, desprevenido *He tried to set his mind on a way to throw the Shoshonis [Indians] off balance.* -LJS,200.

on balance considerando-se todos os aspectos, detalhes etc., levando-se tudo em consideração ... *on balance he feels that the sacrifice is worthwhile.* -BL,viii. ♦ *... his new economic plan is, on balance, both wiser and more promising than his earlier efforts ...* -T/92.

strike a balance estabelecer um equilíbrio satisfatório (entre extremos) *They will have to strike a balance between their rights and their needs.*

tip/turn the balance/scales = tip the SCALE(S) 2 ... *in the South [of the U.S.] groups were formed to tip the balance in favor of slavery.* -SH,23.

BALL ball game 1. qualquer jogo realizado com uma bola *The ball game had already started when we arrived.* 2. [gir] série de circunstâncias, situação, conjuntura, estado de coisas *This is an entirely different ball game.*

ball of fire [gir] pessoa enérgica e arrojada, ativa, empreendedora *He's a real ball of fire, just what our staff needs.*

ball up [gir] tornar(-se) confuso, atrapalhado, desordenado *Now you've balled up the plan.* ♦ *He gets all balled up when he tries to make a speech in public.*

behind the eight ball [gir] em sinuca, em apuros *If this doesn't work out, you're apt to end up behind the eight ball.*

carry the ball [gir] arcar com a maior responsabilidade ou a parte mais difícil em um empreendimento, situação etc.), assumir o comando *Who's going to carry the ball on this project?* ♦ *I want you to carry the ball on this. You did a grand job on that speech – I think I can count on you.* -WSM,230.

drop/fumble the ball [gir] cometer um erro, dar uma mancada *He dropped the ball and everything was lost.* ♦ *It was the Soviets who fumbled the ball.* -T/86.

get on the ball [col] tornar-se mais alerta, eficiente; agir com competência e habilidade *Let's get on the ball, buddy.* -SJD,174.

get/start the ball rolling [col] iniciar o funcionamento, dar início à ação, começar (conversa, atividade etc.) *Let's get the ball rolling before it gets late.* ♦ *Who would like to start the ball rolling ... ?* -SJG,366.

have a ball [gir] divertir-se muito, farrear *They had a ball while the money their father had left them lasted.* ♦ *We went to her pad and had ourselves a ball.*

have a lot/enough/plenty/something etc. on the ball [gir] ser hábil, ágil, eficiente, inteligente; possuir uma qualidade, ter talento *He is sure to succeed as an actor because he has a lot on the ball.* ♦ *... he had something on the ball. At least part of the time he was entirely right.* -SV,116.

keep the ball rolling [col] manter o entusiasmo (da conversa ou da ação), manter o ritmo (de uma atividade) *As he left the meeting he told me to keep the ball rolling.*

on the ball [col] alerta, competente, hábil, eficiente, sagaz *That new employee is on the ball. Watch him handle the customers.*

play ball [col] 1. começar (qualquer atividade) *O.K. Let's play ball.* 2. cooperar *The Mafia was after him because he had refused to play ball.*

BALLPARK [col] aproximado, mais ou menos certo *How much money was transferred from the fund? Woodward was looking for a ballpark figure.* -BC,313. ♦ *... a ballpark guess ...* -T/77.

in the ballpark [col] aproximadamente correto, perto de (valor, cifra etc.) *... machinery credits in ways that will cost in the ball park of $5 billion a year ...* -T/92.

BALLPOINT ballpoint pen caneta esferográfica *[He was] ... taking occasional notes with a gold ballpoint pen.* -T/78.

BANANA banana republic [pej] republiqueta *People must think we have become a banana republic.* -T/84.

drive bananas [gir] deixar doido *Stop that noise! You're driving me bananas!*

go bananas [gir] enlouquecer, endoidecer *... he thought the President might "go bananas"...* -T/76. ♦ *... my parents went bananas ...* -EJP,327.

second banana [gir] 1. comediante secundário de um espetáculo *Now that he has won the award, he is no longer a second banana.* 2. qualquer pessoa que ocupa uma posição secundária, às vezes servil *... burdened as he is with the image of the eternal second banana.* -T/87.

top banana [gir] 1. comediante principal de um espetáculo *... Walter Matthau play-*

ing top banana on the set of Paramount's A New Leaf ... -T/69. 2. a pessoa mais importante de um grupo *The top banana of the establishment was one G. F. W. ...* -BM,26.

BAND band together aliar-se, unir-se ... *they banded together in co-operating groups ...* -LJ,158.

to beat the band/devil [gir] muitíssimo, exageradamente, velozmente, com grande energia e vigor, à beça, pra burro *The girls were giggling to beat the band.* ♦ *Promotion and advertising to beat the band.* ♦ *... my head still aches to beat the devil.* -SLT,69.

BANDWAGON climb/get/jump on the bandwagon [col] aderir a um partido, causa, movimento etc. que tem a preferência da maioria *[The senator] ... habitually a loner, hastened to climb on the bandwagon.* -T/60.

BANG bang away [col] 1. disparar (arma) continuamente; atacar com persistência *They banged away at him with rifles, burp guns and ... machine guns ...* -T/60. 2. trabalhar com afinco (especialmente numa máquina de datilografia), dedicar-se (a alguma coisa) com grande empenho *[She] ... began to bang away on the typewriter.* -RL,14.

bang out [col] produzir (principalmente datilografar) apressadamente *... a journalist can bang out a newspaper column ... in an average ... time of eleven minutes ...* -T/61.

bang up [col] danificar, destroçar *He banged up his new car on the first day on the highway.*

bang-up [col] de primeira, excelente, esplêndido *... he would pass a bangup week at Bill York's Lodge on Bald Mountain ...* -QE,61. ♦ *I should have ... had a bang-up affair with him and let things go at that.* -GE,116.

get a bang out of [gir] divertir-se muito com, obter viva emoção com *He gets a bang out of riding his Harley-Davidson motorcycle on the highway.*

not with a bang but a whimper não com estrondo, mas com um queixume (isto é, que chega ao fim não de maneira dramática, espetacular etc., mas inexpressivamente) *Borrowing the words from T. S. Eliot, we might perhaps say of the Soviet Union that this is the way it ended, "not with a bang but a whimper".*

with a bang [gir] com êxito, com entusiasmo, vigorosamente *[The President] ... hoped to end his tour with a bang ...* -T/66.

BANK bank on [col] confiar em, contar com *You know you can always bank on my being there when you need me.*

break the bank abafar a banca, ganhar todas as reservas do banqueiro (em jogos de azar) *Many gamblers hope to break the bank at Montecarlo.*

BANKROLL [col] financiar *[He] ... is now bankrolling a dozen Hungarian high school graduates each year to study at Oxford.* -T/87.

BAR bar none sem exceção *Kenneth Roberts'* Northwest Passage *is the best historical novel in American literature, bar none.* ♦ *You're the best bugler in this Regiment, bar none.* -JJF,10.

behind bars atrás das grades, na cadeia *[He] ... had spent 23 years behind bars ...* -T/92.

BAREBACK em pêlo, sem sela *[William Faulkner] ... could ride a horse bareback as no other Faulkner could ...* -T/63. ♦ *He's an excellent bareback rider.*

BAREFACED descarado, atrevido, indisfarçado, desavergonhado, deslavado *We caught him in a barefaced lie and won't ever believe him again.*

BAREFOOT descalço, de pés nus *When I was a little boy I liked to go barefoot during the summer.* ♦ *She went barefoot in the park.*

BARGAIN bargain basement seção de loja de departamentos que vende mercadorias a preços de oferta *... Macy's basement [is] one of the first bargain basements in U.S.*

retailing. -T/77. ⇒ **bargain-basement** muito reduzido, baratíssimo *In return for its friendship, Iran sells Syria oil at bargain-basement prices.* -T/87.
bargain for/on contar com, esperar, planejar *[The soldiers] ... are going to get a lot more action than they bargained for ...* -CHT,4. ♦ *My girl and I had planned to go out for a night on the town but we hadn't bargained on such a heavy rain.*
bargain hunter consumidor que procura preço barato *My wife has been a bargain hunter ever since I can remember.*
bargain price preço baratíssimo *They were selling the stolen merchandise at bargain prices.*
drive a (hard) bargain pechinchar em demasia; exigir condições especiais para si em uma negociação, acordo etc. *The old Yankee traders were famous for driving hard bargains.* ♦ *... he had been capable of driving as hard a bargain as any Soviet leader since Joseph Stalin.* -T/80.
in(to) the bargain de quebra, de lambujem, além disso, também *He was a talented pianist and a good singer into the bargain.*
strike a bargain chegar a um acordo, fazer negócio satisfatório a ambas as partes *I haggled with the salesman over the price of the car for a full fifteen minutes but we finally struck a bargain.*
BARGE barge in(to) [col] entrar com ímpeto, sem cerimônia, irromper, arrojar-se, lançar-se, intrometer-se em, interferir, interromper (conversa etc.) com rudeza *She barged in unexpectedly.* ♦ *Tom barged into the house noisily.* ♦ *He knew he couldn't just barge into the political race without assurance of support.* ♦ *He always barges in on any conversation without invitation.*
BARNSTORM 1. fazer turnê (companhia teatral) por cidades do interior exibindo-se em celeiros ou outros locais disponíveis *The theater group barnstormed all over New England.* 2. viajar por regiões rurais, fazendo campanha política ou promocional *... Teng [Chinese Communist leader] went barnstorming through four U.S. cities ...* -T/79.
BARRELL over a barrel [gir] indefeso, à mercê de *OK, I'll have to do it for you. You have me over a barrell.*
BASE not get to first base [gir] não se sair bem na fase inicial de um plano, ação, empreendimento etc., não ter um bom começo, fracassar *He couldn't get to first base with the new girl in the office.*
off base [gir] 1. enganado, equivocado, errado *... they were way off base ...* -BC,82. 2. desprevenido, em desvantagem; surpreendido *The surprise attack caught the enemy off base.*
BASH bash in [col] esmagar *[She]... was found floating in San Francisco Bay with her head bashed in.* -T/78.
BASKET basket case [gir] 1. pessoa que perdeu os quatro membros *He came back from Vietnam a basket case.* 2. pessoa cansada, consumida ou atingida por severa depressão e incapaz de cuidar de si mesma, um trapo; organização, país etc. em condição semelhante *She became a drug addict and wound up a basket case.* ♦ *Poland is an even worse basket case, plagued by perennial food shortages and a foreign debt of $27 billion.* -T/85.
BAT at bat empunhando o bastão, atuando como batedor (no beisebol) *Casey was at bat and doing a very good job of it.*
bat out [gir] criar ou compor rapidamente, datilografar com grande rapidez *My main interest is batting out shapely prose that will inform the reader.* -T/87. ♦ *With an old typewriter ... he batted out articles ...* -T/87.
go to bat for [col] ir em auxílio de, ajudar, defender *When an American businessman is in trouble, we go to bat for him.* -T/61.
have bats in the belfry [gir] ter macaquinhos no sótão, sofrer da bola *Pay no*

attention to what he says or does. He has bats in the belfry.
like a bat out of hell [gir] rapidamente, velozmente *I went down those stairs like a bat out of hell.* -CGT,179.
(right) off the bat/reel [col] imediatamente, sem perda de tempo, sem hesitação *She gave me the bad news right off the bat.* ♦ *Right off the reel he told us that we could not leave without a week's notice.*

BATTLE battle it out → **FIGHT it out**
battle royal luta generalizada; disputa acirrada *There were two pretenders to the throne and a veritabe battle royal ensued.* ♦ *[The two men were] ... Shultz's main adversaries in what he called a "battle royal"...* -T/87.
do/give battle dar combate, lutar *We must do battle with dragons guarding treasures and maidens ...* -KS,63. ♦ *They were ready to give battle to the enemy troops.*
half the battle cinqüenta por cento, a metade do sucesso, meio caminho andado, uma grande parte da tarefa *Getting there is half the battle. Then we'll have to find out where he lives.* ♦ *... I wake up at this same hour each morning ... Which is fine, but is only half the battle, for to wake up is one thing, and to get up quite another.* -OE,2.
losing battle luta sem possibilidade de vitória, batalha que não se pode vencer, esforço inútil *Doctors used heroic measures [to save a patient], but it looked like a losing battle.* -T/63. ♦ *... she felt that she fought a losing battle with ignorance and was overcome with a sense of futility and helplessness.* -MG,17.
pitched battle batalha campal; conflito generalizado, pancadaria *... the insurgents fought increasing numbers of pitched battles with the army ...* -T/85. ♦ *The students and the police had a pitched battle in front of the Washington Monument.*

BAWL OUT [gir] repreender, desancar, descompor, esculachar *The boss bawled him out for arriving late.*

BAY at bay acuado, imobilizado, encurralado, em xeque, mantido a distância, em situação de impotência *Some members of the opposition party supported the demonstration, and their influence kept the police at bay.* -LA,148. ♦ *For more than ten years he [Apache Indian chief Cochise] kept the U.S. Army at bay ...* -MJ,440. ♦ *He stood with his back against the wall holding the attackers at bay.*
bay window 1. janela saliente *It was an old house with two large bay windows.* 2. [gir] pança *Mr. Pickwick has developed a bay window.*
bring to bay encurralar, pôr cerco a, cortar as possibilidades de fuga *The Army of the Potomac had not yet brought its adversary to bay ...* -CB,408.

BE as is [col] no estado (em que algo se encontra), nas condições atuais *I'll sell you the camera as is, OK?*
as it is na realidade, no jeito em que as coisas estão, nas circunstâncias atuais *Don't bother me with your troubles. I've already got enough problems of my own as it is.*
as it were por assim dizer *... women, even in their supposed emancipation, have often been, as it were, prisoners of the male imagination.* -T/72.
as to be/appear/look/seem a ponto de parecer, que chega a parecer, como se fosse *... two flashing eyes, so deeply blue as to seem black.* -SLT,9. ♦ *... scholarship in our culture is so rare as to be highly exceptional.* -JW,12.
be around 1. estar em evidência, em atividade, em circulação, estar vivo *... he looked like he'd be around for a hundred years.* -HA,272. v. **HAVE been around** 2. estar próximo, por perto, à mão, disponível *Tinted contact lenses that make blue eyes appear even bluer have been around for several years.* -T/87.
here you are aqui está (aquilo que você pediu ou quer, aquilo que você está pro-

curando) *When the ticket agent at San Francisco Airport asked for my ticket I said: "Here you are."*.
so be it assim seja *If she insists on helping him, so be it.*
BE-IN [col] reunião pública de caráter informal na qual as pessoas exprimem amor, felicidade etc. ... *loosely programmed outdoor chapel meetings known here and there as love-ins, be-ins or demonstrations* ... -T/87.
BEACH on the beach [gir] desempregado, sem recursos, na pindaíba *He had gone to Hawaii expecting to be a great success but wound up on the beach.*
BEAD draw a bead on [col] 1. apontar para, fazer pontaria sobre *I took the rifle and drew a bead on the shark.* -RQ,69. ♦ *[The detective was] ... drawing a bead on him [a drug pusher] with a .38 special.* -BRF,32. 2. criticar ... *they were drawing beads on more and more of the alleged cultural media every year.* -SEB,129.
BEAM on//off the beam [gir] funcionando bem, alerta, correto, na marca, na mosca//funcionando mal, incorreto, errado, enganado *She's always on the beam.* ♦ *He was off the beam when he said that.*
BEAN full of beans [gir] cheio de energia e vitalidade *The little boy was full of beans and gave his teachers a lot of trouble.*
not know beans about [gir] não entender nada de, desconhecer completamente *Neither he nor his partner knew beans about the restaurant business.*
spill the beans [gir] revelar um segredo (estragando plano, surpresa etc.) *Now that you know the whole story, don't spill the beans.*
BEAR bear down 1. vencer, derrotar *The soldiers bore down all opposition.* 2. exercer pressão, força ... *the twister [tornado] was bearing down at about 70 m.p.h.* ... -T/79.
bear down on/upon 1. aproximar-se de, ir na direção de ... *a police squad car* ... *was bearing down on him.* -WI,227. 2. arremessar-se sobre, investir contra, abater-se sobre, atacar, punir *The soldiers bore down upon the enemy.* ♦ *The hot desert sun bore down on the men* ... -CHT,121. 3. pressionar, esforçar-se, dar toda a atenção a ... *the President is considering ways to bear down harder on his team and improve performance.* -T/79. ♦ *He majored in architecture, minored in physics, bore down heavily on history* ... -T/63. 4. pesar sobre, oprimir, preocupar, inquietar *His responsibility as a father and family man bears down on him.*
bear hug abraço apertado *[He greeted friends and] ... a number of onetime adversaries with handshakes and bear hugs.* -T/77.
bear out apoiar, comprovar, corroborar *I'm sure you will bear me out when I say that our product is of the best quality.* ♦ *His answer simply bears out what I had suspected.*
bear up conservar a coragem, suportar os reveses, manter-se firme *During her husband's funeral, though she looked tense and old and tired, she managed to bear up well.*
bear with ser paciente com, ter condescendência com, tolerar *I can't bear with you another minute. Pack your things and get out, now!* -WR,60.
loaded for bear [gir] preparado para lutar, preparado para qualquer emergência *You must be loaded for bear when you decide to attack that city.*
teddy bear ursinho de brinquedo *Children love teddy bears.*
BEARING get//lose one's bearings orientar-se//desorientar-se *He stood a moment on the sidewalk, getting his bearings.* -SEB, 42. ♦ ... *Khrushchev sounded like a man who had lost his strategic bearings* ... -T/60. ♦ *I intend no pun, but I think Mr. Timken has lost his bearings.*
have a//no bearing on/upon ter//não ter relação com, influir//não influir, vir//não

vir ao caso *Nearly all fields of the biological sciences have a bearing on paleontology.* -SR,14. ♦ *The evidence had no bearing on the case.*
take one's bearings = **get one's BEARINGS** *I could see that he was cooly and deliberately taking his bearings ...* -UJ,74.
BEAT beat back rechaçar, repelir, fazer recuar *[He] ... beat back an attempted Communist coup ...* -T/78.
beat down 1. pechinchar para obter um preço mais baixo *I don't think he's ever bought a single thing without trying to beat the price down.* -MG,400. 2. tentar reduzir, tornar menor, fazer baixar *... the U.S. can only return to economic health once it has beaten down its still dangerous inflation.* -T/80. 3. incidir com violência, cair sobre, projetar seu calor intenso (o sol) *It was noon and the hot sun beat down from overhead.* -SSG,6. 4. derrotar, destruir, suprimir *... he beat down enemies of his plan ...* -T/61. ♦ *The enemy was thoroughly beaten down.*
beat it [gir] dar o fora, retirar-se, sumir-se *The older boys always told the young kids to beat it when they began to tell dirty jokes.* ♦ *Beat it! We don't want you around.*
beat off rechaçar, expulsar, repelir *[He] ... beat off a German attack.* -T/72. ♦ *The country beat off a takeover by the Communist party.* ♦ *... the company beat off a rival bid ...* -T/87.
beat one [gir] intrigar, deixar perplexo, confundir *It beats me how he managed to get away from the police.*
beat out 1. fazer soar (batendo em tambor etc.) *... a lively band beat out a variety of tunes ...* -T/78. ♦ *He beat out the rhythm on a drum.* 2. superar, derrotar *... some of the imitations ... beat out the original.* -T/87. ♦ *She beat out another star for the lead part in that movie.*
beat up surrar, espancar *He was beat up when he resisted arrest.* ♦ *[He] ... may beat his wife up as often as he can catch her ...* -GD,208. ⇒ **beat-up** [col] estragado, arruinado, em péssimo estado *... they owned a couple of beat-up old boats ...* -RE,44. ♦ *a beat-up car*
beat up on [gir] 1. surrar *I'll beat up on you if you do that again.* 2. desancar, espinafrar *[The man] ... who used to beat up on the Democratic Party just four years ago, no longer seems angry.* -T/87.
hear/see the beat of [col] ver/conhecer alguém/algo que seja melhor que, superior a [geralmente neg. e int.] *I never saw the beat of you.* -SCD,9. ♦ *Did you ever see the beat of her? ... she sure is funny.* -LRT,42.
BEAUTY beauty parlor salão de beleza *She works in a beauty parlor down the street.*
beauty sleep [col] sono reparador (iniciado antes da meia-noite) *Well, good night. It's time to get my beauty sleep.*
BEAVER eager beaver [gir] indivíduo extremamente zeloso em seu trabalho ou deveres, caxias *[He] ... was the most trusted of Haldeman's eager beavers.* -BC,178. ♦ *His classmates don't like him because he's such an eager beaver.*
BECK at someone's beck and call à disposição de, às ordens de *People always like a man that's kind, comes at beck and call, and asks nothing.* -HET,446. ♦ *He's always waiting at her beck and call.*
BECOME become of acontecer a, suceder a, ser feito de *I have often wondered what ever became of Rhett Butler and Scarlett O'Hara after he walked out on her.*
BED bed and board cama e mesa *When you go to Europe try to find a pension that gives you bed and board.*
bed down deitar-se, ir para a cama, arranjar lugar para dormir *... you can bed down here tonight.* -SJS,5. ♦ *We decided to bed down under the trees.* ♦ *A traveler who finally beds down in a Moscow hotel after six days on the rails ...* -T/87.

bed of roses mar de rosas, paraíso *A soldier's life is no bed of roses.*
get into bed deitar-se, ir para a cama *I told him to get into bed and get some sleep.*
go to bed deitar-se, recolher-se, ir dormir *She usually goes to bed at eleven-thirty.*
go to bed with the chickens [col] deitar-se com as galinhas, recolher-se muito cedo *My brother used to go to bed with the chickens but always got up just before dawn.*
make one's bed and lie in/on it praticar um ato impróprio e sofrer as conseqüências *I told you to be careful but you wouldn't listen. Well, you've made your bed and now you must lie in it.*
put to bed pôr na cama *Little children must be put to bed early.*
take to one's bed ficar acamado *[He] ... developed an intestinal virus and had to take to his bed.* -SEB,122.
BEDFELLOW strange bedfellows pessoas ou coisas muito diferentes que as circunstâncias freqüentemente põem em contato ou em cooperação e que, de outra maneira, nunca se relacionariam *... politics makes strange bedfellows.* -T/76. ♦ *In The Tempest, Shakespeare says that "misery acquaints a man with strange bedfellows".*
BEDRIDDEN acamado *... he had been bedridden for six weeks while suffering with bronchopneumonia ...* -WD,99.
BEE (as) busy as a bee ocupadíssimo *I'm sorry that I can't help you now. I'm (as) busy as a bee.*
have a bee in one's bonnet [col] ter uma idéia fixa, uma obsessão *She has a bee in her bonnet about cleanliness and punctuality.*
BEEF beef up [gir] fortalecer, reforçar, robustecer *[He] ... beefed up his police force with more men and riot equipment ...* -T/66. ♦ *Security is being beefed up with the addition of more guards.* -T/87.

BEELINE make a beeline [col] tomar o caminho mais curto (para), ir em linha reta (para) *... he started to make a beeline for the door ...* -SJD,102. ♦ *The pursued animal made a beeline for its hole in the rocks.*
BEER beer and skittles divertimento, prazer, boa vida, sombra e água fresca [geralmente neg] *In her candid autobiography she says that being a movie star is not all beer and skittles.*
BEG beg off excusar-se (de um compromisso, promessa etc.), pedir para ser dispensado *[The Shah of Iran] ... had asked to call on Jordan's King Hussein, but the King had begged off, explaining that the Shah's presence would create too much dissension.* -T/79.
BEGGAR beggars can't be choosers pé de pobre não tem tamanho, a cavalo dado não se olham os dentes *Beggars can't be choosers, so you'd better take the job he's offering you.*
BEGIN begin to [em orações negativas ou interrogativas] ser muito difícil, estar longe de, quase não poder, quase não conseguir *... their intelligence was so low that they not only couldn't grasp my questions, but didn't even begin to understand their own motivations.* -SJSN,14. ♦ *We cannot even begin to say how much of our drinking water ... may have been contaminated.* -T/80.
to begin with primeiramente, em primeiro lugar, antes de mais nada *At least to begin with, Lenin put the cause of worldwide revolution ahead of any one nation's self-interest.* -T/64.
BEHALF in/on behalf of em nome de, no interesse de, a favor de, em defesa de, em benefício de *... I was called as a witness in my own behalf.* -BL,152. ♦ *[He] ... spoke in Schlesinger's behalf ...* -T/76. ♦ *I speak to you on behalf of your sister ...* -CTT,41.
BEHAVIOR on one's best behavior na mais bem-comportada das atitudes *Lee*

had been on his best behavior lately. -MW,157. ♦ *Western observers had a close look at Soviet justice on its best behavior* ... -T/87.

BEHEST at someone's behest por ordem de, a mando de ... *he made his appeal at the behest of [the Admiral]* ... -T/86.

BEHIND-THE-SCENES → behind the SCENES

BEHOOVE it behooves compete a, cabe a, é da alçada de *It behooves all physicians to be on the lookout for any influenza patient whose condition suddenly worsens.* -T/87.

BEING come into being/existence começar a existir, vir a ser, nascer ... *we do not know when, where, or by whom language came into being.* -LCT,23. ♦ *We don't know how the world came into existence.*

BELIEF cherished beliefs crenças tradicionais ... *our most cherished beliefs are matters of opinion* ... -MHJ,47.

BELL ring a bell [col] trazer à lembrança, fazer lembrar *Your name seems to ring a bell. Haven't we met before?* ♦ *When asked about the girl, he said, "I can't exactly place her, but the name does ring a bell.".* -T/73.

ring the bell [col] servir exatamente, ter bom resultado, obter aprovação, alcançar sucesso *That rings the bell. It is just the kind of boat I've been looking for.*

(as) sound as a bell [col] muito bem de saúde; em perfeitas condições *I feel as sound as a bell.*

BELLYFUL have a bellyful [gir] estar farto de, ter experimentado mais que o suficiente de algo, da companhia de alguém etc. *I've had a bellyful of you and your silly ideas.*

BELONG ter seu lugar apropriado (em), formar parte (de), ser próprio (de) *Who wants media censorship? That belongs in a dictatorship.* -T/85. ♦ *Go back to that place where you belong!*

BELT belt down [gir] beber, entornar *He poured himself a drink with trem-*bling hands and belted it down quickly. -NE,387.

belt out [gir] cantar dando grande potência à voz, cantar com voz bem alta *Don't just belt out a song, because that's impersonal* ... -HA,36.

black belt comunidade negra, área onde vivem muitos negros *[Presidential candidate Bill Clinton] ... carries [i.e., has the majority of votes of] the black belt easily, with more than 90% of the African-American vote, in every election.* -T/92.
v. BIBLE Belt; CORN belt; COTTON belt; FARM belt; Sunbelt

hit below the belt [col] aplicar um golpe baixo, ser desleal *When he used my wife's past to injure me politically, he was really hitting below the belt.*

pull in one's belt [col] apertar o cinto, economizar, reduzir as despesas *We will have to pull in our belts if we want to survive this economic crisis.*

red-light belt → red-light DISTRICT

tighten one's belt = pull in one's BELT ... *instead of tightening their belts, Israelis have gone on a buying binge* ... -T/84. ⇒ **belt-tightening** comedido nos gastos, regrado ... *a belt-tightening program* ... -T/84.

under one's belt [col] em sua posse, em seu currículo, em sua experiência, como suas qualificações *[Beginning actor James] Cagney only had three pictures under his belt [when Warner Brothers gave him the lead in* The Public Enemy*].* -BAJ,24.

BENCH bench mark referência de nível; ponto de referência a partir do qual se podem fazer medições ou avaliações; padrão de referência ... *the prime rate remains the bench mark by which most people measure the cost of credit.* -T/81. ♦ *... Roots [a 1977 TV series is] a potentially important bench mark in U.S. race relations.* -T/77.

BEND around the bend louco, doido, furioso, enraivecido *If she annoyed her* *parents ... with her debut novel ... she's sure to send them around the bend with her second book ...* -T/89. ♦ *Take it easy, Jim. Don't go around the bend now.* -KJ,11.

bend/lean over backward(s) [col] fazer grande esforço (no sentido de agradar, não cometer um erro, ou uma injustiça etc.) *The Army is leaning over backward to be fair to these men.* -NE,51. ♦ *... liberal churchmen have been bending over backward to avoid criticizing the film ...* -T/88.

BENDER on a bender [gir] "de porre" *[He] ... went on a bender with his wife.* -T/63. ♦ *Louie was on a bender last night and couldn't find his way home.*

BENEATH beneath one indigno de, inapropriado para, abaixo da dignidade de *... there was a time when figures like Edmund Wilson and Mark Van Doren did not consider it beneath them to comment on Disney creations.* -T/73.

BENEFIT give someone the benefit of the doubt supor que alguém é inocente, que esteja dizendo a verdade etc., quando não há prova em contrário *Some legal experts say that white jurors are often inclined to give police the benefit of the doubt in cases involving brutality ...* -T/92.

BENT bent on/upon disposto a, decidido a *The terrorists were bent on destroying the plane on the field.* ♦ *... the rapist [was] bent on another attack ...* -T/81.

BERRY (as) brown as a berry bronzeado, queimado pelo sol *The boy returned from his vacation at the beach as brown as a berry.*

BERTH give a wide berth to evitar, guardar distância de, esquivar-se ao encontro com *Victorio and Delshay [Apache Indian chiefs] distrusted the white intruders and gave them a wide berth.* -BD,11.

BESIDE beside oneself desvairado, fora de si *Utterly beside himself, he reached for his gun.* -LB,11. ♦ *She was beside herself with anger ...* -JEP,160.

BEST as best one can da melhor maneira possível *He packed all his clothes as best he could.* ♦ *... his only possible course of action was to play the part of ... [the other man] as best he could.* -HEB,25.

at best na melhor das hipóteses, se tanto, quando muito *... the lay person ... at best can hope to have only a very general awareness of how his body works.* -SEE,xvii. ♦ *... the central government's efforts ... have been halfhearted at best.* -T/92.

at one's/its best no apogeu, no maior prestígio, forma, condição etc. *Alan Ladd was at his very best when he played the hero in Shane.* ♦ *Hemingway's indirect way of narration is at its best in his short stories...* -HL, 205.

do one's (level/very) best fazer o melhor possível, fazer tudo o que estiver ao alcance, esforçar-se ao máximo *... he did his level best to incite another crisis.* -T/63. ♦ *She did her best to locate the missing document.*

(all) for the best para um bem ulterior, visando ao melhor dos resultados, com a melhor das intenções *Under the circumstances, it will be all for the best if you get a divorce.* ♦ *... it was perhaps for the best that he was away so much.* -HA,15.

get/have the best of levar vantagem sobre, levar a melhor, superar, vencer, derrotar *... his nervousness was getting the best of him ...* -HEB,8. ♦ *Whenever my son and I play chess, no matter how hard I try, he always has the best of it.*

get/have/make the best of both worlds fruir dois benefícios, duas vantagens de aspectos diferentes sem nenhuma desvantagem *... Japanese businessmen concede that they are trying to get the best of both worlds: improved relations with North Korea in a way that would not greatly damage their commercial and political links with Seoul.* -T/72.

hope for the best esperar que o melhor aconteça, que o resultado seja bom *Let's do all we can and hope for the best.*

look one's best apresentar-se da melhor maneira possível *I want to look my best when I meet her again.*

make the best of a bad bargain/job/it/ something fazer o melhor possível em circunstâncias desfavoráveis com aquilo que se tem à disposição, aceitar as limitações de uma situação, conformar-se *Looking back over his first 3 ½ months on the job ... [he] thinks that he has made the best of a bad situation ...* -T/73. ♦ *You may not like this state of affairs, but you must make the best of it.* ♦ *What is done cannot be undone. All you can do now is to make the best of a bad bargain.*
to the best of one's ability da melhor maneira possível *I'll try to carry out my duties to the best of my ability.*
to the best of one's belief segundo se acredita *To the best of my belief, that island has never been visited by a white man.*
to the best of one's knowledge; to one's knowledge segundo consta, até onde se sabe *To the best of our knowledge, Democritus was the first to think of the atom.* -HHO,20. ♦ *The data on [Brazilian] population by color and on occupation and color from the 1960 census, to my knowledge, is not available.* -WC,124.
to the best of one's recollection se a memória não falha *To the best of my recollection, I last saw her five years ago.*
with the best (of them) tão bem quanto qualquer um, igual aos melhores *He could sight-read [written music] with the best ...* -T/92.
BEST-SELLER mercadoria, artigo, especialmente livro, que alcança grande vendagem *Frederick Forsyth's* The Day of the Jackal *was a best-seller for many weeks.* ⇒ **best-selling** de grande vendagem, muito popular *Sidney Sheldon and Milan Kundera are best-selling authors.* ♦ *a best-selling novel*
BET best bet [col] a melhor escolha, a melhor possibilidade ou probabilidade, a coisa mais provável *... a system of free and open trade remains the best bet for global prosperity.* -T/92.

safe bet [col] certeza, coisa de sucesso certo *In an inflated economy, there is no safe bet in trying to invest your money.*
you bet! Pode apostar! Não tenha dúvida! Esteja certo! *When he asked me if I could do the job, I said: "You bet!".*
BETTER all the better melhor ainda, muito melhor *If she comes on Wednesday it will be all the better for us.*
better off em melhor situação financeira; mais feliz, mais confortável, mais seguro etc. *... the Russians are better off today than ever before.* -T/67. ♦ *Between the ages of forty and fifty ... most of us are better off with reading glasses.* -BN,17. ♦ *You're better off without him, believe me.* v. **WELL-off**
better than mais de *It's better than five miles to the river.* ♦ *In the movie* Violent Saturday, *Lee Marvin says about his former wife: "I caught better than fifty colds from that broad [woman]".*
for better or (for) worse bem ou mal, seja qual for o resultado *... for better or worse, our feelings often condition our thinking.* -VC,4.
for the better//worse para melhor//pior *... an old man who has seen the whole world change – and not for the better.* -CT,15. ♦ *The already delicate relationship between the press and politicians changed profoundly, and probably for the worse ...* -T/87.
get/have the better of levar a melhor a, levar vantagem sobre, sobrepujar *Anger got the better of the Corporal in that instant and he started to backhand Wladislaw's face.* -NE,404. ♦ *My wife always gets the better of me in an argument.*
BETWIXT betwixt and between em uma posição intermediária, entre um e outro, nem uma coisa nem outra *When he asked me whether I was a liberal or a leftist I replied jokingly: "Something betwixt and between".*
BEYOND beyond one além da capacidade de compreensão de *Why ... [he] can do*

something in five minutes that the CIA cannot do in two days is beyond me ... -T/87. ♦ How can space ever end? The riddle is beyond us. -MRMT,10.

BIBLE Bible Belt regiões do sul dos EUA onde predomina o fundamentalismo cristão *In 1925, in a Bible Belt town in Tennessee, a biology teacher was arrested for breaking a state law against teaching Darwin's theory of evolution.*

BID bid fair to dar esperanças, oferecer probabilidade de, prometer *... Mohammed's revelation burst upon the world in 622 A.D., and through the following millenium bade fair to become the ultimate religion of mankind ...* -CJM,5. ♦ *As a politician ... [he] already bids fair to become the most powerful Democrat in the nation's second most populous state.* -T/61.

make a bid for fazer um esforço, uma tentativa (para atingir um objetivo) *She was the first woman to make a bid for the position of Prime Minister.*

BIDDING at someone's bidding por ordem de *We are only doing this at his bidding.*

do someone's bidding obedecer a, cumprir as ordens de *They do his bidding without question.* ♦ *... radicals that stand ready to do the Ayatullah's [religious leader of Iran] bidding.* -T/87.

BIG-GAME → big GAME
BIGGER-THAN-LIFE → **larger than LIFE**
BIGMOUTHED → **have a big MOUTH**
BIG-TICKET [col] caro, dispendioso, de alto preço *The Israeli arms industry is pinning its hopes on two big-ticket items.* -T/84.

BIG-TIME → big TIME
BIGWIG [gir] = **big SHOT** *The company's bigwigs hurried into the conference room.* ♦ *... he was a political bigwig in the area ...* -WI,247.

BILL fazer promoção, anunciar em público (em cartazes etc.), apregoar, divulgar *Clark Gable was billed as the only actor who had enough aplomb and sex appeal to play the part of Rhett Butler in* Gone With the Wind.

a clean bill of health 1. relatório ou declaração de médico que atesta o estado saudável do paciente, atestado de saúde *He was given a clean bill of health by the examining doctors.* 2. [col] isenção de culpa, parecer favorável, aprovação (principalmente após investigação, exame etc.) *The police gave him a clean bill of health, so he's no longer a suspect in the murder case.*

fill/fit the bill [col] preencher os requisitos, estar à altura da situação, dar conta do recado, ser apropriado *Do you suppose the new football coach will fill the bill?* ♦ *This piece of tough plastic fits the bill as a replacement for the broken windowpane.*

foot the bill [col] pagar a conta, arcar com as despesas *He put an announcement in the newspaper that he would no longer foot his wife's bills.* ♦ *... he's the one who foots the bills.* -BH,101.

sell someone a bill of goods [col] ludibriar, fraudar, engabelar, vender gato por lebre *It is the commonest technique of propaganda to use symbols ... to sell the public a bill of goods by exploiting already established values regarding "good" and "bad".* -CH,17.

BILLING top billing o nome que aparece em primeiro lugar na relação de atores (em filme, peça teatral, show etc.), papel principal *[James] Stewart, with top billing [in* Two Rode Together*], played a ... frankly mercenary frontier sheriff ...* -TH,114.

BIND double bind situação ou problema que apresenta duas saídas igualmente indesejáveis, dilema *... farmers in those states will face a double bind of low prices and small harvests ...* -T/86. ♦ *... double-bind situations lead to the more serious "confusion" of insanity, and especially schizophrenia.* -WA,144.

in a bind [col] em aperto, em dificuldades, em apuros *He found himself in a* very serious financial bind when the stock market crashed.

BINGE [col] 1. bebedeira *He has been on a binge since he lost his job.* 2. esbanjamento, prodigalidade, gastos exagerados (com compras etc.); algo em que não há moderação ... *Israelis went on a buying binge with their new foreign cash, and inflation went skyward.* -T/92.

BIRD the birds and the bees [col] educação sexual básica *When parents tell their children about the birds and the bees, they leave out the information that the male bee always dies after making love.* -T/63.

bird in (the) hand (mais vale um) pássaro na mão (que dois voando) *They say that a bird in hand is worth two in the bush.*

birds of a feather indivíduos da mesma laia, farinha do mesmo saco, vinho da mesma pipa [geralmente na expressão **birds of a feather flock together**, i.e., cada qual com seu igual, pessoas da mesma categoria estão sempre juntas – sentido freqüentemente depreciativo] *Kinsey, Rabelais and Boccaccio are birds of a feather [i.e., they have a deep interest in the sexual behavior of people]* ... -GD,287. ♦ *So he has gone into partnership with his good-for-nothing cousin! Well, I'm not surprised. Birds of a feather flock together.*

early bird [col] pessoa que se levanta ou chega cedo, madrugador *Ma Kettle was an early bird, always up with the sun.* ♦ *Whenever there is a big sale at that store, my mother is always one of the early birds in line.*

the early bird catches the worm Deus ajuda a quem cedo madruga *Be sure that you talk to Mr. Simpson about that job first thing in the morning. Remember what they say, "It's the early bird that catches the worm".*

eat like a bird lambiscar, debicar, comer muito pouco *In the movie* Psycho, *there is a scene in which Norman Bates says that to eat like a bird is an inaccurate expression, because birds really do eat very much.*

(strictly) for the birds [gir] inútil, inaceitável, improvável, desprezível, insignificante, sem valor, ridículo *Being a public prosecutor was perhaps the best trial training a young lawyer could get ... but as a career it was strictly for the birds.* -TR,17.
♦ *That story is strictly for the birds.*

give the bird [gir] vaiar, ridicularizar *They gave him the bird when he began his speech.*

kill two birds with one stone matar dois coelhos de uma cajadada *We can kill two birds with one stone by testing our new car on a trip to Rio and seeing Carnival at the same time.*

a little bird told me um passarinho me contou (i.e., alguém cujo nome não digo revelou-me um segredo) *"How did you know that?" "A little bird told me."*

bird's-eye view 1. perspectiva aérea, vista do alto *From the top of the Empire State Building you get a bird's-eye view of New York.* ♦ 2. visão de conjunto, resumo *Read each chapter of the book in a cursory way first, so that you get a bird's-eye view of it.*

BIRTH give birth dar à luz *On the night of June 7, Flora gave birth to the twins Victor and Paul.*

BIRTHDAY in one's birthday suit [col] nu *The police arrested three people for bathing in the park fountain in their birthday suits.*

BIT a bit um tanto, um pouco, um pouquinho *I feel a bit tired today.* ♦ *... he was really a good actor, and a bit of a con man ...* -JEP,327.

bit by bit gradualmente, pouco a pouco *We watched the river wash away the planted fields bit by bit.* ♦ *... bit by bit ... [he] produced the evidence that finally sent [the other man] to jail ...* -T/61.

bits and pieces [col] miudezas, coisas pequenas, miscelânea, fragmentos, retalhos *What little education he has came*

in bits and pieces; he has missed so much school he'll have to repeat his present school year. -T/92.
champ/chomp at the bit [col] estar impaciente para iniciar uma atividade *A generation of young Americans is chomping at the bit wanting to carry the flag into space.* -T/81.
do one's bit fazer a sua parte, dar a sua contribuição *I've done my bit. Now you must do yours.*
every bit inteiramente, totalmente, exatamente como, igualmente *... the Democrats are keenly aware that a black vote counts every bit as much as a white one ...* -T/76. ♦ *The Godfather, Part II was every bit as compelling as Part I .*
four bits [gír] 50 centavos de dólar *What can you possibly buy with four bits these days?*
not a bit; not the least bit [col] de forma alguma, nem um pouco *"Are you ready for lunch?" "I'm not a bit hungry."* ♦ *I'm not the least bit interested in what our so-called friends might think.* -GE,118.
take the bit into one's mouth; take/get the bit in one's teeth rebelar-se, tomar as rédeas nas mãos, assumir o controle, agir por conta própria *Mr. Trumbell is a forceful man when he takes the bit in his teeth.* -OFW,41. ♦ *He took the bit into his mouth and drove into his new project.*
two bits [gír] 25 centavos de dólar *I can remember when two bits would take you to a movie, but nowadays twenty-five cents won't buy much.* ⇒ **two-bit** insignificante, inferior, medíocre *a two-bit politician* ♦ *a two-bit gangster* ♦ *... two-bit producers and distributors [of motion pictures] ...* -T/84.
a wee bit um pouquinho, um mínimo *He is a physicist in the tradition of Galileo and Fermi, with only a wee bit of Machiavelli thrown in.* -T/87.
BITE **be bitten by** entusiasmar-se por, deixar-se tomar por *She was bitten by a desire to be a fashion designer.*

bite off 1. cortar com os dentes, decepar com uma dentada ou mordida *The dog bit off the tip of Tom's forefinger.* 2. arrancar, arrebatar, tirar à força *... it is Serbia's determination to bite off parts of the other republics [in former Yugoslavia] peopled by Serbs that keeps the war going.* -T/92.
bite off more than one can chew [col] tentar abarcar o mundo com as pernas, subestimar as dificuldades *When you went after that contract, you bit off more than you can chew. That business belongs to Ajaax.* -HWR,68. ♦ *He bit off more than he could chew when he challenged the champion.*
get/grab/have a bite to eat fazer uma refeição leve, tomar um lanche, fazer uma boquinha [col] *He likes to have a bite to eat every night after the show is over.* ♦ *[We] ... all went to get a bite to eat, as we often did ...* -HA,17. ♦ *Let's go back to the hotel's café and grab a bite to eat.*
have a (quick) bite [col] = **get a BITE to eat** *... he could have a quick bite somewhere and go to his office ...* -SEB,143.
I'll bite estou preparado, pronto (para o resto da história ou da pergunta), consinto em ser a vítima da piada, admito que não consigo adivinhar o resto (do que você tem para contar) [diz-se em resposta a uma pergunta capciosa] *"Do you know what the elephant said to the ant?" "OK, I'll bite. What did he say?"*
once bitten, twice shy gato escaldado tem medo de água fria *You can be sure he'll never do that again. You know, once bitten, twice shy.* ♦ *"Once bitten, twice shy", goes the old saying ...* -T/92.
put the bite on [gír] dar uma facada em, pedir dinheiro emprestado a *He put the bite on me for twenty dollars.* ♦ *He's always putting the bite on his friends.*
BLACK **black and blue** com equimoses, cheio de contusões *Did you get a good look at her? She's black and blue from head to foot.* -LRW,106.

black and white preto e branco (fotografia, filme, televisão etc.) *The movie Schindler's List was beautifully photographed in black and white.* ⇒ **black-and-white** 1. em preto e branco (fotografia, filme, televisão etc.) *black-and-white movies* ♦ *black-and-white television* 2. que só admite dois valores, dois princípios, dois lados (como bem-mal, certo-errado etc.), maniqueísta *... no philosophy that reduces [certain things] ... to black-and-white simplicities is being faithful to the integral human vision.* -WP,13.

black out 1. escurecer, privar de luz *The city was blacked out during the air raid.* ♦ *Manila was blacked out by a power failure.* -T/86. ⇒ **blackout** escurecimento produzido por falta de energia elétrica, blecaute, apagão; cessação total de operações em um sistema de comunicações *Two power blackouts cut off electricity for 100,000 people ...* -T/78. ♦ *... a computer blackout.* -T/84. 2. perder temporariamente a consciência ou a visão, apagar, desmaiar; perder temporariamente a memória *He hit me on the head and I blacked out.* ♦ *... maybe he had blacked out and didn't remember a thing.* -TR,60. ⇒ **blackout** perda temporária de consciência, visão ou memória *He seems to have had another blackout shortly after he left his apartment.* 3. impedir a divulgação de informação ou comunicação, censurar ... *the central government in Peking reacted with total silence, blacking out all news of the protests.* -T/87. ⇒ **blackout** proibição de divulgação de notícias ... *he then imposed a blackout on all official comment.* -T/88.

in black and white preto no branco, por escrito *Let's put our agreement in black and white.*

in the black [col] sem dívida, com ativo superior ao passivo, solvente, em boa situação financeira *[The company] ... lost about $50 million ... and today is nearly in the black.* -T/85. v. **in the RED**

not as black as one is painted não é tão feio ou mau quanto dizem *He has a bad reputation as a businessman, but he is really not as black as he is painted.*

BLACK-AND-WHITE → **BLACK and white**

BLACKLIST 1. lista negra *Many American companies are on the Arab blacklist because they have done business with Israel.* 2. colocar em lista negra *He was blacklisted by the leading Hollywood producers in the late forties.* ♦ *In the 1950s, he fought against the blacklisting of supposed Hollywood Communists ...* -T/67.

BLAH [gir] apático, sem vida, sem interesse, medíocre ... *a built-in sense about clients ... lets me know whether they're going to be interesting or blah ...* -AK,200.

BLAHS [gir] sensação de apatia, tédio, insatisfação, desagrado, desalento *I get the morning-after blahs when I drink too much at a party.*

BLAME be to blame merecer censura, ser culpado (de), ser responsável (por) *Who's to blame for the accident?* ♦ *... he denied in a firm voice that he was directly to blame for the death of any plant workers.* -T/87.

blame it on [col] pôr a culpa em *You've made a mess of everything we ever had between us, and now you want to blame it on me.* -SEB,162.

blame one for culpar alguém de, responsabilizar por *They have blamed him for the crime.*

shoulder the blame assumir a responsabilidade, a culpa *He had to shoulder the blame when his wife threw rocks through the British Embassy windows.*

BLANK blank out apagar, riscar, obliterar *Some of the words in the text had been blanked out.* ♦ *Much of his past is permanently blanked out ...* -T/92.

draw a blank [col] 1. obter resultado negativo, não conseguir o que se deseja ou se procura *I have tried to grow orchids but I always draw a blank.* 2. não conseguir lembrar-se de *He tried to remember the name of the small town his sister had mentioned on the phone but kept drawing a blank.*

BLANKET coletivo, amplo, lato, de grande alcance, que abrange tudo *He has a blanket policy on his car, including even hurricane damage.* ♦ *He was given a blanket endorsement by the Senate.*

wet blanket [col] 1. coisa que provoca desencorajamento, desânimo *They threw a wet blanket over our plans.* 2. desmancha-prazeres *Melinda is a wet blanket at any party she goes to.*

BLARE blare out soar com força, emitir som alto, bradar *... he could pretend he was slightly deaf and not hear the ... music the radio was blaring out.* -SCD,12. ♦ *A female voice blared out ...* -WJT,164.

BLAST blast off levantar do solo, iniciar vôo, deixar a plataforma de lançamento *... mighty ... rockets blasting off ...* -T/87. ♦ *The movie [2010 is], about a U.S.-Soviet astronaut team that blasts off to investigate a series of mysterious events at one of Jupiter's moons ...* -T/84. ⇒ **blast-off** lançamento de foguete ou míssil *Four seconds before blast-off, a faulty valve stalls [space shuttle] Discovery ...* -T/84.

(at) full blast (à) plena força, (a) todo o vapor, com toda a intensidade, a pleno funcionamento *The radio was going full blast.* ♦ *... the air conditioner going full blast ...* -CGT,13. ♦ *His business is going at full blast.* ♦ *... the poker tables [at the Bitterroot Saloon] were going full blast ...* -HJ,43.

BLAZE blaze away abrir fogo e manter o tiroteio contra o inimigo, atirar continuamente *[He] ... took out his Colt [pistol], leaned against the window jamb and blazed away at the surprised Germans.* -CL,299.

go to blazes [gir] ir para o inferno *You can go to blazes for all I care.*

BLEED bleed someone white extorquir todo o dinheiro de uma pessoa, depenar, deixar sem nada *After she had bled him white, she left him for a richer man.*

BLEEP bleep out → **BLIP out**

BLESS blessed with afortunado por (ter algo), ser agraciado com *He is blessed with a good wife and two lovely children.* ♦ *The Jicarilla Apaches in northern New Mexico, [are] blessed with rich oil and gas deposits on their lands ...* -T/73.

BLESSEDNESS single blessedness estado de solteiro, celibato *He lived all his life in single blessedness.*

BLESSING a blessing in disguise graça, bênção ou ventura disfarçada; um mal aparente que vem a ser algo bom *He felt hurt when he was released from his job and took a lesser paid position with another company, but when his old company failed, he realized his dismissal had been a blessing in disguise.*

count one's blessings abençoar a sua estrela, bendizer os fados, ser grato por aquilo que se tem, levantar as mãos para o céu *As Dale Carnegie once said, we should count our blessings, not our troubles.*

mixed blessing algo que apresenta grandes vantagens e também desvantagens; misto de virtudes e defeitos, de altos e baixos, de bons e maus elementos, qualidades etc. *The winning of a lottery can be a mixed blessing to the winner.*

BLINK on the blink/fritz [gir] enguiçado, quebrado, desarranjado, funcionando mal *My TV set is on the blink most of the time.* ♦ *... the telephones went on the blink with great regularity.* -JEP,253. ♦ *The battery in my car is on the fritz.*

BLIP blip/bleep out [col] censurar (som, palavra, trecho) de gravação em uma fita magnética substituindo a parte eliminada por um som eletrônico (bip) *The incriminating words had been blipped out from the tape.* ♦ *Certain words from his jokes were often blipped out on the TV program.*

BLISS wedded bliss felicidade conjugal *It may be that wedded bliss happens most of the time in fiction, but it can also happen in real life.*

BLOCK building block → BUILDING block
knock one's block off [gir] dar uma surra em *I'll knock your block off if you don't stop talking.*
on the block em leilão *Renaissance sculpture and impressionist paintings ... on the block ...* -T/78.
stumbling block → STUMBLING block
blockhead [gir] pessoa estúpida, bronco, cabeça-dura *"Charley Brown, you're nothing but a blockhead!", said Lucy.*
BLOOD bad blood animosidade, antipatia profunda, inimizade, ressentimento, ódio *Part of the bad blood [existing between the two candidates] is a basic personality clash.* -T/80.
blood and thunder muita ação, sensacionalismo, violência e melodrama *As a boy I loved reading stories full of blood and thunder.* ⇒ **blood-and-thunder** em que há muita ação, sensacionalismo, violência e melodrama *While in prison during the war he [Ned Buntline] had used his spare moments to write three blood-and-thunder novels.* -RR,613.
blood is thicker than water a voz do sangue fala mais alto, os laços de família são muito fortes *Even though his brother was a bum, Charles stood behind him when people began to express their disapproval of him. Blood is thicker than water indeed.*
draw blood 1. fazer sangrar, tirar sangue *The small piece of broken glass drew blood from his finger.* 2. ofender, magoar *Phil's unkind remarks drew blood.*
have someone's blood in one's hands/head ser responsável pela morte de *The soldier said he didn't want to have the blood of an innocent man on his hands.*
in cold blood a sangue frio *He knew they would try to shoot him down in cold blood.* -HO,138. ⇒ **cold-blooded** 1. de sangue frio *Snakes and lizards are cold-blooded animals.* 2. desapiedado, cruel, frio, insensível *Raven was a cold-blooded killer.*
♦ *... cold-blooded realism.* -T/92.
in(to) one's blood no sangue, na natureza de alguém *... once it [the American frontier in the 1880s] got into your blood there was a fascination and you didn't want to give it up.* -CEB,40.
make someone's blood boil fazer ferver o sangue de, deixar alguém furioso *It makes my blood boil to see what you're doing to that poor woman.*
make someone's blood run cold fazer gelar o sangue *He can tell you stories that would make your blood run cold.*
new blood sangue novo, gente nova, renovação de pessoal *This organization needs new blood.*
out for blood [gir] 1. disposto a qualquer coisa, a ir às últimas conseqüências, topando tudo *He has been out for blood ever since people said he was incapable.* 2. em busca de vingança *He's out for blood, so be careful.*
run in the blood/family estar no sangue, ser uma característica herdada de família, fazer parte da natureza de *For four generations there have been army officers in their family. A devotion to army life seems to run in their blood.* ♦ *Psychiatrists have argued for generations about the cause of manic-depressive illness, although it is known to run in families.* -T/72.
set someone's blood boiling = **make someone's BLOOD boil** *When he [General William Tecumseh Sherman] reached Fort Richardson word [news] waited him that set his blood boiling ...* -BR,665.
shed blood derramar sangue, matar ou ferir *Kid Curry [a notorious western outlaw] seemed to delight in shedding human blood ...* -BE,93. ⇒ **bloodshed** derramamento de sangue; matança *[Alfred] Hitchcock's* Psycho *inaugurated America's cinema of cruelty, with a demonic amalgam of bloodshed and violence ...*

-T/67. ♦ *There was bloodshed when the soldiers opened fire on the agitators.*
stir someone's blood causar emoção em, despertar o entusiasmo de *The martial music and the flags flying stirred my blood.*
sweat blood [gir] 1. trabalhar com afinco, dar duro *I really sweated blood at that job.* 2. estar impaciente, apreensivo, ansioso, preocupado, amedrontado *He sweated blood waiting for the jury to return a verdict.*
BLOOD-CURDLING pavoroso, assustador *The Indians gave a blood-curdling yell when they advanced on the wagonload of women and children.* ♦ *a blood-curdling story*
BLOODLETTING [col] = **bloodshed** *The chaos and bloodletting ... have turned the republic [Bosnia] into a killing field ...* -T/92.
BLOODSHED → shed BLOOD
BLOOM in (full) bloom florido, em flor *The violets are in bloom now.*
BLOOMER late bloomer pessoa que chega tardiamente à maturidade ou à competência plena *Some students are late bloomers.*
BLOSSOM blossom into desabrochar, transformar-se em *Flora has blossomed into a beautiful girl.* ♦ *[He]... has blossomed into a first-rank [orchestra] conductor since moving to the U.S. in 1974.* -T/76.
blossom out desenvolver-se, amadurecer, expandir-se *We practice loving in the narrow confines of the family before we blossom out to include strangers.* -KS,74. ♦ *He has blossomed out into a talented painter.*
in blossom em flor (árvore frutífera) *The cherry trees are in blossom now.*
BLOT blot out 1. obstruir, cobrir, apagar *... a great cloud had come over the town, blotting out the sunshine.* -HW,11. ♦ *... tiredness blots out your feelings ...* -SEB,5. 2. destruir, eliminar *When Mao Tse-Tung seized power in China, he tried to blot out all traces of foreign influence.*
BLOW at a/one blow/stroke de um só golpe, com uma pancada; de uma só vez, com um único ato *The police succeeded in capturing the kidnappers and rescuing the hostages at a single blow.* ♦ *... the authorities were accused of trying to withdraw more than $400,000 in funds at a stroke.* -T/67.
blow away 1. dissipar(-se), ser levado pelo vento *The curtain of smoke blew away.* ♦ *The darkest political clouds hanging over [the Prime Minister's] ... head have blown away.* -T/86. 2. arrancar, derrubar, levar (diz-se do vento) *He tied his tent to a tree so that it wouldn't be blown away.* ♦ *The wind blew away his hat.* 3. [col] matar a tiros *... confusing groups of [Lebanese] militants who seem united only in their determination to blow themselves and their country away.* -T/87.
blow down arrancar, derrubar (diz-se do vento); ser derrubado pelo vento *The storm blew down the old barn.* ♦ *The old barn blew down.*
blow hot and cold vacilar, mostrar-se inconstante, ficar indeciso, não saber o que quer *In the broader area of foreign policy, the Administration has blown hot and cold on dealing with the Soviet Union ...* -T/81.
blow in(to) [gir] chegar, entrar, aparecer inesperadamente *She just blew in from Chicago.* ♦ *[He] ... blew into the Hotel Ambassador carrying a little bag.* -T/69.
blow off arrancar, derrubar (diz-se do vento); ser derrubado pelo vento *The wind blew off the woman's hat.* ♦ *The woman's hat blew off.* 2. arrancar por explosão *[His] ... left leg had been blown off by an assassin's bomb in Shanghai ...* -TJ,980.
blow one to [col] obsequiar, regalar, presentear, oferecer *He blew his family to a European vacation.*
blow out 1. apagar(-se), extinguir(-se), (geralmente pela ação do vento ou sopro),

desligar(-se) (luzes, eletricidade) *The wind blew out the fire.* ♦ *She got up and blew out the candle.* ♦ *If the lights in your house blow out every time you turn on your toaster, you know something is wrong.* -T/79. 2. estourar, rebentar (pneu etc.); queimar, derreter (fusível etc.) *They were driving across the desert when a tire blew out.* ♦ *The fuse blew out.* ♦ *The bulb in the tent had blown out ...* -HJC,358. ⇒ **blowout** a. estouro ou ruptura de pneu *We had a blowout on the highway.* b. [gir] festa com fartura de comida e bebida *He gave a blowout for his friends.*
blow over 1. passar, dissipar-se (nuvens, tempestade etc.) *After the storm had blown over we went home.* 2. dissipar-se, abrandar-se, ser esquecido (dificuldade, problema, desavença etc.) *We had better wait until her rage blows over.* ♦ *... by the time he came back everything [all the trouble] would have blown over.* -AIM,131.
blow up 1. explodir, ir pelos ares; fazer explodir, dinamitar *The stick of dynamite blew up.* ♦ *The terrorists ... have blown up police stations, banks and TV stations ...* -T/92. 2. [col] perder a calma, ficar irritado *Suddenly he finds himself in a traffic jam – and he simply blows up.* -T/86. 3. encher de ar, inflar *blow up a tire* ♦ *blow up a balloon* 4. ampliar (fotografia) *Can you have this photograph blown up?* ⇒ **blowup** ampliação de fotografia, negativo etc. *In Los Angeles, blowups of those [Marilyn Monroe's] photographs sold for $250 apiece.* -T/73. 5. exagerar, expandir-se, (fazer) sair dos limites, (fazer) atingir proporções exageradas *It was only a small international incident, but it was blown up to unbelievable proportions.* ♦ *She gave us a blown up version of the story.* 6. formar-se repentinamente (tempestade, ventania etc.) *When we reached the top of the mountain, one of those freak summer storms blew up.*

come to blows atracar-se, pegar-se, ir às vias de fato (dois adversários) *They had long been buddies, but they almost came to blows that night.*
deal a blow golpear, desfechar pancada, bater; abalar *He dealt his antagonist a hard blow on the head.* ♦ *Charles Darwin's theory of evolution dealt a serious blow to the traditional idea of creation.*
strike a blow for//against ir em auxílio de//opor-se a, tomar uma atitude a favor de//agir contra *Instead of striking a blow for freedom [he] ... had meekly betrayed a professional confidence ...* -FJH,35. ♦ *In his new book she strikes a blow against the enemies of democracy.*
with one blow = at a BLOW *By closing all the newspapers he eliminated with one blow all opposition.*
BLOW-BY-BLOW detalhado, minucioso *a blow-by-blow account of what had happened* ♦ *a blow-by-blow description of the plan* ♦ *... a blow-by-blow narrative.* -T/87.
BLUE indecente, impróprio, obsceno, pornográfico *Blue material [i.e., a performer's repertoire] is so common now that people are no longer shocked by it.* ♦ *He's always telling blue jokes.*
the blue and the gray os soldados da União e os soldados da Confederação na Guerra de Secessão norte-americana; o exército da União e o exército confederado; nortistas e sulistas *The blue and the gray engaged in hostilities after southern troops attacked Fort Sumter, South Carolina, on April 12, 1861.*
the (wild) blue yonder o imenso céu azul, a imensidão do céu, o espaço ilimitado *The flyboy [i.e., a pilot] – perhaps from spending so much time in the wild blue yonder – acted as though his head were still in the clouds ...* -BM,202.
out of the blue = out of a clear (blue) SKY *... and then, out of the blue, I'm supposed to stop [smoking] just because the boss says so.* -T/87. ♦ *Freud's discovery*

of the connection between sexuality and illness did not spring out of the psychic blue. -FLS,109.

BLUE-CHIP designativo de ações de capital de primeira qualidade *That is a blue-chip investment and will give a small but steady profit for years.* ♦ *Walt Disney Production has become the only blue-chip stock in show business.* -T/73.

BLUE-COLLAR relativo ou referente aos trabalhadores, à classe operária *Blue-collar workers were outnumbered by those in the so-called white-collar occupations ...* -TA,23. ♦ *... blue-collar jobs.* -T/85. v. **WHITE-collar**

BLUENOSE [col] indivíduo puritano, moralista *... bluenoses who want to force their prudish ways of life on other people.* -CG,61. ⇒ **bluenosed** puritano, moralista *... bluenosed censors ...* -T/66.

BLUE-PENCIL suprimir ou alterar (parte de texto); revisar e preparar para publicação *In 1818 Thomas Bowdler, a retired physician, blue-penciled what he regarded as the Bard's [Shakespeare's] blue lines and produced a Shakespeare without blushes for the family reading hour ...* -T/60.

BLUE-RIBBON [col] da melhor qualidade, de primeira água, excelente *... he had appointed a blue-ribbon commission to report to him on state taxes ...* -T/78. ♦ *... a blue-ribbon candidate to run for Governor ...* -T/73.

BLUES the blues [gir] 1. tristeza, depressão, melancolia *He has had the blues ever since she went away.* 2. estilo melancólico de jazz *Some jazz critics have remarked that no one could sing the blues like Billie Holiday.*

BLUE-SKY [col] inútil, sem valor, sem nenhuma aplicação prática *... blue-sky schemes ...* -T/66.

BLUFF call someone's bluff [col] desafiar alguém a cumprir sua ameaça (quando se acredita que ele está blefando), não se deixar intimidar; pagar para ver (no pôquer) *I knew he had nothing to support his threat, so when he said he was going to bring legal action against me, I called his bluff and told him I was not going to be intimidated.* ♦ *He never expected you to call his bluff when you bet one hundred dollars.*

BLURT blurt out proferir abrupta e impulsivamente, dizer (algo) sem pensar, revelar algo inadvertidamente *"My name is John Smith and I want my lawyer", he blurted out when the police arrested him.* ♦ *The girl blurted out what was supposed to be a secret.*

BLUSH at first blush à primeira vista, segundo as aparências indicam *At first blush Gorbachev's latest offer seemed to be a major concession to the U.S.* -T/87. ♦ *At first blush everything seemed to be in order.*

BOARD above board → **ABOVEBOARD** across the board de cabo a rabo, de alto a baixo, sem exceção, aplicável a todas as classes, grupos, categorias, membros etc. *[The Chinese military] ... really need everything [in the matter of weapons] – right across the board.* -T/78. ♦ *I came back to make a business deal, straight across the board.* -FC,14. ⇒ **across-the-board** indiscriminado, geral, coletivo, que inclui todos os grupos, classes etc. *... the members declined to issue an across-the-board condemnation.* -T/87. ♦ *... an across-the-board tax hike.* -T/66. ♦ *... across-the-board opposition ...* -T/87.

come on board → **COME aboard**
go by the board não receber atenção, ser negligenciado, abandonado, esquecido, ser desperdiçado *... in today's sculpture, both traditional subject matter and traditional techniques have gone by the board.* -T/64. ♦ *... I decided to let my reservations at the Hotel Windsor go by the board.* -SJD,162.
on board a bordo (de) (navio, trem, avião, ônibus etc.) *There were 2,223 passengers on board when the* Titanic *went down in 1912.* ♦ *The sailors went on board the ship.*

BOARDINGHOUSE boarding house casa de pensão ... *he took a room at a boarding house* ... -T/79.

BOAT boat people refugiados, indivíduos que fogem de seu país (devido a revolução, falta de liberdade política etc.) em pequenas embarcações ... *the number of people fleeing Viet Nam, whose inhumane policies have generated the bulk of the boat people, has dropped sharply.* -T/79. ♦ ... *all the Haitian boat people – there are more thant 30,000 in South Florida alone – are political refugees* ... -T/80.

burn one's boats/bridges tomar uma atitude definitiva e irrevogável, tornar impossível uma mudança de planos, uma retirada ou um retorno à situação anterior *He had burned his boats and a turning back was impossible now.* ♦ *Leaving school is like burning all your bridges.* -T/64.

in the same boat no mesmo barco, em situação idêntica *They're all in the same boat and will probably end up in jail together.* ♦ *[President] Carter is in the same boat as [former President] Nixon, looking good abroad while facing a sea of domestic troubles.* -T/79.

miss the boat/bus [col] dormir no ponto, bobear, lerdear *You missed the boat when you didn't accept his offer to go into business with him.* ♦ *He's the kind of guy who never misses the bus.*

rock the boat [col] perturbar a paz, romper o equilíbrio de uma situação *Women just don't want to rock the boat. They're afraid of change and men aren't.* -AK,259. ♦ ... *the President is taking extreme pains not to rock the boat with any overly controversial decisions before Election Day.* -T/66.

BOB bob up surgir inesperadamente, subir ou voltar à tona *[He] ... made one prediction that kept bobbing up in my mind* ... -SWLM,22. ♦ *He bobbed up at the party at about midnight.*

BOBBY-SOXER [col] garota adolescente *I can still remember Frank Sinatra singing to bobby-soxers at the old Paramount Theater in New York.*

BODY body blow revés, decepção, desapontamento, frustração, fracasso, adversidade *She suffered a severe body blow when she was dropped from the basketball team.*

body count 1. contagem de corpos (verificação do número de soldados inimigos mortos em combate) *In the [battle] field [in Vietnam] the Americans were encouraged to lie about their "body counts"* ... -T/85. 2. contagem de pessoas em determinado local *The body count at a street riot and its reporting in the newspapers are never the same.*

body English 1. contorções corporais instintivas que alguém faz após efetuar arremesso de bola (de boliche, de golfe, de bilhar etc.) na esperança de que ela siga na direção desejada *His body English was superb but his technical ability was lacking.* 2. contorções ou movimentos que ajudam a manter o equilíbrio ou a controlar a postura do corpo durante exercício, atividade etc. ... *men like Bobby Clark, Bert Lahr, Harold Lloyd and Buster Keaton, ... clowned in flawless body English.* -T/74.

body forth dar corpo ou forma a, simbolizar, representar *[Actor] Paul Scofield seems to body forth all the virtues of Sir Thomas More [in the play* A Man for All Seasons*].* -T/62.

body language comunicação realizada por gestos, movimentos, expressões faciais etc., linguagem corporal *Manners are always simultaneously something more and something less than they seem. They are the body language of a culture, the gesticulations of its soul* ... -T/78. ♦ *[French painter Toulouse Lautrec's] ... ability to capture pose, expression, the slightest nuance of body language in a single inflection of line was extraordinary* ... -T/92.

body politic organismo político, estado *The recognition that rebellion is a necessary impulse within the psyche and the*

body politic is largely a modern western idea. -KS,75. ♦ *... our body politic is sick from war and urban blight ...* -T/69.
in a body em conjunto, em grupo *Half the women rose up in a body ...* -NE,168. ♦ *The strikers came to the street in a body.*
keep body and soul together manter-se vivo, sobreviver *Despite these hard times, he manages to keep body and soul together.*
over my dead body [col] contra minha total oposição, não enquanto eu viver, só passando por cima do meu cadáver *When sixteen-year-old Maureen said she was leaving home, her mother snapped: "Over my dead body!".*
BOG   bog down atolar(-se), encalhar, emperrar, estar impedido de prosseguir, chegar a um impasse *The peace negotiations have bogged down.* ♦ *[The Soviet economy is] ... bogged down in a morass of bureaucratic paper work.* -T/85. ♦ *Let's hope that the recent border incident will not bog down the peace talks between the two countries.*
BOIL   boil away ser reduzido a nada, evaporar *Put out the fire before the soup boils away.*
boil down resumir(-se), sintetizar, reduzir(-se) *My answer boils down to a simple no.* ♦ *[The two men] ... boiled down the essence of what the working groups had accomplished.* -T/86. ♦ *... hundreds of pages ... boiled down to a few sheets.* -T/81.
boil over   1. transbordar, espalhar(-se); chegar a um ponto crítico *... the people's revulsion against crime and gangsterism finally boiled over ...* -WD,106. ♦ *[His] ... dissenting views on modern culture have frequently boiled over into newspapers and magazines.* -T/80. 2. ficar agitado, nervoso, irritar-se *He boiled over when he heard the news.*
BOILING   boiling hot [col] extremamente quente *It was a boiling hot day in early July when he arrived in Tucson.*

boiling mad [col] irritado, furioso *He got boiling mad when I told him what had happened.*
boiling point   1. ponto de ebulição *At sea level, the boiling point of water is 212° F, or 100° C.*   2. [col] ponto crítico, ponto em que um indivíduo perde o controle emocional *Al reaches the boiling point easily.*
BOLD-FACED → **put a bold FACE on**
BOLT   a bolt from the blue algo totalmente inesperado, um imprevisto *In 1944, the news of the invasion of Normandy came like a bolt from the blue.* v. **out of the BLUE**
bolt upright → **SIT bolt upright**
shoot one's bolt jogar a última cartada, esgotar as possibilidades ou os recursos (em um esforço inútil) *Napoleon shot his bolt when he invaded Russia and gradually went into defeat.*
BOMB   bomb out   1. ser bombardeado, ser destruído por explosão *... a Tennessee high school that was bombed out in 1958.* -T/69. ♦ *... concrete was a practical material for rebuilding bombed-out, impoverished Japan.* -T/87.   2. [gir] falhar, fracassar, ser malsucedido *If we try to make a television series out of this idea of yours and the series bombs out, we stand to lose a lot of money ...* -WS,39. ♦ *He bombed out in his second year at the university.*
BONE   the bare bones o essencial, o fundamental, os fatos básicos *I'll give you the bare bones of the plan.* ♦ ⇒ **bare-bones** essencial, fundamental *... President Johnson sent to Congress ... a foreign aid message asking for a bare-bones $3.4 billion for fiscal 1965.* -T/64.
bone [col] inteiramente, completamente, totalmente, positivamente, francamente *After nine hours of the hardest ... work, both of us were bone tired ...* -CJC,135. ♦ *... he was bone cold ...* -FP,6. ♦ *His parents were kindly, God-fearing and bone poor ...* -T/65.
bone of contention pomo de discórdia *This subject has always been the bone of*

contention between us. ♦ *Another bone of contention was the $7.9 million paid by Iran for U.S. weapons and left in Swiss accounts.* -T/87.
bone up on [col] estudar intensivamente (determinado assunto, matéria etc.) *He went into the commercial department of the foreign office, boned up on economics at night ...* -GJI,69. ♦ *He had boned up on the artist's work ...* -T/86. ♦ *... boning up on too many subjects ...* -T/87. v. **BRUSH up**
bred in the bone; bred-in-the-bone congênito, imutável, inextirpável, intrínseco, inerente à natureza de alguém *His honesty is bred in the bone.* ♦ *bred-in-the-bone integrity* ♦ *bred-in-the-bone honesty*
cut to the bone reduzir drasticamente (custos, despesas etc.) *All our expenses have been cut to the bone.*
(as) dry as a bone totalmente seco *Every canteen in their company was dry as a bone ...* -KM,411. ⇒ **bone-dry** *... coastal areas that were bone-dry ...* -T/80. ♦ *... bone-dry desert ...* -T/61.
feel/know (it) in one's bones pressentir, intuir *Something about the circumstances of Burke's death was wrong, he felt in his bones, but what it was he simply could not diagnose.* -QE,58. ♦ *He knew in his bones that his end was near.*
funny bone 1. região do cotovelo atravessada pelo nervo cubital que produz uma sensação desagradável de formigamento quando recebe uma batida *I just hit my funny bone on the door.* 2. senso de humor *His jokes didn't hit our funny bones.* ♦ *[He] ... had no funny bone whatsoever ...* -JEP,438.
have a bone to pick with [col] ter uma queixa, uma reclamação contra, ter uma questão desagradável a resolver com *I have a bone to pick with you. Why have you been telling lies about me?*
know (it) in one's bones → **feel/know (it) in one's BONES**

make no bones about [col] falar francamente sem temer as conseqüências, não ocultar, não hesitar, não fazer cerimônia *[He] ... made no bones about his right-wing beliefs.* -T/81.
to the bone até os ossos, inteiramente *... his joints ached and he was cold to the bone.* -AT,9. v. **cut to the BONE**; **work one's FINGERS to the bone**
BONE-DRY → **(as) dry as a BONE**
BONER pull a boner [gir] cometer uma gafe, dar uma mancada *You certainly pulled a boner when you said you had been with me last night.*
BOOBY booby trap 1. armadilha para pregar peças em incautos; perigo oculto, alçapão, escolho *The pharaoh's tomb had many booby traps to foil grave robbers.* 2. armadilha explosiva (mina, bomba, granada etc.) *The soldiers were afraid to go in the house because it was full of booby traps.* ⇒ **booby-trap** preparar armadilha (de qualquer tipo) *The Western Allies were afraid to accept the Russian plan because they felt that it was booby-trapped.* ♦ *The car had been booby-trapped and might explode at any moment.*
BOOK 1. reservar (passagem, bilhete, lugar etc.) *The airlines have many passages booked for their transcontinental flights.* ♦ *... that afternoon I booked a reservation for Cincinnati ...* -HA,104. ♦ *[She] ... booked all the seats in the business section of a jumbo jet ...* -T/86. ♦ *He has booked two seats for a new show on Broadway.* 2. contratar (alguém para tarefa, serviços, compromissos, apresentações etc.) *... he was booked for a three-month lecture tour that was to take him all over the U.S.* -T/65. ♦ *We were booked to play at The Strand, a big Broadway showplace ...* -HA,53. 3. autuar *I wound up being booked on a narcotics possession charge.* -BL,207.
the (Good) Book a Bíblia *... I'll see if I can find the answer in the Book.* -NE,201.

♦ *The Good Book says, "Thou shalt not kill.".*
bring to book chamar a contas, pedir explicações pela conduta; punir *He was finally brought to book when the police caught up with him in New Orleans.*
by the book [col] de acordo com as normas ou com o regulamento, da maneira correta *... Webster ... is likely to run the CIA as he did the FBI – by the book ...* -T/87. ♦ *When you do everything by the book, you'll never do anything that hasn't been done before.* -GM,285.
closed book coisa que não se compreende, sobre a qual nada se sabe, mistério, enigma *Her behavior is a closed book to me.*
comic book → **comics**
crack a book [gir] abrir um livro para ler ou estudar *... every person who has ever cracked a book on elementary electricity [is familiar with the phenomenon of magnetic force].* -UM,61. ♦ *... I was 26 years old before I cracked a book in the field to which I have devoted my career ...* -T/86.
hit the books [col] estudar com afinco *I have to stay home tonight and hit the books for the big exam tomorrow.*
in one's book na concepção de, na opinião de, na cartilha de *I had you down all wrong in my book.* -CEP,121 ♦ *... I know what you were before, and that's the way you stay in my book.* -CHT,26.
in one's good//bad books nas boas graças de alguém//mal com alguém *He's in the mayor's bad books now and nothing can save him. It's the end of his political career.*
keep books fazer escrituração mercantil *... she kept the books for his peanut and fertilizer business, while raising four children.* -T/78.
know/read someone like a book [col] conhecer alguém muito bem, ser capaz de predizer-lhe as ações e o pensamento, conhecer-lhe o caráter *... he knew them like a book, he said, and they were not bad people.* -LA,19. ♦ *He knew Emily. He could read her like a book.* -HWL,40.
make book [gir] agenciar apostas clandestinas em corridas de cavalos *The police raided the club and arrested all who were suspected of making book.* ⇒ **bookmaker** corretor de apostas clandestinas em corridas de cavalos *New York bookmakers were always extravagantly dressed in expensive suits.*
one for the book(s) [col] algo totalmente inesperado ou extraordinário, grande surpresa *That would be one for the books, the White House chief of staff hauled before the Congress he so despised.* -BC,277. ♦ *His coming home after a thirty-five year absence was certainly one for the books.*
read someone like a book → **know/read someone like a BOOK**
talking book livro (ou trecho) gravado em disco ou fita magnética destinado principalmente a pessoas cegas *Blind people can learn much from talking books.*
throw the book at [gir] formular todas as acusações possíveis contra, sentenciar à pena mais severa, punir rigorosamente *We've got a lawyer waiting in New York ... We're going to throw the book at you.* -BAS,53. ♦ *If he doesn't cooperate with the police, they'll throw the book at him.*
BOOKMAKER → **make BOOK**
BOOM boom out ressoar, estrondar; proferir em voz estrondosa *Every Christmas ... [Irving] Berlin's song White Christmas booms out of department store loudspeakers ...* -CBC,12. ♦ *... distant cannons boomed out 21-salvo salutes ...* -T/80. ♦ *His powerful voice boomed out a string of obscenities.*
boom town; boomtown cidade de grande desenvolvimento, que cresce rapidamente *The legislation ... proposed granting loans to boom towns to build the schools, hospitals and other facilities needed to accommodate new settlers.* -T/80.
lower the boom [gir] descer a lenha, punir, tratar rudemente, conter, criticar

severamente, pôr fim *I can lower the boom on you any time I want to ... -GES,112.* ♦ *The police are going to lower the boom on all the bars that cater to teenagers.*

BOOT bet one's boots ter absoluta certeza, estar seguro, convicto *... you can bet your boots on that. -GA,7.*

boot camp campo de treinamento de fuzileiros navais *Boot camp separates the men from the boys.* ♦ *... Marine recruits en route to boot camp at Parris Island, S.C. -T/60.*

boot hill; Boot Hill cemitério das cidades primitivas do Oeste americano *According to Ramon F. Adams, Boot Hill was "a name given to the frontier cemetery because most of its early occupants died with their boots on".*

boot out [gir] expulsar, pôr na rua *If you start any of your old tricks around here, you'll get booted out of Fort Buchanan just as fast as you were booted out of Fort Apache. -CHT,26.*

die with one's boots on morrer em atividade, em ação, morrer lutando *It was said of Lieutenant-Colonel George Armstrong Custer and his men that they died with their boots on in the Battle of the Little Bighorn.*

get//give the boot [gir] ser despedido// despedir *He got the boot yesterday.* ♦ *The boss gave him the boot.*

lick someone's boots lamber as botas de, agir de maneira servil, bajular *He may be the boss but I'm not going to lick his boots.*

to boot bem como, além disso, a mais, de inhapa, de quebra *[Joseph Conrad became] ... one of England's greatest novelists, and a stylist to boot ... -SV,61.* ♦ *Many problems face the citizens of big cities: traffic, robbers, lack of good transportation, and pollution to boot.*

too big for one's boots/breeches/britches [col] orgulhoso demais, presunçoso, arrogante, pomposo *He had grown too big for his boots and the rival gang decided to get rid of him.* ♦ *He has grown too big for his breeches. I guess I'll have to tell him a thing or two.* ♦ *You may get too big for your britches. -DJ,18.*

BOOTSTRAPS pull oneself up by one's (own) bootstraps alcançar sucesso por esforço próprio *Mr. Jenkins is a self-made man. He pulled himself up by his own bootstraps.*

BOOZE booze it up [col] embebedar-se, encher a cara *You going to booze it up like this all night? -SEB,108.* ♦ *He gets boozed up on weekends.*

BORDER border on/upon 1. confinar com, fazer divisa com *All the countries bordering on the former Soviet Union are buying heavy equipment from the arms merchants.* 2. aproximar-se de, tocar as raias de *Perhaps the most marked of all ... [his] characteristics is a self-assurance that ... borders on arrogance. -T/81.* ♦ *... some of [his] ... ideas border on the demagogic. -T/92.*

BORED bored stiff [gir] totalmente entediado *We get bored stiff by political speeches on TV.*

BORN be born nascer *Hector was born in 1990 and Octavius in 1994.*

not born yesterday não ser ingênuo, saber das coisas, ter experiência da vida *When someone tried to trick my father or deceive him in any way, the old man used to say: "I wasn't born yesterday".*

BORN-AGAIN 1. que se converteu a uma seita evangélica ou que fez nova profissão de fé a sua religião (geralmente cristã) *A born-again Christian ... -T/87.* 2. que adotou ou voltou a professar certa filosofia de vida, certa concepção do mundo, determinada atividade *A born-again conservative, he tends to hold fervent and dogmatic views. -T/80.* ♦ *... a born-again marketing expert ... -T/88.* ♦ *... a one-time moderate who is now a born-again right-winger ... -T/87.*

BOSS boss about/around [col] = OR-DER about *Don't get the idea that you can come here and boss my kid around.* -MWL, 64. ♦ *He showed them he couldn't be bossed around.*

BOTCH botch up realizar um trabalho malfeito, medíocre, cheio de imperfeições (por desatenção ou negligência), consertar toscamente, fazer um serviço porco, fazer trapalhada, arruinar, estragar *He botches up every job that he tries to do.*

BOTTLE UP bottle up 1. encurralar, bloquear, obstruir, confinar, restringir *Government forces claimed to have captured one boat and bottled up the invaders in the beach area ...* T/81. ♦ *Traffic was bottled up for miles along the highway.* 2. conter, refrear (emoções, sentimentos etc.) *Agnes bottled up her anger.* ⇒ **bottled-up** contido, reprimido *... bottled-up anger can lead to acts of unexpected and sometimes enormous violence.* -T/84.

hit the bottle/sauce [gír] beber em excesso, encher a cara *We have heard that his wife hits the bottle secretly.* ♦ *He hits the sauce every once in a while, but nothing serious.* -BC,330.

BOTTLE-FEED alimentar com mamadeira *She both breast-feeds and bottle-feeds her baby girl.* v. **BREAST-feed**

BOTTOM at bottom na realidade, fundamentalmente *He's really a very nice man at bottom.*

be at the bottom of ser a verdadeira causa de *[He] ... had concluded that sexual inhibitions were at the bottom of most aberrations and the cause of most social hypocrisy ...* -DDT,459.

the bottom (of something) drops/falls out [col] 1. ocorrer uma perda no valor ou no preço de, ocorrer um colapso *In 1921, the bottom fell out of the rubber market.* -DJ,9. ♦ *In 1970 the bottom fell out, profits plunged, and an estimated 10% of the [advertising] agency business work force lost their jobs.* -T/72. 2. acabar-se o mundo (para), ser o fim do mundo (para), mostrar-se adversa a fortuna (para) *In Somerset Maugham's novel* The Razor's Edge, *the bottom drops out of Sophie's world when her husband and little daughter are killed in an automobile accident.*

bottoms up! [gír] esvaziem os copos (ou a garrafa)! vamos beber! à nossa *OK, everybody, bottoms up!*

Foggy Bottom [col] o Departamento de Estado dos EUA *... some advisers ... insist on getting the Pentagon and Foggy Bottom into harmony.* -T/87.

from the bottom of one's heart → **from the (bottom of one's) HEART**

get to the bottom of buscar a causa de, ir ao âmago de *... to get to the bottom of the mystery.* -T/92. ♦ *... we want to get to the bottom of your total problem ...* -SHS,2.

hit/touch bottom [col] chegar ao ponto mais baixo, chegar ao fundo do poço, abater-se, perder as esperanças *In the Great Depression of the early thirties, they hit bottom but survived.* ♦ *... in the late 70s, business hit bottom.* -T/87. v. **ROCK bottom**

knock the bottom out of [col] provocar o colapso de, retirar o apoio, suporte etc., fazer cair, derrubar, invalidar, frustrar, fazer malograr *They have knocked the bottom out of our plans.*

scrape the bottom of the barrel [gír] ser obrigado a utilizar artigo de qualidade inferior, mão-de-obra insatisfatória etc., quando não se dispõe de algo melhor *They must have been scraping the bottom of the barrel when they picked you for this job.*

touch bottom → **hit BOTTOM**

BOUNCE bounce back [col] recuperar-se rapidamente após derrota, fracasso, queda, doença etc. *Everyone is waiting for the automobile business to bounce back to normal.*

get//give the bounce [gír] 1. = **get//give the AX 1** *He got the bounce last week.* ♦ *They gave him the bounce.* 2. = **get//give**

the AX 2 *He got the bounce from his girl friend.* ♦ *Ted and Liz quarreled and she gave him the bounce.*

BOUND bound for a caminho de, rumando para *"Where are you bound for this year?", he asked his well-traveled friend.* ♦ *The pirate ship was bound for Tortuga.*

bound to 1. fadado a ... *controversial problems are bound to arise.* -T/74. 2. decidido a, resolvido a, disposto a *Woodward was bound not to use the information in a story [i.e., in a news article in a newspaper] ...* -BC,26.

bound up in absorto em, ocupado com, interessado em *She's so bound up in her teaching activities that she has no time for social engagements.*

bound up with ligado a, relacionado com *... he had a strong, unsurprised sense of evil in human nature – and an even stronger conviction that it is inextricably bound up with good.* -T/78. ♦ *Madeleine's fears were all bound up with certain childhood memories.*

out of bounds fora dos limites prescritos, proibido, que não pode ser adentrado *Nobody goes near that place, understand, Corporal! ... It's off limits and out of bounds.* -NE,191. ♦ *All the bars in that area are out of bounds to American soldiers.*

BOW bow and scrape mostrar-se excessivamente cortês e cerimonioso, descomedir-se em mesuras servis *In Alfred Hitchcock's* Strangers on a Train, *Bruno Anthony says that he is sick and tired of bowing and scraping to his father.* ♦ *She was always bowing and scraping for social approval.*

bow down bajular, agir com servilismo, dobrar-se *He will never get far in politics because he will bow down to no one.*

bow out 1. retirar-se, desistir de participar, renunciar *He bowed out as a possible candidate for President.* 2. aposentar-se, deixar cargo, emprego etc. após longo tempo de atividade *[He] ... bowed out after 29 years in government ...* -T/81.

take a bow [gir] fazer uma reverência em agradecimento ao aplauso do público *She came slowly back to the center of the stage and took a bow.*

BOWEL bowel movement defecação, evacuação *Roy began to develop a fierce stomachache, one which could not be relieved by a bowel movement ...* -WJT,337. ♦ *His bowel movements are difficult and infrequent.*

move one's bowels obrar, defecar *He can't move his bowels regularly.*

BOWL bowl along [col] mover-se, rodar, rápida e suavemente (veículo) *We bowled along the coastal highway and enjoyed the marine sights.*

bowl over [col] pasmar, causar grande surpresa a *I was bowled over when she appeared at the door.* ♦ *The shocking news of his death bowled me over.*

BOX box office 1. bilheteria (de teatro, cinema etc.) *Get your tickets at the box office.* ♦ *The ... documentary movie ... is the smash of the summer, drawing thousands to the box offices ...* -T/77. ♦ *Back to the Future, was the box-office champ of 1985 ...* -T/87. 2. [col] capacidade de atrair público (filme, peça, espetáculo, ator, diretor, escritor etc.); probabilidade de ser popular; certeza de êxito financeiro *She had been good box office since the seventies ...* -JEP,30. ♦ *It's good box office to have movie stars involved in scandals.*

in a box [gir] em dificuldades, em um dilema *Inflation has us in a box.* -T/77. ♦ *It won't be my fault if you get in a box.*

BOY bad boy pessoa de comportamento e opiniões chocantes *[He was] ... the bad boy of '60s journalism.* -T/76.

the boys in the back room [col] os políticos que ficam por trás dos bastidores e realmente tomam as decisões *The boys in the back room decide who is going to get the jobs before the open election at the presidential conventions.*

boys will be boys os meninos são naturalmente cheios de energia e, conseqüentemente, ativos, barulhentos, travessos e não devem ser criticados com muito rigor *When Victor and Paul smashed the living room window, their mother refused to be too severe on them saying, "Boys will be boys".*

whipping boy bode expiatório *Just as some American politicians blame Japan for the recession, the U.S. is a popular whipping boy in Europe.* -T/92.

BOYFRIEND [col] namorado *I hear she's got a new boyfriend.* v. **GIRLFRIEND**

BRACE brace oneself preparar-se (para receber um impacto, choque, surpresa, algo desagradável etc.) *When my cousin and I realized that the Ford automobile he was driving was going to hit the wall, we braced ourselves for the impact.* ♦ *[He] ... told his countrymen to brace themselves for hard times.* -T/86.

brace up [col] armar-se de coragem, ganhar ânimo *Brace up and do what I'm telling you to do. Now!*

BRAIN beat one's brains (out) matutar, pensar muito, dar tratos à imaginação, fatigar o cérebro, quebrar a cabeça *He beat his brains out all evening trying to find a solution to his problem.* ♦ *You don't have to beat your brains out on this job.* v. **rack one's BRAINS**

blow one's//someone's brains out suicidar-se com um tiro na cabeça//atirar na cabeça de alguém *He blew his brains out when he lost his fortune in the stock market.* ♦ *In the heat of the moment he blew the man's brains out.*

brain drain [col] migração intelectual, evasão de recursos intelectuais e científicos de um país para outro, especialmente para um país mais desenvolvido *... the much publicized "brain drain" – the mass migration of European scientists to the United States and Canada.* -TA,44. ♦ *... Moscow restricts emigration in order to thwart Western atempts to create a brain drain ...* -T/87.

brain trust grupo de técnicos de várias áreas que assessoram o governo, especialmente em questões de estratégia e política *He will create a group of intellectual and knowledgeable businessmen in a brain trust to solve economic problems.*

brain wave [gir] = **BRAINSTORM** *He had a brain wave which got us out of the stalemate our enemies had brought about.*

have something on the brain pensar continuamente em, não tirar da cabeça, ser obcecado por *That lieutenant on duty last night has got spies on the brain. He sees one under every stone.* -HG,64.

pick someone's brain(s) [gir] conseguir informação (especializada) de alguém para utilizá-la em proveito próprio, servir-se do conhecimento de alguém *[He] ... picked my brain for background detail.* -T/77.

rack one's brains quebrar a cabeça, tentar lembrar-se de *They are racking their brains for a solution for the fuel shortage.* ♦ *I racked my brains but could not remember where I had last seen the suspect.* v. **beat one's BRAINS (out)**

BRAINCHILD [gir] qualquer idéia, plano etc. produzido pela criatividade de alguém *The reform movement in Czechoslovakia was the brainchild of liberal intellectuals.* -T/80. ♦ *He was a brilliant strategist and the whole invading operation had been his brainchild.*

BRAINSTORM [col] idéia-mãe, idéia brilhante *The problem had baffled us for many days when Chuck had a brainstorm that solved all our difficulties.* ⇒ **brainstorming** técnica de solucionar problemas, criar novas idéias etc. mediante idéias e sugestões oferecidas pelos componentes de um grupo *We had a brainstorming session yesterday.*

BRAINWASH fazer uma pessoa mudar de opinião, crença etc. pelo processo de lavagem cerebral *Isn't it sad the soldiers have been so brainwashed that they can't even think for themselves?* -T/69. ♦ *John Frankenheimer's [movie] The Manchurian Candidate ... explored the mind of a brainwashed assassin ...* -T/67. ♦ *[They] ... had been brainwashed into silence.* -T/61. ⇒ **brainwashing** lavagem cerebral *... I met people who had gone through brainwashing in the communist satellite countries of Europe.* -HE,12.

BRAKE put the brakes on; put on the brakes 1. frear, brecar (veículo) *As the car sped around the curve, I carefully put on the brakes.* 2. reduzir a velocidade, movimento, ritmo, atividade etc., retardar *[It is necessary to] Find a way to put the brakes on the world's spiraling population, which will otherwise double by the year 2050.* -T/92. ♦ *... when senior officials of the [Communist] party and state saw how the reforms might threaten their power and positions, they put on the brakes.* -T/92.

BRANCH branch off desviar-se da estrada principal, sair de um tronco central, bifurcar-se *The road to Apache Wells branches off from the highway after you pass Eagle Mountain.*
branch out ampliar-se, expandir as atividades *The company has branched out all over the western states.* ♦ *... it is time for South Korea to branch out into new markets.* -T/89. ♦ *The Collector [a novel], by John Fowles ... [is the] story of a weird, solitary young man who branches out from butterflies to young girls for his chloroformed collection.* -T/63.

BRAND brand name nome comercial de um artigo, produto, mercadoria etc. *That article is sold under different brand names, of course, by the various manufacturers that produce it.* ⇒ **brand-name** que tem nome comercial conhecido *... Americans ... [wear] 200 million pairs of brand-name athletic shoes a year.* -T/89. v. **NAME brand**

BRAND-NEW novíssimo, novo em folha *He owned a knife which was not a secondhand hand-me-down, but a brand-new shining thing ...* -HJE,16.

BRASS [gir] 1. oficiais militares de alta patente *... a lot of military brass and scientists from Los Alamos.* -RE,75. ♦ *Marshal Ogarkov was a controversial choice among the top brass.* -T/87. 2. pessoas que ocupam cargo importante, como executivos, diretores, políticos etc. *The top brass of CBS ... had gathered to cheer the TV network's narrow victory over rival ABC ...* -T/80.
brass hat [gir] 1. = **BRASS** 1. *The brass hats in the army often forgot that many a soldier had more education than they had had.* 2. = **BRASS** 2. *The brass hats have decided to close down the factory in Boston.*
double in brass [gir] ser capaz de exercer dois tipos diferentes de trabalho, servir tanto para uma coisa como para outra, ter duas utilidades *He can double in brass in an emergency.*
get down to brass tacks [gir] ir ao que interessa, discutir o cerne da questão, começar a trabalhar, começar a fazer (o que precisa ser feito) *Let's stop our foolish arguments and get down to brass tacks.* ♦ *... an almost nude man and woman [in a magazine ad] unequivocally getting down to brass tacks ...* -EA,23.

BRAZEN brazen it out enfrentar (acusação, repto, suspeita etc.) com impudência e ousadia, embora sabendo-se merecedor da acusação; agir com ousadia, como se nada tivesse a temer *Though confronted by his accuser, he brazened it out and refused to admit his guilt.*

BREAD bread and butter o pão de cada dia, sustento, ganha-pão *This work is my bread and butter.* -WI,17. ♦ *The West has provided a tremendous store of material for men and women who earn their bread and butter by writing.* -RR,609.

take the bread out of someone's mouth privar alguém de seu meio de vida *If you go ahead with that crazy plan, you'll be taking the bread out of the poor workers' mouth.*

BREAD-AND-BUTTER bread-and-butter letter/note carta de agradecimento pela hospitalidade recebida *Cindy stayed with her relatives in Oregon for a week. After she went home, she wrote them a bread-and-butter letter.*

BREAK bad//good break acaso feliz// infeliz, sorte//má sorte *He's been having some bad breaks lately.* ♦ *He got a good break when he was offered that job.* ♦ *He had a better start in life, and got better breaks, than thousands of other boys ...* -SV,53.

big break grande oportunidade *John Wayne's big break in movies came in 1939 with* Stagecoach.

break apart romper-se, desfazer-se, separar-se *... if he doesn't lead the reform ... the organization may break apart.* -T/92.

break away 1. fugir (de), escapar (de), livrar-se (de); afastar-se ou ir-se subitamente *Strong hands seized her and she struggled to break away.* ♦ *He kissed her tenderly. Then he broke away, saying: "I have to go now".* ♦ *Ivan broke away from his Russian group that was touring abroad.* 2. romper (com), separar-se (de) *He broke away from the traditional dance routines common in classical ballet.* ♦ *... break away from all civil authority ...* -SER,24.

break down 1. demolir, derrubar; vencer (oposição, resistência etc.) *break down walls* ♦ *break down defenses* ♦ *... break down old geographical barriers ...* -T/66. ♦ *They [the fur traders] broke down Indian self-sufficiency, accustoming red men to the guns, knives, and firewater of the white men's higher civilization.* -BR,4. 2. abrandar, fazer perder a intensidade, o vigor; tornar-se ineficaz, sem efeito *... the old taboo on the mention of death is breaking down.* -T/80. ♦ *... the accord had long since broken down ...* -T/87. ♦ *... a time in history when the traditional order is breaking down ...* -GS,174. 3. deixar de funcionar, enguiçar, quebrar (máquina, motor, aparelho etc.) *His car broke down again and he had to take a taxi to work.* ⇒ **breakdown** pane, desarranjo, falha mecânica *My car had another breakdown this morning.* 4. fracassar, falhar, declinar, deteriorar-se, debilitar-se (saúde) *The Byzantine Empire broke down about the year 1000 ...* -MHJ,16. ♦ *... moral controls break down.* -WC,119. ♦ *Bob's health broke down ...* -HA,323. ⇒ **breakdown** falha, fracasso, cessação *... the breakdown of railroad transportation.* -T/60. ♦ *... the breakdown of East-West relations.* -T/81. ♦ *... the breakdown of family life ...* -T/72. ⇒ **broken-down** em péssimas condições, gasto, usado, deteriorado, debilitado, doente *a broken-down bus* ♦ *... a broken-down former newspaper reporter ...* -T/86. ♦ *a broken-down old man* 5. sucumbir à aflição, ao desespero, perder o autodomínio, chorar *She broke down in tears.* ♦ *After a while they [wives] break down and tell us about the beatings their husbands give them.* -LRW,11. ♦ *... he broke down and wept.* -WJT,224. 6. sofrer um colapso nervoso *Because of financial worries Mr. Lane finally broke down and had to take a long rest.* ⇒ **breakdown** colapso físico ou mental *[He was] Continually drunk, perpetually on the verge of a physical and mental breakdown ...* -CS,496. ♦ *In 1929 he suffered a nervous breakdown ...* -T/75. 7. separar em partes, dividir em categorias, classificar *The file was broken down into three categories.* ⇒ **breakdown** divisão em categorias, classificação *Please give me a breakdown of all expenses for the last quarter.* 8. decompor-se, desintegrar-se *Radioactive minerals break down spontaneously ...* -PR,50.

break even [col] não ganhar nem perder (em atividade industrial, comercial, jogo etc.) ... *most toymakers now feel that they'll be doing well if they can simply break even with last year.* -T/80. ⇒ **break-even** relativo ao ponto de equilíbrio, em que não há ganho nem perda ... *my business is operating at well below the break-even point.* -T/81.
break forth irromper, prorromper *A terrible scream broke forth from the woman.*
break free libertar-se *[They] ... saw India break free from British rule ...* -T/91. ♦ *... human consciousness ... continually breaks free of yesterday's dogmas.* -KS,128. ♦ *She broke free from conventions.*
break in 1. arrombar (porta), forçar a entrada (em uma emergência) *The police broke in the door of the old house and found two corpses on the floor.* 2. entrar à força em, invadir (casa etc. para roubar) *She had bolted both doors of her house, but a burglar managed to break in.* ⇒ **break-in** entrada forçada, violação de domicílio *There are many break-ins during the vacation months when whole families go away for a long time.* ♦ *Watergate has become the most famous break-in in the U.S. political history.* 3. estrear, começar a usar (algo), tirar a rigidez de, amaciar (máquina, equipamento, veículo etc.) *I've just begun breaking in a new pair of boots.* ♦ *My wife and I are breaking in our new car.* 4. domar, amansar, amestrar (animal); treinar (principiante) para um trabalho *She's breaking in a new pony for the circus.* ♦ *Mrs. Roberts left her job and her boss had to break in a new secretary.* 5. iniciar-se em uma atividade, começar a trabalhar em *[He] ... goes home to Key West and decides to break in as a professional fishing guide.* -T/73. 6. interromper (conversa, fala), intrometer-se *Nancy and I were having a quiet conversation when Jim broke in.*

break in on/upon interromper (conversa etc.), intrometer-se em *Every time I tried to talk to Mary, he kept breaking in on us.* ♦ *He has an irritating habit of breaking in on private conversations.*
break into 1. romper em (choro, lágrimas, riso etc.); começar subitamente a (rir, chorar, cantar, correr etc.) ... *his whole face broke into a smile.* -RQ,142. ♦ *She broke into tears.* ♦ *The children broke into wild shouts and war cries.* ♦ 2. forçar a entrada em, arrombar *Burglars broke into her home last night.* ♦ *... violence is breaking into the lives of the secure and comfortable.* -T/80. 3. [col] iniciar-se em uma carreira, atividade etc. ... *he tried to break into show business.* -T/87. ♦ *She was only fourteen when she broke into the movies.* 4. interromper (conversa etc.) *Helen kept breaking into our conversation.*
break loose 1. soltar-se, libertar-se, escapar, desprender-se ... *a monkey broke loose last week in the baggage hold of a 727 [plane] about to take off ...* -T/87. 2. desoprimir-se, livrar-se de restrições, explodir, irromper *Unrestrained joy broke loose when the news of the Allied victory reached London.*
break off 1. quebrar (parte ou pedaço de um todo), separar quebrando *She broke off a small branch from the tree.* 2. calar-se abruptamente *He started to say something but broke off when his wife came in.* 3. pôr fim (a um relacionamento, negociação, amizade, namoro etc.), romper, terminar, interromper *The boy is trying to take up the normal life that was broken off by the death of his brother.* -T/80. ♦ *Tom and Mary have broken off their engagement.* ♦ *... the two nations broke off relations last month.* -T/87.
break open abrir ... *he broke open a few of the envelopes.* -SJD,142.
break out 1. irromper, aparecer inesperadamente, começar ou surgir de repente ... *a sweat broke out on his face.* -LR,7. ♦

... *a cholera epidemic broke out in Naples* ... -T/78. ♦ *World War Two broke out in 1939.* 2. fugir, evadir-se, escapar *[He] ... broke out of another [penitentiary] under a hail of bullets.* -T/61. ⇒ **breakout** fuga, evasão *[The Great Escape, a movie, is] ... a wholesale breakout from a Nazi P. W. [prisoner of war] camp* ... -T/63. 3. sofrer uma erupção cutânea (pessoa); manifestar-se em erupção (doença) *I broke out with a rash of goose-pimples* ... -T/73. ♦ *... my face broke out with a rash known as acne.* -FLF,5. ♦ *A severe rash broke out on the boy's face.* 4. ficar coberto de *He broke out in a sweat when the police started questioning him.* 5. aprestar (algo) para uso *The spies broke out the equipment and started bugging the secret conversation between the ambassador and the Prime Minister.* 6. tirar (algo) de onde estava guardado, estocado, acondicionado, recolhido etc. para usá-lo ou consumi-lo ... *he broke out champagne to celebrate* ... -T/87. ♦ *[He] ... broke out his pipe and lit up ...* -T/87. 7. falar em altos brados, exprimir com impulsividade ou violência, dar vazão à emotividade reprimida *He suddenly broke out in a string of obscenities.*

break through 1. atravessar, transpor, penetrar, romper, abrir caminho *After two days of stalemate [in the Iran-Iraq war], the Iraqis broke through and punched toward the east forcing the remaining Iranians back to the shores of the marshes.* -T/85. ♦ *The tanks broke through the enemy lines.* ⇒ **breakthrough** ofensiva que rompe as linhas inimigas, brecha, ruptura *a breakthrough in the enemy lines* 2. aparecer (o sol) *The sky had cleared, the clouds raveled to tatters, and at four o'clock the sun broke through* ... -FS,9. 3. realizar nova(s) descoberta(s), um grande avanço, um grande progresso *He knew he had broken through some important barriers* ... -WCG,76. ♦ *It seems that scientists are finally breaking through in their fight against AIDS.* ⇒ **breakthrough** grande avanço na área do conhecimento, descoberta importantíssima, revolução, transformação radical, ação diplomática que remove obstáculos ... *an age when technological breakthroughs occur almost overnight* ... -T/60. ♦ *... the agreement was hailed as a breakthrough* ... -T/86. ♦ *Practically any breakthrough in knowledge carries with it the possibility that it will be used for evil.* -T/78. 4. alcançar êxito após muito trabalho *In 1953, after starring in* Stalag 17 *and* The Moon is Blue, *William Holden broke through to superstar status.*

break up 1. quebrar(-se) em pedaços *She used an ice pick to break up the ice cake.* 2. dispersar(-se) *Police broke up a group of people being interviewed by a radio reporter.* -T/77. ♦ *The crowd broke up when it started raining.* 3. (fazer) cessar, dissolver(-se), terminar, pôr fim a *The party broke up before midnight.* ♦ *... break up a fight* ... -WJT,46. ♦ *They broke up their marriage after living together for twenty years.* ⇒ **breakup** desintegração, dissolução *With the breakup of Christendom, the Popes lost much of their secular power.* -T/68. 4. [col] afligir, angustiar *When he received the news that his sister had lung cancer he was badly broken up.* 5. [col] terminar um relacionamento, uma união, uma amizade *They got married in 1982 but broke up soon afterward.* ⇒ **breakup** separação, rompimento (de casal, amigos etc.) *They had a breakup after twenty years of marriage.* 6. [col] fazer rir; entregar-se ao riso, dar gargalhadas *Bob Hope's jokes always broke me up.* ♦ *At the end of his story his listeners broke up in hysterics.*

break with 1. romper com (tradição, costume, prática etc.) *She broke with her past.* 2. cortar relações com, separar-se de *Jung broke with Freud and developed his own school of psychotherapy.*

clean break separação completa, rompimento total *[He] ... has to make a clean break with the past ...* -T/77.
even break [col] oportunidade justa, imparcial *If he were given an even break he would be a great success.*
get/have a break [col] ter sorte, ter uma oportunidade, uma chance *He had a better start in life, and got better breaks, than thousands of other boys ...* -SV,53. ♦ *He's a poor guy who has never had a break.*
get the breaks [col] ter sorte, ser um felizardo *He seems to get all the breaks in life.*
give a break [col] dar uma oportunidade, propiciar uma ocasião favorável *Give me a break, will you?*
make a break 1. romper, terminar (relacionamento, vínculo etc.) *C. G. Jung made a break with S. Freud and developed his "analytical psychology".* 2. [col] cometer um erro, uma gafe *Don't make any breaks when you talk to his family.* 3. [col] fugir da prisão *The convicts are planning to make a break tonight.* ♦ *The convicts will try to make a break for it tonight.*
take a break fazer um intervalo (no trabalho, atividade, escola etc.), fazer uma pausa *At noon three students are taking a break ...* -T/87. ♦ *Let's take a break for a cigarette, huh?*
BREAKING breaking point limite máximo da resistência, ponto crítico, momento crucial em que uma pessoa sucumbe à tensão, ao estresse etc. *... these men had reached the breaking point of rage and frustration ...* -T/87.
BREAKNECK vertiginoso, perigoso *Women who expect the police to come rushing at breakneck speed to their aid are usually disappointed.* -LRW,160. ♦ *... breakneck pace ...* -T/87. ♦ *... breakneck schedules.* -T/84.
BREAST make a clean breast of confessar (culpa etc.), desabafar *Why don't you make a clean breast of it? We know you stole the jewels.* ♦ *... they had made a clean breast of the affair ...* -MMA,51.

BREAST-FEED amamentar *Do you breast-feed or bottle-feed your baby?* v. **BOTTLE-feed**
BREATH a breath of fresh air novo alento, mudança bem-recebida *Stanley Kubrick's 2001: A Space Odyssey was a breath of fresh air.*
catch one's breath tomar fôlego, descansar, fazer uma pausa *There are moments when the audience can catch its breath [when seeing* Raiders of the Lost Ark*], but they are brief and shrewdly calculated.* -T/81.
draw/take a deep/long breath descansar após um esforço; respirar aliviado *[He] sat down and took a deep breath.* -DJ,50.
hold one's breath manter-se em expectativa, ficar ansioso, aflito *[He] ... seemed to hold his breath while he waited.* -FL,5.
in the same breath praticamente ao mesmo tempo, quase simultaneamente *As Gunnar Myrdal, the Swedish Nobel laureate, once pointed out, Americans will say, practically in the same breath, "No one can tell me what to do" and "There ought to be a law against that".* -T/86.
out/short of breath ofegante *After an hour, he came back dishevelled and out of breath.* -T/66. ♦ *She walked so fast that she was soon short of breath.*
save one's breath poupar palavras (que não serão ouvidas) *Save your breath because I won't listen to you.*
take someone's breath away causar grande surpresa, admiração, emoção, deslumbramento, maravilhar, deixar boquiaberto *The pristine beauty of the Colorado Rockies always take my breath away.* ⇒ **breathtaking** emocionante, eletrizante, sensacional *breathtaking excitement* ♦ *a breathtaking scenery*
under one's breath em um sussurro, entre dentes *The students didn't talk back to the teacher, but some of them muttered obscenities under their breath.*

waste one's breath falar inutilmente, perder tempo *You're wasting your time if you think you can convince me.*
with bated breath com a respiração contida (devido a medo, emoção, expectativa etc.), quase sem respirar *We stood with bated breath waiting for the bomb to explode near the speaker.*
breathtaking → **take someone's BREATH away**
BREATHE **breathe easily/freely/again** tranqüilizar-se, sossegar, sentir sensação de alívio *You can breathe freely now. The policemen are gone.*
breathe in//out inspirar//expirar *... breathe in through your nose, out through your mouth.* -WCG,19. ♦ *Plants and animals breathe in oxygen and breathe out carbon dioxide.*
breathe into insuflar, instilar *Mr. Wright breathed new life into the plan.* ♦ *She breathed courage into her son.*
BREATHER take a breather [col] = **take a BREAK** *I need a rest. Let's take a breather.*
BREATHING breathing space/spell pausa para repousar, avaliar a situação, reorganizar-se etc. *I told the men there would be no breathing spell until we finished the work.*
BRED-IN-THE-BONE → **bred in the BONE**
BREECHES too big for one's breeches → **too big for one's BOOTS**
BREEZE breeze in(to) [col] entrar despreocupadamente, chegar subitamente *My aunt always breezed in from New York when we least expected her.* ♦ *... a big, bluff man with a jovial grin came breezing into the office ...* -GES,4.
in a breeze [col] sem esforço, facilmente *He can do that in a breeze and not even get tired.*
shoot the breeze/bull [gír] bater papo *After classes we usually went into a small bar near the university and drank beer and shot the breeze.* ♦ *... he was forever dropping by the CIA office to shoot the bull.* -LA,234.
BRICK make bricks without straw realizar um trabalho sem as condições, os materiais e os elementos necessários *In this job, you often have to make bricks without straw.*
run into a brick/stone wall não conseguir atravessar uma barreira ou vencer uma dificuldade, ver-se impedido de prosseguir seu caminho, ser tolhido *[Two reporters] ... kept running into brick walls as they tried to check the story out.* -T/76. ♦ *... when I asked them to prove it by showing me the secret sighting reports [on UFOs], I ran into a stone wall.* -KD,17.
BRIDGE burn one's bridges → **burn one's BOATS**
cross a bridge when/before one comes to it lidar com um problema quando ele surgir, não se preocupar antecipadamente *We'll cross that bridge when we come to it.* -LRW,149. ♦ *That is a bridge we'll cross when we come to it.* -GES,147.
BRIEF fazer um resumo, dar todas as informações ou instruções necessárias a uma pessoa para ela desempenhar satisfatoriamente suas atividades (em uma organização, nas forças armadas etc.) *We all checked our watches after we had been briefed on the procedure for battle.* ♦ *... he would be briefed as to what to say.* -BC,158. v. **briefing**
hold a brief for apoiar, defender, ser a favor de, interceder por *We hold no brief for Western colonial imperialism.* -T/60.
in brief em síntese, em resumo *This, in brief, is what happened.*
BRIEFCASE pasta de couro para documentos *He's carrying a small gun in his briefcase.*
BRIEFING informações e instruções detalhadas necessárias ao bom desempenho de tarefa, missão etc. transmitidas por superiores ou especialistas no decorrer de uma

reunião rápida *Before the meeting with the Russian Prime Minister, the President was given a thorough briefing on the subjects to be discussed.*

BRIGHT bright and early bem cedo pela manhã *We got up bright and early to go on an excursion to White Rock Mountain.*

BRIGHTEN brighten up alegrar(-se), animar(-se), avivar(-se) *You need someone to brighten up your life.* ♦ *She brightened up when she heard the good news.*

BRIM brim over (with) transbordar (de) *He brims over with confidence.* -T/77.

BRING bring about 1. causar, motivar, ocasionar, provocar *How did they bring about such a change in government without a revolution?* ♦ *... bringing about the collapse of the Soviet economy ...* -T/92. 2. fazer um barco a vela mudar de rumo *It is difficult to bring about a boat when the sea has big waves.*

bring around/round 1. fazer recuperar os sentidos, devolver à consciência *The girl had fainted but Dr. Jones brought her around.* 2. persuadir, convencer (por meio de argumentação) *He brought around the other cabinet members to his way of thinking.*

bring back 1. trazer de volta, devolver *I brought back the book I had taken by mistake. I brought it back.* 2. fazer lembrar, trazer à lembrança *Begin the Beguine brings back many pleasant memories.*

bring down 1. diminuir, reduzir, fazer baixar *... a long-term economic revival that would bring down the unemployment rate.* -T/92. 2. abater, derrubar, derrotar, provocar a queda de *The storm brought down many trees.* ♦ *What forces conspired to bring Salvador Allende down?* ♦ *The plane was brought down while flying over enemy territory.* 3. fazer descer, provocar (castigo, ira divina etc.) *When he refused to marry the girl, he brought down on his head the wrath of an outraged father.* 4. [gír] rebaixar, humilhar, diminuir (alguém) *He likes to make remarks that bring down his friends.*

bring forth 1. dar à luz *... Yahweh [Jehovah] cursed the woman to bring forth in pain and be subject to her spouse ...* -CJM,29. 2. dar, produzir *The trees brought forth fruit.* ♦ *Research is systematic investigation which brings forth the logical answer to a specific question.* -VC,112. 3. apresentar, dar a conhecer *In his speech he brought forth intelligent proposals to reduce unemployment.*

bring forward expor, propor, apresentar *A very unusual matter was brought forward at the meeting.*

bring home fazer compreender, fazer sentir, deixar bem claro, bem nítido, dar ênfase *For many Americans, the 1973 oil shock brought home for the first time the fact that the U.S. economy was vulnerable to conditions in distant parts of the world.* -T/92. ♦ *How can I ever forget that sad fact, with you here to bring it home to me?*

bring in 1. introduzir, incluir *Don't bring in points that are not pertinent to our problem.* 2. render, produzir, dar de lucro *... no matter how much the show brought in, he [Buffalo Bill] was always in debt.* -RR,616. ♦ *Her new movie has already brought in upwards of $40 million.* 3. dar, apresentar, anunciar (veredito, relatório etc.) *Don't be surprised if the jury brings in a verdict of not guilty.* 4. fazer entrar, levar para dentro, levar (para determinado lugar) *"Bring him in", the doctor said.* -RP,17. ♦ *... a campaign to bring in foreign investment.* -T/87. ♦ *Her bags were brought in.*

bring off realizar (tarefa etc.) com êxito, levar a cabo, fazer dar certo (apesar de dificuldades) *How did he ever brought off that deal?* ♦ *He's trying to bring off a significant social reform in his country.*

bring on 1. ocasionar, causar, provocar, resultar em, conduzir a *We will bring on*

a precipitous deflation if we persist in high interest practices ... -T/66. ♦ *[He] ... died of shock brought on by ... poison.* -T/64. 2. apresentar, trazer (ao palco, à cena) *Bring on the dancing sisters.* ♦ *Bring on the clowns.*
bring oneself to persuadir-se a fazer algo ou agir de determinada maneira *It is difficult for a man to bring himself to be a martyr when he is afraid he might look a fool instead.* -HO,120. ♦ *I couldn't bring myself to shoot the little dog that was sick.*
bring out 1. destacar, salientar, mostrar claramente, revelar, evidenciar, pôr em relevo *A juror alleged that the jury had knowledge of "other evidence" not "brought out" in the trial ...* -BL,209. 2. publicar (livro, revista, peça etc.) *Margaret Mitchell's novel* Gone With the Wind *was brought out in 1936.* 3. produzir, oferecer ao consumidor, colocar no mercado *Manufacturers are furiously bringing out new clothes and shoes ...* -T/89. ♦ 4. fazer surgir, trazer à tona, desenvolver (traço de caráter, qualidade, habilidade, faculdade, aptidão) *[He] ... has brought out the best in his collaborators.* -T/78.
bring over = BRING around 2 *His persuasive argument finally brought her over to our side.*
bring to = BRING around 1 *... he rushed over to his unconscious daughter and brought her to.* -SJD,72.
bring to bear aplicar (algo) eficientemente (contra), pôr (algo) em ação (contra), aplicar, pôr em vigor *[The U.S.] ... has little military power to bring to bear in the region.* -T/80. ♦ *They were bringing to bear all their leverage ... to get ... [the ambassador] freed.* -LA,181. ♦ *[Margaret Mead] ... brought a keen, insatiably curious mind and anthropological insights to bear on the problems of her own society ...* -T/78.
bring together 1. juntar, unir, reunir *... the distant shouts and barks of dogs were brought together in the single melody of night.* -LJS,39. ♦ *... two persons who are married may be brought together at an emotional level which transcends that to be found in any other type of human contact.* -KAC,12. 2. reconciliar *Robert tried to bring John and Mary together after they separated.*
bring under 1. dominar, subjugar, derrotar *The Indian uprising was quickly brought under.* 2. colocar sob (supervisão, controle, autoridade, categoria etc.) *... the project had to be brought under the aegis of an advisory agency.* -LA,48. ♦ *... the Kremlin is determined to bring the KGB [security police] under control.* -T/87.
bring up 1. criar, educar *... General Douglas MacArthur, an authentic hero brought up by military tradition and brought down by private arrogance.* -T/79. ♦ *He was brought up on a small farm in the Midwest.* ♦ *I was brought up a Lutheran ...* -WJT, 346. 2. levantar (questão) para discussão, apresentar (assunto) para ser debatido, trazer à baila *... Charlie seemed to have something he wanted to say to Mart, without knowing how to bring it up.* -LM,201. 3. [col] (fazer) parar subitamente, deter(-se), despertar a atenção [geralmente **bring up short/sharply/with a start** etc.] *A loud scream brought me up as I walked along the dark road.* ♦ *She brought me up with a start when she said that I must be responsible for her debts.* ♦ *The ambiguous question brought him up short and he said: "Would you mind rephrasing the question?"* 4. vomitar *Joey ate too much at dinner and brought it all up.*
BRINK on the brink of à beira de, na iminência de *The new government is on the brink of collapse.* ♦ *[He] ... is on the brink of going insane.* -T/73.
over the brink para além do limite de segurança, para um estado ou condição de declínio, ruína, fracasso, desgraça, falência, prejuízo, irreparabilidade etc. *Many*

more borrowers could go over the brink along with their bankers. ♦ Low prices and small harvests have pushed many farmers in that area over the financial brink. ♦ ... years of sexual abuse had pushed her over the brink. -T/87.

BRINKMANSHIP a prática de uma política temerária – que visa conseguir determinados objetivos – até os limites de segurança ou à iminência de um conflito *There was a time when actions like our now admitted intervention in Cuba [the Bay of Pigs invasion] were called "brinkmanship".* -T/61. ♦ *In the early 1970s, many political leaders were of the opinion that Kissinger was playing brinkmanship.*

BRISTLE bristle with 1. mostrar (raiva, indignação, agressividade etc.) *The customer bristled with indignation.* ♦ *She bristled with irritation when I mentioned the incident.* 2. ter em grande quantidade, em grande número, estar repleto de *Our task bristles with many difficulties.* ♦ *... a gang of teenagers bristling with weapons.* -T/92. ♦ *[He] ... bristled with versatility.* -T/64.

BRITCHES too big for one's britches → **too big for one's BOOTS**

BROADLY de maneira geral *In foreign policy, broadly speaking, the situation is the same.* -T/87.

BROAD-MINDED tolerante, sem preconceitos ou fanatismo, que fecha os olhos a pequenos desvios do convencionalismo *They're more original, more broad-minded than they used to be.* -T/62.

BROKE (dead/flat/stone) broke [gir] sem dinheiro, liso, duro *I'm almost always broke at the end of the month.* ♦ *He's always flat broke when you ask him for a loan.*

BROKEN-DOWN → **BREAK down**

BROKENHEARTED → **break one's/someone's HEART**

BRONX the Bronx cheer [gir] som grosseiro e ultrajante produzido com a língua entre os lábios, vaia *A loud Bronx cheer came from the crowd.*

BROOM a new broom um novo funcionário costuma demonstrar grande entusiasmo para introduzir mudanças, mostrar eficiência etc. *He won the election because of his slogan: "A new broom sweeps clean. Out with the grafters".*

BROTHER Big Brother o chefe de um regime totalitário; o sistema totalitário como um todo que invade a privacidade do indivíduo e o domina *George Orwell warned: "Big Brother is watching you".*

BROW knit one's brow(s) franzir a(s) sobrancelha(s), a testa *Marsile's brows were knit, his keen black eyes preoccupied.* -PM,14.

BROWN-BAG (it) levar lanche em um saquinho de papel para comer (no trabalho, na escola etc.) *He doesn't eat in elegant restaurants but brown-bags it in the small office that he has to himself.* ♦ *... office workers brown-bagging lunch on the grass ...* -T/73.

BROWNOUT blecaute parcial, redução de fornecimento de energia *During the past three summers, there have been scattered brownouts across the nation.* -T/73.

BRUNCH [col] primeira refeição do dia realizada mais tarde do que o normal, mais reforçada do que um simples desjejum e que substitui *breakfast* e *lunch Saturday we stay in bed late and when we get up around twelve we eat brunch.*

BRUNT bear the brunt suportar a parte mais intensa de um impacto, choque, embate, ataque; sofrer as piores conseqüências, arcar com a parte mais difícil *The Philippine military feels it bears the brunt of criticism for failing to curb the rebels ...* -T/87. ♦ *[The horsemen] ... do not stand their ground to bear the brunt of an attack.* -DM,42.

BRUSH at first brush ao primeiro encontro ou contato *The kiss of your lover, as you may recognize at first brush, is entirely different from that of him who does not truly adore you.* -EA,74.

brush aside/away recusar-se a dar atenção a, não tomar conhecimento de, rejeitar, repelir *She brushed aside any insinuation that her husband might be involved in political corruption.* ♦ *... evidence which we cannot set aside or brush away.* -HGI,24.

brush off [gir] repelir, repelir sumariamente, recusar-se a dar atenção a *Their experiences are not to be brushed off lightly ...* -EM,x. ♦ *She felt she could not brush off the doctor's recommendation.* ⇒ **brush-off** rejeição, repúdio, recusa, acolhimento frio, contestação, rompimento brusco *Am I to assume ... that you want me to give him the brush-off?* -SEB,126.

brush up recordar (conhecimento, habilidade etc.), recapitular, recuperar, refrescar (a memória) *I can still remember Keenan Wynn and James Whitmore singing "Brush Up Your Shakespeare" in MGM's* Kiss me Kate. ♦ *I've been brushing up on Brazilian Portuguese as I'm planning a business and cultural trip to Rio and São Paulo.* ♦ *My son has been brushing up on his chess lately.* ⇒ **brush-up** recapitulação, renovação, revisão de conhecimentos *He needs a good brush-up on English grammar.* ♦ *... after a one-year brush-up course at New York's Manlius School, Carpenter was admitted to the Point [West Point – United States Military Academy].* -T/66.

have a brush with ter um encontro inamistoso, um desentendimento, um atrito, um embate com *After he quit school he had a brush with juvenile authorities.* ♦ *... his closest brush with death came during a typhoon that nearly washed him overboard ...* -T/74.

tarred with the same brush que tem os mesmos defeitos de caráter, que é da mesma laia *He and his cousin must have been tarred with the same brush.*

BUBBLE bubble over ferver, ficar em estado de agitação intensa *... if he was the kind of man who could not keep information to himself, he would be bubbling over like a pot, ready to give it away.* -HW,19.

bubble over with estar cheio (de euforia, jovialidade, animação, entusiasmo etc.) *He seemed to be bubbling over with enthusiasm when he answered her phone call.*

BUCK almighty buck → **almighty DOLLAR**

buck for [gir] empenhar-se (em algo), mostrar serviço (com a intenção de conseguir promoção, vantagem etc.) *Hal is bucking for promotion.* ♦ *He is bucking for Tom's job.*

buck naked [col] completamente despido, nu *We saw her buck naked at a secluded beach.*

buck private [col] soldado raso, recruta *[He] ... was drafted as a buck private into the U.S. Army.* -T/63.

the buck stops here [col] a responsabilidade é aceita aqui, a responsabilidade é nossa e não será transferida a mais ninguém *On his desk, he [President Harry Truman] placed a sign: The Buck Stops Here.* -T/73. v. **pass the BUCK**

buck up [col] animar(-se), encorajar(-se) *For God's sake, buck up!* -CGU,122. ♦ *His drink was beginning to buck him up.* -SEB,108.

a fast/quick buck [gir] dinheiro ganho rápida e facilmente *He is always ready to pick up a quick buck.* ♦ *Always alert for a fast buck, he went to Hollywood in 1926 ...* -T/64.

pass the buck [col] fugir à responsabilidade ou à culpa transferindo-a a outra pessoa *Passing the buck is said to be the art of passing responsibility on to the next fellow, but when Harry Truman took up office as President of the U.S. he placed a sign on his desk that read: "The Buck Stops Here".*

BUCKET bucket of bolts [gir] carro velho e barulhento, calhambeque *You call that old bucket of bolts an automobile?*

bucket seat assento anatômico individual (em automóvel ou avião) *Bucket seats*

seem to have been introduced in automobiles in the sixties.
kick the bucket [gir] esticar as canelas, bater as botas *The old man kicked the bucket last night.*
rain buckets → rain CATS and dogs
BUCKLE buckle down [col] atacar (tarefa etc.) com vigor, dedicar-se (a), concentrar-se (em), aplicar-se (a) *The young people must buckle down if they want to succeed in life.* ♦ *We have an important task ahead. Let's buckle down to it.* ♦ *All right, boys, buckle down to work.*
buckle under ceder, submeter-se, render-se *He buckled under when we told him he must accept the salary cut or resign.*
BUD nip in the bud eliminar (mal etc.) antes que cresça, corrigir (algo) no início, cortar pela raiz ... *I nipped their plan in the bud.* -CGU,127.
BUFF in the buff despido, nu *[They] ... frolic in the buff at exclusive North Sea beaches.* -T/62.
BUG [gir] 1. aborrecer, irritar *What's bugging you?* ♦ *Big Government isn't what is bugging everyone these days ...* -T/87. 2. assediar (alguém) constantemente até conseguir seu intento *Bug him until he agrees to do the job for us.* 3. grampear telefone ou ocultar microfone em um ambiente *This telephone has been bugged.* ♦ *... the bugging of Democratic National Committee headquarters at the Watergate complex.* -T/72. 4. aparelho de escuta (em telefone ou ambiente) *[He] ... used bugs for political spying.* -T/76.
the bug [col] entusiasmo súbito, idéia fixa, obsessão, mania, paixão *[Actress Annette] ... Benning caught the theater bug in college.* -T/91. ♦ *[Clark Gable] ... saw* Bird of Paradise *[when he was about seventeen years old] and was immediately bitten by the acting bug.* -JR,17.
bug/buzz off [gir] dar o fora, se mandar *Bug off, bud.* ♦ *Buzz off before you get hurt.*

bug out [gir] tornarem-se salientes, protuberantes (os olhos) *His eyes bugged out when he heard the news.*
put a bug in someone's ear [gir] fazer uma insinuação a alguém, despertando-lhe a curiosidade e incitando-o à ação *I will put a bug in her ear and we'll see what happens.*
snug as a bug in a rug [col] bem instalado, muito confortável, aconchegado *After a hot bath I felt as snug as a bug in a rug.*
BUG-EYED [gir] 1. que tem globos oculares protuberantes *In the 1950s Hollywood produced a lot of movies about visitors from other planets and bug-eyed monsters.* 2. que está com os olhos esbugalhados (de surpresa, espanto etc.) *Benny was bug-eyed, watching us.* -CGU,143.
BUGHOUSE [gir] 1. manicômio *They took him to a bughouse.* 2. louco, doido *Her son is driving her bughouse.*
BUILD build (something) into 1. servir-se de (algo) para construir ou formar, transformar (algo) em parte permanente de *[He] ... began working at the turn of the century in the ... leather firm owned by his uncle. He eventually built it into one of the finest such companies in Europe.* -T/78. 2. ser parte integrante de *They say that safety is built into their cars.*
build on/upon basear(-se), fundar(-se), edificar(-se) *The basic institutions of marriage and the family are built in our society primarily on sexual atraction, love, and sexual expression.* -RC,54.
build up 1. desenvolver, aumentar, intensificar, criar, formar gradualmente, acumular, estabelecer firmemente, consolidar *Pressure was built up by the escaping gas until the explosion blew out the windows.* ♦ *We must build up an oil reserve in case there is another boycott.* ♦ *He built up his company into one of the most powerful in the nation.* ♦ *Historians have built up an immense body of factual knowledge ...* -MHJ,37. ♦ *The Soviet Union has been building up*

its military forces ... -T/81. ⇒ **buildup** aumento gradual, desenvolvimento, intensificação *... two months after the convention, Jack Kennedy began the long buildup for his 1960 campaign.* -T/60. ♦ *... the stimulation ... [of many parts of the human body] contribute to the buildup of sexual awareness, arousal, and fulfillment.* -GD,24. 2. restaurar (a saúde), melhorar (a condição física) *Dr. Smith is building her up with proper food and vitamins.* ♦ *You must build up your health.* 3. cobrir de prédios, edificar (área) *The huge area on the other side of the river has been built up.* ⇒ **built-up** coberta de prédios, edificada (área) *The built-up areas of most large cities eventually revert to slums.* 4 [col] dar publicidade a, fazer propaganda de, louvar, elogiar *When an egghead [i.e., intellectual] runs for political office, his backers ordinarily try to build up his image as a regular guy.* -T/62. ⇒ **buildup** publicidade favorável, elogio, encômio, campanha publicitária, promoção *Some of the press gave his new book a big buildup.*

BUILDING building block elemento constitutivo, unidade componente, unidade estrutural básica *... basic hydrocarbon building blocks ... have provided the framework for life on the surface of our globe.* -HD,116. ♦ *The tiny electron, and two sister particles [the proton and the neutron], are the building blocks out of which all matter in the world is constructed.* -JRR,13.

BUILT-IN 1. embutido *The ship has built-in fire-fighting equipment ...* -T/61. ♦ *Portable radios have a built-in antenna.* 2. inerente, intrínseco, integrante, incorporado *... there are built-in limits to what man can do.* -T/77.

BUILT-UP → **BUILD up** 3

BULL bull in a china shop pessoa que causa estragos, prejuízos etc. com suas maneiras estabanadas, pessoa desajeitada, inepta *Mrs. Macgillicuddy was so clumsy and tactless that people said she was like a bull in a china shop.*

bull session [col] discussão informal em grupo (principalmente de estudantes) *He spent hours in what he called "delightful bull sessions" in students' rooms or at the Young Men's Christian Association ...* -NEW,41. ♦ *The strictly unofficial bull-session-type discussion that followed took up the entire lunch hour ...* -RE,78.

shoot the bull → **shoot the BREEZE**

take/seize the bull by the horns enfrentar uma dificuldade resolutamente, pegar o touro à unha *The General Secretary [Mikhail Gorbachev] decided to take a more active, direct and public role in advancing the [modernization] process. He resolved to seize the bull by the horns.* -T/87. ♦ *They finally decided to take the bull by the horns and present their problem to the president himself.*

BULLET bite the bullet aceitar com resignação e coragem uma situação desagradável, algo doloroso *Since she didn't know where to reach him, she bit the bullet and took the decision herself.* -JEP,285.

magic bullet droga capaz de destruir bactérias patogênicas sem produzir efeitos colaterais nocivos *I often dream of a day when science will develop a magic bullet to eliminate most infectious diseases that plague mankind.* ♦ *Interferon, it seems, was not a magic bullet.* -T/85. v. **SILVER bullet**

BULLETIN bulletin board quadro de avisos *He was in charge of keeping the bulletin board up to date in his class.*

BULLHEADED teimoso, obstinado, cabeça-dura *You bullheaded idiot! D'you realize what you've done?*

BULLHORN megafone *The officials had to use bullhorns to control the people seeking exit visas.*

BULL'S-EYE hit the bull's-eye acertar na mosca, atingir o alvo em cheio *His*

comments hit the bull's-eye. ♦ *He hit the bull's-eye when he said that we are to blame for the accident.*
BUM bum around [gir] perambular na ociosidade *He bummed around looking for roustabout jobs ...* -T/92.
give//get the bum's rush [gir] expulsar// ser expulso à força de um lugar *The drunk was given the bum's rush and the bar was again quiet.* ♦ *The man who was making a nuisance of himself got the bum's rush.*
on the bum [col] desocupado, à toa, sem trabalhar, na vadiagem *He's been on the bum since he lost his job.*
BUMP bump into 1. colidir com, chocar-se com *The rewards of having two eyes are intensely practical. They keep us from bumping into things and enable us to judge the speed of approaching cars.* -SHR,18. 2. [col] encontrar casualmente *I bumped into him when he came to Boston a few years ago.*
bump off [gir] matar friamente, despachar *He was bumped off by a rival gang.*
bumps and grinds [gir] movimentos sensuais ao dançar que consistem em rebolados da pélvis e meneios de quadris *The old style of bumps and grinds so popular with striptease dancers has now become the popular style of accepted dancing.*
BUMPER bumper crop colheita abundante, grande produção *... the bumper crops have kept the grain prices low ...* -T/87. ♦ *Big farm producers harvest a bumper crop of federal funds.* -T/86.
BUMPER-TO-BUMPER em fila indiana, um imediatamente atrás do outro (veículos) *... the bumper-to-bumper procession of flashy cars ...* -T/87.
BUNCH bunch up agrupar(-se), juntar(-se), amontoar(-se), aglomerar(-se) *... the muscles in his bronze, rocklike jaw bunching up into quivering knots.* -HJC,309. ♦ *The students bunched up in groups as they left the school.*
BUNDLE bundle off/out [col] expulsar sem cerimônia, mandar embora, mandar sair, despachar às pressas; sair às pressas *... two years ago ... [he] would have been bundled off to a labor camp.* -T/87. ♦ *He was bundled off by helicopter to the nearest hospital.* ♦ *The impudent witness was bundled out of the courtroom at the judge's command.*
bundle up agasalhar(-se) bem *She was bundled up in sweaters and skirts and wore a dark shawl about her head.* -HJC,415. ♦ *He was short and looked fat bundled up in his greatcoat.* -KJ,14.
BUOY buoy up levantar o ânimo de, encorajar *We will feel buoyed up by the noble stream of Western civilization of which we are a part.* -FCT,14. ♦ *We did what we could to buoy up his hopes – and ours, too.* -RK,209.
BURN be burning to estar com grande desejo de, estar ansiando por *... the 36-year-old soldier was burning to be President of the U.S.* -T/66.
burn down 1. queimar até o alicerce, queimar até o fim, destruir//ser destruído pelo fogo *... the Yankee soldiers burned down our house, in Missouri ...* -GFT,46. ♦ *... a library has burned down.* -T/86. ♦ *How long does it take a typical king-size cigarette to burn down?* 2. diminuir de intensidade (o fogo, à medida que o combustível ou o material é consumido) *The fire has burned down.*
burn out 1. extinguir-se, apagar-se (o fogo), queimar (o fogo) até consumir o combustível; chegar ao fim, extinguir(-se), (fazer) cessar *The fire has burned out.* ♦ *... the matches burned out in 15 seconds.* -BL,99. ♦ *John's uncontrollable jealousy burned out Sally's feelings for him.* 2. desintegrar-se, derreter-se, fundir-se (pelo calor, pelo atrito) *The light bulb has just burned out.* 3. ser destruído//destruir (o interior de) pelo fogo *The old building was burned out.* ⇒ **burned-out; burnt-out** carbonizado, destruído pelo fogo, queimado *... burned-out hulks of Iraqi*

tanks ... -T/85. ♦ *Burned-out buildings smell of smoke.* -T/77. 4. exaurir(-se), estafar(-se), arruinar a saúde (por excesso de trabalho ou qualquer outro descomedimento) *He was a spectacular football player for a few years but was burned out before he was twenty-five.* ♦ *I feel burnt out, emotionally and physically exhausted.* -MAT,281. ♦ *Mr. Knox has worked so hard during the past few years that he has burned himself out.* ⇒ **burned out; burnt-out** gasto, estragado pelo uso; exausto, esgotado, alquebrado ... *a burnt-out cliché.* -T/64. ♦ *[Giorgio de Chirico, Italian painter] ... died a burnt-out case at 90 ...* -T/78.
burn up 1. queimar inteiramente *All the incriminating documents were burned up.* ♦ *... a dying star ... that has burned up its fuel ...* -T/86. 2. avivar-se (o fogo) *The fire burned up when we put some more wood on it.* 3. [gír] irritar(-se) *He was burned up when she told him she had wrecked his car.* ♦ *It burns me up to be asked silly questions.*
slow burn [gír] ato de encolerizar-se, gradualmente demonstrando-o em expressões faciais *Edgar Kennedy was famous in silent movies for his perfect rendition of the slow burn.*
BURNER cooking on the front burner [col] fazendo a coisa certa, saindo-se bem, correto, no rumo certo *Now you are really cooking on the front burner.*
put on the back burner [col] deixar (problema, tarefa, trabalho etc.) para outra ocasião, aguardar melhor oportunidade *Police complain that they have so many killings to investigate that they must concentrate on the simplest cases and put more complex slayings on the back burner.* -T/92. ♦ *The ... idea [for a business merger] was put on the back burner ...* -T/72.
BURST burst forth irromper *A loud cry burst forth in the still of the night.*

burst in on/upon chegar subitamente e interromper, entrar com violência *The SS [Nazi elite troops] burst in on the Gleiwitz radio station ...* -T/89.
burst into 1. entrar sem cerimônia, precipitar-se em, invadir *As she burst into the living room we all turned to look at her.* ♦ *... the growing mob burst into the two-story villa.* -T/87. 2. irromper em (lágrimas, risos etc.) *I felt like bursting into tears when my husband said that.* ♦ *The audience burst into laughter.*
burst out 1. surgir subitamente, irromper *It was June and flowers were bursting out all over the place.* ♦ *... new leaders and new organizations began bursting out all over.* -T/63. 2. começar a (chorar, rir, gargalhar, cantar etc.) *The clown's jokes made the children burst out laughing.* ♦ *My sister burst out crying when I broke the news to her.*
BUS miss the bus → **miss the BOAT**
BUSH beat about/around the bush rodear o assunto, usar de subterfúgios, ladear a questão *Above all, he hates long-winded analysis and beating around the bush.* -T/87. ♦ *Stop beating about the bush. Tell me exactly what happened.*
bush league [gír] 1. de segunda categoria (time de beisebol) *He played on a bush league team before he got on one of the big national teams.* 2. de pouca importância, inferior *He's just a bush league member of the State Department.*
BUSINESS be nobody's business não ser da conta de ninguém *[She] ... warned that her husband's fidelity was nobody's business.* -T/87.
big business 1. o mundo dos altos negócios, as grandes empresas poderosas e influentes *[His] ... opponents charge that Big Business is the real force behind the government's policy.* -T/92. 2. empreendimento muito lucrativo *By the turn of the twenties, Hollywood had become big business as well, the newest major industry in the United States.* -KA,107.

the business end of (something) [gir] a parte, extremidade etc. de um instrumento, arma, máquina etc. que exerce a função específica desse objeto ... *too often, Soviet power still comes from the barrel of a gun or the business end of a truncheon.* -T/87. ♦ *[He] ... had the business end of a pistol suddenly thrust in his face by one of a gang of teenagers ...* -T/92. ♦ *The business end of the .38 automatic had a cold and deadly look.*
business hours horas de expediente ... *hourly costs [for using a computer network] can vary from $6 at night to as high as $15 during business hours ...* -T/86. ♦ *... business hours are over.* -T/81. v. **after HOURS**
do busines with negociar com *We can't do business with that man.*
funny business [gir] 1. atividade ou ato suspeito, ilegal ou desonesto; trapaça, chicana *There is some funny business going on here after dark.* 2. libidinagem, safadeza *If he tries any funny business with you, let me know.*
get down to business arregaçar as mangas, começar a trabalhar, pôr mãos à obra *The group got down to business just after 8 p.m.* -T/86.
get the business [gir] 1. ser surrado, ser maltratado, ser vítima de violência *He got the business from the rival gang.* 2. ser repreendido com severidade, enfrentar dificuldades *Sean got the business from his father for coming home late.*
give the business [gir] usar de violência contra, surrar, maltratar *When I asked them to return my money, they gave me the business.* 2. repreender severamente, desancar, causar dificuldades *If he attempts to sell the fake stock the government will give him the business.*
go about one's business cuidar da própria vida *He went about his business and tried not to meddle into other people's affairs.*
have no business não ter o direito de, estar errado (em agir de determinada maneira, praticar determinado ato etc.) *I told him he's got no business hitting a pregnant woman ...* -LRW,104. ♦ *He was an optimist when he probably had no business being an optimist.* -T/78.
in business em atividade, em ação ... *50 per cent of these stores were not in business five years ago.* -TA,67. ♦ *A quarter century after Dr. No [the first James Bond story], Ian Fleming's spy is still in business.* -T/87.
know one's business [col] = **know one's STUFF** *I guess you know your business, miss ...* -SLT,108.
make it one's business to propor-se a, chamar a si, estabelecer a intenção de *[They] ... make it their business to know what should be done to give their work its best shot ...* -AJ,6. ♦ *He had made it his business to learn the youngsters' names when he came to town.* -AI,19.
mean business [col] falar a sério, com determinação, não estar gracejando *The new President has stated that he intends to fight corruption and he means business.*
mind one's own business tratar da própria vida, não se meter nos negócios alheios *[He] ... had always minded his own business ...* -NE,111.
none of one's business nada que lhe diga respeito, que seja de sua conta *It's none of my business, Mr. Rath, but aren't you going to make a lot of trouble for yourself?* -WSM,268. ♦ *It's none of my business. But have you got something on your mind?* -MAT,40.
on business a negócio, para tratar de negócios ou assuntos profissionais *Tony flew to Japan on business.*
(not) one's business (não) ser da conta de, (não) dizer respeito a *What an individual does on his own time is his business, not that of his employer or the U.S. Government.* -T/86.
out of business [col] fora de ação, desativado, sem mais que fazer *A 25% cut won't*

put us out of business ... -T/81. ♦ *World War I put the Prussian military machine out of business ...* -T/91.
send about one's business mandar plantar batatas, mandar às favas *They sent him about his business when he became too inquisitive.*
that's your business [col] isso é problema seu *... if you'd rather rot in prison for thirty years that's your business.* -NE,116.
BUSMAN a busman's holiday feriado ou dia de folga em que se exerce atividade igual ou semelhante à do trabalho diário *[He] ... was on a busman's holiday.* -T/73.
BUST [gir] 1. rebaixar de posto *He got busted from sergeant to private.* 2. socar, esmurrar *Shut up or I'll bust you.* 3. soco, murro *Keep quiet or I'll give you a bust on the mouth.* 4. prender, deter *Three mafiosi got busted for carrying firearms.*
bust up [gir] dissolver(-se), terminar, pôr fim a, separar-se *Sammy and Rachel busted up after twenty years.* ♦ *He wants to bust up his marriage.* ♦ *They decided to bust up their partnership.* ⇒ **bust-up** separação, rompimento, dissolução *Marital bust-ups are not unusual these days.*
BUSTLE bustle with fervilhar de, pulular de, abundar em *At that early hour the streets of Manhattan were already bustling with activity.* ♦ *When we got to the building where we were supposed to meet her, the place was bustling with people.*
BUT but for (se) não fosse (por), não fora *But for the [Viet Nam] war, [Lyndon] Johnson might have served two terms [as President].* -T/85. ♦ *[They] ... would have stayed forever [there] but for the war.* -NE,119.
BUTT butt in (on)/into [gir] intrometer-se (na vida de), interromper (conversa etc.) *I don't like to butt into a man's business.* -SL,24. ♦ *She hates it when somebody butts in on her privacy.*
BUTTER butter up [gir] bajular, adular

Hank always butters up people he hopes will help him get a better job.
look as if/though butter wouldn't melt in one's mouth [col] aparentar inocência e recato, fazer-se passar por santo *She looks as though butter wouldn't melt in her mouth but when angered, she is a monster.*
BUTTERFINGERS [col] pessoa descuidada, que deixa cair tudo que pega *... I snatched at pencils and books, succeeding only in dropping everything so often that I was nicknamed "Butterfingers".* -RLI,18.
BUTTERFLY butterflies in one's stomach [col] sensação de medo, nervosismo, ansiedade, tensão *He gets butterflies in his stomach when he goes down a dark road alone.*
social butterfly pessoa que freqüenta muitas festas, sempre presente a reuniões sociais *... she asked her host ... for a job. He, taking her for a social butterfly, refused.* -T/87. ♦ *Zelda McCallister was a social butterfly who flitted from one party to the other.*
BUTTON button down [gir] apurar, identificar, delinear, estabelecer com exatidão *This time we want to be damned sure we've got everything buttoned down [before we voice our opinion].* -T/73. ⇒ **button-down** com botões (colarinho), abotoado nas pontas *... button-down shirts.* -T/80. ⇒ **buttoned-down** conservador, tradicional *... Wall Street's buttoned-down moneymen.* -T/85. ♦ *Smith is a fastidiously groomed, buttoned-down Establishment figure ...* -T/80. ♦ *The Press Secretary ... in his dark business suit and buttoned-down attitude ...* -T/73.
button up 1. abotoar (qualquer peça de vestuário) *He buttoned up his collar and tightened his tie.* 2. [gir] ficar de bico calado *Now, remember: button up when the police begin to ask you questions.*
not have all one's buttons/marbles [gir] ter uma telha de menos, sofrer da bola *He*

still has all his buttons. You can discuss any subject with him. -BS,14. ♦ *The way he acts, he doesn't seem to have all his marbles.*
(right) on the button [gir] 1. exatamente a tempo, na hora, no alvo etc. *... tomorrow at 3:30 a. m. on the button.* -QE,118. ♦ *The rocket came down on the sea right on the button.* 2. exatamente correto *You're right on the button.* ♦ *... her analysis of the ... motive is right on the button.* -T/66.
BUTTONHOLE abordar (pessoa) para dizer-lhe ou pedir-lhe algo, obrigá-la a ouvir o que se tem a dizer etc. *... [French director] Alain Resnais ... buttonholed some businessmen for money and flew off to Japan to shoot a picture called* Hiroshima, Mon Amour. -T/63. ♦ *[The reporter] ... raced to buttonhole civic leaders and senior White House aides as they arrived back in Washington.* -T/79.
BUY [gir] aceitar como válido, verdadeiro, prático etc., aprovar, acreditar *I don't buy that idea at all.* ♦ *The lawyer said: "No jury will ever buy that story".*
buy off subornar *They bought off the Indians in colonial days with presents of glass beads and other inexpensive trinkets.*
buy out adquirir as ações, direitos, propriedade etc. de (sócio, sociedade, negócio, empresa etc.) *[They] ... entered into trade agreements with those firms they could not buy out.* -KA,188. ♦ *He made so much money the first year that he bought out his partner.* -T/60. ♦ *Thompson allowed his partners to buy out his shares in the business.* ⇒ **buyout** aquisição (de empresa, controle acionário etc.) *They began arranging buyouts of small companies ...* -T/86. ♦ *... the proposed $3.9 billion buyout of Dome Petroleum by the Canadian ...* -T/87.
buy up 1. comprar todo o estoque de, a totalidade de *... the great American electrical industries bought up the basic patents on existing, competing sound systems [for sound films] ...* -KA,188. 2. comprar em grande escala, comprar largamente *The Japanese have bought up banks in the U.S. and Australia ...* -T/86.
BUZZ buzz off → **BUG off**
give someone a buzz → **give someone a RING**
BY by and by logo, dentro em breve *By and by the pain went away ...* -TR,16.
by and large de modo geral *By and large, each case of sexual deviation is an individual case.* -DDT,479. ♦ *By and large ... [parrots] are among man's warmest friends in the animal world.* -GET,200.
BYE-BYE [col] adeusinho, tchau-tchau *I'll see you tomorrow. Bye-bye.*
BYGONE let bygones be bygones esquecer o que passou, não pensar mais em, passar uma esponja sobre *Despite the fight we had had, we let bygones be bygones and shook hands.* ♦ *... he's ready to let bygones be bygones.* -FL,89.
BYLINE nome do autor de artigo de jornal ou revista que aparece em destaque acima da matéria *He finally made the big time with a byline on the sports page.* ♦ *[She] ... was a byline writer for the Chicago American ...* -GD,286.
BY-PRODUCT subproduto, efeito secundário *The money has come as a by-product.* -WSM,215. ♦ *All victorious creeds and policies have unintended by-products ...* -MHJ,31.
BYWORD alguém que personifica um tipo; indivíduo ou coisa que se tornou proverbial em virtude de suas qualidades ou defeitos *Carmen Miranda became a byword in American movies.* ♦ *The name of Buffalo Bill became a byword for bravery and sharpshooting.*

CAHOOTS in cahoots [gir] em sociedade, de parceria; em conluio, mancomunado *The sheriff of Apache Wells was in cahoots with a gang of rustlers.* ♦ *[He] ... is in cahoots with drug traffickers ...* -T/87.

CAIN raise Cain/cain/hell/the devil [gir] 1. festejar com algazarra, farrear, divertir-se; fazer muito barulho, causar tumulto, agitação *They went out last night and really raised hell.* ♦ *He raised hell before he married, but now is very quiet and orderly.* ♦ *The children raised Cain when the teacher was out of the room.* ♦ 2. enfurecer-se, causar encrenca; protestar violentamente, reclamar, repreender *He raised Cain when he discovered his girlfriend with another guy.* ♦ *She raised the devil when she found out what her husband had been up to.* ♦ *Papa will raise hell when he finds out you smashed the front window.* 3. causar perturbação, desordenar, danificar, arruinar, destruir *... [the storm] is going to raise the devil with the trees. Tomorrow there'll be branches all over the place.* -OJ,294. ♦ *[Meteors] ... can raise cain with radio reception all over the world.* -SRS,135. ♦ *The cold weather has raised hell with my fruit crop.* ♦ *The German tanks raised hell with the infantry.* ♦ *... a coastal gun [placed] ... on that high ground ... could raise hell with our ... [landing] at Omaha beach ...* -SLS,240.

CAKE have one's cake and eat it too; eat one's cake and have it too fazer com que dois proveitos caibam em um saco [geralmente neg] *... she isn't someone who thinks she can have her cake and eat it too.* -T/72.

go/sell like hot cakes [col] vender-se rapidamente, vender-se em grandes quantidades *... a world where weapons are sold like hot cakes ...* -T/84. ♦ *Her new novel is going like hot cakes.*

take the cake [gir] levar a palma, superar tudo, meter no chinelo, bater o recorde, ser inacreditável *Of all the stupid things I've ever seen, that takes the cake.* ♦ *All is vanity, Portnoy, but you really take the cake!* -RP,145.

CALL call away 1. chamar (a determinado lugar) *Dr. Williams was called away a minute ago.* 2. gritar *Call away all you want. No one can hear you in this deserted area.*

call back 1. pedir que (alguém) volte, chamar de volta *Don't let her go away. Call her back.* 2. telefonar em resposta (a

um telefonema) *Mr. Richardson is not in, but I'll ask him to call you back as soon as he comes in.*
call down [col] repreender *The foreman called him down for his blunders.*
call for 1. exigir, requerer, pedir *The recipe calls for sugar and we don't have any in the house.* ♦ *[Edna Ferber's books] ... are realistic, too, when realism is called for.* -SV,55. *This calls for a celebration.* ♦ *... it was [Fidel] Castro who called for the current negotiations ...* -T/72. v. **UNCALLED-for** 2. ir buscar *She takes the children to school every morning and calls for them in the afternoon.*
call forth evocar, suscitar *It was a task that called forth all his energies and he accepted it wholeheartedly.*
call girl prostituta que marca encontros por telefone; garota de programa *She came to New York to work as a secretary but wound up as a high-priced Park Avenue call girl.*
call in 1. chamar para uma consulta, requerer o auxílio de (médico, especialista, técnico, polícia etc.) *... he was going to call in a heart specialist.* -HA,263. ♦ *When it comes to solving crime, it is still elementary to call in Scotland Yard.* -T/63. 2. tirar de circulação, recolher (notas, moedas, bônus etc.) *... these [bank] notes had been called in by President Roosevelt in April, 1933 ...* -WD,111. ♦ *Argentina called in its pesos in 1985 and launched the austral ...* -T/91.
call it quits [col] 1 = **call it a DAY** *It was past six o'clock when they called it quits and went home.* 2. desistir de prosseguir (uma tentativa, uma disputa, um esforço etc.); dar-se por satisfeito *... I made it very clear to them that either I do what I believe I should do, or else let's call it quits.* -T/87.
call it square [col] considerar algo satisfatório para ambas as partes *If you will fix my radio for me, I will do your typing for you and we can call it square, OK?*

call off 1. cancelar *Our trip to New York had to be called off.* 2. ler ou anunciar em voz alta *Call off all the names on this list and put a check against anyone missing.* 3. mandar retirar-se, ordenar o recuo de (tropa, perseguidor, cão etc.) *"Call off your policemen and I'll give myself up", the thief said.* ♦ *Call off your dogs.*
call on/upon 1. visitar *... it was not until September that I called upon the Judge, and then it was to tell him goodbye.* -CTT,141. ♦ *I called on Mr. Collins the other day.* 2. recorrer a, valer-se de, chamar em auxílio, solicitar, requisitar *... [Mikhail] Gorbachev called on the party to approve a series of reforms ...* -T/87. ♦ *... she was sometimes called upon to speak before civil rights groups ...* -T/63.
call one's own considerar (algo) como seu, ter, possuir *He doesn't even have a pair of good shoes to call his own.*
call out 1. gritar; chamar em altos brados *His wife called out from the kitchen that lunch would be ready in a moment.* ♦ *... a railroad conductor calling out station stops ...* -T/80. 2. convocar para entrar em ação, para enfrentar uma emergência etc. *... the government had to call out the army to quell the disturbances.* -T/84. ♦ *Dr. Smith is often called out in the middle of the night.* 3. convocar (trabalhadores) para entrar em greve *The union has called out the autoworkers.* 4. desafiar para um duelo *In western movies the sheriff is often called out by a gunslinger.*
call up 1. trazer à lembrança, fazer lembrar *The very mention of her name called up images of a distant past.* ♦ *... a smell of leaves and smoke ... called up thoughts of other autumns ...* -CTT,51. 2. convocar para serviço militar *The government is going to call up young men aged between 18 and 22.* ⇒ **call-up** convocação para o serviço militar *... men who are now ... liable for call-up only in a national emergency ...* -T/66. 3. convocar para compa-

recer perante uma autoridade, um tribunal etc. *He was called up by the Un-American Activities Committee to testify against alleged Communists in the government.* 4. telefonar para *I called up the hotel but Mrs. Flynn had already left.* ♦ *Linda called me up just to say hello.* 5. invocar (espírito) *In voodoo, spirits are called up to punish one's enemies.*
call upon → **CALL on**
close call/shave [col] algo indesejável que só não aconteceu por um triz, uma quase-ocorrência, um quase-acidente, derrota, fracasso etc. *The falling rock missed me by a few inches. It was a close call.* ♦ *He had a close shave when his boat sank near the beach and that was enough.*
have no call não ter razão, motivo, justificativa etc. para, não ter o direito de ... *Sergeant Morgan had no call to do some of the things he'd been doing.* -NE,209. ♦ *Helen has no call to meddle in her sister's life.*
make/place a (telephone/phone) call telefonar, dar um telefonema *Tania made a call to her mother in Toronto.* ♦ *[He] ... had placed a call from the motel room to his home ...* -T/72.
on call disponível, à disposição, pronto para atender (chamado, convocação etc.) *... 500 state patrolmen are on call to move into the city on two hours' notice ...* -T/67. ♦ *If you should need any help, I'll be always on call.*
pay a call/visit fazer uma visita, visitar alguém *... the Archbishop of Canterbury ... intends to pay a courtesy call on Pope John XXIII.* -T/60. ♦ *Let's pay a visit to uncle Fred.* ♦ *He paid his mother a visit.*
within call/hail ao alcance da voz, ao alcance de um chamado, à pequena distância, nas imediações *He seems to be always within call whenever I need him.*
CALM the calm before the storm a calmaria que precede a tempestade, a tranqüilidade que dá lugar a uma explosão de raiva *We were living a period of relative peacefulness but I knew it was just the calm before the storm* ♦ *When my father read the letter from my professor he became very quiet, the calm before the storm, and I began to worry.*
calm down acalmar(-se) *... we'd better calm down and talk this over like normal humans.* UL,167. ♦ *... the medication helped calm him down.* -T/92.
CAMERA on camera diante de uma câmera de televisão em transmissão ao vivo *It's no secret that [he] ... didn't like to go on camera ...* -T/86. ♦ *... his on-camera manner is no act ...* -T/84.
CAMP break camp levantar acampamento, partir *[The major] ... sensed an uneasy feeling among his men as they broke camp.* -CHT,140.
camp [gir] 1. comportamento, atitude, interpretação etc. premeditadamente exagerado, artificial, teatral *[Movie star John Wayne] ... carries with him the unmistakable aura of camp and comic strip ...* T/69. 2. de mau gosto, extremamente artificial ou exagerado, cafona, brega *Actor Vincent Price was once called the king of camp horror.* 3. próprio de homem efeminado, homossexual *His camp gestures and walk made it clear that he was gay.* 4. apresentar comportamento e maneirismos femininos (homem homossexual), desmunhecar *When the fag saw the young man he started camping.*
camp it up [gir] = **camp 4** *Some queers try to get attention by camping it up.*
camp out acampar *They camped out in the mountains all week.*
CAMPY [gir] de mau gosto, extremamente artificial, cafona, brega *In his book,* TV Movies, *Leonard Maltin says that Dr. Phibes Rises Again is a "Campy sequel to The Abominable Dr. Phibes ..."*
CAN can afford poder permitir-se, dar-se ao luxo de, ter condições para *That car*

costs a lot of money, but he can afford it. ♦ *He couldn't afford to lose all that money.*
can I help it if ... ? é minha culpa se ...?, sou responsável se ...? *Can I help it if it rains?*
cannot but não poder deixar de, não poder senão *All things exist as bundles of energies subject to the impact of environmental energies. They cannot but change continuously.* -MRMT,5.
cannot/can't help não conseguir abster-se de, não conseguir deixar de *She can't help loving that man.* ♦ *No one can help liking him.* -LRT,25.
cannot/can't help but não poder deixar de, ser obrigado ou compelido a *... one can't help but wonder what the outcome of the evening would have been ...* -T/81.
cannot/can't help it 1. não ser responsável por, não ser culpa de *I can't help it if Margie never arrives on time.* 2. não conseguir deixar de fazer algo, ou deixar de agir, de determinada maneira etc. *She left us and left my father. I guess she was in love and couldn't help it ...* -LRT,67.
cannot/can't help oneself não conseguir se conter *I shouldn't have done that but I just couldn't help myself.*
carry the can [col] levar a culpa, assumir a responsabilidade *Some people were of the opinion that the army had singled out Lieutenant Calley to carry the can for the My Lai massacre in Vietnam.*
it/that cannot/can't be helped isso não pode ser evitado, impedido, remediado *Certain things cannot be helped.* ♦ *Kevin was an editor, and if he was bourgeois, that couldn't be helped.* -SEB,132.
not if I can help it não se eu puder evitar, impedir (algo); não tenciono fazer isso *When I asked her if she wanted to talk to the reporters, she said: "Not if I can help it".*
CANCEL cancel out cancelar(-se), contrabalançar(-se) *When you return a favor, you cancel out a debt.*

CANDLE burn the candle at both ends desperdiçar energias sem repousar, exaurir as forças, estafar-se *... the attractive red-haired poet [Edna St. Vincent Millay] burned her candle at both ends ...* -SV,62. ♦ *If you burn the candle at both ends it will be bad for your health.*
not hold a candle/stick to não se comparar a, ser inferior a *... the current mayor cannot hold a candle to [Fiorello] La Guardia [a former mayor] ...* -T/81.
not worth the candle → **the GAME is not worth the candle**
CAN-DO [col] que tem uma disposição ávida para enfrentar desafios *... he has a confident can-do attitude ...* -T/92. ♦ *... a can-do optimism ...* -T/87.
CANNON loose cannon [col] pessoa ou coisa perigosamente imprevisível, irrefreada, que não está sujeita a condições restritivas *One major concern at the NATO meeting was what [Caspar] Weinberger – regarded by Europeans as a loose cannon – would do and say at a gathering this week of the Atlantic Alliance's defense ministers.* -T/81.
CANOE paddle one's own canoe [col] não depender de ninguém, dirigir a própria vida *When he left his family and went to live in Brazil, he had to learn how to paddle his own canoe.*
CAP set one's cap for [col] tentar conquistar (homem) para ser marido ou amante *He wondered if she had set her cap for anyone else in town.* -OFW,36.
CAPACITY in the capacity of na qualidade de, na posição de *I had seen him several times previously in the capacity of an observer only.* -CCT,29.
CAPITAL make capital (out) of valer-se de, tirar proveito de, lucrar com *Too many times had he seen family quarrels that healed when an outsider stepped in to make capital of them.* -HJ,78.
CAPITOL Capitol Hill; the Hill o Congresso dos EUA, o Capitólio, o poder legis-

lativo do governo americano ... *a debate is going on in the Kremlin, as it is on Capitol Hill, about the value and aim of foreign aid.* -T/67. ♦ *They were old friends when they were both on the Hill.* ♦ *... Capitol Hill conservatives ...* -T/87.

CARD card up one's sleeve → **ACE up one's sleeve**

green card cartão de identidade de um estrangeiro não-naturalizado mas legalmente autorizado a residir permanentemente e trabalhar nos EUA *He carries a green card entitling him to permanent residency in the U.S. ...* -T/85.

hold all the cards → **have/hold all the ACES**

in/on the cards fadado, predestinado, previsível *It was in the cards that he would marry her some day.* ♦ *He was a marked man. It was in the cards [that he was going to be killed].* -SG,23.

lay/put one's cards on the table pôr as cartas na mesa, abrir o jogo, falar com franqueza *He put his cards on the table when she asked him what he was going to do.*

play/hold one's cards close to one's chest [col] não revelar suas intenções, esconder o jogo *... he is playing his cards close to his chest ...* -T/64.

play one's cards well/right [col] agir inteligentemente, saber tirar proveito da situação, aproveitar ao máximo uma oportunidade *Play your cards well in this job and you will get ahead.* ♦ *Maybe you can entice ... [her] to your pad if you play your cards right ...* -WJT,211.

show one's cards → **show one's HAND**

stack the cards/deck dispor as cartas do baralho em certa ordem a fim de trapacear *The card players knew by the way they received their cards that the cards had been stacked.*

stack the cards against someone//in someone's favor arranjar de antemão e de maneira injusta as circunstâncias contra//a favor de alguém; ter as coisas contra si//a seu favor; estar em grande desvantagem//vantagem; tratar injustamente//com favoritismo *All the cards were stacked against Nick Romano, but as long as he had a gun he didn't care.* ♦ *He constantly failed at each and every job that he tried. He felt that he had the cards stacked against him.*

CARD-CARRYING 1. que tem carteira de associado, que é membro registrado de uma organização, especialmente do Partido Comunista *... [Senator] McCarthy ... said he had in his hand a list of 205 card-carrying State Department Communists ...* -LW,94. ♦ *[He was] ... a card-carrying Communist ...* -T/63. 2. [col] genuíno, completo, "de carteirinha," plenamente identificado com um grupo, idéias etc., que apóia determinada causa *... card-carrying liberals ...* -T/81.

CARE care about 1. mostrar interesse por, importar-se com *Clara Barton, founder of American Red Cross Society, cared about less fortunate people than herself.* 2. preocupar-se com *Little children don't care about the results of overeating when it is cake and ice cream.*

care for 1. gostar de, apreciar, querer *Do you think your wife would care for a new handbag?* ♦ *Do you care for Italian cooking?* 2. cuidar de, tratar de, prover a *Florence Nightingale cared for the wounded during the Crimean War.* ♦ *Who cares for the cleaning of the house while you work?* 3. ter amor, afeição, predileção por, importar-se com *Tom cares for his wife very much.*

for all I care é-me indiferente, não ligo a mínima, tanto faz *He can wrap his daughter in cellophane and pack her in mothballs for all I care.* -SM,17.

in care of aos cuidados de *I'll send him a letter in care of his uncle.*

intensive care terapia intensiva *Jim had had a motorcycle accident and was in in-*

tensive care. ♦ *In the intensive-care unit after the operation ... [he] was never left alone with the hospital staff.* -T/68. ♦ *... the intensive-care period that followed the operation.* -T/73.

one couldn't care less não se importar absolutamente, não dar a mínima ... *she has tried to commit suicide, and he couldn't care less about her condition ...* -T/60.

take care tomar cuidado, ser cauteloso *Take care when you cross the street.*

take care of 1. vigiar, tomar conta de, proteger, preocupar-se com *Mrs. Dundee is assured that her baby is well taken care of.* ♦ *... you're a sick man and need somebody to take care of you ...* -OF,140. 2. prover de, suprir (as necessidades de), providenciar *Two thousand dollars should take care of your plane fare and your personal expenses.* 3. [col] lidar com, tratar de *Let me take care of this matter.* 4. [gir] matar, assassinar *Big Louie will take care of the night watchman.*

what do I care? que me importa? *What do I care? This is none of my business.*

CAREER career girl/woman [col] moça/mulher que escolhe dedicar-se a uma carreira profissional dando importância secundária ao casamento *She is a career girl who wants her boss's job.* -MG,377.

CARPET (call) on the carpet [col] (ordenar que compareça) perante uma autoridade, um superior, chefe etc. para ser repreendido *A waitress ... is called on the carpet for being suspected of having affairs with the customers ...* -EA,31. ♦ *[He was called] ... on the carpet for letting the crisis get out of hand.* -T/81.

roll out the red carpet dar uma acolhida real, receber com a máxima hospitalidade *They literally rolled out the red carpet when we arrived.* ⇒ **red-carpet** afável, hospitaleiro, cortês, cheio de atenções *When he arrived in Paris, they gave him the red-carpet treatment.* ♦ *... a red-carpet reception ...* -T/81.

CARRY carry/sweep all/everything before one/it levar tudo de vencida, vencer todos os obstáculos, conseguir êxito pleno *Where school sports were concerned, Danny carried all before him.* ♦ *[He was] ... a confident gregarious young man with a rollicking personality that swept all before it.* -SJ,75.

carry away enlevar, arrebatar, entusiasmar, comover, emocionar [geralmente pas] *McDougal was carried away by emotion when the band began to play* Danny Boy. ♦ *Walter Mitty got carried away by his daydreams and often had unpleasant results in reality.*

carry it/something/too far exagerar, levar ao extremo, ir longe demais *When he called the man a thief, he carried it too far.*

carry off 1. levar à força, roubar, raptar *Helen [of Troy] was twelve years old when Paris carried her off from Sparta.* -KAC,13. ♦ *... a thief carrying off more than $1,000 in merchandise.* -T/86. 2. realizar (tarefa etc.) com êxito, lidar habilmente com uma situação embaraçosa, desagradável etc. *[His awareness] ... enables him to carry off situations that seem outrageous.* -T/60. ♦ *... he was still uncertain if he could carry off the lie ...* -WJT,227. 3. matar, causar a morte de *Plagues frequently carried off whole populations ...* -T/80. ♦ *Frail as she was, the shock of hearing the news could carry her off.* -LA,8. 4. conquistar (prêmio, louvor, honraria etc.) *The first Indian team to enter the Olympics, in 1928, carried off a gold medal.* -T/84.

carry on 1. continuar, prosseguir sem interrupção (trabalho, tarefa, atividade etc.), não se deter (especialmente diante de obstáculos ou dificuldades) *Carry on with your work.* ♦ *... they are fundamentally decent persons caught in the stupid tragedy of war ... carrying on courageously ...* -SV,127. 2. gerir, administrar, conduzir,

manter, ocupar-se com *The sons now carry on the business of their father.* ♦ *... it was impossible for him to carry on a conversation.* -GES,128. 3. [col] comportar-se de maneira tola, infantil, extravagante, ruidosa etc., portar-se mal; demonstrar raiva, aborrecimento, desagrado com relação a, queixar-se com veemência *"Do your boys always carry on like this?", he asked Mrs. O'Hara.* ♦ *Meg carries on about her husband to anyone who will listen to her.* ⇒ **carrying-on** comportamento suspeito, impróprio, ocorrência esquisita, atividade anormal; agitação, barulho, bagunça *There have been strange carryings-on in their apartment lately.* 4. [col] manter relação extraconjugal, ter um caso *He is said to be carrying on with his secretary.* 5. lamentar-se, afligir-se, chorar, ficar histérico *She carried on terribly when she heard her son had been seriously injured in a motorcycle accident.*
carry out executar, cumprir, desempenhar, levar a cabo, completar *Please carry out my orders.* -HRA,36. ♦ *... Winston must be sentenced to death and the sentence must be carried out promptly.* -FH,13. ♦ *[He] ... had never been asked to carry out an investigation ...* -T/73.
carry through 1. executar, realizar, pôr em ação, levar a cabo *Their plan was carefully carried through.* ♦ *How long could he hope to carry it [his impersonation of another man] through?* -HEB,32. 2. ajudar, auxiliar (em uma dificuldade etc.), amparar *His unconquerable will carried him through.*
CART cart off remover, retirar; levar [geralmente] à força [para a cadeia etc.] *... pieces [of the Berlin Wall have been] carted off to a huge depot for resale as art ...* -T/91. ♦ *... the Gestapo ... carted him off to a concentration camp.* -SWLR,373. ♦ *I insisted that either he call a doctor or ... [we] would pick him up and bodily cart him off to the hospital.* -HA,279.

put the cart before the horse pôr o carro adiante dos bois *You're putting the cart before the horse when you say that he took to drinking after his wife left him.*
CARVE carve out criar, fazer, construir (com trabalho árduo e persistência) *[He] ... was 25 and had already set about carving out a career ...* -T/69. ♦ *[He] ... carved out a large but financially troubled empire ...* -T/87.
carve up [col] dividir, partilhar, desmembrar *[King Lear] ... proposes to carve up the map of England for his daughters.* -T/68. ♦ *Today's models [of sneakers] are a mixture of fashion and technology and are carving up a $9 billion market.* -T/89.
CASE as the case may/might be conforme o caso *We don't know what will happen to Jim. He may either be discharged from his job or moved to another department, as the case may be.* ♦ *... she had recognized a force against which she could and would fight, fairly or unfairly, as the case might be.* -SEB,114.
a case in point um caso ilustrativo, uma situação que serve de exemplo *Some people just can't keep their mouth shut. Dan's wife is a case in point.*
get down to cases [gír] tratar do essencial, dos detalhes importantes, ir ao que interessa *This meeting is urgent. Let's get down to cases without wasting time.* ♦ *When the film [The Alamo] finally gets down to historical cases, it proves to be shamelessly inaccurate.* -T/60.
in any case de qualquer maneira, seja como for, aconteça o que acontecer ou possa ter acontecido *No one knows what will happen to Endicott, but in any case, you can be sure that he'll be punished.*
in case se, caso *In case Mr. Shannon brings the money, you know what to do.*
in case of na hipótese de *In case of an emergency, you can always turn to Paul.*
just in case por via das dúvidas, por precaução, para a eventualidade (de) *There*

were always a number of high-speed limousines kept handy ... just in case ... -NE,463. ♦ *All recruits go through rugged basic training, learning to shoot and strip rifles (just in case they ever have to in an emergency) ...* -T/76.
make a federal case (out) of [gir] fazer tempestade em copo d'água, exagerar *Don't make a federal case of it, please. Marriage isn't for me, that's all.* -MJA,1062.
make (out) a/one's case provar, estabelecer a prova de, provar as suas alegações, apresentar argumentos a favor de *In order to make his case, [Walter] Mondale last week challenged [President Ronald] Reagan to a series of six televised debates ...* -T/84. ♦ *Dr. [Edward] Wagenknecht, in [his book]* Utopia Americana, *makes out an excellent case for the* Wizard [of Oz] *[an American fairy tale] as an important item of Americana ...* -SV,48. ♦ *[They] ... have apparently been unable to make a case against him.* -T/87.
overnight case → **overnight BAG**
rest one's/the case dar por encerrada a apresentação de provas ou a argumentação (em um julgamento) *The defense rests its case.*
CASH cash crop safra destinada à comercialização, não a consumo próprio *... sugar cane continues to be the most important cash crop in the region [northeastern Brazil].* -WC,30.
cash in 1. converter (fichas, ações etc.) em dinheiro *His lawyer instructed him to cash in all his bonds.* 2. obter bom lucro, ganhar dinheiro, faturar *Everyone hopes to cash in this summer when an army of tourists ... marches in.* -T/81. 3. [gir] esticar a canela, morrer *The old man cashed in last night.*
cash in on [col] tirar bom proveito de, auferir vantagem de, lucrar com *He had decided to cash in on the fame of his brother who was a famous writer.* ♦ *[They] ... cash in on their experience and contacts by becoming private dealers.* -T/87.
cash on the barrelhead [col] pagamento à vista, contra a entrega da mercadoria *He wants cash on the barrelhead.*
cash on the line pagamento à vista, imediato *It's cash on the line or we won't do business with you.*
cold cash [col] grana, dinheiro na mão, dinheiro disponível *[He] ... wasn't making this movie for an Oscar award, just for cold cash.* -CG,29.
hard cash moeda corrente, dinheiro *... their efforts were going to pay large dividends in hard cash.* -HRW,5. ♦ *Some 50% of the total will be in hard cash ...* -T/60. v. **hard CURRENCY**; **hard MONEY**
petty cash pequeno fundo para despesas menores *How much petty cash is there left?*
ready cash → **ready MONEY**
spot cash dinheiro à vista, dinheiro disponível *He paid spot cash for his car and received a considerable discount.*
CAST be cast away sofrer naufrágio, ser lançado numa praia solitária *In the novel* Lord of the Flies, *a group of boys are cast away on a desert island.* ⇒ **castaway** náufrago; naufragado *They became castaways on a desert island.* ♦ *... a band of castaway boys high and dry on a desert island.* -T/63.
cast about/around procurar, buscar, tentar encontrar (saída, solução, explicação, desculpa etc.) *[They are] ... desperately casting about for a way to restore peace.* -T/87. ♦ *[He] ... cast about for another candidate ...* -T/64. ♦ *Casting desperately around for someone else ...* -T/65.
cast aside afastar, pôr de lado, rejeitar, abandonar *He cast aside his old friends when he became rich and famous.* ♦ *... the old traditions that have been cast aside ...* -MM,14.
cast down deprimido, desalentado, triste *Jenny was cast down after I gave her the bad news.*

cast off 1. soltar as amarras de um barco do ancoradouro *Just after we cast off, we realized we had forgotten to put the oars in the boat.* 2. abandonar, rejeitar, repudiar, descartar *In later years, when she became rich and famous, she cast off some of the people who had helped her.* ♦ *The exuberant humanists, it might seem, were in fact casting off all authority, not merely that of the medieval church ...* -BCS,36. ♦ *... cast off the plagues of racial politics.* -T/87. ⇒ **cast-off** refugado, enjeitado, descartado, abandonado, repudiado *They'd been dressed in ... cast-off clothing, indescribably dirty.* -HWR,15. ♦ *a cast-off mistress* ⇒ **cast-off** pessoa ou coisa enjeitada, abandonada, repudiada, descartada etc. *He was wearing an old coat, a castoff from a friend.* ♦ *... the Committee for the Re-Election of the President ... [is staffed] in part with castoffs from the White House ...* -T/72.
cast out expulsar, excluir, escorraçar, banir *Many pets are cast out into the streets by their owners.*
CAST UP 1. lançar à superfície, trazer à tona *The sea had cast up the remains of the torpedoed ship.* 2. levantar, elevar *She cast up her eyes in a silent prayer.*
CASTLE (build) castles in the air (construir) castelos no ar (entregar-se a) devaneios, (acalentar) sonhos *His hopes to marry Helen were just castles in the air.*
CAT cat got your/his tongue? o gato comeu sua língua? *What's the matter with the boy? Cat got his tongue?*
fat cat [gir] pessoa rica e influente, especialmente alguém que doa vultosas importâncias a partido político *... Republican fat cats ...* -T/87. ♦ *What fat cat paid his expenses?*
holy cats → **holy COW**
let the cat out of the bag [col] revelar um segredo (nem sempre involuntariamente) *I promised myself you'd never know, Emily, but I guess I've let the cat out of the bag, haven't I?* -HWL,44.

like a cat on a hot tin roof [col] muito apreensivo, nervoso, inquieto, agitado *She is like a cat on a hot tin roof when her husband goes on a trip.*
look like something the cat dragged in [gir] estar com péssima aparência *What happened? You look like something the cat dragged in.*
rain cats and dogs/buckets/pitchforks [col] chover a cântaros, chover torrencialmente *It had been clear and sunny when suddenly it began to rain cats and dogs from clouds that seemed to have burst.* ♦ *It was raining buckets when I left her apartment.*
CATBIRD the catbird seat [col] posição vantajosa, lugar privilegiado *... because I could see the cards my opponents were dealt, I was plumped squarely in the catbird seat.* -CGU,40.
CATCH catch flat-footed [gir] apanhar (alguém) desprevenido, apanhar de surpresa *They're caught flat-footed this time.* -FL,35. v. **FLAT-footed**
catch/get it [col] levar uma bronca, receber uma descompostura; ser punido, receber um castigo *If your mother sees you doing that, you'll certainly catch it.* ♦ *We're getting it from all sides.* -T/81.
catch napping apanhar (alguém) desprevenido *Nobody ever caught him napping.* -HJC,193.
catch on [col] 1. compreender, apreender *His statement was so confusing that I failed to catch on.* 2. adquirir popularidade, entrar em moda, pegar *The public liked her new song and it caught on.* ♦ *[She] ... caught on as a model.* -T/81.
catch out apanhar em erro, flagrar *Frank's a smart one. You'll never catch him out.*
catch phrase; catchphrase expressão que cai no agrado do público e passa a ser usada amplamente *Some interesting catchphrases are: "We like Ike." "Give'em hell, Harry." "Diamonds are a girl's best*

friend." "Just what the doctor ordered." "I shall return.".
catch-22 situação paradoxal ou dificuldade (também lei, estatuto, regulamento etc.) da qual é impossível o indivíduo escapar ou livrar-se, já que isto é impedido por uma condição inerente à situação original (a um artigo da lei etc.) *[He, a patient] ... is caught in a vexing catch-22. ... he is now well enough to resume his career as an actor. But if he works, he may lose his Medicaid benefits.* -T/80.
♦ *People can't find work to pay for their education, because they cannot afford an education to get a job. Catch-22!* -T/92.
♦ *[They] ... are caught in a catch-22 dilemma.* -T/80.
catch up 1. enredar, envolver, tolher [geralmente pas] *Billy and Ted were caught up in the barbed wire.* ♦ *He got caught up in his own web of intrigue.* 2. encantar, fascinar, cativar [geralmente pas] *The tourists were caught up in the magic and beauty of Rio's carnival.* ♦ *The two men were caught up in the spirit of the occasion and sang loudly and merrily.*
catch up on pôr em dia, atualizar, completar (algo que ficou faltando, que não foi terminado etc.), recuperar *Jack will try to catch up on all the things that he missed while in prison.* ♦ *I have to catch up on my reading.* ♦ *[They] ... wanted to catch up on some sleep.* -BC,333.
catch up with 1. alcançar, emparelhar-se com, atingir a mesma igualdade, situação, estado, de; pôr-se em pé de igualdade com *Young Jim Thorpe runs fast. You'll never catch up with him.* ♦ *He turned out to be a slow learner and was unable to catch up with the other kids in school.* ♦ *Shaw is trying to catch up with his well established competitors in the food selling business.* 2. produzir um efeito inevitável, um efeito inexorável do qual não se pode fugir *His past eventually caught up with him when his secret life was brought out into the open.* ♦ *I'm afraid old age is beginning to catch up with me.* 3. deter, capturar, prender *The FBI finally caught up with the spy in Miami.*
wouldn't be caught/found dead não seria visto nem morto (em determinado lugar, na companhia de, usando determinada roupa etc.), recusar-se-ia terminantemente a *I wouldn't be found dead in that place.*
♦ *Girls play "school" as readily as they play "house", whereas any normally robust boy would not be caught dead playing either game.* -AD,482.
CATER cater for suprir, fornecer (comida, provisões, serviços) *They run a restaurant and also cater for banquets and parties.*
cater to 1. suprir, prover (alguém com aquilo que é necessário ou que satisfaz seus desejos, gosto popular etc.) *Ralph's mother catered to all his likes and dislikes in food but his wife fed him what she liked.*
♦ *... as he became increasingly incapacitated, she devoted herself to catering to his every need.* -T/92. ♦ *This shop caters to discriminating people.* 2. mostrar favoritismo, tratar com consideração especial *When jobs are given he always caters to his friends.*
cater-cornered; cater-corner; catty-corner diagonalmente situado; diagonal(mente), oblíquo, obliquamente *The drugstore is cater-cornered from the new twenty-storied building.* ♦ *At the corner he started cater-cornered across Main Street toward the jail ...* -HO,106. ♦ *... there's a bar catty-corner, across the street.* -SEB,182.
CAUSE lost cause movimento, ação, ideal, esforço etc. que não terá êxito ou que já foi derrotado, causa perdida *Has the survival of planet Earth become a lost cause?*
CAUTION throw (all) caution/discretion to the wind(s) abandonar toda a cautela, agir com audácia *Al was ready to throw all caution to the wind and tell Marcia how much he loved her.*

CAVALIER cavalier (attitude/manner/way etc.) (atitude) arrogante, (maneira) rude, (acolhimento) desdenhoso, despótico etc. *... Indonesia's Moslems ... were becoming increasingly resentful of the cavalier treatment they were getting ...* -T/66. ♦ *They were treated in a cavalier manner.*

CAVE cave in 1. (fazer) ceder, desmoronar, afundar *There was an explosion and the roof of the house caved in.* 2. sucumbir, não resistir, ceder, admitir a derrota, falir, fracassar, desistir *Many small businesses caved in during the monetary crisis.* ♦ *The producers of the film caved in and altered its ending to satisfy the star.*

CEILING hit the ceiling/roof [gir] enfurecer-se, protestar violentamente *When I told my father that I had quit school, he hit the ceiling.* ♦ *Max hit the roof when he found out his car had been stolen.*

CELLAR the cellar [col] o último lugar (na classificação de clubes que disputam o campeonato), a lanterninha *I think my team is going to wind up in the cellar this year, the way they are playing.*

CENT feel like two cents [gir] sentir-se insignificante; sentir-se humilhado, envergonhado *Mr. Murray felt like two cents when he was unable to help the poor families in his district.*

red cent um vintém furado, um tostão [geralmente neg] *When it came time to pay the bill, he found that he didn't have a red cent.*

two cents worth [gir] opinião, palpite, comentário (não-solicitado) *Herbie always has to get in his two cents worth in any argument.* ♦ *Let me put in my two cents worth.*

CEREMONY stand on ceremony fazer cerimônia, portar-se com formalidade *Don't stand on ceremony. Relax. You're among friends.*

CERTAIN for certain com certeza, sem dúvida, por certo *Could they say for certain that the games [strategies] were White House sponsored?* -BC,140.

CHAIN chain gang grupo de prisioneiros acorrentados uns aos outros (quando executavam trabalhos forçados) *He was a fugitive from a chain gang.* ♦ *... black convicts on a Mississippi chain gang.* -T/78.

chain of command a hierarquia de autoridade nas forças armadas *... he was regarded as a painstakingly efficient officer who paid scrupulous attention to the chain of command ...* -T/87.

chain stores cadeia de lojas *There are lots of chain stores all over the country.*

CHAIN-SMOKE fumar continuamente, fumar sem parar *He chain-smoked so frantically that he sometimes had two or three cigarettes going at the same time.* -T/69. ⇒ **chain-smoker** pessoa que fuma sem parar *Chain-smokers often ruin their health at an early age.*

CHAIR easy chair poltrona *[They] ... sat in a semicircle of easy chairs facing the empty fireplace.* -MD,63.

rocking chair cadeira de balanço *... patients who had spent all day in a rocking chair ...* -T/69.

CHALK chalk out delinear, esboçar *Buddha was the rare mystic able to chalk out clearly to others the signposts leading out of reality, in the form of easily remembered shorthand formulas.* -T/64. ♦ *He chalked out a clever plan of attack.*

chalk up 1. registrar, anotar *The club has chalked up losses totaling $13 million since 1989 ...* -T/92. 2. atribuir, imputar, creditar *If I've been rude, I apologize. Chalk it up to my being tired and ignorant.* -NE,178. 3. conseguir, atingir, conquistar *The firm chalked up a record volume of sales last year.*

walk the chalk/chalk mark/line andar na linha, comportar-se, proceder bem *He makes his employees walk the chalk.* ♦ *In one of his songs, Johnny Cash says: "Yes,*

I'll admit that I'm a fool for you./ Because you're mine, I walk the line".

CHANCE by chance por acaso, fortuitamente, sem planejar, a esmo *He says that nothing happens by chance.* ♦ *The killers operate at night ... apparently picking their victims by chance.* -T/72.

chance it correr o risco, arriscar *With all the snow on the mountain road, I wouldn't chance it if I were you. Wait a few days for better weather.*

chance/happen on/upon encontrar por acaso *... in 1953, I chanced upon a book by Frederick Pohl, who had spent many years trying to solve the riddle of the Vikings and their voyages to New England.* IBCMT,xiv. ♦ *Peaceably strolling along a London street, Ryan happens on a terrorist attack on a cousin of the royal family's.* -T/92.

(the) chances are [col] provavelmente, de acordo com as probabilidades *If you do not understand language well and cannot use it effectively, the chances are that you will not do very well in college.* -BCM,3. ♦ *Chances are he'll be arrested before long.*

fat chance [gir] diminuta probabilidade, remota possibilidade *Fat chance I have of becoming rich.* ♦ *Fat chance that we will be invited to her party.*

fighting chance [col] possibilidade de sucesso, vitória, realização etc. que depende de um grande esforço *If I do what must be done, I think I have a fighting chance of saving his life.*

not a chance [col] de jeito nenhum, nem por sombra *When I asked him if he could lend me fifty dollars, he said: "Not a chance".*

not have a chance (in hell) [col] não ter a mínima probabilidade *... Colonel Cathcart did not have a chance in hell of becoming a general.* -HJC,220.

on the (off) chance na probabilidade (remota ou improvável) *He hated to leave the apartment on the chance that Lakla might show up any minute.* -SLT,65. ♦ *Tommy passed by Jackie's house on the off chance of seeing her.*

stand a chance ter probabilidade *He stands a good chance of getting that job.* ♦ *He hopes to win the race but he really doesn't stand much of a chance.*

take a chance arriscar-se, aventurar-se *Jordan took a chance when he crossed the bridge.*

CHANGE the change → **the CHANGE of life**

change of heart mudança de opinião, sentimento, atitude etc. *He had a change of heart while he was in prison.* ♦ *The reason for the change of heart is not clear ...* -T/87.

the change (of life) menopausa *Mrs. Brown is going through the change of life.*

for a change para variar, para fugir à rotina *Maybe you are going to sleep alone for a change ...* -HG,234.

ring (the) changes variar as maneiras de fazer ou dizer uma coisa ou de agir, reiterar algo de muitas maneiras, insistir no mesmo tema empregando variações *... he rang very inventive changes on his basic material.* -T/73.

small change 1. moedas de baixo valor, troco miúdo *I have no small change right now.* 2. [col] pessoa insignificante, mediocridade; coisa sem valor, ninharia *He was considered small change in the organization.* ♦ *That is small change, however, compared with a program begun in 1976 ...* -T/87.

work a change produzir uma mudança, alterar *The new decree worked a change in the habits of the government workers.*

CHANGEOVER viravolta, transição, conversão, mudança de um sistema, método, processo, programa, condição etc. para outro *A changeover in moral attitudes is under way.* -HEW,5. ♦ *... a changeover [from black-and-white TV] to color is planned ...* -T/78.

CHANNEL go through channels passar pelos meios oficiais de comunicação, tramitar pela forma legal, pelos canais competentes *We wasted a lot of precious time going through channels.* ♦ *This will have to be done through the proper channels.*

CHAPTER **give/cite/quote chapter and verse** ser preciso e explícito (em uma citação), citar textualmente, dar referências exatas *She not only stated all the facts clearly, but quoted chapter and verse.*

CHARACTER **a character** pessoa excêntrica, esquisita, "figura" *He's a character. My guess is you won't like him.* -RL,15.

character actor ator que interpreta personagens incomuns ou excêntricas *Walter Huston was a distinguished character actor whose performance in* The Treasure of the Sierra Madre *was simply superb.*

character assassination difamação do caráter de uma pessoa *... I have not enough tears to weep for ... those others who ... while still living, suffer character assassination.* -T/68.

in//out of character consistente//inconsistente com o comportamento habitual ou a natureza de uma pessoa *His act was in character for a man who has always fascinated public opinion.* ♦ *... an affection that seemed out of character and incongruous to the cynical gambler he professed to be.* -JJ,131.

CHARGE **charge account** conta-corrente (em loja) *Mrs. Van Hopper has charge accounts in all the best stores in New York.*

charge with 1. dar tarefa ou responsabilidade, encarregar, incumbir *The committee charged him with a very important task.* 2. acusar de, culpar/responsabilizar por *I'm going to charge you with this murder ...* -MMA,22. 3. saturar, impregnar, carregar *His voice was charged with grief.* ♦ *... Billy's words were charged with a deep Biblical faith.* -T/63.

free of charge(s) sem despesas, grátis, gratuito *She received a full-color catalogue free of charge.*

get a charge out of [gir] = **get a BANG out of** *He gets a charge out of all the beautiful girls that come to his office.*

have charge of ser responsável por, estar encarregado de, administrar, gerenciar *Mr. Smith has charge of the Educational Department.*

in charge (of) responsável (por), encarregado (de) *His position placed him in charge of all public works and public money ...* -EMW,12. ♦ *Who's the officer in charge?*

take charge (of) tomar conta (de), encarregar-se (de), assumir a direção (de) *He is definitely the boss, the authority, the expert, the one who takes charge and tells people what to do.* -MA,15 ♦ *[President] Reagan ordered the State Department to take full charge of any future relations with Iran.* -T/87.

CHARLEY **charley horse** [col] rigidez muscular, câimbra *He was kicked in the upper leg and had a charley horse that put him out of the game.*

CHASE **chase after** ir em perseguição de, ir atrás de, buscar, procurar *Larry and I were crossing a field on my father's farm when a bull chased after us.* ♦ *... Farrah Fawcet-Majors is the girl that every boy chased after in high school but could never quite find.* -T/78.

chase down buscar, procurar, tentar localizar *The policeman chased down all clues that might lead to the murderer.* ♦ *... chasing down elusive documents ...* -T/87.

give chase dar caça, ir em perseguição *The pilot of an F-94 plane spotted an unknown object at 26,000 feet and gave chase but the object managed to get away.*

lead someone a merry chase evitar ou tornar difícil ser alcançado ou capturado por, dar muito trabalho (a alguém) em uma perseguição, busca, procura etc. *Though wounded, the escaped prisoner led his pursuers a merry chase.*

CHEAP on the cheap [col] a baixo custo, com pequeno orçamento, na bacia das almas *[He] ... operates out of Pittsburgh, making his films on the cheap.* -T/73.

CHEAPSKATE [gir] pessoa sovina, pão-duro, unha-de-fome *He is such a cheapskate that he makes guests in his house pay for their food.*

CHEAT ON [gir] ser infiel ao cônjuge, enganar, trair *Mrs. Robinson was said to cheat on her husband.*

CHECK blank check liberdade completa de ação, plenos poderes, carta branca *He was given a blank check to take any action he deemed necessary to carry out the program of reforms.*
check in 1. registrar a entrada num hotel *He checked in at the São Paulo Hilton on July 27.* 2. apresentar-se para embarque em avião *What time must you check in for your flight?* ♦ *Make sure you check in at the airport by 3 o'clock p.m.* ⇒ **check-in** balcão onde os passageiros (de avião) se apresentam para embarque *You're supposed to be at the check-in by 4 o'clock p.m.* 3. [col] apresentar-se (ao serviço etc.), marcar o ponto, registrar sua presença (no local de destino), chegar *As soon as you check in, come up to my office.* ♦ *[The plane] ... checked in with the approach control tower ...* -T/64. 4. devolver ou receber a devolução de (algo que é emprestado – livro, ferramenta, aparelho etc.) mediante o devido registro *Tom returned the books to the librarian and she checked them in.*
check into 1. registrar-se em, dar entrada em (hotel etc.) *We checked into the Miami Hilton on a Saturday morning and checked out on the following Tuesday.* ♦ *[Ernest] Hemingway checked into Minnesota's Mayo Clinic, where he was treated for 53 days last winter.* -T/61. 2. investigar ... *he would have to check into the facts before he could approve the statement.* T/62.
check off conferir, assinalar, ticar, marcar com um sinal de "conferido" indicando exatidão ... *they checked off each item carefully.* -MW,668. ♦ *He checked off all the names on the list.*
check on averiguar, examinar, fazer investigações sobre *A suspicious sheriff checked on a Cadillac parked on the street ...* -WD 102.
check out 1. pagar a conta e deixar um hotel *He had slipped from the hotel's rear door without checking out, without taking his luggage.* -HJ,60. 2. [col] partir *Marge and Bill were supposed to stay with us for three or four days but they decided to check out on Saturday.* 3. inspecionar, examinar, averiguar, verificar *Last year the civil rights staff checked out more than 250 complaints of police brutality ...* -T/73. ♦ *We'll do everything we can to check out your claim that you're innocent.* -NE,337. 4. estar de acordo (com), condizer (com), bater (com), ser verdadeiro, corresponder aos fatos *When several details in his story checked out with the known facts, we realized he was telling the truth.* 5. [gir] morrer *He checked out last night.* 6. retirar ou entregar ao solicitante (algo que pode ser emprestado – livro, ferramenta, aparelho etc.) mediante o devido registro *Audrey checked out three books from the school library.* ♦ *Some of the material [books and papers] had been checked out from the White House library ...* -BC,32.
check up = **CHECK on** *The police checked up his story carefully.* ⇒ **checkup** exame, inspeção, exame médico geral ... *your stepmother came to my office for her semiannual checkup.* -QE,13. ♦ ... *candidates should have a complete medical checkup ...* -T/78.
check up on = **CHECK on** *We assume you are adults. We won't check up on you to see that you are in a given place at a given time.* -T/60. ♦ *He gave me vague references that I couldn't check up on.*
check with 1. corresponder exatamente com, conferir com, estar conforme com

His story checked with what his partner had said. 2. consultar, aconselhar-se com, falar com ... *the reporters checked regularly with a half-dozen persons in the Justice Department and FBI who were sometimes willing to confirm information that had been obtained elsewhere.* -BC,105.
double check uma segunda verificação, um novo exame para certificar-se de que algo está correto, seguro ou funcionando normalmente etc. *His wife always makes a double check on all doors and windows of the house at night before going to bed.*
⇒ **double-check** examinar novamente, verificar uma segunda vez *Their report had been checked and double-checked.* -RCT,57.
hold/keep in check reprimir, conter, controlar, impor restrições a *She held her anger in check.* -TD,245. ♦ *... she kept herself in check ...* -T/73. ♦ *[Lenin] ... was determined to keep popular stirrings in check, especially nationalistic ones.* -T/92.
keep a close check vigiar cuidadosamente, manter sob observação contínua *The FBI has kept a close check on his activities.*
rubber check [col] cheque sem fundos, cheque-borracha *I didn't realize that he had given me a rubber check until the bank refused payment.*
CHECKLIST lista de verificação, de conferência, de controle ... *a long checklist of international subjects ...* -T/81.
CHECKPOINT barreira (em estrada etc.), posto de fiscalização, posto de controle *The 300-km car trip took two days because of checkpoints where he had to stop to show militiamen the travel documents ...* -T/92.
CHEEK cheek by jowl muito próximos, lado a lado, juntos, em intimidade *It was the kind of place where the houses stand cheek by jowl.* -T/64.

turn the other cheek dar a outra face, não revidar à violência *I have been taught to turn the other cheek, and I definitely believe in this philosophy.* -T/66.
CHEER cheer up animar(-se), encorajar(-se) *"Cheer up," he said. "It can't be as bad as you think."* ♦ *I felt low and my friends tried to cheer me up.*
CHEESE big cheese [gir] = **big SHOT** *He managed to get an interview with the big cheese.*
CHEESECAKE [gir] fotografia de mulher nua ou seminua, geralmente em pose sensual *[During World War II] ... there was one cheesecake photo of [Betty] Grable for every twelve men in uniform.* -T/73. ♦ *... photographs of girls with big breasts he had torn out of cheesecake magazines ...* -HJC,322.
CHESHIRE grin like a Cheshire cat rir fixamente, rir sem motivo *He ... stood grinning like the legendary Cheshire cat.* -CGU,9.
CHEST get something off one's chest [col] desabafar, abrir-se, revelar o que sente ou pensa *After he had gotten everything off his chest, he felt much better.* ♦ *I'd like to get a lot of things off my chest.* ♦ *Tell me what happened. Get the load off your chest.*
CHESTNUT pull someone's chestnuts out of the fire prejudicar-se para livrar alguém de um problema, dificuldade etc. *You're in trouble because of your own neglect. I'm not going to pull your chestnuts out of the fire.*
CHEW chew out [gir] repreender severamente, esculachar *He's really going to chew you out ...* -HJC,287.
chew over [gir] discutir, debater, examinar detidamente *Let's stop talking for a while. We've chewed over the matter time and time again and still we haven't come to an agreement.*
chew up 1. mastigar completamente *Chew up your food before you swallow*

it. 2. danificar, esmagar, destruir ... *costly battles that chewed up whole divisions without gaining ground for either side.* -T/66.

CHICKEN chicken feed [gír] dinheiro miúdo, ninharia, quireras *[NASA's] ... $7,7 billion budget is not chicken feed.* -T/86.

chicken out [gír] perder a coragem, acovardar-se *Tommy chickened out and ran when he saw the big guy coming toward him.*

chickens come home to roost sobrevir como punição por qualquer ato malévolo, hostil etc. cometido no passado *Curses, like chickens, come home to roost.* ♦ *[Commenting on the assassination of President John F. Kennedy, civil rights leader Malcolm X said it was] ... "a case of the chickens coming home to roost".* -T/92.

count one's chickens before they are hatched fazer planos com base em acontecimentos futuros e incertos, contar com o ovo na galinha *When I realized I would never have the money I had counted on, I learned a lesson: never count your chickens before they are hatched.*

CHICKENHEARTED; CHICKEN-HEARTED [gír] covarde, temeroso, tímido *He's so chickenhearted that he's afraid of his own shadow.*

CHILD a burnt child dreads the fire = **once BITTEN, twice shy** *She was attacked by a Doberman pinscher once and has learned to stay away from dogs. A burnt child dreads the fire, you know.*

child's play tarefa simples, coisa fácil de ser realizada *Swimming across that channel is child's play. I can do it any time.*

with child grávida *"I'm with child", the woman said ...* -SWS,19.

CHILDHOOD second childhood segunda infância, caduquice, senilidade *My grandfather always wanted to go home to a home which no longer existed when he was in his second childhood.*

CHIME chime in 1. expressar concordância com algo que foi dito, fazer coro *The two hoodlums pointed their guns at the secret agent. "We know who you are", one of them said. "We've been expecting you", the other chimed in.* 2. harmonizar-se, concordar, condizer, combinar *Elmer's ideas on the subject chime in with mine.* 3. [col] interromper conversa, entrar na conversa, assunto etc. (principalmente para dar sua opinião), participar, tomar parte *He will chime in on any conversation he happens to hear.*

CHIN keep one's chin up [col] enfrentar (algo) com coragem, agir com resolução, não desanimar, não desistir *Keep your chin up. We know you can win.*

take it on the chin [col] sofrer derrota, revés; fracassar, prejudicar-se; suportar castigo, injúria, humilhações, sofrimento *Bert always seems to have to take it on the chin.*

CHIP cash in one's chips [gír] bater a caçoleta, morrer *As things now looked I would probably cash in my chips in battle and dissolve into soil and air ...* -CRST,94. ♦ *Joe cashed in his chips because he wouldn't give up drinking.*

chip in [col] contribuir (com) *[They] ... had agreed to chip in a modest $50 million each.* -T/85. ♦ *... the President ... invited all Cabinet members to chip in with ideas.* -T/79.

a chip off the old block [col] filho que sai ao pai *Timmy is a chip off the old block and is the pride of his father.*

a chip on one's shoulder [col] índole agressiva, provocadora, propensão a ser belicoso *[Movie star] Alan [Ladd] admitted in later years that he was a kid with a chip on his shoulder, ready to read insults into almost anything that was said to him.* -HMT,21. ♦ *He had a chip on his shoulder, a grudge against the world ...* -CD,7.

in the chips [gír] endinheirado, rico, opulento *Ernie is now in the chips. A rich uncle died and left him a bundle.*

let the chips fall where they may doa a quem doer, sejam quais forem as conseqüências *Mr. MacKaye was a tough public official who did his duty and let the chips fall where they might.*
when the chips are down [col] quando a situação é crítica ... *when the chips are down, they do their jobs like men.* -MAT,190.
CHISEL chisel in on [col] introduzir-se em, intrometer-se em, entrar sem ser convidado *Stop chiseling in on my business.*
CHOCK-FULL completamente cheio, pleno, repleto, transbordante *[Did you keep] ... notebooks chock-full of all the new words you ever heard or read?* -LNW,12. ♦ *As a boy, I read Classics Illustrated Editions which featured stories chock-full of thrilling adventures such as Ivanhoe, Robin Hood, The Last of the Mohicans and so many others.*
CHOKE choke back/down reprimir, conter (lágrimas, emoções, palavras etc.) *He started to speak then choked back the words.* -FP,78. ♦ *She choked back her tears.* ♦ *I tried to choke down the joy that welled up into my throat.* -RQ,114.
choke off 1. pôr fim a (desenvolvimento, atividade etc.), causar a súbita cessação de, suprimir, obstruir, bloquear, silenciar *Actor [Richard] Burton took on a virus that almost choked off his singing voice ...* -T/60. 2. ficar com a garganta obstruída, sufocar, engasgar-se *There was something in the older man's voice and eyes that made Richey choke off and turn away.* -TD,181.
choke up 1. bloquear, obstruir, entupir *I'm so choked up and congested anyway I can't see straight.* -BS,40. ♦ *It had rained hard during the night and the drain in the garden was choked up with leaves.* 2. [col] emocionar-se a ponto de não poder falar, ficar com um nó na garganta *I was so choked up I couldn't speak.*
CHOP chop down derrubar cortando *The white colonists chopped down the tropical forests to enlarge their fields ...* -BD,6. ♦ *Many trees in that area have been chopped down.*
chop up picar, cortar em pedaços pequenos *Chop up your meat before you put it into your mouth.* ♦ *They chopped up the big logs.*
lick one's chops [col] ter ávida antecipação de um prazer, lamber os beiços *In the 1960s the Communists were licking their chops over the trouble inside the African countries that had just been formed.*
CHORD hit/strike/touch a chord comover, sensibilizar, tocar o coração, causar viva impressão *Her quandary struck a resonant chord in men and women across the nation ...* -T/87. ♦ *Her story was so poignant that it touched a universal chord in the minds of all readers.*
CHRIST for Christ's sake → **for Christ's SAKE**
CHRISTMAS Christmas Eve véspera de Natal, noite de Natal *As Christmas Eve approaches, the kids get all excited looking forward to the beautiful toys Santa Claus will bring them.* ♦ *I'll never forget that sorrowful Christmas Eve many years ago when my mother died.*
CHUCK chuck it (*all*) [col] desistir de, abandonar, renunciar a, livrar-se de, largar (tudo) *In the letters from home the Tunstall family never understood why John didn't chuck it all and come back to England.* -CEB,40. ♦ *[A] ... 45-year old guy who decided to chuck it all ... [and] move to an island ...* -T/87.
chuck out atirar fora, livrar-se de *She's always chucking old clothes out.* ♦ *Henry was chucked out of his job.*
chuck up [col] abandonar, renunciar a *Wes chucked up his old job and moved to a small town in California.*
CHUM chum around with [gir] tornar-se amigo de, andar em companhia de *Khrushchev was reduced to chumming around with Cuba's Fidel Castro ...* -T/60.

CHURN churn/grind out [col] produzir, fabricar, publicar etc. (algo) em grandes quantidades e de maneira automática, sem inspiração ou criatividade ... *to churn out goods for the American consumer.* -T/87. ♦ *... it is hard to defend the bulk of salacious literature being churned out today.* -T/69. ♦ *She ... ground out radical books and pamphlets ...* -T/60. ♦ *... grinding out screenplays ...* -T/87.

churn up produzir, causar, (algo) por agitação, agitar violentamente, perturbar *The storm ... still churned up waves four and five feet high ...* -T/84. ♦ *... the Democrats churned up bitter disputes at home about the war.* -T/72.

CIRCLE come full circle completar o ciclo, voltar à posição ou estado original, voltar ao ponto inicial ... *the sound film seems to have come full circle, from the early, awkward imitation of theater back to the theater's emphasis on dramatic performance ...* -KA,187.

go/run around in circles estar desorientado, confuso, andar às tontas, esforçar-se inutilmente ... *I was going around in circles, talking to myself half the time.* -AIM,153. ♦ *Joslyn was just running around in circles, getting nowhere.*

run circles around → **run RINGS around**

vicious circle círculo vicioso *The rise in prices and the rise of the minimum wage results in a vicious circle and solves no problem.*

CITY inner city o núcleo antigo de uma cidade grande, a área original, principalmente em se tratando de zonas densamente povoadas, empobrecidas e deterioradas *Police and fire protection are especially important in the inner city.* -GJK,5. ♦ *... Chicago is losing population as people leave the decaying inner city for the suburbs.* -T/87. ⇒ **inner-city** relativo a, ou característico de tais áreas *Inner-city black males are America's newest lost generation.* -T/86. ♦ *Many black Americans live in inner-city ghettos.*

CLAIM lay claim to reivindicar (um) direito a *[He] ... had laid legal claim to a vast tract of land.* -WC,81. ♦ *... Monterey [a city in California] can now lay claim to being the country's classiest jazz display case.* -T/60.

stake (out) a claim reivindicar a posse (de terras), demarcando-as, reivindicar um direito *[He went to Kansas in 1854 and] ... staked out a claim as a settler ...* -SH,19. ♦ *... a hot young newcomer, Tom Cruise, staking his claim to authentic stardom in the best part he has yet had [*The Color of Money*].* -T/86.

CLAM clam up [gír] calar a boca, ficar de bico calado *Stan clammed up and refused to answer further questions.*

CLAMP clamp down [col] reprimir, coibir, agir com rigor, dar uma prensa *The order to clamp down on organized crime came from the mayor himself.* ♦ *... clamping down on the import of luxury items ...* -T/60. ⇒ **clampdown** [col] proibição, impedimento, medida repressiva, interdição *There is a clampdown on exporting alligator hides.*

CLASS cut a class [col] matar aula *He cuts class frequently ...* -T/73.

have class [col] ter classe, distinção, educação, ser refinado no trajar e no comportamento *President Kennedy had a lot of class.*

in a class by itself/oneself único, sem igual, *sui generis The Rolls Royce automobile is in a class by itself.*

CLASSIFIED confidencial, secreto (documento etc. que só pode ser lido ou visto por certos oficiais de alta patente ou funcionários de alto escalão do governo) *... highly classified documents ...* -T/87. ♦ *... classified information that could be of value to the enemy.* -T/81.

CLEAN clean off limpar a superfície de *She cleaned off the table after breakfast.*

clean out 1. limpar (o interior de), esvaziar *[Boris] Yeltsin ... moved into Gorbachev's Kremlin office before the ex-President had even had time to clean out the desk.* -T/92. 2. eliminar, expulsar, despedir *... his former staffers were cleaned out of the NSC [National Security Council] after his departure ...* -T/87. 3. [gir] tirar todo o dinheiro ou bens de, limpar, depenar *The thieves cleaned out his house while he was traveling in Europe.* ♦ *Her second husband cleaned her out.*

clean up 1. limpar, remover a sujeira de, pôr em ordem *... a sweeping 20-year plan to clean up Southern California's atmosphere.* ♦ *Clean up the mess in the kitchen.* ⇒ **cleanup** limpeza, faxina *... 27 villages [in Ukraine, after the Chernobyl nuclear accident] are still so heavily contaminated that workers have abandoned cleanup efforts.* -T/87. 2. [col] pôr fim a, concluir, liquidar, erradicar *I still have to clean up a few pending matters at the office before I leave on my vacation.* 3. limpar, livrar de características indesejáveis, corrupção etc. *Lawman Wyatt Earp was said to have cleaned up Dodge City.* ♦ *The new mayor has promised to clean up the government.* ⇒ **cleanup** limpeza (eliminação de corrupção, crime etc.), devassa *The white-collar crime wave is spurring a determined cleanup operation.* -T/88. 4. lavar-se, limpar-se, arrumar-se *In the morning, they cleaned up, and each got ready for work.* -LRW,15. ♦ *I have to go home and clean up. I feel dirty.* 5. [gir] ter grande lucro, ganhar muito dinheiro *Chuck's father really cleaned up in the stock market.* ♦ *... to clean up fifty or sixty thousand dollars a year.* -KRI,597.

CLEAN-CUT 1. bem-formado, bem-proporcionado *... a clean-cut face ...* -T/87. 2. bem-definido, distinto, claro, nítido *... his good looks and clean-cut behavior have made him popular.* -T/87. ♦ *... a clean-cut scientific method ...* -WN,8. 3. de boa aparência, bem-cuidado, esmerado, apurado *Larry is a clean-cut young man with sandy hair.* 4. íntegro, de bem, de caráter, incorrupto *... she can also be pretty sure you're a fairly clean-cut individual.* -WJT,43.

CLEAN-SHAVEN bem barbeado *His hair was black, his eyes dark... and ... he was clean-shaven.* -HJ,10.

CLEANER take to the cleaners tirar todo o dinheiro de (em jogo, trapaça, assalto etc.), depenar *He was taken to the cleaners by a dishonest partner.*

CLEAR clear away 1. retirar, remover, afastar, limpar *All the obstacles to the agreement had been cleared away.* ♦ *The trees that had fallen during the storm were now being cleared away.* 2. desaparecer, dissipar-se *When the mist cleared away, we could see the ship in the harbor.*

clear of longe de, afastado de *She likes to remain clear of public opinion.* v. **KEEP clear of**

clear off limpar, retirar, remover *... they cleared off a little spot about ten by twenty feet for the shack ...* -LMT,32. ♦ *The barman cleared off the counter and served the new customers.* 2. [col] ir-se, retirar-se, evadir-se, dar o fora *The boys cleared off when they saw the police coming.* ♦ *They were told to clear off her property by my angry grandmother.*

clear out 1. esvaziar, limpar, pôr em ordem *He cleared out his desk before leaving his job.* ♦ *The room had to be cleared out before he moved into it.* 2. retirar, tirar *She cleared out all her clothes from the closet.* 3. [col] partir, ir-se embora, dar o fora *Tony Romano cleared out when he was fourteen and has never returned to see his parents.* 4. expulsar, mandar sair *... his troops had been clearing out the last fighters ...* -T/82. *Clear out all the people from the building. There has been a bomb warning.*

clear up 1. clarear (o tempo) *The weather cleared up after the rain and we went out.*

2. esclarecer, elucidar, solucionar, resolver, explicar *If we sit down and talk, we can clear things up.* -T/87. ♦ *He cleared up a number of mysteries that had long puzzled the police.* 3. pôr em ordem, arrumar, limpar *... clear up the mess ...* -T/87. ♦ *Clear up the kitchen.*

in the clear 1. [col] inocentado, livre de suspeitas *[He had murdered the two men but the sheriff] ... still didn't have anything on him. He was in the clear.* -HWR,136. 2. livre de dívidas, dificuldades etc. *At last we're in the clear. Our business is a success.* 3. livre, a salvo, fora de perigo, desimpedido, não mais sob restrições *He meant to shoot his way out if necessary, but it would be far better if he could get the girl [who was with him] in the clear before the firing started.* -HJ,139.

CLEAR-CUT bem demarcado, exato, nítido, inequívoco *... a clear-cut policy ...* -T/92. ♦ *His duties were clear-cut ...* -LA,74. ♦ *... questions that seldom have clear-cut answers.* -T/87.

CLEAR-EYED; CLEAR-SIGHTED perspicaz, arguto, sagaz, que enxerga longe *[Doris] Lessing is one of the most clear-eyed, humane yet relentless novelists alive.* -T/73.

CLIFF-HANGER [col] 1. filme cinematográfico seriado, principalmente das décadas de 1930 e 1940, no qual cada capítulo terminava em uma situação de suspense *The cliff-hangers of the 1930s and 1940s – such as* Flash Gordon, The Adventures of Captain Marvel, Drums of Fu Manchu, Zorro's Fighting Legion*, to name but a few – are among the most vivid images of my boyhood.* 2. qualquer situação em que haja suspense *Any U.S. presidential election is a stirring drama, but the election of 1960 is without doubt the political cliffhanger of the century.* -T/61.

CLIMAX cap the climax ir além do limite esperado, não ter par, sobrepujar a tudo *What you did last night certainly capped the climax.*

CLIMB climb down descer *The cat would not climb down from the tree.*
climb into vestir (roupa) *She sat up, watching her husband climb into his dark suit.* -HJD,2.

CLIMBER social climber indivíduo que busca elevar sua posição social travando relações com pessoas ilustres, famosas, ricas etc. *His wife was a social climber who enjoyed each new and more expensive house until there were no more guests to impress ...* -KF,122.

CLIP at a clip de uma vez, de cada vez *Lieutenant McPherson found out that Shelby Carpenter had been withdrawing sums of money from the bank, sometimes $1,500, sometimes $1,700 at a clip.*
at a fast/lively/rapid/etc. clip a passos largos, à rédea solta, depressa *... Iraq has been printing money at a rapid clip ...* -T/92. ♦ *... the people who pass at an ever faster clip through our lives.* -TA,11.
clip joint [gír] boate de baixa reputação *The clip joints in New York are only patronized by tourists.*

CLOAK-AND-DAGGER de capa e espada, relativo a intriga e espionagem, característico das atividades de agentes secretos e espiões *Spies are thought to be like the cloak-and-dagger men of the Borgia days.*

CLOCK against the clock; against time contra o tempo, rapidamente, a todo o vapor *Racing against the clock, scientists develop a drug that is at least partly effective against AIDS ...* -T/87. ♦ *The tide was coming and we had to work against time to get our boat ready to take advantage of the rising sea.*
around/round the clock o tempo todo, dia e noite, sem cessar *Working around the clock ...* -T/60. ♦ *... some 1,000 employees worked round the clock in three shifts ...* -T/67. ♦ *We have bus service*

round the clock. ⇒ **around-the-clock**; **round-the-clock** constante, contínuo, incessante, ininterrupto, que está em efeito dia e noite ... *he needs round-the-clock nursing care.* -T/92. ♦ *... round-the-clock assistance.* -T/87.

clock/punch in//out registrar entrada// saída no relógio de ponto, iniciar//encerrar o dia de trabalho *Those still working have so little to do that they clock in only on Thursdays and Fridays.* -T/84. ♦ *What time do you clock out?* ♦ *He punches in at seven a.m. and punches out at five-thirty.*

put/set/turn back the clock voltar atrás em relação ao tempo, reviver o passado, opor-se ao progresso, regredir, voltar às instituições e idéias antigas *The American presence in the [Persian] gulf has turned back the clock to the years of the hostage crisis ...* -T/87. ♦ *The clock can be turned back but not the time the clock has measured.* -MRMT,7. ♦ *... set back the clock by more than 100 years.* -T/87.

CLOCK-WATCHER [col] funcionário ocioso que não tira os olhos do relógio *He was fired from his job because he was a clock-watcher.*

CLOCKWORK like clockwork como um relógio, com perfeita regularidade e precisão, uniformemente, com exatidão rigorosa *When he put his clever plan into action, everything moved like clockwork*.

CLOSE bring to a close pôr término a, encerrar ... *sensing that the conversation is getting pretty silly, [he] brings it to a close.* -T/87. ♦ *... papers which brought to a close the career in America of General Thomas Gage ...* -SGF,105.

close down encerrar as atividades, cessar o trabalho, deixar de funcionar; fazer cessar as atividades de *The factory closed down last month.* ♦ *The Communist regime had waited weeks before moving to close down the student protests ...* -T/87.

close in avizinhar-se, aproximar-se; envolver, cercar e produzir uma sensação de isolamento, opressão etc. *Night was closing in and they decided to stay where they were.* ♦ *... the sound of engines, drumming, roaring, and the terrible stillness and emptiness that closed in when the engines stopped.* -UJ,101.

close in on/upon cercar de todos os lados, encurralar *The Communists closed in on Saigon.* -T/85. ♦ *They fled Germany in 1936 just before the Nazis closed in on them.*

close out 1. liquidar (mercadorias) *The store closed out its stock of toys.* 2. liquidar (negócio), fechar, encerrar atividades *Phyllis has decided to close out her pet shop.* 3. terminar, descontinuar, cessar, interromper *Early in 1950 the project, for all practical purposes, was closed out ...* -RE,19.

close up encerrar as atividades do dia (e fechar as portas do estabelecimento) *Let's close up the store and go home.* ♦ *What time do you close up?*

come/draw to a close chegar ao fim, findar-se, terminar ... *the lecture is coming to a close.* -T/87. ♦ *He was killed in combat just as World War II was drawing to a close.*

CLOSED-DOOR → **behind closed DOORS**

CLOSEFISTED/TIGHFISTED sovina, avaro *He was so closefisted that he would make old Ebenezer Scrooge look like a spendthrift.*

CLOSE-KNIT; CLOSELY KNIT unido por fortes laços (de crenças, interesses comuns, amor, amizade etc.), coeso *Nixon had a very close-knit group of advisers who gave him too much protection.* ♦ *... a close-knit family ...* -T/87. ♦ *Experts agree that there tends to be less crime in cohesive, closely knit communities with shared values and a strong sense of neighborhood.* -T/81.

CLOSEMOUTHED taciturno, discreto, reservado, retraído, reticente *The Presi-*

dent has a group of loyal, closemouthed advisers.
CLOSET   secreto, clandestino, encoberto *... he is a closet conservative ...* -T/76. ♦ *I think he's a closet homosexual, or to put it more bluntly, a closet queen.*
come out of the closet [col] 1. assumir abertamente sua homossexualidade *Homosexual men and women are coming out of the closet as never before to live openly.* -T/79. 2. revelar-se, manifestar-se abertamente, vir à tona, a público, pôr-se a descoberto *Racists have been led to feel comfortable and are coming out of the closet.* -T/87.
CLOSE-TO-HOME → close to HOME
CLOSE-UP 1. fotografia ou cena de filme tomada bem próxima de seu objeto *It was in 1903 ... that Edwin S. Porter made his celebrated [film]* The Great Train Robbery, *which contained the first recorded close-up.* -FJ,40. ♦ *The famous movie star has said that her right side is better for close-ups.* ⇒ **CLOSE-UP; CLOSE UP** próximo, à curta distância *... a close-up look at some Olympic stars.* -T/87. ♦ *There are thirty-one known moons of Jupiter, Saturn, Uranus and Neptune. None has been photographed close up.* -SC,204.
CLOTH **(out) of whole cloth** fictício, falso, inverídico, sem fundamento, inventado *... the incidents were really invented out of whole cloth by [Thomas] Wolfe [in some of his novels].* -NEW,11. ♦ *His memoirs too were made of whole cloth ...* -T/77.
CLOTHESHORSE [gir] pessoa que se esmera no trajar (com a freqüente implicação de ser este seu único mérito) *Though never a great movie star, she was always a fashionable dresser and people called her a clotheshorse.*
CLOUD **cloud over** 1. nublar, cobrir-se de nuvens (o céu) *The sky was clouding over as I got off the train at Black Rock.* 2. toldar-se, anuviar-se (o semblante) *Ann's face clouded over when I gave her the bad news.*

every cloud has a silver lining   em todo infortúnio há um lado positivo, benévolo, esperançoso etc. *When you have had trouble, many people will tell you that every cloud has a silver lining, in an effort to cheer you up.* v. **silver LINING**
in the clouds   em devaneio, nas nuvens *Linda was in the clouds when Jeff asked her to marry him.*
on cloud nine [gir] eufórico, extremamente feliz *Jay has been on cloud nine ever since he met Daisy.*
under a cloud   sob suspeita *He and three other lawyers quit their jobs under a cloud and may be forced to face trial for misappropriation of company funds.* ♦ *[He] ... resigned from [his job] under a cloud of suspicion ...* -T/87.
CLOVER   **in clover** [col] em situação próspera, na opulência, muito bem de vida, rico *With the fortune his aunt left him, Ben will live in clover for the rest of his life.*
CLUE   **clue in** [gir] pôr (alguém) a par de, dar todas as dicas a *When we arrive at the job, I'll clue you in.*
CLUTTER   **clutter up** juncar, atravancar *Marcel's desk was always cluttered up with papers.*
COAL   **bring/carry coals to Newcastle** levar água ao rio, fazer esforços desnecessários *Little Annie had so many dolls that giving her another one was like carrying coals to Newcastle.*
coal oil   querosene *Don's grandmother always called kerosene coal oil.*
haul/rake over the coals [col] repreender ou criticar com severidade, descompor, esculachar, desancar *... the media routinely rake capitalist countries over the coals.* -T/87. ♦ *He was raked over the coals when his error was discovered.*
COAST   **the (West) Coast** [col] a costa ocidental dos EUA, a região litorânea banhada pelo Oceano Pacífico *I've got to fly back to the Coast ...* -WSM,211. ♦ *When*

we were living on the coast ... -BL,105. ♦ *Have you ever been to the West Coast?*

coast along deixar-se levar (como por uma correnteza, em sentido figurado) fazendo pouco ou nenhum esforço, sem se preocupar etc. ... *you can't coast along on someone else's opinions.* -T/66. ♦ ... *he coasted along on the glory he had left behind.* -LI,11.

the coast is clear não há perigo ou obstáculo à vista, o terreno está livre *James, who stood at the door of the building, gave Ernest the signal that the coast was clear.*

COATTAILS [col] influência, prestígio, popularidade etc. ... *he latched on to the coattails ... of the powerful and rich Soong family.* -LW,35.

hang/ride on someone's coattails valer-se do prestígio ou auxílio de alguém para alcançar seu próprio sucesso, fama etc. ... *the Democrats chose to ride on the coattails of Eisenhower's immense international popularity* ... -T/60.

COCK cock of the walk pessoa autoritária que domina um grupo, uma situação etc. *When he was elected the best student in his class, he began to think he was the cock of the walk.*

COCK-AND-BULL cock-and-bull story história absurda, lorota, história da carochinha *She told him a cock-and-bull story about having met a green man from Mars.*

COCKEYED 1. vesgo, caolho *Ben Turpin was the most famous cockeyed comedian in the movies.* 2. [gir] embriagado *He was cockeyed when he came to our party.* 3. [gir] excêntrico, maluco *You and your cockeyed ideas for making money.*

COCKLE warm the cockles of someone's heart agradar alguém, deixá-lo jubiloso, feliz *It warms the cockles of my heart to hear that you're going to marry such a wonderful girl.*

COCKSURE convicto, confiante, certo, seguro ... *a cocksure combatant who was not too scrupulous about his methods.* -T/68.

COFFEE coffee break intervalo para o café (durante o expediente), hora do café *Maybe they were taking a coffee break* ... -T/86. ♦ ... *the morning coffee break.* -T/87.

coffee house estabelecimento comercial que serve café e outras bebidas ... *a Greenwich Village coffeehouse that serves soft drinks* ... -T/62.

coffee shop pequeno restaurante, restaurante incerimonioso onde se servem café, bebidas e refeições rápidas *[He] ... met the French actress in a Montreal coffee shop* ... -T/87.

COIN pay someone (back) in his own coin pagar na mesma moeda *When his company failed and he was broke and hungry, he was paid in his own coin for his lack of charity and understanding.*

COKE 1. [col] Coca-Cola *How about a Coke?* 2. cocaína ... *they sometimes took coke while on the job* ... -T/86.

COKEHEAD [gir] cocainômano ... *in the old days it was rare for someone to come to work stoned on drugs or for managers to have to worry about cokeheads in the office.* -T/86.

COLD catch/take (a) cold resfriar-se *I was worried now he might catch cold* ... -HEM,128. ♦ *Be careful that you don't take cold when you go fishing.*

leave out in the cold abandonar à própria sorte, desamparar *He was left out in the cold when jobs were awarded to the campaign workers.* ♦ *[They] ... were being left out in the cold.* -T/81.

COLD-BLOODED → **in cold BLOOD**

COLD-EYED frio, friamente imparcial, desapaixonado, de aparência indiferente ... *Manhattan's cold-eyed critics.* -T/66. ♦ ...*cold-eyed calculation* ... -T/66.

COLD-HEARTED insensível, duro, cruel *He was a cold-hearted man.*

COLD-SHOULDER → **give/turn a cold SHOULDER to**

COLLAR hot under the collar [gir]

zangado, irritado *...what's made you so hot under the collar, Wilhelm?* -BS,54.

COLLECTOR **collector's item** coisa rara por sua beleza, qualidade, excelência etc., que vale a pena guardar ou acrescer a uma coleção *... the* Whole Earth Catalog *[a book], may soon become a collector's item.* -T/69. ♦ *The old Chinese vase you got at the auction is really a collector's item.*

COLLEGE **go to college** freqüentar faculdade, fazer curso superior *He never went to college but his son goes to New York University Law School.*

COLOR **call to the colors** convocar para servir nas forças armadas *Seven German schoolboys, all 16, all in the same small-town classroom, are called to the colors on the same day: April 27, 1945.* -T/61.

change/turn color mudar de cor, empalidecer ou enrubescer *Bill turned color each time the pretty young girl spoke to him.*

give/lend color to tornar plausível, admissível, fazer parecer real, verdadeiro ou possível *His bleeding nose gave color to his claim that he had been attacked by two men on a dark street.*

one's (true) colors o (verdadeiro) caráter de uma pessoa, aquilo que ela realmente é; as (verdadeiras) intenções, planos etc. de alguém *He showed himself in his true colors.* ♦ *[He] ... showed his true and natural colors ...* -TRL,9. ♦ *I've awakened to Wallace's true colors: a false prophet and political phony.* -T/73.

sail under false colors pretender ser algo que não é, simular, fingir ser *Wilkins tried to pass himself off as one of the legal heirs to the vast fortune, but he was really sailing under false colors.*

see the color of someone's money certificar-se de que o comprador de algo tem realmente com que pagar *If you really want to buy it, let me see the color of your money first.*

there's no disputing colors and taste → **there's no accounting for TASTE(S)**

with flying colors com grande êxito, plenamente vitorioso *The women knew that their political skills were on trial, and they passed the test with flying colors.* -T/77.

COLOR-BLIND daltônico *Melinda is color-blind and simply can't tell one color from another.*

COMBAT see combat → see **ACTION**

COME **as good/bad/big/strong etc. as they come** [col] muito bom/mau/grande/forte etc. *Big Frankie was no dope, he was as sharp as they come.* -CG,77. ♦ *... a tall, skinny ... lawyer ... who was as bellicose and litigious as they come ...* -JEP,360.

come 1. quando vier (a época), quando chegar (a ocasião) *Come next spring, he'll start building a new house.* 2. caber por justiça, ser devido, ter (algo) a receber *[Most of the maids she had fired had] ... simply vanished ... and often with money coming to them ...* -SEB,19. 3. vamos! deixe disso! *Come, John! You would really like to work with us.*

come aboard; come on board [col] juntar-se a um grupo, organização, empresa etc., começar a participar (de algo) *These events took place before I came aboard.* -BC,46. ♦ *This is Bill Sanderson, our new sales manager. He'll come on board next Monday.*

come about 1. suceder, acontecer, ocorrer *Control of electricity has come about slowly, and there is still a good deal to be learned.* -GH,89. ♦ *How did this come about?* 2. mudar de direção (o vento), virar de bordo (embarcação a vela) *The wind has come about.* ♦ *We had difficulty trying to come about in the strong wind.*

come abreast of entestar com, emparelhar-se com *The three [youths] came abreast of [the man], and the Mexican boy, grinning, stepped directly in front of him.* -MWL,60.

come across 1. encontrar acidentalmente, topar com, achar *He came across an old* *first edition copy of* Ulysses *in a Manhattan second-hand bookstore.* ♦ *You come across a word you don't know and ... you consult a dictionary for its meaning.* -NM,17. 2. [gir] dar, entregar, fornecer, dizer (aquilo que é exigido ou devido); pagar *We want you to come across with all you know.* ♦ *He has failed to come across with the money he owes us.* 3. [col] produzir (determinada) impressão, mostrar-se, mostrar ser ... *[President] Johnson comes across as a sincere and rather simple man ...* -T/64. 4. ser comunicado, ser facilmente compreendido (significado) *She was trying to tell us something, but the meaning of her message didn't come across.*

come again [col] quê? como disse? pode repetir? *Come again? I don't believe I heard what you said correctly.*

come alive despertar da inatividade, mostrar-se ativo, alerta, desentorpecer-se; parecer adquirir vida *Her suspicions came alive when I mentioned I had been to Smith's office.* ♦ *... the loudspeakers ... came alive ... with somber music.* -T/86.

come along 1. acompanhar, ir com *Wait for me. I'm coming along with you.* 2. fazer progresso, desenvolver-se, avançar, melhorar, ter êxito *How are you coming along with your new invention?* ♦ *Grace is coming along well after her breast surgery.* ♦ *The wound on the back of my hand was coming along nicely.* -RQ,35. 3. aparecer, surgir, chegar *Every girl has a dream that sooner or later the right guy will come along.* 4. apressar-se, esforçar-se *Come along, Pete. We'll be late for the show.*

come and get it [col] está servido! está na mesa! (almoço, refeição), venha(m) comer! hora do rancho! *She put the food on the table and called out to the children in the garden: "Come and get it!".*

come apart quebrar-se, romper-se, desfazer-se, desintegrar-se, desmoronar-se

Joseph Wambaugh's novel The New Centurions *tells the story of three Los Angeles cops who have to deal with the unrest and violence of a society coming apart all around them.*

come around/round 1. retornar, reaparecer, voltar (periodicamente) *Christmas has come around again.* 2. mudar de direção *The wind has come around.* 3. restabelecer-se, recuperar-se; recuperar os sentidos, recobrar a consciência *She was so overwhelmed by the news that she collapsed in a swoon but she soon came around.* 4. mudar de opinião, de parecer *[He] ... eventually came around to the President's point of view.* -T/91. ♦ *Lester's experience made the others come around to his view of the political situation.* 5. [col] visitar *Ben came around a week later to see his old friend.*

come at atacar, cair sobre, investir contra *The man came at me with a frightening yell.*

come away voltar, regressar, partir, deixar (alguém ou algum lugar) *I came away from this experience with two disturbing convictions.* -TA,12. ♦ *[He] ... came away empty-handed.* -T/78.

come back 1. voltar, regressar *I came back about an hour ago.* 2. voltar (lembrança) à memória, acudir à mente *Suddenly it all came back to me: the man I was talking with was George Burnett and he had been in high school with me in the early fifties.* 3. retrucar, replicar *I asked him a simple question and he came back with an insulting reply.* ⇒ **comeback** réplica, resposta sarcástica, respostada *He is very clever with the comeback.* 4. voltar a uma situação, condição ou posição anterior, voltar a ser o que era, reabilitar-se *Silent screen movie star Gloria Swanson came back spectacularly in* Sunset Boulevard. ⇒ **comeback** volta, retorno, reaparecimento, reabilitação, recuperação ... *a nation that prides itself on its economic comeback* *from recession ...* -T/87. ♦ *Perhaps the decade's most spectacular comeback was that of Marlon Brando [in* Last Tango in Paris*].* -BRF,64.

come between interpor-se, colocar-se entre (como um obstáculo), dividir *His former wife's money had come between them and had caused them to separate.*

come by 1. adquirir, conseguir, obter, ganhar, receber *The family had come by a tinkly piano, on which the younger girls, Anna and Rosa, liked to play.* -BRS,17. ♦ *... food was hard to come by and expensive.* -WC,49. ♦ *[He] ... came by his religious faith early.* -T/87. 2. visitar *I just came by to say hello.* -SWS,29.

come clean [gír] confessar, contar tudo, dizer a verdade *He finally came clean and told the police the whole story.* ♦ *Honey, why don't you come clean?* -DD,60.

come crashing down despencar com estardalhaço, cair com violência, desabar, vir abaixo, ir por água abaixo *[His meteoric career] ... came crashing down last week.* -T/92.

come down 1. cair, ruir, descer, vir abaixo, ser abatido, ser demolido *... new barriers of fear and hostility between blacks and whites ... might not come down for years.* -T/67. 2. perder sua posição social, riqueza etc. *He was once a rich and proud man but he has come down lately.* ⇒ **comedown** queda, declínio, revés, humilhação *He tried to blame some of his friends for his comedown.* 3. ser transmitido por tradição, passar de uma geração para outra *... a tradition that comes down to the present day.* -AM,114. 4. provir de uma fonte mais alta ou autoridade superior *... verbal orders came down from [the] Major General ...* -RE,19.

come down (hard) on/upon opor-se firmemente a, ir contra, repreender severamente, punir *[The new Economy Minister] ... has come down hard on tax cheats ...* -T/91.

come down to 1. reduzir-se a, redundar em; ser uma questão de, ser na realidade *What it comes down to is that everyone here must conform to the company's rules and act accordingly.* ♦ *What it all comes down to is, what do we want?* -WSM,236. 2. considerar diretamente, encarar cruamente (assunto, questão etc.), refletir friamente sobre *Was she, when you come right down to it, only an evil pretentious, lying old woman who could be expected to beget nothing but evil ...* -WSM,168.

come down with [col] adoecer de *[He] ... came down with a mysterious attack of fever.* -CBC,9. ♦ *... he had come down with a cold ...* -SLS,267.

come easy/natural to ser fácil para *Lying does not come easy to me.* -T/87.

come forth aparecer, surgir à vista, apresentar-se *When he presented his plan to the committee, a clear picture of his ideas came forth.*

come forward apresentar-se, aproximar-se, comparecer, oferecer-se (para prestar auxílio, serviço etc.) *... four other witnesses came forward, all with stories pointing to the same man.* -T/92. ♦ *... the town had to cancel its regular election because no candidate came forward.* -T/77. ♦ *No one has come forward to defend him.*

come from ser nativo de, originar-se de, provir de *He comes from a small Kansas town.* ♦ *This wine comes from France.* ♦ *Sugar comes from various vegetable sources.*

come in 1. entrar *Ask Mr. Burton to come in.* 2. chegar *What time does the train come in?* 3. entrar em uso, entrar na moda *Since psychoanalysis came in, psyche has become the goddess of the conscious and unconscious minds.* -SJJ,424. 4. assumir sua parte em uma função, encaixar-se, participar *They will be needing a new man for the job. That's where you come in.* 5. classificar-se (em determinado lugar, posição) em uma competição, corrida etc. *The horses that I bet on always come in last.*

come in for [col] receber, tornar-se objeto de, ficar sujeito a *She came in for a small fortune when her father died.* ♦ *Casey came in for heavy criticism ...* -T/87.

come in handy/useful ser útil, vir a calhar, ser oportuno *Inexpensive things such as an ice pick, a file, and a ruler often come in handy [when you are collecting rocks and crystals].* -PR,34. ♦ *Don't throw away old towels. They may come in handy to use as rags to clean the floor.*

come into receber como herança, entrar na posse de *... she was an heiress who had come into half a million dollars when she was fourteen ...* -CJC,19.

come into one's own receber aquilo que lhe pertence, que lhe cabe, receber o reconhecimento devido; alcançar seu potencial, importância, valor etc., mostrar do que é capaz *With the beginning of scientific explorations, Egyptian art came into its own as an important part of the heritage of mankind.* -CEO,27.

come of 1. resultar de, advir de *No good will come of that.* 2. descender de *He comes of Irish and German stock.*

come off 1. dar-se, ocorrer, acontecer *An occasion that never came off.* -SG,38. ♦ *Flora and Sergio's wedding will come off on October 23.* 2. [col] ter êxito, dar bom resultado, ser bem-sucedido, ter o resultado esperado *[The] ... plan failed to come off ...* -HJ,43. ♦ *They tried to produce a different kind of show but the novelty didn't come off as expected.* 3. [col] sair-se, desempenhar-se *How did you come off with your new invention?*

come off it [gir] pare com isso, deixe de fingir, não seja pretensioso *Come off it now, we know that you didn't do all these things by yourself.* ♦ *Come off it, Ray, no one is blaming you for the accident.*

come on 1. chegar, aproximar-se gradualmente, avançar pouco a pouco; começar, iniciar *I'm going to bed. I feel a cold coming on.* ♦ *Night was coming on and* he had to go home. 2. aparecer, entrar em cena, em atividade, em funcionamento, começar a trabalhar *The street lights were coming on when we arrived.* ♦ *The emergency diesel generator came on, but in two or three minutes power failed again ...* -T/86. 3. fazer progresso, desenvolver-se, avançar *How is your book coming on?* 4. causar (determinada) impressão, produzir (certo) efeito *[Country singer Willie Nelson] ... comes on like some improbable blend of Celtic bard and Hell's Angel ...* -T/78. 5. = **COME upon** 2. 6. [col] vamos! venha! apresse-se! *Come on! I'm in a hurry.* 7. [col] deixe disso! pare com isso! *Oh, come on, Meg! Are you going to harp on the same subject again?* 8. [col] por favor (como solicitação ou tentativa de persuadir) *Come on, Fred, tell me what happened last night.*

come on strong [gir] falar ou agir de maneira impetuosa, enérgica, mostrar uma personalidade forte e dominadora *[In Funny Girl] Barbra Streisand comes on strong ...* -T/68. ♦ *In the cutthroat competition to sell planes, the Europeans are coming on strong.* -T/87.

come out 1. sair-se *How did you come out on that business deal?* 2. revelar-se, vir a público, tornar-se conhecido *Many of the hidden crimes of the organization came out as a result of the Senate investigation.* 3. ser revelada (a imagem em filme), sair bem (uma fotografia ou o objeto da foto) *Our photos of the Colorado Rockies came out gorgeously beautiful.* ♦ *The Colorado Rockies came out gorgeously beautiful in the photographs.* 4. resultar, terminar *One never can tell how a war will come out.* 5. ser publicado, ser lançado, ser colocado à venda *Ernest Hemingway's novel* The Old Man and the Sea *came out in 1952.* ♦ *In the winter of 1956, not six months after* Mystery Train *[a song] came out, Elvis Presley released* Heartbreak Hotel *and sent American*

popular culture into a collective delirium that came, after a while, to be called "the Rock Era". -T/77. ♦ *... the first Polaroid camera came out [in 1947] ...* -T/63. 6. desabrochar *When spring arrives, all the wild flowers in the forest come out.* 7. debutar, estrear na vida social *Debbie is old enough to come out this year.* 8. desaparecer (mancha) *These stains are difficult to come out.* 9. declarar-se, manifestar-se (a favor ou contra) *The Senator came out strongly against the plan.* ♦ *[He] ... has come out ... for a radical antiobscenity proposal ...* -T/66.
come out with 1. revelar, tornar público; dizer, expressar *Lathrop came out with an unexpected suggestion at the meeting.* 2. publicar *... five national magazines ... came out with articles on [Alfred Kinsey's book]* Sexual Behavior in the Human Female ... -GD,288. 3. pôr no mercado, lançar, oferecer ao público *Sony has come out with a new type of color TV.*
come over 1. afetar, acometer, apoderar-se de, ocorrer a *You would hardly believe the change that has come over Mrs. Wyatt.* ♦ *... a feeling of homesickness came over him.* -LD,149. 2. fazer-se ouvir, ser recebida com clareza (recepção radiofônica) *We turned on the radio and soon the news came over that the President had resigned.* 3. passar-se para, bandear-se (de um lado, opinião etc. para outro) *Dan will soon come over to our side. Just wait and see.* 4. visitar informalmente, vir (de determinado lugar ou distância) para visitar etc., dar um pulo *Come over and see us Friday night.* ♦ *... Harris had come over for a talk ...* -AT,27. ♦ *My wife was not feeling well, so I called Dr. Carson and asked him to come over.*
come round → **COME around**
come through 1. [gír] fazer aquilo que é necessário, esperado, combinado, desejado etc.; dar, entregar; pagar, cumprir *Simon had given them his word on a few things and never came through with them.* ♦ *... she had never come through with any money.* -T/81. ♦ *The U.S. also agreed to come through with additional credits.* -T/60. 2. vencer (apesar de dificuldades), ter êxito, chegar a bom termo *Our team came through very well.* 3. sobreviver, resistir, agüentar, recuperar-se (de doença, crise etc.) *He had come through in a crisis.* ♦ *Neville came through the war without a scratch.* 4. surgir, vir à tona, aflorar, mostrar-se *Cooper, Cagney, Gable, among many other movie stars, played many different roles but their individual personalities always came through.* 5. ser recebida (comunicação, por telefone, telégrafo ou qualquer outro meio) *Ten minutes later, a [phone] call came through from ... the congressman ...* -LA,24.
come to 1. importar em, montar a, totalizar *Your bill comes to $25.75.* 2. tratar-se de, dizer respeito a, ser questão de *He considered himself a shrewd man when it came to politics ...* -GM,7. 3. voltar a si, recuperar os sentidos *When he came to, he had no memory of what had happened.* 4. resultar em, chegar a uma situação, condição, estado etc. [geralmente mau ou desagradável] *... I don't know what our poor country is coming to.* -HG,234.
come together 1. convergir, unir-se, juntar-se, reunir-se *Their needs and the needs of others come together.* ♦ *The Olympics are the only times in the history of the world when so many nations come together in one spot in an association of friendship ...* -T/84. 2. reconciliar-se, fazer as pazes *Will Brad and Elizabeth ever come together again?*
come to pass suceder, acontecer *Don't worry about things that will probably never come to pass.* ♦ *... the prophecy shall soon come to pass!* -WL,68.
come to think of it pensando bem, na realidade, de fato *Come to think of it, he did say something about her.*

come true realizar-se, cumprir-se ... *making his dream come true* ... -T/60.
come under ficar sob, tornar-se alvo de, ficar sujeito a *[He] ... came under political attacks that seriously curbed his effectiveness.* -T/61. ♦ *... another patrol ... came under heavy fire from across the river.* -T/85.
come undone fracassar, falir, falhar, arruinar-se *He has invested in ambitious development projects around the world, several of which have come undone.* -T/87.
come unglued [gír] perder o controle emocional, ficar perturbado, desvairado *He came unglued when his wife died.*
come unstuck [col] ficar desordenado, confuso, incoerente, perturbado *The government's plan to stabilize the country's currency is beginning to come unstuck.*
come up 1. surgir, começar, acontecer, ocorrer; ser mencionado *Something unexpected has come up and I have to fly to Chicago this afternoon.* ♦ *Your name never came up in the discussion.* 2. aproximar-se *The presidential election is coming up.* 3. ser apresentado para discussão, consideração etc. *The bill has come up before Congress and been defeated.* ♦ *... the party nomination for Prime Minister came up in February 1977.* -T/80. 4. atingir uma posição social, condição etc. mais elevada, progredir, melhorar *He came up from the ranks to become president of the company.*
come up against enfrentar, ir contra, fazer frente a *He came up against stiff opposition from the other parties.*
come upon 1. afligir, acometer, atacar, apossar-se de *A sudden desire to get out of the area came upon him and he headed back out of the woods.* 2. [também **come on**] encontrar acidentalmente, topar com, achar *Browsing in a London second-hand bookshop, I came on a 1900 edition of Joseph Conrad's* Lord Jim.
come up to 1. aproximar-se de, chegar-se a *The little boy came up to the group and asked for food and bus fare home.* 2. igualar-se a, equiparar-se a, estar à altura de ... *psychoanalysis failed by a wide margin to come up to its expectation in solving the American problems of love.* -DDT,482.
come up with 1. expor, oferecer, propor, apresentar, encontrar, sugerir *Dave always comes up with a novel idea for decorating the gym for a big dance.* ♦ *... my mother came up with a new voice teacher ...* -HA,35. 2. dar, entregar (aquilo que é devido, exigido etc.) *Warren is having trouble coming up with the $25,000 necessary to pay his debts.*
come what may aconteça o que acontecer *You can be sure he'll never desert her, come what may.*
easy come, easy go água dá, água leva; aquilo que se consegue com facilidade (dinheiro, principalmente) é rapidamente dissipado ou esbanjado *He inherited a fortune from his rich uncle, but, you know, easy come, easy go.*
first come, first served as pessoas a chegar, apresentar-se etc. serão atendidas pela ordem *At present, all those who pass the tough ... exam, are guaranteed admission to a university on a first-come, first-served basis.* -T/86.
how come [col] como é quê? por quê? como se explica? *[He] ... was continually asked how come he was so young.* -T/75. ♦ *How come you don't smoke?*
to come vindouro, futuro ... *economic and social problems ... destined to plague the nation for a half-century to come.* -BR,723. ♦ *... the masses of men were taught to seek their well-being in the life to come.* -MHJ,20.
what is coming (to one) [gír] aquilo a que alguém faz jus, aquilo que é devido a alguém, aquilo que alguém merece (recompensa ou punição) *... and now I want what's coming to me.* -RP,168. ♦ *Now you'll get what's coming to you.* -NE,261.
when it comes to → **COME to** 2

COME-HITHER [col] sexualmente convidativo (olhar, olhos) ... *a seducer-soldier who has his way with any lass who meets his come-hither eyes.* -T/67. ♦ *She gave him a come-hither look when he walked by.*

COME-ON [gír] chamariz, engodo, atrativo, isca *The 20% discount they offered on every buy was the come-on.* ♦ *The girl was the beautiful come-on for the gang of robbers.*

COMEUPPANCE get one's comeuppance [col] ter o que merece, ser castigado, receber uma lição *He'll get his comeuppance so good that he'll never forget it.* -MG,400.

COMFORT cold comfort pouco ou nenhum consolo *He took cold comfort from all the assurance we gave him that he wouldn't be arrested.*

little/small comfort pequeno consolo, certo alívio, lenitivo *To humanists and others who believe that both man and society are perfectible, [anthropologist] Lévi-Strauss extends small comfort.* -T/73.

too close for comfort (algo perigoso, incômodo, desagradável etc.) preocupante por estar muito próximo, por ser uma ameaça, por deixar (alguém) intranqüilo *... his eyes returned to the rearview mirror. The lead car was close – too close for comfort.* -SF,15. ♦ *The ape is man's nearest neighbor on the tree of life ... For man, that hairy presence stands just too close for comfort ...* -T/66.

COMICS 1. (histórias em) quadrinhos *Many of the American comics are used in the newspapers in Brazil under Brazilian names.* 2. [ou] **comic book** revista de (histórias em) quadrinhos *Children like to place comics inside their school books and pretend to be doing their work.* ♦ *The first comic books appeared in 1935.* -MMU,154.

COMING comings and goings 1. idas e vindas, vaivém *... the comings and goings had left the company divided into factions.* -T/92. 2. atividades, ações, faina *The tabloids scream about the comings and goings of the wealthy and the great.* -AK,70.

COMMAND have a good command of dominar bem (idioma), ser fluente em *She has a good command of French.*

COMMENTARY running commentary observações, comentários contínuos proferidos no decorrer de aula etc. *For the students who couldn't understand the Portuguese in the film, the teacher gave a running commentary.*

COMMISSION out of commission inativo, desativado, fora de ação; sem funcionar, desarranjado, quebrado *The destroyer had been heavily hit by enemy fire and was out of commission.* ♦ *My TV has been out of commission since last Saturday.*

COMMON in common em comum *Ideas like "pain" and "hunger" have a fairly good chance of being understood in common because all of us have experienced these things ...* -SWM,4.

COMMUNITY community chest fundo para assistência social coletado por meio de contribuições individuais *The community chest in my city collects funds for, and distributes the money to all the various charitable institutions.*

COMPANY the company one keeps as pessoas com quem alguém se relaciona, o círculo de amizade de alguém, as pessoas com quem alguém anda *... men whose past was never questioned but who were judged by the company they kept.* -BE,18.

good company bom amigo, boa companhia *Ann is always good company.*

keep company with 1. andar constantemente na companhia de *He's been keeping company with the wrong sort of people.* 2. namorar *Guy has been keeping company with the Senator's daughter.*

keep someone company fazer companhia a *... if you get lonesome I know Wade will be glad to keep you company ...* -LRT,60.

mixed company grupo de pessoas de ambos os sexos ... *some things are just not spoken in mixed company.* -T/71. ♦ *He never tells off-color jokes in mixed company.*

part company separar-se, despedir-se, dizer adeus *When the American man and woman part company, as half the newly married couples are expected to do these days ...* -T/86. ♦ *After the war was over we parted company and we have never seen each other since that time.*

COMPARE beyond/past/without compare incomparável, incomparavelmente *Debra Paget was lovely beyond compare when she played an Apache girl in* Broken Arrow. ♦ *When we reached the top of the White Rock, the beauty of the scenery was past compare.*

COMPLAINT lodge a complaint apresentar uma queixa, fazer um protesto *The Secretary was forced to lodge a personal complaint with the President.* -T/87.

COMPLIMENT left-handed/backhanded compliment elogio insincero, malicioso, dúbio, ambíguo *When he told me that he liked me because he felt more intelligent when we conversed, I took it as a left-handed compliment.*

CON [gír] enganar, iludir, lograr, lesar, fraudar; convencer, persuadir (com falsas promessas) *He was always able to con his sister into helping him do his work.* ♦ *... he simply cannot be conned into spending money needlessly ...* -T/81.

CON GAME → **CONFIDENCE game**
CON MAN → **CONFIDENCE man**

CONCERN a going concern empreendimento de sucesso, negócio muito próspero *He began with a small store but now it is a going concern.* ♦ *... their partnership is a going concern.* -T/67.

CONCERNED as far as someone/something is concerned no que diz respeito a, com referência a, no que tange a *As far as I'm concerned she can leave right now.*

CONCLUSION draw a conclusion tirar uma conclusão ... *drawing too many conclusions about the vulnerability of the American Navy.* -T/87.

foregone conclusion conclusão inevitável, resultado previsto *It was a foregone conclusion that the Prime Minister would resign.*

jump to conclusions tirar conclusões apressadas, precipitar-se ... *quit jumping to conclusions; I want facts.* -HRA,17.

CONFIDENCE confidence/con game [col] conto do vigário *Mrs. Macgillicuddy had been the victim of a confidence game.*

confidence/con man vigarista Elmer Gantry ... *Sinclair Lewis' notorious 1927 novel about a con man of religion ...* -T/60.

take someone in one's confidence acolher alguém como confidente, confiar na discrição e lealdade de *As she got to know me better, Mrs. Doyle took me into her confidence.*

CONJURE conjure up 1. fazer aparecer como por mágica; invocar (espíritos) *He was somewhat acquainted with seances, in which a person known as a medium conjures up the spirit of the dead.* 2. trazer à lembrança, evocar, idear, imaginar *To most people, the term technology conjures up images of smoky steel mills or clanking machines.* -TA,32. ♦ *Shakespeare could do anything he wanted with language; the way he talks of a thing conjures up the thing itself.* -T/60. ♦ *He had received a letter from a friend he hadn't seen in a very long time and it conjured up a lot of pleasant, half-forgotten memories.*

CONK conk out [gír] 1. deixar de funcionar, enguiçar *Our engine suddenly conked out because of the poor quality of the gasoline.* 2. adormecer subitamente, adormecer de cansaço *Grandpa conked out right after lunch.* 3. desmaiar *She conked out when she saw the horrible monster approaching her.*

CONSUMER consumer goods bens de consumo *The production of consumer goods in Brazil has expanded enormously.*

CONTRARY contrary to em oposição a, a despeito de, apesar de *Contrary to the popular notion, nobody is born with a fine sense of rhythm – people simply learn it ...* -SMS,13.

on the contrary ao contrário, longe disso *I won't object to staying home tonight. On the contrary, I'll love it.*

to the contrary 1. em contrário *If you don't hear from me to the contrary in 24 hours, go ahead with the plan.* 2. não obstante, em que pese, malgrado *There's no such thing as an elephant graveyard, popular belief to the contrary.* -LAK,47.

CONVENIENCE convenience store loja de conveniência *It was past midnight and I went to a convenience store to buy some beer and snacks.*

CONVERSANT conversant with familiarizado com, conhecedor de, versado em *Mr. Collins is conversant with Irish folklore and mythology.*

CONVERSATION make conversation travar conversação, puxar conversa *The youth was trying to make conversation and the officer ... did not know what to talk about.* -SGT,22.

COOK cook up [col] forjar, fabricar, inventar, planejar *Do you really think she could have cooked up the whole story?*

COOKIE smart cookie homem inteligente e de forte personalidade *... I thought you were a really smart cookie.* -SLS,231.

COOKOUT refeição preparada ao ar livre *During the summer, they have a cookout in their backyard every Saturday.*

COOL blow one's cool → keep one's **COOL**

cool down/off 1. perder calor, esfriar; refrescar *It had been a hot day but it cooled off after the sun went down.* ♦ *Let's wait until the motor cools down.* 2. acalmar (-se), moderar(-se), arrefecer, perder o entusiasmo, a intensidade, o vigor etc. *Cool down! No one is trying to harm you.* ♦ *When the crusade against crime cools off, the crime rate will rise again.*

cool it [gir] 1. acalmar-se, não se irritar *Cool it man! Get hold of yourself.!* 2. trabalhar mais lentamente, não se esforçar muito, ir mais devagar *... factory workers and farmers [in Red China] cooled it on the job ...* -T/66.

keep//lose/blow one's cool [gir] manter// perder a calma, a compostura *Let's keep our cool and maybe we'll all get through this thing alive.* -T/87. ♦ *... a man who never loses his cool.* -T/69. ♦ *Only when forced to take a bath would Billy blow his cool.* -T/67.

COOLHEADED calmo, imperturbável, comedido, inexcitável, de cabeça fria *Colleagues ... consider ... [her] coolheaded style [as managing editor of a newspaper] one of her greatest assets.* -T/76.

COON coon's age → DOG's age

COOP coop up confinar, enclausurar *Cooped up in a hotel room ...* -T/92. ♦ *He was in jail, cooped up like a wild animal.*

fly the coop [gir] dar no pé, escapulir, fugir *When the police arrived, the crooks had flown the coop.*

COP cop out [gir] quebrar promessa, compromisso etc. desdizer-se, recusar a responsabilidade, pular fora *We thought he'd keep his word but he copped out.* ♦ *If you decide to cop out on our cause, you'll live to regret it.* ⇒ **cop-out** evasiva, desculpa (para não se comprometer ou evitar problemas) *He used his illnes as a cop-out to avoid going on trial.*

COPE cope with lidar eficazmente com, enfrentar, encarar, arrostar *He is unable to cope with his financial problems.* ♦ *Knowing nothing of his past, [a person with no knowledge of history] is poorly prepared to cope with the present and the future.* -SJV,x. ♦ *[They] ... must cope* *with their emotions and with the stresses of daily life ...* -T/91.

COPY **copy cat** [col] pessoa que imita outra no aspecto pessoal, maneira, hábitos, trajes etc. *What a copy cat that girl is!*
good copy assunto de interesse para um jornal ou revista, algo que merece ser noticiado *The correspondents here ... want to meet you. ... the Winston affair is a big story, and they know about you and you make good copy.* -FH,60.

CORDON **cordon off** cercar, fechar, demarcar (área, rua etc.) com cordão de isolamento (de soldados ou policiais) *Several roadways were cordoned off by police ...* -T/92. ♦ *... the military cordoned off the crash site ...* -T/86.

CORE **at the core** no âmago, na essência *At the core of his [Carlos Castaneda's] books and Don Juan's method is, of course, the assumption that reality is not an absolute.* -T/73.
to the core inteiramente, completamente, até a medula *... President Eisenhower was ... optimistic to the core.* -PVH,198. ♦ *... a coalition that was rotten to the core.* -T/87.

CORN **corn belt** região do Centro-Oeste dos EUA onde se produz milho em grande escala *... the corn belt ... Indiana to Nebraska and Missouri to Minnesota ...* -T/86. v. **BELT**

CORNER **(just) around the corner** bem próximo; iminente, prestes a ocorrer *The Hatfields live in a large house just around the corner.* ♦ *Airlines and communications satellites foster the impression that the rest of the world is just around the corner.* -T/77. ♦ *[Recession] ... is just around the corner.* -T/92.
the (four/far) corners of the earth/world os lugares mais longínquos da terra *He had traveled to the four corners of the earth in search of spiritual enlightenment.* ♦ *... Joe Kennedy moved out of Boston into the big time of Wall Street ... and the far corners of the world.* -T/60.

cut corners economizar (dinheiro, tempo, esforços etc.) eliminando aquilo que não é essencial; simplificar ao máximo (uma tarefa etc.), cortar caminho *... they have been forced to cut corners on maintenance.* -T/87. ♦ *... the temptation for the manufacturer to cut corners can be strong ...* -T/89.
get/have a corner on ter o monopólio de *The company has a corner on the cotton market.* ♦ *... the U.S. does not have a corner on violence.* -T/81.
get someone cornered encurralar alguém, colocá-lo em uma posição ou situação da qual é impossível sair *We've got him cornered. He can't get away now.*
in a corner em situação difícil, em apuros *He found himself in a corner after he made that statement on TV.*
out of the corner of one's eye de soslaio, de esguelha, com o canto dos olhos *Watching [her husband] out of the corners of her eyes, Gladys went hesitantly from the room to prepare breakfast.* -WR,58.
paint into a corner colocar-se em situação difícil, precária; encurralar-se *... I was not unlike the man who painted himself into a corner.* -CTT,135. ♦ *He painted himself into a corner when he released confidential information.*

CORRIDOR **the corridors of power** a cúpula do poder, o lugar onde se tomam as decisões governamentais *Throughout his career he has shuttled easily between the military outposts and Washington's corridors of power.* -T/87.

COST **at all costs; at any cost** a todo custo, custe o que custar *Environmental damage is a serious problem and must be avoided at any cost.* ♦ *... since primitive societies are disappearing rapidly, it is felt that they must be studied at all costs while they still exist ...* -SWL,21.

COTTAGE **cottage industry** indústria caseira, manufatura de fundo de quintal *Thousands of peasants in [Indonesian]* *cottage industries ... now make textiles for export.* -T/91. ♦ *It is true that women have generally excelled in the "cottage industries" of publishing – mysteries and romantic escape fiction.* -T/72.

COTTON cotton belt região do Sul dos EUA onde se cultiva algodão em grande escala *The cotton belt is that part of the Southern United States where much cotton is grown.*

cotton to [col] afeiçoar-se a, sentir-se atraído por, começar a gostar de, simpatizar com, concordar com, aprovar *I try to avoid him but he cottons to me like a brother.* -MAT,81. ♦ *You may think that idea interesting but I don't cotton to it.*

cotton (on) to [col] compreender, perceber, conscientizar-se de *[The father] ... did not cotton on to the fast, wily ways of the city streets in which his sons got their education.* -T/87.

COTTON-PICKING [gir] maldito, detestável, abominável, desprezível, odioso, reles, vulgar, rústico, próprio de camponês *"Keep your cotton-picking hands off me!", she yelled.* ♦ *Get out of here with your cotton-picking ideas.*

COUCH on the couch [col] recebendo tratamento psiquiátrico *Henry's wife has been on the couch for two years.*

COUGH cough up [gir] entregar, dar (dinheiro), pagar (a contragosto) *When are you going to cough up your share of the bill?* ♦ *[He has the] ... ability to get business firms to cough up contributions.* -T/87.

COUNSEL keep one's own counsel não revelar seus planos, intenções, idéias, pensamentos etc. *[They] ... have always been intensely private people, keeping their own counsel and concealing their innermost feelings.* -T/74.

COUNT count in incluir *Count me in. I'm going, too.*

count on/upon fiar-se em, contar com, depender de, esperar *She's counting on you. Don't let her down.*

count out 1. excluir, deixar de fora, desconsiderar, descartar *He is still in the race and can't be counted out yet.* ♦ *Count me out! I'm not interested in being part of a holdup.* 2. contar (coisas) uma a uma *... they counted out the bills which came to eight hundred dollars ...* -WJT,223. 3. declarar derrotado (boxeador) após a contagem de dez segundos *The referee counted him out in the seventh round.*

count up contar, somar, achar o total de *Count up the cash we still have left.*

COUNTDOWN contagem regressiva *The launch [of Discovery space shuttle], postponed and rescheduled five times, was even delayed during the final countdown ...* -T/85.

COUNTER over the counter sem necessidade de receita médica (diz-se de venda de medicamento) *[The manufacturer of a condom for women] ... expects the device to be sold over the counter ...* -T/88. ⇒ **over-the-counter** vendido sem necessidade de receita médica *... over-the-counter drugs.* -T/87. ♦ *... the sleeping-pill-tranquilizer was approved for over-the-counter sales ...* -T/62.

under the counter de maneira ilegal, sub-repticiamente, clandestinamente *... a very limited amount of sexual material is being sold "under the counter".* -RC,22. ⇒ **under-the-counter** ilegal, sub-reptício (venda, preço, pagamento etc.) *He was arrested for being involved in under-the-counter sale of pornographic material.*

COUNTRY country and western música rural americana, música típica do sul e do oeste *Hazel is fond of classical music but she also likes jazz and country and western.* ♦ *My favorite country-and-western singers are Johnny Cash, Willy Nelson and John Denver.*

the old country terra natal, país [geralmente europeu] de onde se origina um imigrante *His father came from the*

old country but his mother was born in America.
open country área desobstruída, campo aberto, região desabitada *Bill Gordon and four others managed to get away [from the Blackfeet Indians] and they made it through open country ...* -MF,48.

COUPLE a couple (of) dois ou mais, alguns *A couple of years ago I was in debt up to my neck.* ♦ *The police asked him a couple of questions and let him go.*
odd couple parceria inverossímil mas verdadeira, dupla desemparelhada *They [President Richard Nixon and his Assistant for National Security Affairs Henry Kissinger] constitute in many ways an odd couple, an improbable partnership.* -T/73.

COURAGE screw up one's courage armar-se de coragem *He finally screwed up enough courage and broke with his associate.*

COURSE in due course no devido tempo *In due course he won the Democratic nomination for the House of Representatives ...* -SJ,76.
in the course of durante, no decorrer de *I have worked at lots of trades in the course of my life.* -KRI,566.
main course prato principal de uma refeição *... the main course was pasta in a tomato-and-duck sauce.* -T/85.
of course sem dúvida, é claro, naturalmente *They know he is my brother, of course.* ♦ *Of course you realize what I'm telling you is strictly confidential.*
off//on course fora da rota//na rota *A Delta 737 [jet], whose pilots had been thrown off course by thunderstorms ...* -T/87. ♦ *The ship was on course.*
run/take its course terminar sua trajetória, chegar ao seu fim natural, completar seu ciclo *... the month had almost run its course ...* -SGF,153. ♦ *It's always better to let nature take its course.*
stay the course agüentar até o fim, perseverar, não entregar os pontos *... he is determined to stay the course, no matter what.* -T/73.

COURT go to court tomar medidas legais, recorrer à justiça, intentar uma ação judicial *[He] ... went to court three years ago ...* -T/76.
laugh out of court não levar a sério, ridicularizar, rir à custa de *... the case was laughed out of court ...* -SV,71.
pay court to cortejar *In* Hamlet, *the prince of Denmark pays court to Ophelia.*
settle out of court chegar a um acordo (sem necessidade de levar uma demanda à decisão judicial) *He was suing for one million but settled out of court for half the sum.*
take to court levar à justiça, processar *He has been taken to court so often that he greets the judges by their first names.*

COVER blow one's cover trair-se, deixar transparecer algo que não é, dar bandeira *The spy blew his cover when he began to use his knife and fork American style while eating in the German restaurant.*
break cover sair ou ser forçado a sair do esconderijo ou do lugar onde se estava protegido ou abrigado *The wild boar broke cover and attacked the two men.*
cover for 1. substituir, tomar o lugar de uma pessoa durante a ausência desta, assumir as funções de *I'll cover for you while you're out having lunch.* 2. fornecer um álibi para (alguém), ocultar (má conduta, erro, crime de alguém para protegê-lo) *Although he confessed to having stolen the money, the police were sure he was covering for someone.*
cover girl [col] garota da capa, modelo cuja foto estampa capa de revista *She became a famous cover girl after appearing on the covers of many U.S. magazines.*
cover story reportagem ou artigo cujo tema, pessoa entrevistada etc. é estampado na capa da edição de uma revista; reportagem de capa *He wrote thousands of articles [for* Time Magazine*], includ-*

ing more than 50 cover stories, on subjects ranging from British elections to Middle East wars ... -T/92.
cover up [col] ocultar, dissimular; acobertar algo comprometedor, secreto, ilícito *[He] ... has believed that UFO's [unidentified flying objects] are visitors from outer space and that the Air Force and the government are trying to cover up the facts.* -HD,21. ♦ *... to cover up a criminal action ...* -T/77. ♦ *A suspicion will always linger that if Nixon and his men had not tried to cover up, his presidency would have survived ...* -T/81. ⇒ **cover-up** disfarce, camuflagem; tentativa de ocultar algo comprometedor, secreto, ilícito etc. *The Watergate case has been called the most famous cover-up.*
cover up for [col] acobertar (culpa, crime, segredo etc. de alguém) *You wouldn't cover up for a murderer, would you?*
from cover to cover de princípio a fim (de um livro) *Sam seldom reads a book from cover to cover.*
run for cover; take cover fugir correndo (para livrar-se de um perigo), safar-se, escapulir, abrigar-se, procurar proteção *They ran for cover when the madman started shooting.*
under cover 1. oculto, escondido, em segredo *This matter must be kept under cover at all costs.* 2. sob a proteção (de) *The marines went ashore under cover of Navy fighter planes.* 3. sob aparência (de), sob pretexto (de), sob disfarce (de) *Under cover of nationalism, they went to extremes.*
under separate cover em outro envelope, em correspondência separada *In his letter, the manager said that under separate cover he was sending his client a set of new catalogs.*
COW **holy cow/cats/mackerel/Moses/smoke** Santo Deus! caramba! puxa vida! *"Holy cow!" he exclaimed when the shooting started.* ♦ *Holy smoke! Look at those flames!* ♦ *"Holy Mackerel!", said Mrs. Snell.* -SJD,79.
sacred cow pessoa, instituição, coisa etc. considerada acima de crítica *Science has often been called a sacred cow.* ♦ *Until Nixon the Presidency was considered a sacred cow.*
till the cows come home [gir] para sempre, eternamente *You can wait till the cows come home for the fulfillment of his promise.* v. **(un) till HELL freezes over**

CRACK **crack down** [col] tomar severas medidas contra (má conduta, insubordinação, crime etc.), dar uma dura, impor a lei, fazer cumprir o regulamento *The government is cracking down on people who falsify their income tax returns.* ♦ *... authorities have begun to crack down on drug suppliers ...* -T/87. ⇒ **crackdown** repressão severa, aplicação de medidas extremas, força total no combate ao crime, má conduta etc. *... a narcotics crackdown in which more than 4,000 drug dealers were arrested ...* -T/87.
the crack of dawn o raiar do dia, a aurora *We began to climb the White Rock at the crack of dawn.*
crack open abrir *Not a few Americans cracked open bottles of champagne for the event.* -T/74. ♦ *He managed to crack open the hotel safe.*
crack up 1 [col] elogiar, enaltecer *He cracked up his product to us even though he knew it was no good.* 2. [col] sofrer colapso físico ou mental *The experience of war was too much for Danny and he cracked up.* ⇒ **crack-up** a) colapso físico ou mental *He was a difficult patient much of the time, but his crack-up, when it came, was pathetically thorough and thoroughly pathetic.* -HE,15. b) desmoronamento, colapso, desintegração *... Czechoslovakia may be heading toward a crack-up.* -T/92. ♦ *... a marital crack-up ...* -T/60. 3. destroçar(-se), destruir(-se), despedaçar (-se) (veículo, avião) *[He] ... cracked up*

the first [his first car] last summer. -T/64.
♦ *... three of the planes have cracked up on a high, icy plateau ...* -T/76. ⇒ **crack-up** colisão, choque, desastre *He died in the crack-up of an airplane.* -OF,133.
crack wide open 1. solucionar, resolver, esclarecer, revelar *The police cracked wide open the case of the "red-light murderer".* 2. perder o controle emocional *He could no longer stand the pressures on his life and he finally cracked wide open.* 3. ceder, afrouxar, confessar *They kept on questioning her until she cracked wide open.*
have/take a crack [col] experimentar, fazer uma tentativa *May I take a crack at it?* ♦ *... she decided to take a crack at a modeling career.* -T/87.
not be what all/everything/one/it is cracked up to be [col] não ser aquilo que se apregoa, que se acredita ser; não estar com essa bola toda (alguém ou alguma coisa) *Elephant hunting isn't all it's cracked up to be.* -LAK,39. ♦ *He's not the efficient salesman he's cracked up to be.*
CRACKBRAINED insensato, maluco *... he was dismissed as crackbrained ...* -T/92. ♦ *It was a crackbrained plan doomed to fail from the start.*
CRACKER-BARREL rústico, simples, informal (como o diálogo das pessoas que se reúnem para papear em uma venda do interior) *[The movie] True Grit is a creaky western comedy that features a lot of painful cracker-barrel dialogue ...* -T/69.
CRACKPOT [col] 1. pessoa que tem idéias excêntricas, indivíduo maluco *His colleagues called him a crackpot because of his eccentric ideas.* 2. excêntrico, insensato, amalucado *... his crackpot ideas were given short shrift ...* -SWLR,998.
CRADLE from the cradle to the grave a vida inteira, do nascimento à morte *Britain's National Health Service offers free medical care from cradle to grave ...* -T/69. ♦ *Our insurance company will take care of you from the cradle to the grave.*

v. **from WOMB to tomb**
rob the cradle [col] namorar ou casar-se com uma pessoa muito mais jovem *I'm not going to rob the cradle. Jean is only fifteen.*
CRANK crank out produzir ou fabricar (algo) de maneira automática, sem inspiração ou criatividade *... Italian [movie] directors have cranked out 180 eastern westerns.* - T/67.
crank up [col] pôr em movimento, expedir, dar execução, agilizar, apressar, acelerar *The plans to improve the economy are being cranked up at a fast pace.* ♦ *... the Communist regimes ... are also cranking up a noisy new era of ideological confrontation ...* -T/72.
CRAPS shoot craps jogar dados *He was tempted to shoot craps when he went to Las Vegas.*
CRASH de emergência (curso, programa etc.), que visa à produção de algo ou à consecução de um resultado com a maior rapidez possível *They will begin a crash program to teach old people how to read and write.* ♦ *... he felt the need for a crash course in economic theory.* -LA,88. ♦ *... the crash training of legions of doctors, nurses and paramedics ...* -T/78.
CRASH-DIVE fazer mergulho de emergência (um submarino) para escapar a ataque *The submarine crash-dived when a fighter plane attacked it.*
CRASH-LAND fazer aterrissagem forçada, pouso de emergência (às vezes sem a utilização do trem de pouso) causando danos à aeronave *... the plane must have crash-landed near the beach ...* -T/66.
CRASH PAD [gir] um lugar para passar a noite ou para habitar durante algum tempo *He [John Lennon] and [Yoko] Ono lived in a series of elaborate post-hippie crash-pads ...* -T/80.
CRAW stick in one's craw/crop ficar atravessado na garganta de, incomodar, ser difícil de aceitar *When the President said*

that we must sacrifice many luxuries for our country, it stuck in our craw. ♦ *What sticks in my crop about this period when he was so desperately poor and miserable is the air of elegance and fastidiousness which clung to him.* -MH,14.

CRAWL crawling with fervilhando de, repleto de *The streets were crawling with people who had come out to see the visiting President.*

CRAZY crazy/nuts about [col] louco por, apaixonado por, entusiasmadíssimo por *I'm crazy about you, baby.* ♦ *Joe's crazy about jazz.* ♦ *Dean's nuts about girls and cars.*

CREAM the cream of the crop a nata, a melhor parte, o que há de melhor *The short stories in An Anthology of Famous American Stories represent the cream of the crop.*
whipped cream creme chantilly *... a strawberry shortcake smothered with whipped cream ...* -MHH,10.

CREATURE creature comfort coisa que nos proporciona conforto e bem-estar, bem material *Creature comforts are things such as food, clothing, shelter and warmth that promote physical comfort and satisfaction.* ♦ *With success came creature comforts.* -T/87.

CREDIBILITY credibility gap falta de credibilidade, de confiança; a discrepância entre aquilo que é divulgado ou revelado (pelas autoridades, por exemplo) e a realidade *His credibility gap was so obviously great that he could convince no one of his sincerity.* ♦ *... another problem concerns misinformation – commonly referred to as "the credibility gap" or "news management". The misinformation problem takes a variety of forms, such as lies, clichés and rumours ...* -PN,11.

CREDIT credit someone with dar o devido mérito ou crédito a *They credit Mr. Marshall with good sense.*
do credit to; do someone credit honrar, dar valor a, fazer justiça a *Flora and Tony do their parents credit.*
give credit to dar crédito a, reconhecer o mérito de *We must give credit where it is due, and I think that in this case most of the glory goes to you.*
give someone credit for reconhecer o mérito de, louvar *I told them I knew more than they gave me credit for.* -LC,9.
on credit a crédito *He bought his TV on credit.*
take credit for levar as honras de, colher os louros *He was determined to take credit for everything good his department achieved.*
to someone's credit 1. para crédito de, a favor de *... all I'd ever heard of him was to his credit.* -GJH,23. 2. sob seu nome, de sua autoria, de sua realização *[The author has] ... thirteen books to his credit ...* -T/77.

CREEK up the creek (without a paddle) [gir] em uma enrascada, em apuros *If you don't get some money soon, you'll be up the creek without a paddle.* ♦ *... he finds himself right up the creek.* -HJC,179.

CREEP creep in(to) insinuar-se (em), entrar vagarosamente (em), chegar de mansinho *It was nearly eight, now, and dusk was creeping in ...* -CGU,61. ♦ *[She] ... was allowing a little acidity to creep into her voice.* -DD,49.
the creeps [gir] arrepios, calafrios, medo, nervosismo, inquietude *The howling of my neighbor's dog late last night gave me the creeps.*
creep up on 1. arrastar-se, mover-se furtivamente em direção a, aproximar-se sorrateiramente de *The rabbit was unaware that a fox was creeping up on it.* 2. avançar gradualmente, chegar pouco a pouco *He lost his job and soon financial trouble began creeping up on him.* ♦ *... age has crept up on her.* -T/87.

CREW crew cut corte de cabelo bem rente, cabelo à escovinha *Phil ... wore his brown-blond hair in a short crew cut ...* -MWL,60.

CRIMP put a crimp in [col] obstruir, tolher, entravar, fazer emperrar, colocar um obstáculo em *I've put a crimp in their plan ...* -CGU,67.

CRISP burn to a crisp ficar torrado, reduzir-se a carvão, ser carbonizado *In the kitchen of one home [during a volcanic eruption] ... a woman and several children had been burned to a crisp ...* -VA,24.

CRISS-CROSS marcar ou cobrir com linhas que se entrecruzam, entrecruzar-se *His clean-cut features were criss-crossed with worry.* -SSG,7.

CROP crop out vir à superfície, surgir, manifestar-se, ocorrer *Political riots have cropped out all over the country.*
crop up aparecer inesperadamente, surgir sem aviso *[He] ... cropped up in 1967 as the leader of a Communist or semi-Communist guerrilla band in Bolivia.* -GJI,615.
stick in one's crop → **stick in one's CRAW**

CROPPER come a cropper [col] 1. sofrer uma queda, cair de cabeça, ir ao chão *Princess Anne of England was photographed as she came a cropper.* 2. fracassar, ser malsucedido, ser derrotado, sofrer sério revés *[Scotland's overconfident soccer team coach] ... came a cropper in his opening test against Peru.* -T/78.

CROSS cross fire 1. fogo cruzado *... El Salvador and Costa Rica [are] all the more determined not to get caught in the cross fire [exchanged between Honduran and Nicaraguan forces in Honduras].* -T/86. 2. discussão acalorada, troca de acusações, bate-boca *... [President] Carter was caught in a cross fire from most of organized labor ...* -T/76.
cross off/out cancelar, eliminar, riscar, expungir *Jim crossed off all the old names and put new ones on the list.* ♦ *Some of the words in the message had been crossed out.*
cross section corte ou seção transversal; amostra que detalha as características de um todo; grupo ou seleção típica *... the persons who get to the consulting rooms of psychotherapists and psychoanalysts are not a cross-section of the population.* -MRM,16.
cross up [col] trair, enganar, ludibriar *He's not used to people crossing him up.* -HJ,84.

CROSS-COUNTRY 1. de uma extremidade de um país à outra *After a harrowing cross-country chase by car, plane and helicopter, the federal agents finally managed to capture the spies.* 2. através de campos, matas ou terreno acidentado *[They] ... ski cross-country, sometimes covering as many as twelve miles a day.* -T/73. ♦ *[The military] ... unit began to move cross-country toward "Front 698" in south Laos ...* -T/72.

CROSS-EXAMINATION reinquirição de uma testemunha (feita pelo advogado da parte contrária) *I had no fear of being tripped up in cross-examination.* -T/73.

CROSS-EXAMINE 1. interrogar rigorosamente *After landing, both pilots were cross-examined, separately and together.* -KD,15. 2. reinterrogar (testemunha da parte contrária) *The defense saw no need to cross-examine him.*

CROSS-PURPOSE at cross-purposes em desacordo, em divergência, com intenções opostas; sem se entenderem, com pontos de vista diversos *Their principles and fears are at cross-purposes.* -T/81. ♦ *They were arguing at cross-purposes and couldn't reach an agreement.*

CROSSROAD at a/the crossroads na/em uma encruzilhada, em local ou momento de uma decisão vital *He was at the crossroads of his career.* ♦ *... the U.S. economy stands at an important crossroads.* -T/92.

CROSSWORD crossword puzzle problema de palavras cruzadas *Solving crossword puzzles is my wife's favorite pastime.*

CROW as the crow flies em linha reta *When we say "as the crow flies" we mean*

as straight as possible, for it is known that the crow flies in a straight line to its destination. ♦ *As the crow flies, [the city of] Rabaul was only about thirty miles away ...* -RQ,51.
crow over exultar, cantar vitória, rejubilar-se com a derrota ou o infortúnio de *After they had won the game, they crowed over the victory for a long time.*
eat crow [col] admitir o erro, rebaixar-se, humilhar-se *When they showed him how wrong his statement had been, he had to eat crow.*
CROWD crowd out forçar a saída de, expulsar, pressionar para fora, tomar o lugar de *When Negro music became popular, the respectable use of the word [jazz, meaning a kind of music] crowded out the vulgar use [of jazz, meaning sexual intercourse] ...* -LCT,63.
follow/go/move with/the crowd seguir a maioria, fazer como os outros, seguir a moda *Almost all women go with the crowd when the skirt length changes fashion.* ♦ *Very few people have an independent mind. Most just follow the crowd.*
the madding crowd a turba ensandecida, o populacho alvoroçado, a agitação dos grandes centros urbanos *Lou finally made up his mind to move to a quiet place in the country to get away from the madding crowd.*
CRUSH have a crush on [gir] estar apaixonado por *[She] ... has a wild crush on her professor ...* -T/87.
CRUST have the crust/gall/nerve to [gir] ter o descaramento de, o atrevimento de *He had the crust to invite himself to my party.* ♦ *I don't know how you have the nerve to speak to me ...* -SEB,106. ♦ *Gus had the gall to ask for a loan.*
upper crust [col] a classe mais alta da sociedade, a elite, a aristocracia *The party was limited to the upper crust of Washington society.* ⇒ **upper-crust** de elite, de escol *... an audience of upper-crust fans*

that included the Queen Mother herself. -T/80.
CRY cry down 1. abafar com gritos a voz de *He tried to speak to the crowd but they cried him down.* 2. depreciar, menosprezar, desmerecer, desacreditar *They tried to cry down his many achievements.*
cry out gritar, bradar, clamar; queixar-se, protestar *[They] ... awoke from years of resignation to cry out their rage.* -T/87. ♦ *She cried out against the many abuses she had suffered.*
cry out for pedir com insistência, implorar, reclamar, ter grande necessidade de *... millions of people on this planet are crying out for something to eat ...* T/81. ♦ *The violent and passionate young nation had cried out for a poet to express its spirit ...* -SRE,39.
a far cry from uma grande distância de; uma coisa muito diferente de *The seventies were a far cry from the opulent sixties for most middle-class people.* ♦ *[Modern parachutes] ... are a far cry from the old rounded canopies of World War II.* -T/78.
for crying out loud [col] 1. ora vejam! ora essa! que surpresa! *When my niece saw me she said: "For crying out loud! If it isn't uncle Joe!".* 2. com os diabos! que coisa irritante! *For crying out loud, what are you sitting here with me for? Go on out there. There are some other cute boys.* -WH,395.
in full cry demonstrando grande antagonismo, em atitude hostil, ameaçadoramente, dando caça *The critics were at him in full cry after he made his TV speech.* ♦ *[His] ... customary mordant humor is in full cry.* -T/86.
CRYSTAL crystal clear perfeitamente claro, claro como a água, sem nenhuma dúvida, transparente, óbvio *We made it crystal clear that these are alcoholic beverages and must be handled as such.* -T/86. ♦ *... a crystal-clear morning ...*

-MJA,962. ♦ ... *a crystal-clear answer* ... -T/61.
CUCUMBER (as) cool as a cucumber [col] senhor de si, sereno, calmo *He acted as cool as a cucumber and denied his guilt.*
CUE cue one in [gir] pôr alguém ao corrente dos últimos fatos, novidades, informações etc. *Cue me in on what has happened since I left.*
on cue 1. a um sinal convencionado *The TV audience are advised to applaud the performers on cue.* 2. na ocasião precisa, no momento exato ou esperado, na hora certa *He never comes in on cue and the other actors in the show dislike working with him.*
take one's cue(s) from aproveitar a sugestão, a indicação, o exemplo ou a experiência de alguém (e moldar sua ação nesse sentido) *More than in any other art, the artist in film must take his cue from his public* ... -KA,13. ♦ *Local prosecutors and judges, taking a cue from Washington, began pressuring reporters to reveal confidential material.* -T/73.
CUFF on the cuff a crédito, a prazo, fiado *They won't let Mrs. Kendall buy anything on the cuff because she takes too long to pay.*
off the cuff [gir] de improviso, sem ensaiar ... *they were not speaking entirely off the cuff in their critiques.* -T/69. ⇒ **off-the-cuff** improvisado, irrefletido, impensado, espontâneo *[He is] ... an off-the-cuff theologian ...* -T/73. ♦ *... an off-the-cuff remark ...* -T/87.
CULT devoção ou admiração exagerada a uma pessoa, idéia, princípio, livro, filme etc. *... [Ayn Rand, American novelist and philosopher] is more a cult figure than a popular philosopher ...* -T/81. ♦ *Sunset Boulevard has become a cult movie.*
CULTURE culture shock perplexidade, confusão e desorientação provocadas em um indivíduo pelo contato pessoal deste com a cultura de outro país *Since 1985 almost 50 Ethiopians [in Israel] have committed suicide, depressed by both family separations and culture shock.* -T/91.
culture vulture [gir] devoto da arte e de assuntos culturais, pessoa ávida de cultura *I like to go to art exhibits and listen to the culture vultures discussing the merits of the paintings.*
CUP cup of tea [col] coisa, atividade etc. pela qual se tem predileção *Watching a late-night movie on TV is just my cup of tea.* ♦ *Pop art is not my cup of tea.*
in one's cups embriagado *When in his cups, Perkins would often beat up his wife.*
CURE-ALL panacéia ... *ginseng root, the ancient Oriental aphrodisiac and cure-all.* -T/72.
CURIOSITY curiosity killed the cat não seja tão curioso; a curiosidade pode ser perigosa; meta-se com sua vida *Curiosity killed the cat. You shouldn't meddle in other people's affairs.*
CURRENCY hard currency moeda forte, moeda valorizada *Part of the hard currency these firms earn ... may be used to buy badly needed foreign equipment and technology.* -T/87. v. **hard CASH**; **hard MONEY**
CURRENT swim against the current/stream nadar contra a corrente, remar contra a maré *You're just swimming against the current and accomplishing nothing.*
CURTAIN curtain call volta do(s) ator(es) ao palco (após o término do espetáculo) em atenção e agradecimento ao aplauso do público *She had so many curtain calls that they lasted for several minutes.*
curtains [gir] a morte, o fim *... we had to make a crash landing on a beach and, if it hadn't been for some miracle flying by our pilot ... it would have been curtains for us all.* -RQ,24.
ring down the curtain encerrar, pôr fim a *In the summer of 1927 Henry Ford rang*

down the curtain on the immortal Model T and closed his plant to prepare for Model A. -GJKT,8.

CURVE throw someone a curve [gír] colocar em posição difícil, enganar, ludibriar, desorientar, tratar deslealmente, causar surpresa desagradável a *He threw us a curve when he talked us into investing money in his small company.*

CUSTOM-MADE; CUSTOM-BUILT feito ou construído sob especificações, de encomenda ... *custom-made supercomputers more powerful than anything dreamed possible a few years ago.* -T/78. ♦ ... *custom-built communications networks that hum into operation at the flick of a switch.* -T/92.

CUSTOM-TAILOR fazer, construir, planejar (algo) sob encomenda, sob medida ... *custom-tailored work.* -T/81.

CUT a cut above [col] um pouco superior a, melhor que *[He] ... is a cut above all the rest.* -T/87.

cut across 1. atravessar transversalmente, cortar caminho cruzando um espaço diagonalmente *Jesus and his disciples were cutting across a field one Sabbath morning ...* -PJ,18. 2. transcender, ir além de *[Democratic candidate Jesse] Jackson cuts across traditional lines of race, class and party.* -T/84.

cut and run [gír] dar no pé, fugir apressadamente *Nobody would be able to say that Polly Biegler had cut and run when the going got tough.* -TR,19.

cut away eliminar, remover *The first colonists also had to cut away some of the political traditions that entwined them ...* -RR,7.

cut back (on) cortar, reduzir, diminuir, restringir *The company will begin cutting back its labor force next month.* ♦ *John cut back on his alcohol intake when he became sick.* ♦ *Cutting back on oil purchases would reduce federal expenditures ...* -T/87. ⇒ **cutback** redução,

diminuição ... *one group of presidential advisers favors a major cutback in Government spending.* -T/72.

cut dead/cold [col] virar a cara a, não tomar conhecimento de, desprezar *Bill tried to talk to Vera, but she cut him dead.*

cut down 1. derrubar cortando, abater (árvore) *They've cut down all the trees in that area.* 2. [ou] **cut down on** diminuir, reduzir, economizar *You should cut down your drinking.* ♦ ... *in making it [a sentence] short you will instinctively cut it down to its most important parts.* -PL,108. ♦ *He cuts down on sugar and eats only two or three eggs a week.* -T/72. 3. matar *[The 6,000-man army of Saxon King Harold] was cut down by the Norman invaders of William the Conqueror.* -T/66.

cut in 1. interromper (a conversa, a palavra de quem está falando) *He cut in on our conversation and began to expound his views on the subject.* 2. ultrapassar veículo no trânsito e entrar à sua frente, podar; colocar-se indevidamente à frente de alguém em uma fila etc., interpor-se *The taxi cut in fast ahead of our car.* 3. [col] (um homem) cortar um casal que está dançando a fim de dançar com a dama *In the U.S. it is a common custom to cut in on couples who are dancing.* 4. [col] incluir (alguém ou a si mesmo) na distribuição de um benefício, vantagem, ganho etc.; dar (ou tomar) uma parte, porcentagem etc. *Both [firms] were cut in on the profits.* -T/77.

cut into 1. interromper (conversa) *I wish she'd stop cutting into our conversation.* 2. diminuir, reduzir *Most firms have had to hold their prices down, even though it means cutting into their profit margins.*

cut it/that out [gír] pare com isso, fique quieto *Cut it out. You know I can't stand being tickled on the soles of my feet.* ♦ *Cut that out. But immediately.* -SJD,26.

cut loose 1. livrar-se de domínio, coerção ou influência; libertar-se, sacudir o jugo, desfazer-se das amarras *She began to cut loose from her old associates ...* -T/73. 2. desfazer-se de todo constrangimento; comportar-se desregradamente, com impetuosidade; agir ou falar sem restrição; celebrar, festejar sem refreamento *When she is angry, she can cut loose with a string of profanities that would make a top sergeant blush.* ♦ *When the end of World War II in Europe was announced, the people cut loose in the streets.*

cut off 1. remover cortando, decepar, amputar *There is the story of the widow Judith saving the Israelites by cutting off the head of Nebuchadnezzar's general, Holofernes ...* -T/75. 2. interromper, parar, terminar, suprimir, eliminar, fazer cessar *Our gas supply has just been cut off.* ♦ *How do you propose to punish him? Cut off his allowance?* -OJT,288. ⇒ **cutoff** interrupção, corte, impedimento, obstrução, paralisação *The cutoff of military aid to Turkey caused much discussion.* 3. interromper (ligação telefônica, transmissão radiofônica etc.) *We were suddenly cut off by the telephone operator.* ♦ *He gets cut off when he uses vulgar language on the radio or TV.* 4. bloquear, obstruir, separar, isolar *... the airports and other routes of escape are cut off.* -T/81. ♦ *Before he was 15, young Eugene had cut himself off from his church ...* -T/68. 5. interceptar, atalhar, deter *Chief Cochise and his band of Apache Indians cut off the retreating cavalry soldiers.* 6. causar a morte de, levar a um fim prematuro *... lives so suddenly cut off.* -SV,80. ♦ *He was cut off in the prime of life.* 7. deserdar *The famous millionaire cut off his son when he married a girl his father didn't approve of.*

cut out 1. remover cortando, recortar *Maggie cut out several addresses and pictures from the newspaper.* 2. tomar o lugar de, suplantar, levar vantagem sobre *All the other workers were cut out by a newcomer.* 3. [col] omitir, eliminar *Cut out all the superfluous words from your composition.* 4. [col] interromper, descontinuar, fazer cessar, suspender, abandonar, deixar de *He told his noisy children to cut out the racket.* ♦ *You must cut out smoking.* 5. [gir] ir-se, dar o fora, partir subitamente *When they heard the bad news, they cut out for home.* ♦ *Well, guys, I've got to cut out ...* -WR,55. 6. separar (animal da manada) *... the best [wild] horses were cut out from the exhausted band.* -MJ,67.

cut out for/to be talhado para, feito para *... I'm not cut out for a businessman.* -CT,8. ♦ *Maybe this is the sort of thing I was cut out for.* -BL,73. ♦ *In my opinion he is not cut out to be a teacher.*

cut short interromper de repente, encurtar, abreviar *[She] ... didn't finish [what she was going to say] because her husband cut her short with a wave of his hand.* -PJW,87. ♦ *... multiple sclerosis cut short her career.* -T/87.

cut through abrir (passagem) cortando, penetrar, atravessar, cortar, transpor *... the CIA cut through the walls of an employee's apartment to plant seven microphones ...* -T/75. ♦ *... a radar signal can cut through the densest fog.* -T/86.

cut up 1. cortar em pedaços *When the huge tree fell, it took me several days to cut it up to remove it.* ♦ *... she cut up the meat with the long knife she carried in her belt ...* -MET,36. 2. [col] magoar, ferir, ofender [geralmente pas] *Millie was very cut up at the news of her father's illness.* 3. [col] fazer palhaçadas, brincar, gracejar, fazer travessuras; portar-se mal *The twins were cutting up and their mother told them to be quiet.* ⇒ **cutup** palhaço, gracejador, engraçadinho, exibido *Milton was the class cutup, always making jokes and playing tricks on the other students.*

CUT-AND-DRIED; CUT-AND-DRY preparado ou arranjado de antemão; rotineiro, monótono, sem originalidade *The situation may not be quite so cut-and-dried.* -T/87. ♦ *... cut-and-dried answers.* -T/87.

CUT-RATE 1. que vende a preços reduzidos (loja); de preços reduzidos (mercadorias); reduzidos (preços) *There are many large cut-rate stores in New York City.* ♦ *... she cares little for clothes, buying cut-rate bargains.* -T/61. ♦ *... Wal-Mart's cut-rate prices ...* -T/87. 2. inferior, de baixa qualidade, de segunda classe *[He is] ... a cut-rate master of the macabre who seems to work better with spiders than he does with actors ...* -T/66.

CUTTHROAT impiedoso, inexorável *By cutthroat competition they were able to eliminate all their rivals.*

CYLINDER hitting on all cylinders [col] funcionando bem (motor) *The engine was hitting on all cylinders and Ted won the race easily.*

D

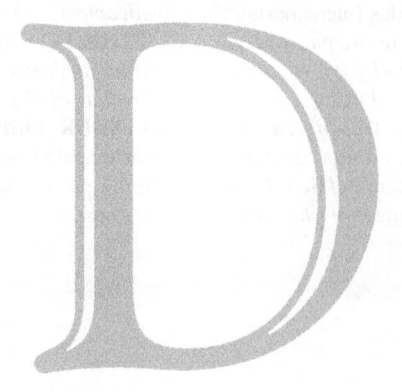

DAGGER look daggers at olhar com ódio ou ameaçadoramente para, fulminar com o olhar *Her husband waved at her and smiled but she looked daggers at him.*

DAISY (as) fresh as a daisy bem-disposto, com boa aparência *Despite the unbearable heat, Alice managed to look as fresh as a daisy.*

push up daisies [gir] comer capim pela raiz, estar morto e enterrado *Many a careless driver is now pushing up daisies.*

DAME Dame Fortune boa fortuna, Dona Sorte *Fate, or Dame Fortune, may also have played a role in my vocation.* -AK,10. v. **LADY Luck**

DAMN damn; damned [col] 1. maldito, amaldiçoado, detestável, odioso *That damned dog is howling again.* 2. completo, total, rematado, perfeito *What a damned fool I was not to listen to her advice.* 3. muitíssimo, extremamente, absolutamente *They're paying me a damn good salary.* ♦ *He was damn sure of himself.* ♦ *There are too damn many journalists analyzing the news.* -T/92.

damn it [col] diabos! diacho! droga! *Damn it! Why don't you watch where you're going?*

I'll be damned/darned; I'm damned macacos me mordam *"Well, I'll be damned", he exclaimed utterly surprised to see her there.* ♦ *When she asked me where Billy was, I said: "I'm damned if I know".*

not care/give a damn/darn não se importar, não ligar a mínima ... *Clark Gable telling Vivien Leigh [in* Gone With the Wind*]: "Frankly, my dear, I don't give a damn".* -T/81. *[He] ... could suddenly act as if he didn't care a damn.* -LMC,9. ♦ *I don't give a darn if you are a government official. You cannot come in here without paying.*

not worth a damn [gir] sem valor, inútil, sem importância *Your opinion isn't worth a damn to me.*

DAMNDEST do/try one's damndest [col] empenhar-se ao máximo, dar o melhor de si *Kevin did his damndest to spoil my plans.*

DAMPER put a damper on [gir] desencorajar, tirar o entusiasmo de, fazer perder o ânimo *Don't put a damper on my idea.*

DANCE lead (someone) a (merry) dance fazer (alguém) andar em uma roda viva, complicar a vida de (alguém) fazendo-o desdobrar-se em muitas atividades, tornar as coisas difíceis para *His first wife, who had been a famous movie star, led him a merry dance.*

DANDER get one's//someone's dander up [col] irritar-se//irritar alguém, perder a calma//fazer perder a calma ... *no need to get your dander up. We were only kidding.* -NE,346. ♦ *Dudley's critical attitude got my dander up.*

DARK in the dark no escuro, às cegas, na ignorância, desinformado *If the Germans were in the dark about the date of the [Allied] invasion [which took place on the Normandy coast], they were also ignorant of where it would take place.* -SWLR,1346. ♦ *... there seemed to be no reason for keeping Blanchard in the dark any longer.* -SBW,5.
whistle in the dark [col] fingir coragem ou confiança em um momento ou situação de perigo, de medo etc. *That girl is whistling in the dark if she thinks he's going to marry her.* -EJ,216.

DARLING you're a darling/doll [gir] você é bacana, legal, formidável, um amor *"You're a darling!", she laughed, kissing him ardently ...* -MJA,991. ♦ *I told him he was a doll, kissed him on the lips, and started off.* -CGU,58.

DARN darn/darned [col] 1. = **damn** 1 *It's that darned dog howling again!* 2. = **damn** 3 *I feel darn weak this morning.* ♦ *You're darn right.*
I'll be darned → I'll be **DAMNED**
not give a darn → not give a **DAMN**

DASH cut a dash [col] fazer figura, causar boa impressão, ser alvo dos olhares e da atenção geral *She cut quite a dash in her lovely light blue dress.*
dash off 1. escrever às pressas, rabiscar; esboçar rapidamente *He can dash off a magazine article in a day.* ♦ *Jeff dashed off a letter to a friend in Toronto.* ♦ *Burt dashed off a rudimentary drawing of a flying fuel tank ...* -T/86. 2. sair apressadamente, correr *Foreign correspondents spend much of their lives dashing off to wars and disasters ...* -T/81.
make a dash correr *... he made a dash for the nearest room ...* -KJ,35.

DATE blind date [col] 1. encontro entre um homem e uma mulher que não se conhecem, combinado por um amigo de ambos *He had met her on a blind date set up by his cousin ...* -T/87. 2. um dos participantes de um encontro dessa natureza *The blind date Preston arranged for me turned out to be a bashful but beautiful blonde.*
bring up to date atualizar, pôr ao corrente, colocar a par ... *they brought him up to date on family news.* -T/86. v. up to DATE
date back (to) remontar (a), datar de, ter origem em, existir desde ... *a series of cultural values dating back to the time of slavery.* -WC,8. ♦ *... a dynastic tradition that dates back seven centuries ...* -T/78.
date from = DATE back to *The Mona Lisa dates from the 16th century.*
double date [col] encontro, saída, programa (de dois casais) *Bob and Carol and Ted and Alice went out on a double date.* ⇒ **double-date** saírem juntos (dois casais) *Jerry and I double-dated with two young movie stars.*
out of date/fashion antiquado, fora de moda, obsoleto *Marxism may be out of date – but so is South America.* -GJI,616. ♦ *an out-of-date theory* ♦ *Long skirts have gone out of fashion, again.*
set a/the date marcar a/uma data *Antonio and Solange have set the date for their wedding.*
to date até o momento, até agora *To date we have had no complaints from dissatisfied customers.*
up to date que inclui o último estilo, idéias, conhecimento, fatos etc.; atual, moderno, recentíssimo, de última moda *What seemed up to date this year will be old-fashioned tomorrow.* ♦ *up-to-date facts/ideas/information/methods*

DAUGHTER-IN-LAW nora *My son's wife is my daughter-in-law.*

DAVY Davy Jones's locker [col] o fundo do oceano (considerado a sepultura daqueles

que morreram no mar) *The ship was sinking, headed for Davy Jones's locker.*
DAWN dawn on/upon começar a ser perceptível para, tornar-se evidente para *The full implications of the situation began to dawn on her and she felt desperate.*
DAY all day o dia inteiro *Hurry up! I haven't got all day.*
all day long durante o dia inteiro *Anna and I stayed there all day long.*
all one's born days [col] toda a vida (de alguém), desde que nasceu *She'd never chewed any tobacco in all her born days ...* -T/75.
call it a day [col] pôr termo ao trabalho do dia, encerrar a atividade *It's five o'clock. Let's call it a day and go home.*
carry/win the day levar a melhor, sair vitorioso *Youth and innovation carried the day at the world championship.* -T/87. ♦ *... to weld the diffident organizations together and win the day for the Democrats.* -T/60.
day after diariamente, dia após dia *Day after day goes by with almost the same routine.* -LAK,26. ♦ *He was kept busy day after day at the hospital.* -T/63.
the day before yesterday anteontem *She came to see me the day before yesterday.*
day by day dia a dia, diariamente, continuamente *Our affluent society grows more infantile day by day.* -T/77.
day care assistência diurna a crianças de pouca idade *... in many major cities only 10% of children needing day care were being provided for.* -T/72. ⇒ **day-care center/facility** creche *... some mothers use day-care centers as a substitute for child rearing ...* -T/72. ♦ *Mothers with children under three years old ... who cannot find day-care facilities ...* -T/81.
day in and day out; day in, day out todos os dias, continuamente *... you must devote yourself day in and day out to learning the spelling, pronunciation, and exact meaning of new words.* -PC,29.

day in court (em uma ação judicial, litígio etc.) dia em que uma pessoa tem a oportunidade de comparecer ao tribunal para apresentar os argumentos de sua defesa, as provas de suas alegações, as acusações contra alguém etc.; oportunidade para (uma pessoa) apresentar seu lado de uma questão *Burr had had his day in court and won.* -VE,99.
day of reckoning dia de ajuste de contas *As the day of reckoning approaches, tensions between the two groups may erupt.* -T/91.
days of grace; grace period; period of grace prorrogação concedida após o vencimento de um título, fatura etc., prazo de tolerância *Your second payment fell due yesterday but they decided to grant you three days of grace.* ♦ *There is a period of grace given on this loan of one month if you have always paid on time.*
dying day dia da morte; o fim, o término, a derradeira etapa, o apagar das luzes *[He] ... was [President] Nixon's closest adviser in the dying days of his Administration.* -T/74. ♦ *He loved his wife to his dying day.*
every other day dia sim, dia não *Please do telephone me at least once every other day.*
every single day todo santo dia, diariamente *Every day, every single day, 34,000 new sets of fingerprints came into the FBI ...* -WI,217.
fall on evil days sofrer revés, infortúnio, desgraça *Thomas Wolfe's [novel] Look Homeward, Angel, a biographer points out, "fell on critically evil days ...".* -LAS,193.
forever and a day para sempre *The George and Ira Gershwin song says that "Love is here to stay/Forever and a day".*
from day to day dia a dia, quotidianamente *The richest source of material for any topic [in writing a composition] is what happens to you from day to day.* -SHS,30.
the good old days os dias felizes do passado, os bons tempos *[He] ... viewed with*

nostalgic sadness the passing of the good old days. -RR,618.

halcyon days dias felizes e tranqüilos, época de paz e serenidade *As in the halcyon days of the 1960s, Americans believe they ought to be able to buy big cars if they feel like it ...* -T/87.

(as) happy/honest/etc. as the day is long muito honesto/feliz/etc. *Nellie [was never] ... too bright, but she was honest as the day is long.* -MG,447. ♦ *... you're as unreasonable as the day is long.* -WCN,242.

have had one's/its day já ter tido sua época de glória, seu período de sucesso etc., estar em declínio, ser coisa do passado *... soon after 1901 it was to be clear that realism and romanticism had had their days in France.* -CS,346.

have seen/known better days ter conhecido dias melhores, já ter sido mais próspero, já ter tido melhor aparência *The coat he was wearing had seen better days.* ♦ *The old gentleman had known better days.*

have/take the/a day off ter o/um dia de folga, ausentar-se do trabalho *My boss said I could have the day off tomorrow.* ♦ *It was best to take a day off.* -LRW,134.

in days of old antigamente, outrora, em tempos idos *In days of old, when knights were bold, the peasant had a very difficult life.* v. **of OLD**

in one's day no tempo de, na época de *What are the major, inner problems of people in our day?* -MRM,13.

in the old days no passado, outrora, em tempos idos *Kit Carson liked Indians. In the old days he had lived with them for months at a time without seeing another white man.* -BD,23.

in this day and age em nossa época, no momento atual *She still believes in fairies and gnomes in this day and age.*

in those days naquela época, antigamente *Few places so spruce and well worked [as the Starrett ranch] could be found so deep in the Territory in those days.* -SJS,3.

it's all in a/the day's work [col] isso faz parte do dia-a-dia, parte da rotina, do labor diário, deve ser aceito normalmente *For the American entrepreneur [talking to half a dozen people at once and also on the telephone making appointments in Rome, Berlin, London and New York City] ... it was all in a day's work.* -T/87.

lose the day ser derrotado, sofrer revés *Our position in the hills is precarious. We're exposed to enemy fire and may lose the day.*

make someone's day [col] fazer o dia valer a pena, dar satisfação, alegria ou felicidade a alguém *O.K., Santa [Claus], make my day.* -T/86. ♦ *Go ahead, voters, make my day.* -T/86. ♦ *Detective Dirty Harry [Clint Eastwood] pointing his magnum .375 at a terrorist and daring him to resist arrest: "Come on, make my day!".*

many a day ⇒ **MANY a/an/another**
many's the day ⇒ **MANY's the**

name the day marcar o dia do casamento *Zillah and Lou have named the day for the wedding.*

off day [col] dia aziago, dia em que nada parece dar certo *This must be an off day for me. Everything that I have tried to do today has gone wrong.*

of its/one's/ the/ day da (sua) época, daquele/de seu tempo *... The Virginian [a western novel by Owen Wister] became the outstanding best seller of its day.* -SV,38. ♦ *... the rugged individualists of the day understood increasingly complex commercial operations.* -RR,3.

the old days os velhos tempos, os tempos que se foram, os tempos de outrora *They like to get together and talk about the old days.*

one fine day um belo dia, certo dia *... [François] Truffaut got a loan from his father-in-law and one fine day in 1958 got cracking on a film called* The 400 Blows. -T/63.

one of these days um dia destes, qualquer dia (no futuro), logo mais *One of these days you're going to land in jail.*
one of those days um dia daqueles, isto é, um dia aziago, em que nada parece dar certo *First the car wouldn't start. Then when I was on the highway I was fined for speeding. It seemed I was going to have one of those days.*
the other day outro dia, recentemente, há dias *I ran into Jackie's sister the other day.*
palmy days época de abundância, dias prósperos *... the palmy days of 1957 ...* -T/72. ♦ *... it had been all very well for me in my more palmy days of money earning ...* -KRI,590.
rainy day época de dificuldades, tempos difíceis *I still have some money left over for a rainy day.*
red-letter day dia memorável, que marca um acontecimento muito importante *The most important red-letter day for me was the day World War II ended and I knew that I was finished as a soldier.*
save the day alcançar a vitória, ganhar a batalha, levar a melhor (principalmente quando a derrota é quase certa) *Not even Lieutenant Colonel Custer's military know-how and experience could save the day in the Battle of the Little Big Horn.*
someone is/must be 40/50/55/etc. if someone is a day fulano tem/deve ter pelo menos 40/50/55/etc. anos *... the bleached fat one who was fifty-five if she was a day ...* -WJT,231. ♦ *People are always telling me that I must be 50 if I'm a day ...* -T/66.
someone's days are numbered seus dias estão contados, a morte ou o fim se aproxima *... he received ... a note ... warning him that his days were numbered.* -WL,31.
take the day off v. **have the DAY off**
that'll be the day nunca, jamais, em hipótese alguma, é pouco provável *In John Ford's* The Searchers, *after an exchange of angry words with Ethan Edwards, Martin Pawley shouts at him: "I hope you die". Edwards replies matter-of-factly: "That'll be the day".*
these days nos dias atuais, na atualidade, hoje em dia *He dealt with the problem in a thoroughly honest way, which is unusual in his profession these days.*
those were the days aquele foi um período áureo, uma época feliz *Remember when love at the movies was as simple, and romantic, as boy meets girl? Those were the days.* -T/87.
to this day até hoje, até agora, até este momento *To this day, the movie* Captain Horatio Hornblower *reminds me of the old Colonial movie theater.*
win the day → **carry the DAY**
DAYDREAM 1. devaneio, fantasia, sonho *In Hollywood movies, sex is a daydream for people who are scared of the real thing.* -T/63. 2. devanear *... the poor kids have no time to lie on their beds and daydream.* -T/60.
DAYLIGHT beat/knock/etc. the (living) daylights out of [gir] surrar, bater em; nocautear *He knocked the daylights out of two bigger kids.* ♦ *Mr. Burgess would grab something and flail the living daylights out of you if he heard you saying things like that ...* -CEP,166.
in broad daylight à luz do dia, em plena luz do dia *According to the FBI ... [he] walked into the Soviet embassy three times in broad daylight ...* -T/81.
scare the (living) daylights out of [gir] dar um grande susto em, apavorar *Unemployment still scares the daylights out of me.* -T/87. ♦ *He scared the living daylights out of me when he whipped out a gun.*
see daylight [col] 1. divisar o fim ou a solução (de tarefa, dificuldades, provação etc.), ver que o fim está próximo *The amnesty may never see daylight.* -T/78. 2. entender, compreender finalmente (a

natureza de algo que nos parecia obscuro) *At first I didn't understand, but finally I saw daylight.*
DAY-TO-DAY diário, rotineiro, do dia-a-dia ... *the day-to-day struggle for security* ... -T/81.
DAZE in a daze aturdido, assombrado, pasmo, perplexo *[They] ... were walking around in a daze, too shocked to realize [what had happened]* ... -T/86.
DEAD 1. completamente, inteiramente, absolutamente *She was dead right when she said that.* ♦ *I'm dead tired.* ♦ *He came home dead drunk.* 2. diretamente *When the fog lifted, the fishermen saw a lifeboat dead ahead of them.*
in the dead of night/winter na calada da noite/no período de frio mais intenso do inverno *The soldiers marched in the dead of night.* ♦ *Why would he want to go to Canada in the dead of winter?*
wouldn't be caught dead → **wouldn't be CAUGHT dead**
DEADBEAT [gir] caloteiro *He was always known as a deadbeat in the business world.*
DEAD-END → **dead END**
DEAD-LETTER dead-letter office departamento do Correio para onde são enviadas as cartas cujos destinatários não podem ser localizados *Jones is a mailman and his brother works in the dead-letter office.*
DEADLINE data-limite, prazo final para a consecução de tarefa ou entrega de alguma coisa *The weekly newsmagazines have a Wednesday night deadline.* ♦ *The deadline for paying your income tax is May 15th.*
DEADLOCK 1. impasse, paralisação, beco sem saída *The crisis in the Middle East has come to a deadlock; neither side will give in a little.* 2. chegar ou levar a um impasse *Labor and Industry often are deadlocked over the questions to be solved in a labor dispute.*
DEADPAN [gir] inexpressivo, sem emoção, impassivo ... *he sometimes had a deadpan expression that told exactly nothing.* -KD,16.
DEAL big deal [col] 1. algo importante, especial, sensacional etc. *I just didn't want to make a big deal out of getting married.* -HA,140. 2. grande coisa! [exprime ironia] *So you think you're special now that you're president of your class. Big deal!*
clinch/swing a deal [col] fechar o negócio, negociar uma transação com êxito *Try to clinch the deal today.* ♦ *Instead of a simple deal, he has swung a deal whose complications are infinite, and infinitely surprising* ... -T/87.
cut a deal chegar a um acordo, fazer um trato, uma negociação *Every President sooner or later has to cut a deal with that thing we call Washington* ... -T/87.
deal in vender, comerciar com (determinado artigo) *They deal in imported books.*
deal out distribuir, dar (algo) a um número de pessoas *The lieutenant has not yet accepted the fact that we have been put into the field [of combat] to deal out death.* -MAT,14.
deal with 1. negociar com (pessoa), ter negócios, relações comerciais ou sociais com *They deal directly with the manufacturers.* 2. tratar de, versar sobre, ter que ver com *Last Tango in Paris dealt with the bizarre sexual odyssey of an embittered middle-aged man and a modish young woman.* -BRF,65. 3. lidar com, agir com relação a, enfrentar, tratar com ... *the psychologist is dealing with the most mysterious of natural phenomena: the mind of man.* -DR,174. ♦ *She dealt with the problem squarely and bravely.*
a good/great deal grande quantidade, alto grau; muito, bastante *A good deal of food is spoiled by rats in storehouses.* ♦ *Keefer and his wife quarrelled a great deal about money.*
make a deal fazer um acordo *If you make a deal you're expected to abide by it.*

new deal 1. reforma para melhor, remodelação, mudança, novo começo *Franklin D. Roosevelt promised the country a "new deal" when he accepted the democratic nomination for President in 1932.* 2. [maiúsculas] programa de reformas econômicas e sociais introduzidas por Franklin D. Roosevelt na década de 1930 *... the New Deal focused public attention upon the need for improving the living conditions of thousands of families ...* -WJ,380. 3. nova distribuição de cartas no jogo *Let's put all the cards together and shuffle them better for a new deal.*
no deal [col] nada disso, não há acordo, nada feito *He tried to offer money to the police officer, but the lawman said: "No deal".*
raw deal [col] tratamento muito injusto e cruel *They gave him a raw deal when he refused to cooperate.*
see a great deal of/a lot of encontrar-se com (alguém) freqüentemente, estar quase sempre em companhia de *He had been seeing a great deal of Paula.* -WJT,256. ♦ *We used to see a lot of each other in those days.*
square deal tratamento justo, bom acolhimento, negócio honesto, transação insuspeita *We expect that he will give us a square deal even though he is not very fond of us.*
strike a deal chegar a um acordo, a um entendimento, fazer um trato *... the U.S. could strike a deal for reduction of Soviet aid to Nicaragua ...* -T/87.
think a great deal of/a lot of ter em alta consideração, ter grande estima por *The students think a great deal of their English teacher.*
DEATH at death's door próximo à morte, perto do fim *He thought he was at death's door.* -LAK,80.
be the death of causar a morte de; afligir, causar profundo sofrimento a *Tom's trouble with the police was the death of his father.*

death throes estertores da morte, agonia final *The end came quickly for the Third Reich in the spring of 1945. The death throes began in March.* -SWLR,1426.
do to death matar *... millions of hapless persons were done to death [in the Nazi concentration camps] ...* -SWLR,375.
frighten/scare (half) to death dar um grande susto em, matar de susto *Primitive peoples are frightened to death of spirits.* ♦ *... Two bad little boys scared half to death ...* -MMA,51.
meet one's death morrer *[Wild Bill Hickock] ... met his death at the hands of a coward who shot him in the back.* -RR,615.
put to death matar, executar *[He] ... disclosed that the monarch was actually put to death by lethal injections of morphine and cocaine ...* -T/86.
sign one's (own) death warrant assinar sua sentença de morte, condenar-se *He signed his own death warrant when he refused to cooperate with the CIA.*
starve to death morrer de fome, definhar de inanição *[They] ... have been slowly starving to death for years ...* -SV,123.
tickled to death; tickled pink [gir] contentíssimo, extremamente satisfeito *He was tickled to death when he heard the news.* ♦ *Cathy was tickled pink when she found out she had won first prize.*
to death 1. extremamente, muitíssimo *Any one that came fooling around his property would get scared half to death.* -LRT,48. ♦ *She bores me to death.* 2. até matar, até a morte *... men in uniform shot and bayoneted to death 46 [people] ...* -T/87.
to the death até o fim, até a morte *You really believe in segregation? You'll fight for it to the death?* -BL,237. ♦ *When Shane and Wilson met in Grafton's saloon, it was a duel to the death.*
DEATHBED on one's deathbed em seu leito de morte, em seus últimos instantes

... in *[the movie]* Citizen Kane ... *there is an enormous close-up of the lips of the protagonist as on his deathbed he murmurs the mysterious word, "Rosebud!"*. -FJ,183.

DECISION make a decision tomar uma decisão *He had the greatest difficulty in making decisions* ... -NEW,12.

DECK clear the decks preparar-se para agir, trabalhar etc. removendo quaisquer empecilhos *Let's clear the decks and get ready for what's coming.*

deck out [geralmente pas] vestir-se com apuro, adornar-se *She was all decked out in an elaborate oriental costume.*

hit the deck [gir] levantar-se da cama *OK, everyone hit the deck and be out on the parade grounds in five minutes.*

on deck [gir] presente, no local *Everyone was on deck when they heard that a famous movie queen was to be at the dance.*

stack the deck → **stack the CARDS**

DEEP deep down no íntimo, no fundo, na realidade *Did he feel deep down, as I did, that little bite of fear?* -SSG,6.

DEEP-DYED = DYED-in-the-wool ... *a "radically liberal" politician whose "personal beliefs seem to indicate a deep-dyed conservatism".* -T/63.

DEEP-ROOTED arraigado, profundo, entranhado ... *a deep-rooted psychological disturbance.* -T/60. ♦ ... *deep-rooted hostilities* ... -T/87. ♦ *deep-rooted traditions*

DEEP-SEATED = deep-rooted ... *a deep-seated prejudice* ... -DJ,xii. ♦ ... *deep-seated neurotic conflicts* ... -EA,55. ♦ *[He] ... had a number of deep-seated personal problems that only some form of psychological therapy might cure...* - MJV, 6.

DEEP-SET fundo, encovado, entrado ... *he had dark deep-set eyes and hollow cheeks* ... -PRT,24.

DEEP-SIX [gir] livrar-se de, dar sumiço a ... *suggested to him that some "politically sensitive" documents ... be "deep-sixed".* -T/73. ♦ *Graham told his secretary to deep-six all the files that might cause trouble.*

DEGREE by degrees gradualmente, pouco a pouco *His knowledge of the subject is improving by degrees.*

third degree [gir] interrogatório rigoroso usado pela polícia (freqüentemente acompanhado de tortura) *The third degree was prohibited by law throughout the state* ... -DJ,10.

to a/certain/some/etc. degree até certo ponto, um tanto, um pouco *[He] ... had been cooperating to some degree with the Government* ... -T/87.

to the nth degree ao máximo, ao extremo *He tried to the nth degree to achieve something new in his field.* ♦ ... *you're unreasonable to the nth degree, I'm not joking* ... -WCN,244.

DELIVERY special delivery entrega (de correspondência) por via expressa *She sent the letter special delivery.*

DENT not make a dent não ter efeito apreciável, quase não deixar marca, impressão etc., quase não produzir redução ... *it is clear we have not made a dent in the problem.* -T/87.

DEPARTMENT department store loja de departamentos *Macy's, Sears Roebuck and Mappin are well-known department stores.*

DEPLANE desembarcar de um avião ... *they would deplane in San Francisco at twelve thirty.* -WI,308.

DEPTH in depth em profundidade, em detalhes, minuciosamente *Campbell's new book examines in depth the influence of psychoanalysis on modern literature.* ⇒ **in-depth** detalhado, minucioso, profundo *Time Magazine is famous for its in-depth reporting.*

out of/beyond one's depth além do limite de entendimento, conhecimento ou habilidade de; fora de seu elemento, no escuro, desnorteado *Nuclear physics is beyond my depth.* ♦ *I'm just out of my depth. I should have known that my ignorance [of the subject] would get me into some disaster ...* -HEB,55.

DERRING-DO bravura, ousadia, coragem indômita, proeza, arrojo *Burt Lancaster's fantastic feats of derring-do, archery and acrobatics in* The Flame and the Arrow *are still something to see.*

DESIGN have designs on/upon ter más intenções, querer apossar-se de (propriedade, dinheiro, cargo etc.); estar a fim de alguém (sexualmente) *Turner had designs on the widow's property.* ♦ *He confessed later that he had designs on the girl.*

DEUCE what the deuce que diabo *What the deuce is going on here?*

DEVICE leave someone to his own devices deixar alguém fazer como achar melhor, dar plena liberdade de ação a, deixar alguém resolver seus próprios problemas *Tom was left to his own devices and fell hopelessly in love with ... a twenty-one-year-old girl ...* -NEW,35.

DEVIL between the devil and the deep (blue) sea entre a cruz e a caldeirinha, entre dois fogos *Now that both the police and the Mafia are after him, he is between the devil and the deep blue sea.*
the devil take the hindmost os mais fracos, os menos capazes, os mais vagarosos, os últimos etc., que se danem *I'm going to look after myself, and the devil take the hindmost.*
the devil/hell to pay encrenca, barulho, briga; castigo, penalidade severa, conseqüências desagradáveis *If these documents ever fall into the hands of the Senator, there will be the devil to pay.* ♦ *There will be hell to pay when papa finds out what you've done.*
play the devil with [col] perturbar, transtornar, estragar, danificar, prejudicar, arruinar *... spooks, bogies and supernatural agents start moving the furniture about,* *playing the devil with the shapes of common objects.* -T/60.
raise the devil → **raise CAIN**
speak/talk of the devil (and he appears/is sure to appear) fala-se de uma pessoa (e ela aparece) *Mr. and Mrs. Miller were talking about their son Tommy when the front door banged and the boy walked in. "Talk about the devil and he's sure to appear", observed Mr. Miller.*
to beat the devil → **to beat the BAND**
to give the devil his due a bem da verdade, justiça seja feita *Now, to give the devil his due, I must make it clear that Fred never said that.*
what/where/who the devil [como expletivo, para dar ênfase] que diabo, onde diabo etc. *What the devil are you doing here?* ♦ *Where the devil have you been?* ♦ *Who the devil are you?*

DEVIL-MAY-CARE descuidado, indiferente, inconseqüente, estouvado, jovial *In Wild West fiction and films the Arizona cowboy ... is a reckless, devil-may-care individual who is ready for trouble, even looking for it ...* -MJ,69.

DICE no dice [gir] nada feito, nada disso *When I asked him for fifty dollars, he said: "No dice".*

DIE be dying for/to estar com grande vontade de, estar morrendo de desejo (por algo) *I'm dying for a cup of coffee.* -SLT,169. ♦ *I thought you were dying to go to the ball.* –UL,12.
die away/down diminuir aos poucos, desaparecer gradualmente *The shouts died away in the distance.* ♦ *The night wind had died away.* -DD,115. ♦ *... the thunder of the cavalcade died down to a whisper.* -BW,10. ♦ *The dust died down.*
die hard custar a morrer ou desaparecer, perdurar *Old habits die hard.* -T/86. ♦ *[His] ... prejudices died hard ...* -LA,279.
⇒ **diehard** conservador extremo, indivíduo que não admite mudanças (políticas, sociais etc.) *A few diehards refused to*

accept the new realities. → **die-hard** extremamente conservador, avesso a mudanças, teimoso, obstinado, irredutível ... *a die-hard fascist* ... -T/81. ♦ ... *die-hard Marxism* ... -T/64.

the die is cast a sorte está lançada *When the Allied forces landed in Normandy, the German generals knew that the die was cast.*

die off morrer em seqüência, um após outro *[Brazilian Indians] ... died off rapidly from small pox, measles [and other infectious diseases transmitted by the white man]* ... -WC,18.

die out 1. deixar de existir, extinguir-se *Isaac Asimov once said that dinosaurs died out about 65 million yeas ago.* 2. diminuir aos poucos, cessar gradualmente *... he stood silently in the moonlight until the echoes of the pounding hoofs [of the troopers' horses] died out.* -CHT,85.

DIEHARD → **DIE hard**

DIFFERENCE split the difference [col] dividir em partes iguais a diferença entre duas importâncias, rachar *He wanted $2,000 for the car and I wanted to pay $1,800. So we split the difference and I gave him $1,900.*

DIG dig in 1. cavar trincheiras, entrincheirar-se *The military force dug in to await the enemy.* 2. [col] entregar-se ao trabalho com determinação *Let's dig in and finish the task we were assigned.* 3. [gír] começar a comer *Sit yourself down, Captain, and dig in.* -SLS,236.

dig into [col] procurar, investigar, pesquisar *The investigating committee dug freely into the affairs of the accused businessmen.*

dig out 1. procurar e (re)tirar (algo de onde estava) *When the [school] principal dug out our records ... he sized up all those forged signatures ...* -HA,173. 2. descobrir, encontrar, desenterrar, trazer à tona, revelar *She wants to dig out all the facts.*

dig up [col] desenterrar, descobrir, encontrar, trazer à tona, revelar *You certainly know some strange men ... I don't understand where you dig them up.* -EJ,97.

DIME a dime a dozen [col] abundante, disponível em grande número, muito comum, barato *When the French began to flee from Algeria, cars were a dime a dozen and many Arabs bought them to sell later at a high price.*

on a dime 1. em um espaço muito pequeno *The modern compact cars can turn on a dime.* 2. em um átimo, instantaneamente *[A bicycle] can sprint like a cat, then stop on a dime ...* -T/87.

DINT by dint of a poder de, à força de, por meio de *We were keen, sharp, perspicacious, and superior by dint of hard work and good business sense.* -KS,141.

DIP dip into 1. examinar ou estudar superficialmente (assunto, tema, tópico), ler trechos (de um livro), correr os olhos por *She likes to dip into philosophy.* ♦ *Henry didn't read the book, he merely dipped into it.* 2. tirar dinheiro de (bolso, reservas, fundo etc.), recorrer a (fundo, reservas etc.) para obter dinheiro; apropriar-se de, apossar-se de, apoderar-se de (dinheiro, fundos etc.) *Now I am having to dip into my own savings ...* -T/87. ♦ *... her guardian ... had dipped into ... [an ample bequest that her father had left her].* -T/87.

take a dip dar um mergulho, nadar um pouco *Let's take a dip in the lake to cool off.*

DIRT dirt poor muito pobre *Once dirt poor, Trinidad and Tobago are awash in petrodollars ...* -T/81.

dish the dirt [gír] mexericar, falar mal da vida alheia *When two or more women get together, they like to dish the dirt.*

do/play someone dirt [gír] prejudicar, fazer mal a, lesar, fazer jogo sujo com; caluniar maldosamente, difamar, ser infiel a, atraiçoar *... She enjoys doing dirt to people, even those she doesn't know very well.* ♦ *He played his girl friend dirt by taking another girl to the school dance.*

hit the dirt [gir] atirar-se ao chão e permanecer de bruços para evitar rajada de balas, estilhaços de bomba etc. (durante um ataque do inimigo) *In combat, [his] first instinct was to attack, not hit the dirt.* -T/87.

DIRT-CHEAP [col] baratíssimo *He got his new car dirt-cheap.*

DISAGREE disagree with fazer mal a, ter efeito nocivo sobre, produzir mal-estar (alimento ou o clima) *Poorly cooked pig meat disagrees with many people.* ♦ *The cold Boston winters disagree with him.* v. **AGREE with**

DISCRETION throw discretion to the wind → **throw (all) CAUTION to the wind(s)**

DISFAVOR fall in/into disfavor cair em descrédito, em desagrado ... *after his death from tuberculosis in 1938 at the age of 38, he [Thomas Wolfe] fell into disfavor ...* -T/87.

DISH dish it out [gir] repreender, censurar, criticar severamente *He can dish it out but he can't take criticism.*

dish out [col] distribuir, dar, suprir, servir *He's always dishing out advice to his employees.* ♦ *Texas Catholics are dishing out $2.5 million for ... [the Pope's] visit to San Antonio.* -T/87.

dish up [gir] fornecer, apresentar, oferecer *The TV newscasters often dish up rumor as fact and never apologize for their misinformation.*

do the dishes lavar a louça, lavar os pratos ... *details like who does the dishes or whose turn it is to clean the bathroom.* -T/72.

one's dish [gir] algo de que muito se gosta; predileção, interesse especial *The songs of Cole Porter and George Gershwin are just my dish.*

DISPOSE dispose of 1. dar fim a, desfazer-se de, remover, livrar-se de; matar ... *the company failed to comply with a state order to dispose of the [dangerous] chemicals ...* -T/80. ♦ *The dictator has disposed of his enemies most efficiently.* 2. vender, liquidar *Mr. Buchanan has disposed of his property.*

DISTANCE keep at a distance manter distante, não permitir intimidade *Stop trying to keep me at a distance and let's be friends.*

long distance serviço telefônico interurbano *The sisters communicate by long distance at least once a week.* T/60. ⇒ **long-distance** interurbano (telefonema) *[He] ... received a long-distance phone call.* -RE,41.

within hailing/hearing/shouting distance ao alcance da voz, à pequena distância, próximo *I live within hearing distance of the nearest neighbor.* ♦ *Mike's house is within shouting distance of Mustafa's ...* -T/91.

within striking distance a uma distância que possibilita um ataque, que um alvo ou objetivo se torna vulnerável ... *the U.S. aircraft carrier* Kitty Hawk *moved to within striking distance of newly installed Iranian missile batteries ...* -T/87.

within walking distance à pequena distância, a uma distância que pode ser percorrida a pé ... *the red Audi parked within walking distance of the [border] checkpoint.* -T/87.

DISTINCT as distinct from em contraste com, diferentemente de, em contraposição a, em vez de ... *the writer who deals with financial, as distinct from military, history.* -GJKT,xiv.

DISTRICT district attorney promotor público *[He was] ... a twenty-nine-year-old assistant district attorney from Massachusetts.* -LA,91.

red-light district/belt zona de meretrício ... *the red-light districts of Amsterdam ...* -T/92.

DITCH last ditch [gir] a última cartada, o último recurso *The Cambodians were fighting to the last ditch.* ⇒ **last-ditch**

derradeiro e desesperado (esforço, recurso, defesa, tentativa etc.) ... *last-ditch attempts to avoid a nationwide railway strike.* -T/63.

DIXIE; DIXIELAND os estados do sul dos EUA *He traveled all over Dixie and no one ever knew that he was a Negro passing for a white man.*

DO do away with 1. abolir, eliminar, pôr fim a *[The barber] ... did away with the sideburns that Mr. Krank treasured so dearly.* -BL,10. 2. assassinar *A Mafia killer did away with the witness.*

do (well//badly) by tratar (bem//mal) *He had done well by his mother.* -WI,52. ♦ *... the press had not done so badly by him ...* -T/66.

do fine realizar (algo) satisfatoriamente, sair-se bem *... he has been doing just fine on his own.* -T/81.

do in 1. [gir] assassinar, causar a morte de *He was done in by bandits while crossing the Gobi desert.* 2. [geralmente pas] estafar-se, fatigar-se *After a day in the hot sun we were done in.* 3. arruinar, destruir, derrotar *The people sympathized with a military man done in by the politicians.* -T/92. 4. ludibriar, enganar, lesar *A confidence man did her in.*

do out of [col] lesar, esbulhar, trapacear *He did me out of ten thousand dollars.*

do over 1. repetir, refazer *She had to do her homework over.* 2. [col] redecorar *She's looking for a decorator to do over her apartment.*

do's and don'ts regras, regulamentos, instruções, orientação (o que se deve fazer e o que não se deve fazer; obrigações e proibições) *We all must learn the do's and don'ts of our profession.*

do (someone) proud causar orgulho a alguém *Jim's athletic and scholastic achievements did his parents proud.*

do up 1. embrulhar, amarrar *The books were done up in a neat package.* 2. arrumar, pôr em ordem, limpar *He had to do up his room this morning.* 3. lavar e passar *I have two suits to be done up this week.* 4. arranjar, amarrar (cabelo) no alto *... a woman with her black hair done up to look like a crow in flight ...* -T/86.

do up brown [gir] fazer (algo) por completo, empenhar-se totalmente, não medir esforços, dar o máximo de si *Well, we sure did that job up brown.*

do well ter ou dar bom resultado, ser bem-sucedido, sair-se bem, dar-se bem *Philippe entered into his new duties with zeal and tried to do well in his appointment.* -EMW,34.

do well to convir, ser aconselhável, ser a coisa certa a fazer *You'd do well to take his advice.*

do with 1. tratar com, lidar com *He's a difficult man to do with.* 2. arranjar-se com (algo inferior ou não adequado na falta de coisa melhor ou mais apropriada) *This isn't the right tool for the job but we will have to do with it unless we find something better.* 3. [precedido de **can/could**] beneficiar-se de, fazer boa utilização de, empregar bem, achar salutar, útil, gostar de *She has principles, let her stick to them. You could do with a few principles yourself.* -WH,77.

do without passar sem, dispensar, não querer, não precisar de *Metaphysics is a human drive or appetite, and to ask men to do without metaphysics is as pointless as to ask them to do without sex relations.* -BCS,13.

easy does it [col] tome cuidado, vá devagar, vá com calma, não force, com jeito vai *Now, don't push too hard. Easy does it.*

it/that won't do isso não serve, não é satisfatório, não basta, não é apropriado *... it won't do for us to be seen together.* -CJT,16.

that does it! agora basta! chega! *That does it! I can't stand you any longer! Get out of here now!*

that will do! chega! pare com isso! *That will do! I've had enough of your rudeness.*

what's doing? quais são as novidades? que há de novo? *Hi, kid. What's doing?* ♦ *What's doing at the club tonight?*

you can do better than that você pode se sair melhor, você é capaz de fazer ou dizer coisa melhor, superior, mais apropriada etc. (ao que você acaba de fazer ou dizer) *When Lois Lane told Perry White she suspected Clark Kent to be Superman, White told her: "Oh, come on, you can do better than that".*

DOCTOR just what the doctor ordered [col] aquilo de que alguém estava precisando *This trip to Hawaii is just what the doctor ordered.*

DOG die like a dog ter uma morte miserável, morrer na desgraça *He was to die like a dog, an unpleasant and unheroic death.*

dog days dias extremamente quentes do verão, dias de canícula *... the dog days of August ...* -T/80. ♦ *... the dog days of summer.* -T/87.

a dog's/coon's age [col] um tempão *I haven't seen her in a dog's age.*

a dog's chance [col] possibilidade remota *He doesn't have a dog's chance of ever becoming the President.*

dog tags duas placas metálicas de identificação usadas pelos soldados e marinheiros americanos em uma corrente em volta do pescoço *The soldiers who volunteered to go behind enemy lines in civilian clothes and act as spies had to leave their dog tags behind.*

every dog has his day cada um tem seu dia (de glória, de sorte, de sucesso), sua vez, sua oportunidade *Don't despair. Every dog has his day.*

give a dog a bad name and hang him uma pessoa que é caluniada ou adquiriu má reputação dificilmente limpará seu nome *Some people still ask: was the Caryl Chessman affair a case of give a dog a bad name and hang him?*

go to the dogs [col] arruinar-se, degenerar-se, decair *[He] ... went to the dogs early in life.* -T/60.

lead a dog's life levar vida de cachorro, vida infeliz, enfrentar muitas dificuldades *He's been leading a dog's life ever since he lost his job.*

let sleeping dogs lie evitar encrencas, não procurar sarna para se coçar *Don't tell her anything about this. Let sleeping dogs lie.*

love me, love my dog quem me ama tem de amar também tudo o que é meu ou o que me diz respeito *Love me, love my dog. That's the way I see it.*

no one (ever) kicks a dead dog ninguém dá importância a um joão-ninguém ou a quem é desconhecido *He paid no attention to his critics and often said that no one ever kicks a dead dog.*

put on the dog [gir] bancar o importante *You can't stand his wife when she puts on the dog.*

you can't teach an old dog new tricks é difícil convencer pessoas idosas a adquirir novos hábitos, idéias etc. *... the old saw that claims you cannot teach an old dog new tricks is a baseless, if popular, superstition.* -LNW,15.

DOG-EARED que tem os cantos dobrados pelo uso [diz-se das páginas de um livro] *... a newly published 653-page book is already badly dog-eared ...* T/63.

DOG-EAT-DOG caracterizado por competição ou concorrência implacável *As the republics [of former Soviet Union] ... attempt to assert control over their natural resources and manufacturing facilities, a chaotic dog-eat-dog economy has developed ...* -T/91.

DOGGONE; doggoned [col] muito, extremamente *We know doggoned well we can't stay in this crisis forever.*

I'll be doggone/doggoned macacos me mordam, quero ser mico de circo *Well, I'll be doggone.* ♦ *I'll be doggoned if I ever talk to him again!*

DOGHOUSE in the doghouse [gir] em descrédito, em desgraça, em situação desfavorável *... he should have put us – and*

kept us – in the doghouse for some of the dreadful things we did ... -RJ,17.
DO-GOODER → **do GOOD**
DOG-TIRED [col] cansadíssimo, exausto *Pietro was dog-tired.* -YF,37.
DOING take some doing dar um trabalhão, ser muito difícil *The FBI agents have vowed to catch all the spies involved in the case but that'll take some doing.*
DOLDRUMS in the doldrums 1. em estado de inatividade, em estagnação *... the Tokyo stock market is in the doldrums ... because investors are demanding greater returns on their money.* -T/92. 2. em estado de desalento, depressão, melancolia *Sharon has been in the doldrums ever since her husband walked out on her.*
DOLE dole out distribuir parcimoniosamente, repartir *She assembled the orphans and doled out the food.* ♦ *... funds doled out to higher education ...* -T/67.
on the dole recebendo seguro-desemprego (subsídio oficial a desempregados) *In some neighborhoods more than three-quarters of the families are on the dole ...* -T/87.
DOLL doll up [col] 1. vestir-se bem, embonecar-se *She gets all dolled up when she goes out with her beau.* 2. enfeitar, decorar *They dolled up the city for the festive occasion.*
you're a doll → **you're a DARLING**
DOLLAR almighty dollar/buck [col] veneração ou interesse exagerado pelo dinheiro, o poder do dinheiro *The only thing he ever cared about was the almighty dollar.*
bet one's bottom dollar [gir] apostar o derradeiro vintém; ter toda a certeza, não ter dúvida *I'll bet my bottom dollar that he won't arrive on time today.*
feel like a million dollars → **feel like a MILLION (dollars)**
look like a million dollars → **look like a MILLION (dollars)**
the sixty-four thousand dollar question a pergunta crucial, o *x* da questão, a grande incógnita *Now that his father has died, the sixty-four thousand dollar question is whether he'll be able to take the old man's place.*
DONE be done for [col] estar arruinado, destruído, estragado, liquidado; próximo à morte, cansadíssimo, exausto *He was done for. His time was up.* -MF,103.
be done in [col] estar exausto, cansadíssimo *I was pretty done in, and I just lay there bathing my head in the cold water.* -RQ,35.
be done with não ter mais nada a ver com, não ter mais serventia para, dar por terminado, cessar, encerrar, dispensar *I'm done with all the papers in that pile. You may return them to the files.* ♦ *Don't go away. I'm not done with you yet.*
get (something) done levar algo a cabo, fazer, realizar (trabalho, tarefa etc.) *... they're unable to get the job done.* -T/87. ♦ *... he looks to me like a man who can get things done.* -WSM,148.
have done with livrar-se de, encerrar um assunto, dar por terminado (algo) e não mais ter de lidar com (isso) *Let's have done with this nonsense.*
it isn't done isso não se faz, é impróprio, é de mau gosto, não é de bom-tom *Drinking with your spoon still in the cup isn't done in polite society.* ♦ *"My dear girl", James Bond tells a new conquest [in the movie Goldfinger], "there are some things that just aren't done. Such as drinking [champagne] Dom Perignon '53 above a temperature of 38° F. That's as bad as listening to the Beatles without earmuffs."* -T/87.
now you've done it você cometeu uma gafe, você fez uma boa *Now you've done it! We'll never get another invitation to dine here.*
over and done with completamente acabado, encerrado, liquidado *Let's get the job over and done with as quickly as possible.*
that's done it isso estragou tudo *That's done it. I've caught a fish hook in the rubber raft and made a hole.*

DOOR **at one's door/doorstep** contíguo, pegado, vizinho *When she paid a visit to Mr. Prendergast she noticed there is a bus stop at his door.*

behind closed doors a portas fechadas, em particular, com o acesso vedado à imprensa e ao público ... *they like to operate in secret and behind closed doors.* -T/72.

⇒ **closed-door** particular, vedado à imprensa e ao público ... *a closed-door hearing* ... –T/80.

close one's doors 1. vedar o acesso, não permitir, proibir a entrada, impor restrições *Iran has closed its door to Western influence.* 2. falir, fechar as portas *Business was so bad that the firm had to close its doors.*

close the door 1. fechar a porta, erguer uma barreira *To reduce another [a human being] to an object is by that very act to rob him of his humanity and to close the door between you and him.* -SJH,39. 2. impossibilitar, impedir, recusar-se a considerar *The manager's obstinate position closed the door to negotiations.*

lay (something) at someone's door/at the door of pôr a culpa em, responsabilizar *The responsibility for the accident was laid at his door.*

leave the door open deixar a porta aberta, oferecer uma saída *His doctor told him he had cancer but also left the door open for hope.*

next door (to) 1. na/da casa ao lado; no/do vizinho do lado *the girl next door* ♦ *The treasurer lives next door to you.* -T/87. 2. quase, bem próximo *It would be next door to impossible to foresee the many difficulties that cropped up later.* ⇒ **next-door** vizinho, contíguo ... *his next-door neighbor.* -T/86.

open the door abrir a porta, facultar, desobstruir o caminho, deixar livre trânsito *We have ... opened the door to a consideration of the structure and meaning of life.* -SHO,7.

out of doors; outdoors ao ar livre *Some peoples think of women as too weak to work out of doors ...* -MM,16.

pull the door to fechar a porta *Pull the door to when you leave the room.*

show one the door; show the door to expulsar alguém de casa, pôr na rua, mostrar a porta a ... *there were times when a less tolerant and loving father would have shown some of us the door ...* -RJ,18.

shut/slam the door in someone's face dar com a porta na cara de, negar-se a receber ou ouvir alguém *She slammed the door in my face before I could finish explaining why I had rung the doorbell.*

slam the door trancar a porta, rejeitar qualquer contato, recusar-se a ouvir ou atender *America ... slammed the door against new immigration.* -T/87.

DOORNAIL **dead as a doornail** [col] bem morto *He was dead as a doornail when the police arrived.*

DOORSTEP **at one's doorstep** → **at one's DOOR**

DOPE **dope out** [gir] entender, compreender, calcular, imaginar, conceber, encontrar a solução, resolver *Read this mathematical problem and see if you can dope out the answer.*

inside dope/information informação especial ou confidencial *He says he has some inside dope about the election results.*

DOSE **give someone some/a dose/a taste of his own medicine** dar a alguém o mesmo tratamento recebido, pagar na mesma moeda *The biggest boy in school who had always beaten the smaller children was given some of his own medicine by the new boy who had just arrived.*

DOT **on the dot** [col] em ponto (na hora certa), no momento exato, na hora convencionada *She left at 9:00 p.m. on the dot.*

DOUBLE **double as** exercer duas funções, desempenhar uma ocupação adicional, ter uma segunda atividade *Marcia doubles as telephone operator and receptionist.* ♦

[He is] ... a practicing doctor from San Francisco who doubles as a news photographer. -T/78.

double back [col] voltar sobre os seus passos, voltar ao lugar de onde partiu *The soldiers went north because the enemy was watching but they doubled back when night fell.*

double for substituir (ator/atriz) *Yakima Canutt, one of the most famous stuntmen in movie history, doubled for John Wayne in dangerous scenes in* Stagecoach.

double over = DOUBLE up 2 *They doubled over in agony and dropped.* -HJC,264.

double up 1. usar em conjunto (quarto, aposento, cama etc.) *We moved into an empty campsite, and within 15 minutes we were surrounded by campers, all doubling up on the same site.* -T/66. 2. dobrar-se, curvar-se, inclinar-se *... Tom punched her in the stomach and ... she ... doubled up in pain ...* -LRW,149.

on the double [col] rapidamente, a passo corrido *Come here now, and on the double!*

DOUBLE-BREASTED trespassado (paletó jaquetão, terno com paletó jaquetão) *His gray double-breasted suit was rumpled and stained ...* -DP,19.

DOUBLE-CHECK → double CHECK

DOUBLE-CROSS [col] trair (agindo de maneira contrária ao que foi combinado) *It was one thing for Stalin and Hitler to double-cross third parties, but quite another when they began do double-cross each other.* -SWLR,1049.

DOUBLE-DATE → double DATE

DOUBLE-DEALING 1. duplicidade, velhacaria *... you have no grounds for accusing me of double-dealing.* -FL,45. 2. insincero, velhaco *He's a double-dealing character and nobody likes him.*

DOUBLE-EDGED; TWO-EDGED 1. de dois gumes *a double-edged knife* ♦ *a two-edged sword* 2. ambíguo, contraditório, de dupla interpretação *a double-edged remark* ♦ *a two-edged argument.*

DOUBLE-HEADER duas partidas de beisebol jogadas em sucessão no mesmo programa *... he had gone downtown to pick up tickets for the baseball game on Saturday (a doubleheader ...)* -BS,77.

DOUBLE-PARK estacionar veículo em fila dupla *... a cab double-parked in front of a hotel.* -WJT,22.

DOUBLE-TALK linguagem ambígua, evasiva, confusa, conversa mole *Advertising men have invented a double-talk to entertain each other and to impress clients.* -CH,28.

DOUBT beyond doubt fora de qualquer dúvida, incontestável, incontestavelmente *Her honesty is beyond doubt.*

call in(to) doubt pôr em dúvida, questionar *Man has become so dangerous to himself that his continued existence has been called into doubt.* -T/72.

cast doubt on levantar dúvida sobre, tornar incerto *His record of arrests cast doubt on his testimony.*

no doubt 1. sem dúvida *There's no doubt that Murdock was in the building at five o'clock. He was seen there.* 2. muito provavelmente *You are, no doubt, aware of the facts.*

without doubt sem dúvida, certamente *Glenda is, without doubt, the prettiest girl in the office.*

DOWN down and out acabado, vencido; liquidado financeiramente, sem recursos, sem perspectivas *... he was down and out in Mexico, New York, Hollywood and British Columbia.* -T/77. ♦ *The man with the Charlie Chaplin mustache [i.e. Adolph Hitler] ... had been a down-and-out tramp in Vienna in his youth, an unknown soldier of World War I ...* -SWLR,19.

down on [col] irritado com, zangado com, ressentido com *They were down on us when they should have been down on the people who sent us there [i.e., Vietnam].* -T/79.

down to 1. com apenas (alguns, uns poucos, um pouco etc. de qualquer coisa especificada) *I was down to my bottom dollar and didn't know what to do.* 2. até (uma categoria inferior, quantidade menor etc.) *Every officer from the general down to the lieutenant were there.* 3. até (uma pessoa ou época posterior) ... *[mystic] beliefs nourished the science of alchemy throughout the Middle Ages down to the time of Isaac Newton.* -JRR,44.

down with 1. doente, atacado de *Their two children are down with the flu.* 2. abaixo! fora! morra! *... men bearing placards that said DOWN WITH U. S. ...* -T/87.

DOWN-AT-THE-HEELS → **down at the HEELS**

DOWNBEAT [col] pessimista, desalentador *a downbeat mood.* v. **UPBEAT**

DOWNFALL queda, derrocada, ruína *It was the Communist Party that created the Soviet Union and also brought about its downfall.* -T/92.

DOWNPLAY = **PLAY down** *The CIA often try to downplay some of their clandestine activities.*

DOWNPOUR chuvarada, aguaceiro, toró *... a torrential downpour ...* -T/87.

DOWNSIZE reduzir o tamanho de, diminuir, redimensionar *Now the [automobile] industry's favorite new verb is "downsizing", and the products that will begin appearing in showrooms ... will define what that means: cars that are shorter, lighter and, if not cheaper to buy, at least easier on gas.* -T/77.

DOWN-THE-LINE → **down the LINE**

DOWN-TO-EARTH → **come back/down to EARTH**

DOZE doze off cochilar, dormitar *At a special performance of The Magic Flute by the Vienna State Opera, he dozed off to sleep ...* -T/60.

DRAFT on draft de barril (chope) *They serve beer on draft here.*

DRAG drag in(to) introduzir (assunto estranho ou irrelevante) em uma discussão ou conversa *Must you always drag in your right-wing bias when we discuss religion?*

drag on prolongar-se monotonamente ... *the summer dragged on.* -T/81. ♦ *... [a] long imprisonment, which dragged on for nearly four years.* -HE,15.

drag out prolongar mais do que o necessário, alongar enfadonhamente *The speaker dragged out the session for two hours.*

drag up [col] relembrar assunto desagradável, desnecessário etc. *Each time Ron's wife fights with him she drags up the time she caught him kissing the maid.*

the main drag [gír] a rua principal de uma cidade *Washington Street is the main drag in Boston.*

DRAIN go down the drain ir por água abaixo, perder-se, terminar, fracassar, dar em nada *After a few bad movies his acting career went down the drain.*

DRAW beat to the draw/punch [gír] fazer (algo) antes que outro o faça, tomar a dianteira, antecipar-se *We were going to buy the old farm, but the Craigheads beat us to the draw.* ♦ *... Chase [Manhattan Bank] beat Citibank to the punch, opening the first U.S. banking office to appear in Moscow since 1922.* -T/73.

draw away afastar-se *I drew away when he pulled a knife.*

draw back recuar, retirar-se *We all drew back in alarm when he threatened to hit us with the iron bar.* ⇒ **drawback** impedimento, empecilho, desvantagem, obstáculo *One important drawback to our plan is that we lack money.*

draw close/near aproximar-se, acercar-se, avizinhar-se *They were drawing close to the river now.* ♦ *... a historic presidential election draws near.* -T/87.

draw in 1. retrair, recolher *The dog drew in its tongue.* 2. induzir, incitar, levar a (participar de algo) *Her sisters had a quarrel but she refused to be drawn in.*

3. inalar, aspirar, absorver *[He] ... drew in the fresh night air of the city ...* -CL,277.
♦ *... he drew in a long breath.* -LJS,175.
draw near → **DRAW close**
draw off 1. drenar, esgotar, desviar *They drew off the water from the flooded room.* 2. retirar-se *The enemy forces drew off when our tanks came in.*
draw on 1. aproximar-se, avizinhar-se *It started to rain as the afternoon drew on.* 2. sacar (dinheiro) *Mrs. Donnelly drew on her savings because she needed money in a hurry.* 3. induzir, levar a *She drew Walt on to tell her what had happened.* 4. [também **draw upon**] valer-se de, utilizar-se de, fazer uso de *His article drew on his personal experience as a Navy frogman.* ♦ *Writers inevitably draw upon their experience [to write more expressively]...* -WW,3.
draw oneself up empertigar-se (especialmente por altivez ou ira) *... General Johnston ... drew himself up in the saddle ...* -FS,11. ♦ *He drew himself up angrily when I said he was a fool.*
draw out 1. prolongar(-se), alongar(-se) *Most politicians like to draw out their speeches.* ⇒ **drawn-out** = **LONG-drawn-out** *The senator's conference was long and drawn-out.* ♦ *...this drawn-out agony of dying.* -MAT,61. 2. induzir a falar, ajudar a vencer a timidez *When we were finally able to draw him out, we found him a most interesting person.* 3. sacar (dinheiro) *He had drawn out all the money he had in the bank.*
draw up 1. parar, fazer alto; parar, deter, interromper a marcha de *A taxi drew up to let out a young man ...* -SWS,23. ♦ *Helen drew up the car outside her mother's house.* 2. redigir (documento etc.), compilar, minutar, preparar *He felt so sick that he decided to draw up his will.* ♦ *By the last week in July [1940], the Nazi plan to kidnap the Windsors had been drawn up.* -SWLR,1034. 3. dispor em posição (tropas) *The troops were drawn up at 6 a.m.* 4. v. **DRAW oneself up**
quick on the draw/trigger [col] rápido no sacar do revólver, ágil no gatilho *They say that Johnny Ringo was so quick on the draw that no one could defeat him in a gunfight.* 2. ágil no raciocínio, rápido nas decisões *Mr. Collins was so quick on the draw that it was very difficult to trap him in an argument.* ♦ *You didn't have to explain anything to him more than once because he was quick on the trigger.*
DRAWING drawing card grande atração (em espetáculos), ator popular *In the mid-1950s William Holden became a hot drawing card in Hollywood.*
DREAM the American dream ideal social dos norte-americanos que preconiza igualdade de condições e prosperidade econômica para todos *Another theme found almost invariably in [Arthur] Miller's work, connected to his interest in the family, is the American Dream of material success – the cult of the dollar.* -HDR,401.
beyond one's wildest dreams muito além do que se poderia imaginar, esperar etc. *[The experiment] ... has succeeded beyond our wildest dreams.* -HEB,15.
dream of sonhar com, fantasiar, imaginar *... he has dreamed of going to America ever since he was a boy.* -T/76.
dream up [col] conceber, inventar, imaginar *Once in a while someone will ask me where Stan [Laurel] and I [Oliver Hardy] dreamed up the characters we play in the movies.* -MJM,42.
not dream of [col] considerar impossível, não imaginar sequer em sonhos, não pensar em *I wouldn't dream of doing anything to hurt the Republican Party.* -T/86.
DREDGE dredge up trazer à superfície, fazer vir à tona, revelar (geralmente algo desagradável) *The expanding investigation ... will inevitably dredge up revelations ...* -T/86.

DRESS dress down [col] repreender severamente, censurar *I called you up here to dress you down good and proper.* -LLN,16.
⇒ **dressing-down** repreensão severa ... *Mitchell gave her a dressing-down such as I never heard in my life.* -T/72.
dressed fit to kill [col] muito bem vestido, elegantíssimo *They came to the dance dressed fit to kill and created a sensation.*
dress rehearsal ensaio final (de uma peça teatral, cerimônia etc.) *Preliminary to the public hearing I was questioned, as though in dress rehearsal, in a small committee room ...* -KRI,610.
dress up 1. vestir-se com apuro, vestir as melhores roupas; vestir traje a rigor *She dressed up to go to a party.* ♦ *The dictator dressed up in his fanciest uniform to attend the parade.* 2. disfarçar sob falsas aparências, fazer parecer diferente, mais atraente ou aceitável; enfeitar *The plan is little more than the Soviet Union's propaganda points customarily aimed at the U.S. and now dressed up as a "peace doctrine".* -T/80.
DRIB dribs and drabs pequenas quantias, porções diminutas *He paid back his loan in dribs and drabs.*
DRIFT drift off 1. derivar, ir com a corrente *The boat became untied and drifted off downstream for miles.* 2. afastar-se aos poucos, retirar-se displicentemente, ao acaso, sem destino *The crowd began to drift off toward something more interesting at the County Fair.* 3. desviar-se (do assunto, curso, rumo etc.) *The history professor would begin by discussing the early Greek statesmen but would gradually drift off into a discussion of Greek myths.*
get the drift [gír] compreender o sentido, manjar, sacar *[Regionalisms] ... were new words to Jeff, but he got the drift of them, and marked them for remembering.* -LD,25.
DRINK drink deep of sorver grande quantidade de, absorver muito de *Mother drank deep of Scotch virtue, but not whisky ...* -KS,141.
drink down beber de um só gole *Lem drank down a tumbler of whisky ...* -PRT,70.
drink in absorver (pelos sentidos), deleitar-se com, extasiar-se com, ouvir ou contemplar com prazer *The tourists drank in the lovely scenery.* ♦ *Both men were looking at Riley Gratton with rapt expressions, earnestly drinking in his every word.* -TRW,33.
drink to brindar, beber à saúde de *Let's drink to Murphy's health.*
drink up beber de uma só vez, beber completamente *She gave the little boy a glass of milk and said: "Drink up".*
drive someone to drink atazanar alguém levando-o a beber *Vincent's nagging wife drove him to drink.*
soft drink bebida sem álcool, refrigerante *The favorite soft drink in Brazil is guaraná.*
DRIVE drive at insinuar, dar a entender *What are you driving at?* ♦ *He was driving at something I couldn't understand.*
drive back 1. repelir, rechaçar *The Indians were driven back by the soldiers who came to the rescue of the besieged settlers.* 2. voltar, regressar (dirigindo automóvel) *We flew to Rio but drove back.*
drive crazy/insane/mad/nuts apoquentar, irritar, atormentar, deixar maluco *That girl's driving me crazy.* ♦ *... the monotony [was] driving us insane.* -UL,3. ♦ *Kelly's nagging wife is driving him nuts.*
drive (something) home fazer compreender, deixar bem claro, salientar *The recession has driven home the fact that big cars are no longer economical with the inflated fuel prices.*
drive off 1. partir, ir-se (pessoa em automóvel) *They ... drove off in the car of a waiting accomplice.* -T/78. 2. repelir, rechaçar *The Indian attack was driven off by the cavalry.*
drive out expulsar, fazer sair *Love can drive out hate.*

drive up 1. elevar, fazer subir, aumentar *Crop failures have driven up cereal prices in many countries.* 2. chegar, parar (em um veículo) *... the police car drove up ...* -WJT,319. ♦ *He drove up to the nearest motel.*

DRIVE-IN designativo de organizações em que os clientes entram com seus automóveis e são atendidos dentro deles *a drive-in theater.* ♦ *a drive-in restaurant.* ♦ *a drive-in bank.*

DRIVER be in the driver's seat [col] ter o poder nas mãos, estar no comando, ser aquele que manda *He's in the driver's seat and, naturally, he gives the orders.*

DROP at the drop of a hat 1. sem demora, sem hesitação, imediatamente *I'd move out of this neighborhood at the drop of a hat if I had the means to afford it.* 2. à menor provocação, por dá cá aquela palha, sem nenhuma razão plausível *[The American cowboy] ... is still a lone rider, taking orders resentfully, literally quitting [his job] at the drop of a hat.* -T/61.

drop around/by/in/over fazer uma visita informal ou impremeditada, aparecer inesperadamente, dar uma passada (em determinado lugar) *Drop around anytime you feel like.* ♦ *[He] ... dropped by for a chat ...* -T/87. ♦ *Drop in and see us sometime.*

drop back 1. retirar-se *The captain ordered his men to drop back.* 2. = **DROP behind** *He began to pant and gradually dropped back until all the other runners were ahead of him.*

drop behind (deixar-se) ficar para trás (de), não acompanhar a velocidade, a marcha ou o progresso de; ser ultrapassado *He has dropped behind the other students.*

drop by → **DROP around**

drop dead 1. morrer de repente *He dropped dead of a heart attack this morning.* 2. [gír] não me amole, vá pro inferno, vá se danar *When he began to talk to the girl she just said, "Drop dead", and then ignored him.*

drop everything largar tudo, deixar o que está fazendo (para dar atenção a outro assunto) *They are willing to drop everything, serve you coffee and try to explain themselves and their country.* -T/84.

drop in → **DROP around**

a drop in the bucket [col] quantia muito pequena, insignificância, migalha, gota *The $275,000 our department will get is only a drop in the bucket.*

drop it pare com isso, pare com essa conversa, deixe de falar nisso *Drop it! Drop it now! You're driving me crazy with all this talk!*

drop off 1. diminuir, escassear, declinar *... cases of drug abuse have dropped off suddenly from last year.* -T/72. 2. cair *The leaves began to drop off when the cold weather set in.* 3. entregar, deixar, largar; deixar (passageiro de um veículo) em determinado lugar *[She] ... dropped off the phial of blood at the lab.* -JEP, 171. ♦ *... a driver for the Yellow Cab Co. had just dropped off two men at a movie ...* -T/67. 4. [col] [também **drop off to sleep**] adormecer *My brother-in-law often drops off while watching baseball on TV.* ♦ *Paul was very tired and dropped off to sleep almost immediately.*

drop out 1. cair, tombar *The money dropped out of her handbag when she got on the bus.* 2. abandonar (uma atividade, escola, curso, a sociedade etc.), deixar de ser membro, deixar de participar, desistir *Close to forty percent of those who begin high school drop out before they finish.* -HJH,15. ♦ *... some of his parishioners have dropped out ...* -T/87. ⇒ **dropout** aluno que abandonou a escola antes de se diplomar; indivíduo que abandonou a sociedade convencional, uma atividade, carreira etc. *[He is] ... a college dropout ...* -T/72.

get/have the drop on [gír] 1. ter (alguém) sob a mira de um revólver, sacar a arma antes do adversário *When the agent and*

Turkish police got the drop on the crooks, they tried to shoot their way. -T/64. 2. levar vantagem sobre, suplantar *With your knowledge of French and Spanish you have the drop on the other foreign language students.*
   take a drop 1. tomar um gole *He likes to take a drop of whiskey now and then.* 2. sofrer uma baixa (de preços) *The price of his stock took a drop after the news came out in the paper.*

DROWN drown out abafar (som, voz etc.), encobrir, não deixar ouvir *Their conversation was drowned out by the roar of planes and thunder of bombs ...* -TJ,287.

DRUG drug on the market mercadoria de pouca procura, artigo que ninguém quer *So many companies began to manufacture the article that it soon became a drug on the market.*
   hard drugs drogas pesadas, que viciam, que causam dependência (cocaína, heroína, ópio) *... 53 Israelis have died from hard drugs ...* -T/81.

DRUM drum into incutir (algo por repetição persistente) *The captain had it drummed into his men not to fire the first shot.*
   drum majorette garota que vai à frente de um desfile fazendo acrobacias e manejando um bastão, baliza *[She was] ... the head drum majorette of the high school band.* -RP,37.
   drum up 1. chamar, convocar, reunir, aliciar *Drum up enough people so that we can vote on the proposed law.* 2. promover, atrair, criar entusiasmo, encorajar *... drum up support for his plan ...* -T/87.

DRY dry out secar(-se) pela evaporação *Put your wet shoes near the fire to dry out.*
   dry up 1. secar(-se) completamente *The lack of rain caused the soil to dry up and blow away with the first strong wind.* 2. cessar, acabar, desaparecer, deixar de produzir, não estar mais disponível *... international sales started to dry up in the face of slowing foreign economies ...* -T/84. 3. [gir] parar de falar, calar-se *Will you dry up? I'm trying to listen to this TV program.*

DUB dub in colocar som em um filme, dublar (diálogos ou trilha sonora) *The English dialog was dubbed into the Italian film.*

DUCK duck out [col] 1. sair ou fugir às escondidas, sorrateiramente, de mansinho *Jim ducked out just before the police entered the bar.* 2. retirar-se, livrar-se *He ducked out of the deal when he suspected something was wrong with it.* 3. abandonar, desertar, desamparar, fugir à responsabilidade etc. *He ducked out on his friends.* ♦ *Maisie ducked out on her responsibilities.*
   duck soup [gír] tarefa fácil, canja *This job is duck soup for me.*
   lame duck [col] detentor de qualquer cargo público eletivo que está em fim de mandato e não conseguiu reeleger-se, ou então que está impossibilitado por lei de concorrer a um terceiro mandato; pessoa incompetente *... as a lame duck he has precious little political capital to spend.* -T/87. ⇒ **lame-duck** próprio ou característico dessa condição *A lame-duck President ...* -T/87.
   sitting duck [col] vítima fácil, alvo acessível *The slow [German] Stuka dive bomber ... was proving to be a sitting duck for British fighters ...* -SWLR,1019.

DUCKLING ugly duckling patinho feio, criança desgraciosa, feia, que ao crescer se transforma em uma pessoa de belas feições, cheia de encantos etc. *She has come a long way from the willowy, luminous-eyed, adolescent girl who deprecated herself as an "ugly duckling"...* -RJ,13.

DUDE dude ranch fazenda de criação (no Oeste dos EUA) transformada em local de recreio onde os turistas montam a cavalo e observam de perto a vida dos vaqueiros *Pete went to a dude ranch in Wyoming for his vacation.*

DUE due to 1. por causa de, devido a, atribuível a *Her success is due to her versatility.* 2. comprometido, que deve (fazer determinada coisa) *[He] ... is due to leave the state presidency on May 16.* T/80. 3. que deve chegar (ou é esperado) em determinada hora, dia etc. *The ship is due to arrive on September 12.*
to give someone his due dar a alguém aquilo a que tem direito, ser justo para com *To give the author his due, we can say that he drew a good picture of the complicated Irish nature.*
pay one's dues [gir] conquistar certos direitos, privilégios etc. com trabalho duro, sacrifícios etc. *He has paid his dues as an essayist and reviewer.* -T/58.
DUMBBELL [gir] indivíduo tolo, paspalhão *He looked like a dumbbell but few people realized how intelligent he really was.*
DUMMY dummy up [gir] recusar-se a falar, ficar de bico calado *You think you can dummy up and stand us off.* -BAS,53.
DUMP dump on [gir] criticar severamente, tratar desrespeitosamente, descompor, esculachar *[They] ... calculatedly dumped on the opposition.* -BC,227.
(down) in the dumps [col] deprimido, abatido, triste *God only knows how bad in the dumps I get sometimes.* -CEP,139. ♦ *I was down in the dumps that night.*
DURATION for the duration enquanto (algo) durar ou estiver em curso, principalmente uma guerra *Her husband was a private in the U.S. Infantry, stationed in Iceland for the duration.* -BL,24.
DUST bite/lick the dust [col] ser morto; ser derrotado *A famous cowboy saying in frontier days was: "And another Indian bit the dust".*
dust bowl região extremamente seca onde tempestades de poeira são freqüentes *The Oklahoma dust bowl of the thirties and its social consequences were poignantly chronicled by John Steinbeck in his novel* The Grapes of Wrath.

dust jacket sobrecapa de livro *Dust jackets are often works of art.*
dust off 1. espanar, tirar o pó, limpar a superfície de *He dusted off the chair and sat on it.* 2. [col] voltar a praticar (algo que se deixou de usar, fazer etc.), preparar-se para usar novamente *The Moscow veterans dusted off their copies of the Soviet criminal code and looked up Article 65.* -T/86.
shake the dust from/off one's feet partir de um lugar com desagrado ou desprezo, com a intenção de nunca mais voltar *He was disgusted, tired of the town. He wanted to shake its dust from his feet.* -BFW,27.
DUTCH be/get in Dutch [gir] encrencar-se, meter-se em apuros *He always seems to get in Dutch when he tries to help other people.*
get one's/someone's Dutch up [col] irritar-se; irritar alguém *Don't get your Dutch up. I was only kidding.* ♦ *If you get her Dutch up there'll be hell to pay.*
go Dutch [col] pagar cada um a sua parte, as suas despesas (em restaurante etc.) *"If we go to the movies, will you go Dutch?", he said. "I don't have much money."*
DUTY do duty for servir de, desempenhar a mesma função que, fazer as vezes de *This room will do duty for a study.* ♦ *... a great number of Chinese words do duty for both nouns and verbs ...* -WAW,19.
(in) duty bound; duty-bound compelido pela consciência ou pelo dever *... he felt sure that his father would feel in duty bound to scold and berate him ...* -DJ,22. ♦ *... man is duty-bound to resist the state if it encroaches upon his integrity.* -HMJ,1135.
off//on duty de folga// de serviço, em seu posto, de plantão *[The policeman] ... happened to be off duty ...* -T/80. ♦ *He was arrested by an off-duty policeman.* ♦ *... the dark figures stood like silent soldiers on duty.* -MRI,17.

DUTY-FREE 1. isento de taxas ou direitos alfandegários *Some foreign products that come into the country are duty-free.* 2. referente a mercadorias isentas de taxas ou à sua venda *Taxis whisk tourists to the duty-free shopping district.* -T/72.

DWELL dwell on/upon repisar, insistir em, estender-se sobre, alongar-se, salientar constantemente, ter sempre no pensamento *Must you dwell on unpleasant subjects?*

DWINDLE dwindle away/down definhar, minguar, decrescer, diminuir, reduzir-se *... the American Army at Valley Forge dwindled away through death, desertion, and disgust.* -SGF,349. ♦ *... when her income dwindled down [she] found a job ...* -WF,34.

DYED-IN-THE-WOOL completo, extremo, radical, inflexível, fanático, consumado, duro, implacável *... such dyed-in-the-wool Romans as Actress Gina Lollobrigida ...* -T/87. ♦ *His father was a dyed-in-the-wool Communist and hated capitalists.*

EACH each and every cada *"I am looking forward to working with each and every one of you" [the President told the members of his Cabinet].* -T/74.
each other um ao outro, reciprocamente *... father and the stranger looked at each other a long moment, measuring each other ...* -SJS,5.
EAR about/around someone's ears a um estado de ruína, derrota, fracasso, destruição, colapso total etc. (trabalho, esforços, esperanças, planos etc.) *... he could not risk inquiries which could well bring disaster about his own ears!* ♦ *His political campaign was collapsing around his ears.*
be all ears [col] ficar muito atento, ser todo ouvidos *You can tell me what happened now. I'm all ears.*
bend someone's ear [gir] falar demais, aborrecer o ouvinte com conversa excessiva *... a former college football player who bends your ears about all those touchdowns he scored.* T/72.
box someone's ears dar bofetão ou soco (especialmente na orelha) de *He boxed the boy's ears.*
by ear de ouvido, sem ler as notas musicais *He plays the piano by ear because he doesn't know how to read music.* v. **play by EAR**

fall on deaf ears passar despercebido, não ser ouvido (conselho, aviso etc.) por displicência, descaso etc. *Her warning fell on deaf ears.*
give/lend an ear ouvir, dar atenção *Mark Antony asked the Romans to lend an ear to what he would say about Julius Caesar.*
go in (at) one ear and out (at) the other [col] entrar por um ouvido e sair pelo outro (conselho, advertência, recomendação etc.) *Time and again we gave him a lot of advice but it went in one ear and out the other.*
have an ear for ter boa percepção auditiva, bom ouvido para (línguas, música, ritmos etc.) *Because he has a good ear for Latin American rhythms, he was able to learn to dance the samba very rapidly.*
have/keep an ear to the ground [col] estar atento aos últimos acontecimentos, às tendências da opinião pública *He keeps an ear to the ground at all times so he is always aware of things.*
have someone's ear ter a atenção, a confiança, os favores de alguém *... he had the ear of the President.* -HRA,20. ♦ *... he has the President's ear ...* -T/72.
not believe one's ears/eyes não acreditar naquilo que se ouve/vê por ser algo muito surpreendente, chocante etc. *I couldn't*

believe my ears when she said that. ♦ *I could hardly believe my eyes when I saw her at the club.*
not dry behind the ears; wet behind the ears [col] inexperiente, imaturo *The job is not for him. He's not dry behind the ears yet.* ♦ *... he was ... one of those lightweight intellectuals, still wet behind the ears.* -WI,103.
over the/one's ears até as orelhas, completamente *Over the ears in debt.* -T/87. ♦ *... probably over his ears in debt and desperately needing [money] ...* -QE,131.
pin someone's ears back [col] repreender severamente, puxar as orelhas de *You'd better get busy or the boss will pin your ears back.*
play by ear 1. tocar de ouvido *When he was five, he learned to play the piano by ear.* -T/87. 2. [col] improvisar, fazer (qualquer coisa) sem preparação, sem planejamento, agir segundo as exigências da situação *In situations like that one, I always played things by ear.* -AK,125. ♦ *I'm going to have to play this by ear.*
prick up one's ears levantar as orelhas (o cão ou outro animal); prestar atenção, ficar vigilante *Our German shepherd dog had pricked up his ears long before we realized that someone was at the door.*
talk someone's ear off [gir] falar demais, incomodar alguém com conversa sem fim *My sister-in-law can talk your ears off any time of day ... or night.*
to the ears/gills totalmente, completamente, até as orelhas *[The man was] ... fed up to the gills with the stinks of the city ...* -OC,1. ♦ *Doyle had been drinking all evening and he was now drunk to the ears.*
turn a deaf ear não dar atenção a comentários, observações etc., não dar ouvidos *[He] ... hopes that you will turn a deaf ear to empty praise ...* -T/87. v. **turn a blind EYE**
up to one's/the ears/eyes/neck profundamente ocupado, imerso ou absorto em; profundamente envolvido em ou comprometido com *I can't help you now. I'm up to my ears in unanswered complaints.* ♦ *Mr. Shaw is up to his eyes in debt.* ♦ *Glenda is always up to her neck with unfinished work at the end of the month.*
wet behind the ears → **not dry behind the EARS**
EARFUL get an earful [col] 1. ouvir uma torrente de informações, novidades, mexericos etc. (especialmente quando não solicitados), ouvir mais que o suficiente ou necessário *The spy listened to the secret conference with a hidden microphone and got an earful.* 2. ouvir, atentar para *"Get an earful of this", he said.*
EAR-SPLITTING altíssimo, estridente, ensurdecedor (som) *... the ear-splitting shriek of jetliners ...* -T/69.
EARLY as early as já em *As early as 1933 he became convinced that another world war was inevitable.* v. **as LATE as**
early on logo no começo, no período inicial *He knew early on about the frauds in the company.* ♦ *[He] ... served early on as a secretary to Monsignor ...* -T/78.
in one's early twenties/thirties etc. aos vinte e poucos/trinta e poucos anos etc. *Zee was eighteen and Lou was in his early twenties when they met and fell in love.* v. **in one's LATE twenties; in one's MID-twenties**
EARMARK 1. marca identificadora, sinal, traço, feição característica *The Fall of the Roman Empire has all the earmarks of a great movie but some of the critics didn't seem to like it.* 2. reservar, destinar, indicar, designar *The European Community earmarked $1.35 billion to help rebuild the devasted region.* T/80.
EARNEST in earnest 1. sério, sincero, de boa-fé *He was so in earnest about becoming a painter that he spent three years in Paris.* 2. a sério, com determinação *At last he has begun to study in earnest.*
EARSHOT out of//within earshot fora do alcance//ao alcance da voz, som de algo

etc. *She was out of earshot and couldn't hear me.* ♦ *Scientists have long suspected that living or working within earshot of a major airport can be dangerous to health.* -T/78.

EARTH come back/down to earth voltar à realidade, parar de sonhar *It's high time you stop daydreaming and come down to earth.* ⇒ **down-to-earth** prático, simples, trivial, sensato, realista, comum ... *a small-town Texas lawyer, old-fashioned and down-to-earth...* -T/64. ♦ *... a down-to-earth fellow ...* -T/87.

how/what/where/who/why on earth/in the world [col] [para dar ênfase] como é que ... ? *How on earth am I to know where she is?* ♦ *How in the world do you expect your wife to believe that?* que diabo ... ? *What on earth were you doing in Casablanca?* -WH,528. ♦ *What in the world are you doing here?* onde diabo ... ? *Where on earth did you go?* ♦ *Where in the world have you been?* quem diabo ... ? *Who on earth will know where she is?* ♦ *Who in the world can answer that question?* por que diabos/cargas d'água ... ? *... American merchandisers began doing some serious wondering. They wondered why on earth customers act the way they do.* -PVH,18. ♦ *Why in the world should we pay for the company's mistakes?* -T/79.

run to earth/ground caçar, procurar até encontrar *Hundreds of thousands of dollars were spent by the Government in attempts to run him [Apache Indian Chief Victorio] to earth.* -FL,vii. ♦ *Coogan [the deputy sheriff in the movie* Coogan's Bluff*] ... sets out to run Ringerman [the fugitive] to ground in an attempt to salvage his personal and professional honor.* -T/68.

EASE at ease à vontade *Being at ease with himself put him at ease with the world.* -SJST,13.

ease into deslizar ou fazer deslizar para dentro com cautela, entrar ou fazer entrar lentamente *The news media eased Billy [Carter] into the limelight, and now it's their responsibility to ease him out.* -T/79.

ease off/up moderar(-se), afrouxar, diminuir, relaxar, tornar(-se) menos tenso *The press had eased off the attacks on Nixon.* ♦ *[They] ... have never eased off the pressure on our officers ...* -T/66. ♦ *... friends ... urged her to ease up ...* -T/66.

ease out afastar (alguém) diplomaticamente de cargo ou posição *[President Ronald] Reagan eased Secretary of State Alexander Haig out of office.* -T/87.

ill at ease constrangido, inibido, pouco à vontade *He suddenly felt embarrassed and ill at ease.* -JJ,122.

EASY easier said than done → **easier said than done** (em **SAY**)

easy come, easy go → **easy COME, easy go**

easy does it → **easy does it** (em **DO**)

EASYGOING calmo, natural, desembaraçado, despreocupado, pachorrento, imperturbável *[His] ... style of decision making is very easygoing ...* -T/87. ♦ *... he was the easygoin' sort – too easygoin' for this world ...* -QE,125.

EAT be eating someone [gir] estar preocupando alguém *... what's eating Ellen is she's afraid she's gonna lose you.* -SM,13.

eat away corroer, carcomer, roer, causar erosão em, desgastar, consumir *Even Athens' ruins are in ruin: sulfur dioxide eats away at the marble of the Parthenon, the Erechtheum and other treasures on the Acropolis.* -T/79.

eat in//out almoçar ou jantar em casa// comer fora, comer em restaurante *Let's eat in tonight, OK? I'm not in the mood to go out.* ♦ *Flora and Sergio like to eat out at least once a week.*

eat into corroer, carcomer *The acid slowly ate into the steel plate.*

eat out 1. v. **EAT in//out** 2. [gir] espinafrar, descompor *The boss will eat you out if you make any more mistakes.*

eat up 1. comer (tudo), limpar o prato

Eat up. There's plenty of food left. 2. consumir, absorver, devorar ... *the high interest is eating up profits.* -T/84. ♦ *[Police officer] Winslow [driving a patrol car] ate up the ground which separated [his car from the one he was chasing]* ... -WJT,341. 3. [gir] demonstrar grande entusiasmo, interesse ou prazer por, aceitar avidamente *Flanagan ate up all the flattery they lavished on him.*

EBB at a low ebb em declínio, em decadência, em má fase, em deterioração, em dificuldades, minguante *In early 1948, his popularity was at a low ebb.* -T/73. ♦ *I was at a very low ebb when I met Oliver* ... -T/87.

ebb and flow 1. fluxo e refluxo, avanço e recuo, aumento e declínio, variação alternada (ora mais, ora menos intensa) ... *the ebb and flow of the tides* ... -T/73. 2. baixar e subir (a maré), intensificar-se e decrescer alternadamente ... *the sea ebbs and flows* ... -CR,88. ♦ *During the Middle Ages, the political strength of Popes ebbed and flowed with the tides of growing nationalism* ... -T/68.

ebb away retroceder, recuar, refluir, diminuir, declinar, decair *Their political power is ebbing away and there's nothing they can do about it.* ♦ *... the infant's life ebbed away.* -T/63.

EDGE cutting edge a frente mais avançada, vanguarda, posição de liderança, de pioneirismo ... *the concentration of resources on the cutting edge of technology may result in important spinoffs in peaceful and military fields* ... -T/87. ♦ *U.S. colleges ... are so responsive to cultural currents that they are often on the cutting edge of social change.* -T/92.

edge away afastar-se vagarosamente ou cautelosamente *I found myself edging away from the man closest to me* ... -HRA,37.

edge in on introduzir-se em *Many companies try to edge in on a successful business.*

edge out empurrar para fora, deslocar, desalojar, fazer sair para tomar o lugar de; vencer, derrotar por pequena diferença *He very quietly and very slowly edged out his business partner.*

edge up to aproximar-se lenta e sorrateiramente de *He edged up to the bank teller's window and drew his gun.*

have an/the edge [col] levar vantagem, estar em posição de superioridade *Students with some factory or military experience have an edge in the selection.* -T/66.

have an edge on [col] estar embriagado *O'Hara had an edge on when he made the speech.*

on edge 1. apreensivo, inquieto, tenso, nervoso, irritado *Tim was on edge the night he was to appear before a TV camera.* ♦ *Her nerves were on edge.*

on the edge of à beira de, a ponto de, no limiar de *[She] ... was on the edge of tears.* -T/71.

take the edge off abrandar, suavizar, tornar fraco, minorar *He can take the edge off the most uncomfortable situations.*

EFFECT give effect to pôr em prática, executar *We don't think she will give effect to her threat.*

in effect 1. na realidade, de fato, virtualmente, praticamente *He is, in effect, no longer able to earn his living as an intellectual.* 2. em vigor *The new law has been in effect since January.*

into effect em ação, em execução *He and I made plans ... and they were almost immediately carried into effect.* -RQ,87.

personal effects objetos de uso pessoal *The soldiers photographed the dead Americans and retrieved some of their personal effects.* T/92.

take effect 1. fazer efeito *In a few minutes the liquor began to take effect.* -LJS,126. 2. começar a vigorar *The new law will take effect next month.*

to no effect sem resultado, inutilmente, em vão *We all tried to bring him to reason but to no effect.*

to that/this effect nesse sentido, com esse significado, para essa finalidade, visando a esse objetivo *They called him a liar, or words to that effect.*
to the effect that no sentido de que, com a informação ou o significado de que, que equivale a *A legend has been going around to the effect that I never had much schooling.* -MHH,13.

EGG **egg on** incitar, instigar, atiçar, provocar, encorajar *The older boys egged him on to break the school windows.*
lay an egg [gir] falhar, fracassar, não produzir o efeito desejado, fazer fiasco *The play had been successful on Broadway, but laid an egg on its cross-country tour.*
put all one's eggs in one basket arriscar tudo em um só empreendimento, em uma tacada *They say you should never put all your eggs in one basket, so I bought an apartment, a house on the beach and an interest in a small business.*
walk on eggs pisar em ovos, ser extremamente cuidadoso, proceder com toda a cautela *[They] ... walked on eggs through the last weekend ... responding instead of telling, implying more than explaining.* -T/74.

EGGHEAD [gir] [pej] pessoa intelectual *Many intellectuals who work for the government are called eggheads by their critics.*

EGO **ego massage** [gir] bajulação do ego, da vaidade *He needs an ego massage to feel better.* ⇒ **massage someone's ego** bajular a vaidade de, afagar o amor próprio de *... a writer who massages the egos of the rich and famous in New York and Europe.* -T/87.
ego trip [gir] ato ou procedimento egocêntrico, algo que visa à satisfação do ego *[He] ... had turned a tour abroad into an ego trip ...* -T/84.

EITHER-OR [col] escolha inevitável entre duas alternativas *The only either/or that confronts us is the choice between psychology as a physical science and psychology as a human science.* -JRE,10.

EKE **eke out** 1, suprir o que falta em, ampliar, suplementar *Lon will do any job to eke out his meager salary.* 2. ganhar (a vida, o sustento) com sacrifício *For the last dozen years of his life he [Edgar Allan Poe] eked out a meager living in Philadelphia and New York, as journalist, editor and general hack writer ...* -HL,353.

ELBOW **at one's elbow** junto de, ao alcance de, à mão *His aides were always at his elbow to whisper counsel.*
bend the elbow [gir] ingerir bebidas alcoólicas, entornar *I hear that he bends the elbow too much for his own good.*
elbow aside/out afastar, tirar do caminho, distanciar, pôr de lado, desconsiderar *In major medical centers the family doctor is elbowed out by specialists and house physicians who have their elaborate and expensive gadgets.* -T/73.
elbow grease [col] força, energia, trabalho árduo *If you work a little harder and use some elbow grease, you will get the job done.*
elbow room espaço amplo para ação ou movimento, campo livre *We need more elbow room here.*
out at the elbows malvestido; em má situação financeira *Although he gives an appearance of elegance at first glance, a careful look shows that he is out at the elbows.*
rub elbows/shoulders with misturar-se socialmente com, fazer amizade com, relacionar-se com *Many snobs like to rub elbows with prominent and successful people.* ♦ *In a small town you rub shoulders with almost all the local inhabitants at one time or another.*
up to the/one's elbows ocupadíssimo, totalmente imerso *... I'm up to my elbows in foreign policy ...* -T/86.

ELEPHANT **white elephant** elefante branco, algo que requer muito trabalho e oferece pouca vantagem ... *Togo's [Togo, country in West Africa] state-owned steel mill, a notorious white elephant ...* -T/87.

ELSE or else 1. senão, ou, ou então *Let's get out of here, or else it will be too late.* 2. ou sofra as conseqüências *You better tell me you're sorry, ... or else!* -RP,85.

EMPTY-HANDED de mãos vazias, sem levar ou trazer coisa alguma *She had returned empty-handed.*

EMPTY-HEADED tolo, desmiolado, imbecil *Where is that empty-headed husband of yours?*

END at loose ends confuso, incerto, indeciso, desorganizado, sem saber o que fazer *They had thought themselves at loose ends.* -MW,573. ♦ *The main character in the film seems completely at loose ends at times.*

the end of one's rope/tether o limite de suas forças, recursos etc. *Didn't Margaret know that he was at the end of his rope?* ♦ *... a mind approaching the end ot its tether ...* -T/86.

bring//come to an end pôr fim a, acabar com//chegar ao fim, encerrar-se, terminar *... Korea brought [General Douglas] MacArthur's military career to a dramatic but unhappy end.* -T/64. ♦ *We say that the Neolithic Age came to an end with the introduction of metal tools and weapons.* -SJV,9.

dead end beco sem saída, situação crítica *... populism and militarism [in Latin America] are dead ends.* -T/91. ♦ *... negotiations are at a dead end.* -T/80. ⇒ **dead-end** 1. sem saída (rua etc.) *a dead-end street* ♦ *... a dead-end canyon of brown rock.* -T/72. 2. sem perspectiva de melhoria, promoção etc. *[She was] ... tired of her dead-end job as a railway clerk ...* -T/76.

the end [gir] o fino, o melhor que existe *That show was the end.*

the end of the line/road o fim, o fim da linha, ponto final *He has reached the end of the line.* ♦ *It looks like the end of the road for you, my friend.*

end up acabar, terminar (como desfecho ou desenlace de um processo) *Iconoclasts always end up needing more icons than anyone else.* -T/64. ♦ *He ended up in prison.*

get the dirty/short end of the stick [gir] ficar com a parte mais difícil ou desagradável (de uma tarefa etc.), levar a pior, ser prejudicado, receber tratamento injusto, pagar o pato *I was always giving him orders and he was always getting the short end of the stick.* -MJM,44.

go off the deep end [col] 1. agir com precipitação e sem pensar, deixar-se levar pelo entusiasmo *Teenagers go off the deep end when they see their favorite singers.* 2. zangar-se, perder a calma; ficar pancada *Now don't go off the deep end because you failed to pass the examination.* ♦ *[They] ... thought the colonel had finally gone off the deep end.* -SLS,239.

hold/keep one's end up [col] fazer suas obrigações, realizar sua parte (de tarefa, dever etc.) *We must try to hold our end up even though we find it very difficult.*

make (both) ends meet viver dentro do orçamento, conciliar as despesas com a receita *More than 7 million Americans hold two or three jobs to make ends meet.*

no end [col] 1. muito, muitos, um sem-fim, um grande número *Her unkind words caused no end of grief to my mother.* 2. enormemente, sobremaneira *He enjoyed himself no end at the surprise party.*

on end 1. ereto, em pé, apoiado em uma das extremidades *Her hair stood on end when she saw the ghostly figure.* 2. ininterruptamente, a fio *... you may sail [the sea] for days on end without seeing anything you could recognize as life ...* -CR,19.

on the receiving end [col] como alvo, como a vítima (que experimenta algo desagradável) *[He found himself] ... on the receiving end of some pointed questions.* -T/92.

put an end/stop to pôr fim a, fazer cessar *He wanted to put an end to his loneliness ... -PRT,10.* ♦ *They were determined to put a stop to all that nonsense.*
to end para superar, exceder, desbancar os demais, os congêneres *Movie critic Steven H. Scheuer said that in* Born Yesterday *actress "Judy Holliday copped [won] an Oscar for her hilarious performance as Billie, the dumb blonde to end all dumb blondes".*
to the bitter end até o fim, até tudo acabar, até que nada mais possa ser feito *He clung to his beliefs to the bitter end.*
ENGLISH broken English inglês mal falado ou mal escrito *It was always a delight to watch S. Z. Sakall in Warner Brothers movies and to listen to his broken English.*
(in) plain English (em) linguagem clara, (em) termos diretos *In plain English, my answer is no.* ♦ *How can you teach me anything if you don't even understand plain English? -HE,276.*
ENOUGH enough is enough já é demais, agora chega, basta, nada mais precisa ser dito *Enough is enough, boys! This has gone too far! Stop it!*
ENTITLE be entitled to ter direito a, fazer jus a *[They] ... gave him the job I was entitled to. -KJS,7.*
entitle to dar direito a, habilitar, autorizar *The services he rendered to his country entitles him to a distinguished place among the great political leaders of his time.*
ENVY green with envy morrendo de inveja *Linda was green with envy when she was told about Abigail's success.*
EQUAL equal to capaz de, à altura de, suficientemente apto, hábil ou corajoso para (fazer ou enfrentar algo, lidar com etc.) *In* The Wonderful World of Books, *Bennett Cerf says that some people "... shy away from books because they're afraid they are not equal to them."*
ERRAND on an errand em uma incumbência, missão etc. (a mando de alguém) *The boy was out on an errand.* ♦ *... Mr. Blair is leaving on an errand to the West for me tomorrow morning. -EW,24.*
run an errand cumprir pequenas incumbências (como levar recados, fazer pequenas entregas, retiradas ou executar qualquer outro propósito específico para alguém) *When I was a boy, I ran errands for the neighbors who had no children.*
ERROR in error 1. errado, equivocado, inexato; por equívoco *Future research [in biology] will undoubtedly prove some concepts to be in error. -SEE,2.* ♦ *That letter was sent to you in error.* 2. em erro de crença *The Church found Joan of Arc in error and burned her at the stake as a heretic.*
ESCAPE have a narrow escape escapar por um triz *When the bus crashed he had a narrow escape and was the only person uninjured.*
ESSENCE of the essence da maior importância *We are creatures of time in more ways than one, and time is of the essence. -BN,14.*
ESTABLISHMENT the Establishment os membros que compõem a estrutura de poder de uma sociedade, grupo, instituição etc., a autoridade institucional, a classe dirigente *... a spartan prep school designed to groom likely lads for their destined place in the Establishment. -T/68.*
ESTATE real estate/property bens de raiz, imóveis *[He] ... was making himself a small fortune in real estate in this town. -HW,19.*
EVEN even out parar no mesmo nível, manter-se em equilíbrio, regularizar-se *[He] ... waited for his heartbeat to slow, his breathing to even out ... -NE,247.*
even so mesmo assim, ainda assim *It is the correct thing to do, but even so I don't like to do it.*
even though ainda que, mesmo que *... even though she believes the acts of others are wrong, she usually withholds judgment ... -WPT,68.*

EVENHANDED imparcial, justo ... *the new policy is more evenhanded toward foreign nations* ... -T/76.

EVEN-TEMPERED calmo, tranqüilo *Tom Jobim was an even-tempered man who loved nature and composed wonderful music.*

EVENT **at all events** aconteça o que acontecer, seja como for, de qualquer maneira *No matter what happens, at all events call me immediately.*

in any event = **at all EVENTS** *War or famine, in any event life will continue as before.*

in the event of em caso de, na eventualidade de *In the event of fire, call 411.*

EVER **ever after** para sempre *Hal married Madge and they lived happily ever after.*

ever since desde então *You began the process of learning language when you were an infant, and the process has continued ever since.* -BCM,9.

ever so [col] muito, extremamente *... a stranger ... tugs at his elbow and says ever so sweetly, "Thank you for not smoking".* -T/86.

ever so much muito *Thank you ever so much.*

hardly/scarcely ever raramente, quase nunca *You hardly ever see a man wearing a hat these days.*

EVERYTHING and everything → **and ALL**

EXCEPT **except for** 1. com exceção de, excluindo *Except for Mildred, all the girls came to the party.* 2. se não fosse por, não fora *Groucho Marx used to say that except for Karl [Marx] he'd be the most famous of all Marxes.*

EXCEPTION **take exception to** fazer objeção a, censurar, desaprovar *There are many free individuals who take exception to what you say.* -T/91.

EXCESS **to excess** excessivamente, demais, exageradamente *... I'm not doing anything to excess except enjoying life.* -HA,342.

EXCLUSION **to the exclusion of** de maneira a excluir, barrar, deixar de fora *... in a free society men should be able to band together in social or fraternal organizations to the exclusion of whom they please, without stigma.* -T/66.

EXISTENCE **come into existence** → **come into BEING**

EXPENSE **at the expense of** à custa de, com sacrifício de *We'll have to cut down costs but not at the expense of quality.*

meet one's expenses fazer face às despesas *He tried all kinds of extra work to supplement his salary, but still could not meet his expenses.*

EXPLAIN **explain away** dar explicação satisfatória, convincente ou persuasiva na tentativa de atenuar o significado ou a importância de algo; justificar algo dissipando dúvidas, problemas, dificuldades etc. *... scientists have tried to explain the expanding universe, or to explain it away.* -T/60.

EXTENT **to a great/large extent** muito, grandemente, em grande parte *To a great extent the success of his career was due to his wife.*

to some/a certain extent até certo ponto *To a certain extent, all of us are to blame for what she did.* ♦ *The monsters Sade conceived in his writings ... live to some extent in each and every one of us.* -GD,208.

to such an extent that a tal ponto que *He wants to keep his family in the background and he has carried that feeling to such an extent that he refuses to allow his wife and children to pose for photographs.*

to the extent of na quantia de, no valor de, até o limite de, até o ponto de *He owes me money to the extent of $5,000.*

to the extent that na medida em que *Religion was important to the extent that the ancient Egyptian believed in a life after death.* -CEO,31.

EYE **be all eyes** ficar vigilante, concentrar toda a atenção em; ficar cheio de curiosidade, observar bem de perto *Hector was* *all eyes when he opened* The Big Book of Dinosaurs *his father gave him on his birthday.*

believe one's eyes → **not believe one's EARS**

black eye [col] estigma, má fama, desonra, mácula *The fact that he had once been involved in corruption gave his political record a black eye.*

cast a cold eye on censurar, desaprovar, condenar *... cast a cold eye on the use of lie detectors and mail interception.* -T/66.

catch someone's eye/attention atrair a atenção de *He caught the girl's eye as he was drinking his beer.* ♦ *... as an astronomer with special interest in the moon, the early reports of flying saucers caught my attention.* -JM,2. ⇒ **eye-catching** atraente, vistoso, que chama a atenção *... an eye-catching school uniform of red, white and blue.* -T/81.

close/shut one's eyes to não querer ver, fechar os olhos para, não tomar conhecimento de, fazer vista grossa para *She knew perfectly well what was going on, but she closed her eyes to it.*

cry one's eyes/heart out chorar copiosamente, debulhar-se em lágrimas *Gwen cried her eyes out when her lover ditched her.* ♦ *When she didn't get apple pie with the rest of us one time, she cried her heart out.* -ST,24.

easy on the eyes [gir] atraente, belo, agradável à vista *As every tourist knows, this place [San Francisco] is very easy on the eyes.* -T/91.

the eye of the hurricane/storm o centro do furacão, zona de calmaria cercada de grande agitação e turbulência *... Poland seemed to be in the eye of the hurricane.*

feast one's eye on olhar com prazer para, deleitar os olhos em *Clint feasted his eyes on the wonderful beauty of the Colorado Rockies.*

give (someone) the (glad) eye olhar com interesse ou admiração (para), olhar convidativamente (para) *The lovely girl gave me the eye as she walked by.*

have an eye for estar atento para, saber apreciar, ver, avaliar etc. *He had ... an eye for the ladies ...* -T/64.

have one's eye on estar de olho em, estar interessado em, estar desejando, ter pretensões a *He has his eyes on the pretty coeds ...* -T/72. ♦ *... Mr. Barlowe had his eye on him [for a promotion] ...* -BH,19.

have/keep an eye on/to the main chance colocar seu interesse em primeiro lugar, reconhecer uma boa oportunidade (principalmente para ganhar dinheiro) *He's a shrewd businessman and always has an eye to the main chance.*

have an eye to ter em vista, ter por finalidade, objetivar, dedicar-se a *Mr. Parkinson always has an eye to good business opportunities.*

have eyes in the back of one's head [col] saber tudo o que se passa à sua volta, saber o que acontece quando não se está olhando *She must have eyes in the back of her head. How else could she know he had taken the money from her purse?*

have eyes only for; only have eyes for estar apaixonado por; só se interessar por, dar toda sua atenção a *At the square dance, Lou only had eyes for Zee.*

in the eye of the beholder nos olhos do observador, segundo a concepção do circunstante, de acordo com cada um *Is eros, like beauty, in the eye of the beholder?* -T/69.

in the eyes of; in someone's eyes aos olhos de, do ponto de vista de, na opinião de *In the eyes of the law, Marian was just as guilty as the man who pulled the trigger.* ♦ *Dave loved Ann very much and, in his eyes, she could do no wrong.*

in the public eye que aparece freqüentemente em público, nos noticiários etc.; amplamente conhecido, que está sempre em evidência, à vista de todos *... he has spent 46 of his 64 years in the public eye ...* -T/92.

jaundiced eye visão parcial, opinião preconceituosa *He tends to view things with a jaundiced eye.*

keep an/one's eye on vigiar cuidadosamente *[They] ... were still talking guardedly among themselves, at the same time keeping an eye on him.* -TRW,37.

keep an eye out [col] ficar atento, prestar atenção, ficar de olho *... he said he was expecting a friend from out of town and wanted to keep an eye out for him.* -TR,288.

keep one's eyes open/peeled/skinned estar atento, ficar alerta, vigilante *When you do business with him, you must keep your eyes open.* ♦ *We'll keep our eyes peeled tonight ...* -LMT,27.

lay/set eyes on ver *Liz was the most beautiful woman I had ever laid eyes on.* ♦ *I haven't set eyes on any of my Army buddies since I left the service.*

look in the eye/face olhar de frente, encarar sem medo, de cabeça erguida *... he looked Fred in the eye with his crinkly smile.* -HG,83. ♦ *She was unable to look me in the face and tell me what I wanted to hear.* ♦ *... I gave that girl enough backbone to stand up straight and look the world in the eye.* -AK,199.

make eyes at dirigir olhares amorosos a, flertar com *... soon she is making eyes first at Stiglitz and then at Mark.* -T/63.

meet someone's/the eye ser visto, apresentar-se aos olhos *... other [concessions] sounded good, but were less than met the eye.* -T/92. ♦ *When we got to the top of the ridge, the first thing to meet our eyes was the Doge's palace.*

never/not bat an eye/eyelash/eyelid [col] não pestanejar, não se surpreender, não demonstrar seus sentimentos, manter a calma *She saw him come in but she didn't bat an eye.* ♦ *Al never batted an eyelid.* -T/81.

open (up) someone's eyes revelar, mostrar, fazer ver, fazer perceber *They say that love is blind but marriage opens your eyes.* ⇒ **eye-opening** surpreendente, revelador *In his new book he gives an eye-opening account of criminal organizations now at work all over the world.*

private eye [gír] detetive particular *Sam Spade and Philip Marlowe are unquestionably the most famous private eyes in American detective stories.*

see eye to eye estar de pleno acordo, ter opiniões idênticas *... we need not see eye to eye in order to walk hand in hand.* -T/84.

see with half an eye ver ou compreender claramente por ser evidente *I could see with half an eye that they were in love.*

set eyes on → **lay EYES on**

shut one's eyes to → **close one's EYES to**

someone's eyes are bigger than his/her/someone's stomach [col] ter o olho maior que a barriga, ser guloso *Go easy on the food, Mac. It seems your eyes are bigger than your stomach.*

there is more to someone/something than meets the eye alguém/algo é mais complexo do que aparenta ser, não é só aquilo que se percebe *There's more to that ... boy than meets the eye.* -UJ,204. ♦ *There's much more to his amazing success than meets the eye.*

turn a blind eye fingir não notar, fechar os olhos *[He] ... voiced his disapproval, but turned a blind eye because the money helped keep the family from going hungry.* -T/87. v. **turn a deaf EAR**

up to one's eyes → **up to one's EARS**

weep one's eyes out = **cry one's EYES out** *Grace wept her eyes out when she received a negative reply to her application to Bryn Mawr College.*

with an eye to com um objetivo definido em mente, com o propósito ou a intenção de *[John Steinbeck's] ... Of Mice and Men, a short novel written with an eye to both stage and movie adaptation.* -SRE,218.

EYEBALL [gír] olhar cuidadosamente ou fixamente, examinar com toda a atenção

He [John Kennedy] exercised superpower machismo by eyeballing the Soviet Union over its Cuban missiles until Khrushchev blinked. -T/92.

eyeball to eyeball [gir] cara a cara, frente a frente ... *a hunter and a mountain lion eyeball to eyeball.* -T/74.

EYEBROWS raise (one's) eyebrows chocar, provocar surpresa ou reprovação, escandalizar; mostrar espanto, desagrado etc., escandalizar-se *The film's [The Postman Always Rings Twice] steamy sex scenes – will raise eyebrows and temperatures.* -T/81. ♦ *They will make suggestions that raise my eyebrows and my respiration level.* -HS,325.

EYEFUL get/have an eyeful [col] olhar (para), dar uma boa olhada, abranger com a vista, ter uma visão total (de) *Get an eyeful of those girls swimming in the lake.*

EYE-OPENING → **open (up) someone's EYES**

EYESHOT within eyeshot ao alcance da vista *There wasn't anyone within eyeshot as I crossed the street at that early hour.*

EYESORE algo desagradável à visão *Many unfinished apartment buildings have been an eyesore as well as a potential danger.*

EYETEETH cut one's eyeteeth/teeth adquirir experiência, tornar-se competente, proficiente, traquejado, tornar-se conhecedor do mundo, iniciar-se (em) *[She] ... is a no-nonsense woman who cut her teeth on the board of the village library.* -T/86.

give one's eyeteeth dar qualquer coisa (por), dar tudo (para) *Plenty of girls would give their eyeteeth to marry someone with George's money ...* -AK,61.

EYEWITNESS testemunha ocular ... *he was an eyewitness to the crime ...* -T/64.

FACE **at face value** ao que aparenta ser, pelas aparências *He [Galileo] refused to accept the theories of Aristotle at face value as his colleagues had done for centuries.* -HHO,25.
face about dar meia-volta *She faced about and came after me.*
faced by/with diante de, perante, frente a frente com *The emerging nations are faced by a lack of investment capital.* ♦ *Sarah was faced with a serious problem.*
face down enfrentar resolutamente *He bravely faced down his opponents.*
faced with 1. v. **FACED by** 2. revestido de *The building was faced with Italian marble.*
face off confrontar-se, defrontar-se *Cuban prisoners and lawmen face off in a tense hostage drama.* -T/87. ⇒ **face-off** confronto *Iran has been locked in a face-off with France since the two nations broke off relations ...* -T.87.
face up to reconhecer (dificuldade, adversidade, os fatos da vida) *Most people don't like to face up to the realities of life.*
fall (flat) on one's face ser malsucedido, fracassar, quebrar a cara *The financial fellows think we're going to fall on our faces ...* -T/73. ♦ *... he has fallen flat on his face a few times because of that attitude.* T/87.
fly in the face/teeth of desafiar, contestar, opor-se a *Many theories that try to explain the UFO phenomenon fly in the face of all logic.*
have one's face lifted ser submetido a cirurgia plástica facial *She has had her face lifted and looks much younger now.* ⇒ **face-lift; face-lifting** 1. cirurgia plástica facial *He always looks as if he had just had a face-lift.* 2. reforma, remodelação, restauração, modernização *The Eastern side [of Berlin] is now undergoing a much needed face-lifting.* -T/86.
have the face to [col] ter o descaramento de *He had the face to say that to me.*
in the face of em face de, diante de, à vista de *[Hamlin] Garland worked long and hard as a farm boy, and managed to obtain an education only in the face of severe handicaps.* -RR,620.
keep a straight face permanecer impassível, não demonstrar nenhuma emoção; conter o riso *... the authorities have been uneasy and have tried, like all uneasy people in control, to keep a straight face and say as little as possible.* -HGI,15. ♦ *I could hardly keep a straight face as I told him what had happened.* v. **straight FACE**

let's face it sejamos francos, encaremos os fatos *Let's face it, she's a a much smarter girl than any of us.*
long face aparência tristonha, infeliz *That long face of yours gets everybody depressed.* -HJC,289. ⇒ **long-faced** triste, melancólico *Those close to Humphrey are determined not to be long-faced ...* -T/77.
look in the face → **look in the EYE**
lose face desprestigiar-se, perder o bom conceito *... he could not reverse himself without losing face.* -T/80.
make/pull a face fazer careta *Little children like to make faces when they're angry.* ♦ *He always pulled a face when he was told to do an unpleasant job.*
on the face of it a julgar pela aparência, aparentemente *On the face of it, Dr. Warren and Paul Revere seemed unlikely associates.* -SGF,15.
pull a face → **make a FACE**
pull a long face entristecer-se, mostrar expressão de desânimo *The children pulled long faces when they were told that they had to have an oral examination.* v. **long FACE**
put a bold/brave/firm/good/etc. face on mostrar destemor, confiança, segurança, enfrentar (algo) corajosamente *She tried to put a bold face on when she realized her friends had deserted her.* ♦ *[The dictator] ... last week tried to put the best face on his disintegrating hold on national power.* -T/79. ⇒ **bold-faced** insolente, atrevido, deslavado *A bold-faced lie ...* -T/78.
put on one's face [col] aplicar cosméticos no rosto, maquiar-se *Rose sat for hours in front of her mirror putting on her face.*
save (one's) face evitar uma humilhação, proteger sua reputação, manter sua dignidade *After that terrible blunder he tried to find a way of saving face.* ⇒ **face-saving** que salvaguarda as aparências, que protege a dignidade *... Mikhail Gorbachev [Secretary of the Communist Party] is looking for a face-saving settlement in Afghanistan.* -T/85.
set one's face against opor-se fortemente a, mostrar-se totalmente contra *... men of outstanding achievement and those who live full, happy lives usually set their faces against drastic innovation.* -HETB,19.
shoot off one's face → **shoot off one's MOUTH**
show one's face aparecer, comparecer, mostrar-se *I wouldn't show my face around here if I were you.*
shut one's face → **shut one's MOUTH**
someone's face falls demonstrar decepção, frustração, desalento etc. *His face fell when I told him what had happened.*
stare someone in the face ser óbvio, evidente, estar bem à vista; estar iminente *People who enjoy learning seem to be able to learn what stares them in the face.* -JW,175. ♦ *Though bankruptcy was staring the old man in the face, he fought on to try to save his business.*
straight face expressão facial séria, que não demonstra hilaridade ou nenhuma outra emoção *He ... can tell the biggest lies with a straight face.* -T/86. ⇒ **straight-faced** de expressão facial séria; sóbrio, sisudo, circunspecto, que não denota hilaridade ou nenhuma outra emoção *[In silent movies, Buster] Keaton was straight-faced, a poignant automaton caught up in a world that was beyond his control or understanding.* -KA,121.
throw in someone's face lembrar (algo) constantemente (a alguém), jogar na cara *She's always throwing my faults in my face.*
to someone's face na presença de alguém, diretamente, abertamente *... you cannot say you hate him to his face, because it hurts his feelings.* -JEP,249.
FACE-LIFT → **have one's FACE lifted**
FACE-SAVING → **save one's FACE**
FACE-TO-FACE frente a frente, cara a cara, em contato direto *... he came face*

to face with a male lion. -LAK,7. ♦ *... a face-to-face interview ...* -T/86.

FACT the fact is o fato é que, a verdade é que *The fact is, most smokers want to quit.* -T/87.
a fact of life fato da vida, realidade que não pode ser descartada *Violence is a fact of life to the children of West 116th Street ...* -T/69.
the facts of life os detalhes da vida sexual, reprodução, nascimento etc. *As a bride of 16, Catherine the Great was ignorant of the facts of life ...* -T/61.
for a fact [col] com toda a certeza, sem sombra de dúvida *I know for a fact that he went to Brazil in the late fifties.*
the hard facts os fatos inegáveis, verídicos, exatos, a verdade nua e crua *... the press is so convinced that the American people don't want the hard facts of foreign affairs ...* -LW,vii.
in (point of) fact na verdade, na realidade *Be here at eight-thirty sharp or you won't be taken. In fact, you'd better be here by eight ...* -WCN,279. ♦ *I haven't seen Frances today. In point of fact, I haven't seen her since Monday.*
FACT-FINDING que busca os fatos, que pretende apurar a verdade *Dr. Kinsey and his co-workers [in their books on human sexual behavior] sought to act as a fact-finding board of inquiry ...* -HEW,6.
FADE fade away 1. desaparecer gradualmente *They heard her voice calling for help until it faded away.* 2. definhar, morrer aos poucos *The old man is fading away.*
fade in aumentar em intensidade (som ou imagem em rádio, TV e filme) *The sound on my radio fades in slowly, but fades out rapidly.*
fade out 1. decrescer em intensidade (som ou imagem em rádio, TV e filme) *The radio program was loud but began to fade out after a few minutes.* 2. [col] desaparecer, perder proeminência *He was a famous star in the 1920s but faded out in the 1930s.*

FAIL without fail sem falta, infalivelmente *Bring me the money tomorrow without fail.*
FAIL-SAFE à prova de falhas [diz-se de um mecanismo ou sistema provido de um dispositivo eletrônico que impede a ocorrência de mau funcionamento ou possível acidente] *... the system is not fail-safe.* -T/87.
FAINT not have the faintest (idea) → **not have the faintest IDEA**
FAINTHEARTED tímido, covarde, medroso *They were a fainthearted group and failed to help him when he needed their support.*
FAIR fair and square [col] 1. leal, honesto, justo *O'Shea is fair and square in all his business deals.* 2. honestamente, lealmente *Joe won the fight fair and square.*
FAIR-HAIRED [col] protegido do(s) superior(es), favorito do(s) chefe(s) *Robertson was always considered the fair-haired boy in our office and we were shocked when he was fired.*
FAIR-MINDED imparcial, justo *He's got a reputation for being fair-minded ...* -PRT,68.
FAITH in good faith de boa-fé *... your warning was unnecessary. However, you gave it to me in good faith, and I thank you for it.* -MET,155.
keep//break faith with ser leal//desleal com, cumprir//não cumprir a palavra, o compromisso *You must always keep faith with your friends.* ♦ *You must not break faith with those who are risking their lives on every continent, from Afghanistan to Nicaragua ...* -T/85.
on faith sem questionar, sem prova, baseado simplesmente na confiança *His word was taken on faith and we never questioned his reasons.*
pin one's faith/hopes on depositar fé em, confiar em *We have all pinned our faith*

on you. ♦ *Shirley pinned her hopes on a speedy recovery.*
FALL fall afoul of → **FALL foul of**
fall all over oneself → **FALL over backward**
fall all over someone → **FALL (all) over someone**
fall apart 1. desmoronar-se, romper-se, desintegrar-se, desfazer-se *The jeep looks dilapidated enough to fall apart.* -CN,76. ♦ *... rocks and their minerals decay and fall apart to become soil.* -PR,15. ♦ *His marriage fell apart.* 2. perder o controle emocional, sofrer colapso nervoso *She divorced when he [her son] was nine and she seemed to fall apart.* -WCG,17.
fall asleep adormecer *As he fell asleep he was remembering what Delafield had told him ...* -PF/27.
fall away 1. afastar-se (de), abandonar, renunciar, renegar *Our one hope of salvation, [Arnold J.] Toynbee asserts, is a return to the "One True God", from whom we have fallen away.* -MHJ,8. 2. reduzir-se, diminuir, dissolver-se, desaparecer *All his troubles have fallen away.* 3. emagrecer, definhar *He became sick and fell away to eighty pounds.*
fall back recuar, retirar-se *The crowd fell back in confusion ...* -T/63. ♦ *... they didn't want to fall back into their old habits.* -T/86.
fall back on/upon recorrer a, utilizar-se de (algo) em uma emergência *In economics writing, you can always fall back on statistics.* -T/79.
fall behind 1. ficar para trás *The stagecoach rolled on and the miles fell behind.* 2. atrasar-se *He ... fell behind in paying his income taxes.* -T/80.
fall down 1. cair, ir ao chão *He always falls down when he drinks too much.* 2. [col] falhar, fracassar, ser malsucedido *Most students fall down in the oral exams.*
fall due vencer-se (dívida, conta, fatura etc.) *The rent falls due on the fifth of each month.*

fall flat não produzir o efeito desejado, falhar, fracassar *The movie has an interesting story but falls flat because of its improbable ending.*
fall for [col] 1. tomar-se de amores por, apaixonar-se por *They fell for each other when they were working in the same film.* 2. ser logrado por (algo), cair como um patinho *Ron is so gullible that he will fall for any scheme to get rich quickly.*
fall foul/afoul of encrencar-se com, desavir-se com *Don't fall foul of the law in an Arab country. You'd never survive jail.*
fall guy [gír] bode expiatório, aquele que paga o pato *... in Laurel and Hardy [movies], I [Oliver Hardy] always am the fall guy.* -MJM,44.
fall in 1. ruir, desmoronar *The walls of the bombed building fell in.* 2. entrar em forma, enfileirar-se (militar); fazer entrar em forma *Sergeant Stryker ordered his men to fall in.* ♦ *The corporal was told to fall the men in.*
fall in for receber, ser alvo de, ficar sujeito a *She fell in for severe criticism.*
fall into começar, entregar-se a, empenhar-se em *The 25 participants quickly fell into heated disagreements ...* -T/87.
fall in with 1. encontrar casualmente *When we were hiking Mount Washington we fell in with a group of German tourists who were climbing the Presidential Range in New Hampshire.* 2. unir-se a, associar-se com *... the girl had fallen in with a bad crowd ...* -T/60. 3. concordar com, aquiescer *If he agrees to your plan, all the other companies will fall in with you.*
fall off 1. cair, desprender-se, soltar-se *... the plane's engine fell off ...* -T/80. 2. diminuir, escassear, declinar, abrandar, serenar *Sales have fallen off during the last few months.* ♦ *The wind fell off at last.* 3. deteriorar-se, piorar, decair *The quality of many television programs has fallen off considerably.* ⇒ **falloff** queda, declínio

... *the falloff in British oil production from the North Sea.* -T/87.
fall on/upon 1. atacar, assaltar *The Indians fell on the colonists and killed all of them.* 2. ocorrer em (dia, data), cair em *Christmas falls on the 25th of December.* 3. caber a, tocar a, ser da responsabilidade de *It fell on me to pay all her bills.* 4. experimentar, sofrer, suportar, passar por *The family has fallen on hard times.*
fall out 1. desentender-se, cortar relações ... *he fell out with both the President and the National Democratic Party.* -T/72. ⇒ **falling-out** desentendimento, desavença, separação ... *the youngster had a falling-out with his father* ... -T/72. 2. sair de forma (militar) *On long marches, at least ten percent of the soldiers had to fall out and rest.*
fallout 1. precipitação radioativa *Fallout consists of radioactive debris produced by a nuclear explosion and borne into the air.* -T/61. 2. conseqüência secundária, efeito derivado *Most other companies were anxiously waiting to see how much fallout the stock crash would generate.* -T/87.
fall over tombar, cair, ir ao chão ... *the leather-backed swivel chair behind the desk had fallen over on its side* ... -QE,126.
fall over backward; fall (all) over oneself [col] agir com afoiteza, precipitação, esforçar-se excessivamente (na tentativa de fazer algo, agradar alguém etc.) *People were falling over backward to join the rescue workers during the flood.* ♦ *The boys fall all over themselves trying to get a date with Madge.*
fall (all) over someone [col] mostrar-se demasiadamente atencioso para com *He will flatter and fall all over anyone he thinks might be able to get him a better job.*
fall over each other; fall over one another apressar-se em fazer ou conseguir algo antes de outrem *The fans fall over each other to get the players' autographs.*

fall short ser insuficiente, deficiente ... *he [President Ronald Reagan] fell short in the performance.* -T/87.
fall short of não atingir (objetivo, nível, padrão etc.), não corresponder (ao desejado), ficar aquém de ... *the program fell short of its objective* ... -T/91.
fall sick/ill adoecer *He fell sick just as he was about to leave for France.*
fall silent calar-se, emudecer ... *Dakin fell silent.* -QE,125.
fall through fracassar, dar em nada *In 1970 the Soviets invited IBM to set up a plant in Russia, but the deal fell through.* -T/73.
fall to 1. começar, dar início (a uma ação, trabalho etc.) *[He]* ... *fell to work, puffing and talking to himself.* -LLN,25. ♦ *Billy, Ayrton, Milt, and Lou met for lunch on Saturday and fell to talking about old times.* 2. começar a lutar *When Scaramouche and his archenemy, the Marquis de Maynes met accidentally in the theater, they drew their swords and fell to.* 3. começar a comer *It was a jovial lunch as we fell to at table.* -T/78. 4. ser dever de, caber a, competir a ... *it fell to her to arrange new rooms for the fugitive PCBR members* ... -LA,203. 5. fechar-se (por si próprio – porta, portão etc.) *The door fell to noiselessly.*
fall upon → FALL on
ride for a fall procurar encrenca, arriscar-se, expor-se a perigo *Henry is riding for a fall if he thinks that he can arrive late for work and get away with it.*
FALLING-OUT → FALL out
FAMILY broken family → broken HOME
in a/the family way [col] grávida *He has been very happy since his wife told him she's in the family way.*
run in the family → run in the BLOOD
FAN fan out espalhar-se (a partir de um ponto central) ... *some 60* ... *FBI men had fanned out through the area.* -T/64.
FANCY catch/strike/take someone's fancy cair no agrado de, deleitar, granjear o afeto, a simpatia de *It was her hair that*

caught my fancy ... -SHE,17. ♦ *I bought an abstract painting at the art show because it took my fancy.*
fancy que surpresa, quem diria, imagine só *Fancy meeting you here, of all places in the world.* -JJF,229.
take a fancy to ficar gostando de, agradar-se de, afeiçoar-se a *... he took a great fancy to me ...* -MJM,45. ♦ *Tom has taken a fancy to cowboy boots and hats.*
FANCY-FREE que não está enamorado, que não tem compromisso, livre para fazer o que quiser *... you are still fancy-free?* -CT,10.
FAR as far as 1. até (a distância, o lugar, ou ponto mencionado), até onde *... grasslands rolled away in all directions as far as eye could see.* -LD,16. v. **GO as far as** 2. na medida em que, tanto quanto, até o ponto em que *As far as it has been possible to ascertain, the Loch Ness monster is a figment of the imagination.*
as far as someone/something goes; as far as someone/something is concerned no que diz respeito a, com referência a, no que tange a *I was having my own troubles as far as women went.* -AIM,94. ♦ *As far as I'm concerned she can leave right now.*
as far back as já em, desde *As far back into the earth's history as records in the rock take us, volcanoes are found to have been present.* -VA,26.
by far sem dúvida, por grande margem de diferença, incomparavelmente *The Neolithic Age was by far the shortest of the three stone ages ...* -SJV,7.
far afield a uma grande distância, muito além, bem longe (de casa, do assunto em questão etc.) *[In* To Have and Have Not*] Director Howard Hawks guided [Humphrey] Bogart through a performance that was not far afield .. from that of Rick in* Casablanca *...* -BA,101. ♦ *The church sends missionaries far afield.*
far and away = **by FAR** *... depression [is] far and away the most common of the emotional disorders ...* -T/64.

far and near/wide de toda a parte, por toda a parte *Thousands of people came from far and near to see the book fair.* ♦ *Brooklyn is famed far and wide as the City of Churches.* -TB,19.
far be it from me longe de mim (fazer, pensar etc. determinada coisa ou agir etc. de determinada maneira) *Far be it from me to question Valerie's sincerity.*
far from longe de, quase o oposto de, longe disso, de maneira alguma *We know you've tried very hard, but the results are far from satisfactory.* ♦ *... the findings were far from complete.* -T/87.
far gone 1. muito avançado, em adiantado estado (de), muito comprometido, em situação crítica *Toward the end of his life, the old man often seemed far gone in alcohol.* 2. cansadíssimo, exausto; deteriorado *... she is too far gone to recognize the hellish landscape that surrounds her.* -T/72. 3. muito doente, próximo à morte *The doctor said that the patient was too far gone from loss of blood.* 4. apaixonado, enamorado *Ginny was much too far gone to hear what her father had to tell her about her boyfriend.*
how far 1. a que distância, quão longe *How far is it to Timbuktu?* 2. até que ponto *The question is, how far can we trust him?*
in so far/insofar as no que concerne, no que diz respeito a, na medida em que *The [Kinsey] Report, then, is a study of sexual behavior in so far as it can be quantitatively measured.* -GD,219. ♦ *Insofar as writing is a science, almost any person can learn to write with grammatical acceptability ...* -VC,3.
so far 1. até agora, até o momento, até aqui *So far, man has only limited control of the atom.* -GH,87. 2. até certo ponto, até determinado limite *Steve will help you just so far, and from then on you must help yourself.*
so far as até, até onde, até o ponto em que, tanto quanto *So far as is known, he*

was the first white man to set foot in New Guinea. v. **GO so far as**
so far, so good até aqui não há dificuldades, até o momento tudo é satisfatório *"How's your new book coming along?" "So far, so good."*
thus far = so FAR 1 *Thus far he has managed to elude the police of seven states.*
FAR-FETCHED forçado, artificial, improvável, implausível, exagerado *... the notion of using solar satellites to capture vast amounts of energy may not be very far-fetched at all.* -T/80. ♦ *a far-fetched hypothesis*
FAR-FLUNG 1. remoto, distante *... in far-flung corners of the world.* -T/87. ♦ *far-flung places* 2. amplo, vasto, que cobre uma grande área *[He] ... said he had never even discussed his far-flung secret operations .. with the President.* -T/87. ♦ *... far-flung crises ...* T/92.
FAR-OFF longínquo, distante *far-off planets* ♦ *... a far-off land ...* -T/69. ♦ *Our close friendship with the Barotti brothers started in the far-off fifties when we were in high school.*
FAR-OUT [col] avançado, de vanguarda, não-convencional *Kitty always dresses in far-out style.* ♦ *... far-out films ...* -T/66. ♦ *He was a far-out liberal on domestic issues, yet carried the conservative aura of his father ...* -T/60.
FAR-REACHING de importância; de amplo alcance, efeito ou conseqüência *Is it possible that the impact of Freud will in the end prove to be more decisive and far-reaching than the discoveries of Planck and Einstein?* -NB,9. ♦ *... far-reaching reforms.* -T/91.
FARM farm belt região de grandes fazendas no centro norte dos EUA, cinturão verde *Across the farm belt last week, it was clear that another bumper crop was on the way.* -T/86.
farm out 1. delegar, distribuir, terceirizar *... large manufacturing companies ... farm out the production process to suppliers of components, as in the automobile industry.* -T/92. 2. enviar (criança ou pobre) a uma instituição para ser cuidado *[The mother] ... went to work seven days a week in a sewing shop; the children were farmed out to friends for a year.* -T/77. 3. enviar (jogador de beisebol para um time de segunda divisão, subsidiário do primeiro time) para treinamento *He was farmed out to a small town baseball team for two years.* 4. arruinar (o solo) por uso excessivo *The area had been farmed out.*
FASHION after/in a fashion sofrivelmente, assim-assim, nem bem nem mal, à sua moda, de maneira insatisfatória *Despite the stress of modern life, most people still manage to "muddle through," worrying along and solving their problems after a fashion.* -CJ,5.
fashion designer estilista (de moda) *Agnes became a successful fashion designer.*
in fashion na moda *Short skirts are in fashion again.*
out of fashion → **out of DATE**
FAST fast food comida preparada e servida rapidamente *You'd better cut down on fast food.* ⇒ **fast-food** designativo de organização ou local que serve esse tipo de comida *a fast-food restaurant.* ♦ *Milan has become the fast-food capital.* -T/87.
FAST-PACED ligeiro, de ação rápida, que se desenrola à rédea solta (história, narrativa, filme etc.) *The movie* Raiders of the Lost Ark *was truly a thrilling fast-paced adventure story.*
FAST-TALK [col] persuadir (alguém) mediante conversa fluente e aprazível que é também convincente e enganadora *... [Julius Henry] Groucho [Marx] was an appealing rogue capable of fast-talking his way out of any difficulty.* -T/77.
FASTEN fasten on/upon fixar(se) em, cravar(se) em, agarrar, pôr, colocar; impor *[His] ... eyes fastened upon a spare and distinguished-looking gentleman of respectable*

years. -HM,13. ♦ *She fastened the responsibility for the accident on Riley.* ♦ *[His name was] Percival, fastened upon him by a doting, romantic-novel-reading mother ...* -DJ,10.

FAT **chew the fat/rag** [gír] bater papo *His wife can chew the fat over the phone for hours on end.* ♦ *Don came to see me the other day and we chewed the rag for quite a while.*

fat farm [col] clínica de emagrecimento no campo *He has attempted to leave 50 excess pounds on fat farms in the U.S. and Europe ...* -T/78.

the fat is in the fire [col] vai haver barulho, o mal está feito, é tarde para evitar complicações *The fat's in the fire now. Let's wait and see what happens.*

live on/off the fat of the land viver regaladamente, desfrutando fartamente os melhores alimentos, bebidas, confortos etc., ter do bom e do melhor *The soldiers entered the captured city and lived off the fat of the land.*

FATHER **like father, like son** tal pai, tal filho *You can't blame Dave for following in his old man's footsteps. You know, like father, like son.*

FAULT **at fault** errado, em falta, culpado, responsável *You were at fault when you asked Mrs. Kirkpatrick how old she was.*

find fault (with) procurar falhas ou defeitos (em), censurar, criticar *I wish you'd try listening once in a while instead of always finding fault.* -HJC,288. ♦ *The boss found fault with my work.* ⇒ **faultfinding** 1. censura, crítica, repreensão *Faultfinding is his worst characteristic.* 2. detrator, reprovador, crítico *... a faultfinding wife ...* -T/73.

to a fault excessivamente, demasiadamente *[They] ... are good-hearted and generous to a fault.* -MR,12. ♦ *... Germans have always been proud to a fault of their craftsmanship ...* -T/63.

FAVOR **curry favor (with)** adular, bajular *... her apartment now is filled with flowers sent by reporters trying to curry favor.* -T/73. ♦ *... the desire of politicians to curry favor with the military.* -T/87.

drop/fall from favor cair em desgraça, incorrer no desagrado, cair do pedestal, impopularizar-se, ficar malvisto *[He] ... was an army general who had dropped from favor during the Eisenhower years ...* -LA,50.

fall out of favor cair em descrédito, em desagrado *George had fallen out of favor with his boss.*

find favor ter aprovação, receber boa acolhida *The proposal did not find favor.*

in favor favorecido, protegido, que tem aprovação, boa acolhida *His doctrines are no longer in favor.*

in favor of a favor de, pró *Are you in favor of capital punishment?*

in favor with apoiado por, bem considerado por, nas boas graças de *He's no longer in favor with the President.*

in someone's favor 1. nas boas graças de *Becky is trying desperately to get back in her rich aunt's favor.* 2. a favor de *The judge decided the case in her favor.*

out of favor em descrédito, em desagrado, sem apoio *[He] ... is currently out of favor with both the electorate and his party.* -T/80.

FEAR **for fear of/that** por medo de que, para evitar que, para prevenir, para que não *I am afraid to open my mouth for fear that if I do no words will come out – or the wrong words.* -RP,105. ♦ *He complied with their orders for fear of incurring their anger.*

in fear of temeroso, com medo de *As a young boy he lived in constant fear of his tyrannical father.*

FEATHER **a feather in one's cap** feito notável, motivo de orgulho, honra, distinção *Among the many feathers in his cap was his election as Man of the Year.*

in fine/good/high/etc. feather em boa condição física, mental etc., bem-disposto,

bem-humorado *Gloria was in fine feather this morning.*
ruffle someone's feathers [col] irritar, perturbar, fazer perder o controle *[Though he is getting old] ... he just doesn't let birthdays ruffle his feathers.* -T/80.
show the white feather demonstrar covardia, amedrontar-se *If he shows the white feather in battle, it will bring shame on his father, the Duke.*
you could have knocked me down with a feather [col] fiquei perplexo, pasmo *You could have knocked me down with a feather when I opened the door and set eyes on my father whom I hadn't seen in over twenty years.*
FEATURE double feature sessão cinematográfica na qual se exibem dois longas-metragens *... spending his boyhood watching double features at the neighborhood movie palace.* -T/78.
feature film 1. filme de longa metragem *Paths of Glory was director Stanley Kubrick's fourth feature film.* ⇒ **feature-length** de longa metragem *... a feature-length film ...* -T/64. ♦ *... feature-length cartoons.* -T/92. 2. o filme principal de uma sessão cinematográfica *The feature film is on first and will finish at 6:30.*
feature story reportagem ou artigo que recebe destaque especial *[She] ... was awarded a Pulitzer [prize] this year for three feature stories ...* -T/81.
FED fed up [col] aborrecido, entediado, farto, cheio *There are a lot of high executives in this studio who are fed up with you.*
FEED feed on/upon alimentar-se de, nutrir-se de *Most chameleons feed on insects and other small invertebrates ...* -SK,91.
off one's feed [gir] indisposto, abatido, adoentado *... you're a bit off your feed ... this morning.* -BH,104.
FEEL feel bad sentir-se pesaroso, consternado, desolado *I lied to Louise and felt bad about it.*

feel cheap sentir-se vulgar, vil, desprezível *He made me feel cheap.*
feel for 1. tatear, procurar às apalpadelas *Eloise got up from the window seat and felt in the dark for her shoes.* -SJD,35. 2. sentir, ter pena de, condoer-se de *The compassionate person does not only feel for others, but acts to alleviate or remedy their pains or injustices.* -JS,11.
feel great sentir-se muito bem, estar muito bem disposto; produzir ótima sensação *I feel great this morning.* ♦ *It feels great to be in a house full of people who care ...* -T/87.
feel like 1. ter vontade de, estar disposto a, estar inclinado a *I don't feel like eating this morning.* ♦ *... sometimes I just feel like screaming!* -DP,8. ♦ *I just don't feel like cold snacks this evening.* 2. produzir (determinada) sensação *This material feels like glass, doesn't it?*
feel low sentir-se abatido, deprimido, andar triste *Maybe it's this weather or maybe I'm overworked, but I feel low this week.*
feel out inquirir com cautela, sondar *Let's feel out Mr. Kent's reaction to the ethical aspects of our plan.*
feel small sentir-se envergonhado *Johnny felt small when the teacher caught him looking for the answers in his book.*
feel sorry lamentar, estar desolado *What else can I say except that I feel sorry?*
feel sorry for condoer-se de, ter pena de *He was an unfortunate man and we felt sorry for him.* -OJ,4.
feel strongly acreditar com plena convicção *We feel strongly about some of our beliefs ...* -VC,4. ♦ *... if [she] ... feels strongly about something, she stands up for it.* -T/72.
feel up to [col] sentir-se capaz de, à altura de *You'd better let Wilson take the job if you don't feel up to it.*
get the feel of familiarizar-se com, acostumar-se a, compreender, aprender a (usar

etc.) *Todd picked up his new gun and fired a few shots just to get the feel of the weapon.*
how does it feel? qual é a sensação ou a impressão que dá? *... how does it feel to live in the White House?* -FLF,2.
FEELING hard feelings ressentimento, rancor, má vontade *When Logan and Gomez ended their partnership, there were no hard feelings between them.*
hurt someone's feelings magoar alguém, ferir a sensibilidade de *If you tell Carol the truth, you'll hurt her feelings.*
mixed feelings sentimentos ambíguos, opiniões ambivalentes ou conflitantes *I have mixed feelings about it all [the war in Vietnam].* -T/85. ♦ *... his feelings about his profession were mixed.* -T/78.
FEET → **FOOT**
FELLOW fellow traveler simpatizante de partido político, especialmente do partido comunista *In the 1950s, he was accused of being a fellow traveler by the Senate anti-communist investigators.*
FENCE fence in cercar, restringir, prender *"Don't fence me in", he said. "I want to be as free as a bird."*
mend one's fences [col] melhorar um relacionamento (principalmente político), reconciliar-se *... [The king of Jordan] ... has lately been mending his fences with [the President of Egypt] ... to secure his shaky throne ...* -T/61.
on the fence [col] em cima do muro, indeciso *He was on the fence too often on vital questions concerning his country.*
sit on the fence [col] permanecer em uma posição de neutralidade, não se comprometer, ficar em cima do muro *Many politicians sat on the fence in the early days of the Nixon impeachment proceeding.* ♦ *Whenever you must write about a controversial topic, don't sit on the fence.* -SHS,45.
FEND fend/shift for oneself cuidar de si mesmo, arranjar-se, não depender de ninguém *You will have to fend for yourself from now on.* ♦ *... Mark Twain had less than ten years' schooling before he had to shift for himself.* -HL,271.
fend off desviar, afastar, rechaçar, manter a distância *... he fends off real and imagined enemies ...* -T/78. ♦ *... he fended off attacks from both the Communist left and jingoist right ...* -T/67.
FERRET ferret out desentocar, fazer sair, forçar a saída de; descobrir, chegar (à verdade, aos fatos etc.) *They are trying to ferret out the disloyal citizens in government offices.* ♦ *The investigation ferreted out the facts.*
FETCH fetch up [col] chegar (a lugar ou posição), aportar, terminar *A woman and a faceless lover fetch up at a "white lakeside hotel ..."* -T/81.
FETTLE in fine/good fettle são, bem, disposto, saudável *I was in fine fettle for the day's work.*
FEVER at/to fever pitch intensamente, freneticamente, com veemência, com ímpeto, a um alto nível de emoção, agitação etc. *The air force was working at fever pitch to rescue the stranded people in the flooded areas.* ♦ *Their excitement rose to fever pitch.*
run a fever/temperature ter febre *Despite feeling poorly and running a fever, he constantly got up to get cigarettes ...* -SEB,122. ♦ *When you run a temperature, it is your body's signal that an infection is being fought by body cells.*
FEW a few alguns *Dan and I had a long talk a few days ago.*
few and far between raros, infreqüentes, escassos *With civil war raging, alternatives of any kind in El Salvador are few and far between.* -T/84. ♦ *... surprises are few and far between.* -T/87.
not/quite a few muitos *Not a few people answered the priest's request for old clothes for the poor.* ♦ *Quite a few people turned up at the meeting.*

what few os poucos que *I showed them what few photographs we had ...* -RE,29.

FIDDLE fiddle around [col] 1. perder tempo, ficar à toa *I don't have time to fiddle around with their ideas ...* -T/80. 2. bulir, mexer, brincar (com) *I wish you'd stop fiddling around with that watch.*

fiddle away desperdiçar, esbanjar *Don't fiddle your time away.*

(as) fit as a fiddle em ótima forma, muito bem disposto *... the next morning [he was] ... looking fit as a fiddle ...* -HJC,243.

play second fiddle desempenhar papel secundário, ocupar posição subordinada *... he didn't like playing second fiddle ...* -LMT,23. ♦ *He is playing second fiddle to the new leader of the conservatives.*

FIELD come out of left field ser inesperado, ilógico, muito surpreendente, contrário à opinião geral *Campbell's remarks on the subject under discussion came out of left field.*

have a field day ter um dia de grande atividade, agitação etc.; ter um dia cheio, profícuo; ter grande êxito ou oportunidade *The reporters had a field day covering the visit of Mikhail Gorbachev to the U.S.* ♦ *Our team had a field day with our rival school.*

lead the field liderar, ir na dianteira, caminhar à frente, fazer-se seguir *The great nobles [of 18th century France] led the field in voluptuous living ...* -GD,196.

(way) out in left field [gir] errado, enganado, equivocado; deslocado, extraviado, ilógico, contrário à opinião geral *Listen, boy, you're way out in left field.*

play the field [col] namorar mais de uma pessoa ao mesmo tempo, namorar por diversão *Joe never sticks to one girlfriend. He likes to play the field.*

take the field sair a campo, entrar na arena, iniciar combate ou ação contra, ir à luta *[President] Nixon took the field against his critics in his November 3 plea to the silent majority for backing of his Viet Nam policy ...* -T/69.

FIFTH take the Fifth invocar a Quinta Emenda à Constituição dos EUA [ao depor num tribunal] para justificar recusa em responder a determinada(s) pergunta(s) *Many political criminals avoid conviction by taking the Fifth, which gives them the right to refuse to answer an incriminating question.*

FIFTY fifty-fifty [col] meio a meio, em partes iguais *He said, "Let's split the bill fifty-fifty".*

FIG not care/give a fig não dar a mínima importância, ser totalmente indiferente *I don't give a fig for your opinion.*

not worth a fig sem o menor valor *Your opinion isn't worth a fig.*

FIGHT fight back 1. reagir, revidar *The man was too old to fight back.* ♦ *The soldiers fought back to recapture the bridge.* 2. reprimir, sufocar, conter *[The women were] ... fighting back tears ...* -UL,6.

fight down = FIGHT back 2 *Angie tried to fight down the anger that was welling up in her.*

fight/battle it out lutar até que um dos contendores vença, resolver pela luta *In the last battle they had to fight it out without the aid of airplanes.* ♦ *The Prime Minister resigns as Muslim factions battle it out.* -T/85.

fight off 1. repelir, rechaçar *John tried to hold Vicky's arms but she fought him off.* 2. reprimir, refrear *I had to fight off the urge to sleep.*

fight shy of afastar-se de, evitar *Glenn fought shy of the reporters by refusing to answer the telephone or the doorbell.*

pick a fight/quarrell procurar briga, entrar em conflito *When we're bored in a relationship, we pick fights ...* -WCG,12. ♦ *Mrs. Leslie was always picking a quarrell with her neighbors.*

show fight resistir, enfrentar, reagir *Most animals show fight when cornered or captured.*

throw a fight/game/race [gir] perder (jogo/corrida/luta etc.) deliberadamente (porsuborno, acordo etc.) *He threw the fight and was barred from fighting in New York State.* ♦ *If a jockey is caught throwing a race, he is suspended for at least a year.*

FIGHTING fighting mad [col] colérico, irado *By the time ... [he] showed up on Monday, they were fighting mad ...* -T/84.

FIGURE cut a (fine/sorry etc.) figure fazer (ótima/triste etc.) figura *He knew he cut a fine figure there on the platform with his open shirt collar ...* -HJC,338. ♦ *... she never realized what a ridiculous figure she cut.* -T/92.

figure in [col] acrescentar, incluir em uma soma ou cálculo *Try to figure in all the possible expenses we will be likely to have in our trip.*

figure of speech figura de linguagem *When I called him a "rat", I was just using a metaphor, one of the most common figures of speech.*

figure out [col] 1. apurar, averiguar, verificar, descobrir, calcular *When scientists try to figure out how life got started on earth, they are forced into many assumptions that they cannot prove.* -LJ,151. ♦ *Try to figure out how much we will have to pay.* 2. compreender, entender *I can't figure out what has happened to Baby Jane.*

figure on [col] 1. contar com, fiar-se em *You can always figure on Joan to help you.* 2. calcular, planejar, levar em consideração *I figured on getting Kerrigan to support our candidate.*

figure up calcular o total de, computar *Have you figured up how much I owe you?*

in round figures → **in round NUMBERS**

it/that figures [col] isso faz sentido, é lógico, é razoável, é de esperar *That figures. Blake would have to be a friend of the police to know that.*

FILE file away 1. arquivar *All the letters had been filed away.* 2. limar, desbastar com lima *The imprisoned men filed away at the bars on their windows.*

file for fazer petição, requerer, solicitar *Four computer firms have filed for protection from creditors this year ...* -T/87. ♦ *... she filed for divorce ...* -T/80.

file in//out entrar//sair (de) em fila *An endless procession of newsmen filed in and out of the conference room.*

on file arquivado (e disponível para qualquer referência) *Your application is on file for consideration when we have a vacancy in our chemical department.*

FILL eat/drink/get/have one's fill comer, beber, ter etc. (alguma coisa) até fartar-se *Did you get your fill of beer?* -BF,21. ♦ *Over the past week, Ray had had his fill of rumor and speculation.* -LA,23.

fill in 1. completar, preencher (formulário etc.); acrescentar detalhes, suprir o que está faltando *The teacher told the class to fill in the blanks with the missing words.* 2. substituir, fazer as vezes de, servir de substituto *She filled in for the teacher on Monday.*

fill (someone) in on [col] dar as informações mais recentes e necessárias (a alguém), atualizar, pôr (alguém) a par de *Fill me in on what really happened at the airport this morning.*

fill out 1. completar, preencher (formulário etc.) *... he filled out the application forms for U.S. citizenship in 1963 ...* -T/66. 2. engordar, ganhar corpo, adquirir peso; avolumar(-se) *She will fill out when she gets older.*

fill up encher totalmente; encher-se *Fill up the glass.* ♦ *The football stadium was filling up quickly.*

FIND find for julgar ou decidir a favor de *The judge found for the defendants.*

find it easy//difficult//hard conscientizar-se de que (algo) é fácil//difícil *Although exhausted each night, I found it difficult to sleep.* -FLF,8.

find it in oneself → **find it in one's HEART**

find oneself 1. dar consigo, ver-se, achar-se *The children suddenly found themselves on a strange, unfamiliar street.* 2. descobrir a sua vocação *Jeff found himself at last when he decided to study medicine.*

find out 1. descobrir, apurar, decifrar, ficar sabendo *Find out the reason why he lied to us.* ♦ *To find out the facts about appropriateness in American English usage, we sometimes consult grammar books.* -MJL,24. 2. desmascarar, apanhar *When Jennings was found out, he denied all the accusations.*

FINE-TUNE ajustar ao máximo, ajustar com precisão, tornar estável *Anyone who is convinced that he can fine-tune the economy doesn't know what he is talking about.*

FINGER **burn one's fingers; get one's fingers burned** meter-se em encrencas por ser curioso, intrometido etc.; sofrer um prejuízo por ser precipitado, imprudente etc. *One day he'll get his fingers burned playing in the stock market.*

cross one's fingers; keep one's fingers crossed cruzar os dedos (na expectativa de que seus planos se realizem, de que suas expectativas dêem certo), torcer para que o melhor se realize *They crossed their fingers as they watched the mighty Saturn rocket lift off from its launching pad.* ♦ *Keep your fingers crossed and hope for the best.*

have a finger (in the pie) ter um interesse, ter participação, estar metido *[He] ... had a finger in everything, from top-level staffing to deciding who should be invited to the ... [President's] parties.* -T/73. ♦ *Hollis has a finger in every lucrative pie in the city.*

lay a finger/hand on maltratar, bater, levantar um dedo ou a mão contra *If you lay a finger on that poor dog once more, I'll clobber you.* ♦ *[He told his stepfather] ... never to lay a hand on his mother again.* -T/92.

lay/put one's finger on indicar com precisão, localizar, achar, encontrar, definir com exatidão *Something is wrong with the electrical system in your radio but I can't put my finger on the exact defect.*

not lift/raise a finger/hand não fazer o mínimo esforço, a menor tentativa, não mover uma palha (para ajudar) *She didn't lift a finger to help me.* ♦ *Vic wouldn't lift a hand when we needed his help.*

put the finger on [gír] trair, acusar, delatar *Your pal has put the finger on you.*

slip through one's fingers 1. fugir, escapar *... the authorities allowed ... [the terrorist] and his comrades to slip through their fingers.* -T/78. ♦ *... the liberties they seek might easily slip through their fingers ...* -T/92. 2. desaparecer, esvair-se, dissipar-se, perder-se *The fortune that he had inherited slipped through his fingers in two years.*

snap one's fingers estalar os dedos *Norman loves me. All I have to do is snap my fingers and he'll come running.*

snap one's fingers at tratar com indiferença, não dar importância a *Don't snap your fingers at the dangers we may encounter on a trip to another planet.*

twist/turn someone around one's (little) finger conseguir (com habilidade) tudo o que se deseja (de outra pessoa), ter grande influência sobre, dominar *There's no man in the world you can't twist around your finger.* -MN,232.

work one's fingers to the bone trabalhar arduamente, mourejar *Leo's father worked his fingers to the bone to get extra money for his son's schooling.*

FINGER-POINTING imputação (às vezes desleal) de culpa *There is always too much finger-pointing when a big disaster occurs.*

FINGERTIPS **at one's fingertips** à mão, ao alcance de, disponível, pronto para ser utilizado *Cheryl has all the information she needs right at her fingertips.*

to one's/the fingertips totalmente, completamente *She was a lady to her fingertips.*
FINISH finish off 1. terminar, pôr fim a; concluir, rematar, completar *... TV ... did much to finish off the golden age of Hollywood ...* -T/65. ♦ *Finish off your drink.* 2. liquidar, matar, destruir *... the gunmen were about to finish off the girl ...* -T/72.
finish up 1. acabar, terminar, concluir *He hopes to finish up the painting next week.* 2. usar ou consumir completamente *Let's finish up the bottle of wine.*
finish with 1. terminar de usar, ocupar, trabalhar, falar com etc., não mais necessitar de *Have you finished with that tool?* ♦ *My crew of boat makers had finished with their task ...* -DM,37. 2. cortar relações com *Doug thought he had better finish with Millie.*
FINISHING finishing touch toque final, últimos retoques, acabamento *... the leaders returned to the conference room to put the finishing touch on their communiqué.* -T/86.
FIRE between two fires = between the DEVIL and the deep (blue) sea *Jim was caught between two fires and there was no escape for him.*
catch fire 1. pegar fogo, incendiar-se *The old building caught fire rather fast.* 2. despertar entusiasmo, provocar agitação, emoção *Their plan to incite the population against the dictator caught fire.*
draw fire provocar crítica, ser alvo de comentários etc. *The show started drawing fire even before it went into production.* -T/87.
fire away [col] começar a falar, dizer o que tem a dizer, fazer perguntas em rápida sucessão etc. *OK. Fire away! We will listen to you for no more than five minutes.*
fire off 1. desfechar rapidamente (perguntas, acusações etc.) *He fired off so many questions at the same time that he had me confused.* 2. escrever e enviar (carta etc.) às pressas ou movido por súbito impulso,

emoção etc. *Duke [i.e., John Wayne] ... was also good at firing off angry letters to friends, including Ronald Reagan.* -T/87.
fire up 1. entusiasmar, estimular, inflamar *He was fired up to begin his political campaign in the small towns.* 2. [col] irritar-se, exaltar-se *... she does fire up a little when she gets rattled ...* -WPI,43.
hang fire atrasar-se, demorar-se, custar a se realizar ou desenvolver-se, ficar pendente *The plan will have to hang fire until there are sufficient funds to carry it out well.*
hold (one's) fire fazer trégua, suspender as hostilidades *[Her] ... critics within the party are holding their fire during the election campaign.* -T/86.
miss fire fracassar, falhar, não produzir o resultado esperado *His pallid joke missed fire.* -DJ,12.
on fire 1. em fogo, em chamas *The house was on fire and people were running up and down the street looking for help.* 2. exaltado, emocionado, cheio de entusiasmo, de ardor *Sister Sarah was on fire with a mystical vision.*
open fire abrir fogo, começar a atirar *We ran for cover when the enemy opened fire.*
play with fire brincar com o perigo, arriscar-se *If you try to work for both the candidates, you're playing with fire.*
set fire to incendiar, atear fogo a *... the skyjackers set fire to ... [the plane].* -T/73.
set on fire 1. = **set FIRE to** *... lightning had set a part of the forest on fire.* -SJV,4. 2. exaltar, inflamar, excitar *The breathtaking potentialities of mechanization [introduced by the Industrial Revolution] set the minds of manufacturers and merchants on fire.* -HETB,20.
under fire 1. sofrendo ataque à bala, sob o fogo da metralha *Under fire he was a bold man of great ingenuity.* -MF,7. 2. sob crítica, sofrendo censura severa *... personalities in radio and television were coming under fire ...* -PV,194. ♦ *... the President*

is under heavy fire from the Democrats ... -T/84.
FIRST at first em princípio, de início *At first I couldn't understand him when he spoke to me.*
first and foremost primeiramente, antes de mais nada *Some critics have seen myth and metaphor in George Stevens' Shane, but let's not forget that it is first and foremost a western movie.* ♦ *First and foremost, we need not, we must not, become panicky.* -HGI,24.
first of all em primeiro lugar, antes de tudo *Architecture is not only an art, it is also a science, for first of all it is building, and as building it must be understood.* -WJ,4.
first off [col] primeiramente, antes de mais nada, imediatamente *First off, I want you to tell me everything that happened at the party last night.*
from the first desde o início *She had been warned against him from the first, and there were enough bad stories about him to condemn him completely.* -WPI,25.
FIRST-CLASS ótimo, excelente, de primeira classe *Steven Spielberg's E.T. The Extra-Terrestrial is first-class family entertainment.*
FIRSTHAND → at first HAND
FIRST-RATE excelente, ótimo, de primeira *[Henry James's] ... novels are first-rate contributions to the study of inhibitions.* -DDT,452. ♦ *a first-rate job*
FIRST-STRING 1. titular, efetivo *Cameron used to play on the first-string team.* 2. excelente, da maior importância *Lionel Trilling was certainly a first-string literary critic.*
FISH big//small fish pessoa importante, graúda; chefão//pessoa subordinada, de graduação inferior, sem importância *The FBI found out that Boettiger was the big fish in the spy ring.* ♦ *... two Communist agents described as "small fish".* -T/87.
drink like a fish [col] beber habitualmente, ter o vício da bebida, beber como um gambá *They say those two drink like a fish ...* -HWL,33.
fish for procurar, tentar apanhar ou alcançar *[He] ... fished in his pocket for another cigarette.* -AT,2. 2. tentar obter (por artifícios ou meios indiretos) *When Carla talks to you, beware. She's always fishing for information.*
fish out puxar, tirar *[He was] ... fishing out his papers ... [from] the pocket of his jacket ...* -TRL,9.
fish out of water pessoa fora de seu elemento *When he arrived in the Senate for his first day, he felt like a fish out of water.*
fish story [col] história exagerada, caso inverossímil *Cole told a fish story to cover the loss of the money that he had spent.*
have other fish to fry ter coisas mais importantes, prementes etc. a considerar *We tried to talk Costello into joining us but he seemed to have other fish to fry.*
queer fish [col] pessoa esquisita *Langley was a queer fish but had many interesting qualities.*
FIT by/in fits and starts de maneira irregular, intermitentemente, com entrepausas, por saltos *The work is progressing by fits and starts and will probably never be finished.* ♦ *Evolution may occur in sudden fits and starts ...* -T/81.
fit for 1. adequado, próprio para, digno de *This food is not fit for pigs.* 2. em boas condições físicas para, competente para, preparado para, capaz de *Do you suppose he is fit for the job?*
fit in/into adaptar-se (a), ajustar-se (a), enquadrar-se (em), encaixar-se (em) *Although he was good at his job, he didn't fit in because he lacked the social background and education of the rest of the executives.* ♦ *There is a very basic belief that man somehow fits into the universe ...* -BCS,37.
fit in with harmonizar-se com, estar de acordo com, afinar-se com *[He] ... went*

by rail to San Francisco on a vital mission which also fitted in with his plans for his own security. -BE,15.

fit out equipar, prover, suprir *We fitted out two trailers for our long trip in the Arizona Indian country.*

fit to be tied [col] extremamente zangado, colérico *When Harry realized he had been told a lie, he was fit to be tied.*

have/throw a fit/tantrum [col] enfurecer-se, encolerizar-se, ter um acesso de raiva *Bailey threw a fit when he saw that his wife had banged up his car.* ♦ *[She] ... threw a tantrum when ... [her secretary] asked for a raise ...* -T/69.

FIVE-AND-TEN; FIVE-AND-DIME loja que estoca ampla variedade de mercadorias baratas (originalmente vendidas a 5 ou 10 centavos de dólar) *[He] ... decided that the future was in discounting [i.e., discount stores] rather than in five-and-dimes.* -T/87. ♦ *She was working behind the counter at a five-and-ten ...* -AIM,94.

FIX artful fix [gir] jeito, jeitinho *For all their recurrent economic and political crises, the Brazilians are traditionally a gentle, urbane people who believe that any problem on earth can be solved by* jeito, *the artful fix.* -T/64.

fixed for suprido (do que é necessário) *Before we leave on our trip I want to find out how we are fixed for money.*

fix on/upon escolher, decidir-se por *Norman and Vicky have fixed on a date for the wedding.*

fix over reformar, renovar *Each spring the housewife likes to clean or fix over her living room in a different decor.*

fix up [col] 1. consertar, reparar, renovar *Joe, our best mechanic, will fix up your car in a few minutes.* 2. ajustar, pôr em ordem, resolver, solucionar *What's wrong with you is something any girl could fix up quick.* -HET,39. 3. dispor, fazer preparativos, providenciar, tomar medidas *All the arrangements for the wedding have been fixed up.* 4. suprir (aquilo que é necessário), fornecer, proporcionar (algo de que alguém necessita) *Horace can fix you up with any tool that you need.* 5. arranjar (parceiro do sexo oposto para uma pessoa) *Greg fixed his friend up with a lovely girl who works for his boss.* 6. curar, restaurar a saúde de *Dr. Mortimer fixed Rachel up in a short time.*

in a fix [col] em dificuldades, em apuros *Sue will be in a fix when her husband finds out she ran the car into a tree and ruined the front fender.*

quick fix [col] solução de emergência, quebra-galho *Why can't technology rescue the world from the mess that technology created? Isn't there a quick fix?* -T/92.

FIZZLE fizzle out [col] fracassar, falir, falhar, malograr, perder importância *... the "free university" movement ... has fizzled out.* -T/73. ♦ *The play fizzled out after a few weeks.*

FLAG flag (down) fazer sinal (a um veículo) para pará-lo *Mrs. Bennett flagged down a taxi near the Guggenheim Museum.* ♦ *... children would ... flag down passing vehicles, begging for food.* -T/80.

FLAG-WAVING alarde jactancioso ou sentimental de patriotismo, nacionalismo exagerado *... a land that had grown weary of flag-waving.* -T/73. ♦ *... flag-waving crowds shouted their approval.* -T/81.

FLAKE flake off [gir] dar o fora, ir-se *The cars began to flake off until none were left.*

flake out [gir] 1. sucumbir ao sono ou à exaustão *I find it difficult to flake out if the lights are on.* 2. fracassar *The show flaked out.*

FLAME burst into flames incendiar-se subitamente *There was an explosion in the old building and it burst into flames.*

go down in flames ser abatido, ser derrubado (aeronave); malograr-se, ser malsucedido *Baxter's plane went down in flames over enemy territory.* ♦ *He's not* *going to go down in flames for the activities of others.* -BC,326.

go up in flames incendiar-se, ser destruído pelo fogo ... *a family watches in horror as their house goes up in flames.* -T/87.

old flame [col] ex-namorado(a) *Everything is right in this World War II classic [Casablanca] ... with elusive nightclub owner Rick (Humphrey Bogart) finding old flame (Ingrid Bergman) ...* -ML,86.

FLARE flare up 1. rebentar em chamas, acender-se *The fire had died down but flared up with the sudden wind.* ⇒ **flare-up** súbita explosão ou intensificação de chamas, fulgor *There was a sudden flare-up of the smoldering fire.* 2. manifestar-se subitamente, irromper, surgir repentinamente ou intensificar-se *The fears that Mago had expressed flared up again ...* -DM,43. ⇒ **flare-up** manifestação súbita de cólera, violência, distúrbio, doença etc., explosão, intensificação *[She had] ... a painful flare-up of bursitis ...* -T/77. 3. [col] encolerizar-se *[He] ... flared up angrily.* -HJC,179.

FLASH flash in the pan [gir] 1. esforço ou tentativa promissora que termina em fracasso, sucesso efêmero, fogo de palha *[The] ... resounding success [of John Ford's movie* The Iron Horse, *in 1924] proved that the "big Western" was no mere flash in the pan.* -KA,121. 2. pessoa que inicia algo de maneira muito promissora mas logo fracassa ou causa decepção *He was a flash in the pan. One great picture and the rest were failures.*

flash point ponto de erupção de ira, violência etc. *The Middle East has more crisis flash points than any other place in the world.* -T/80.

in a flash em um momento, em uma fração de segundo *In a flash he understood how to solve the problem that had been bothering him all week.*

FLASHBACK cena ou seqüência de um fato ocorrido anteriormente que é intercalada na narrativa de obra de literatura ou de filme *Her new book has a series of brilliant flashbacks that add meaning to the story.* ♦ *The story of* The Man Who Shot Liberty Vallance *is told in a long flashback by [James] Stewart ...* -TH,115.

FLAT flat broke → (dead/flat/stone) **BROKE**

flat out 1. abruptamente, de supetão, à queima bucha, de maneira totalmente franca e direta, abertamente, sem rebuços, categoricamente *[They] ... say flat out what they think.* -T/85. ⇒ **flat out** total, completo, absoluto, categórico, inequívoco, franco e aberto *Kevin was a flat-out failure all his life.* ♦ *... flat-out contradictions ...* -T/87. ♦ *Women of flat-out sin.* -T/60. 2. à velocidade máxima, a todo vapor; com grande presteza, com a maior energia, com todo o esforço ou empenho *He had the car going flat out when the cops grabbed him.* ♦ *... people who go flat out for this particular President.* -T/78.

FLAT-FOOTED [col] 1. inepto, inábil, desajeitado, despreparado *... the U.S. diplomatic maneuvers looked a bit flat-footed ...* -T/87. v. **CATCH flat-footed** 2. firme, decidido, positivo, franco *a flat-footed denial* 3. de maneira direta, abruptamente, de supetão, categoricamente, com determinação *You can't just come out flat-footed and tell Joyce her mother is dead!*

FLEA a flea in one's ear repreensão severa, reprimenda mordaz, observação desfavorável *If he bothers me again, I'll send him away with a flea in his ear.*

FLESH flesh and blood ser humano; o corpo humano, a natureza humana *I'm only flesh and blood, you know. There's a limit to what I can do.* ⇒ **flesh-and-blood** real, de carne e osso *... a real flesh-and-blood person.* -WS,43.

flesh out 1. ampliar, aumentar, tornar mais cheio, mais extenso; acrescentar detalhes, dados, informações, substância etc.

... you flesh it [a story, subject etc.] out with examples, images, anecdotes, facts and characters. -AJ,12. 2. engordar, criar corpulência, encorpar *Mrs. Hughes began to flesh out when she aged.*
in the flesh em carne e osso, em pessoa *He shook hands with Harry Truman ... the first President he saw in the flesh.* -T/76.
make one's/someone's flesh creep apavorar, arrepiar, causar temor a *Ghost stories always made my flesh creep.* ♦ *A shriek of terror in the pitch-black night made Laura's flesh creep.*
one's own flesh and blood parente consangüíneo *Scaramouche didn't realize that the Marquis des Maynes was his own flesh and blood until after he had wounded him in a duel.*
press the flesh [gir] apertar a mão de alguém em cumprimento, trocar um aperto de mão *[He was] ... touring neighborhoods, pressing the flesh ... in a successful last-minute campaign ... for the job of mayor ...* -T/87.
FLIGHT flight of stairs/steps lanço de escada *Jerry went up two flights of stairs to his apartment.* ♦ *... Nellie came down the flight of steps from her room ...* -MWL,61.
put to flight pôr em fuga, afugentar *The thief was put to flight by the hungry, barking dogs.*
take (to) flight fugir *All the animals seemed to take flight when he went into the woods with his gun.*
FLING have a/one's fling [col] experimentar um período de diversões, prazeres sensuais, aventuras etc. geralmente breve e típico da juventude, que antecede uma vida mais responsável *You've had your fling and it's time to settle down.* -TM,84. 2. ter um caso amoroso *... he have a brief extramarital fling five years ago with a former secretary ...* -T/92.
have/take a fling at [col] fazer uma tentativa, experimentar (fazer algo) *Mel says he's willing to try anything, even have a fling at a new job.* ♦ *"Let me have a fling at it", Dick said when I showed him my broken radio.*
FLIP flip out [gir] perder o uso da razão, alucinar-se, pirar *A family man who "flipped out" is executed in Louisiana.* -T/87.
FLIRT flirt with entreter-se com, brincar com, considerar (idéia etc.) *When man destroys large numbers of insect species with mass spraying he is flirting with disaster.* -GET,10. ♦ *In Rome he ... flirted with the idea of becoming a painter ...* -SRE,34.
FLOODGATES open the floodgates abrir as comportas, dar vazão a algo que se encontrava reprimido ou sob controle (emoção, força destrutiva, idéias, mudanças violentas etc.) *Kierkegaard and Bergson opened the floodgates of existencialism in philosophy ...* -JRE,57.
FLOOR get/have the floor estar com a palavra, ter o direito de falar *Let me talk a while, you had the floor, you and George, now let me say something.* -WCN,148. ♦ *Western delegates [at the Geneva meeting] clamored to get the floor.* -T/60.
mop (up)/wipe the floor with [gir] derrotar fragorosamente; surrar, dar uma sova em *Reed wiped the floor with his opponent.* ♦ *Someone was always wiping the floor with Charlie Chaplin in his movies.*
take the floor tomar a palavra, começar a falar, dirigir-se a uma platéia *As soon as the Congressman from Massachusetts took the floor all talking and coughing ceased.*
FLOORWALKER funcionário de loja de departamentos que supervisiona vendas, orienta clientes etc., gerente de seção *Kerr was a floorwalker in one of the big department stores.*
FLOP flop down on deixar-se cair pesadamente (por cansaço) em (cadeira, sofá, etc.) *He flopped down on a couch ...* -BC,164.
take a flop levar um tombo *Ray was walking along smoothly with an arrogant

air when suddenly he took a flop and caused everyone to laugh.

FLOTSAM flotsam and jetsam 1. destroços, restos, detritos, lixo etc. flutuando no mar ou levados à praia pela maré *Quite a lot of flotsam and jetsam had been washed ashore.* 2. pessoas sem teto, sem trabalho que perambulam pela vida, párias, refugos da sociedade *[The Wapshot Chronicle, a novel by John Cheever, depicts] ... the richly detailed human flotsam and jetsam of a tidewater town ... -T/64.*

FLOW flow in vir, chegar, afluir em grande número ou volume *Mrs. Langdon often helps her husband with the sometimes amazing volume of mail which flows in from all over the country.*

FLOWER flower child indivíduo *hippie [She] ... converses with a bunch of flower children who teach her the power of Love. -T/69.*

flower power o amor e a não-violência como ideais de vida segundo a filosofia dos *hippies San Francisco's Haight-Ashbury, the communal temple of flower power, became a seedy slum of strung-out addicts. -T/86.*

in flower em flor, florido *Our roses are now in flower.*

FLUNK flunk out [col] ser reprovado em colégio ou faculdade e ter de deixar a escola *[He] ... flunked out of Oxford and worked in a variety of jobs ... -T/84.*

FLY drop/die like flies morrer às dúzias, morrer em grandes números *[I'm 82 years old.] How many d'ye know can say the same? ... Not many ... They're droppin' like flies around me but I feel grand. -OE,7.*

fly at atacar violentamente *The enraged animal flew at her.*

fly back regressar de avião *Mr. Collins has flown back to the States.*

fly in viajar, ir, vir de avião *[She] ... flies in from Hollywood once a month. -WSM,30.*

fly in the ointment pessoa ou coisa desagradável, incômoda, importuna etc. que estraga uma situação feliz, uma circunstância agradável etc. *That was the fly in the ointment, that husband of hers. -LRT,65.*

on the fly [col] em movimento, em atividade, ocupado *Grant is always so busy that he eats his meals on the fly.*

there are no flies on (someone) [col] (fulano) não é tolo, (ele) sabe das coisas, é inteligente, sagaz etc. *There are no flies on Luke, you can be sure.*

FLY-BY-NIGHT 1. indivíduo que prega calotes, que não cumpre seus compromissos comerciais, que não é confiável, vigarista; arapuca, estabelecimento comercial que comete fraudes e desaparece da noite para o dia *The fly-by-night opens a small office, gets business and is gone in a few days with all your money.* 2. suspeito, escuso, desonesto; instável, irrresponsável, indigno de confiança *It was a fly-by-night business and many people were cheated.*

FOB fob off 1. impingir, empurrar, fazer passar (coisa falsa por legítima); fazer-se passar por *The crooks tried to fob off the paintings as genuine works by Rubens.* ♦ *[John Lennon] ... might travel incognito for a change, or fob himself off as Peter Sellers. -T/66.* 2. afastar, pôr de lado, excluir *Don't try to fob me off with excuses. Tell me the truth.*

FOG in a fog perplexo, aturdido, confuso *... he's in a fog ... -T/81.* ♦ *[He is] ... with his mind in a fog. -HE,231.*

FOGGY not have the foggiest (idea) → **not have the faintest IDEA**

FOGY old fogy/fogey pessoa de idéias antiquadas, retrógradas, indivíduo conservador; caturra, fóssil *[The show] ... was made for teenagers, not old fogies... -T/66.* ♦ *... Dan was acting like a typical father, or as Cindy had chided, "a conservative old fogy". -HJD,7.*

FOLD fold up 1. dobrar *He spent Saturday folding up bandages for the Red Cross.* 2.

curvar-se, dobrar-se *When the man hit him he folded up and dropped to the floor.* 3. [col] falir, quebrar, fracassar *I know of one bank that may fold up ...* -BF,16.

FOLKS [col] 1. membros da família *"These are my folks", he said as he introduced me to his family.* 2. pessoas *The young folks like to sing and dance at family parties.*

FOLLOW as follows como segue, o(s) seguinte(s) *The 20th century American novelists on the required reading list are as follows: F. Scott Fitzgerald, Ernest Hemingway, William Faulkner, John Steinbeck, Sinclair Lewis and Thomas Wolfe.*

follow out 1. executar, levar a cabo *Ross always makes wonderful plans on paper but he never follows them out.* 2. levar até o fim, seguir, cumprir, obedecer a (instruções, planos etc.) *... follow out our instructions to the letter ...* -LMC,24.

follow through 1. continuar o movimento (da jogada no tênis, golfe etc.) *In the golf swing, it is necessary to follow through after you hit the ball.* 2. persistir em uma atividade, ação etc. e levá-la a término, completar *... the government ... produces grand designs for family planning but fails to follow through.* -T/92. ⇒ **follow-through** o ato de levar a cabo (projeto, plano etc.), execução, efetuação *His welfare reforms ... while well conceived, have suffered from a lack of follow-through.* -T/92.

follow up 1. seguir de perto e persistentemente, acompanhar diligentemente, ir no encalço de, buscar, investigar atentamente *The case histories of the children to whom the vaccines had been given, were followed up for ten years.* ⇒ **follow-up** a. acompanhamento (de paciente, tratamento etc.) *She is recovering from a stroke and needs intensive follow-up.* b. que vem depois, que complementa, que secunda (contato, visita, oferta, proposta etc.), subseqüente, consecutivo, adicional, que vai em aditamento *... recovering [drug] addicts need follow-up care and counseling ...* -T/86. 2. continuar (algo já iniciado, um processo já começado) prosseguir, levar avante *The first shot is followed up by a series of reaction tests.* ⇒ **follow-up** seqüência, continuação, seguimento, aditamento *[The author is going] ... to write a follow-up to his super best-seller.* -T/87. 3. aumentar a eficiência (de algo, ação etc.) tomando novas providências; reforçar, secundar *He followed up his initial letter with a personal visit to his prospective client.* ⇒ **follow-up** carta, circular etc. *In addition to his first letter, he wrote a follow-up three days later.*

FOND be fond of ter afeição, carinho por, gostar muito de *Maurer had become more than fond of Monique.* ♦ *We were very fond of singing.* -MJM,42.

FOOD food for thought estímulo para reflexão, algo que faz pensar *The subject of magic and medicine can ... provide us with much food for thought.* -NJ,107.

FOOL act/play the fool agir como bufão, bancar o bobo, fazer palhaçadas *Stop acting the fool and be serious for a while.* ♦ *He played the fool until his father died, then suddenly assumed control of the business in a creditable manner.*

a fool and his money are soon parted um tolo logo esbanja ou perde seu dinheiro *A fool and his money are soon parted, and I don't want you to be a fool.* -DJ,58.

fool around [col] 1. matar o tempo, ficar à toa, fazer hora, ocupar-se com futilidades *... he was just fooling around to kill time ...* -HG,58. 2. ocupar-se (com), mexer, bulir, brincar (com) *Chuck likes to fool around with old clocks.* ♦ *You'll be wise not to fool around with drugs.* 3. divertir-se, namorar para passar tempo, tratar displicentemente *Mike fools around with many girls.*

fool away [col] desperdiçar *We fooled away the time watching the ships come into the harbor.*

fool's paradise estado de felicidade ilusória, falsas esperanças, crenças etc. *Some*

people seem to live in a fool's paradise.
fool with [col] mexer com, brincar com, bulir em *Don't fool with the TV.* ♦ *Stop fooling with that shotgun.*
make a fool of fazer (alguém) de bobo *Cole made a fool of the boss at the party.* ♦ *... I could make a big fool of myself if the truth came out.* -RE,85.
be no/nobody's fool não ser bobo, ser sagaz, hábil *Fowler was nobody's fool as his adversaries soon found out.*
no fool like an old fool quanto mais velho o tolo, maiores as tolices que comete *Lloyd was 64 when he married Jenny, who was only 22. The end of the story was sad but predictable. There's no fool like an old fool.*
play the fool → **act the FOOL**
FOOLPROOF à prova de erro ou de acidente, perfeitamente seguro, infalível *The plan seemed foolproof and had the full support of every man who was to participate.* -RE,83. ♦ *a foolproof system*
FOOT at the foot of ao pé de, na parte mais baixa de, no sopé de (colina, montanha) *Ella was standing at the foot of the stairs.* ♦ *The town nestles at the foot of a steep hill.*
carry/sweep (someone) off his/her/their feet empolgar, arrebatar, deslumbrar (alguém) *He met her at a dance in Boston and he started right in to sweep her off her feet.* -CT,11.
cold feet [col] medo, insegurança, falta de coragem *[He] ... got cold feet and refused to come out publicly on the side of the rebels.* -T/66.
come/get/jump to one's feet levantar-se, ficar em pé *Calder pushed back his chair and came to his feet.* ♦ *... he got to his feet and moved groggily toward the door.* -EW,64.
dead on one's feet → **out on one's FEET**
drag one's feet [gir] agir com deliberada lentidão, demorar-se propositadamente, recusar-se a cooperar *... the FDA [Food and Drug Administration] is dragging its feet on approval of potentially more effective AIDS drugs.* -T/87.
feet of clay falha de caráter, imperfeição, fraqueza humana *The boys were disappointed when they found out that their hero had feet of clay.*
foot in the door primeiro passo (em direção a um objetivo), iniciação, introdução, primeira etapa, ponto de partida, abertura *... sometimes [the religious organization] ... hand out religious calendars and books to get a foot in the door.* -T/87.
get off on the wrong foot [col] iniciar mal um relacionamento, entrar com o pé esquerdo *He didn't like the way he and the beautiful Cushman girl had got off on the wrong foot.* -HWW,48.
get to one's feet → **come to one's FEET**
have one foot in the grave estar com um pé na cova, entre a vida e a morte *The old man had one foot in the grave and the other on a banana peel.*
have/keep one's/both feet on the ground ser objetivo, realista, prático, ter os pés fincados na terra *Mr. Fuller will know what to do because he has both feet on the ground.*
have two left feet ser desajeitado, desastrado, inábil *She wanted to be a famous dancer but unfortunately she had two left feet.* ♦ *A big dumb musclebound Swede with two left feet.* -UL,4.
in one's stocking(ed) feet de meias (calçadas), mas sem sapatos *I asked him to take off his shoes and walk in his stockinged feet.* -RQ,115. *[He] ... slowly paced the corridor in his stocking feet ...* -T/87.
jump to one's feet → **come to one's FEET**
keep one's feet não cair, permanecer em pé, manter o equilíbrio *Anne found it difficult to keep her feet on the slippery sidewalk.*
land on one's/both feet sair-se bem de uma situação perigosa, empreendimento

arriscado, aventura etc. *It was a risky business undertaking, but Hughes managed to land on his feet and have a big profit.*
on foot 1. a pé ... *Kelly and his men were on foot. They would find it hard to escape from the town without ... [horses].* -HJ,141. 2. em andamento, em curso, em planejamento, em movimento, em atividade *Dr. Heywood has a new project on foot.*
on one's feet 1. em pé, andando *He was weak and very uncertain, but he was on his feet.* -ST,23. 2. com a saúde restaurada, restabelecido, são *After a brief illness, Angie is now back on her feet.* 3. reconstruído, restaurado, em seu estado original, em bom estado ... *I'm here to put this company back on its feet ...* -GM,282.
out/dead on one's feet [col] cansadíssimo, exausto *Lucy was out on her feet by the time we got back to the hotel.*
put one's best foot forward [col] fazer o melhor possível, dar o máximo de si, aplicar-se diligentemente *Always put your best foot forward when applying for a job.*
put one's foot down [col] opor-se firmemente, dizer não *Leonard's wife wanted to move into a bigger house but he put his foot down and that was that.*
put one's foot in(to) it/one's mouth [col] cometer uma gafe, dar mancada, dizer a coisa errada, dizer o que não deve *Every time she opens her mouth she puts her foot into it.* ♦ *Jack's always putting his foot in his mouth.*
set foot pôr os pés, ir, entrar, visitar *Don't ever set foot in this house without first telling me ...* -WR, 60. ♦ *According to history books, Europeans first set foot on American soil in the 15th century.*
set on foot começar, dar início *The election set on foot all types of false, malicious stories about both candidates.*
shoot oneself in the foot fazer ou dizer algo que cause problema a si, prejudicar-se *He shot himself in the foot when he admitted that he was an atheist.*
six feet under [gír] sete palmos debaixo da terra, morto e sepultado *Do you want your wife and kids to find you six feet under because of your wallet?* -T/87.
stand on one's own (two) feet ser capaz de cuidar de si mesmo, ser independente *[He was] ... able to stand on his own two feet ...* -BH,5.
sweep someone off his feet → **carry/ sweep someone off his FEET**
think on one's feet pensar depressa, ter grande agilidade mental, saber o que fazer, como agir, ter jogo de cintura *He will succeed as Secretary of State because he has, among other things, an unusual ability to think on his feet.*
vote with one's feet deixar um lugar (país, assembléia, reunião etc.) quando não se concorda com o que está sendo votado, proposto etc. *Many of those present voted with their feet and the meeting soon ended.*

FOOTING **on a footing with** em pé de igualdade com ... *in ability, energy and commitment, male and female politicians meet on an equal footing.* -T/84.

FOOTLOOSE **footloose and fancy-free** livre, desembaraçado, independente, livre de qualquer responsabilidade, livre e desimpedido *Norman had been footloose and fancy-free all his life and marriage was the last thing on his mind.*

FOOTSTEPS **follow in someone's footsteps** seguir os passos, o exemplo de *In La Strada ... [Federico Fellini] followed in Chaplin's footsteps but couldn't quite fill the little fellow's shoes.* -T/63.

FOR **for all (that)** a despeito de, apesar de, não obstante *In his best films [John] Wayne, for all the machismo he displayed, only rarely played a loner – a scout or gun fighter.* -T/79. ♦ *He may have his shortcomings, but for all that, he's the most suitable man for this job.*

FORCE in force 1. em grande número *When the students came back in force, they found 20,000 police from all over Rio at the ready.* -LA,151. 2. em vigência, válido, ativo ... *the new regulations were in force* ... -T/88.

FORE to the fore em proeminência, em evidência, na ordem do dia, em primeiro plano *A few pertinent questions have been brought to the fore.* ♦ *Old, unsolved problems are now coming to the fore and are demanding solution.*

FOREFRONT the forefront of a vanguarda de, a frente de *[Saul] Bellow is at the very forefront of American writing today.* -T/68. ♦ *Canadians ... have been in the forefront of the global struggle to protect the environment ...* -T/91.

FOREIGN-BORN nascido em outro país, estrangeiro ... *a foreign-born Jew with a well-deserved reputation as a radical advocate of liberal causes.* -T/62. v. **NATIVE-born**

FOREST not see the forest/wood(s) for the trees; unable to see the forest/woods for the trees concentrar-se em pequenos detalhes e não ver o conjunto, a totalidade; criticar pequenas coisas e não perceber o que é importante *The danger of scholarship is always that, in extreme specialization, it may be unable to see the forest for the trees.* -WAW,42.

FOREVER forever and ever para sempre *Dan said he'd love Marcia forever and ever.*

FORGET forget oneself comportar-se de maneira inconveniente, perder a cabeça, descontrolar-se *Erica forgot herself and slapped the woman who had called her a liar.*

FORGIVE forgive and forget perdoar e esquecer, não guardar ressentimentos, reconciliar-se *Sam and Joe had quarreled bitterly but both men were now prepared to forgive and forget.*

FORK fork out/over/up [col] pagar; entregar, passar às mãos de outrem (freqüentemente a contragosto) *I always complain when I have to fork out money for taxes.* ♦ *The thug made me fork over all my valuables.* ♦ *Carl had to fork up ten dollars for parking in a restricted area.*

FORM good//bad form boa//má conduta relativamente às convenções sociais, boas maneiras//falta de boas maneiras *It was good form among the villagers to offer refreshment. It was bad form to accept.* -AI,18.

(run) true to form (agir) consoante as expectativas, como era de esperar, (ser) consistente com a experiência anterior etc. *His design for a new Tokyo city government complex seems a remarkable departure. True to form, it will be big ... and orderly* ... -T/87.

FORT hold the fort 1. não ceder terreno, manter-se firme *Stan held the fort in spite of strong opposition from his family and in the end he proved to be right.* 2. [col] encarregar-se de, assumir a responsabilidade, tomar conta de (lugar etc.) na ausência de outrem, manter (algo) em funcionamento *Take the rest of the day off ... I'll hold the fort.* -TR,20. ♦ *Hold the fort while I go out and get the latest newspapers.*

FORTUNE read/tell someone's fortune ler a sorte de, prever o futuro de *If we could read our own fortune, we would not do many of the foolish things that are often a pleasure.*

FOUL foul up [col] estragar, arruinar, tornar confuso, desorganizar, desordenar, bagunçar *Don't get things fouled up around here.* -RL,17. ♦ *Switchboard operators, unfamiliar with the personnel, fouled up phone calls.* -T/66. ⇒ **foul-up** erro, confusão, embrulhada, mancada *Because of a postal foul-up, only 50 or so invitations were delivered.* -T/92.

FOUL-MOUTHED boca-suja, desbocado, que usa linguagem obscena *The husband ... is a foul-mouthed, beer-bellied, wife-belting brute.* -T/60.

FOUR on all fours 1. de gatinhas, de quatro, sobre as mãos e os joelhos *Even when they have learned to walk, many children prefer to go on all fours.* 2. coincidente, idêntico, que corresponde exatamente *Your assessment of the crisis is on all fours with mine.*

FOUR-LETTER referente ou relativo a palavra obscena ... *the poorly educated individual may have no sexual vocabulary beyond the four-letter English vernacular.* -KAC,61. v. **four-letter WORD**

FOX crazy as/like a fox [col] muito inteligente, sagaz, astuto *People who knew him well knew that he was as crazy as a fox.*

FRAME frame of mind disposição de ânimo, estado de espírito, humor ... *one aspect of the way he was received [in Moscow] reveals a great deal about Soviet bureaucracy and the Russian frame of mind.* -T/67.

frame of reference conjunto de conceitos (princípios, idéias, fatos, conhecimentos, experiências, circunstâncias, padrões etc.) que servem de base à compreensão ou à abordagem de algo *Fletcher's limited frame of reference prevents him from fully understanding the problem.*

FRAME-UP [col] falsa acusação, conspiração, trama, armação ... *I had reflected sufficiently to determine not to chance another frame-up.* -KRI,610.

FRAUGHT fraught with repleto de, cheio de, carregado de *Lee's mission was fraught with great danger.*

FREAK freak out [gír] 1. perder o contato com a realidade, experimentar as reações provocadas pelo uso das drogas alucinógenas *Some workers get so freaked out on drugs that they become a menace to everyone around them.* -T/86. ♦ ... *counterculture youths of the '60s proudly called themselves "freaks" and spent a good deal of their time "freaking out".* -T/78. 2. perder o controle, ficar sob intensa emoção ou arrebatamento, ficar agitado, agir anormalmente, pirar ... *she ... really freaked out.* -HS,368.

FREE for free [col] de graça, grátis; gratuitamente *Are these samples for free?* ♦ *I got this book for free.*

free and easy informal, descontraído, incerimonioso, despreocupado, liberal, generoso *Politicians are often free and easy with government money.*

FREE-FOR-ALL briga, rolo, pancadaria generalizada; competição aberta a qualquer pessoa *The demonstration quickly turned into a free-for-all with the police.*

FREEWHEELING [col] que age ou se comporta quase sem responsabilidade ou restrições, sem dar muita atenção a regras, atitudes, formalidades etc.; irresponsável, despreocupado, desinibido, não-reprimido *The Pink Panther is a freewheeling comic farce in which Peter Sellers plays a clumsy, blundering French police inspector.* ♦ ... *his freewheeling practices as a private banker.* -T/84. ♦ ... *the freewheeling anarchy of New York street life ...* -T/80.

FREEZE deep freeze 1. suspensão de atividades, negociações, acordo etc. *The plans were put in deep freeze until a more opportune time.* ♦ ... *the deep freeze between Washington and Moscow ...* -T/84. 2. congelamento, estado jacente ... *a promise for possible life [for a dead person] after years of deep-freeze.* -KR,16.

freeze out [col] eliminar por meio de concorrência, excluir, expulsar *[They] ... kept threatening to freeze out their old partners ...* -T/63.

freeze over cobrir(-se) de gelo, congelar(-se), congelar a/na superfície *In the winter the lake freezes over.*

put a/the freeze on/to [col] pôr término a; refrear, restringir ... *many of the President's critics favored putting a freeze on farm-commodity prices ...* -T/73.

FRENCH pardon my French [col] com perdão da (má) palavra, desculpe minha linguagem chula ou imprópria *Where's that goddamned – er – pardon my French, ma'am.*

FRESH   fresh from/off; fresh out of recém-chegado de, recém-saído de, recém-vindo de *She is fresh from a convent and very naive.* ♦ *Director Billy Wilder fresh off the boat from Europe and without a bean in his pocket, picked up his first salary check in Hollywood by hiring out as a stunt man ...* -T/60.

fresh out of 1. sem, privado de, desprovido de, com falta de (algo que terminou há pouco) *I'm fresh out of cigarettes.* 2. = **FRESH from** *[He] ... was a second lieutenant fresh out of West Point.* -CHT,11.

FRESHEN   freshen up lavar-se ou banhar-se e trocar de roupa (especialmente após trabalho, viagem etc.) *I came home at six, freshened up and went out again at seven-thirty.*

FRET   fret and fume bufar de raiva e impaciência *Because he could not do as he wished, he would fret and fume for hours.*

FRIDAY   Good Friday Sexta-feira Santa *Good Friday, the Friday before Easter, commemorates the Crucifixion of Jesus Christ.*

FRIEND   be/become/make friends with fazer amizade com, ser/tornar-se amigo de *He wanted to be friends with me.* ♦ *I have become good friends with him.* ♦ *It's not difficult to make friends with Brazilians.*

bosom friend amigo do peito *We played the piano and sang and danced, and everyone became bosom friends.* -CBC,3.

fair-weather friend amigo só nas horas felizes, amigo que nos abandona na adversidade *Leo turned out to be a fair-weather friend.*

friend at/in court pessoa influente, em posição de auxiliar ou apoiar alguém *[America's European allies] ... had a friend in court in Alexander Haig, the hard-charging Secretary of State who had been NATO commander in the Ford and Carter Administrations.* -T/87.

friend in need amigo em uma necessidade, amigo na adversidade, amigo leal *The saying goes: "A friend in need is a friend indeed". That is, a true friend will stand by you when you need him.*

make friends with → **be FRIENDS with**

FRIGHTEN   frighten into compelir pelo medo, intimidar *They tried to frighten her into submission.*

FRINGE   fringe benefit benefício extra oferecido a empregado (seguro, assistência médico-social etc.); qualquer vantagem adicional *... the university is replacing full-time workers with part-timers to avoid paying fringe benefits.* -T/77.

FRITTER   fritter away desperdiçar, dissipar, esbanjar, torrar *All the reserves in the Treasury have been frittered away by mismanagement.* ♦ *[They] ... frittered away fortunes ...* -T/63.

FRITZ   on the fritz → **on the BLINK**

FROG   frog in the throat rouquidão produzida por irritação na garganta, pigarro *... a clean-cut fellow with a frog in his throat.* -T/63.

FRONT   front for [col] atuar como testa-de-ferro de *He passes for a respectable businessman but he actually fronts for criminal activities.*

front man testa-de-ferro *Maybe I was just playing the front man to a big cover-up.* -RE,85.

out front em posição de liderança, à frente de todos *[He is] ... the man [President] Carter wants to be out front as articulator of American foreign policy.* -T/78.

put up a front [col] aparentar, mostrar na aparência (caráter, sentimentos, atitude, comportamento, imagem, posição social, riqueza, importância, porte etc., geralmente simulado ou estudado) *... American diplomats put up a good front about their feelings toward him ...* -T/78. ♦ *You can always be sure that Raquel Welch and Dolly Parton will never put up a false front.*

up front 1. na frente, na parte dianteira *We got into the car and Frank sat up front with the driver.* 2. [col] adiantadamente, antecipadamente, previamente ... *he's not required to pay cash up front.* -T/91. v. **UP-front**

FRONT-PAGE 1. de primeira página (de jornal), que vale a pena noticiar, importante, sensacional (notícia) ... *a front-page story* ... -T/87. ♦ *front-page headlines* ♦ *The scandal made front-page news.* 2. imprimir (notícia) na primeira página (de jornal) ... *Detroit papers front-paged the shocking report that he had gotten married* ... -T/66.

FROWN frown on/upon desaprovar, não ver com bons olhos *Most colleges officially frown on student sex on campus* ... -T/76.

FRUIT bear fruit dar resultados ... *his labors will bear fruit and you will learn the true story of his heroism and courage.* -T/92.

fruit salad [col] fitas de campanha, condecorações que representam medalhas *Soldiers often referred to the small bar-shaped ribbons that represented medal awards as fruit salad.*

FRY small fry [col] 1. crianças, criançada *There were two swimming pools. The pool for the small fry was beautiful and safe.* 2. pessoas sem importância, arraia miúda; coisas insignificantes ... *the spy couple who escaped to East Germany last week were small fry.* -T/85. ⇒ **small-fry** sem importância, insignificante ... *small-fry mobsters.* -T/78.

FUDDY-DUDDY [gír] indivíduo antiquado, conservador *She's no old fuddy-duddy like the other mothers. She wears turtlenecks and ski pants just like us.* -JE,152.

FUEL add fuel to the fire/flames jogar lenha na fogueira *Things are bad enough already. Let's not add fuel to the fire.*

FULL full well plenamente, muito bem *[He] ... knew full well what he was doing.* -T/87.

in full 1. integralmente, totalmente *My debt has been paid in full.* 2. por extenso, sem abreviar *Write your name in full.*

to the full ao máximo *Those poor people have been exploited to the full.* ♦ *Mr. Rogers was willing to cooperate to the full in the production of the film.*

FULL-BLOODED de raça pura, não-mestiço, autêntico *Ira Hamilton Hayes was one of the marines who helped raise the American flag on Iwo Jima and he was a full-blooded Pima Indian.*

FULL-BLOWN 1. completamente desabrochado *A full-blown cactus flower is truly a lovely sight.* 2. maduro, completamente desenvolvido ou formado *The Bolshevik and Nazi revolutions are ... full-blown nationalist movements.* -HETB,27.

FULL-BODIED de sabor rico e forte, de ótima qualidade, encorpado (vinho) *a full-bodied French wine*

FULL-FLEDGED maduro, pleno, total, completo, completamente desenvolvido ou plenamente habilitado *a full-fledged pilot* ♦ ... *a full-fledged battle* ... -T/86. ♦ *[She was] ... not merely a starlet but a full-fledged star* ... -BM,89.

FULL-LENGTH → **at full LENGTH**

FULL-SCALE amplo, pleno, total, completo, global, ilimitado, absoluto ... *the [German] generals couldn't make up their minds whether or not a full-scale assault was being aimed at the Normandy coast.* -SLS,275. ♦ *[President Ronald] ... Reagan holds a full-scale news conference.* -T/87.

FULL-SIZE de tamanho natural ... *a full-size replica of a 9th century Viking ship* ... -T/92.

FULL-TIME → **full TIME**

FUME in a fume com raiva, irritado *She was in a fume when her husband refused to take her to the party.*

FUN for/in fun de/por brincadeira *The practical joke was done for fun, but it had tragic results.* ♦ *I only said it in fun, there's no need to be cross with me.*

for the fun of it = **for FUN** *[They] ... don't write letters like this one just for the fun of it.* -SEB,147.

fun and games [col] 1. diversão, divertimento, entretenimento, prazer, brincadeira; coisa divertida ou engraçada, experiência agradável, festa etc. *The nation this week [January,1981] is mesmerized by the fun and games of the Inauguration, but for Ronald Reagan it is obvious the serious work of being President has already begun.* -T/81. 2. carícias, beijos e abraços como atividade preliminar ao ato sexual; o próprio ato sexual *[Robin Hood] ... was simply an outlaw who had deserted his lawful wife for fun and games in the greenwood with Marian.* -T/63.

have fun divertir-se *We had a lot of fun at the party.*

make fun of zombar de, caçoar de, ridicularizar *... no one made fun of the husky boy, who got into fights easily.* -T/78.

poke fun at = **make FUN of** *... some of [Bernard] Shaw's plays were permitted to be performed in Nazi Germany – perhaps because he poked fun at Englishmen ...* -SWLR,335.

FUNERAL it's not my funeral; that's/it's your funeral [gir] (isso) não me diz respeito, não é de minha conta, não é meu problema, você é quem vai se dar mal, azar seu *Have it your way, kid. It's your funeral.* -JJF,16.

FUNNIES the funnies [col] (histórias em) quadrinhos *Most students, and most of the rest of us too, seem not to read the morning paper much beyond the sports pages and the funnies.* -JW,7.

FUR make the fur fly armar barulho, causar encrenca *Your wife will make the fur fly if she finds out that you went to a party last night.*

FUSE blow a fuse/gasket [gir] perder a calma, zangar-se *Clint blew a fuse when he found out that his money had been stolen.* ♦ *[He] ... will blow a gasket when he hears this.* -T/63.

have a short fuse [col] irritar-se facilmente, ter pavio curto *People have a short fuse these days. There's a lot of aggression and hostility.* -T/80. ⇒ **short-fused** facilmente irritável *He was always known as a short-fused basketball player.*

FUSS kick up a fuss [col] provocar distúrbio, armar barulho, protestar com veemência *He kicks up a fuss when his lunch does not arrive on time.*

make a fuss 1. queixar-se, protestar com veemência *He will make a fuss if he is served cold soup in a restaurant.* 2. dar excessiva atenção (a), dar demasiada importância (a) *... she couldn't understand why anyone made a fuss about housekeeping ...* -SEB,31.

FUTURE future shock estresse, angústia, tensão, desorientação etc. experimentados pelos indivíduos que não conseguem adaptar-se às mudanças sociais e tecnológicas bruscas e profundas *... for many people, the pace of change is simply too fast, resulting in what has been termed "future shock".* -CJ,3.

in future de agora em diante, para o futuro *In future, I hope you will be more cautious about spending money.*

GAFF **stand the gaff** [gír] agüentar o rojão, agüentar a mão, suportar maus-tratos, situação aflitiva, adversidade, provação etc. *With luck, his plan was going to work. Feretti's driver couldn't stand the gaff.* -SF,18. ♦ *If you can't stand the gaff you won't succeed in politics.*

GAIN **gain on** aproximar-se de, ganhar terreno sobre *His pursuers were gaining on him.*

GALL **have the gall to** → **have the CRUST to**

GALLERY **play to the gallery** [col] exibir-se, impressionar a platéia *Roy is a good athlete but not a team player because he likes to play to the gallery.*

GALLOWS **gallows humor** humor que utiliza cinismo, morbidez etc. diante de sinistros, tragédias, calamidades ou circunstâncias assustadoras em que haja perigo de vida *There were funny parts always and she liked them and also what the Germans call gallows-humor stories.* -HEM,24.

GAMBLE **gamble away** esbanjar, perder no jogo *Arthur gambled away all the fortune his father had left him.*

GAME **ahead of the game** [col] em posição de superioridade, em vantagem, na liderança, triunfante *When Greg opened his store he was already ahead of the game because his father was able to give him merchandise below cost.*

beat someone at his own game superar, sobrepujar, derrotar, alguém em alguma atividade, habilidade etc. em que este se distingue *[He] ... had set out to beat his persecutors at their own game.* -T/63. ♦ *Do you really believe you can beat Langdon at his own game?*

be game topar (o que seja proposto), estar disposto, estar pronto, preparado (para um desafio etc.) *I'm game to try anything with you ...* -MJA, 988.

big game caça grossa (os grandes animais – leões, tigres, elefantes etc. – caçados por esporte) *In his last years ... [he] continued to hunt big game in Africa ...* -T/73. ⇒ **big-game** relativo à caça grossa, de caça grossa *He traveled widely and was an enthusiastic big-game hunter.* -T/73.

early//late in the game no início//à determinada altura, já próximo ao fim (de uma atividade, iniciativa, empreendimento, lida, tarefa, luta, jogo etc.) *... just remember this, and remember that I said it very early in the game ...* -WH,173. ♦ *It was pretty good advice but it came a little late in the game.* -HWW,6.

fair game caça lícita, permitida por lei; qualquer pessoa, assunto, tema etc. que seja objeto legítimo de ataque, crítica etc. *... any subjects were fair game ...* -T/72. ♦ *... oil installations [in the Iran-Iraq war] became fair game ...* -T/80.

the game is not worth the candle o resultado não vale a pena, não compensa o trabalho que dá *Getting ... Helen [to grant him her sexual favors] ... was going to be a long, hard process, and he was not at all sure that the game was going to be worth the candle ...* -MG,433.

the game is up é o fim, acabou-se tudo, não há mais esperança de êxito *After we [American troops] cross the Rhine, ... a flood of men and arms pours over Germany. Even the most fanatic Nazis must now see that the game is up ...* -MAT,362.

make game of zombar de, caçoar de *The bigger kids at school were always making game of him.*

off one's game fora de forma, desempenhando mal uma atividade esportiva, jogo etc. *I'm off my game today.*

play games engodar, levar no bico, fingir, embalar com promessas, esconder a verdade, agir de má-fé *Look, Dean, don't play games with me. Tell me the truth.*

play the game [col] agir de acordo com as regras, comportar-se com lisura *I am not interested in politics. But if it serves my business interest, I'll play the game.*

someone's (little) game propósito, intenção, objetivo, artimanha *... I don't know what your game is and I don't care.* -FC,14. ♦ *So that's your little game!*

throw a game → throw a FIGHT

GAMESMANSHIP arte ou habilidade de vencer (jogo, disputa etc.) ou alcançar determinado objetivo empregando com grande perícia métodos dúbios ou impróprios ainda que não ilegais *... as always, he was relying almost as much on gamesmanship as on power to preserve his reputation as the world's best sculler.* -T/60.

GAMUT run the gamut cobrir toda a escala, gama, série etc., abarcar (algo) de ponta a ponta, abranger de cabo a rabo *My reading matter ran the gamut from a technical book on intercontinental ballistic missiles to Jean-Paul Sartre's study of anti-Semitism ...* -BL,199.

GANDER take a gander at [gir] olhar para, dar uma olhadela em *Take a gander at the new car our neighbors have.*

GANG gang up [col] 1. formar-se numa multidão, reunir-se em turma, bando etc., formar uma multidão *The people began to gang up in front of the speaker.* 2. unir-se contra, em oposição a *... the big-city Democratic leaders ganged up on him.* -T/63. 3. agrupar-se para atacar alguém *... teen-agers ganged up on policemen ...* -T/64.

GANGBUSTER like gangbusters [gir] com impacto, com grande energia, vigor, rapidez etc. *The movie [Jaws] moves like gangbusters ...* -T/75.

GAP bridge/fill the gap preencher a lacuna, eliminar o vácuo, a distância, a divergência, a deficiência etc. *Education of parents may help to bridge the communication gap between them and their children ...* -RC,36. ♦ *... to bridge the gap between AIDS sufferers and an indifferent public.* -T/92.

GARDEN garden; garden-variety vulgar, comum, ordinário *[He] ... was notorious as a rake, and not of the garden-variety (kind) ...* -T/78.

GAS cook with gas [gir] fazer, sentir ou pensar a coisa certa ou desejada; estar a par, estar bem informado, alerta *That's the way to do it. Now you're cooking with gas.*

gas/filling/service station posto de gasolina *American gas stations are famous for their sanitary toilet facilities.* ♦ *[She] ... had run out of gas and had to walk to a service station ...* -GES,6.

gas up [col] abastecer de gasolina (o tanque do automóvel) *Traditional to any*

U.S. holiday is a national urge to gas up the family car and take to the road ... -T/61.

step on the gas [col] acelerar, ir mais depressa *You had better step on the gas if you want to get there in time to catch the plane.*

GASKET blow a gasket → **blow a FUSE**

GASP at one's/the last gasp no último suspiro, nas últimas, no fim *He was at his last gasp and no one believed he would live to see daybreak.*

GATE crash the gate/party [col] entrar (em festa, recepção, baile etc.) sem convite ou ingresso *Many of the people at the party had crashed the gate.* ⇒ **gate-crasher** indivíduo que entra (em festa etc.) sem convite ou ingresso, penetra *He became famous for being a gate-crasher at all the big society parties.*

get//give the gate [gir] 1. = **get//give the AX** 1 *Two more men from our department got the gate yesterday.* ♦ *Brad was given the gate when they found out that he could not do the job competently.* 2. = **get//give the AX** 2 *Harry got the gate from Sally last night.* ♦ *Edwina gave her boyfriend the gate.*

GATHER deduzir, inferir, concluir *From what I've heard, I gather he's no fool.*

gather together reunir, coligir, recolher *The stories gathered together in* Famous Science Fiction Stories *were written between 1934 and 1945.*

gather up pegar, apanhar, recolher *Mother told the children to gather up their toys.*

GAUNTLET pick/take up the gauntlet aceitar o desafio *None of the knights were ready to pick up the gauntlet the Black Knight had thrown down.*

run the gauntlet 1. passar correndo no meio de duas fileiras (de soldados, guerreiros ou outros), os quais golpeiam a vítima/o condenado com cacetes, varas, chicotes etc. [antigo método de punição] *The Indians made the white prisoners run the gauntlet between the lines of armed warriors who struck at them.* 2. passar por uma série de tarefas, provações, experiências ou críticas rigorosas, aflitivas etc. *To be accepted as a candidate he must run the gauntlet set up by Congress.*

throw down the gauntlet/glove lançar desafio *The President has thrown down the gauntlet. What are we going to do now?* -T/73. ♦ *Davis was told that he couldn't win the election, but he threw down the glove.*

GEAR be geared to/for estar ajustado a, adaptado a, organizado de forma a atender uma situação etc. *The old economy was geared to coffee but now is geared to industrial exports and sugar and soya bean.* ♦ *... his music is geared for U.S. audiences ...* -T/66.

gear up 1. aprontar-se, preparar-se, organizar-se *... some groups are gearing up for action [against AIDS].* -T/87. 2. aprontar, preparar, organizar, pôr em execução *They are gearing up plans for the next presidential campaign.*

high//low gear 1. alta//baixa velocidade; marcha acelerada//lenta *The truck moved without lights, groaning along in low gear ...* -SSG,26. 2. [col] grau máximo de esforço, eficiência etc.//diminuto esforço, eficiência etc. *Advertising got into high gear only at the end of the last century, with the invention of photoengraving.* -MMU,204.

in gear engrenado (veículo), com a marcha engatada *Mitch put the car in gear and drove off.*

out of gear 1. desengrenado (veículo), em ponto morto *The car was out of gear.* 2. desorganizado, inativo, sem funcionar *The economy seems to be out of gear.*

shift gears [col] mudar a maneira de encarar uma coisa, abordar (problema, situação etc.) de outro ângulo, mudar de atitude *Many are seeing ... [the upcoming*

presidential election] as a once-in-a-lifetime chance to shift gears and start off in a new direction toward democracy. -T/87.
throw out of gear 1. desengrenar (veículo) *He threw the truck out of gear, jammed his foot on the brake and pulled up at the curb.* 2. desorganizar, prejudicar, tornar ineficaz, impotente *They succeeded in throwing the economics of the Western World out of gear ...* -T/74.
GENERATION generation gap conflito de gerações caracterizado pelas divergências de idéias, atitudes etc. entre pais e filhos *There will always be a generation gap as long as there are parents and children.*
GENTLEMAN gentleman's/gentlemen's agreement acordo de honra, acordo de cavalheiros *... there was a sort of gentlemen's agreement among reporters who covered public figures that certain matters were off limits.* -T/87.
GEORGE let George do it [col] deixar (para) outra pessoa fazer (algo que deve ser feito); quem quiser que o faça *"Let George do it" is an expression used by people who refuse to accept responsibility.*
GET 1. [col] compreender, entender *"You're not to go out this evening, you get me?", his father said.* 2. [gir] emocionar, sensibilizar, causar viva impressão *We were watching the beautiful sunset over the lake when my friend said: "It really gets you, doesn't it?".* 3. [gir] irritar, exasperar *Her strange behavior is beginning to get me.* 4. [col] desorientar, intrigar, confundir, deixar perplexo *This new type of music gets me.* 5. persuadir, convencer, induzir *Get Victor to help us.*
get about 1. andar, locomover-se, andar para lá e para cá, circular, viajar *[He had missed] ... a lot of fun out of life by not getting about more in his young manhood.* -OJT,7. 2. espalhar-se, tornar-se público, propagar-se (notícia, boato etc.) *The scandal got about more rapidly than if it had been broadcast by radio.*

get above oneself imaginar-se mais importante do que realmente é *He was getting above himself, so we told him off properly.*
get across [col] esclarecer, explicar, fazer compreender, comunicar *Fraser was a skillful politician who knew how to get his ideas across.*
get ahead 1. obter bom êxito, ser bem-sucedido, fazer progresso, avançar *Poverty and racial prejudice are obviously powerful incitements to violence, but so ... is the classic American emphasis on getting ahead.* -T/66. 2. passar à frente; ir além de, superar *May I get ahead of you in this line?*
get along 1. arranjar-se; conseguir o intento; fazer face às necessidades; ter meios de subsistência suficientes *How will Nancy get along now that her husband has left her?* ♦ *Many Americans cannot get along without French clothing, wine and perfume ...* -T/87. 2. dar-se bem, cooperar, viver harmoniosamente *He gets along well enough with other boys ...* -SH,7. ♦ *He was a pleasant guy who got along with people.* -T/73. 3 [col] ir embora, partir, retirar-se *Well, I must be getting along now.* 4. progredir, prosseguir, avançar, desenvolver-se; ir (passando), sair-se (de determinada situação), prosperar *How is your business getting along?* ♦ *How are you getting along with your wife?* 5. envelhecer *Mother is getting along and needs all our attention and care.* v. **get along in YEARS**
get anywhere/anyplace [col] [neg] alcançar bom resultado, sair-se bem, ser bem-sucedido, levar a bom termo *Linda had always wanted to be in showbiz but she never got anywhere.* ♦ *... neither of us is ever gonna get anyplace.* -CHT,37. ♦ *You need my help as much as I need yours. If you refuse to cooperate, it won't get us anywhere.*
get around 1. = **GET about** 1 *... the family gets around in a white Mercedes*

convertible. -T/69. 2. = **GET about** 2 *Bad news gets around very fast.* 3. estar sempre em atividade, ter vida social ou profissional intensa, relacionar-se com muitas pessoas, adquirir muita experiência e conhecimento *[Anthropologist] Margaret Mead was a small woman, but she got around.* -T/78. ♦ *Dinah used to lead a very busy social life, but she doesn't get around much any more.* 4. contornar, evitar, burlar, esquivar-se a *Anyone who wants to get around the law knows that the first person to consult is a lawyer.* -T/73. 5. sobrepujar, ludibriar, persuadir, conseguir (algo) com lisonjas ou astúcia *Young girls can always get around their fathers when they want money for a new pair of shoes or a dress.*

get around to 1. achar ocasião, tempo ou oportunidade para ... *I've been lucky enough, in my time, to do a number of things that most people never get around to doing.* -MHH,9. 2. tratar de fazer, realizar etc. (algo) ainda que tardiamente, dar (afinal) a devida atenção ou consideração a *When she gets around to calling us, she's desperate and looking for a way out.* -LRW,11.

get at 1. alcançar, atingir, chegar a ... *he withdrew into himself. I tried to get at him; but I couldn't.* -UJ,99. 2. dar atenção para, dedicar-se a, concentrar-se em *It will be a difficult job and we must get at it immediately.* 3. averiguar, descobrir, apurar, chegar à verdade, descobrir o significado de *Cliff was getting at something very important when he was mysteriously murdered.* 4. = **DRIVE at** *It was easy to understand what Eloise was getting at.* 5. [col] subornar, intimidar, ameaçar *The lawyer fears someone may get at the witness before the trial begins.* 6. atacar, agredir, ferir *Madeleine was furious and trying to get at the woman who she thought was having an affair with her husband.*

get away 1. fugir, escapar *I go to the mountains to get away from the noise of the city.* ⇒ **getaway** fuga ... *the [holdup] men had made their getaway with about $300.* -T/81. ♦ *Policemen are still looking for the getaway car which is believed to be heading south.* 2. partir, ir embora, sair, deixar um local, sair de férias, afastar-se *Everyone needs to get away once in a while, have some fun and forget everything.* ⇒ **getaway** local ideal para passar férias ... *the getaway cottage the family keeps in Majorca.* -T/87.

get away from it all [col] passar férias em lugar exótico, diferente; fugir do tumulto, das preocupações e demais problemas da cidade grande, buscar alívio *Even with inflation, many Americans are getting away from it all on cruises to the West Indies where they can forget the financial crisis.*

get away with 1. roubar, levar (produto de roubo) *Five men held up a bank and got away with over $150,000.* 2. [col] escapar impunemente a, livrar-se de culpa, responsabilidade ou conseqüências (por cometer ato criminoso, ilegal etc.), safar-se *Perkins thought he could get away with the perfect crime he planned to commit.* 3. [col] não ser questionado, não sofrer conseqüências, evitar censura ou punição, safar-se *The things some people do, and get away with.*

get back 1. voltar, regressar; voltar a um assunto, conversa etc. *When did you get back from Chicago?* ♦ ... *let's get back to Joby. How do you propose to punish him?* -OJT,288. 2. recuar, afastar-se *The firemen shouted at the crowd near the burning building, "Get back!"* 3. reaver, recuperar *You'll never get your money back.*

get back at [gir] vingar-se de, desforrar-se de *Edmond Dantes, the future Count of Monte Cristo, swore that someday he'd get back at the men who had betrayed him.*

get behind 1. ficar para trás, atrasar-se *Connie is getting behind in her work.* 2. [col] apoiar, aprovar, favorecer *The new*

President has managed to get the country solidly behind him.
get better//worse melhorar//piorar (de saúde, condição etc.) *Ruth is getting better now, thank God.* ♦ *The political situation in Ruritania seems to be getting worse.*
get bombed [gír] tomar um pileque, encher a cara *It's easy to get bombed on vodka without realizing it.*
get busy ocupar-se, aviar-se, atacar (tarefa, serviço etc.), começar a trabalhar com disposição, mexer-se *Let's get busy or we'll never finish this work.*
get by 1. passar, ir de um lado para o outro *The snow was so deep that the cars could not get by to the cleared main roads.* 2. conseguir (fazer algo geralmente censurável, ilegal etc.), sem ser descoberto ou punido, safar-se *They apparently thought they could get by with the hoax...* -T/72. 3. conseguir viver (financeiramente), sobreviver; arranjar-se, sair-se bem (apesar de problema, dificuldade etc.) *How will your wife get by if you die?* ♦ *... gorillas and cats sleep about 14 hours out of every 24, while elephants and short-tailed shrews get by on a positively neurotic two hours.* -T/78. 4. conseguir ser aceito, aprovado etc. por diminuta margem ou com um mínimo de esforço *He got by on the examination.*
get cracking [gír] ocupar-se, começar a trabalhar ativamente; apressar-se, mexer-se, sair, partir *[Director François Truffaut] ... got cracking on a film called* The 400 Blows. -T/63. ♦ *Let's get cracking or we'll miss the first act of the new play.*
get down 1. descer, apear, desmontar *Help me to get down from the tree.* 2. deprimir, desanimar, fatigar *The loneliness is the only thing that gets him down.* -T/84. 3. engolir (com certa dificuldade) *She gave the boy all the apple pie he could get down.* 4. anotar *Before Scott starts writing a report, he always gets all the facts down on paper.*

get down to dar atenção a, ocupar-se com, concentrar-se em, atacar (trabalho etc.) com energia *[He] ... had never really got down to the work he had dreamed of and planned.* -CS,500.
get even (with) [col] vingar-se (de), ajustar contas (com) *Sheila had made a fool out of Burt, but he got even.* ♦ *Jay got even with the two men who had betrayed him.*
get going começar, dar início, pôr(-se) em ação, em movimento, partir, apressar-se *He first got going on his present studies back in 1985.* ♦ *Let's get going before it begins to rain.* ♦ *... he refilled his pipe and got it going again.* -KD,29.
get high → HIGH
get home regressar ao lar, chegar em casa *What time did you get home last night?*
get/be hooked [gír] 1. viciar-se (em droga) *Bob ... was so hooked on cocaine that he lost his job ...* -T/86. 2. ficar vidrado, gamar, encantar-se *I was hooked on Honey [a girl].* -BL,66. ♦ *[He] ... got hooked on flying in 1961...* -T/66. 3. casar-se *Ryan got hooked to a rich widow.*
get hurt ferir-se, magoar-se *There's no reason for a war correspondent to get hurt, if he's careful.* -CN,14.
get in 1. entrar, ingressar em *The door was locked and she couldn't get in.* 2. chegar *What time did you get in?* ♦ *I just got in from Boston.* 3. receber *Did the bookstore get in any new books by John Updike or Philip Roth?* 4. interpor, inserir, introduzir, encaixar, colocar *Each of the six Senators present seemed to want to get in a few words ...* -T/79.
get in on participar de *In the late 60s he got in on the guerrilla movement.*
get into 1. entrar *Get into the car.* 2. entrar para, ingressar em, iniciar carreira em *[He] ... got into a leading New York City law firm after graduation.* -T/62. 3. afligir, atormentar, acometer, apoderar-se de *What in the world has got into you, Ross?* -PF,10. 4. tornar-se entusiasta de,

começar a gostar de, dedicar-se vivamente a, viciar-se em *Tom and Jeff got into surfing at a very early age.* ♦ *Nick got into hard drugs.* 5. meter-se em, enredar-se em *Luke got into a fight with the other boy.* 6. vestir, calçar *He was struggling to get into his coat.* ♦ *He got into his shoes without putting on socks.*
get in with 1. tornar-se amigo de, fazer amizade com *Try to get in with the new mayor and then we can get some contracts.* 2. envolver-se com *He got in with the wrong people and landed in jail.*
get in wrong [col] colocar (alguém) em dificuldade, em situação crítica *He helped get many young children in wrong with the police by teaching them how to steal.*
get it [col] 1. entender, compreender *I don't get it. What does it mean?* 2. → **CATCH it** 3. ser morto, levar um tiro *... before this night's over some cop will get it from a single shot from a handgun ...* -WJT,318.
get/have it bad estar muito apaixonado, muito entusiasmado *I didn't realize you got it so bad. Why don't you tell her you love her?*
get it/something straight → **get THINGS straight**
get lost 1. perder-se, errar o caminho *He went for a walk downtown and got lost.* 2. [gir] dar o fora, ir-se, sumir *Get lost! Don't bother me with your troubles.*
get married casar-se *She wants to get married to Dewey ...* -JJ,134.
get moving começar, dar início, pôr-se a caminho, apressar-se *Don't you think it's time we got moving?*
get next to [gir] travar uma relação muito amistosa com, tornar-se íntimo de, ganhar as boas graças de *He is trying to get next to the boss.*
get nowhere/no place não alcançar bom resultado, ser malsucedido, não chegar a lugar algum *... the U.S. got nowhere [in the Vietnam war] as long as it tried to defeat guerrillas with massed firepower ...* -T/85. ♦ *... we'll get no place shooting at each other. We've got to hang together ...* -HJ,108.
get off 1. descer (de), apear (de), sair de (veículo) *Daisy got on the bus at 8 o'clock and got off at her destination fifteen minutes later.* 2. sair, partir, ir embora *Jimmy wants to get off before dark.* 3. tirar, retirar, remover, despir *Cindy's finger was so bruised after the accident that the doctor had difficulty getting her ring off.* 4. escapar, livrar-se de, safar-se, ser absolvido, perdoado *He got off scot-free.* 5. livrar, absolver, isentar de mal, perigo etc., salvar *If you come with me quietly, I might be able to get you off with no punishment ...* -BRT,160. 6. enviar, despachar *Get off a telephone call or message to Connally.* -T/72. 7. contar (piada), expressar (opinião) *Our professor gets off a good joke now and then.* 8. v. **TELL someone where to get off**
get off easy receber castigo ou penalidade leve *You got off easy. That judge usually puts you in jail for speeding in this city.*
get off with 1. roubar *The robbers got off with all the woman's jewelry.* 2. escapar, safar-se, livrar-se (pagando multa, sofrendo diminuta penalidade etc.) *The driver got off with a small fine.*
get on 1. embarcar em *The detective got on the train at 11:45 p.m.* 2. vestir *It was raining and Mr. Ladd got his trench coat on before leaving.* 3. = **GET along** 3 *I must get on if I expect to see the parade.* 4. = **GET along** 1 *He would never get on in this job without my help.* 5 = **GET along** 4 *Let's get on with the show.* 6. = **GET along** 2 *Miss [Vivien] Leigh did not get on well with [Director Victor] Fleming [during the shooting of* Gone With the Wind*] ...* -BRSP,55. 7. = **GET along** 5 *Mr. Wilkinson was getting on and decided that the time to retire had come.* 8. v. **get along in YEARS**
get one's [col] sofrer castigo, sofrer as conseqüências, levar o seu *Some day ... that*

bastard will get his. -MG,400. ♦ *You'll get yours when father finds out that you broke his best fishing pole.*
get one's own back [col] vingar-se, ajustar contas *[He was] ... a disappointed man who wanted to get his own back ...* -T/77.
get on for/to/toward aproximar-se de, estar perto de (hora, tempo, idade) *It was just getting on for three in the afternoon ...* -HGI,15. ♦ *It was getting on to midnight and still there was no sign of Paul.* ♦ *It was getting on toward evening now ...* -UJ,200. ♦ *John's father must be getting on to ninety.*
get on to/onto [col] compreender, entender, ficar ciente, ficar por dentro *His mother never gets onto his tricks.* ♦ *... the magazine that first got on to the story.* -T/86.
get on with continuar com, prosseguir com *You have the courage and ability to lead the world. In heaven's name, get on with it.* -T/61.
get out 1. partir, sair, desembarcar, ir embora, escapar; fazer sair, mandar embora, libertar, tornar livre *I think you'd better get out now.* ♦ *Pratt took a train to Albuquerque but got out at Black Rock.* ♦ *Whitney's lawyer got him out of jail.* 2. publicar, apresentar (ao público), produzir, mostrar *The publisher was in a hurry to get the new book out for the Christmas season.* 3. tornar-se público, transpirar *The word got out that there was a new kid in town.* -T/87. ♦ *Rumors soon got out that the island would be invaded.* 4. tirar (algo, de onde estava), trazer (para fora) *She got out the whisky bottle and poured him a drink.* 5. conseguir dizer, emitir (com certa dificuldade) *Sullivan managed to get out a few words before he died.*
get out from under [col] livrar-se de dificuldade, problema, perigo etc. iminente *[If Saddam Hussein, Iraq's dictator, were ousted] Iraq would have a better chance of getting out from under intrusive United Nations sanctions ...* -T/92.
get out of 1. evitar, escapar de *Boyd will try to get out of any work you give him.* 2. receber de, ganhar de, extrair de *How much money did you get out of the insurance company?*
get out on one's own não depender de ninguém, ser senhor de si, tornar-se independente *Young people are always eager to get out on their own.*
get over 1. recobrar-se de (surpresa, choque etc.), superar, esquecer (crise, problema, revés, adversidade etc.) *I couldn't get over my surprise when I saw her come in.* 2. sarar de, curar-se de *You'll get over your cold in a few days.*
get (something/it) over (with) terminar, completar (algo) *... he was anxious to get the job over with quickly.* -MRI,19. ♦ *My lawyer said I'd just better plead guilty and get it over with.* -LR,9.
get (something/it) over to fazer compreender, transmitir, comunicar (idéia, informação, fato etc.) a *It is hard to get the idea of sanitation over to people who do not understand microscopic organisms.*
get/have/know (down) pat/cold [col] decorar, reter (algo) na memória, saber ou conhecer com perfeição, saber de cor *I want you to get this story down cold so that the district attorney won't be able to trap or confuse you.* ♦ *Prescott had his speech down pat but when he looked into the television cameras, he suddenly forgot everything.* ♦ *... he had the whole case [of a mysterious murder] cold: he knew who gave the orders, who fired the shots ...* -T/92.
get/become personal fazer observações ofensivas ou críticas hostis, descer a alusões pessoais *[He] ... got personal in his criticism of President Reagan's tax program.* -T/81.
get rattled ficar confuso, atrapalhado, nervoso *When the police began to question Natalie she got rattled and forgot the story her lawyer had rehearsed with her.*
get ready 1. preparar, arranjar *Get your things ready. I'll pick you up at seven a.m.*

2. preparar-se, aprontar-se, ficar pronto *Get ready. We're leaving in ten minutes.*

get/be rid of livrar-se de, desfazer-se de, eliminar, descartar-se de *... we'll just have to get rid of him.* -AI,22. ♦ *... get rid of falseness in order to live more fully.* -DDT,459. ♦ *They were now rid of their unpleasant visitor.*

get set ficar preparado, pronto (para qualquer emergência, ação etc.) *Get set for a possible change in our plans.*

get sick 1. adoecer, ficar doente *Tim got sick all of a sudden and we had to take him to a hospital.* 2. ficar enjoado, sentir ânsia de vômito *She got sick in the car.*

get somewhere ser bem-sucedido, sair-se bem, alcançar seu objetivo *After the long meeting, the leaders of the two blocs were finally getting somewhere.*

get started 1. começar, dar início, encetar (atividade, trabalho, vida nova etc.) *... a moviemaker who cannot get started on a new project.* -T/63. 2. sair, partir, pôr-se a caminho *We'd better get started. It's almost five o'clock.*

get stoned [gir] encher a cara *Phil got stoned on vodka last night.*

get stuck → STUCK

get there [col] ser bem-sucedido, atingir seu objetivo *Gordon will get there sooner or later, you can be sure of that.*

get through 1. terminar, completar, chegar ao fim de *We got through playing football at six o'clock.* 2. passar (exame, teste etc.); aprovar ou ser aprovado por (órgão legislativo, comissão etc.) *As realists, we want to get as much of our [political] program through [Congress] as we can.* -T/61. 3. passar, atravessar, chegar ao seu destino *His urgent radio messages for arms had, after all, gotten through.* -CL,187. ♦ *The soldiers never got through the enemy lines.*

get through to 1. chegar a, alcançar (fisicamente) *Do you think you could get through to your target?* -T/81. 2. alcançar, atingir (principalmente por telefone) *Claire just couldn't get through to her husband by telephone.* 3. fazer-se compreender (a), estabelecer comunicação (com) *Because information [in an organization] is so important, managers need to know whether they're getting through [to employees].* -BJ,103. ♦ *The psychiatrist felt that, at last, he was getting through to his patient.*

get through with terminar, completar *Once we get through with this task we can rest for a few days.*

get tired cansar-se *I'm getting tired of all this.*

get to 1. chegar a (lugar etc.), alcançar, ter acesso a *They got to Boston at seven p.m.* ♦ *... places that are difficult to get to ...* -CEO,17. 2. começar (a), chegar ao ponto de, conseguir (fazer algo), ter a oportunidade de, começar a lidar com, tratar de *You'll get to like this job after you have been here for a few days.* ♦ *Stan never got to know his father.* ♦ *That's not so important. We'll get to it tomorrow morning.* 3. [col] fazer-se compreender a, conseguir comunicar-se com, contatar *Andy is very shy and the teacher finds it difficult to get to him.* 4. [col] afetar, incomodar, produzir determinado efeito ou impressão em, sensibilizar *The sight of thousands of children starving to death in East Africa really got to her.* 5. [col] subornar, intimidar, ameaçar *When Maynard began to answer our questions with evasions, we realized that someone had gotten to him.*

get to be chegar a certa condição, posição etc., tornar-se *Someday you'll get to be boss if you keep working at this rate.* ♦ *... he finally faced up to the reality that drinking was getting to be a problem, and quit.* -T/66.

get together 1. reunir, juntar, acumular *It took months to get together the pictures we'd use ...* -T/87. 2. reunir-se *William, Milton, Ayrton, John, Octavius, Peter and*

Louis got together after many years and talked about the good old times. ⇒ **get-together** [col] reunião social informal, festinha *He held a get-together last Christmas for neighbors and friends.* -T/87. 3. [col] chegar a um acordo *Fred and Rosie don't seem to get together on the real merits of John as a painter.*
get up 1. levantar-se, pôr-se de pé *They all got up when I came in.* 2. levantar-se (da cama); fazer levantar-se (da cama) *Danny usually gets up at seven.* ♦ *Please get me up at eight.* 3. organizar, preparar, aprontar *I never thought you'd get up a decent party for us tonight.* -CEP,128. 4. [col] vestir(-se), enfarpelar(-se), apresentar(-se) *Amanda got herself up as a gypsy girl for the fancy dress ball.* ⇒ **getup** [col] roupa, traje, vestes *Sue always has some strange getup for the carnival party.* 5. subir em, montar, escalar *We used to get up on the wall that separated our neighbor's orchard from our yard to reach the apples high on the tree.* 6. munir-se de, estimular ou despertar (coragem etc. em si próprio) *Michael got up enough courage to tell his boss what he thought of him.*
get used to acostumar-se a *You'd better get used to that idea.*
get well recuperar a saúde, o bem-estar *The doctor said Jean will get well soon.*
get wet molhar-se *Chris had been walking in the rain and got wet.*
get what's coming → **what is COMING to one**
get wise [gír] 1. ficar alerta, ficar atento aos fatos, abrir os olhos, ficar por dentro *Karen will fool you if you don't get wise.* 2. comportar-se de maneira insolente *Keith tried to get wise with the girl.*
get wise to [gír] perceber, ficar ciente, ficar sabendo (da verdade, dos fatos, da verdadeira razão) *She got wise to her husband's frequent trips to Philadelphia after she found hairpins in his suitcase.* v. **WISE to**

get with it [gír] ficar alerta, ativo, esperto, tornar-se mais eficiente, mais habilidoso, adaptar-se, ficar por dentro da situação, afinar-se com a atualidade *You must get with it to be successful.* v. **WITH it**
get worse → **GET better**
get (someone/something) wrong entender mal, interpretar mal (pessoa, acontecimento, assunto, fato etc.) *Don't get me wrong.* ♦ *You've got me wrong. That's not what I said.* ♦ *... Washington's leaders are getting it wrong about China.* -T/91.
you've got me there [col] você me pegou *You've got me there. I wish I knew the answer to that question.*
you've got something there [col] o que você diz é verdade, você tem razão, você está certo *When Carl made that statement, I said: "Well, you've got something there. I agree with you".*
GET-UP-AND-GO [col] energia, ímpeto, ambição profissional, entusiasmo *Kevin will never be a success because he has no get-up-and-go.*
GHOST ghost of a chance a mais remota possibilidade *Gene doesn't have a ghost of a chance of going to Boston this year.*
ghost town cidade abandonada (geralmente no oeste dos EUA, construída perto de garimpo que depois se exauriu) *Many old western towns became ghost towns when the mines no longer held gold or silver.*
give up the ghost 1. entregar a alma, morrer *Mr. Conway gave up the ghost after fighting to live for many days.* 2. deixar de funcionar, parar, cessar, chegar ao fim *The tires on the old truck are just about to give up the ghost.*
GHOSTWRITE escrever discursos, artigos, livros etc. para outra pessoa que assume a autoria *She is credited with having ghostwritten her husband's best seller ...* -T/87.
GI 1. fornecido pelas forças armadas dos EUA *GI clothes* ♦ *GI shoes* ♦ *All his*

equipment was GI. 2. [col] soldado das forças armadas dos EUA durante a Segunda Guerra Mundial, pracinha *... Americans who'd been officers and GI's in Japan during the Occupation ...* -WPT,61.
GI Joe = GI 2 *The American GI was known in Europe as GI Joe.*
GIFT don't/never look a gift horse in the mouth a cavalo dado não se olham os dentes *Never look a gift horse in the mouth. Be content with what you receive and accept it gratefully.*
(the) gift of (the) gab [col] dom da palavra, poder da eloqüência e persuasão, lábia, falas melífluas *I learned to trust in words and cultivate the gift of gab.* -KS,144. ♦ *... youngsters with a good voice and a gift of gab.* -T/87.
GILL to the gills → **to the EARS**
GILT-EDGED da melhor qualidade; do maior valor e segurança (papéis, títulos, ações etc.) *... a gilt-edged reputation ...* -T/64. ♦ *... gilt-edged industries ...* -T/72. ♦ *... a gilt-edged education ...* -T/79. ♦ *Mr. Blake only buys gilt-edged securities issued by the U.S. government.*
GIN gin mill [gir] bar de baixa categoria *The gin mills are always full on Saturday night.*
GIRL girl Friday → **MAN Friday**
GIRLFRIEND [col] namorada *Jerry came to the party with his new girlfriend.* v. **BOYFRIEND**
GIVE don't give me that não venha com essa, deixe-se disso *Don't give me that! You knew from the start what this was all about!*
give and take fazer concessões mútuas, ser tolerante *If you learn to give and take in life, you may succeed.* ⇒ **give-and-take** concessões mútuas, troca de idéias, tolerância *[He had a good] ... sense of give-and-take.* -MMA,44.
give as good as one gets retaliar, revidar, responder ao pé da letra, reagir à altura da ofensa *... he proved in 1988 that he can give as good as he gets.* -T/92.

give away 1. doar, fazer dádiva de, presentear, distribuir *The Rockefeller Foundation has given away many millions of dollars to charity.* ⇒ **giveaway** artigo ofertado ou vendido quase de graça pelas lojas comerciais para atrair clientes *The stores always have a giveaway item to entice customers.* 2. [col] trair(-se), denunciar(-se), revelar (segredo) *At first we thought she was an American, but her Spanish accent gave her away.* ♦ *He gave himself away when he said he'd seen Glenda the day before.* ⇒ **giveaway** qualquer coisa que involuntariamente revela um segredo; traição ou revelação inconsciente *His voice on the telephone was a giveaway to his identity.* 3. entregar (a noiva ao noivo na cerimônia de casamento) *The proud father gave away his daughter in marriage to the prince.*
give back devolver, restituir *Give him back the money. Give it back to him.*
give forth emitir, soltar, produzir *The old mission bell gives forth a strange sound.*
give in 1. entregar *Give in your examination papers at the end of the class.* 2. render-se, dar-se por vencido; ceder, fazer a vontade de *Don't give in to your children's pleading when you have forbidden them to do something.* 3. desabar, desmoronar *The roof gave in from the weight of the snow.*
give it to [col] 1. criticar, repreender, censurar, castigar, soltar os cachorros em cima de *Your father is going to give it to you because you lied to him.* 2. surrar *Though Tommy was a smaller boy, he gave it to Ed when Ed called him a liar.*
give it to (someone) straight [col] falar (a alguém) com franqueza, dizer a verdade, ser claro *Just give it to me straight and in detail, the way it happened.* -T/73.
given to dado a, propenso a, habituado a *He wasn't a man given to brooding ...* -PF,1. ♦ *Jones was not given to much talk.*
give off emitir, soltar, exalar, produzir *As the atoms disintegrate and change to other*

elements, they give off energy. -PR,50. ♦ *This gadget gives off an electronic signal that can be picked up many miles away.* ♦ *This stuff gives off an awful smell.*

give on/onto/out on/out to/upon dar para, oferecer vista ou passagem para *Our rear windows give out on a beautiful lake.* ♦ *The door of the living room gives onto a large patio.*

give oneself over to abandonar-se a, entregar-se a *Becky gave herself over to despair when her husband was killed.*

give oneself up entregar-se, render-se *Give yourself up or the police will shoot you.*

give oneself up to entregar-se a, dar-se a, dedicar-se a, abandonar-se a *When Bailey's wife died, he gave himself up to utter despair.*

give out 1. emitir *The wounded animal gave out piteous cries.* 2. anunciar, proclamar, declarar, divulgar, fazer saber *They gave out incorrect information to confuse any spies.* 3. distribuir, dar, oferecer *The company gave out samples of their product to all the housewives.* 4. cansar-se, sucumbir, ceder *Lee gave out before the end of the race.* 5. acabar-se, esgotar-se, chegar ao fim *The little money he had gave out and he had to look for a job.* 6. deixar de funcionar, desarranjar-se, parar, enguiçar *The program was at its peak when the TV gave out.* ♦ *His heart gave out before he was 42.* 7. v. **GIVE on**

give out on → **GIVE on**

give over 1. destinar, reservar (a uma finalidade específica) *Most of their time was given over to reading ...* -T/77. 2. v. **GIVE oneself over to**

give someone to understand/believe dar a entender, levar a crer *Martha gave us to understand that she would cooperate with us.*

give up 1. renunciar a, desistir (de), abandonar, abrir mão de, deixar de *In 1951, he gave up a career as an army officer ...* -T/62. ♦ *... I wish you'd give up this foolish idea of trying to be a writer.* -HJT,49.

♦ *Ken has given up cigarette smoking.* 2. entregar-se, render-se *The criminal gave himself up.* 3. entregar, ceder *Cole was forced to give up the secret documents to the government.* ♦ *[Macbeth's] ... soldiers refuse to follow him and they give up the castle to the invaders.* -CMSS,179. 4. perder a esperança de ver ou rever (alguém), dar (alguém ou algo) por perdido, irrecuperável etc. *... many civilians began to give up the cause [of the American Revolution] for lost.* -SGF,349. 5. dedicar, consagrar, devotar *Jackie's spare time is given up to collecting recipes for a cookbook.* 6. abandonar-se a, entregar-se a, dar-se a, consagrar-se a *Mrs. Leslie has had many ups and downs in her life, but has never given herself up to despair.* 7. revelar *Jennings refused to give up the hiding place of the stolen money.*

give up on desistir de, renunciar; não prosseguir (num intento), não mais esperar por (alguém) ou que algo ocorra, não mais contar com *I'd just about given up on you ... What happened?* -WI,310. ♦ *... they were not ready to give up on democracy.* -T/92.

what gives/goes? [gir] que é que há? que se passa? que está acontecendo? *... I have a right to know what gives between you two.* -TR,89. ♦ *Hi, girls. What goes?*

GLANCE at a glance em um relance de olhos, imediatamente *The new teacher saw at a glance that she'd have trouble handling the class.*

at first glance → **at first SIGHT**

glance off resvalar, desviar-se, ricochetear *The bullet glanced off when it hit the windshield.*

GLORY in one's glory em um estado de exaltação, absoluta satisfação, felicidade etc. *The prophet [Joseph Smith] was in his glory. More and more he thought of himself as a messiah ...* -BR,536.

GLOVE fit like a glove assentar como uma luva, ajustar-se perfeitamente *Anna bought a new dress that fits her like a glove.*

throw down the glove → throw down the GAUNTLET
GO anything goes tudo é permitido, válido etc., não há restrições, vale tudo *When she gives one of her wild parties, anything goes.*
as far as someone/something goes no que diz respeito a, com relação a, no que tange a *I was having my own troubles as far as women went.* -AIM,94.
as (people/someone/something/things etc.) go/goes em comparação com o que são (as outras pessoas/coisas típicas, comuns etc.) *Miss Hayden was a good teacher, as teachers go.* ♦ *... the Appalachian Mountains ... are no youngsters as mountains go.* -T/76.
go about 1. circular, ir de um lugar para o outro, ir de pessoa para pessoa *There's a rumor going about that Hughes might be involved in the corruption scandal.* 2. ocupar-se de/com, desempenhar, fazer *How does he go about his work?* 3. atacar (tarefa etc.), começar a trabalhar, começar a fazer (algo) *Freud went about tackling the interpretation of dreams as though he were assailing the devil.* -FLS,95.
go ahead começar ou continuar, prosseguir; ir avante sem vacilar *Go ahead, young man! Your mother and I are waiting for an explanation!* ♦ *He decided to go ahead with his plan.* ⇒ **go-ahead** 1. vigor, energia, ambição *Jimmy has more go-ahead than the rest of my employees.* 2. permissão ou ordem para iniciar algo *[The President] ... has given the armed forces the go-ahead to fight the guerrillas ...* -T/87.
go all out [col] fazer um esforço supremo *Our team is going all out to win the championship.* ♦ *The financial crisis has forced Brazil to curb imports and go all out on the export front.* -T/87.
go along 1. avançar, prosseguir (em uma atividade), continuar (fazendo algo) *... they [the artisans that built the cathedral of Hagia Sophia] did not work to exact specifications, but improvised as they went along.* -MHJ,13. 2. fazer progresso, evoluir, desenvolver-se, avançar, melhorar *After all the troubles she had last year, she's going along fine, now.* 3. acompanhar *Whenever Flint goes on a trip, his wife goes along.*
go along with 1. acompanhar ... *responsibilities that go along with fathering a child.* -T/86. 2. concordar com, cooperar com *We will go along with you in your effort to improve the educational program.*
go around 1. ir de um lugar para outro, de pessoa para pessoa, ir pra lá e pra cá, circular *... rumors are going around that residues of pesticides have been found on some supposedly organic foods ...* -T/71. 2. suprir a demanda, a necessidade *When Dr. Watts spoke at our school last summer there weren't enough chairs to go around.* 3. contornar, desviar-se de, passar por cima da autoridade de *You can't go around your boss and take your problem directly to the department manager.*
go around with estar freqüentemente em companhia de *She was going around with Bovard, riding in his carriage, having meals with him ...* -HWR,104.
go as far as ir até (determinado lugar, certo ponto) *They went as far as Tierra del Fuego.*
go astray 1. sair do caminho, extraviar-se *Didn't you get my letter? Then it must have gone astray.* 2. desencaminhar-se, perder-se, corromper-se *Pat went astray when she met the wrong kind of people.*
go at 1. atacar *[They were] ... going at each other with knives.* -LJS,44. ♦ *... go at them! Don't back off!* -T/87. 2. abordar, achegar-se a, empreender *... as I flew back to the States I decided I'd go at things differently.* -AK,265. ♦ *Gus went at the job enthusiastically.*
go away 1. partir, ir embora *Go away! Can't you see I'm busy?* 2. sair, partir (de férias) *Charles and Fay are going away for*

two weeks. 3. desaparecer gradualmente, passar *The pain still hasn't gone away.*

go back 1. voltar, regressar *He went back to Boston.* 2. remontar a, datar de, ter origem em, existir desde *Belief in nature spirits goes back beyond written history.*

go back on [col] 1. abandonar, quebrar (palavra, promessa etc.) *The government shouldn't give its word and then go back on it.* -T/77. 2. trair, ser desleal a *Carpenter was not a man to go back on his friends.*

go bad 1. estragar-se, deteriorar-se *The meat has gone bad.* 2. corromper-se, perverter-se *When a boy goes bad, his mother often blames the other boys who are his friends.*

go begging [col] estar em baixa demanda (coisas), não ter procura, não achar quem o queira *... many of the jobs are going begging ...* -T/77.

go berserk ser tomado de fúria incontrolável *One reads occasionally about someone running berserk and shooting down a lot of people whom he does not even know ...* -HC,66.

go bonkers [gír] = **go BANANAS** *... my kids were really going bonkers...* -T/81. ♦ *Have you gone bonkers?*

go broke [col] falir, ir à bancarrota *Carmichael went broke several times before he finally became a success in business.*

go bust [gír] falir; fracassar *... thousands of new businesses are launched every year while thousands go bust.* -T/87. ♦ *Donna's dream of having a husband, a happy home and children went bust.*

go by 1. passar, ir-se (tempo, oportunidade, ocasião) *As time went by, Rick fell in love with Ilsa.* ♦ *Don't let this chance go by. Act now!* 2. passar (por) (determinado lugar) *Your father wondered if you would go by the bank and pick up the money for the payroll ...* -SJE,75. ♦ *Frank likes to watch the girls go by.* ⇒ **give the go-by** [col] desprezar, fazer pouco caso de, fingir não ver, fingir desconhecer, deixar de lado *Brenda always gives me the go-by when we see each other on the street.* 3. seguir, obedecer, guiar-se por, orientar-se por *I just had to go by the jury decision.* -T/88. 4. julgar por, avaliar, formar uma opinião (em razão de algum fato, dado etc.) *Going by the length of the shadows, I would say it is after three o'clock.* 5. v. **go by the NAME of** 6. fazer breve visita (a) *Bruce knew that his uncle and aunt were home, so he went by to say hello to them.*

go crazy/mad enlouquecer *... in [the movie] Empire of the Sun a boy goes to war and nearly goes mad.* -T/87. ♦ *I'll go crazy if I stay here.*

go down 1. baixar, descer; decrescer, diminuir *Prices should go down when the supply of eggs increase.* 2. ir ao chão, cair *... a DC-7B [airplane] went down ... in the Gulf of Mexico ...* -T/60. 3. afundar, naufragar *The Titanic went down on April 14, 1912.* 4. desaparecer no horizonte, pôr-se (o sol, a lua) *The night was clear and cool after the sun went down.* -HWR,58. 5. sofrer derrota *... they preferred to go down fighting on American soil ...* -T/87. 6. encontrar aceitação, ter receptividade *The new rules that he annnounced don't go down well with me.* 7. deteriorar-se, decair *... the Byzantine Empire had every reason to go down as Rome did ...* -MHJ,21. 8. ser registrado (na História), ser perpetuado, ser lembrado pela posteridade *Will the Twentieth Century go down in History as the Freudian Century?* -NB,9. 9. ser deglutido, descer ao estômago (comida, bebida) *The salmon salad was delicious and went down well with the Riesling wine.*

go downhill ir ladeira abaixo, deteriorar-se, estar em decadência *While there has been some environmental progress in individual countries, the state of the world has mostly gone downhill.* -T/92.

go easy ir devagar, não abusar, proceder com cautela, moderar *Go easy on the Scotch, young man.*

go far 1. ser de grande auxílio, ajudar muito, contribuir grandemente *These talks should go far to make a lasting peace in the Middle East.* 2. ser de amplo uso ou utilidade; comprar bastante (diz-se do dinheiro) *Fifty dollars will not go far in these days of inflation.* 3. ter grande êxito, ser muito bem-sucedido *We expect this new generation to go far in the financial world.*

go for 1. procurar, ir buscar; tentar pegar ou alcançar, esforçar-se para conseguir; visar a, tencionar *At the Olympics, she went for the gold medal.* ♦ *The maddened [natives] had gone for their knives.* -SLT,126. 2. favorecer, aprovar, apoiar, aceitar *I can't go for your plan.* 3. [col] atacar; censurar energicamente, repreender *The bull will go for any color that moves in front of him.* 4. aplicar-se a, servir para, valer para *This law goes for you as well.* 5. [col] sentir atração ou interesse por, gostar de *He goes for young, blond girls, with money.* 6. ser vendido por (determinado preço) *The book goes for $24,95.* -T/86.

go for broke [gir] fazer um esforço supremo, ir com tudo, botar pra quebrar *If I was going to achieve something, I'd really have to go for broke.* -T/76.

go forward prosseguir, ir adiante, avançar, progredir *Unable to restore the primal union with nature, man must always go forward.* -SJH,43.

go from bad to worse ir de mal a pior, deteriorar-se *They say that the political situation in Ruritania is going from bad to worse.*

go hang [gir] ir embora, desaparecer, não perturbar *If you don't like the way we do things, go hang.*

go hard with ser difícil, severo, doloroso para *Let me ketch [catch] you foolin' around any of them [those] Cherokee gals and it'll go hard with you ...* -TD,31.

go haywire [gir] 1. deixar de funcionar, desarranjar-se; desorganizar-se, ficar em confusão *Everything has gone haywire in our office.* ♦ *Our instruments went haywire ...* -RQ,25. 2. ficar perturbado emocionalmente, enlouquecer *Ralph went haywire when his wife died.*

go in for [col] participar de, interessar-se por, entregar-se a, regalar-se com *Mrs. Kendall goes in for civic activities in her home town.* ♦ *Hal goes in for all the competitive sports.*

going on quase, perto (de), próximo (de) *It was going on ten o'clock p.m. when we got to our destination.* ♦ *The little girl is three going on four.* ♦ *It's going on for a year since I last saw her.*

going strong em plena atividade, bem de saúde, sem mostrar sinais de debilidade, declínio etc. (apesar da passagem do tempo); sólido, firme *[He] ... has been writing about health for almost 50 years, [and] is still going strong.* -T/72. ♦ *... a Pennsylvania Dutch [food product] ... that has been going strong for 45 years ...* -T/87.

go into 1. examinar, investigar, discutir, tratar de *There's no need for you to go into those previous events in your life.* 2. dedicar-se a (profissão, ocupação, carreira, estudo) *[He] ... went into public relations ...* -T/73. 3. ter um acesso de, entrar em (estado, condição), ser acometido por *Frances went into a coma last night.* 4. caber em *Five goes into twenty-five five times.* 5. fazer parte de, estar incluído em, entrar na composição ou construção de *... the many and marvelous things that can be done with sentences and with the words that go into them.* -PL,11.

go it alone [col] agir por conta própria, enfrentar ou fazer (algo) sem ajuda ou assistência *... conservatives who believe that the U.S. essentially must go it alone in enforcing world peace.* -T/92.

go mad → **GO crazy**

go nuts [gir] ficar maluco *I'll go nuts if I listen to you for another minute.*

go off 1. explodir, detonar, disparar *At that precise moment ... the bomb went off.* -SWLR,1366. ♦ *... a gun went off as a signal.* -HET,21. 2. partir, ir embora, sair *They are worried as everybody else that their sons will go off and never come back.* -T/87. 3. acontecer, ocorrer, resultar, realizar-se *Everything went off as planned.* 4. soar (despertador, alarme etc.) *The alarm clock went off at 7 o'clock.*

go off half-cocked agir ou falar impetuosamente ou sem ponderação, agir com precipitação *He knew the people who made these sightings [of UFOs] and said that they weren't the kind to go off "half-cocked".* -RE,35. v. **HALF-cocked**

go on 1. prosseguir, continuar *The bell went on ringing.* ♦ *Discussions about the existence of flying saucers have been known to go on all night.* 2. continuar (a andar, avançar etc.) *Go on a little beyond the woods and you will come to a beautiful lake.* 3. acontecer, ocorrer, realizar-se *When they got home, there was a big party going on next door ...* -LRT,48. ♦ *What's going on here?* ⇒ **goings-on** [col] a. ocorrências, acontecimentos, eventos *[The art exhibit] ... is a limited survey of recent goings-on in plastics as used by contemporary artists.* -T/69. b. conduta censurável, comportamento leviano, episódio reprovável *The goings-on in Hyde Park were a scandal.* 4. [também **go upon**] basear-se em, usar como prova *Today, with enough scientific data to go on, we can be fairly sure that life as we know it does not exist on Venus.* ♦ *This is all the evidence I have to go upon to solve such a difficult case.* 5. aparecer em cena, entrar no palco *When the star of the show got sick, Esther was told to go on in her place.* 6. [col] tagarelar, soltar-se em palavras *When Tuttle starts lecturing on his favorite subject – air pollution control – he can go on for hours.* 7. passar, ir-se (o tempo) *As the years went on, I got to*

know him better. 8. entrar em operação, começar a funcionar (sistema elétrico, motor, lâmpada etc.) *A light went on in the living room.* 9. deixe-se disso! pare com isso! não tente me enganar! *Oh, go on! You're kidding!* 10. v. **GOING on**

go (someone) one better [col] superar, sobrepujar fazer melhor que (alguém) *No matter what you do or say, Clem can always go you one better.*

go on to prosseguir (após uma pausa); dizer ou fazer (algo) a seguir, passar a *Hopkins went on to discuss ... other letters, while Tom took notes.* -WSM,244. ♦ *In spite of his humble origins, he went on to become a respectable citizen.*

go out 1. sair, ir para fora (de casa, sala etc.) *Mrs. Rawlings isn't home. She has gone out.* 2. sair (para ir a cinema, restaurante, festa etc.), passear, divertir-se *... she seldom goes out except for dinner with married friends.* T/72. 3. extinguir-se, apagar-se (fogo, chama, luz etc.) *Mr. Morley's pipe had gone out.* 4. sair de moda *The Hollywood musical seems to have gone out.*

go out for tentar conseguir vaga (em uma equipe) *In high school, he went out for football and track.*

go out to simpatizar com, sentir afeição ou inclinação por, sentir-se atraído emocionalmente por *The way Donna looked at me made my heart go out to her.*

go over 1. examinar cuidadosamente, analisar, ponderar *The policeman went over Jim's clothing.* 2. repetir, refazer, rever, reler, estudar novamente, repassar *There isn't a single detail of [this case] ... I haven't gone over a hundred times.* -OJT,49. 3. [col] ter bom êxito, ser bem recebido, sair-se bem, ser aprovado *The corporate style that works for Americans at home may not go over with their new [Japanese] colleagues or competitors.* -T/85. ♦ *He told the audience a couple of good jokes that went over well.* 4. ir

(para, até) *We went over to the gym to play basketball.*
go overboard [col] entusiasmar-se muito, ir a extremos, fazer (algo) com excesso, com exagero *"I guess I go overboard to avoid taking credit for the image I have", says [Henry] Fonda.* -T/78.
go past passar junto ou ao longo de, passar (por), ir além de, deixar para trás *We were watching the cars go past.* ♦ *Ferguson carefully went past the sleeping guard and entered the empty building.*
go shopping/dancing/hunting etc. → **go SHOPPING**
go short (of) ficar com menos (de algo) do que o necessário ou do que se desejaria *If you eat apples now, Mama will go short when she starts to make pies.*
go so far as (to do something) ir até o ponto de, chegar ao extremo de ... *he went so far as to say that democratic freedom very largely consists in ignoring politics ...* -MMU,203. ♦ *... the authorities went so far as to dissolve the organization ...* -T/87.
go sour [col] falhar, dar errado, ser malsucedido ... *investors who put $15 million into a May shipment [of arms] that went sour ...* -T/87.
go sour on [col] ficar descontente com, desiludir-se com *You didn't go sour on marriage?* -WJT,351.
go steady [col] namorar um só rapaz ou uma só garota, namorar firme *Bruce and Fay are going steady.*
go straight regenerar-se, corrigir-se reabilitar-se *[He] ... devoted his life to helping released convicts in St. Louis get jobs and go straight ...* -T/63.
go through 1. examinar meticulosamente, verificar, estudar detidamente, discutir, dar busca em ... *give me a few minutes to go through my mail ...* -QE,84. 2. sofrer, experimentar, passar por ... *he is gentle and sweet and has gone through so much ...* -SLS,244. 3. ter êxito, ser aprovado, passar (lei etc.), ser concluído, completar *If the plan went through, a lot of Americans were due for a big surprise.* -KD,16. 4. efetuar, realizar, desempenhar, cumprir, executar, ensaiar *The orchestra went through the new number several times and the singer rehearsed the vocal.* -T/65. 5. gastar, desperdiçar, consumir ... *he has gone through most of her family fortune ...* -T/65. 6. ter (certo número de edições) (livro) *Margaret Mitchell's novel* Gone With the Wind *has gone through countless editions and is still selling.*
go through with levar a cabo, completar, concluir ... *he refused to go through with the agreement ...* -DDT,442.
go to freqüentar (escola) *Julia goes to New York Law School.*
go to make/prove/show etc. contribuir para, colaborar para, levar a cooperar para (resultado, finalidade etc.) *Part of the knowledge which goes to make up an art is theoretical and part of it is practical.* -SJH,27. ♦ *The unexpected success of my candidate for President goes to show you that organizing carefully gets results.*
go to it [col] mexer-se, aviar-se, ocupar-se, atacar (tarefa, trabalho) com energia e disposição, pôr mãos à obra *Too late for me, but you, young ones – go to it. Work your way up. Fight like hell.* -T/72.
go together 1. combinar-se, harmonizar-se *The feelings of emptiness and loneliness go together.* -MRM,24. 2. [col] namorar, manter um relacionamento afetivo *Louise and Ben have been going together for several months.*
go too far ir longe demais, exceder-se, passar dos limites *Government officials think that he has gone too far in his criticism.*
go under 1. afundar, naufragar *The* Andrea Doria *liner went under off the coast of the U.S.* 2. fracassar, falir, arruinar-se *Many small businesses go under because of poor management.*

go undercover disfarçar-se, assumir falsa identidade (policial, agente secreto etc.) ... *an agent who went undercover for nearly ten years* ... -T/87.

go up 1. subir, ir para cima *The plane went up.* 2. aumentar (de preço, custo, valor, número, nível etc.) *Everything goes up these days, even the price of a place in the cemetery.* 3. ser construído, ser erigido *A spanking new museum has gone up near by* ... -T/76. 4. fazer-se ouvir, irromper *A cheer went up from the crowd assembled in front of the building.* 5. v. **go up in FLAMES**; **go up in SMOKE**

go upon → **GO on** 4

go up to aproximar-se de, chegar-se a *Donovan went up to the mayor and shook his hand.*

go wild manifestar alegria, entusiasmo etc. com grande intensidade, delirar, vibrar efusivamente *The audience went wild when Judy began to sing* Over the Rainbow.

go with 1. harmonizar-se com, combinar com *Peggy had black hair and green eyes to go with it.* 2. [col] namorar com *There's a woman in Roxbury that I went with.* -BS,49.

go without passar sem, ficar sem, ser privado de ... *his broken leg went without medical attention for five days.* -T/76. ♦ *[Ostrichs] ... can go without water for days* ... -GET,21.

go without saying ser óbvio, ser evidente, não precisar ser dito *It goes without saying that his generosity is to be admired.*

go wrong 1. falhar, fracassar, dar mau resultado, malograr-se ... *something had gone wrong with the mechanism [of his wristwatch].* -SLS,273. 2. afastar-se do bom caminho, desencaminhar-se, perverter-se *Minnie can't explain why her children have gone wrong.* -T/87.

have a go at [col] fazer uma tentativa, uma experiência, esforçar-se por (conseguir ou fazer algo) *I'm not sure I can fix this thing, but I'll have a go at it.*

here goes [col] aqui vou eu, lá vai *I don't like to swim in icy water, but here goes!*

how goes it [col] como vão as coisas? *How goes it with the wife and new baby?*

it's no go [col] nada feito, é inútil *We tried to interest Shannon in our plan, but it was no go.*

make a go of [col] ser bem-sucedido em, transformar (algo) em triunfo, bom êxito *Emily tried to make a go of her marriage but it was all to no avail.*

on the go [col] muito ocupado, em grande atividade *That young mother is on the go from morning until night.*

to go 1. por terminar, por completar, faltando *We have only six more months to go on our three-year contract.* 2. [col] para viagem, para levar (comida comprada em restaurante, lanchonete etc.) *One more pizza to go!*

what goes → **what GIVES**

where do we go from here que faremos a seguir? qual é o próximo passo? *We have got here so far, but where do we go from here?*

GO-AHEAD → **GO ahead**

GOAT get someone's goat [col] irritar, encolerizar *Barry's cynical remark really got my goat.*

GO-BETWEEN mediador, intermediário, agente *Bailey acted as the go-between for the two rival groups.*

GO-BY → **GO by**

GOD for God's sake → **for Christ's SAKE**

God/heaven forbid Deus nos livre *God forbid that the day should come when we would have to face such a crisis.*

God/goodnes/heaven knows 1. sabe Deus (i.e., é impossível dizer) *The world picture has changed dramatically in the past ten years, and goodness knows what's ahead.* -T/86. 2. Deus é testemunha, é verdade, não há dúvida *God knows, I've tried to make her happy.* ♦ *Heaven knows I tried to give that boy a good education.*

God willing se Deus quiser *God willing, at the opportune time we shall deal with her.* -T/87.
honest to God [col] sinceramente, no duro, é verdade *I didn't lie to you, honest to God.* ⇒ **honest-to-God/goodness** genuíno, autêntico, verdadeiro *... you're a real honest-to-goodness soldier ...* -FL,45. ♦ *Archie had a big, honest-to-God smile on his face.*
hope to God depositar as esperanças em Deus, esperar em Deus *I hope to God I never see such a thing again.* -T/84.
so help me God Deus é testemunha *I will tell them the truth, so help me God.*
GODDAMN 1. **goddamned/goddamn/goddam** [col] maldito, amaldiçoado, detestável, execrável, odioso *Where did you put that goddamned book?* 2. **goddamn [God damn] it** diabos, diacho, maldição, droga *Goddamn it, kid, I told you not to do that!* ♦ *Just leave us alone, God damn it ...* -RP,86. 3. **goddamn you** dane-se, vá pro inferno *Goddamn you, shut up!* -AIM,173.
GO-GETTER [col] pessoa ambiciosa e cheia de vigor, empreendedora, que procura o sucesso a qualquer custo *Kincaid was always known as a go-getter and we were sure that he would be a big success.*
GOING 1. existente, em atividade, disponível *In the 30s and 40s Dashiell Hammett and Raymond Chandler were the best mystery writers going.* 2. corrente, atual *What's the going price?*
the going gets/is rough/tough a situação se complica ou se agrava, as coisas ficam feias *... a man who doesn't run away when the going gets tough.* -T/63. *When the going is good everything is OK, but when the going gets rough you won't like it.* ♦ *The going was tough for the Danes when the Nazis occupied the country on April 9, 1940.* -T/66.
hard/rough/tough going circunstâncias desfavoráveis, caminho difícil, entrave, dificuldade, osso duro de roer *... the flight over the Andes proved to be rough going.* -T/73. ♦ *It was tough going when they first started their business.*
GOING-OVER [col] 1. exame minucioso, inspeção severa *The experts gave the old map a good going-over.* 2. repreensão, bronca; surra, espancamento *Sammy got quite a going-over from his father.* ♦ *A rival gang had given the boy a going-over.*
GOINGS-ON → **GO on** 3
GONE gone on [col] apaixonado por *Milly is ... gone on a young German groom.* -T/60.
GOOD all to the good vantajoso, conveniente, favorável, benéfico *It's all to the good that things turned out that way.*
as good as quase, virtualmente, praticamente, a bem dizer *When he was in the Naval Hospital, he thought he was as good as dead.* -RK,184. ♦ *[He] ... as good as called me a liar every time I opened my mouth.* -GES,29.
be good at ser apto, hábil, competente, eficiente (em determinada atividade) *Polly is good at her job.* ♦ *Clyde is very good at crossword puzzles.*
be good enough to; be so good as to ter a bondade de, fazer o favor de *Would you be good enough to tell Mr. Forster that I'm here?*
be/get/stand in good with ter boas relações com, gozar das boas graças de *Brewster stands in good with many important people in the government.*
be no good 1. de nada adiantar, de nada valer, ser inútil *I tried to persuade him but found out that it was no good talking to him.* 2. não prestar, não ter caráter (pessoa) *That boy is no good. Stay away from him.*
but good [gir] de maneira extrema, com todo o vigor ou força, intensamente, eficazmente, totalmente [para dar ênfase ao que foi dito anteriormente] *You're in trouble, but good.*

come to no good terminar mal, não chegar a bom resultado, fracassar *[My teacher] ... liked to predict, in front of the class, that I would come to no good.* -MHH,14.

do good fazer o bem, auxiliar ao próximo; ser benéfico, útil, vantajoso *You don't have to be a better person than you already are in order to do good.* -T/92. ♦ *It doesn't do any good to worry about something that may never happen.* ⇒ **do-gooder** [col] pessoa bem intencionada que procura fazer o bem, corrigir erros sociais etc., mas de maneira ingênua e ineficaz e com indevida intromissão *[He is a] ... self-professed "do-gooder" who has worked for various liberal and humanitarian causes ...* -T/81.

do (someone) good fazer bem (a), ser benéfico (para) *Maybe it would do you good to go home for a while.* -CN,22.

for good para sempre, definitivamente *... say you'll stay home this time, for good, and never go away ...* -BRT,93.

get in good with cair nas boas graças de *... he began to smile at the Captain, trying to get in good with him.* -BW,35.

good and [col] muito, bem, bastante, excessivamente *"How do you want your coffee?" "Good and hot."* ♦ *We'll get to that topic when I'm good and ready.*

good for you parabéns, ótimo, muito bem *So you have received a promotion? Good for you!*

good gracious Santo Deus! *Good gracious, it's that woman again!*

no good → **be no GOOD**

to the good de lucro, de vantagem, a seu favor, benéfico *After we paid salaries and other incidental expenses, we found that we were ten thousand dollars to the good.*

what good de que vale, de que serve *What good is it talking to Les again? He has made up his mind and won't listen to us.*

GOOD-BYE; GOOD-BY kiss (someone/something) good-bye 1. despedir-se (de alguém) com um beijo, dar um beijo de adeus a *... she kissed me good-by – and married him.* -CRS,26. 2. [col] renunciar a, dizer adeus a, dar por perdido *Kiss those seven hundred bucks good-by ...* -BS,70.

GOOD-FOR-NOTHING imprestável, inútil *Nora's good-for-nothing father was out drinking with his friends again last night.*

GOOD-HEARTED bondoso, generoso, de bom coração *[They] ... are good-hearted and generous ...* -MR,12.

GOOD-LOOKING → **good LOOKS**
GOOD-NATURED → **good NATURE**
GOODNESS for goodness sake → **for Christ's SAKE**
goodness knows → **GOD knows**
honest to goodness → **honest to GOD**
my goodness nossa! puxa! meu Deus! *... my goodness, when you think of all the unhappiness you've had ...* -HA,4.

thank goodness graças a Deus! *Thank goodness! The child is still alive!*

GOODS catch with the goods [col] apanhar com a boca na botija, pegar em flagrante delito *Big Harry was caught with the goods and was sent to prison.*

deliver the goods [col] executar eficientemente sua função ou tarefa, cumprir o prometido, fazer o que é esperado *If you deliver the goods you will get ahead in this job.*

dry goods tecidos, roupas *He took a summer job in a local dry goods store ...* -LI,14.

get/have the goods on [col] conseguir ou ter prova incriminadora contra *[She is] ... a British agent who has just about got the goods on a big international spy ring.* -T/60.

GOOD-SIZED de bom tamanho *... larger [crocodiles] ... have a gruesomely efficient means of tearing up a good-sized animal.* -SK,44. ♦ *... a good-sized crowd of people ...* -HO,131.

GOOF goof around [gír] matar o tempo, fazer hora *Rocky has been goofing around with a friend all afternoon.*

goof off [gir] esquivar-se ao trabalho, fugir à responsabilidade, matar o tempo *I've been goofing off since the day I was born.* -HJC,175.

goof up [gir] cometer um erro crasso, pisar na bola, dar mancada, baralhar, misturar, confundir, pôr (algo) a perder por incompetência, descuido etc. *We thought he'd do a competent job but he goofed up.* ♦ *They goofed things up.*

GOOSE cook one's/someone's goose [col] arruinar a reputação, as esperanças etc. de, deixar em apuros [mais comum na passiva: *one's goose is cooked*] ficar em apuros, arruinado etc., estar frito *Eddie knew his goose was cooked when the police found cocaine in his apartment.*

goose egg [gir] zero (nota escolar ou resultado de jogo) *Too many goose eggs and you're no longer a student at this school.*

goose flesh/bumps/pimples pele arrepiada (de medo ou frio), pele anserina *Each time he went to see a war movie and heard the air raid siren he got goose flesh.* ♦ *... I broke out with a rash of goose-pimples ...* -T/73.

kill the goose that lays/laid the golden eggs matar a galinha dos ovos de ouro *Don't kill the goose that lays the golden eggs by asking for more money than you have already been given.*

wild-goose chase → **WILD-goose chase**

GORGE make one's gorge rise causar nojo, repulsa, indignação ou raiva a *The cruelties to which the soldiers were subjecting the civilians made my gorge rise.*

GOSPEL gospel truth a verdade absoluta, afirmação ou fato inquestionável *[The novels of Thomas Wolfe] ... suddenly depart into the realm of pure fiction just when a reader is inclined to accept everything in them as the gospel truth.* -NEW,11.

GRAB grab bag 1. aglomerado de coisas dissimilares, conjunto de coisas várias e diferentes, miscelânea *[South America] ... is a grab bag of contrasts and conflicting tendencies ...* -GJI,604. ♦ *The book is undeniably awkward at times, a grab bag of facts and fancy ...* -T/87. 2. fonte de lucros, vantagens e proveitos (às vezes duvidosos) *When the government decided to award contracts for airfields it was a grab bag for graft and corruption.*

how does that grab you? [gir] qual é sua reação a isso? que acha disso? que tal? *And our deal would be satisfactorily concluded [if you would agree to my proposal]. How does that grab you?* -WI,157.

up for grabs [gir] disponível a quem quiser tomar posse, pagar o preço exigido ou fazer o esforço necessário para conseguir *... the party's highest prize [is] up for grabs ...* -T/64. *The business was up for grabs after the head of the company killed himself.*

GRACE fall from grace cair no desagrado, cair do pedestal, impopularizar-se, perder o conceito *The presidential candidate fell from grace when his sexual liaison with a starlet became known.*

grace period = **DAYS of grace**

in someone's good//bad graces nas boas graças de//em descrédito, sem apoio, mal com alguém *Wilbur was trying to get back in his girl's good graces.*

saving grace predicado redentor, a boa qualidade que redime as outras deficiências *[His] ... only saving grace is his love for a young girl ...* -SLE,133.

say grace orar (antes da refeição) agradecendo a Deus pelo alimento *We usually said grace at our Thanksgiving meal.*

There, but for the grace of God (go I) não fosse pela graça de Deus, sorte, circunstâncias etc. (poderia ser eu/você/ele a vítima, o réu, a pessoa em questão, quem vai sofrer as conseqüências etc.) *Watching Noel's coffin being carried out of Washington's National Presbyterian Church, Elbrick thought, There, but for the grace of God.* -LA,303. ♦ *There, but for the*

grace of God go you and I. It could happen to any of us. -T/64.
with (a) good//bad grace de boa//má vontade, cortesmente//grosseiramente *Virginia took her husband's comments with good grace.*

GRADE grade school → **GRAMMAR school**
make the grade superar os obstáculos, alcançar seu objetivo, alcançar o padrão exigido, tornar-se apto, capaz, sair-se bem, vencer *Although Crane doesn't have much ability, his personal charm will help him make the grade in his new job.*

GRAIN against one's/the grain a contrapelo, a contragosto, contra a própria vontade, de mau grado [geralmente **go against one's/the grain**, ser contra a índole de uma pessoa, irritar alguém] *It goes against my grain to let someone cheat me openly.* ♦ *No man is to be forced to believe in something that goes against the grain of his conscience.* -BL,94.
with a grain of salt com cautela, com ceticismo, com reserva *His words are to be taken with a grain of salt.*

GRAMMAR grammar/grade school escola primária *Generally including the first six or eight grades of the common school system, ... [elementary school] has been called the "grade school" or the "grammar school".* -HH,231.

GRANDSTAND grandstand play; grandstanding [col] jogada exibicionista, lance para a platéia aplaudir; exibicionismo, teatralidade *When he stopped making grandstand plays and settled down to organization teamwork, his team began to win games.* ♦ *... his blunt language and grandstanding earned him enemies.* -T/87.

GRAPE sour grape(s) algo pretensamente desprezado por não poder ser alcançado ou possuído, desculpa fingida, uvas verdes *Henry Clay, who spent 20 years trying to occupy the White House, finally produced that famous sour grape: "I would rather be right than President".* -T/68.

GRAPEVINE (the) grapevine [col] meio de transmissão de informações; boato, rumor *[The gangsters] ... soon knew, through the underworld grapevine, exactly where he [a rival gangster] had settled.* -TB,13. ♦ *I've heard by the grapevine that Fred will soon be dismissed.*

GRASP have a good grasp of ter bom domínio de, entender bem de, estar a par de *He has a good grasp of nuclear physics.*

GRASS the grass is (always) greener on the other side of the fence a galinha do vizinho é (sempre) mais gorda *Although his wife is young and lovely, Adam seems to think that the grass is greener on the other side of the fence.*
grass roots os cidadãos comuns, especialmente as populações de áreas rurais, consideradas um grupo sociopolítico-econômico e apoio fundamental, a fonte básica de um movimento etc.; as regiões agrícolas e rurais *The President's plea for help [on the war against drugs] at the grass roots has not gone unheeded.* -T/86. ♦ *... grass-roots organizations ...* -T/87.
grass widow mulher divorciada ou separada *Frances has been a grass widow since the war.*
not let the grass grow under one's feet não perder tempo, não ficar na expectativa, agir rapidamente, despachar-se *Don't let the grass grow under your feet! Be an active worker and you will succeed.*

GRASSHOPPER knee-high to a grasshopper [col] da altura de uma criança pequena, baixo, pequenino *... I've never set foot in a church since I was knee-high to a grasshopper ...* -HJE,176.

GRAVE turn in one's grave; turn over in one's grave ficar profundamente magoado ou irado (alguém já falecido), não descansar em seu túmulo *Your Irish grandmother would turn over in her grave if she knew you had married an English girl.*

GRAVEYARD SHIFT [col] período de trabalho noturno, turno da noite *I never liked to work from 11 at night to 7 in the morning, on the so-called graveyard shift.*

GRAVY **gravy train** [gir] mamata, trem da alegria *When a politician takes over a government, all his friends get on the gravy train and help themselves to well-paid jobs.*

GREAT **great at** hábil em, perito em *Farley is great at games where agility and not strength counts.*

great big [col] bem grande *... he wanted to ... live in the great big outdoors.* -GE,116.

GREEK **be Greek to** [col] ser obscuro, ininteligível para, ser grego para *I'm sorry but I can't make out the note he left. It's all Greek to me.*

GREEN-EYED ciumento, invejoso *Green-eyed, tempestuous, unscrupulous, false-hearted Scarlett O'Hara is one of the bitchiest heroines of fiction ...* -SV,90. v. **green-eyed MONSTER**

GREENHOUSE 1. estufa (para cultivo de plantas) *In the glass greenhouse, flowers will grow even in winter.* 2. relativo a *greenhouse effect*, causado pelo efeito-estufa *... carbon dioxides and other greenhouse gases.* -T/92.

greenhouse effect efeito-estufa *... scientists are also concerned about the "greenhouse effect," a long-term warming of the planet caused by chemical changes in the atmosphere.* -T/87.

GRIEF **come to grief** falhar, fracassar, arruinar-se, sofrer um desapontamento ou acidente, ter um resultado infeliz *Wright's attempts to explain flying saucers and other similar phenomema soon came to grief.* ♦ *Mat came to grief when he was racing around in his sports car.*

good grief meu Deus! puxa vida! credo! *Good grief! Here comes Charlie Brown!*

GRIN **grin and bear it** sorrir em face da adversidade, suportar com estoicismo *Regret it as he may, [he] will have to grin and bear it.* -T/64.

wipe the/that grin/smile off one's face [col] parar de rir, de brincar (e concentrar-se no que está fazendo), ficar sério, prestar atenção etc. *Wipe that grin off your face, soldier!*

GRIND **daily grind** o trabalho ou a rotina diária monótona e cansativa *... the daily grind that keeps them (a man and a woman) from getting together.* -WCG,14.

grind down enfraquecer, destruir gradualmente, oprimir, reprimir, manter submisso *... most women among the common people before our own century were ground down by the sheer struggle for existence ...* -SE,xii.

grind out → **CHURN out**

GRIP **at grips with** a braços com *The detective was at grips with a puzzle he couldn't solve.*

come to grips 1. empenhar-se em luta, atracar-se *I knew that they would come to grips sooner or later.* 2. ver-se a braços, começar a lidar (com problema etc.) *... many religions involve at their cores an attempt to come to grips with profound mysteries of our individual life histories ...* -SC,xii.

get a grip on 1. agarrar, segurar *Get a grip on the back of the canoe and I'll get the front so that we can lift it out of the water.* 2. controlar, dominar *... good God, you're acting as if it's the first girl you ever knew. Get a grip on yourself.* -WCN,288.

in the grip of sob o domínio de, nas garras de *Poland was in the grip of a nationwide strike.* -T/82.

keep//lose one's grip manter//perder o poder de compreender ou fazer (algo), manter//perder o controle, a habilidade, o jeito *... scientists who become so obsessed with their theories that they lose their grip on real life.* -T/91. ♦ *Guy was a famous tennis player but heavy drinking made him lose his grip.*

GRIST **grist to/for one's/the mill** algo que pode ser útil, vantajoso, profícuo, aproveitável etc. para alguém *When Reynolds lived in Italy he saw plenty of material which was grist to his mill and later he wrote a fine book on Italian architecture of the Renaissance.*

GROOVE **in the groove** [gir] em ótima forma, indo muito bem, funcionando perfeitamente *[After the successful rocket flight, NASA project manager said] "We feel we are back in the groove."* -T/86.

GROSS **gross out** desagradar, insultar, ofender *Ted said something that grossed me out.*

GROUND **break ground** 1. escavar o solo (para iniciar construção), dar início à obra *In 1966 [he] broke ground for his 13-story Tower of Hope ...* -T/85. 2. iniciar (um empreendimento) *... Nixon ... broke diplomatic ground just by arriving in Bucharest.* -T/69.

break new ground inovar, introduzir novos métodos etc., iniciar algo novo e diferente *... professional articles that often break new ground.* -T/64. ⇒ **groundbreaking** original, inovador, novo *... a groundbreaking film ...* -T/87. ♦ *... a groundbreaking idea ...* -T/87.

cover a lot of ground 1. abranger grande extensão ou área, percorrer grande distância, viajar *The congressman covered a lot of ground on his trip to the Southwest.* 2. discutir (algo) de maneira ampla, tratar de muitos assuntos, abranger muita coisa *His field of expertise is reality and that covers a lot of ground.*

from the ground up do início, desde o começo, inteiramente *... the company practically rebuilt our product from the ground up.* ♦ *We want you to learn the manufacturing process from the ground up.*

gain//lose ground ganhar//perder terreno *In his attempt to stop the river from flooding his property, Simmons would gain ground for a time and then lose it in one day.* ♦ *[He] ... has lost ground among voters ...* -T/87.

get in on the ground floor [col] ser dos primeiros a participar de um negócio, empresa etc. obtendo assim uma posição vantajosa ou oportunidade excelente *We get in on the ground floor of investments.* -GES,108.

get off the ground começar a concretizar-se, ter início, ocorrer, decolar *... it is doubtful that ... the cease-fire will get off the ground this week.* -T/87.

give ground retirar-se, ceder terreno *The two boys began to fight fiercely and neither of them gave ground.*

ground rule regra básica, princípio fundamental *Under the ground rules, ... [the CIA Director] refused to discuss sources or methods of covert operations.* -T/86.

ground zero início, começo, estaca zero *The campaign goes back to ground zero.* -T/87.

happy hunting ground campos de caça do além [o conceito de paraíso dos guerreiros e caçadores de certas tribos de indígenas americanos] *When Indians died, they were said to go to the happy hunting grounds.*

hold/stand one's ground não ceder terreno, permanecer firme, resistir, não mudar de atitude *The platoon was told to try to hold its ground until relief could be sent to their aid.* ♦ *He turned on her ... but she stood her ground ...* -LM,168.

lose ground → **gain GROUND**

on the ground(s) of/that; on grounds of sob a justificativa de, em razão de, com o pretexto de *... he petitioned for release [from prison] on the grounds of ill health.* -SGF,105. ♦ *[He] ... was discharged from the Army in World War II on grounds of mental instability.* -T/77.

run into the ground [col] esgotar, exaurir, estragar (à força de tanto usar etc.), levar à exaustão, ao desgaste, à deterioração etc. *... the socialist National Liberation Front ... has run the country's economy into the ground through corruption, mismanagement, nepotism and sloth.* -T/92.

run to ground → **run to EARTH**

shift (one's) ground mudar de atitude, assumir outra posição, adotar argumentação diferente ... *they became convinced that Wilson, for political reasons, had actually shifted ground* ... -T/72.

stamping/stomping ground [col] hábitat, ambiente natural, lugar normalmente freqüentado *All athletes normally play better on their own stamping grounds.*

stand one's ground → **hold one's GROUND**

suit (right) down to the ground [col] satisfazer plenamente *We got a place that'll suit you right down to the ground.* -PRT,9.

to the ground completamente, totalmente, por inteiro ... *the house of one friend had already burned to the ground.* -EM,23.

worship the ground someone walks/ stands on amar imensamente, idolatrar, ter profunda devoção por *I worship the ground she walks on.* -KS,71. ♦ *Monica about worships the ground he walks on.* -WH,281. ♦ *He worshipped the ground she stood on.* -HJC,225.

GROUNDBREAKING → **break new GROUND**

GROW grow (cold, dark, old etc.) tornar-se, ficar (frio = esfriar, arrefecer; escuro = escurecer; velho = envelhecer) *The fires of radicalism have grown cold.* -T/61. ♦ *I'm growing weary of all this.*

grow into crescer e transformar-se em, tornar-se, fazer-se *The boy soon grew into a man.*

grow on/upon 1. ter crescente influência ou efeito sobre, cair no gosto ou apreciação de, agradar mais e mais a *After you have been in Brazil for a while, the country grows on you and you don't want to leave.* 2. arraigar-se em, tornar-se mais forte, intensificar-se *The conviction has grown on me that I shall never express myself dramatically.* -NEW,63.

grow out of 1. resultar de, provir de, ser conseqüência de ... *many serious arguments, even fights and wars, grow out of misunderstandings* ... -LCT,17. 2. crescer demais para (usar suas roupas etc.) *Many children grow out of clothes so rapidly that their shoes never need to be repaired.* 3. perder com a idade, livrar-se de (hábito, complexo etc.) com o passar do tempo *[President Ronald] ... Reagan declared that the country had grown out of its "Vietnam syndrome"...* -T/81. **v. OUT of**

grow up 1. crescer, tornar-se adulto *Beth grew up in Canada.* ♦ *[They] ... grew up with American rock music and Hollywood movies ...* -T/92. ⇒ **grown-up** a. pessoa adulta *The magic world of moviemaker Steven Spielberg fascinates children and grown-ups alike.* b. adulto, próprio de adultos *grown-up daughter* ♦ *grown-up behavior* 2. vir a ser, surgir, desenvolver-se *That strange custom seems to have grown up during World War I.*

GRUDGE bear/harbor/have/hold/nurse a grudge nutrir ressentimento, guardar rancor ... *some enemy who bore him a grudge and sought revenge.* -CEO,32. ♦ *[He] ... harbored a grudge against [them]* ... -T/72.

G-STRING tanga reduzidíssima, tapa-sexo, fio dental (usado principalmente por *strip-teasers*) *A young woman slowly strips down to her G-string, thrusting her naked breasts toward the audience.* -T/91.

GUARD off//on (one's) guard desprevenido, desprotegido, distraído//vigilante, prevenido, preparado ... *catch them off guard.* -FV,23. ♦ ... *he was ... very much on his guard.* -T/86.

stand guard estar de guarda, ficar de sentinela ... *together (they) stood guard over America's secrets for much of the postwar era.* -T/80.

GUESS anybody's/anyone's/ guess coisa que ninguém sabe, da qual ninguém tem certeza *What such creatures [from other planets] would look like and act like is anyone's guess.* -LJ,156.

educated guess hipótese, conjetura, palpite etc. apoiado em fatos, informações, conhecimento ou experiência *None of the experts ... would [venture] ... much more than an educated guess about what Europe will look like [in a few years' time].* -T/91.

guess at fazer conjeturas, arriscar um palpite *... they could only guess at the extent of the collaboration.* -T/92.

have another guess coming [gir] estar errado, enganado, estar cometendo um equívoco *"If you think you can do as you please", his angry father shouted at him, "you have another guess coming."*

wild guess conjetura, suposição ou palpite sem fundamento, sem lógica *Any guess about it was a wild guess.* -FV,23.

your guess is as good as mine seu palpite vale tanto quanto o meu, i.e., ninguém sabe nada *We don't know what happened there. Your guess is as good as mine.*

GUEST be my guest fique à vontade! por favor! não faça cerimônia! [exprime afirmação cordial a uma solicitação] *"May I borrow your dictionary just for a minute?" "Of course! Be my guest!"*

GULP gulp down comer ou beber às pressas ou vorazmente, engolir *Bert gulped down the coffee and left in a hurry.* ♦ *[His] ... idea of a meal is to gulp down a hamburger and french fries in three minutes flat.* -T/80.

GUN big gun [gir] = big SHOT *[The two new executives have been described as] ... a finely matched pair of big guns.* -T/73.

give it the gun [gir] acelerar à velocidade máxima (veículo, motor) *When we saw the police coming after us, we gave it the gun and roared away in a cloud of dust.*

great guns [col] com grande intensidade, vigorosamente; com eficiência, com pleno êxito, muito bem *... the wind blowing great guns.* -SLT,124. ♦ *Their business is going great guns.*

gun down alvejar, abater a tiros *They were gunned down by a rival mob.*

gun for procurar (alguém) com intenção de matar (com arma de fogo) *... Terry was gunning for Johnny ...* -SB,266.

jump the gun 1. iniciar prova (corrida etc.) antes do sinal *The runners jumped the gun and were called back by the starter.* 2. começar antes do tempo devido, antecipar-se aos outros, agir prematuramente *The holiday doesn't begin until Friday but many jumped the gun and quit work Thursday at noon.*

smoking gun [col] evidência clara e inequívoca de algo, principalmente da perpetração de um delito *... the investigators had not found a "smoking gun" in the President's hand.* -T/87. ♦ *The so-called smoking-gun tapes that prompted Nixon's resignation were released in August 1974.* -T/91.

spike one's guns inviabilizar os planos ou as intenções de, frustrar *We spiked his guns before he went through with his crazy plan.*

stick to one's guns manter-se firme, opor resistência, não ceder *No matter what happens, he will stick to his guns.*

under the gun submetido a coerção, sob pressão ou coação, sob a ameaça de ataque *An old Italian longshoreman who was under the gun in Jersey City and afraid even to sign his name ...* -SB,266.

GUNG gung ho, gung-ho [col] extremamente zeloso, ardoroso, ansioso, impaciente, cheio de otimismo e entusiasmo incontidos e freqüentemente ingênuos *He was gung ho just like the marines in the movies.* ♦ *... a gung-ho patriot ...* -T/86.

GUNPOINT at gunpoint; at the point of a gun sob a ameaça de uma arma de fogo *Grady's specialty was jewel robbery at gunpoint ...* -QE,97. ♦ *[He was] ... holding his pursuers off at the point of a gun ...* -WM,187.

GUN-SHY 1. que se assusta facilmente com o som do disparo de uma arma ou com outros estrondos *In Destry [a western movie], Audie Murphy plays a pseudo* *gun-shy sheriff who brings law and order to a frontier town.* 2. desconfiado, cauteloso, receoso *[The U.S.] ... began to feel gun-shy about protecting its national interests even in the strategically critical Persian Gulf.* -T/87.

GUSSY gussy up [gir] vestir-se bem, vestir roupas vistosas, embelezar, decorar *Nanette got all gussied up for the party.* ♦ *The city is all gussied up ...* -T/87.

GUTS [gir] coragem, ousadia, perseverança, vigor *It takes guts to do what he did.*
hate someone's guts [gir] detestar, odiar intensamente, não ir com a cara de *She hates my guts ... She thinks I killed her husband.* -HJ,84.
spill one's guts [gir] abrir o bico, desembuchar, confessar, cagüetar *He changed his mind at the last minute and spilled his guts.*

GUY bad//good guys [col] bandidos//mocinhos, vilões//heróis *If you cannot tell the good guys from the bad guys in the western, your reactions will be all wrong ...* -CCC,11.
a regular guy [col] um cara legal *... even if he is a millionaire's son, he is the most regular guy you ever knew.* -MMA,48.
wise guy [gir] indivíduo convencido, sabichão, espertinho *Don't try to be a wise guy with me.*

HABIT be in the habit of ter o hábito de *Len is in the habit of smoking in bed.*
fall/get into the habit of adquirir o hábito de, acostumar-se a *He fell into the habit of dropping in at night clubs ...* -DJ,85.
kick the/a habit [gir] livrar-se de droga, vício, cigarro, hábito etc. *... companies can help employees kick the drug habit ...* -T/86. ♦ *... 30% of the group had kicked the habit completely or had cut down to ten or fewer cigarettes a day.* -T/73.
set in one's habits → **set in one's WAYS**

HAIL hail from provir de, vir de *Fuller hails from a small town in Idaho.*
within hail → **within CALL**

HAIL-FELLOW; HAIL-FELLOW-WELL-MET 1. amistoso, amigável, sociável, amável no trato, urbano, afável *[He was] ... a hail-fellow, stogie-smoking Kansan ...* -T/87. ♦ *Drake was always hail-fellow-well-met with all of us.* 2. bom amigo, camarada *In college, they were always hail-fellows-well-met.*

HAILING hailing distance → **within hailing DISTANCE**

HAIR by a hair; by a hair's breadth por um triz, por pequeníssima margem, por um fio de cabelo *... he could still win [the election] by a hair ...* -T/87. ♦ *The first bombs missed their objective by a hair's breadth.* -T/89. v. **hairbreadth**
get in one's hair [gir] enervar, irritar *... do business with them ... without letting them get under your skin or in your hair.* -KJS,192.
in one's hair [gir] amolando, incomodando, importunando *That guy is still in my hair.* ♦ *[The Air Force] ... didn't want [him] ... or any other [flying] saucer fans in their hair.* -RE,93.
let one's hair down [gir] 1. ficar à vontade, agir sem cerimônia *Let your hair down, relax and have a good time.* 2. falar com toda a franqueza, fazer confidências *When we were alone, Debbie let her hair down and I understood her problems.*
not turn a hair não demonstrar medo, surpresa etc., estar senhor de si, não se perturbar *Monique didn't turn a hair when the police started questioning her.*
out of one's hair [gir] já não importunando, já não incomodando *Margot's maid keeps the children out of her hair.*
split hairs exagerar nas distinções, discutir sobre minúcias insignificantes *Let's not split hairs over unimportant points.*
to a hair exatamente, com precisão, com

exatidão rigorosa *Maggie's new dress fits her to a hair.*

HAIRBREADTH estreito, pequeníssimo, exíguo ... *after a hairbreadth defeat to John F. Kennedy for the presidency in 1960, [Nixon] left Washington an unhappy man.* -T/87.

HAIRPIN hairpin bend/curve/turn curva muito fechada, curva em forma de *U* *They would soon reach the hair-pin turn.* -SF,32.

HALE hale and hearty saudável e vigoroso *He was hale and hearty after a good rest on a farm.*

HALF better half [col] cara-metade, esposa *"This is Zillah, my better half", Lou said as he introduced his wife to a friend.*

by halves pela metade, incompletamente, imperfeitamente *She could do nothing by halves. She loved desperately and hated desperately.* -JEP,234.

go halves repartir igualmente, dividir meio a meio (despesas etc.) *Let's go halves on the lunch.*

not half bad [col] = **not (so) BAD** *The movie was not half bad.*

not know the half of it não saber da missa a metade, saber menos do que pensa *You think you know what this is all about, don't you? Well, you don't know the half of it!*

HALF-BAKED [col] incompleto, imperfeito, mal-acabado, falho *a half-baked plan* ♦ *half-baked thoughts*

HALF-BREED; HALF-CASTE mestiço; indivíduo mestiço ... *no one will ever take you for an Injun [Indian] – or a half-breed either.* -LMT,9. ♦ ... *a half-breed boy on an odyssey of vengeance ...* -T/66.

HALF-COCKED deficientemente planejado, sem preparo ou reflexão prévia, malesboçado, prematuro, precipitado *Shaw often rushes into things in a half-cocked manner.* ♦ *a half-cocked plan*

HALFHEARTED; HALF-HEARTED irresoluto, tíbio, desanimado, sem ardor ... *the central governments's efforts ... have been halfhearted at best.* -T/92. ♦ ... *halfhearted objections ...* -T/64.

HALF-MAST at half-mast a meio-pau [bandeira] *The flags flew at half-mast in honor of the deceased President.*

HALT bring to a halt fazer parar, pôr fim a *Lack of funds brought to a halt the completion of the new highway.* ♦ *[He] ... brought the car to a screeching halt ...* -T/72.

call a halt pôr fim a, encerrar, dar por terminado ... *he urged [President] Reagan to make a public statement calling a halt to the arms sales [to Iran].* -T/86.

come/draw to a halt parar, cessar, fazer alto, deter-se *After capturing Leipzig, the U.S. First Army drew to a halt along the Mulde River ...* -T/85.

grind to a halt 1. diminuir gradualmente a velocidade até parar (veículo) ... *when the German convoy ground to a halt, the partisans began searching the trucks.* -T/85. 2. cessar gradualmente (ação, atividade, processo etc.) até parar *As the official economy has virtually ground to a halt, the illegal underground economy has boomed.* -T/87.

HAMMER hammer and tongs [col] com grande energia, vigor, força, barulho etc. [freqüentemente na frase *go at it hammer and tongs*, discutir violentamente, brigar; iniciar ou fazer algo com todo o vigor, energia etc.] *Wright enters every new project hammer and tongs.* ♦ *Early the next morning my father and mother were at it hammer and tongs trying to work out what to do.* -TRL,11.

hammer away at trabalhar com afinco em, concentrar esforços em, reiterar, insistir, malhar (no mesmo assunto) *A good detective hammers away at any slight discrepancy in a suspect's story.* ♦ *[He] ... hammered away at his typewriter ...* -T/73.

hammer home enfatizar, dar grande importância a (argumento, questão etc.) a fim de que seja bem compreendido *The health authorities are trying to hammer home the fact that children must be kept clean and well-nourished.*

hammer into fazer gravar (na mente) por repetição incessante, repetir (algo) com insistência, repisar *I'm going to hammer into you all the facts you must know to pass the test.*

hammer out formar, elaborar, criar, produzir, realizar, discutir (algo) e chegar a uma decisão *[He] ... insisted on hammering out a detailed agreement ...* -T/84.

under the hammer em leilão *Melinda cried when she saw all her family heirlooms go under the hammer.*

HAND at close hand de perto, à pequena distância *... for the first time in his life Shig was able to study at close hand a refined human mind at work.* -MJA,1015.

at first hand diretamente da fonte original, por experiência própria, pessoalmente *... the shabby world that ... [she] knew at first hand ...* -T/60. ⇒ **firsthand** direto, pessoal; diretamente, pessoalmente, de experiência própria *firsthand observations* ♦ *firsthand experience* ♦ *... I have experienced firsthand the many problems of California ...* -T/91.

(close/near) at hand próximo, à mão; prestes a acontecer *The Christmas season is close at hand.* ♦ *This is a good place for a family to live with stores, school and parks at hand.*

at second hand por vias indiretas, por meio de um intermediário, indiretamente, não por experiência própria *I had this information at second hand.* ⇒ **secondhand** 1. de segunda mão, usado, inferior *a secondhand car* 2. indireto, derivado, feito ou recebido por intermédio de outrem *secondhand information* 3. que vende mercadorias usadas (loja) *a secondhand bookstore* 4. = **at second HAND** *... the mass of people obtain ideas secondhand ...* -DR,13.

at the hand(s) of por meio da ação de, por ato de, pela mão de *... you have nothing to fear at our hands.* -WL,99.

a big hand aplauso caloroso *Let's give this next singer a big hand to show that we appreciate her.*

bite the hand that feeds one retribuir com ingratidão, levantar as mãos contra o seu benfeitor, cuspir no prato em que come *You'll be most ungrateful if you bite the hand that feeds you.*

by hand à mão, manualmente *[The interviews] ... were copied by hand ...* -HE,46.

change hands passar à posse de outra pessoa, mudar de dono *It seems as if some money has changed hands in the agreement.*

come to hand estar próximo, à mão, acessível *Jack grabbed everything that came to hand and hurled it at the mad dog that was trying to attack him.*

die by one's own hand suicidar-se *[His father] ... had died by his own hand in 1928.* -T/61.

eat out of someone's hand fazer o que outra pessoa quer, tornar-se extremamente dócil e servil, submeter-se totalmente *He's even got the governor ... eating out of his hand.* -CEB,35.

force someone's hand forçar alguém a agir, a tomar uma atitude ou a revelar suas intenções prematuramente *[They hoped that] ... public pressure would force the President's hand.* -T/73.

a free hand carta branca, plena liberdade de ação *If we are to do a good job, we must be given a free hand.*

full hand → **full HOUSE**

gain the upper hand → **get the upper HAND**

get one's hand in familiarizar-se com uma ocupação, um processo, acostumar-se com uma atividade, adquirir prática *I'm sure I won't find it difficult to operate that machine once I've got my hand in.*

get one's hands on → **lay one's HANDS on**

get out of hand fugir ao controle, desgovernar-se, exceder-se *The meeting got out of hand and the police were called in to restore order.* v. **out of HAND**

get/gain/have/take the upper hand ter/assumir o controle, o poder, dominar, mandar *It is difficult to tell which political party has the upper hand in that country.*

give/lend a hand dar uma mão a, ajudar *Come here and give me a hand with this heavy box.*

the glad hand [gir] cumprimento cordial (nem sempre sincero) *A politician always gives the glad hand to his prospective voters.*

a good/skillful//poor hand at pessoa hábil//inábil em (determinada atividade, assunto etc.) *Ward is a good hand at giving advice, but a poor hand at doing anything practical.* ♦ *I'm a good hand at sleeping.* -RQ,27.

hand down 1. passar, transmitir (de pai para filho), legar (de geração para geração) *The formula has been handed down from father to son.* 2. pronunciar (veredicto, decisão) *... the Supreme Court handed down a decision ...* -T/63. ♦ *This is not a trial. We're not handing down verdicts.* -T/87.

hand in entregar, dar, apresentar *Mr. Powell handed in his resignation.*

hand in/and glove em estreito acordo ou cooperação, estreitamente ligado, em íntimas relações *[They] ... had once worked hand in glove for a Communist spy ring ...* -T/61. ♦ *The organization is working hand in glove with the police.*

hand in hand 1. de mãos dadas, um segurando a mão do outro *The song It's Magic, by Styne and Cahn, says: "When we walk hand in hand/The world becomes a wonderland".* 2. em cooperação, junto(s), conjuntamente *Population increases have gone hand in hand with the emergence of many new nations.* -MJL,99.

hand it to someone [gir] dar o devido crédito a, reconhecer o mérito de *Hank had to hand it to Glenn: he could certainly handle Robish.* -HJD,5.

hand out distribuir, dar *Pat was handing out leaflets to passersby.* ⇒ **handout** esmola, donativo (roupa, alimento, dinheiro etc.) *[They] ... want handouts from the Government ...* -T/84.

hand over entregar, ceder, dar, passar para outrem *... military regimes have voluntarily handed over power to civilian governments ...* -T/87. ♦ *[He] ... handed over his wallet [to the robbers] ...* -T/80.

hand over fist [col] com rapidez e em grande abundância *They're making money hand over fist in their new business.*

handpicked; hand-picked escolhido a dedo *... respected statesmen hand-picked by the President.* -T/87.

hands down facilmente, sem esforço *They won the game hands down.* ⇒ **hands-down** fácil *It was a hands-down victory.*

hand to hand corpo a corpo, a curta distância *They fought hand to hand.* ⇒ **hand-to-hand** de corpo a corpo, de homem para homem *hand-to-hand combat*

hand up entregar (indiciação, acusação formal) a um juiz ou autoridade superior [diz-se de um júri] *... the Washington grand jury ... handed up its major indictments in the Watergate cover-up case.* -BC,366.

have/take a hand in tomar parte em, estar metido em *[He] ... had a hand in Joey's murder.* -T/72. ♦ *[He] ... took a hand in the effort to break the siege [of the city].* -T/72.

have one's hands full estar muito ocupado, ter muito trabalho, ter muito que fazer *Anyone who tries to control inflation will have his hands full.*

have the upper hand → **get the upper HAND**

helping hand ajuda, auxílio *She often lends a helping hand when there's work to be done.*

hold a good hand ter boas cartas na mão *A good card player doesn't need to hold a good hand to win the game.*

hold hands segurar a(s) mão(s) um do outro, dar as mãos *It was their last night together, and they were holding hands under the table ...* -FP,5.

in hand 1. na mão, disponível, em sua posse *We still have a large sum of money in hand.* 2. sob controle *They seem to have the situation pretty well in hand.* 3. em curso, em andamento, recebendo atenção *We must not be distracted from the task in hand.*

in one's/someone's hands sob o controle ou sob os cuidados de alguém *We ... have it in our hands to determine the future appearance of the planet's land areas ...* -WCB,162. ♦ *I leave this matter in your hands.*

keep one's hand in manter a forma ou habilidade, manter-se treinado, adestrado *Tommy plays a little basketball each week to keep his hand in.*

lay a hand on → **lay a FINGER on**

lay hands on 1. localizar, apanhar, agarrar, segurar, prender *If I lay hands on that guy I'll wring his neck.* 2. usar de violência com, maltratar, atacar *Don't you dare lay hands on that boy!*

lay one's hand on achar, encontrar *I can never lay my hand on a literary quotation when I want to check the correct wording.*

lay/get one's hands on 1. apanhar, pegar, obter, conseguir, achar *... he had read everything he could get his hands on ...* -NEW,29. 2. maltratar, bater em *I'm warning you, don't ever lay your hands on my children again!*

lend a hand → **give a HAND**

live from hand to mouth viver ao acaso, viver ao deus-dará *In India, more than half the population live from hand to mouth.* ⇒ **hand-to-mouth** precário, penurioso, minguado *Judson has been leading a hand-to-mouth existence for the past three years.*

not lift a hand → **not lift a FINGER**

off//on one's hands não mais sob os cuidados ou responsabilidade de, fora das mãos de//sob os cuidados de, sob a responsabilidade de, nas mãos de *Thank God, that problem is off my hands now.* ♦ *When Bendix described the situation, we knew we had a difficult job on our hands.*

an old hand pessoa experiente, indivíduo traquejado *Griffin is an old hand at this job.*

on hand perto, próximo, presente; em estoque, disponível, à disposição, à mão *This is a book to be kept on hand for ready reference ...* -SJJ,xi. ♦ *We don't happen to have any imported speakers for your hi-fi on hand this week.*

on (one's) hands and knees de quatro *Gail was on her hands and knees looking under the bed.*

on (the) one hand//on the other hand por um lado, de um ponto de vista//por outro lado, de outro ponto de vista *[He was] Sensitive and introspective on the one hand but aggressive and sensual on the other ...* -CS,501. ♦ *Rio is a very beautiful place, but on the other hand, it is warm and humid.*

on one's hands → **off//on one's HANDS**

out of hand 1. desgovernado, sem controle *Some people believe that the economy is out of hand in the U.S.* 2. imediatamente, sem perda de tempo, prontamente *[They] ... rejected the idea out of hand.* -T/87. ♦ *[He] ... dismissed the proposal out of hand.* -T/87.

overplay one's hand superestimar a própria força (seguindo-se possíveis resultados negativos) *Carey was so sure of himself that he overplayed his hand and lost the confidence of the voters.*

play a hand tomar parte ativa, ter atuação, cooperar (para uma finalidade) *Lafayette played a hand in the American Revolution.*

play a lone hand agir sozinho, não estar associado a ninguém, ser independente *[He was] ... a man playing a lone hand against heavy odds ...* -HJ,42.

play into someone's hands fazer algo ou agir de maneira que inadvertidamente beneficie ou dê vantagem a um adversário *I told them they were playing themselves into the hands of people who don't care about them.* -T/92. ♦ *Stan played into the hands of his critics when he admitted that he had knowledge of the document.*

put/set/turn one's hand to dedicar-se a, empreender, atacar (tarefa, serviço etc.) *Every enterprise to which he had set his hand had come to a dismal conclusion.* -DR,28. ♦ *Matthews can turn his hand to any job and make it a success.*

shake someone's hand(s); shake the hand(s) of; shake hand(s) (with) apertar a mão de (alguém) em cumprimento, cumprimentar (alguém) com um aperto de mão *When Mrs. Hayward came into my office I stood up and shook her hand.* ♦ *... the two Democratic candidates moved onto the floor to shake the hands of delighted delegates ...* -T/84. ♦ *Hayden and I shook hands again when he left my office.*

show one's hand/cards [gir] mostrar as cartas, revelar as intenções *... Trumbell would eventually be forced to meet his demands when he showed his cards.* -OFW,24. ♦ *... she would show her hand when she was ready.* -DD,41.

sit on one's hands [col] 1. recusar-se a aplaudir *The audience were not impressed by the comedian's jokes and sat on their hands.* 2. ficar de braços cruzados, não prestar auxílio *You sat on your hands when I needed you.*

someone's hands are tied as mãos de alguém estão atadas, alguém está impedido de agir *My hands are tied. There's nothing I can possibly do in this matter.*

take a hand in → **have a HAND in**

take in hand assumir o controle, a responsabilidade; tomar a seu cargo e lidar severamente com *This is a serious problem and you must take it in hand without delay.*

take (something) off someone's hands comprar (algo) de alguém *I'll take that old boat off your hands if you will sell it at a good price.*

take the upper hand → **get the upper HAND**

throw up one's hands levantar as mãos em sinal de desistência, desânimo, renúncia *Sam threw up his hands in disgust and refused to continue the discussion.*

tip one's hand [gir] revelar suas intenções, "telegrafar" *The gang thought everything was under control, but Shaughnessy got drunk and tipped his hand.*

try one's hand (at) fazer uma tentativa (em algum empreendimento, atividade etc.), experimentar *... he wanted to try his hand at sports journalism ...* -T/75.

turn one's hand to → **put one's HAND to**

wait on someone hand and foot atender a alguém de maneira servil, estar sempre à disposição de *... she graciously permits her spinster sister ... to wait on her hand and foot ...* -T/63.

wash one's hands of lavar as mãos de, eximir-se de qualquer responsabilidade *It was as if he had washed his hands of the whole business ...* -DK,113.

with a heavy hand 1. de maneira abrutalhada ou desajeitada, sem habilidade ou sensibilidade, desgraciosamente, sem delicadeza, com inépcia *Wayne conducted the meeting with a heavy hand.* ⇒ **heavy-handed** desgracioso, desajeitado, insensível, inábil, inepto, sem tato *... the tactics seemed abrupt and heavy-handed.* -T/86. 2. severamente, rispidamente, de maneira opressiva, com rigor, com mão

de ferro, despoticamente *The Communists put down the Czech rebellion with a heavy hand.* ⇒ **heavy-handed** opressivo, cruel, impiedoso, desagradável, rude *The country is ruled by a heavy-handed theocracy.*
with a high hand com arrogância, com arbitrariedade, despoticamente *Mr. Fuller ran his business with a high hand.* ⇒ **high-handed** discricionário, arbitrário, despótico *a high-handed decision* ♦ *a high-handed act*
HANDLE fly off the handle [col] irritar-se subitamente, perder a calma *My father flew off the handle when I asked him if I could have the car.*
too hot to handle perigoso, delicado, difícil de lidar com, de tratar de, de mexer em *The situation became too hot to handle.*
HAND-ME-DOWNS 1. roupa usada, roupa de segunda mão *The youngest child always gets the hand-me-downs that are too small for an older sister or brother to wear.* 2. qualquer coisa usada ou de segunda mão *He owned a knife which was not a second-hand hand-me-down, but a brand-new shining thing ...* -HJE,16. 3. usado, de segunda mão; inferior, ordinário *... hand-me-down clothes ...* -T/87.
HANDS-OFF relativo a ou caracterizado por uma política de não-interferência ou não-intervenção *... the government's hands-off policy spells economic doom.* -T/80.
HANDS-ON prático, relativo a ou caracterizado por experiência ou contato direto, sem intermediários, pessoal *... hands-on training to medical, nursing, dental, and allied health personnel ...* -T/87.
HAND-TO-MOUTH → **live from HAND to mouth**
HANDWRITING (read/see) the handwriting/writing on the wall (perceber) um aviso de advertência para o futuro, (prever) adversidade iminente *The Republican Party did not read the writing on the wall and*

the Watergate trial was the unpleasant result. ♦ *By 1950, the handwriting was on the wall. By 1955 the message was clear. Millions of people had abandoned the movies for television.* -SLE,119.
HANG get the hang of [col] compreender, acostumar-se a pegar o jeito de (fazer algo etc.) *... he has begun to get the hang of foreign policy.* -T/64.
hang around [col] deixar-se ficar (em determinado lugar ou em suas vizinhanças), ficar por perto, fazer hora, passar o tempo, freqüentar *Let's hang around and see what happens.* ♦ *Tommy and the other boys are always hanging around the poolroom.*
hang around with [col] andar na companhia de, relacionar-se com *Eddie is hanging around with the wrong sort of people.*
hang back/off relutar (em avançar, prosseguir etc.), hesitar *I hoped she would come with me, but she hung back.* ♦ *We all tried to get Cathy to come to the party, but she hung off.*
hang heavy arrastar-se monotamente, custar a passar (o tempo), pairar opressivamente *Time is beginning to hang heavy on my hands.* ♦ *The unasked question [the question that everyboby at the meeting was afraid to ask] hung heavy over the quiet room.* -SLS,242.
hang in (there) [gir] não se deixar intimidar ou desanimar, persistir, agüentar a mão *[President] Reagan hung in, ... a bit unsteady at times but improving.* -T/87. ♦ *It's tough to hang in there when we don't get quick results.* -WCG,25.
hang it (all) diacho!, droga! *Hang it! I left my keys in the car.* ♦ *Hang it all! Can't you be quiet for a minute?*
hang off → **HANG back**
hang on 1. segurar-se firmemente *This is a bumpy road. Hang on or you'll be thrown from your seat.* 2. continuar (uma atividade), perseverar, persistir, perma-

necer firme, resistir, perdurar *In spite of the advanced state of his disease, he is hanging on very well.* 3. esperar, aguardar; não desligar (o telefone), continuar na linha *Hang on while I get Mr. Edwards to help you.* ♦ *Hang on a minute until I find a pencil to take your message.*
hang on to 1. segurar firmemente, agarrar-se a, não largar de *I used to hang on to my mother's skirt when we crossed the street.* 2. aferrar-se a, não se desfazer de *The military are trying hard to hang on to power.*
hang/tie one on [gir] tomar um pileque, encher a cara *Saturday nights they usually hang one on.*
hang out [gir] freqüentar, passar muito tempo (com) *I usually hang out at the Park.* ♦ *[He] ... exiled himself to Santa Monica, ... where he hung out with movie people ...* -T/87. ⇒ **hangout** local de encontro, ponto de reunião de pessoas *... the most popular teen-age hangout in Glendale.* -T/60. 2. morar *Where do you hang out?*
hang together 1. permanecer juntos, unidos, agir de comum acordo *We've got to hang together, and we've got to get out of here, fast.* -HJ,108. 2. ser consistente, lógico, fazer sentido, ter coerência, unidade *... when he tried to put the story into words, it did not hang together ...* -LD,21.
hang tough [gir] não desistir, não esmorecer, enfrentar a adversidade *... as long as everyone hangs tough there will be no problems.* -T/92.
hang up 1. pendurar, colocar em um gancho *In the army, he learned to hang up his clothes.* 2. [geralmente pas] encalhar, atolar, imobilizar-se, ficar detido, impedido de prosseguir; adiar, suspender ou interromper temporariamente, reter *He got hung up in a traffic jam.* v. **HUNG up** 3. [gir] [geralmente pas] dedicar-se a, ocupar-se com, ficar absorvido por *Sid is often hung up on more projects than he can handle.* 4. recolocar o fone no gancho ao encerrar a conversa telefônica *Flora said good-bye to her mother and hung up.*
hang up on recolocar o fone no gancho enquanto o interlocutor ainda está falando *[He] ... hung up on her during telephone arguments.* -T/87.
HANGDOG envergonhado e servil, intimidado, acovardado, furtivo, abjeto (expressão facial, olhar) *He wore a hangdog, hopeless look.* -HJC,166. ♦ *... his characteristically hangdog expression ...* -T/80.
HANGOVER 1. algo que sobreviveu ao passado, remanescente, resto, resíduo *Physically punishing a wife, a hangover from earlier days, is generally frowned upon today.* -LRW,52. 2. indisposição após bebedeira, ressaca *I get a hangover if I drink too much beer.* v. **HUNG over**
HANG-UP [gir] problema emocional, bloqueio psicológico *He has so many psychological hang-ups ...* -T/69.
HANKY-PANKY [col] 1. atividade questionável, furtiva, fraudulenta, suspeita etc. *There is some hanky-panky going on around here.* 2. comportamento sexual impróprio *[He] ... might have been doing a little hanky-panky with his secretary.* -T/87.
HAPPEN happen on/upon → **CHANCE on**
it so happens that acontece que, a verdade é que *It so happens that I know Mr. Higgins personally.*
HAPPY-GO-LUCKY despreocupado, livre de inquietações *His general reputation on the [university] campus was that of a humorous, happy-go-lucky boy ...* -NEW,41.
HARD hard by próximo *... a small hotel hard by the shipyard ...* -DJ,viii.
hard up [col] 1. duro, sem dinheiro *I need that money ... I'm hard up.* -HWR,108. 2. necessitado, carente *The reporter ... was hard up for a human-interest story around Christmas time ...* -BL,73.
HARD-AND-FAST estrito, severo, rigoroso, inflexível *No hard-and-fast rules apply to this case.*

HARDBITTEN duro, rude, rijo, violento, tenaz, ferrenho *In the movie From Here to Eternity, Frank Sinatra played Angelo Maggio, a hardbitten soldier.*

HARD-BOILED [col] rude, severo, insensível, realístico *[W. R.] Burnett is one of the leading exponents of hard-boiled fiction, usually laid in the world of gangsters.* -HMJ,125.

HARD-CORE 1. irrestrito, incondicional, absoluto, total, convicto, inveterado, conservador *... hard-core criminals ...* -T/81. ♦ *... hard-core conservatives ...* -T/87. ♦ *[She is a] ... hard-core New Yorker ...* -T/81. 2. explícito, claro, cru, sem retoque (filmes, revistas, livros etc. pornográficos) *... hard-core porno films.* -T/73. ♦ *Hard-core written pornography can be purchased anywhere in the U.S. now.* -RC,483.

HARDCOVER 1. encadernado, de capa dura (livro) *Margaret Mitchell's novel Gone With the Wind has sold many millions of hardcover copies.* 2. livro encadernado *Hardcovers are, of course, much more expensive than paperbacks.*

HARDHEADED 1. teimoso, obstinado *MacBride is so hardheaded that he will not admit a mistake even if he knows he is wrong.* 2. astuto, sagaz, prático, realista *... hardheaded scientists see some purpose in space flight ...* -GH,199.

HARD-HEARTED empedernido, impiedoso, insensível, cruel *[The Front Page] ... the most famous play ever written about newspapermen [is] ... a sardonic portrait of hard-boiled, hard-hearted journalists ...* -T/87.

HARD-HITTING vigoroso, possante, impetuoso, enérgico, intenso, eficaz *Hollis is a hard-hitting business manager.* ♦ *... a hard-hitting speech ...* -T/87. ♦ *a hard-hitting novel*

HARD-LINE → hard LINE

HARD-NOSED [gir] duro, inflexível, obstinado, realista, sagaz, prático, sensato *Hughes is a hard-nosed pragmatist who knows how to get things done.* ♦ *... hard-nosed leadership style.* -T/89. ⇒ **hardnose** indivíduo duro, inflexível, realista, prático *... he is not the hardnose he seems ...* -T/81.

HARD-PRESSED 1. extremamente necessitado, com muita falta (de algo), em dificuldades (por não ter dinheiro, tempo etc. suficiente) *Turner is hard-pressed for money this week with so many bills coming due.* 2. pressionado, premido pelas circunstâncias, constrangido *[He] ... was hard-pressed to explain the failure of history to record the changes which nature seemed to bear witness to.* GJ,59.

HAREBRAINED tolo, insensato, estouvado, irresponsável *Where's that harebrained brother of yours?* ♦ *... the idea [was] a harebrained plot likely to end in disaster ...* -T/92.

HARK hark back to voltar (em pensamento ou em palavras) ao passado, a alguma origem, circunstância etc., retomar um assunto etc., fazer lembrar *Today's difficulties have led many West Europeans to hark back with nostalgia to the '50s and '60s ...* -T/85.

HARM in harm's way//out of harm's way em perigo, em situação precária, desprotegido, vulnerável//fora de perigo, em lugar seguro, a salvo *... a deliberate decision to go in harm's way ...* -T/87. ♦ *Simpson had helped many refugees out of harm's way.*

mean no harm não tencionar fazer mal, ter boas intenções *Why am I being treated this way? I mean no harm to you.* -VR,33.

HARNESS in harness trabalhando, exercendo sua atividade, cumprindo sua rotina *... U. S. forces intend to arrive back on the mainland before any enemy can fully get in harness.* -T/66.

HARP harp on repisar (assunto), falar com insistência, bater na mesma tecla *He*

keeps harping on the same theme again and again.
HAS-BEEN [col] pessoa ou coisa que já foi célebre, popular etc. *Once in a while we see an old movie star who is now a has-been in some small part.*
HASH hash out/over [col] discutir (questão, problema, diferença etc.), debater, rever, (visando a uma solução) *He can hash out a complex issue until it can be stated as simply as A, B, C.* -T/80. ♦ *... to hash out a problem.* -T/78.
settle someone's hash [col] silenciar, desancar, reprimir, dominar, domar, dar uma lição em *They'll settle your hash when they discover what you've done.*
HASTE haste makes waste a pressa é inimiga da perfeição *Haste makes waste. So let's make our plans very carefully and not let anything go wrong.*
in haste depressa, rapidamente; às pressas, sem reflexão *Marcia was in great haste and had to leave.* ♦ *He did it in great haste.*
make haste apressar-se, agir com prontidão *Gail made haste to clarify her remark.*
HAT I'll eat my hat [col] quero ser mico de circo, macacos me mordam, darei a mão à palmatória *I'll eat my hat if that isn't the same dance group that we saw in at least five night clubs on our tour.*
keep under one's hat [col] manter em segredo, guardar sigilo *Will you keep this under your hat?* -TRL,332.
knock into a cocked hat [gir] estragar, arruinar *There's a reasonably good chance that business investment will not be knocked into a cocked hat [despite the risk of recession].* -T/78.
old hat [gir] antiquado, fora de moda *... the discussion of extramarital relations is practically old hat in American literature...* -EA,238.
pass the hat [col] fazer coleta, solicitar contribuição *[He] ... passed the hat among his underlings for contributions to the Republican campaign ...* -PVH,198.
take one's hat off tirar o chapéu, mostrar admiração, aprovação etc. *... I take my hat off to those men for the nobility of that gesture.* -T/84.
talk through one's hat [col] dizer asneiras, cometer disparates *You're talking through your hat when you say that French and Portuguese are almost alike.*
HATCHET bury the hatchet cessar as hostilidades, fazer as pazes, reconciliar-se *Though Eric and Ronnie had a serious quarrel years ago, they have finally buried the hatchet.*
hatchet job [col] ataque difamatório, injúria *His book on the Democratic candidate is really a hatchet job.*
hatchet man [col] político, jornalista etc. que faz ataques difamatórios contra adversários políticos, demolidor de reputações *Most political parties have their hatchet men.*
HATTER mad as a hatter louco, maluco, pancada *He was friendly, talented and good fun but mad as a hatter.*
HAUL haul in [gir] prender; levar à presença de um juiz *... he was hauled in on gambling charges ...* -TB,10. ♦ *[The judge] ... once hauled in nearly 30 postal workers for contempt of court ...* -T/77.
in/over the long haul com o passar do tempo, com a sucessão dos anos, após um longo período *[The novel* Gone With the Wind*] ... was a sensation when it appeared, and over the long haul it became the nation's largest-selling novel.* -SV,91.
long//short haul 1. um longo//curto período de tempo; uma longa//breve espera *He could see that he and his colleagues were in for a long haul, but he did not mind.* -T/87. 2. uma longa//curta distância, viagem, jornada etc. *It's only a short haul to the river.*
HAVE had best/better seria melhor, seria aconselhável *We had better do something*

while there is still time. -T/75. ♦ *... you'd better have the doctor take a look at you ...* -WR,56.

had/would rather/sooner preferiria *I would rather have my salary in weekly payments than in one monthly sum.* ♦ *I'd rather stay home this evening.* ♦ *Jones'd sooner fight than surrender.*

have at atacar *Bereft of conventional weapons [an American marine (Lee Marvin) and a Japanese officer (Toshiro Mifune) in the movie* Hell in the Pacific*] ... have at each other with sticks, fire, traps and maledictions.* -T/69.

have been around [col] ser experiente, saber das coisas, conhecer os fatos da vida *Olivia seemed older and wiser, as though she had been around and seen it all.*

have been had [col] ter sido enganado, tapeado, lesado *Carla has been had by a clever con man.*

have (someone) do (something) mandar (alguém) fazer (algo) *I'll have Harry drive you to the airport, Mr. Jones.*

have done with → **have DONE with**

have (someone) down/in/out/over/up convidar (alguém) *We had the office crowd down to our beach cottage last Saturday.* ♦ *We're having the Smiths over for dinner next Friday.*

have got [col] 1. ter *Mr. Vanderbilt's got a lot of money.* 2. ter de, precisar, necessitar *It's getting late. I've got to go now.*

have had enough estar farto, estar cansado, não agüentar mais *I've had enough of your silly remarks.*

have had it [gir] 1. estar acabado, liquidado, sem conserto, sem esperanças, não ter mais salvação *... we've got to get these men up and going [away from the enemy line], because if we stay here we've had it.* -FP,3. ♦ *You've had it, buster! You're finished here as far as I'm concerned!* 2. estar cansado de sofrer, de passar por maus bocados, não agüentar mais, estar farto *Not another word! I've had it with all your constant complaining.*

have it 1. ouvir dizer, ficar sabendo *We have it on reliable authority that she worked as a call girl once.* 2. afirmar, asseverar, garantir *Rumor has it that he will not be president for long.* ♦ *Word has it that Tony will be head of the Electrical Design Department.* 3. permitir, tolerar [geralmente em orações negativas com **will** e **would**] *Don't talk to me like that! I won't have it!*

have it bad → **GET it bad**

have it easy/good etc. [col] levar boa vida, viver confortavelmente, ter boa situação econômica *Those people don't have it easy.* -WSM,146. ♦ *... in every sphere of American life the white guy has it better.* -T/62.

have it in for [col] ter rancor, mágoa de (alguém) e desejar vingar-se *... he had it in for me right from the start.* -UJ,210.

have it in one ser capaz, ter capacidade ou habilidade *... he had it in him to be a "consistently great" movie artist.* -T/87.

have it/something coming merecer, estar para receber (aquilo que acontece a alguém, recompensa ou punição) *... whatever Zeb did to Slim, Slim probably had it coming.* -LLN,20. ♦ *... he still would dress down [his friend] ... when he thought he had it coming.* -RJ,185. ♦ *Mat has a lot of money coming to him.*

have it made [gir] não ter preocupações, estar em situação tranqüila, estar assegurado de êxito infalível *I had it made. A good job, a beautiful house, a new car, money in the bank and not a single worry. Then I woke up.*

have it out decidir uma questão, resolver uma pendência, um desentendimento etc., tirar (algo) a limpo mediante discussão ou briga *The Irish boys and the Italian boys met at the empty lot to have it out.*

have it (all) over ser superior, ter vantagem, sobrepujar *Wilbur has it all over the other candidates as far as intelligence and capability are concerned.*

have (something) left ter (algo) de sobra, de resto *I've only got one bullet left.*

have none of não aprovar, não permitir, não querer saber de *Now please, Mr. Ward, we'll have none of that. You'll have to control yourself.* -CHT,92.

have nothing on 1. não ter superioridade sobre, não ser mais capaz que, não levar vantagem a *The younger generation has nothing on the older.* -CE, 109. 2. não ter nenhuma evidência incriminadora contra *The F.B.I. has nothing on him. He's clean.*
♦ *... you haven't anything on me except the flimsiest circumstances ...* -MMA,22.

have on 1. estar vestindo, estar trajando *She had on her coat and hat.* -SJE,86. 2. ter um compromisso, plano etc., ter (algo) planejado, combinado, marcado *Do you have anything on tonight?*

have on one ter em seu poder (dinheiro etc.) *... I gave [him] ... fifty dollars, which was all the cash I had on me.* -HA,291.

have (down) pat/cold → **GET (down) pat/cold**

have something/a thing/a lot/much etc. going for one [gir] ter algo, uma vantagem, muito, muita coisa etc. a seu favor *... mature men who have something going for them – life experience.* -T/68. ♦ *Jennifer has a lot going for her.* ♦ *Earl seems to have everything in life going for him.*

have something on (someone) saber de algo incriminador contra *Sloan has something on the boss and gets raises and all sorts of favors.*

have (anything/little/nothing/something etc.) to do with 1. tratar de, ter a ver com, estar ligado a, ter relação com *Most of my books have to do with philosophy, psychology, and religion ...* -WA,ix. ♦ *Luck had nothing to do with her success.* 2. lidar com, relacionar-se com, estar em convivência com *I refuse to have anything to do with her group.*

have what it takes [col] ter a necessária coragem, inteligência, habilidade, capacidade, virtude etc. (para conseguir realizar algo) *Many doubt that either the President or the Arkansas Governor has what it takes to lead the nation.* -T/92.

never had it so good as coisas nunca foram tão boas, a vida nunca foi tão farta, sem dificuldades econômicas *Financially, I've never had it so good. I'm not overworked and I can travel.* -T/91.

(and) what have you [col] algo dessa espécie, coisas semelhantes, e outras coisas do gênero *In an old country store you could find food, clothes and what have you.*

HAVE-NOTS → **the HAVES**

HAVES the haves//the have-nots os ricos//os pobres (indivíduos ou nações) *Everywhere the have-nots are vocal about their anxiety to have, and the haves are doubly anxious to hang on to what they have.* -T/61. ♦ *[Byzantium] ... history was marked by no class struggle between the haves and have-nots ...* -MHJ,28.

HAVOC play/raise havoc (with); wreak/work havoc destruir, devastar, arruinar, causar grande dano, desordenar *The frost played havoc with the coffee and vegetables.* ♦ *... the famous Indian chief Geronimo ... for several years wrought havoc among the ranches and settlements of Arizona and New Mexico.* -MJ,52. ♦ *... [gas] compounds that wreak havoc on the ozone.* -T/87.

HAY hit the hay → hit the SACK

make hay [gir] [ou] **make hay while the sun shines** aproveitar-se de oportunidade, situação etc. para realizar seus objetivos, não desperdiçar a ocasião *Let's make hay while we can.* ♦ *Now is your chance to make hay while the sun shines. The demand for this article is great at the moment.*

HAZE in a haze em confusão, desorientado, alheio, aturdido *Jeanne was in a haze, as if she didn't know anybody anymore.*

HEAD at the head of no topo de, à frente de, na vanguarda de, em primeiro lugar *He was always at the head of his class, but made very few close friends.* -MMA,45.

beat (something) into someone's head meter (algo) na cabeça de alguém, inculcar *I'd like to beat some sense into his head.*

beat/bang/knock one's head against a (stone) wall dar murro em ponta de faca *I'm tired of beating my head against the wall ...* -T/67.

bite someone's head off [col] responder agressivamente, retrucar com raiva, com mau humor *There's no need to bite my head off. All I want is an answer to my question.*

blow one's/someone's head off = **blow one's//someone's BRAINS out** 1. *Tuttle took a handgun out of the drawer and blew his head off.* 2. *He's a mad killer. Beware or he'll blow your head off.*

bring to a head causar uma crise, fazer atingir o apogeu, fase decisiva, ponto culminante etc. *The U-2 spy plane incident in 1960 almost brought the international situation to a head.*

bury/have/hide one's head in the sand iludir-se, não querer ver a realidade *Burying your head in the sand won't help it.* ♦ *... the U.S. State Department has its head in the sand when it comes to understanding what is really happening in Haiti.* -T/92.

come to a head chegar a um ponto crítico, atingir o apogeu, fase decisiva, ponto culminante etc. *The situation has come to a head.*

count heads/noses [col] contar o número de pessoas presentes num grupo, local etc. *Count noses to see if we are ready to leave.*

cry one's head off → **one's HEAD off**
eat one's head off → **one's HEAD off**
get/take (it/something) into one's head [col] meter (algo) na cabeça, apegar-se à idéia de, vir a acreditar, dar na veneta *He got it into his head that he should become an actor.* ♦ *If Joan takes it into her head to go to New York, off she goes and leaves a note for her husband.*

get (it/something) through one's/someone's head compreender, perceber, conscientizar-se; fazer (alguém) compreender, perceber ou conscientizar-se *... I'll give you a comparison that perhaps you can get through your thick head.* -MET,437. ♦ *You must get this important fact through her head before it is too late.*

go to one's head 1. provocar tontura, embriaguez *Champagne goes to my head almost immediately.* 2. tornar (alguém) presunçoso, vaidoso; subir à cabeça (sucesso) *It seems that his great success has gone to his head.*

hang one's head baixar a cabeça, ficar cabisbaixo *[They] ... should hang their heads in shame for their part in the fiasco.* -T/62.

have a (good) head on one's shoulders ter (boa) cabeça, bom senso, ser inteligente *Lorene has a head on her shoulders and she certainly knows how to use it.*

have one's head in the sand → **bury one's HEAD in the sand**

head and shoulders above/over muito superior a, mais capaz que, muito acima de *Three men towered head and shoulders over the rest in the city ...* -DJ,26. ♦ *Standing head and shoulders above all other men who wrote about the West in the generation after the Civil War was ... Mark Twain.* -RR,610.

head for dirigir-se para, rumar para, ir na direção de *... they were headed for Alexandria ...* -SBW,2. ♦ *The two countries are headed for a confrontation.*

head off 1. evitar, prevenir, impedir que aconteça *... he knew of the invasion in advance and had tried unsuccessfully to head it off.* -T/78. 2. bloquear, interceptar, deter *In the usual run-of-the-mill western, the sheriff is always ready to organize a posse and head off the bank robbers at the pass, or canyon, or whatever.* 3. ir embora, partir *[He] ... headed off to Iowa ...* -T/86.

head over heels 1. desordenadamente, de atropelada, de pernas para o ar, de ponta-cabeça, em confusão *Joe always goes head over heels when he tries to mount a horse.* 2. completamente, totalmente *Sue fell head over heels in love with Bob.*

heads or tails os dois lados de uma moeda, cara ou coroa *Let's toss a coin, heads or tails to see who pays for the beer.*

head start vantagem inicial *I have a head start on you ...* -WJT,295. ♦ *We need all the head start we can get.* -CRS,38.

head up chefiar, dirigir *Who is heading up the new Department for Pollution Control?*

hide one's head in the sand → **bury one's HEAD in the sand**

hold one's head up levantar a fronte, ter altivez, ter orgulho justificado, mostrar dignidade *We're mad as hell that we cannot hold our heads up with pride as our parents were able to.* T/92.

keep//lose one's head manter//perder a calma *He was afraid of liquor and knew that he would have to keep his head about him at all times.* -DJ,85. ♦ *She ... kept her head in every crisis.* -HJC,301. ♦ *Bud lost his head when Jimmy called him a liar.*

keep one's head above water sobreviver à crise, ser capaz de satisfazer seus compromissos comerciais e financeiros *Despite the severe slump in business, we have been able to keep our head above water.*

laugh one's head off → **one's HEAD off**

lose one's head → **keep one's HEAD**

make head or tail of compreender [geralmente neg] *He couldn't make head or tail of the enigmatic remark.* -SLT,116.

off one's head/nut/rocker [col] doido, louco *You're off your head if you think I'm going to do that.* ♦ *Is the President off his rocker?* -T/76.

(have) an old head on young shoulders (ser) pessoa jovem, mas de muito bom senso *He was the youngest President the country ever had, but he soon proved he had an old head on young shoulders.*

one's head off [precedido de verbo: cry/eat/laugh/run/scream/talk/work etc.] demais, extremamente, exageradamente *She cried her head off when her husband divorced her.* ♦ *Our new maid eats her head off but does practically no other physical effort.* ♦ *He was making a monkey of himself and the people near him were laughing their heads off.* ♦ *The boy screamed his head off when the dog bit him.*

out of one's head [col] fora de si, maluco *They had seen him sick before, out of his head with malaria.* -UL,438.

over one's/someone's head 1. além da compreensão, do intelecto de *Isn't that problem a little over the boy's head?* ♦ *... he was too intellectual ... he talked over the heads of the voters ...* -T/65. 2. por cima da autoridade, cargo, posto etc. de, sem consultar (quem de direito) *Do you mean to say that you actually went over my head to the colonel without asking my permission?* -HJC,288. 3. apesar do direito maior de, por cima de, em lugar de *... they promoted McLennan right over my head and gave him the job I was entitled to.* -KJS,7. 4. além da capacidade financeira de, sem poder saldar seus débitos *Paige is in over his head in this new commercial enterprise.*

put heads together trocar idéias, conferenciar, debater planos, buscar soluções *... it seems time that people of all professions and religious backgrounds put their heads together before our society becomes so petrified that it has to destroy itself.* -KR,16.

put out of one's head → **put out of one's MIND**

run one's head off → **one's HEAD off**

scratch one's head dar tratos à bola, tentar compreender algo ou o significado de, refletir muito *I'm still scratching my head*

trying to figure out what Bob meant when he said that.
scream one's head off → **one's HEAD off**
shake one's head abanar a cabeça, discordar, negar ... *Robin shook his head when I suggested that we wade across [the river].* -RQ,118.
stand/turn (something) on its head inverter a ordem natural, virar de cabeça para baixo *The Protestant work heritage is being stood on its head because making money has become a good unto itself.* -T/88. ♦ *The judge has stood the First Amendment [to the Constitution] on its head.* -T/87.
stick one's head in the sand → **bury one's HEAD in the sand**
swelled head [col] vaidade exagerada, presunção *When Steve was voted the best player on the team, he got a swelled head and became disliked by everyone.*
take (it) into one's head → **get (it/something) into one's HEAD**
talking head [col] a imagem televisionada que mostra a cabeça e os ombros de uma pessoa que fala diretamente à câmera ... *CNN [Cable News Network] delivers raw news. It features live events, bulletins and studios full of talking heads ...* -T/92. ♦ *[He] ... has become one of the most sought-after talking heads ... who appear on Japanese television talk shows ...* -T/92.
talk one's head off → **one's HEAD off**
throw oneself at someone's head → **THROW oneself at**
turn (something) on its head → **stand (something) on its HEAD**
turn someone's head virar a cabeça de, tornar orgulhoso, convencido *Success can turn the head of even the most cautious and conservative person.*
two heads are better than one duas cabeças pensam melhor do que uma só *I thought that two heads might be better*

than one, so I asked the bank manager to help me work out my financial problem.
HEADACHE a splitting headache dor de cabeça atroz *I never get a splitting headache from drinking but I get one from reading too much.*
HEAD-HUNTING [gir] 1. recrutamento de pessoal altamente especializado, principalmente para a área de administração *Crane is engaged in head-hunting for several top corporations.* 2. tentativa de destruir ou anular o poder ou a influência do inimigo político, do competidor etc. *A period of headhunting now [after the 1964 coup in Brazil] began.* -GJI,50.
HEAD-ON 1. de frente *A truck ... crashes head-on into a car coming the other way ...* -T/88. 2. diretamente oposto, direto; diretamente ... *a head-on attack against pornography ...* -T/87. ♦ *... science undertaking to deal head-on with a uniquely difficult matter ...* -GD,218.
HEADWAY make headway progredir, avançar ... *the rebels appeared to be making little headway on the battlefield.* -T/87.
HEALTH in good//poor health bem de saúde//enfermo ... *he is already in poor health from meningitis and years of eating deficient prison food.* -T/73.
HEAR hear from receber carta, notícia ou telefonema de, ter notícias de *He simply walked out of our lives, and we never heard from him again.* -MAT,9.
hear of/about ouvir falar de, ser informado sobre, ficar sabendo de *Anna Livia? No, I've never heard of her.* ♦ *What did you hear about the hurricane in Florida?*
hear out ouvir (o que alguém tem a dizer), ouvir (alguém) até o fim ... *he has won the respect of subordinates, as he has in all previous jobs, by hearing them out.* -T/81. ♦ *Hear me out first before you make up your mind.*
will/would not hear of it não consentir, não permitir, não concordar com, re-

cusar-se a considerar, não querer tomar conhecimento de *Wade offered to help her with the dishes but she wouldn't hear of it.* -LRT,45.
HEARING hard of hearing quase surdo, duro de ouvido *Harris was ... somewhat hard of hearing.* -AT,15.
hearing distance → **within hailing DISTANCE**
HEART after one's own heart que possui afinidades com, que tem gostos e interesses semelhantes (aos de alguém), que agrada ou satisfaz (a alguém) *You're a woman after my own heart ...* -JJF,802.
♦ *When he said he liked English poetry of the Romantic period I realized he was a man after my own heart.*
at heart no fundo, no íntimo, fundamentalmente *... he was really a romantic at heart.* -RR,620.
at the heart of no âmago de, no cerne de *... the honorable creation of wealth is at the heart of a healthy democracy.* -T/87.
break one's/someone's heart magoar (-se) extremamente, cortar o coração (de) *When she began to tell me a sad story about her many problems, I said: "Stop it! You're breaking my heart".* ♦ *It broke my heart to see the poor kid crying like that.*
⇒ **brokenhearted** amargurado *The little boy was brokenhearted when his dog died.*
⇒ **heartbreak** desgosto, dor, sofrimento *Love has brought Jean many heartbreaks.*
⇒ **heartbreaking** angustiante, doloroso *... heartbreaking struggle ...* -SWLM,24.
⇒ **heartbroken** desgostoso, amargurado *Tom was heartbroken when his wife left him.*
by heart de memória, de cor *... she continued [reading] as though she knew the words by heart.* -SHE,47.
cross my heart (and hope to die) juro que estou dizendo a verdade (palavras acompanhadas do sinal da cruz sobre o coração) *When I asked nine-year-old Wendy if she was telling the truth, she said: "Cross my heart and hope to die".*

cry one's heart out → **cry one's EYES out**
do one's heart good fazer feliz, alegrar *It would do your heart good to see the expression of happiness on the faces of the poor children who received your gifts.*
eat one's heart out sofrer, afligir-se profundamente *Cliff has been eating his heart out since his wife died.*
find it in one's heart/oneself sentir-se capaz de, ter a coragem, a perversidade de, ser cruel a ponto de [geralmente na negativa e na interrogativa com **can** e **could**] *Mark Antony [a character in Shakespeare's* Julius Caesar] *looks down on the dead body of his foe [Brutus] and cannot find it in his heart to hate him.* -CMSS,134. ♦ *I'm sorry, but I just can't find it in myself to forget what she did to us.*
from the (bottom of one's) heart do (fundo do) coração, com toda a sinceridade *Only here [in the U.S.] can I speak from the heart ...* -T/76. ♦ *... I want to apologize from the bottom of my heart.* -CEP,121.
get to the heart of chegar ao âmago de, à parte mais importante de *[Albert Einstein] ... learned to get to the heart of a problem and to decide quickly if ideas were valid.* -T/79.
have a heart ser compassivo, piedoso, ter pena *Have a heart. Don't fire me. I need the job to feed my family.*
have one's heart in one's mouth estar temeroso, apreensivo, aflito *The first time I went down in a mine I had my heart in my mouth.*
have one's heart in (something); one's heart is in (something) ter animação, interesse, entusiasmo, disposição, vontade etc. por algo, identificar-se com (tarefa, ocupação etc.) *Polly is a well-paid secretary but her heart isn't in her job.*
have one's heart in the right place ser bem-intencionado, praticar o bem, ter bom coração *You can see that he has his heart*

in the right place the way he treats children and animals.
have one's heart set on desejar intensamente (fazer ou ter algo) *You had your heart set on that Civil Engineering course. Why the sudden change?* -UL,9.
have the heart to ter a coragem de, sentir-se capaz de [geralmente neg] *I didn't have the heart to tell Ellen she was going to be fired.*
the heart of the matter o âmago da questão, o cerne do problema, o aspecto central ou mais importante de algo *After a long discussion of the problem, they seemed to be getting to the heart of the matter.*
in one's heart intimamente, no fundo ... *in our hearts we know that all men are brothers ...* -BN,179.
lose//take heart perder o ânimo//criar coragem, animar-se *When Brad saw that his friends had crossed the river, he took heart and began to swim across.* ♦ *He lost heart when things went wrong.*
lose one's heart apaixonar-se *He lost his heart to a lovely brunette from Hot Springs.*
my heart stood still gelei de medo, fiquei extremamente preocupado *My heart stood still when the stranger pulled a gun on me.*
one's heart goes out to → **GO out to**
one's heart misses/skips a beat sobressaltar-se, assustar-se, ter grande surpresa *My heart skipped a beat when I saw Jane at the party.* ♦ *Stephanie's heart missed a beat when she heard the bad news.*
one's heart sinks abater-se, sucumbir, desalentar-se, perder toda a esperança, ficar deprimido *My heart sank when Cathy said she was leaving me.* ♦ *... the minute she saw that man, her heart sank.* -WCN,271.
soft place in one's heart sentimento de ternura *Nan has a soft place in her heart for stray dogs and cats.*
take heart → **lose HEART**

take to heart 1. tomar a sério, refletir seriamente sobre *Taking to heart the adage that a prophet is always without honor in his own country, he [Joseph Smith, founder of the Mormon Church] decided to move to a less-prejudiced region ...* -BR,536. 2. preocupar-se com, afligir-se com, sentir-se profundamente afetado por *Many people take to heart words that were not meant to be spiteful.*
take to one's heart afeiçoar-se a *Anita took the homeless baby to her heart the minute she saw it.*
to one's heart's content à vontade, à saciedade, como lhe aprouver, até fartar *... all his [Thomas Wolfe's] hopes and thoughts were bent on going abroad and writing to his heart's content.* -NEW,89.
wear one's heart on one's sleeve ser incapaz de ocultar os sentimentos, intenções etc. *Don't try to tell me Lulu isn't crazy about you. That girl is wearing her heart on her sleeve.* -MN,230. ♦ *Diane wears her heart on her sleeve so that everyone can feel sorry for her.*
weep one's heart out → **cry one's EYES out**
with a heavy heart com dor no coração, pesarosamente *[He declared] ... that he would vote for impeachment "with a heavy heart".* -T/74.
with all one's heart de todo o coração *I hope with all my heart that Judy has found a solution to her problem.*
young at heart jovem em espírito (apesar da idade) *While militantly young at heart, ... [she] refuses to reveal her exact age.* -T/87.
HEART-TO-HEART 1. sincero, franco *Mrs. Brown wanted to have a heart-to-heart talk with her daughter.* 2. conversa franca sobre assuntos pessoais *[After the quarrel she] ... took her children aside for a heart-to-heart.* -T/92.
HEARTWARMING animador, reconfortante, gratificante, enternecedor, que

inspira simpatia ... *a heartwarming New Year's card* ... -TR,19.
HEAT the heat [gir] 1. arrocho policial total contra malfeitores, crime etc. *The heat is on, so stay off the street and away from policemen.* ♦ *The police put the heat on the drug pushers.* 2. pressão, coerção, intimidação *Washington [i.e., the military establishment] keeps putting the heat on me to step up training, grind out fighting men.* -RL,15.
heat up 1. aquecer, esquentar *When the cars climb the steep mountain road, the engines often heat up.* ♦ *"Heat up my dinner, will you?" he said to his wife.* 2. acirrar-se, agravar-se *Another ... African conflict was heating up in ... Eritrea.* -T/78.
HEAVEN for heaven's sake → **for Christ's SAKE**
good heavens céus! Deus do céu! *Good heavens, Mr. Richards! What do you think you're doing?*
heaven forbid → **GOD forbid**
heaven knows → **GOD knows**
move heaven and earth mover céus e terras *He'll move heaven and earth to get his son into that university.*
seventh heaven o sétimo céu, o paraíso *When the movie star kissed him, the young boy was in seventh heaven.*
HEAVY-DUTY resistente, próprio para serviços pesados, feito para agüentar grande tensão, esforços etc. *... heavy-duty trucks.* -T/91. ♦ *heavy-duty lubricating oil*
HEAVY-HANDED → **with a heavy HAND**
HEAVYSET atarracado, entroncado *Morris was a heavyset man in his mid-forties.*
HEEBIE-JEEBIES = the CREEPS *I get the heebie-jeebies if I'm alone on cloudy, rainy days.*
HEEL at someone's heels; on/upon someone's heels; on/upon the heels of seguindo bem de perto, logo atrás de, acompanhando, na cola de *It is a dangerous life we live when hunger and cold are at our heels.* -HETB,17. ♦ *[The cavalry soldiers] ... were close upon the heels of the Apaches ...* -FL,36. ♦ *The death of his wife came on the heels of his business failure.*
bring to heel submeter à disciplina, dominar pela força, controlar *Many [lawmen] ... had tried without success to bring the bandit to heel.* -HJ,2.
come to heel submeter-se à disciplina, obedecer, sujeitar-se *Billy came to heel when his father threatened to cut his allowance.*
cool one's heels [gir] esperar longo tempo, ficar plantado *Martin had to cool his heels in the doctor's waiting room for some forty minutes.*
down at the heel(s); down-at-(the)-heel(s) malvestido, desleixado; necessitado, em dificuldades financeiras *Tucker looked so down at the heels that we all felt sorry for him.* ♦ *He had a down-at-the-heels look.* ♦ *a down-at-the-heel artist*
kick up one's heels demonstrar efusão, jovialidade, júbilo, animação etc., divertir-se *I think everyone needs to kick up his heels once in a while, just get away, have some fun and forget everything ...* -LR,106.
show one's heels; show a clean pair of heels; take to one's heels fugir ligeiro, dar aos calcanhares *Fred took to his heels when the three men came toward him.*
to heel logo atrás do dono (o cão), sob controle, sob domínio, em obediência, em sujeição *It takes a long time to train a dog to heel.*
turn on one's heel virar-se abruptamente e seguir na direção oposta, fazer meia-volta, recuar *... he turned on his heel and walked out.* -T/74.
HELL as hell [gir] muito, grandemente *She was mad as hell when they called her a liar.* ♦ *It's hot as hell here.*
be hell on [gir] 1. ser desagradável, doloroso, difícil para, severo com *Sergeant*

Croft was hell on his men. 2. ser prejudicial, danoso, lesivo para *The cold weather was hell on my fruit crop.*
beat/knock hell out of [gir] bater, surrar, espancar, agir com violência contra *The two kids had a fight and Tommy knocked hell out of Bobby.*
catch/get hell [col] = CATCH it *Youl'll catch hell if you don't do as he says.* ♦ *He's going to get hell from the boss.*
come hell or high water aconteça o que acontecer, haja o que houver *He is optimistic, come hell or high water.* -PVH,198. v. **HELL or high water**
(just) for the hell of it [gir] = for the FUN of it ... *Bonnie and Clyde ... robbed banks mostly for the hell of it.* -T/72.
give hell [gir] criticar severamente, descompor, desancar *[Harry Truman was once quoted as saying:] "I never did give anybody hell. I just told the truth, and they thought it was hell."* -T/75.
go through hell enfrentar grandes dificuldades, amargar sofrimentos, passar maus bocados *Mitch went through hell to get that job.*
(all) hell broke loose criou-se um pandemônio, estabeleceu-se o caos total, houve grande agitação *All hell broke loose when Captain Reisman and his twelve men raided the Chateau de la Vilaine, where German generals and high-ranking officers were gathered.*
a/one hell of a; a helluva [gir] 1. muito; extremamente *$500,000? Wow! That's a hell of a lot of money!* ♦ *That was a helluva nasty thing to say!* 2. péssimo, árduo, desagradável, incômodo, dificultoso, dos diabos *It had been one hell of a day. Nothing had gone right at the office.* ♦ *We had a hell of a time trying to find out what was going on.* -T/79.
hell on wheels [gir] 1. irascível, birrento, genioso, encrenqueiro, mal-humorado *His wife is hell on wheels when he comes home after having a few drinks.* 2. situação muito difícil ou desagradável *The job turned out to be hell on wheels for him.*
hell or high water dificuldades de todo tipo *He'd go through hell and high water for me.* -TR,94.
hell to pay → the DEVIL to pay
how in/the hell [como expletivo, usado para dar ênfase] como diabo ... *Tell me, man, how the hell are you, anyway?* -TR,71. ♦ *How in hell am I supposed to know the answer to that question?*
like hell [gir] muito, extremamente, como o diabo *Everybody's working like hell ...* -T/60. 2. não, nunca, de nenhuma maneira *When he said he wanted me to be nice to Brenda I said: "Like hell I will".*
raise hell → raise CAIN
scare hell out of [gir] apavorar, causar terror a *I won't have you ... raising your voice to scare hell out of her.* -HET,43.
shot to hell/pieces [gir] arruinado, gasto, esgotado, destruído *Everything I've worked for ... is shot to hell now.* -CHT,117. ♦ *His business was shot to pieces because of neglect and petty thievery.*
sure as hell [gir] com toda a certeza ... *this sure as hell was no cold winter night.* -BRSR,30. ♦ *Ross was no millionaire, but he sure as hell had a lot of money.*
the/to hell with it [gir] ao diabo com, que se dane *The hell with your lousy career.* -SJD,22. ♦ *... we'll get married right away and to hell with your father ...* -LI,9.
(un)till hell freezes over [gir] para sempre *Suckers will be betting on the horses or buying lottery tickets until hell freezes over.* -AIM,101.
what in/the hell [gir] [como expletivo, usado para dar ênfase] que diabo ... *What the hell is Mr. McLuhan trying to say?* ♦ *What in hell is going on here?*
what the hell [gir] que importa? e daí? *What the hell! Never mind what she said!*
when hell freezes over [gir] nunca, jamais *I'll believe that story when hell freezes over.*

where in/the hell [gir] [como expletivo, usado para dar ênfase] aonde/onde diabo ... *Where in hell do you think you're goin'?* -HM,1. ♦ *Where the hell have you been?*
who in/the hell [gir] [como expletivo, usado para dar ênfase] quem diabo ... *Who'n hell do you think you are?* -LRW,22. ♦ *Who the hell are you?*
why in/the hell [gir] [como expletivo, usado para dar ênfase] por que diabo ... *Why in hell would Clyde do a thing like that?* ♦ *After you guys left for town I got to wondering why the hell I should stay home.* -JJF,230.
HELL-BENT [gir] 1. resoluto, firme; resolutamente, firmemente, decididamente *A well-equipped, well-disciplined force, hell-bent on quashing their foes.* -T/86. ♦ *[The Sioux Indians] ... fought [Lieutenant Colonel George Armstrong Custer at the Little Bighorn] simply because Custer with typical recklessness was riding hell-bent to attack them.* -T/66. 2. rapidamente, velozmente *Somebody was coming hell-bent ...* -BW,7.
HELL-FOR-LEATHER [gir] rapidamente, velozmente, à disparada *The cowboy was riding hell-for-leather toward the ranch.*
HELP be of (some/any) help//no help ser//não ser de (alguma) ajuda ou utilidade; ser//não ser útil *As a friend of your father's I thought I might be of some help to you ...* -OJT,34. ♦ *If I can be of any help, let me know.*
cannot help → CANNOT help
help oneself to 1. servir-se de (comida, bebida etc.) *Bernard helped himself to one more drink ...* -CHT,117. ♦ *He helped himself to another piece of meat, to more potatoes and gravy.* -LL,16. 2. pegar, usar etc. sem permissão *Cohn helped himself to some of my best Scotch.*
help out ajudar, socorrer, ser útil, prestativo *He was almost sixteen and big enough for his age: he would work and help out with the expenses ...* -LR,15.

so help me juro, o que digo é a verdade *"So help me, it's the truth", he said to his unbelieving wife.*
HELTER-SKELTER desordenado, confuso, precipitado; desordenadamente, a torto e a direito, precipitadamente *The crowd ... rushes forward in helter-skelter fashion ...* -FJ,124. ♦ *... helter-skelter planning ...* -T/63. ♦ *... the troops [were] retreating helter-skelter through the difficult ... terrain ...* -MJA,966.
HEM hem in 1. rodear, cingir, circundar *[The city] ... is hemmed in by mountains and the sea ...* -T/79. 2. confinar, cercar, restringir, pôr cerco a *He was simply too unsure of himself, too hemmed in by doubt and contradictions and too immature.* -NEW,16.
HEP hep to → HIP to
HERE neither here nor there irrelevante, sem importância *They call me Marianne ... and my full name is neither here nor there.* -T/87.
HERRING red herring pista ou indício enganoso, despiste, engodo *Many red herrings were dragged around to confuse the fundamental issues in the presidential campaign.*
HIDE hide or/nor hair vestígio, traço, sinal [neg] *Thus far no one has brought in hide nor hair of the Abominable Snowman of the Himalayas ...* -EF,12. ♦ *I haven't seen hide or hair of that girl since Monday morning.*
hide out esconder-se, ocultar-se *He had been hiding out in the jungles of Guam ...* -T/72. ⇒ **hideout** [col] = **HIDEAWAY** *We've got to find the rebels' hideout.* ♦ *So, this is your hideout!*
tan someone's hide [col] dar uma surra em *Your father will tan your hide if he finds out what you've done.*
HIDE-AND-SEEK 1. esconde-esconde *Victor, Paul, Hector and Octavius like to play hide-and-seek in their grandparents' house.* 2. evasiva, subterfúgio, pretexto, rodeios *Don't play hide-and-seek with me. Tell me the truth.*

HIDEAWAY [col] esconderijo; refúgio, retiro *No one has been able to locate their hideaway.* ♦ *... a hideaway for a quiet band of nudists ...* -T/66.

HIDING in hiding oculto, escondido *... he has been in hiding in the homes of parents and relatives for four years ...* -T/87.

HIGH [col] 1. sob efeito de álcool ou drogas; embriagado, drogado *[He] ... had been high on drugs and alcohol ...* -T/79. ♦ *[She] ... died at age 20 from the effects of sniffing cleaning fluid to get high.* -T/73. ♦ *He felt high from smoking marijuana.* -HE,46. 2. estado de euforia produzido por álcool ou drogas *... a brownish liquid that when injected produces a potent high.* -T/87. 3. excitação agradável, emoção viva *He gets his high entertaining people with his conversation.*

high and dry 1. em seco, fora do alcance da água ou da maré, encalhada (embarcação) *Creatures that lived only in shallow water were left high and dry by the receding sea and many became extinct.* -VA,36. 2. abandonado, sem auxílio *[Lord of the Flies is] ... a scary adventure story about a band of castaway boys high and dry on a desert island.* -T/63.

high and low em toda a parte *We searched high and low for the missing document but couldn't find it.*

high and mighty [col] arrogante *... I had no high and mighty silk-hatted friends to smooth my way for me.* -FL,4.

high on [col] entusiasmado por, muito interessado em, extremamente a favor de *The President is still high on ... [the] Secretary of State ...* -T/79.

on high 1. no alto, nas alturas, do alto *... the partisans tied Mussolini's heels with wire and then strung him up on high ...* -T/85. ♦ *We have received orders from on high to proceed with the plan.* 2. no céu, para o céu, do céu *... a radiant angel appears from on high ...* -T/92.

HIGHBROW [col] [implica freqüentemente sarcasmo ou menosprezo] 1. intelectual, culto, erudito *... American readers, highbrow and middlebrow alike ...* -T/61. ♦ *... a highbrow publication.* -T/66. 2. pessoa intelectual *He has been called a highbrow.* v. **lowbrow; middlebrow**

HIGHER-UP [col] superior, pessoa de autoridade mais elevada, oficial de hierarquia mais alta *... he said his actions were approved by higher-ups ...* -T/87.

HIGH-FLYING extravagante, exagerado, ambicioso, ostentoso *In 1954, after two high-flying decades ... [Artie] Shaw packed up his clarinet and quit the music business.* -T/92.

HIGH-HANDED → **with a high HAND**

HIGH-HAT [gir] 1. arrogante, soberbo, esnobe, aristocrático *Most new rich act high-hat when they join some exclusive club.* 2. tratar com desdém, menosprezar *When Carson became rich and famous, he high-hatted all his friends.*

HIGH-JACK → **HIJACK**

HIGHLIGHT 1. ponto alto, parte importante *We only read the highlights of the President's speech.* 2. salientar, dar relevo, pôr em destaque *... the press highlighted some of ... [the President's] faults.* -T/87.

HIGH-MINDED magnânimo, nobre, altruísta *[J. F.] Kennedy is widely regarded as a high-minded crusader for religious tolerance ...* -T/60.

HIGH-POWERED 1. possante, de alta potência *Chuck went for a ride on his high-powered Harley-Davidson motorcycle.* 2. enérgico, dinâmico, ativo *High-powered executives have superior vocabularies.* -GR,16

HIGH-PRESSURE 1. vigoroso, enérgico, dinâmico, persistente, incisivo *Don't try to use high-pressure salesmanship on me.* 2. tenso, nervoso, agitado *... high-pressure, fast-paced work environments.* -T/86. 3. [col] pressionar, coagir *When the salesman began to high-pressure me I left the store.*

HIGH-RISE 1. de muitos pavimentos, muito alto (prédio); relativo a, ou típico de tal prédio ... *high-rise apartment buildings* ... -BM,92. ♦ *He is very pleased with their new high-rise apartment.* -T/77. 2. edifício de muitos andares, arranha-céu *Many high-rises have been built along the Jersey shore of the Hudson River.*

HIGH-STRUNG tenso, nervoso, muito sensível ... *a high-strung teacher* ... -T/76.

HIGHTAIL hightail it (out) [col] sair ou ir embora rapidamente, fugir, dar no pé *When he was released from a Washington mental institution ... [he] hightailed it to Italy* ... -T/63.

HIGH-TECH de alta tecnologia, de tecnologia avançada ... *high-tech firms of California's Silicon Valley* ... -T/86. ♦ ... *high-tech instruments.* -T/86. ♦ ... *a high-tech global economy* ... -T/91.

HIGH-TONED [col] aristocrático, excelente, superior, distinto ... *high-toned [television] programs.* -T/61. ♦ *a high-toned party*

HIJACK; HIGH-JACK [col] 1. assaltar, roubar; roubar mercadorias transportadas por um veículo, assaltar veículo em trânsito *The gang hijacked the beer truck.* 2. seqüestrar (veículo, especialmente avião) ... *four armed jewelry-store robbers opened fire at pursuing police before hijacking a taxi and making their getaway.* -T/92. ♦ *The hijacked airliner has landed in Cuba.*

HILL the Hill → **CAPITOL Hill**
over the hill; over-the-hill [col] 1. que já passou da flor dos anos, próximo à velhice, em declínio ... *she dated men around her age, 44, but found them over the hill sexually.* -T/92. ♦ *In* Ride the High Country, *Randolph Scott and Joel McCrea played two over-the-hill former lawmen.* 2. ausente (do quartel, tropa etc.) sem permissão oficial ... *he went over the hill ... to say farewell to [his brother] ... who was about to enter a seminary.* -T/81.

HILT (up) to the hilt completamente, inteiramente *Ferguson is in debt up to the hilt.* ♦ *Norma has documented her thesis to the hilt.*

HINGE hinge on/upon depender de, girar em torno de, ter relação imediata com *The price of vegetables hinges on the whims of the weather.*

HIP be/get hip/hep to [gir] estar/ficar bem informado sobre, ciente de, a par de, por dentro de *Joyce is hep to what you're planning.* ♦ *She told the women in the audience to get hip to politics.* -T/72.
shoot from the hip [gir] falar ou agir impulsivamente, sem medir as conseqüências *I've spent some time thinking about most of the issues I talk about than [other] people who talk about them. And as a consequence I'm not shooting from the hip.* -T/89.

HIRE for hire de aluguel *Those cars are for hire.* ♦ *These killers were not for hire.* -TB,8.
hire out 1. alugar (veículos, roupas etc.) *Mrs. Hayes hires out very elegant hats for weddings.* 2. empregar-se ... *a bored middle-class housewife decided to hire herself out as a maid.* -T/76.

HIS of his/hers/mine etc. dele/dela/meu etc. ... *I was informed that a client of his might consider purchasing a painting of mine* ... -KRI,590. ♦ *Mike is a friend of mine.*

HISTORY ancient history coisa do passado, assunto que já não tem interesse, importância etc. *All that is ancient history now. Let's talk about something else.*
go down in history → **GO down** 8

HIT hit/strike home acertar em cheio, acertar o golpe, o alvo, atingir o íntimo, produzir o efeito visado *[He] ... fired again, and this time we heard the bullet hit home.* -LAK,26. ♦ *The speech he delivered at the United Nations General Assembly struck home with many Third World delegates.*
hit it big [col] conseguir estrondoso suces-

so *[He] ... hit it big as a crooner before the war* ... -T/87.

hit it off [col] dar-se bem, combinar, estabelecer boas relações *[The two women] ... did not hit it off during their first meeting* ... -T/87. ♦ *[He] ... hit it off very well with President Reagan* ... -T/92.

hit on/upon descobrir ou acertar acidentalmente, dar com *Many inventors have hit upon an idea that has made a fortune for them.*

hit out 1. atacar violentamente, golpear com os punhos em todas as direções *He hit out at the natives who swarmed around him menacingly.* 2. agredir verbalmente, criticar severamente *Jessup hit out at the critics in such a stupid manner that the newspapers ridiculed him.*

make a hit [col] fazer sucesso, causar excelente impressão *He made a hit in his new show.*

smash hit [col] grande sucesso (peça, filme, livro, canção etc.) *West Side Story was a smash hit on Broadway.*

HIT-AND-MISS; HIT-OR-MISS aleatório, assistemático, feito ao acaso, impensado, incerto *... developing new substances [is] largely a hit-or-miss process.* -T/87. ♦ *... hit-and-miss methods are not good enough.* -T/91.

HIT-AND-RUN que provoca acidente ou atropelamento e foge (motorista) *Hit-and-run drivers are severely punished when brought to justice.* 2. que visa a ação e resultados rápidos *... hit-and-run raids ...* -T/88. ♦ *a hit-and-run attack*

HITCHHIKE [col] viajar de carona *... he hitchhiked all the way from the West Coast to Dallas ...* -T/92.

HOBSON Hobson's choice nenhuma escolha, falta de opção, ausência de alternativa *... his opponents are left with a Hobson's choice.* -T/71.

HOG be/eat/live high on/off the hog [col] viver com fartura e luxo, estar levando vida próspera; ir às mil maravilhas *She had some money when she came here. Lived high on the hog at the Stockmen's Hotel.* -SG,38. ♦ *[The] ... Times-Herald [a newspaper], was high on the hog.* -T/63.

go (the) whole hog [gir] fazer (algo) até o limite máximo, ir até o fim, não deixar pela metade *Each time that I say that I am going to spend very little, I go the whole hog and spend everything.*

HOLD catch hold of = get HOLD of 1 *He caught hold of the spear and broke it.*

get hold of 1. segurar, agarrar, pegar, apoderar-se de, tomar conta de *Get hold of the rope and pull yourself to safety.* 2. obter, conseguir, adquirir, entrar na posse de *I couldn't get hold of the original manuscript of his play.* 3. contatar, localizar, encontrar (pessoa) *Mr. Williams is not in this morning and his secretary has been trying to get hold of him for hours.*

get hold of oneself controlar-se emocionalmente, conter-se *She stood motionless for a moment, struggling to get hold of herself.* -UJ,71.

have/get a hold ter domínio, poder, autoridade, influência *Actually you must have a firm hold on the realities of your own life before you can expect to translate these realities into prose.* -WW,2.

hold (something) against (someone) atribuir a culpa (de algo) a (alguém), lançar (algo) à responsabilidade de (alguém) *Molly's dubious past has often been held against her.*

hold back 1. conter-se, reprimir-se, abster-se (de agir, falar etc.), retrair-se, conservar-se arredio *Dexter was unable to hold back when the prison guard struck his wife.* 2. reprimir, conter, refrear, deter, controlar, impedir o avanço *Some of the early writers of western fiction saw the Indians as bloodthirsty savages who held back the march of civilization.* ♦ *[She] ... fought to hold back the tears.* -T/86. 3. ocultar, encobrir, manter em segredo

[They] ... believe that Reagan is still holding back what he knows. -T/87.
hold down 1. [col] conseguir manter (emprego) *She ... holds down a full-time public relations job ...* -RJ,14. 2. manter sob controle, conter, segurar no lugar, manter dentro dos limites *It was difficult to hold down the excited prisoners.* ♦ *... hold down energy costs.* -T/87. ♦ *... trying to hold down population growth.* -T/81.
hold everything/it [col] espere! um momento! *Hold everything. If we go off half cocked we've had it. Let's get organized.* -KJ,30. ♦ *Hold it! Don't jump yet. Let me take your picture.*
hold fast manter a posição, agüentar firme, resistir, não ceder *... the Soviets held fast at Stalingrad ...* -T/84.
hold fast to manter-se fiel a, apegar-se a (princípios, idéias etc.) *... the courage to hold fast to what we believe in ...* -T/76.
hold forth 1. propor, oferecer *The company holds forth the prospect of a successful career to bright young people.* 2. expressar suas opiniões, pregar, discursar, discorrer, alongar-se *Wyman is a clever politician and is able to hold forth on television for a long time.*
hold good permanecer válido, em vigor *My offer to buy your business holds good for three months.*
hold it → **HOLD everything**
hold off 1. manter a distância, repelir, rechaçar *Weaver is working night and day to hold off his impending business failure.* 2. resistir *"I can't hold off for much longer. The enemy is almost here", the radio man said.* 3. tardar, demorar, adiar (ação, atitude etc.), protelar, retardar-se *A few other magazines ... held off [publication of the story] until their October issues.* -GD,288. ♦ *[They] ... agreed to hold off on many of their ... experiments ...* -T/77. 4. ficar longe de, manter-se arredio, isolar-se *Millie is very shy and often holds off from the other girls.*

hold on 1. = **HANG on** 1 *Don't let go of the rope. Hold on!* 2. = **HANG on** 2 *South Vietnam did not hold on against the Vietcong after the Americans moved out.* 3. = **HANG on** 3 *Hold on a minute, please. I'll have to ask my boss.* ♦ *Now, hold on a minute! What do you think you're doing?* 4. [col] espere aí! um momento! pare! *Hold on! Don't take another step or I'll shoot.* 5. **hold on to** = **HANG on to** 4 *Hold on to the rope.* ♦ *Hold on to my hand.* 6. **hold on to** = **HANG on to** 5 *... holding on to power ...* -T/86. ♦ *Leonard has never held on to a job for longer than three months.*
hold oneself together manter o domínio de si mesmo, conter-se, dominar-se *You must try to hold yourself together.*
hold one's own manter-se, agüentar-se, sair-se bem, manter a posição *Naturalists tell us that, when cornered, a badger can hold its own against a pack of dogs.*
hold out 1. durar, continuar a existir *Our car will have to hold out for the rest of the year because we have no money to buy a new one now.* 2. agüentar, resistir, manter-se firme, não ceder *... the defenders would hold out for as long as six months ...* -TJ,287. 3. oferecer, apresentar, estender *[He] ... held out his hand.* -SL,22. ♦ *Dr. Welby didn't hold out much hope.* 4. **hold out for** [col] recusar-se a fazer um acordo até que certas vantagens sejam concedidas *Each year there are several players who hold out for bigger salaries.* 5. **hold out on** [col] ocultar, omitir (fatos, informações etc.) *The reporters always say that the President's press secretary holds out on important information which they should get before anyone else.*
hold over 1. adiar, protelar *Our class was to present a play today, but it was held over until next week.* 2. continuar em um cargo além do limite estipulado, permanecer durante um período adicional *Williams was held over from the previous*

administration. 3. prolongar além do período ou prazo normal ou convencional *The show was such a success that it was held over for several weeks.* 4. conservar na mesma condição ou situação de um período anterior *... a remnant held over from the Mezozoic [era] is the tuatara, the lizardlike creature of New Zealand ... -SK,11.*
hold responsible considerar responsável *Drake was held responsible for the accident.*
hold someone to (something) obrigar (alguém) a cumprir (algo) *I hold you to the terms of our contract and will take you to court if you do not keep your promises.*
hold still imobilizar-se, não se mover *The barber told me to hold still when he began to shave me.*
hold tight apertar em um abraço, dar um abraço apertado *Clint held Eileen tight and kissed her.*
hold to ater-se a, apegar-se a *Carey still holds to the story that he found the murder weapon in his pocket when he put his coat on.*
hold together manter(-se) unido, inteiro, intacto, impedir que se separe, desfaça ou desmanche, dar coerência *Without some kind of a religious faith, nothing holds life together ... -HE,270.* ♦ *Education holds our society together only as long as what is taught has value and is important ... -T/87.*
hold true ser válido, verdadeiro *Thoreau's aphorism "The mass of men lead lives of quiet desperation", holds true even today.*
hold up 1. levantar, erguer *He stood up and held up his hands ... -KM,412.* 2. sustentar, apoiar, estear, escorar, manter *The heavy roof is held up by several beams.* 3. expor, apresentar, exibir, apontar *Should he hold Suzanne up as a thief ... ? -LJS,43.* 4. durar, permanecer, resistir, agüentar, passar em um teste, ser aprovado, ter validade, manter-se, manter-se bom (o tempo),

não sofrer alterações, não se deixar abater por circunstâncias adversas, não esmorecer *... as long as my money holds up. -T/88.* ♦ *This material is not strong enough and won't hold up under pressure.* ♦ *For a ruined man he's holding up very well ... -BC,330.* ♦ *His testimony won't hold up in a law court.* 5. parar, fazer parar, cessar, deter, impedir *I was held up in a traffic jam this morning.* ♦ *There's no reason why I should hold you up, though – you can fly back to New York any time you want. -WSM, 263.* ⇒ **holdup** interrupção, paralisação, congestionamento de tráfego *a production holdup* ♦ *a traffic holdup* 6. [col] roubar à mão armada *He was arrested for holding up a bank.* ⇒ **holdup** assalto *... three robbers staged a [bank] holdup. -T/80.*
hold with concordar com, aprovar, apoiar, aceitar [geralmente neg] *I don't hold with violence.*
lay hold of 1. = **get HOLD of** 1 *The man laid hold of the young boy and shook him.* 2. = **get HOLD of** 2 *Where can I lay hold of Salinger's* The Catcher in the Rye?
no holds (are) barred [col] situação na qual se utiliza qualquer expediente, em que não há limites ou restrições, vale-tudo *It was a rough fight in which no holds were barred.* ⇒ **no-holds-barred** que não oferece obstáculos, dificuldades ou restrições; irrestrito, ilimitado, desimpedido *... a no-holds-barred campaign ... -T/66.*
put on hold 1. pedir (ao interlocutor ao telefone) que aguarde na linha enquanto se localiza a pessoa ou a informação desejada *She is less than enthusiastic about recorded music being piped in to entertain a caller who is put on hold. -T/78.* 2. adiar, protelar *... he has had to put all current projects on hold ... -T/87.*
seize hold of = **get HOLD of** 1 *When the air raid began, panic seized hold of a large part of the population of the city.*

take hold impor-se, fixar-se, estabelecer-se, tornar-se aceito *The rumble of the stampede died away gradually, and stillness took hold again.* -LJS,118. ♦ *What are the roots of jazz and how did they take hold in the New World?* -SMS,20.
take hold of = **get HOLD of** 1 *I took hold of Susan's hand and told her how much I loved her.*
HOLE burn a hole in one's pocket fazer cócegas no bolso (o dinheiro), ser rapidamente esbanjado *I've got a couple of 50-dollar bills burning a hole in my pocket.*
hole in/up [col] esconder-se, ocultar-se; refugiar-se, abrigar-se *Let's hole up here until midnight and work out our plan.* -WI,268. ♦ *... he holed up in a Chicago hotel room ...* -T/60.
in the hole [col] em débito, endividado *... he was $275 in the hole ...* -HWW,6.
pick holes in [col] achar erros ou defeitos em, apontar falhas em *Marcia was always picking holes in her husband's plans.*
HOLIDAY the holiday season o período que vai dos dias que antecedem o Natal até o Ano Novo, época natalina *... the atmosphere of the holiday season was almost tangible.* -AK,152.
HOLIER-THAN-THOU [pej] [col] que se julga mais virtuoso que os outros, cheio de virtuosidade fátua, moralmente superior *Don't think you can adopt that holier-than-thou attitude!* -GES,112. ♦ *holier-than-thou preaching*
HOMAGE do/pay homage prestar homenagem, honras, reverência *Wise men from the East, guided by a miraculous star, arrived to do homage with gifts of gold, frankincense and myrrh.* -T/74.
HOME at home 1. em casa, no lar; em sua cidade, em seu país *Ruth works at home.* ♦ *... the Viet Nam War, more than any previous conflict, has helped to foster violence at home.* -T/72. 2. à vontade, confortável, sem constrangimento *He is as much at home at American baseball games as he is in British clubs ...* -LW,28. 3. familiarizado (com), conhecedor (de), versado (em) *Rachel is at home in the biological sciences.*
bring home → **BRING home**
broken home/family lar desfeito *Don was from a broken home, his father having disappeared when Don was in eighth grade.* -KF,115.
close to home bem próximo do ponto que pode afetar, preocupar ou irritar alguém *We're too close to home to have anything go wrong.* -WI, 50. ♦ *His inflammatory rhetoric proved close to home.*
come home to roost → **CHICKENS come home to roost**
feel at home sentir-se à vontade, não estranhar (pessoa, lugar, coisa etc.) *... she felt more at home with him than she ever had with anyone else.* -LL,23. ♦ *... symptoms of pain and nausea ... old nuisances with which I felt at home ...* -KJS,6.
home in on 1. seguir em direção a (alvo, objetivo etc.) *The new robot planes home in on the target under remote control.* 2. dirigir atenção, esforços etc. na direção de, concentrar-se em *It took Carstairs a long time to home in on the source of the trouble.*
make oneself at home ficar à vontade, não fazer cerimônia *Please sit down gentlemen ... Make yourselves at home.* -SWJ,35.
HOMEWORK do one's homework [col] preparar-se para um encontro, entrevista, debate etc. estudando devidamente os assuntos pertinentes, verificando fatos, detalhes etc. *When he failed to give satisfactory answers to some of the questions that were put to him, someone said: "He should have done his homework".*
HONEST-TO-GOODNESS → **honest to GOD**
HONOR do the honors fazer as honras, ser o anfitrião *Will you do the honors and escort the newly chosen beauty queen to the throne?*

HOOK by hook or by crook lícita ou ilicitamente, custe o que custar, de qualquer maneira *We must find out, by hook or by crook if necessary, what happened at that meeting.*
hooked → **GET hooked**
hook, line and sinker [col] completamente, totalmente *He swallowed her story hook, line and sinker.*
hook up ligar, conectar, unir *A quarter of the nation's ... TV homes are hooked up to one of the 4,600 local cable [television] companies ... -T/81.* ⇒ **hookup** conexão de aparelhos, circuitos ou sistemas eletrônicos; cadeia de emissoras ou de rede de emissoras de rádio ou TV *A coast-to-coast hookup willl carry the presidential message tonight.*
off the hook [gir] livre de apuros ou responsabilidade, não mais em dificuldade, desobrigado *[A Soviet spy] ... was a pretty big fish to be let off the hook. -T/61.* ♦ *Cohn doesn't intend to get you off the hook.*
on one's own hook [col] por conta própria, por si só, sem nenhuma ajuda *[He] ... made it clear that ... his country would make it on its own hook, not on U.S. aid. -T/66.*
HOOKY play hooky [col] cabular, faltar à(s) aula(s) ou a obrigações *During his last week in high school, he played hooky and went to a movie. -T/78.* ♦ *He scorned rehearsals [at the theater], frequently played hooky ... -T/73.*
HOOT not give/care a hoot [col] não dar a mínima, não ligar *I don't give a hoot what the police say ... -CTT,108.* ♦ *[They] ... don't care a hoot about him. -T/91.*
HOP hop in entrar (em automóvel) *Hop in. I'll drive you to the station.*
hopped up; hopped-up [gir] 1. furioso, encolerizado *He was all hopped up when he found out that his car had been stolen.* 2. sob efeito de droga *Jack was hopped up when he commited the crime.* 3. emocionado, animado, entusiasmado *Cynthia was all hopped up about her new job.* 4. que teve a potência do motor aumentada; envenenado (automóvel) *a hopped-up car*
hopping mad [col] colérico, furioso *He was hopping mad when I arrived at his office.*
a hop, skip, and jump [col] pequena distância *That accident was a hop, skip, and jump from my house.*
hop to it [gir] começar a trabalhar com energia, dar-se pressa, aviar-se, despachar-se *Hop to it, men! We haven't got all day.*
HOPE beyond/past hope sem esperança, sem remédio, sem probabilidade de êxito, irrecuperável, arruinado, sem expectativa *... any man who today does not know he is lost is lost beyond hope. -SJH,286.*
dash someone's hopes destruir as esperanças de *The stock market crash dashed all his hopes of an affluent future.*
forlorn hope esperança vã, tentativa praticamente fadada ao insucesso *It was his forlorn hope that world peace would come in his lifetime.*
give up hope perder a esperança, desanimar *Apparently he had given up all hope of escape. -HJ,137.*
hope against hope ter esperanças (de que aquilo que se deseja aconteça) apesar de as possibilidades serem remotas *He was hoping against hope that ... there was something wrong with the radar ... -T/86.*
in hopes; in the hope(s) na esperança *The U.S. has been following the South Korean crisis closely in the hope that Washington can somehow help bring it to an end. -T/87.* ♦ *American industry will [make use of the space shuttle] ... in hopes of discovering new ways to produce drugs, crystals and metal alloys. -T/81.*
pin one's hopes on → **pin one's FAITH on**
HORN blow/toot one's own horn/trumpet [col] vangloriar-se, gargantear *I don't like to blow my own horn, but I'm a brilliant*

writer. -BL,107. ♦ ... *the time-honored American taboo against tooting one's own horn.* -T/81.

draw/haul/pull in one's horns retrair-se, moderar-se, comedir-se, recuar *The angry woman suddenly drew in her horns when she heard someone say that she was wearing an attractive dress.*

horn in [col] intrometer-se, ingerir-se, meter o bedelho *The whole family's been trying to horn in on my life since I married Isabel.* -CN,69.

lock horns pegar-se, atracar-se, travar luta, entrar em conflito, desentender-se *In the late 1970s, Libya and Saudi Arabia locked horns over oil prices.*

on the horns of a dilemma entre as duas alternativas de um dilema *Kathleen was caught on the horns of a dilemma when she was asked to choose between two equally unpleasant alternatives.*

HORNET stir up a hornet's nest mexer em casa de marimbondo *The new Senator stirred up a hornet's nest when he said he was going to investigate the Mafia connections in his state.*

HORSE back the wrong horse apostar em cavalo que perde a corrida, apoiar candidato que não vencerá *We backed the wrong horse when we voted for Brady.*

beat/flog a dead horse [col] discutir um assunto já resolvido, liquidado ou esquecido, que não mais interessa, perder tempo com algo inútil *To discuss his theories in this day and age is just flogging a dead horse.* v. **dead HORSE**

change horses in midstream mudar de métodos, meios de ação, orientação etc. durante um empreendimento, atividade ou situação crítica *This is an unusual situation, but it's my considered opinion that we should not change horses in midstream.*

dark horse [col] 1. candidato político pouco conhecido, escolhido inesperadamente pelo partido *The race [Russia's first presidential election] has a dark horse: Bakatin, the former Interior Minister ...* -T/91. 2. concorrente, participante de prova, concurso etc. desconhecido ou com poucas probabilidades de vencer *Cyrano de Bergerac ... lost the Best Foreign Film award to a dark horse ...* -T/91.

dead horse coisa, assunto, tema etc. que já não suscita ou não mais deveria suscitar atenção ou interesse; caso liquidado ou esquecido *Let's put this question aside. It's a dead horse anyway.* -JE,7.

flog a dead horse → **beat a dead HORSE**

(right/straight) from the horse's mouth [col] (diretamente) da fonte original, de fonte fidedigna *For many months reporters and writers had been trying to ... get the UFO story from the horse's mouth, but no luck.* -RE,88.

hold one's horses [gir] ficar calmo, controlar a impulsividade, não se precipitar *"Hold your horses. I haven't finished giving you the directions",* the teacher said to the eager students.

horse of a different color; horse of another color assunto completamente diferente do que está em discussão, outra coisa, outra história, outros quinhentos *I'm not interested in discussing poetry, but if you want to discuss current plays, that's a horse of a different color.*

horse opera filme de faroeste, *western The horse operas became much more interesting with the advent of the widescreen processes such as CinemaScope and Panavision.*

horse sense [col] senso comum, bom senso *Horse sense is a practical quality that most people lack.*

horse trade; horse trading [col] acordo, conchavo (realizado após longas e astutas negociações, concessões etc.) *... the President was at pains to do less preaching than usual and more horse trading with the allies.* -T/80.

off one's high horse [col] menos arrogante, demonstrando uma atitude mais humilde *Come off your high horse. Don't be so uppity.*
on one's high horse [col] petulante, arrogante, orgulhoso *She's ... up on her high horse again.* -JJS,133. ♦ *Don't get on your high horse with me.*
play the horses/ponies apostar em corridas de cavalos *Craig played the horses and lost everything: home, car and business.*
HORSELAUGH gargalhada estrepitosa, rinchavelhada *A horselaugh in the back of the theater startled the actors so that they could not continue for a few minutes.*
HOT not so hot [col] regular, não tão bom, mais ou menos *The movie we saw last night was not so hot.*
HOTBED local que favorece o rápido crescimento, desenvolvimento, atividade etc. de algo, foco, ponto de concentração *... Seoul National University, a hotbed of antigovernment student activism.* -T/87.
HOT-BLOODED ardente, apaixonado; impulsivo, que se enfurece facilmente *... at 17 [movie star Natalie Wood] ... played a hot-blooded young temptress opposite James Dean in* Rebel Without a Cause *...* -RD,230.
HOTFOOT hotfoot it [col] correr, ir às pressas, ir rapidamente *[He] ... hotfooted it to Manhattan.* -T/67. ♦ *When I was anywhere in the vicinity of Baltimore, I would hotfoot it to his home immediately.* -HE,230.
HOTHEAD indivíduo de temperamento agressivo *The hotheads are always looking for a fight.* ⇒ **hotheaded** impulsivo, estouvado, exaltado *Virginia's hotheaded brother was making things difficult for us.*
HOTSHOT [gír] = **big SHOT** *He was a hotshot from a big New York company.*
HOT-TEMPERED → **have a hot TEMPER**
HOUR after hours depois do horário comercial ou convencional, depois do expediente *This bar doesn't serve drinks after hours.* ♦ *... to hold meetings with colleagues, entertain clients and relax after hours.* -T/87. ⇒ **after-hours** que funciona após o horário normal de expediente *... an after-hours bar in Detroit ...* -T/87.
at all hours a qualquer hora *The restaurant serves food at all hours.*
early hours as primeiras horas da madrugada *... a murder that took place in the early hours ...* -T/66.
the eleventh hour a última hora, o último momento *[He] ... saved himself in the eleventh hour ...* -T/87. ♦ *The choice came at the eleventh hour ...* -T/80. ⇒ **eleventh-hour** de última hora *an eleventh-hour agreement*
happy hour [col] hora do aperitivo (após o encerramento do expediente) acompanhado de tira-gostos *The bar across the street has a great happy hour.*
keep early//late hours deitar-se cedo//tarde *Saturday is the only day of the week that he keeps late hours and then not much later than 2 a.m.*
keep good hours deitar-se e levantar-se cedo *If you keep good hours your health will be better.*
of the hour (pessoa, evento etc.) mais proeminente do momento *When Neil Armstrong set foot on the moon he became the man of the hour.*
small/wee hours as primeiras horas da madrugada *The dance lasted until the small hours ...* -CB,3. ♦ *... most flying saucer incidents have been reported at night, often in the wee hours of the morning ...* -HD,11.
strike the hour bater, soar (horas) *I heard the living room clock strike the hour and I began to count. It was three o'clock in the morning*
waking hours horas do dia em que se está desperto *... he spent most of his waking hours watching thriller movies ...* -T/77.

within the hour logo, logo mais *He should be here within the hour.* -SLT,106.
HOUSE bring down the house [col] ser calorosamente aplaudido *In his first cabaret appearance ... he brought down the house ...* -T/76.
count the house contar o número de espectadores presentes a um espetáculo *The play was not very successful and when the manager counted the house he began to worry about making enough to cover expenses.*
eat someone out of house and home 1. comer muito, obrigando a família ou o hospedeiro a ter despesas excessivas [emprego jocoso ou hiperbólico] *My relatives come to visit and stay so long that they eat me out of house and home.* 2. levar à ruína, à insolvência *Donovan's losses at the race track ate him out of house and home.*
full house/hand uma trinca e um par (no pôquer) *I thought Briggs was bluffing but he had a full house – three kings and two aces.*
house of cards coisa sem solidez, coisa malplanejada, castelo de cartas *Their ambitious plan was a house of cards and it crumbled easily.*
keep house cuidar da casa, fazer os serviços domésticos *... his wife kept house ...* -T/85. ♦ *... her husband ... stayed home to keep house and be with their children ...* -T/71.
keep open house ser hospitaleiro, oferecer a casa a todos *At Christmas time, many American families keep open house for all their friends and neighbors.*
like a house afire/on fire rapidamente, facilmente *The new compact cars are selling like a house afire.*
on the house por conta da casa, grátis *"This drink is on the house", the bartender said.*
set up house → **set up HOUSEKEEPING**

HOUSEBROKEN ensinado a defecar e urinar em lugar indicado ou apropriado (cachorro, gato etc.) *An animal is said to be housebroken when it can wait to defecate and urinate outdoors or in a special place.*
HOUSEHOLD household name/term/word palavra ou nome familiar, famoso, que quase todo mundo conhece *After World War II, the name of Albert Einstein became a household word.* ♦ *Arthur Conan Doyle established the hero of his stories, Sherlock Holmes, as a household name.* ♦ *"Flying Saucers" rapidly became a household term.* -HD,12.
HOUSEKEEPER empregada; governanta *Mrs. Robinson decided to hire a housekeeper.*
HOUSEKEEPING set up house/housekeeping montar casa *Why should we live in this place? We'll get an apartment somewhere and set up house.* -WCN,240. ♦ *... they set up housekeeping [in his Village apartment].* -T/64.
HOUSEWIFE dona-de-casa *Many housewives not only cook and clean the house but also work part of the day in an office.*
HOW and how! [col] sem dúvida, muito, grandemente *Do I love her? And how!*
how/what about 1. que tal? que acha (da idéia) de? *What about a juicy steak and a cold beer?* 2. e com relação a, e quanto a *I'm going to have a drink. How about you?* ♦ *What about Mike. Have you spoken to him?*
HOYLE according to Hoyle de maneira correta, como deve ser feito, de acordo com as regras *... anybody who does not conduct himself according to Hoyle will answer to Sky Masterson personally.* -SJG,366.
HUDDLE go into a huddle [col] discutir (algo) em particular ou em segredo, confabular *Let's go into a huddle and decide how we are going to advertise our publication.*

HUE hue and cry clamor de protesto, grita *Even today there is often a hue and cry when a scientist brings forth psychological facts that run counter to the established attitudes.* -MC,6.

HUFF in a huff ofendido, ressentido ... *[Franz Anton] Mesmer left Paris in a huff when the Academy of Medicine refused to endorse his work.* -FLS,9.

HUMOR in a good//bad humor de bom// mau humor *[He] ... did not respond, but he seemed in a good humor.* -EW,55. ♦ *Nan was in a bad humor last night.*

HUMP over the hump 1. [col] com a má fase ou a parte mais difícil superada *We had poor business at first but now we're over the hump and making money.* 2. **over the Hump** sobre o Himalaia *[The Brigadier General] ... had sent a U.S. Air Corps plane, with a medical crew aboard, over the Hump to India ...* -T/78.

HUNG hung over [gir] de ressaca *Oscar is always hung over the day after a big party.* v. **HANGOVER**
hung up 1. atrasado, impedido de prosseguir, retido *Look, I won't be able to meet you at ten. I'm hung up with extra work at the office.* 2. [gir] incapaz de chegar a uma decisão, confuso, preocupado, neurótico, problemático *Carla was so hung up on that problem that she didn't know what to do.* 3. [gir] absorvido, muito entusiasmado, obcecado, apaixonado *I was a complete slave. I was really hung up on her.* -BL,116. ♦ *Everyone is hung up on sex.* -T/67.

HUNGER hunger after/for ter grande desejo de, ansiar por *Horace hungered for companionship.* ♦ *Tina hungered after tenderness.*

HUNKY-DORY [gir] satisfatório, ótimo *Hi, kid. Is everything hunky-dory?*

HUNT hunt down perseguir até alcançar e capturar ou abater *Probably ... [the Neanderthal people] were hunted down and exterminated by a superior race of men [known as Cro-Magnon race].* -SJV,6.

hunt for procurar, buscar *Jennifer hunted for the lost silver bracelet but couldn't find it.*

hunt up procurar, localizar, descobrir (após busca ou esforço) *Hunt up this name in the encyclopedia, will you?*

HURRY hurry away/off ir depressa, partir, ir embora rapidamente ... *the couple hurried off on their honeymoon ...* -T/62. ♦ *... After dinner they announced that they must hurry away as they were expected at the Chateau de Vaudreuil.* -EMW,22.

hurry back voltar logo, regressar sem demora *In the city's silent streets, the last German patrols hurried back to their barracks.* -CL,103.

hurry on with apressar-se com *Try to hurry on with my wedding dress because we have advanced the wedding day.*

hurry up apressar-se, despachar-se, aviar-se *Hurry up! She's waiting for us.*

in a hurry com pressa, apressado; às pressas, apressadamente, sem perda de tempo *Brian was in a hurry and couldn't wait for you.* ♦ *Jane left in a hurry.*

HURT be hurting 1. estar mal de finanças *Not all banks are hurting. Many regional banks ... are in relatively fine shape.* -T/87. 2. estar em apuros, em dificuldades *The Communists are far from defeated. They are hurting but their main forces are intact.* -T/66.

be hurting for estar muito necessitado de *[They] ... are hurting for jobs.* T/75. ♦ *... stores which are hurting for customers.* -T/76.

HUSH hush-hush [col] secreto, sigiloso, confidencial *... a hush-hush operation ...* -T/92. ♦ *Zimmermann was engaged in some hush-hush scientific research.*

hush money dinheiro para suborno, peita *[Hush money was paid] ... to the hired hands who executed the ill-fated Watergate break-in.* -T/91.

hush up encobrir, ocultar, abafar, reprimir

They tried to hush up the scandal but the newspapers printed the whole story.
HUSTLE hustle and bustle barulho ou alvoroço produzido pelo dinamismo de atividades ou grande concentração de pessoas, máquinas etc.; bulício, lufa-lufa *... the noisy hustle and bustle we call our culture and our business.* -WF,vii.
HYPE 1. burla, logro, tapeação, simulação, fingimento *... the hype and shallowness that pervades not only the world of art but the values of the very rich.* -T/87. 2. publicidade exagerada ou espalhafatosa *Special, mini-series, big event: these are the most overused terms in television's absurd lexicon of hype.* -T/78.
hype (up) 1. estimular, excitar, animar, incrementar, exagerar *Before a fight [said an amateur welterweight at the 1984 Los Angeles Olympics], I'm so hyped up I just want to bust. Everything boils up in me.* -T/84. 2. promover, fazer publicidade de maneira exagerada ou espalhafatosa *We'd be very willing to do commercials, provided they didn't hype toxic waste or nuclear plants, whisky or cigarettes [says rock singer Mike Love].* -T/87. ⇒ **hyped-up** que tem os elementos necessários para provocar animação, exaltação ou excitação; incrementado, exagerado *... Midnight Express [a movie], the hyped-up story of an American college boy's escape from a Turkish jail.* -T/79. ♦ *To some, America's hyped-up consumption seems vaguely immoral as well as untenable in the long run.* -T/66.

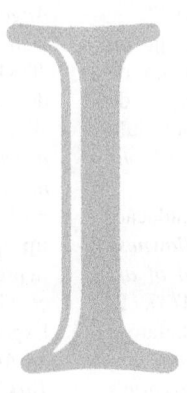

I dot one's i's and cross one's t's pôr os pingos nos is, ser minucioso, exato, suprir detalhes *When you write your report to the boss, remember to dot your i's and cross your t's.*

ICE break the ice [col] quebrar a frieza, a formalidade, vencer a timidez, o acanhamento, dar os primeiros passos para vencer as dificuldades iniciais *Once you break the ice, the rest of the job is easy.*
cut no ice [col] não convencer, não influir, não surtir efeito *All his talks about better conditions for the working class cut no ice with the people.*
on ice [gir] suspenso, pendente, inativo, adiado ... *the agreement is now on ice.* -T/80.
on thin ice [col] em terreno perigoso, em situação difícil, constrangedora etc. *You'll be on thin ice if you do that.*
put on ice [gir] suspender, adiar, afastar, deixar de reserva *They put the plans for a new stadium on ice because they had no money at the present time.*
skate on thin ice arriscar-se, expor-se ao perigo, colocar-se em situação difícil, constrangedora etc. *You'll be skating on thin ice if you try to investigate the Mafia activities in your city.*

IDEA get the idea compreender *I tried to explain to him the rationale behind my decision but he didn't seem to get the idea.*
not have the faintest/first/foggiest/least/slightest idea/notion [col] não saber, desconhecer totalmente, não ter a mínima idéia ou noção *I haven't the faintest idea what he's talking about.* ♦ *I don't have the foggiest idea what happened to him after he left his job.*
one's idea of aquilo que se acredita ser a realidade de, o conceito que se faz de *I'm sure that in a fight Major Roberts would have died very bravely, but he wasn't my idea of a leader.* -RQ,130.
what's the (big) idea que idéia (maluca, estapafúrdia) é essa? que é que você pretende? *Good Lord, what's the idea of running off and leaving me?* -DP,16.

IF if only 1. se ao menos *If only I could see her again and talk to her.* 2. ainda que somente, pelo menos por causa (da razão citada) ... *he'd intended to whip her if only because she'd called him the kind of names he wouldn't take off anybody.* -CTT,87.

ILL terminally ill à morte, moribundo *The question is: should a terminally ill person have the right to choose death rather than long suffering?* ⇒ **terminal illness**

doença fatal, que leva à morte; estágio final de uma doença fatal *[According to Norman Cousins] "The great threat to the health of our people is not cancer or terminal illness but the foreign policies of governments."* -T/84.

ILL-ADVISED imprudente, insensato, desavisado, impensado ... *she realized that her earlier comments ... had been ill-advised ...* -T/79. ♦ *an ill-advised attitude*

ILL-FATED/STARRED malfadado, desditoso, infausto *The ill-fated Titanic hit an iceberg and sank on its maiden voyage.* ♦ *... an ill-starred journey ...* -T/87.

ILL-FAVORED feio, desgracioso *Many ill-favored people are more interesting than their more handsome friends.*

ILL-GOTTEN conseguido por meios ilícitos, ilegítimos, desonestos, espúrios *It is said that people who live on ill-gotten gains willl suffer one day, but for the time being they seem to be very happy.*

ILL-TIMED inoportuno *... the effort was singularly ill-timed ...* -T/63.

IMAGE spitting image → **SPIT** and **image**

IN [col] na moda, da moda; entrosado com o que é novo, moderno, atual, que está em voga *... the endless American preoccupation with what is "in" and what is "out" – clothes, addresses, speeches, schools, cars.* -T/61. ♦ *Apartment living, for a variety of reasons, is "in".* -TA,65. ♦ *What is the in restaurant this year?* ♦ *... what today is the "in" thing to do ...* -T/66.

be in for estar fadado a experimentar (algo geralmente desagradável) *If you think you can do as you please, you're in for a surprise.* ♦ *... they may be in for a shock.* -T/87. ♦ *... none of them really knew what they were in for.* -T/75.

have an in with [col] privar da amizade de, ter intimidade com, desfrutar da simpatia de (pessoa importante, influente, poderosa etc.) *Hayden has an in with a big boss in that company.*

in between no meio, no meio de, de permeio, entre (pessoas, coisas etc.) *Donna and Ellen noticed some flowers in between the trees.* ♦ *[The] ... settings of [Wright Morris's stories] range from Vienna to Brooklyn to Missouri to Northern California, with numerous points in between.* -T/86. ⇒ **in-between** 1. intermediário, interposto, que está de permeio *The word Eros comes from an ancient image of a being who is conceived as neither God nor mortal, an in-between figure ...* -NJ,178. 2. intermediário, mediador, indivíduo que medeia ou intervém *... a President and a Secretary working together with no in-betweens.* -T/80.

in on participante de, conhecedor de, ciente de *There's no doubt that he was in on the deal.* ♦ *You want to be in on everything, don't you?* -OJT,34.

ins and outs pormenores, particularidades, detalhes *Glenn knows the ins and outs of the business.*

in with em boas relações com, íntimo de *Stoddard is in with many influential people and can help your career.*

INCH by inches 1. [ou] **by an inch** por estreita margem, por um triz *When the roof caved in she escaped death by inches.* 2. [ou] **inch by inch** gradualmente, pouco a pouco, passo a passo, a custo *Martin and Carla got to the top of the mountain inch by inch.* ♦ *He will sentence you to die by inches, in Indian fashion.*

every inch inteiramente, da cabeça aos pés, em todos os detalhes *... a tall, ponderous man who seemed every inch the suave man of distinction.* -TW,7. ♦ *... Cassius [Clay] was every inch the grownup pro [professional] prizefighter ...* -T/64.

inch ahead/along/down etc. mover-se lentamente (na direção indicada), avançar vagarosamente *At rush hour, cars inch along Highway 101 ...* -T/78. ♦ *The banner of Spain inched down from the staff to be replaced by that of France.* -VE,15.

♦ *He [was] ... inching forward under the bushes ... -LI,12.*
inch by inch → **by INCHES** 2
not give/yield an inch não ceder um milímetro *Stand up for your ideas and don't give an inch.*
within an inch of → **within an ACE of**
INCOME income tax return → **(income) TAX return**
INCREASE on the increase aumentando, desenvolvendo-se, em ascensão, em expansão ... *the blue whale population is on the increase ... -T/88.*
IN-DEPTH → **in DEPTH**
INDIAN Indian giver [col] pessoa que dá um presente e o toma de volta *My sister would give me a present and in typical Indian giver fashion take it away.*
INFORMATION inside information informação confidencial, secreta, que é do conhecimento de poucos *Police investigators suspect that the thieves probably had inside information. -T/85.*
INK red ink déficit, perda, prejuízo *[They] ... have accumulated $4.5 billion in red ink since the end of last year ... -T/91.*
IN-LAW [col] parente por afinidade (*father-in-law*/sogro; *son-in-law*/genro; *daughter-in-law*/nora etc.) *My in-laws have always been helpful and friendly.*
INNER-CITY → **inner CITY**
INNER-DIRECTED que se pauta por valores e influências interiores, não-conformista *He is far more introspective and inner-directed than most politicians. -T/87.*
INNINGS have one's innings ter sua oportunidade de ação, sua vez, seu momento de expressão, de realização, de autoridade, de poder etc. *[The judge] ... finally had his innings. -T/66.*
INSIDE inside out 1. de dentro para fora, com o lado de dentro para fora, ao avesso *Tommy always puts his undershirt on inside out.* 2. [col] inteiramente, completamente, plenamente *Fay has read that book so many times that she knows its subject inside out.*
INSTANCE for instance por exemplo *You don't like this job? Well, you can let up any time. Now, for instance.*
INSTEAD instead of em vez de, em lugar de *They went to Los Angeles by train instead of by bus.* ♦ *Frank had beer instead of wine.*
INSULT add insult to injury ferir, magoar, prejudicar etc. uma pessoa e ainda por cima insultá-la *Keefer beat up his wife and then, adding insult to injury, called her names.*
INTENT to all intents and purposes para todos os efeitos, virtualmente, praticamente *To all intents and purposes the investigation is over.*
INTO 1. [col] interessado em, dedicando-se a, ocupado com *Alan is into yoga and Zen meditation.* 2. comprometido com, envolvido em, participando de, enredado em *[He] ... was deeply into the ... covert operation ... -T/87.* 3. [col] em débito, devendo dinheiro *Nick is into me already for five hundred dollars.*
IRON have many irons in the fire ter muitas atividades, empreendimentos, interesses, recursos etc. *If McLeod loses money in his cattle business, he won't worry because he has many irons in the fire.*
iron out [col] aplanar, resolver, solucionar (dificuldade, problema etc.) *... trying to iron out the details of a proposed agreement ... -T/73.*
strike while the iron is hot aproveitar a oportunidade, agir enquanto é tempo *Our company is going to change many departments. If you're interested in a new job, ask for it. Strike while the iron is hot.*
ISSUE at issue em questão, em discussão, em debate, a ser decidido *What is really the point at issue here?*
burning issue/question questão de importância primordial, premente, assunto muito discutido, que requer solução urgente *... Neil Armstrong's step in the lunar*

dust will be well remembered when most of today's burning issues have become mere footnotes to history. -T/72.

take issue with discordar de, questionar *Walt takes issue with everything that I propose to help business.*

ITCH be itching to = **have an ITCH to** *... vengeful citizens itching to see serious criminals get their just deserts ...* -T/81. *... I was ... itching to get started.* -KRI,610.

have an/the itch for/to ter grande vontade de, desejar ardentemente *I've always had an itch to travel to faraway places.*

the seven-year itch [col] desejo sexual extraconjugal que, segundo concepção folclórica, manifesta-se acentuadamente após sete anos de casamento *Do you remember the Marilyn Monroe/Tom Ewell movie* The Seven Year Itch?

IVORY ivory tower torre de marfim, isolamento dos problemas do mundo, das realidades da vida, das dificuldades do dia-a-dia *My brother Vasco, never a man to live in an ivory tower, often teases me because of my propensity for philosophy.*

IVY Ivy League 1. referente ou relativo a um grupo de universidades e faculdades antigas e famosas do nordeste americano *The Ivy League schools include: Harvard, Yale, Princeton, Cornell, Columbia, Dartmouth, Pennsylvania and Brown.* 2. característico dessas escolas e de seus alunos, seus padrões, atitudes, moda etc.; conservador, moderado *He has an Ivy League background.* ♦ *Drake wore the standard Ivy League shirt with button-down collar.*

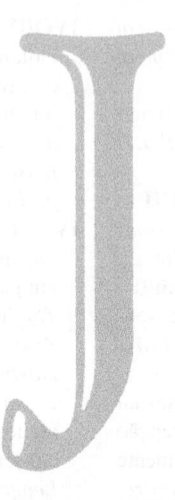

JACK before one can/could say Jack Robinson rapidamente, em um instante *The man went away but came back before we could say Jack Robinson.*
jack up 1. levantar (veículo) com macaco *Ray jacked up the front of the car and changed the flat tire.* 2. [col] elevar, aumentar *[They] ... have jacked up rents as high as possible.* -T/88. ♦ *[He has jacked up] ... the town speed limit from 10 m.p.h. to 25 m.p.h. ...* -T/72.
JACK-OF-ALL-TRADES pau para toda obra, factótum, faz-tudo *... I could end up a jack-of-all-trades and master of none.* -T/72.
JACKPOT hit the jackpot [gír] ganhar muito dinheiro inesperadamente, tirar a sorte grande; sair-se bem, obter bom êxito *Gail really hit the jackpot when she won a new car and a trip to Europe.*
JAM in a jam [col] em dificuldades, enrascado *Whatever the reason, they were in a jam.* -SRU,70.
jam session reunião informal na qual instrumentistas de *jazz* improvisam livremente *The musicians often met in the early morning hours after their work and had a jam session before going to bed.*

JAM-PACKED muito cheio, repleto, apinhado, superlotado *Lecturers on the subject of sexual psychology talk to jam-packed audiences.* -HEW,5. ♦ *The place was jam-packed with teenagers who were eager to see and hear the rock bands.*
JAYWALK [col] atravessar a rua sem respeitar os regulamentos de trânsito *In some American cities it is a punishable crime to jaywalk.*
JAZZ and all that jazz [col] coisas que tais, e tudo mais, e todo esse papo furado; etc. etc. *So she said that we could go to her apartment and drink or smoke pot and all that jazz.*
the Jazz Age a Era do Jazz [Período da História americana que vai do fim da Primeira Guerra Mundial até o Colapso da Bolsa (1929)] *When the novelist F. Scott Fitzgerald labeled the nineteen-twenties "The Jazz Age", he was not particularly interested in the music. He was trying to describe a state of mind.* -SMS,111.
jazz up [gír] tornar atraente, embelezar, ornamentar; revigorar, avivar, animar, estimular; acelerar, intensificar o ritmo *They jazzed up their store to attract more trade among the younger shoppers.* ♦ *They jazzed up their delivery service and*

satisfied customers began to buy more. ♦ *Let's jazz up the music.*

JERRY-BUILT feito às pressas, malconstruído *Construction was being rushed on two jerry-built but air-conditioned hotels.* -T/60. ♦ *... jerry-built vehicles ...* -T/76.

JET jet lag ruptura do biorritmo natural do indivíduo motivada pela mudança súbita de fusos horários (em viagens aéreas muito longas) e que provoca sensação de cansaço etc. *He began this 40,225-km trip with a 20-hour hop to Australia that he admitted gave him jet lag.* -T/92.

the jet set grupo internacional de indivíduos muito ricos e socialmente ativos que viajam com freqüência *The Côte d'Azur is one of the favorite spots of the jet set.*

JIFFY in a jiffy [col] em um instante, rapidamente *I have to change my shoes but I'll be back in a jiffy.*

JIG in jig time [col] rapidamente *[They] ... finished the job in jig time.* -T/66.

the jig is up [gir] acabou-se tudo, é o fim, não há mais esperança *The movie ends as a police car comes on the scene and the fugitive realizes that the jig is up.*

JIM Jim Crow [col] [pej] 1. segregação racial contra o negro americano *Jim Crow demeaned and diminished every Southerner, white or black.* -T/66. 2. próprio de ou relativo a locais onde haja segregação racial contra o negro *... blacks fleeing from the rigid segregation of the Jim Crow South.* -T/87. ♦ *... Jim Crow schools and colleges ...* -T/69.

JIM-DANDY [col] excelente, de primeira qualidade, formidável *They visited a small western town and had a jim-dandy time.* ♦ *... a jim-dandy event.* -T/87.

JITTER the jitters [col] = **the CREEPS** *Adding to the jitters about the dollar is the rising level of U.S. inflation.* -T/87.

JOB do a good/great/nice/thorough etc. job of realizar trabalho, tarefa etc. com eficiência (para o bem ou para o mal) *Our 19th century ancestors did a thorough job of divorcing feeling from intellect.* -T/86. ♦ *I think I do a much better job of just dealing with life as it comes along.* -T/92.

do a job on [gir] causar grande estrago a, danificar, ferir *You really did a job on that guy. He'll never bother us again.*

do the job/trick [col] resolver o problema, apresentar a solução, produzir o efeito desejado *Solving this problem won't be easy. Only a really clever idea will do the job.* ♦ *... the cuts [on his hands] were very superficial and a few Band-Aids did the trick.* -WJT,318.

fall down on the job [col] falhar, fracassar, não dar conta do recado *We expected the new machines to arrive today, but someone must have fallen down on the job.*

give up as a bad job desistir de fazer (algo impossível, impraticável, irremediável etc.) *He strove for an instant to answer [my question] and then gave it up as a bad job.* -VR,32.

have a job [col] ter dificuldade, ter um trabalhão *The last time I was in London, I had a job finding my way in a fog.*

inside job [col] roubo cometido com a necessária participação de alguém que trabalha para a vítima *The police believe that the hotel robbery was an inside job.*

lie down on the job [col] não cumprir sua obrigação, negligenciar uma tarefa *If Stanton isn't watched constantly, he will lie down on the job and produce next to nothing.*

make a good//bad job of cumprir bem//mal sua função, realizar um trabalho bemfeito//malfeito *Palmer had a wife and two kids to support and he intended to make a good job of it.*

odd job trabalho ocasional, biscate *... supporting himself with odd jobs ...* -SC,25. ♦ *... worked at odd jobs ...* -T/66.

one's/someone's job dever de, responsabilidade de, função ou papel de *My job*

is to look after Adele's interests. ♦ It's not her job to wash the dishes.
on the job 1. durante o exercício da função, enquanto trabalha *His training was done on the job.* ⇒ **on-the-job** realizado no decorrer da função, durante o trabalho *... 13 other women have been promoted to management positions after on-the-job training.* -T/72. 2. [col] ocupado, eficiente, alerta, atento ao seu trabalho *Dean is always on the job.*
put-up job [col] trama, conspiração, conchavo, conluio *The robbery at the bank was thought by many to be a put-up job by someone who worked there and knew the daily routine.*
JOCKEY jockey for tentar colocar-se em posição ou situação vantajosa, disputar a primazia *Since the election, party leaders have been jockeying for position.* -T/87. ♦ *... tobacco companies jockey for bigger shares of a market ...* -T/66.
JOHN John Doe homem anônimo, indivíduo comum, fulano de tal *Meet John Doe, a film directed by Frank Capra, tells the story of an average man.*
John Hancock [col] assinatura, rubrica *... putting his own John Hancock on a policy application.* -T/66.
JOHNNY-COME-LATELY [col] adventício, pessoa chegada de outro lugar, indivíduo que ingressou recentemente em um grupo (social, de trabalho etc.), novato *He's a Johnny-come-lately but has already started offering advice to the other employees.*
JOHNNY-ON-THE-SPOT [col] pessoa sempre alerta, sempre presente quando é necessária ou onde quer que haja boas oportunidades para si *He's always Johnny-on-the-spot.*
JOINT out of joint deslocado, desconjuntado, desordenado *What does Shakespeare say to an era that feels that the times are out of joint?* -T/60.
JOKE crack a joke [gir] contar uma piada,

fazer graça *... he had laughed and cracked his jokes ...* -PJW,80.
play a joke on (someone) fazer uma brincadeira com, pregar uma peça em *Carey was always playing jokes on his wife.*
practical joke brincadeira, peça, trote *Nothing is worse than a person who thinks it is funny to play practical jokes like putting lighted matches between the toes of a sleeping man.*
take a joke aceitar uma brincadeira, ser a vítima de uma piada *Most people can't take a joke.*
JOLLIES get one's jollies→ **get one's KICKS**
JONES keep up with the Joneses procurar ter o mesmo padrão de vida dos vizinhos de alto nível social *The great American game is keeping up with the Joneses, that is, trying to live in the same manner as your more affluent neighbors.*
JOT jot down anotar *I always try to jot down the words of new songs when I hear them.*
JOURNALISM yellow journalism/press imprensa sensacionalista, imprensa marrom *... a vulgar, pushy publisher, ... who was known for his yellow journalism.* -T/81. ♦ *... flamboyant stories in the yellow press about sex, murder, and rape.* -KJS,1.
JUDGEMENT pass judgement julgar, formar juízo *An FBI agent is not authorized to pass judgement on the guilt or innocence of a person.* -T/64.
JUICE stew in one's own juice [col] sofrer as conseqüências de algo que se praticou *Stan has brought about this unpleasant situation. Let him stew in his own juice now.*
JUMP get/have the jump on [gir] adiantar-se a, sair na frente de, colocar-se em posição de vantagem sobre *Ford is always trying to get the jump on General Motors and put its new car on display first.*

jump all over/on [gir] repreender severamente *My father would jump on us if he thought we were not spotlessly clean.*
jump at aceitar avidamente *... she'd jumped at a chance for a trip to the moon.* -LMO,9.
one jump/step ahead of [col] um passo à frente de, com ligeira vantagem sobre *Brad is always one jump ahead of everyone.* ♦ *The street gangs were always one step ahead of the police.*
on the jump [col] muito ocupado, muito ativo *Mr. Powell is always on the jump.*
JUNK junk food [col] alimentos ricos em calorias mas sem conteúdo nutritivo, sem proteínas *[She] ... successfully lobbied for a law banning junk food in school vending machines ...* -T/78.
JUST just about [col] quase, aproximadamente, praticamente *Dinner's just about ready.*
just as 1. no momento em que *Sue arrived just as I was leaving.* 2. exatamente como, tal como *Jim behaved just as I thought he would.*
JUSTICE bring to justice instaurar processo contra, levar à justiça *He wondered ... if the bandit would ever be brought to justice for his crimes.* -HJ,129.
do justice to 1. tratar apropriadamente, com dignidade, fazer justiça a *As the author of the screenplay [for* The Maltese Falcon*], [John] Huston made every effort to do justice, and remain faithful, to Dashiell Hammett's novel.* -BA,80. 2. dar o devido valor a, apreciar devidamente *Doug can do justice to a big meal at any hour of the day.*

KEEL keel over 1. tombar, virar, soçobrar *The boat keeled over and several people were drowned.* 2. [col] cair, desmaiar *[He] ... took a bullet in the liver, but operated the gun for over an hour and finally keeled over from loss of blood.* SGT,12.

on an even keel equilibrado, estável, firme *[Population expansion] ... which is hardly sufficient to keep the nation's population on an even keel ...* -WF,26.

KEEP for keeps [col] para sempre, de vez, permanente *Is their marriage for keeps?*

keep at continuar a (fazer algo), persistir em, prosseguir com *Keep at your work and you may learn to like it.*

keep away manter-se afastado, abster-se *Keep away from cigarettes if you wish to get rid of that cough.*

keep back 1. deter, reter, conter, reprimir *[She] ... could not keep back her tears.* -HG,237. ♦ *The police tried to keep back the crowd.* 2. ocultar *Don't keep anything back from me. Tell me what you know.*

keep/stay/steer clear of afastar-se de, evitar, ficar longe de *Keep clear of political groups in your working environment.* ♦ *As a teacher, you should steer clear of arguments involving politics and religion.* ♦ *The soldiers were warned to stay clear of certain sections of the towns near the army camps.*

keep cool permanecer calmo *Keep cool, even if he calls you bad names.* v. **keep one's COOL**

keep dark manter em segredo *[He was] ... keeping dark the personal secret that he was an heir [to the fortune his father and uncles had built up] ...* -T/60.

keep down 1. conter, reprimir, oprimir; manter em nível baixo, não aumentar, não permitir o desenvolvimento de *... there are specific reasons for the nation's incapacity to keep its street crime down.* -T/81. ♦ *... keeping prices down ...* -T/72.
♦ 2. conseguir manter (comida, bebida) no estômago, não vomitar *Clara was unable to keep down the food she had eaten at lunch.*

keep from 1. abster-se de *It was difficult to keep from worrying about my children.* 2. impedir de, não permitir, manter afastado *... keep terrorists from crossing the frontier.* -T/86. *The noise kept Mr. Smith from sleeping.* 3. não revelar a, ocultar de *Dorothy tried to keep her health problem from her husband.*

keep in with [col] ser amistoso com, permanecer em boas relações com *We*

try to keep in with our neighbors as best we can.
keep mum [col] ficar calado, não abrir o bico *Keep mum and nothing will happen to you.*
keep off 1. repelir, afastar, manter à distância *The boy could not keep off the flies that gathered on the sugar.* 2. afastar-se, manter distância de *Keep off the grass is translated into many languages.*
keep on continuar, prosseguir, persistir *John and Mary kept on seeing each other regularly through the long winter.* ♦ *The bell kept on ringing.*
keep out 1. manter-se a distância, não entrar, ficar de fora *The sign read: "Keep Out – Dangerous Explosives Stored Here".* 2. não permitir a entrada, impedir o acesso, excluir *Keep the dog out.* ♦ *... he carefully kept all evidence of astonishment out of his expression.* -MD,56.
keep out of não se envolver em, ficar fora de, evitar; não permitir que se envolva em *Tell your son to keep out of trouble.* ♦ *Try to keep him out of trouble.*
keep plugging along trabalhar com afinco *Joe has never been a great success but he keeps plugging along in hopes of the great day.*
keep (someone) posted manter (alguém) informado, a par de *... I do wish you'd keep in touch, if you can. Keep me posted on what's going on.* -CGC,76.
keep quiet calar-se, ficar quieto; fazer calar-se, manter em silêncio *Keep quiet or you'll wake up the children.* ♦ *Keep that dog quiet.*
keep someone waiting fazer alguém esperar *Vicky kept me waiting for half an hour.*
keep something to oneself guardar algo para si, não divulgar, manter em segredo *[He] ... knew all about [the plans for the air attack on] Pearl Harbor, but kept it to himself ...* -TJ,177.
keep to 1. manter-se fiel a, cumprir, observar *Keep to your ideal no matter how difficult it may seem.* 2. não se desviar de, não se afastar de *Keep to the right when you're driving.* 3. permanecer em (local, posição etc.) *The doctor told Cathy to keep to her bed for three days.*
keep to oneself fugir à convivência, retrair-se, conservar-se arredio, viver isolado *I was also a silent child, keeping much to myself.* -RLI, 9.
keep up 1. continuar, continuar (fazendo, mantendo), prosseguir, persistir *We can't leave if the rain keeps up.* ♦ *I can't keep up working day and night much longer.* 2. conservar, suster, sustentar, manter em boas condições, apoiar, amparar *We try to keep up our garden but find little time to work in it.* 3. manter, observar (costume, tradição etc.) *Ethnic groups in America keep up their old world customs, especially those of Easter and Christmas.* 4. manter, conservar (amizade, correspondência etc.) *... the two men kept up a warm personal correspondence.* -T/64. 5. manter elevado, em alto nível, não deixar cair, diminuir ou esmorecer *Try to keep up your morale.* ♦ *Many families [are] trying to keep up their living standards ...* -T/80. 6. impedir (alguém) de recolher-se à cama, manter acordado *I can't let Bates keep me up all night just because he wants to celebrate.* -CN, 28.
keep up on → KEEP up with 3
keep up with 1. acompanhar (o andar, o ritmo, o desenvolvimento, o progresso de), não ficar para trás *I had to run to keep up with Melinda.* ♦ *He lost his house because he could not keep up with his payments.* 2. manter contato, relações, amizade com *The only friend ... [she] has kept up with ... is Billy Carter's daughter ...* -T/81. 3. [ou] **keep up on** manter-se informado ou atualizado a respeito de *Dictionary makers, it may be pointed out, have a responsibility to keep up with changes in usage status.* -AH,268. ♦ *He reads* Time Magazine *to keep up on domestic and foreign news.*

KEEPING in//out of keeping with de acordo//em desacordo com, em harmonia//desarmonia com *It was dawn now, a gray hopeless dawn that seemed very much in keeping with my mood.* -RQ,68. ♦ *The Senator's behavior was out of keeping with the behavior expected of an important politician.*

KETTLE a fine/pretty kettle of fish confusão, embrulhada, situação problemática *When Gus took his new job in the company and saw the chaos in the Finance Department he said: "This is a pretty kettle of fish".*

KEY importantíssimo, necessário, essencial *He was hired for a key job with General Motors.* ♦ *Simpson held a key position in the Government.* ♦ *Oppenheimer played a key role in the development of the atom bomb.*

keyed up agitado, nervoso, tenso *[He was] ... so keyed up that he couldn't sleep at night ...* -NEW,14.

KICK for kicks [col] por prazer, por divertimento, para sentir uma emoção ou sensação agradável *... Alex, a psychopathic young bully [in the movie* A Clockwork Orange*] who rapes and plunders for "kicks" ...* -BRF,47.

get a kick out of [gir] = **get a BANG out of** *I get a kick out of most of Cole Porter's songs.*

get/have one's kicks/jollies [gir] obter viva emoção, sensação prazerosa, excitação, divertir-se *He gets his kicks out of reading girlie magazines.* ♦ *Many people have strange ways of getting their jollies.*

kick around [col] 1. maltratar, destratar *[President Nixon told reporters] "You won't have Nixon to kick around anymore."* -T/87. 2. discutir, debater, considerar (idéia, plano etc.) *This whole subject has been kicked around for several years now.* -T/75. ♦ *Let's kick this idea around a little before we make any decision about it.* 3. perambular, correr mundo, não parar em um lugar, mudar freqüentemente de emprego ou residência *Roy has kicked around many places and we wonder if he will ever settle down.* 4. estar abandonado, jogado, encostado (em algum lugar); ser negligenciado, esquecido, receber pouca atenção *... this idea had been kicking around in my head for a long time ...* -AK,266.

kick back [gir] dar parte de seu salário ou lucro a outra pessoa em retribuição a emprego ou ganho obtido *To get the job you had to kick back 10% each week to the supervisor of the department.* ⇒ **kickback** comissão ou porcentagem paga a chefe, capataz ou outra pessoa que auxiliou alguém a obter um emprego, a realizar uma venda etc. *... his construction firm had funneled $13,000 in kickbacks to local politicians.* -T/81.

kick in [gir] contribuir com *Each member of the office force had to kick in a day's pay to help the Red Cross.*

kick in the teeth → **kick in the TEETH**

kick off 1. [col] começar, dar início *If Federal help comes too late, it will raise unemployment and kick off a new raise in inflation.* 2. [gir] bater as botas *He kicked off four or five days ago. Had consumption.* -WR,138.

kick oneself sentir-se culpado (por erro cometido), recriminar-se, estar muito zangado consigo mesmo *He kicked himself when he realized the awful blunder he had made.* ♦ *I could have kicked myself for not having been there at the appointed time.*

kick out [col] expulsar *I thought we might all get kicked out ...* -T/87. ♦ *... in 1934 [the Jews] ... were kicked out of the stock exchanges [in Germany] ...* -SWLR,323.

kick up 1. levantar (poeira) ou fazer levantar *The passing trucks kicked up a lot of dust.* 2. [col] provocar, suscitar, incitar, causar *The investigation of the multinationals is kicking up a big controversy.*

kick upstairs [col] promover a cargo mais elevado, mais bem-remunerado etc. mas de menor poder, menor influência etc. *[He] ... was kicked upstairs, losing all operating authority.* -T/85.

KID **handle with kid gloves** [col] tratar com luvas de pelica *In* Singin' in the Rain, *Lina Lamont is a very temperamental star who has to be treated with kid gloves.*

kid brother//sister [col] irmão//irmã mais jovem *... Jack Kennedy sent a crisis message to his kid brother, Ted ...* -T/60.

kid oneself [col] enganar-se, iludir-se *Don't kid yourself. That can't be done.*

kid stuff [col] 1. coisa de criança, criancice, comportamento infantil *Complaints to his parents brought an indifferent shrug from his father and the response, "It's just kid stuff".* -DJ/6 2. coisa muito fácil de fazer, que não oferece nenhuma dificuldade *That's kid stuff. I can do it easily.*

KILL **close/move in for the kill** aproximar-se (da vítima) para destruir, matar, dar o golpe de misericórdia *Gordon's pursuers had driven him into a blind alley and were now closing in for the kill.*

kill off eliminar matando, exterminar, aniquilar *Hunters and fishermen are killing off animal life and depleting the [Brazilian Pantanal] rivers of aquatic life.* -T/91. ♦ *Insecticides kill off useful insects along with the pests.* -T/60.

kill oneself [col] exaurir-se, estafar-se *You're only killing yourself working like that.*

KILLING **make a killing** [col] ganhar muito dinheiro ou ter um grande lucro em curto prazo (especialmente no mercado de ações ou nos negócios) *When his wife asks where the cash came from, he mumbles something about the stock market and adds, ... "I made a killing."* -T/61.

KILTER **out of kilter** [col] quebrado, desarranjado, desordenado, funcionando mal; fora de lugar, desalinhado *That motor sounds as if it were out of kilter.*

KIN **next of kin** o(s) parente(s) mais próximo(s) *We must notify Conrad's next of kin of his sickness.*

KIND **in kind** 1. em mercadorias, em bens, em gêneros *Walsh was paid in kind, not in money.* 2. da mesma maneira, na mesma moeda *The Japanese government could respond to the sanctions in kind with counter-retaliatory steps ...* -T/87.

kind of [col] um tanto, um pouco, meio, mais ou menos, semelhante a *I feel kind of tired this evening.* ♦ *Angela seemed kind of surprised to see me there.*

nothing of the kind nada disso, longe disso *"Why don't you admit it, you were trying to make love to her." "I was doing nothing of the kind."*

of a kind 1. do mesmo tipo, natureza etc., semelhante, igual *You and that lazy brother of yours are two of a kind.* 2. de qualidade inferior, insatisfatório *The guests were served coffee of a kind.*

one of a kind pessoa ou coisa ímpar, singular, especial, inigualável *Carmen Miranda was one of a kind, ... [and] kept movie audiences awake and happy.* -SLE,109.

something of the kind mais ou menos isso, coisa parecida (àquilo que foi dito, mencionado, perguntado etc.) *"Did she actually say she loved you?" "Well, something of the kind."*

KINGDOM **kingdom come** o outro mundo, o reino do céu *... Gardiner listened to him talk about God and Christ and Kingdom Come ...* -NE,18.

till kingdom come para sempre, eternamente *You can count on that [something the speaker is sure of] till kingdom come.* -CEP,182.

to kingdom come para o outro mundo, para a melhor [geralmente precedido de um verbo de ação: *send/blow/blast* etc.] *When the torpedo hit the small ship, it blew all the crew to kingdom come.*

KINGFISH [col] chefe, líder *Mason was the kingfish at work but not at home.*

KINGPIN [col] a pessoa mais importante de um grupo, organização etc. *He is the kingpin in our worldwide organization.*

KING-SIZE(D) [col] de tamanho grande, maior ou mais longo que o tamanho normal ou convencional ... *a king-size cigarette* ... -T/87. ♦ *Architects with the king-sized imagination of a [Frank Lloyd] Wright* ... -T/60.

KISS kiss away dissipar, fazer desaparecer (dor, preocupação etc.), enxugar (lágrimas) com beijos *Gene took Donna in his arms and kissed her tears away.*

kiss of death [col] ato que leva à desgraça, à ruína, ao fracasso etc. *To be perceived as nonrevolutionary in Iran is the kiss of death* ... -T/87.

kiss off [gir] 1. demitir, abandonar, mandar embora *Ellen kissed off her boyfriend and left for New York.* ⇒ **kiss-off** demissão, despedida, adeus, abandono, fim *He was given the kiss-off by his political party after the scandal broke in the papers.* 2. rejeitar, repelir, repudiar, desaprovar, condenar *[He]* ... *kissed off much of U.S. news coverage as "meretricious, superficial and spotty".* -T/69.

KIT (the whole) kit and caboodle/boodle [col] tudo, todos, todo mundo, todo o grupo (de pessoas ou coisas), todos os componentes, todos os pertences, toda a tralha *[The manager of the aircraft company said:] I don't think I have to remind you people of the advantages of building the whole kit and caboodle – the engine, airplane, electronics – the works.* -GM,285. ♦ *The gamblers moved from town to town with kit and boodle.*

KITE go fly a kite [gir] não amolar, ir plantar batatas *They told me to go fly a kite when I asked to play on their team.*

KITH kith and kin amigos e parentes *More kith and kin gathered [at the hospital for news of the patient].* -T/68.

KNEE bring to one's knees subjugar, forçar a se render ... *the German Air Force chief [Goering] thought that the Luftwaffe alone could bring Britain to her knees [in World War II]* ... -SWLR,1017.

KNIFE go under the knife [col] ser operado, entrar na faca *The operation appeared to be successful, but* ... *[he] soon had to go under the knife again* ... -T/85.

KNITTING stick/tend to one's knitting [col] cuidar da própria vida, não se meter em seara alheia *We have stuck to our knitting and used all our weapons.*

KNOCK hard knocks [col] adversidades, reveses, infortúnios, transtornos ... *a realistic preparation for life's hard knocks.* -T/78. v. **SCHOOL of hard knocks**

knock about/around [col] 1. perambular, viajar, ir de um lugar para outro ... *he's been knocking around the Amazon for quite a while.* -UJ,68. 2. maltratar, surrar, socar *Wesley has been known to knock his wife around when drunk.*

knock back [gir] tomar (bebida alcoólica) de um gole *He knocked back a stiff drink.* -AK,104.

knock cold [col] nocautear, deixar inconsciente *The champion was knocked cold.* ♦ *He punched me in the face and knocked me cold.* -LRW,17.

knock dead empolgar, causar grande admiração, viva emoção (a uma platéia) *The new show knocked them dead.*

knock down 1. derrubar (com golpe), lançar ao chão, fazer cair *He was knocked down in the third round.* ♦ *The Berlin Wall ... has been knocked down ...* -T/91. ⇒ **knockdown** a. queda provocada por soco ou golpe violento *He won the fight by a knockdown in the third round.* b. o ato de derrubar, queda; revés, transtorno, baque ... *either the U.S.-Israeli friendship or the Middle East peace process could suffer a knockdown.* -T/92. 2. [col] reduzir, diminuir, baixar ... *Wilson proceeded to knock down one record price after another* ... -T/78. 3. [gir] ganhar, receber (salário) *How much do you knock down at that*

job? 4. arrematar (em leilão) ... *the oil [a Matisse painting] was knocked down for $1,584,000* ... -T/79.
knock it off [gir] deixe de fazer o que está fazendo; pare de falar! pare com isso! basta! chega! *When he began to tell dirty jokes I snapped: "Knock it off!"*
knock off 1. v. **KNOCK it off** 2. [col] cessar o trabalho, encerrar o expediente (ou interromper para o almoço *What time do you knock off?* ♦ *We always knock off for lunch at 11:45.* 3. [col] deduzir, descontar, diminuir *He wants me to knock off $50 on my asking price.* 4.[col] efetuar, realizar, levar a cabo; produzir, compor, escrever ou fazer (algo) apressada ou rotineiramente *Zane Grey knocked off a new western story each year.* 5. [gir] matar, assassinar *A good boy like Joey Doyle could be knocked off and nobody lifts a finger.* -SB,76. 6. [col] eliminar, liquidar, subjugar, livrar-se de *[He was overweight and] ... he figured he needed to knock off a dozen pounds.* -T/87. 7. [gir] roubar, assaltar *The same gang has knocked off three gas stations and a couple of banks.* 8. [col] comer ou beber rapidamente *Mr. Salvatore could knock off two plates of spaghetti and meatballs and still ask for more.*
knock out 1. nocautear, deixar inconsciente *The challenger was knocked out in the fifth round.* ♦ *The powerful drug knocked him out.* ⇒ **knockout** a. nocaute *Ali won the fight by a knockout.* b. [gir] pessoa ou coisa atraente, encantadora, excelente, sensacional *This kid is a knockout. Wait till you hear her sing Over the Rainbow.* 2. destruir, danificar, demolir; inutilizar, avariar, incapacitar, deixar inoperante *The air strike knocked out many tanks along the highways.* 3. **knock oneself out** fazer grande esforço, exaurir-se, extenuar-se *Tuttle knocked himself out working two jobs a day.* 4. [col] = **KNOCK off** 4 *... he [Jack Lon-*

don] decided to knock out a dog story, in about 4,000 words, that would help to pay his wife's doctor bills. -SV, 101. 5. pôr fim a, livrar-se de, acabar com, derrotar, eliminar *[He] ... has every expectation of knocking out his opponents in next January's general elections* ... -T/86.
knock over 1. tombar, derrubar, lançar ao chão *Bobby blamed the cat for knocking over the bottle of milk.* 2. [gir] assaltar, roubar *Jesse and Frank James knocked over many banks in the West before they were stopped.*
knock together fazer ou preparar às pressas, toscamente *Forster had knocked together a table and four chairs.*
KNOT tie the knot [col] casar-se *[He] ... had tied the knot with his 28-year old secretary* ... -T/92.
KNOW before one knows it antes que se dê pela coisa, antes que se perceba, logo *All this unpleasant situation will be over before you know it.*
for all one knows pelo que se sabe, segundo consta *For all I know she might still be living in Italy.* ♦ *For all you know, this could be a paint factory.* -SRU,72.
(someone) has been known to (do something) sabe-se que, é sabido que (alguém às vezes age de determinada maneira, faz isso ou aquilo etc.) *Mr. Peabody has sometimes been known to come home drunk.* ♦ *[They] ... have been known to perform small wonders.* -AJ,133.
in the know [col] bem informado, ciente dos fatos, conhecedor de informações (confidenciais ou que a maioria das pessoas desconhece) *People in the know say that an atomic war is not feasible and therefore an impossibility.*
know best ter o melhor discernimento, saber julgar melhor *Father and mother always know best.*
know better ter bom discernimento, saber julgar, estar mais bem informado, saber que não deve (fazer determinada coisa, ter

determinada atitude etc.) *Don't ask me about preventive medicine when people like you, who obviously know better, smoke two packs of cigarettes a day.* -T/69. ♦ *... no matter how many times they had repeated this exact routine ... they knew better than to trust their memories.* -GE,53.

know differently/otherwise ter informação diferente ou contrária àquela que foi mencionada, estar ciente de que a verdade é outra *The first word to reporters was that mother and child were doing nicely. But in the operating room, doctors knew differently.* -T/63.

know enough (to) ter o necessário discernimento, sensatez, bom senso (para) *I knew enough to check his ability. He was a "fine and capable man", reported my father's relative.* -FLF,20.

know (something) from (something) distinguir, diferenciar *The song says that Ruby Gentry "doesn't know right from wrong".*

know (down) pat/cold → **GET/have (down) pat/cold**

know what's what [col] estar bem-informado, ter experiência, saber das coisas *We must know what's what before we invest our capital in your business.*

know where one stands saber onde pisa, em que situação alguém se encontra *Now you know where you stand insofar as what needs to be done about your desire to improve.* -SHS,23.

little does one know → **LITTLE does one imagine**

not know if/whether one is coming or going [col] estar confuso, desorientado *I've heard so many different stories about Lee's case that I don't know whether I'm coming or going.*

what do you know! [col] ora veja! que surpreendente! quem diria! *When I told Caroline what had happened she said: "Well, what do you know!"*

what you don't know won't hurt you o que os olhos não vêem, o coração não sente *Don't tell her anything. What she doesn't know won't hurt her.*

you know something/what? [col] sabe de uma coisa? *You know something? I've never told this to anybody.*

you never know nunca se sabe *Be careful not to say anything about this to Ann. With redheads like her you never know, she might get mad at you.*

KNOW-HOW [col] conhecimento, habilidade, técnica, capacidade *... technical know-how for oil refineries and petrochemical plants.* -T/87. ♦ *... he shares his financial know-how with students at a Manhattan junior high school ...* -T/92.

KNOW-IT-ALL [col] sabichão, sabe-tudo *... he was a self-important upstart and a know-it-all.* -T/87.

KNOWLEDGE to one's knowledge → **to the BEST of one's knowledge**

KNUCKLE knuckle down = **BUCKLE down** *... he couldn't imagine himself knuckling down to a rigid study program.* -WJT,255.

knuckle under = **BUCKLE under** *[The prisoner refused] ... to knuckle under to the sadistic guards.* -T/67.

rap one's knuckles censurar, criticar, castigar *The Christian Herald [a Protestant periodical] sometimes raps Catholic knuckles ...* -T/64.

L

LABOR labor of love tarefa ou empreendimento realizado por amor ou satisfação *Collecting all the material for the dictionary was a labor of love but it was also a herculean task.*
  labor under 1. estar oprimido ou atribulado etc. por dificuldade, desvantagem, limitação, risco etc. *In world affairs [in 1960] Japan still labored under the inferiority complex of a conquered nation.* -T/66. 2. incidir em engano, equívoco, ilusão etc. *... you labored under the delusion that I was different ...* -WH,405.

LADY ladies'/lady's man homem galanteador, homem que gosta da companhia de mulheres e procura agradá-las *... Bill, with his reputation as a ladies' man.* -T/92.
  ladies' room toalete, sanitário feminino *The ladies' room in the U.S. has many names including: the powder room, the rest room, the John.*
  Lady Luck Dona Sorte, boa fortuna *Lady Luck had been with me so often ... that perhaps I had begun to rely on her as a friend and ally, forgetting she is blind.* -SHE,11.
  the lady of the house a dona da casa, a patroa *The lady of the house is not home today. Just her husband.*
  the old lady/woman [col] 1. esposa *Mr. Haynes and his old lady haven't been getting along very well lately.* 2. mãe *[Movie star] ... Angela Lansbury was the girl to play everybody's old lady.* -T/66.

LADY-KILLER [col] homem atraente; sedutor *Wendell thinks he's an irresistible lady-killer.*

LAKE go jump in a/the lake [gir] ir plantar batatas, ir lamber sabão *[The President] ... told him to "go jump in a lake".* -T/61.

LAM on the lam [gir] em fuga, escondendo-se (da lei, principalmente) *[He] ... has been on the lam from Britain since 1963 ...* -T/92.
  take it on the lam [gir] fugir, foragir-se, dar aos calcanhares *Benson took it on the lam when he thought he had killed a man.*

LAND land on [col] censurar, criticar severamente *Craig's wife landed on him when she found a letter from another woman in his pocket.*
  see how the land lies reconhecer o terreno, examinar a situação *Before you buy shares in that company I advise you to see how the land lies.*

LAND-OFFICE BUSINESS [col] negócio lucrativo, de rápida prosperidade; grande volume de negócios *Both stores did a land-office business last year.*

LANDSLIDE maioria esmagadora de votos de um candidato ou partido; vitória esmagadora *He won the election by an unprecedented landslide.* ♦ *... Mulroney and his party swept into office with a landslide victory.* -T/87.

LANE fast lane [col] estilo de vida extravagante, estróina, excitante etc., de ritmo frenético e que busca a satisfação imediata *... she lived a short life in the fast lane.* -T/87.

LANGUAGE strong language linguagem chula, palavras rudes, grosseiras, xingação *When the two men began to argue, they used very strong language.*

   watch one's language não proferir palavrões, não ser desbocado *The men watched their language when I was around.* -T/76.

LAP drop/dump into someone's lap jogar nas mãos de, passar a responsabilidade (de algo difícil ou espinhoso) para alguém *[The police] ... have dumped the collective evidence in the lap of the district attorney.* -DJ,xi.

   in the lap of luxury em grande riqueza, luxo, conforto *Carson's been living in the lap of luxury ever since he hit the jackpot.*

LARGE at large 1. solto, não-confinado *A homicidal maniac was at large ...* -T/79. 2. no todo, em conjunto, de um modo geral *Viet Nam veterans have higher rates of suicide, divorce and mental breakdown than the population at large.* -T/79. 3. por extenso, na íntegra, em detalhes *We have already discussed this matter at large.*

LASH lash out 1. escoicear, arremeter contra, golpear, bater *The young boy lashed out at his tormentors who stood in a circle around him.* 2. atacar duramente, criticar severamente *[He] ... lashed out at the Reagan Administration for its lack of ethical leadership.* -T/87.

LAST at (long) last afinal, finalmente *At long last the war has ended.*

   breathe one's last dar o último suspiro, morrer *... after agonizing years of gasping and wheezing, [coal miners] finally breathe their last.* -T/81.

   (and) last but not least (por) último (na ordem) mas não menos importante *And last but not least I must mention Mr. Fred Powell, who has helped us so much.*

   last out sobreviver a, resistir a, durar tanto quanto ou mais que *The old man was very sick and we thought he wouldn't last out the night.*

   to the (very) last até o fim, até o último momento *Curtis remained loyal to the last.*

LAST-MINUTE de última hora *... Brazilians like to reaffirm their abiding faith in last-minute miraculous rescues. "God", they say, "is a Brazilian."* -T/80. ♦ *... they wouldn't appreciate any last-minute help from me.* -EW,55.

LATCH latch on/onto [col] 1. pegar, agarrar, obter, entrar na posse de *It seems as though he has latched onto a good thing.* 2. ligar-se a, unir-se a, não desgrudar de *... it has been my job to latch on to a suspect in a major crime ...* -DJ,viii. 3. compreender, entender *Try to latch on to what I'm explaining to you.*

LATE as late as tão recentemente quanto, ainda em *As late as 1956 there were German schools in Brazil ...* -WC,78.

   at the latest o mais tardar *I'll be there on Wednesday at the latest.*

   in one's late twenties/thirties etc. aos vinte/trinta e tantos anos etc. *Frank was in his late twenties when I met him.* v. **in one's EARLY twenties**

   of late recentemente, ultimamente *Several accidents have occurred at that factory of late.*

LATE-BREAKING de última hora (notícia); que acontece ou chega quase na hora do fechamento da matéria a ser impressa ou televisionada *TIME [Magazine] often goes to extraordinary lengths to cover late-breaking events.* -T/86.

LATHER (all) in a lather [gir] 1. muito agitado, emocionado, nervoso *He came* *rushing into the office in a lather.* 2. impaciente, apreensivo, ansioso *They were all in a lather to leave when the bus came up the road.*

LATTER-DAY de nossos dias, de época recente, moderno *... latter-day pioneers.* -T/78. ♦ *... a latter-day attempt to prove once again that the earth is flat.* -HRW,10.

LAUGH for laughs por prazer, por diversão, por satisfação, de brincadeira *Calder says he works just for laughs, but he is always waiting in line to receive his salary at the end of the month.*

get/have the last laugh rir por último, levar a melhor *One of the most satisfying of life's pleasures ... is having the last laugh at the expense of one's critics.* -SV,17.

get/have the laugh on triunfar sobre uma situação totalmente adversa, rir-se de alguém por terem-se trocado os papéis *When Carl received the unexpected gift of a trip to Europe given by his company, he had the laugh on his fellow workers who had ridiculed him for working so hard.*

laugh at rir de, zombar de, ridicularizar *They all laughed at him when he began to sing.*

laugh away não dar importância a, menosprezar (algo molesto, incômodo etc.) com risos *Frank tried to laugh away his wife's apprehensions.*

laugh down zombar de, silenciar (alguém) com riso *They tried to laugh him down.*

laugh off não dar importância a, tratar com menosprezo *Funny as his plan may seem, we cannot laugh it off.*

laugh one out of fazer alguém esquecer mágoa, tristeza, aflição etc. animando-o com risos, bom humor, otimismo etc. *Brian's friends tried to laugh him out of his sad mood when he found out that his girl had left him.*

that's a laugh [gír] essa é boa! isso é ridículo! *You're telling me? That's a laugh!*

LAUGHTER roar with laughter rir às gargalhadas *Whenever I saw a Danny Kaye movie I'd roar with laughter most of the time.*

LAUNDRY laundry list [col] lista (geralmente longa, de tópicos, coisas, artigos, objetos, itens etc.) *... the voters' laundry list of complaints ...* -T/72.

LAUREL rest on one's laurels dormir sobre os louros, estar satisfeito com o que já conquistou *His first book was a work of art, but his recent one makes us think that he's resting on his laurels and not doing any really creative writing.*

LAW blue laws leis puritanas da Nova Inglaterra colonial, estabelecidas em 1630-1700 *In Massachusetts, an old blue law says that you can't kiss your wife on Sunday.*

break the law violar a lei *Don't break the law or we will put you in jail.* -T/92.

a law unto oneself algo auto-suficiente, que se basta a si próprio, que se guia por seus próprios princípios ou inclinações, que age de maneira incomum ou imprevisível *... the [U.R.S.S.] Communist Party ... always acted as a law unto itself.* -T/92.

lay down the law [col] dar ordens de maneira severa, autoritária, repreender com rigor, mostrar sua autoridade *The professor laid down the law to the students who arrived late for class.*

take the law into one's own hands fazer justiça com as próprias mãos *... a powerful historical personality like Napoleon, or others who have, so to speak, taken the law into their own hands.* -LMC,5.

LAW-ABIDING cumpridor da lei, que obedece à lei *We're law-abiding, God-fearing people ...* -SCD,15. ♦ *... law-abiding citizens have been known to break the law under the pressure of neurotic anxiety.* -HC,67.

LAY lay aside 1. pôr de lado, abandonar, largar *... barbarities that had supposedly been laid aside for all time.* -SRE,186. 2. economizar, guardar *Hutton lays aside fifty dollars each week for his son's college education.*

lay bare revelar, desnudar *The trials will lay bare all the dirty political intrigue.*
lay by economizar, guardar para uso futuro *Each week I lay by a few dollars for a rainy day.*
lay down 1. declarar, afirmar categoricamente, asseverar; enunciar, prescrever, dispor *All the rights of the citizen are laid down clearly in the Constitution.* 2. depor, entregar (armas); abandonar, pôr de lado, renunciar a, sacrificar (a vida) *The soldiers laid down their arms and returned to their homes.* ♦ *[They] ... seemed ready to lay down their lives for the cause of their homeland.* -T/86. 3. assentar, instalar, estabelecer, firmar, fundar *[They] ... worked through the night to lay down a crude barrier of cinder blocks, mortar and barbed wire.* T/86. ♦ *The marketing leaders of today are laying down the basic lessons for the marketers of tomorrow to follow.* -PVH,198.
lay for [col] pôr-se em emboscada *[He] ... had been laying for her in the foyer of her apartment house.* -CJC,139.
lay in prover, armazenar *Before her husband had left, he had ... laid in a large supply of groceries ...* -LRT,65.
lay/light into [gir] 1. investir contra, lançar-se sobre; começar a fazer algo com grande energia ou disposição, "atacar" *Call an Irishman a "bogtrotter" and he will lay into you.* ♦ *... I was really lighting into the lyrics of such songs as "Old Black Magic", "St. Louis Blues", "Beale Street Mama", and "Day After Day" ...* -HA,43. 2. criticar asperamente, atacar verbalmente *He lit into his opponents in Congress.*
lay it on [col] lisonjear excessivamente, bajular, exagerar *When Peggy said that her mother-in-law was truly a marvelous, wonderful person, her husband said: "I wish you wouldn't lay it on so thick".*
lay low 1. derrubar, fazer cair, lançar ao chão *Elmer was laid low by a blow from the strong man.* 2. abater, debilitar, prostrar *Sandra was laid low with pneumonia.* 3. matar *He laid the two killers low with two bullets.* 4. [col] = **LIE low** *Big Harry will lay low for a while and the police won't find him.*
lay off 1. demitir ou dispensar (trabalhadores) temporariamente *So far, between 100 and 150 employees have been laid off.* -T/86. ⇒ **lay-off** dispensa temporária de trabalhadores *The big company lay-offs have caused unemployment to rise 7% in Massachusetts.* 2. [gir] cessar, parar, deixar, abandonar *Why don't you lay off smoking?* 3. [gir] parar de criticar, de falar, de amolar *Lay off, will you? You're beginning to annoy me.*
lay of the land a topografia, a configuração do terreno; o estado da situação, as condições existentes *Joshua sent spies to Canaan to get the lay of the land.*
lay oneself (wide) open expor-se, arriscar-se, ficar vulnerável, desprotegido *The President laid himself open to a lot of criticism after that incident.*
lay oneself out [col] fazer um esforço extraordinário, empenhar-se sobremaneira *Mr. Burns lays himself out to provide for his large family.*
lay out 1. estender, arrumar, dispor, pôr à vista, deixar pronto (para uso, inspeção, exibição etc.) *It is only when all of the facts are laid out that a correct evaluation can be made.* -RE,8. 2. planejar, providenciar *I want you to go over these plans I've laid out ...* -CHT,139. 3. projetar, esboçar, delinear *English gardens are beautifully laid out.* ⇒ **layout** plano, planejamento, planta, esboço, traçado, diagrama *The garden had a beautiful layout.* ♦ *The layout of the advertisement was approved by the president himself.* 4. gastar, despender *I know Haarland hasn't got enough cash to lay out.* -PF,20. 5. preparar (corpo) para funeral *They laid him out in an expensive coffin.* 6. [gir] derrubar com um golpe;

nocautear, deixar inconsciente *One hard blow on the head will lay him out.* 7. [gír] censurar, repreender *The boss laid him out because of the big mistake he had made.*

lay over parar, interromper viagem, fazer escala *We laid over in a small town for two days for lack of transportation.* ⇒ **layover** escala, parada *This is a direct flight. There are no layovers unless the weather forces us to land.*

lay up 1. confinar à cama, deixar incapacitado temporariamente *Edwina broke her collarbone roller-skating and was laid up for two months.* ♦ *... when I was twenty years old and working a carnival, I broke my leg. It laid me up ...* -BRT,3. 2. retirar de serviço, desativar (embarcação, automóvel etc.) *Because of the oil boycott many oil tankers have been laid up.* 3. guardar, armazenar, acumular *They have laid up a lot of supplies for the winter months.*

lay waste devastar, destruir, arruinar *... demolition squads laid waste everything in the city that might be used by the oncoming enemy.* -SSG,17.

LEAD¹ [rima com *need*] **follow the/someone's lead** seguir o exemplo de, o precedente estabelecido por *The women of France laid aside their corsets because these garments interfered with their work in industry. Women in other countries followed their lead.* -DDT,439.

have the lead 1. [ou] **play the lead** ter o papel principal (em peça teatral, filme etc.) *John Wayne played the lead in* The Big Trail. 2. liderar, ocupar o primeiro lugar, superar *This brand of cigarettes has the lead over all the other brands.*

lead astray induzir em erro, desencaminhar, desviar do bom caminho *We are often betrayed by ideals, or led astray by poetry which we too seriously take for eternal truth.* -CH,16.

lead off começar, dar início, abrir, principiar; ir à frente, ir na vanguarda *They mounted and Clint led off at a gallop.* -LLN,28. ♦ *The manager led off with a lot of technical talk on the subject.*

lead on 1. guiar, conduzir, dirigir, liderar *Who will lead us on if he dies?* 2. engodar, atrair, induzir, enganar com falsas promessas *Ruby led him on until all his money was gone.*

lead up to 1. preparar o caminho para, levar a *... events leading up to the final breakthrough ...* -T/81. 2. abordar (assunto, tema etc.) de maneira sutil, indireta, gradual etc. *... she knew what Madgie was leading up to now, as well as what she would eventually ask.* -CEP,60.

take the lead assumir o comando, a liderança, tomar a dianteira, a iniciativa *... nothing much could happen unless the army took the lead ...* -GJI,47.

LEAD² [rima com *bed*] **get the lead out of one's pants/shoes/feet** [gír] apressar-se, ativar-se, ocupar-se, aviar-se *Get the lead out of your pants and get this job done now!* ♦ *O.K., get the lead out of your feet ...* -SM,10.

LEAF leaf through folhear *As a teenager, I enjoyed leafing through the copies of* The Saturday Evening Post *that my brother Oswald passed on to me.*

shake like a leaf tremer como vara verde, tremer de susto *Nan was so frightened by the explosion that she shook like a leaf.*

take a leaf out of someone's book seguir o exemplo de, imitar o comportamento de *Sam took a leaf out of his friend's book and went skiing in Sun Valley, Idaho.*

turn over a new leaf recomeçar, regenerar-se, reabilitar-se, tornar-se uma pessoa melhor e responsável *He decided to turn over a new leaf and be true to his wife.*

LEAGUE in league mancomunado, em conluio *He was in league with the corrupt lawyer and was also arrested.*

LEAK out vir a público, transpirar, dar a conhecer (informação, segredo etc. por acidente, descuido ou de propósito) *The story then leaked out that proposals had* been put forward for a secret agreement ... -GJI,72.

leak spring a leak sofrer rombo, rachadura, fenda; começar a fazer água subitamente (embarcação) *When the waves began to pound against the boat, it sprang a leak in the bow.*

LEAN lean over backward → **BEND over backward**

LEAP by leaps and bounds rapidamente, a passos largos *Computer intelligence is growing by leaps and bounds, with no natural limit in sight.* -T/78.

leap year ano bissexto *Every fourth year is leap year, that is, February has 29 days instead of 28.*

LEASE a new lease on life vida nova, novas esperanças, ressurgimento *After Will came back from the war he felt that he had a new lease on life.*

LEAST at (the) (very) least pelo menos, ao menos, no mínimo *... in any analogy the differences are at least as important as the resemblances.* -WP,8. ♦ *... they do hope to ... at the very least give every youngster a good idea of what the science [of biology] is all about.* -T/60.

least of all muito menos *No one, least of all Arthur, would be foolhardy to call Neville a liar.*

not in the least de maneira alguma, nem um pouco, absolutamente não *... she didn't understand him at all, not in the least ...* -WCN,161. ♦ *Lester wasn't in the least annoyed when we told him the news.*

to say the least para dizer o mínimo *Hollis was, to say the least, courteous to us even though he disliked us.*

LEAVE leave/let alone deixar em paz, não amolar; não tocar em, não mexer em *Leave her alone. She's had a bad day at the office and is not in the mood for jokes.* ♦ *All I want is to be let alone.* ♦ *Leave that gun alone.*

leave behind 1. esquecer, deixar de levar ou trazer *Mr. Halsey found a handbag in a taxi, obviously left behind by its last oc-* cupant. 2. abandonar, deixar para trás, deixar (como sinal de que algo ocorreu ou de que alguém produziu algo) *He was left behind in enemy territory.* ♦ *... artifacts, relics, and monuments that ... [prehistoric man] left behind.* -SR,16.

leave for partir para, sair para *He left for his office half an hour ago.* ♦ *They're leaving for Japan tomorrow.*

leave it at that deixar por isso mesmo, deixar pra lá, dar por encerrado *I don't wish to antagonize you further. Let's leave it at that and not prolong the argument.*

leave off 1. terminar, chegar ao fim, parar (de), cessar (de), deixar (de), desistir (de) *Throughout the ages each succeeding generation has been able to start learning where the previous generation had left off.* -FI,4. ♦ *What time do you leave off work?* 2. deixar de lado, abandonar, deixar de usar, vestir, empregar *I'm always glad to leave off the long, itchy wool underwear when winter is over.*

leave out 1. omitir, não incluir, deixar de fora *... ancient Egypt can hardly be left out of a history of Western art.* -CEO,27. 2. desconsiderar, rejeitar, não tomar conhecimento de *I felt left out when I wasn't invited to the picnic.*

leave up to deixar a responsabilidade, decisão etc. para *Don't worry about the details of your trip. Leave it up to me. I'll plan it for you.*

leave/let well enough alone deixar as coisas como estão, não tentar melhorar o que já é satisfatório *... there are times when it is best to leave well enough alone.* -T/92.

on leave de licença *... a young man who was on leave from Vietnam ...* -KR,13. ♦ *[He] ... had been on leave since January ...* -T/66.

take French leave sair à francesa, sair de fininho *She took French leave from her job for a few days.*

take (one's) leave despedir-se, dar adeus, partir, abandonar *He took leave of his*

family. ♦ *The discredited young man takes his leave ...* -T/81. ⇒ **leave-taking** despedida, adeus *At last the final leave-taking took place, the final meeting of relatives.* -BRS,118.
take leave of one's senses ficar maluco, perder o bom senso, o juízo *Have you both taken leave of your senses?* -HJC,461.
LEFT-HANDED → **left-handed COMPLIMENT**
LEFT-WING//RIGHT-WING de ala esquerda, socialista//de ala direita, conservador *Nick had been involved with left-wing activists in the mid-1950s.* ♦ *[He is a] ... well-known supporter of right-wing causes ...* -T/85.
LEG **first/second/third/final etc. leg** primeira/segunda/terceira/final etc. etapa *On the first leg of its transcontinental trip to Toronto ... [the express train] crosses spectacular mountain ranges ...* -T/87. ♦ *... I was on the final leg of a two-week's walking tour ...* -BRT,1.
leg up [col] ajuda, auxílio, mão *He gave me a leg up when I was younger and I'll never forget it.*
not have a leg to stand on [col] não ter qualquer defesa, justificativa etc., estar em má situação *Weir won't have a leg to stand on when all the incriminating evidence against him has been gathered.*
on one's last legs [col] a ponto de cair, quase no fim, nas últimas *That business was on its last legs when it merged with a national chainstore group.*
pull someone's leg [col] caçoar de alguém, fazer alguém de bobo *Somebody's been pulling your leg, my friend.* -BW,68.
shake a leg [gír] apressar-se *You'd better shake a leg if you want to catch that train.*
stretch one's legs andar, caminhar, esticar as pernas *After the long bus ride I found it wonderful to stretch my legs.*
take to one's legs dar no pé, fugir *He took to his legs when he saw the policeman coming in his direction.*

LEGWORK [col] o ato de andar, viajar, locomover-se, ir à procura de pessoas, informações etc., como parte essencial da rotina de repórter, policial etc. *A competent reporter often gets a good story after much legwork.*
LEND **lend oneself/itself to** prestar-se a, acomodar-se a, colaborar para, ser adaptável para *I'm sure he'd never lend himself to such an unworthy cause.* ♦ *The whole plan lends itself to too many unforeseen complications.*
LENGTH **at full length** de comprido, estirado (o corpo) *He lay down at full length, and closed his eyes.* -CRS,26. ⇒ **full-length** 1. de corpo inteiro, que retrata ou mostra o corpo inteiro *a full-length portrait* ♦ *a full-length mirror* 2. de duração ou extensão convencional (livro, artigo etc.), de longa metragem (filme) ... *a full-length biography.* -T/87. ♦ *Snow White and the Seven Dwarfs was Walt Disney's first full-length cartoon.*
at length 1. minuciosamente, em detalhes, extensamente ... *I have discussed this [the Chinese philosophy of nature] at length in my previous book,* The Way of Zen ... -WA,xi. 2. finalmente, afinal *After a seemingly unending journey, they arrived at length at a mountain village.*
at some length com certa minuciosidade, com alguns pormenores *He described at some length the inhabitants [of Britain], their resources, and methods of mining.* -BCMT,28.
go to any/great lengths fazer qualquer esforço, não obedecer a limites, ir a quaisquer/grandes extremos, servir-se de quaisquer meios ... *I am perfectly willing to go to any lengths to explain [what I mean] ...* -KRI,600.
the length and breadth of por toda a extensão de, toda a parte de *The environmental ravages of modernization [in China] scar the length and breadth of the land.* -T/91.

LET **let alone** 1. → **LEAVE alone** 2. muito menos, quanto mais ... *a reality that could not be named, let alone explained.* -T/73.
let be = **LET alone** 1 *Let your sister be. She's too small for you to hit.*
let down 1. baixar, arriar; encompridar, descer (roupa, bainha) ... *the West cannot afford to let down its guard.* -T/87. ♦ *Rachel has let down her blue skirt.* 2. aquietar-se, livrar-se da tensão, descontrair-se *I let down after work ...* -T/73. 3. decepcionar, desapontar, abandonar *You can trust Homer. He won't let you down.* ⇒ **letdown** decepção, desapontamento *The speech was a letdown to some reform-minded Soviets ...* -T/87.
let down easy dizer não (a alguém), negar-lhe algo ou dar-lhe más notícias com diplomacia, com amabilidade *Everett is so kind that he would let even his worst enemy down easy.*
let drop 1. revelar, deixar escapar (algo, como por acidente, mas na verdade feito de propósito) *Kelland casually let drop the news that he would run for office if someone asked him.* 2. deixar de lado, esquecer, não falar mais em *Let's drop the subject.*
let fall 1. deixar cair *Let the blame fall where it should.* 2. = **LET drop** 1 *In his speech he let fall a hint that he would run for President.*
let fly 1. atacar (com arma, objeto etc.), disparar, lançar *... with bows and guns [the Indians] let fly at the running men.* -MF,21. 2. atacar (verbalmente), verberar, desfechar insultos, vociferar *When Corey had finished his speech, the irate audience let fly at him with all sorts of angry questions.*
let go 1. soltar, largar, deixar de segurar; libertar, liberar, deixar ir ou sair *Don't let go of the rope or the cow will run away.* ♦ *When their demands had been met, the terrorists let the hostages go.* ♦ *[The prisoners] ... will be let go.* -T/81. 2. abandonar, renunciar a, alhear-se, tornar-se indiferente, apático *For four weeks [after a serious operation] he fought tenaciously to live ... Then at last he let go, drifted into a coma.* -T/64. 3. demitir, despedir *... 1,200 of [the firm's] ... 5,850 employees were let go.* -T/85. 4. relevar, deixar passar, dar por encerrado, esquecer *She talked back to me but I let it go.* 5. = **LET fly** 1 e 2 *Joe picked up a stick and let go at the man who had tried to kill him.* ♦ *Quinn let go at his opponent with angry words.* 6. [ou] **let oneself go** abandonar-se aos seus impulsos ou entusiasmo, descontrair-se, desinibir-se; abandonar restrições ou limites; cair na folia *In the Polynesian paradise of Tahiti ... [the] tourist really let go.* -T/66. ♦ *... a reporter detected a desire in a man to let go with his true feelings and tell what he had seen and suffered ...* -HE,9. ♦ *Lester finds it difficult to let himself go and relax at a party unless he has had a few drinks.*
let (someone) have it [gir] surrar, bater em, atacar, agredir (com arma, objeto etc.); castigar, repreender *Get out of my way or I'll let you have it.* ♦ *Chuck whipped out a gun and let the other guy have it.*
let in deixar entrar, permitir a entrada de *Jill locked her husband out of the house and wouldn't let him in.* ♦ *[They] ... seem to be opening a window, letting in the fresh air ...* -BCS,30.
let (someone) in for [col] colocar em situação difícil, causar algo (geralmente desagradável) a *You're letting yourself in for a lot of trouble.*
let (someone) in on permitir participar de, compartilhar de (segredo, idéia, plano etc.) *If you'll buy me a drink, I'll let you in on the secret.* -SLS,23.
let it all hang out [gir] contar toda a verdade, não esconder nada, pôr tudo para fora, desinibir-se *Fred and Bill let it all hang out and enjoyed themselves.*
let it/things go at that = **LET go** 4 *I resented Clara's rude remark but I was in*

no mood to argue so I let it go at that. ♦ *I should have ... had a bang-up affair with him and let things go at that.* -GE,116.

let know informar, fazer saber *Let me know if you need any help.*

let loose 1. soltar, libertar *... we fear letting loose of our competitive relationships with each other.* -KS,121. 2. [col] = **LET go** 6 *It was a wild party and we were having a good time. It made us feel like kids letting loose.* 3. = **LET fly** 1 e 2 *[Terrorists] ... let loose with 150 rounds at close range.* -T/88. ♦ *At first Sean held his tongue, but finally, he decided to let loose.*

let off 1. fazer explodir, detonar, disparar *Only authorized persons are allowed to let off fireworks.* 2. perdoar, não castigar, isentar de pena, prisão, multa etc., deixar livre *Cassidy was let off for lack of conclusive evidence.* 3. dispensar (de trabalho, tarefa, obrigação etc.) *The children were let off in the afternoon to see the parade.*

let on [col] 1. revelar, contar, dar a conhecer, quebrar um sigilo *... Manhattan papers let on that the new Mrs. Hartford was a coal miner's daughter ...* -T/62. 2. fingir, fazer de conta, simular *Mrs. Wingate likes to let on that she's a sick woman.* 3. admitir, reconhecer *She never let on that she had had an affair with Mr. Hart.*

let oneself go → **LET go** 6

let out 1. libertar, liberar, soltar, deixar sair *The prisoners were let out at dawn.* 2. emitir, soltar (grito etc.) *He let out a scream of pain.* 3. revelar (segredo), divulgar, contar *We are not sure they are letting out all they know.* -T/81. 4. alargar (roupa), afrouxar, soltar *Martha has gained so much weight lately that she's had to let out her dresses.* 5. outorgar *The big company lets out many contracts to smaller companies.* 6. terminar, findar, encerrar a atividade, a sessão etc. *School lets out at five o'clock.* ♦ *The meeting let out two hours ago.* 7. [col] demitir *Ferguson was let out of his job without any notice.*

let pass deixar passar, fechar os olhos a, transigir *Mrs. Van Hopper would never let a remark pass without making some caustic comment.*

let ride [col] aceitar (situação etc.), não tomar nenhuma atitude no momento, deixar o barco correr *Don't worry about the trouble Martin is causing us now. We'll let it ride for a while and see what happens.*

let slide negligenciar cumprimento (de tarefa, função etc.), descuidar-se de, deixar correr à revelia *Don't let the quality of your work slide until it loses its value.*

let slip 1. deixar escapar (oportunidade etc.) *It was a golden opportunity and he let it slip.* 2. divulgar (segredo etc.) involuntariamente *Without realizing it, Sturges had let slip the information that the enemy intelligence had been searching for.*

let someone have it [gír] 1. censurar, repreender *Lucy's mother let her have it when Lucy came home late again.* 2. agredir, surrar, atacar (com arma, objeto etc.) *Margot was afraid of her husband when he threatened to let her have it.*

let up [col] 1. diminuir, abrandar, amainar, esmorecer; moderar (a atividade, o trabalho etc.) *When is this rain going to let up?* 2. parar, cessar *The two women went on talking for hours and didn't let up a second.* ⇒ **letup** atenuação, declínio, descanso, afrouxamento, pausa, diminuição; cessação *For eight months without letup he passed economic and military information of the highest importance to the Allies ...* -CL,199.

let up on ser menos severo com, tratar com mais tolerância *Why don't you let up on him? He's not a bad boy.*

let well enough alone → **LEAVE well enough alone**

LETTER the letter of the law a letra da lei, o sentido textual da lei *I'll hold to the letter of the law ...* -YF,9.

open letter carta aberta, declaração pública *The Pope sent an open letter to all the Catholics in Latin American countries.*

to the letter ao pé da letra, aos termos exatos, com precisão ... *follow out our instructions to the letter* ... -LMC,24.
♦ *Mrs. Brooks held the tenants of her apartment to the letter of the contract when they tried to leave without paying for damages.*

LETTER-PERFECT 1. correto nos mínimos detalhes, preciso, perfeito *Hayes is always letter-perfect in any action he undertakes.* 2. com toda a exatidão, palavra por palavra, decorado com perfeição (papel, texto, lição etc.) *Mason knows his country's laws and constitution letter-perfect.*

LEVEL level off nivelar-se, estabilizar-se, aplainar-se *At the bottom of the hill ... the ground abruptly leveled off onto a gravel path* ... -T/81. ♦ *... population growth will not level off significantly in the near future.* -T/72.
level with [gir] ser franco com, falar sinceramente com *You can level with me, I'm your friend.*
on the level [gir] sério, sincero, honesto *Are you on the level?* ♦ *... she had been on the level all along.* -HJ,60.

LEVELHEADED; LEVEL-HEADED sensato, equilibrado *... he is considered [by his political peers] pragmatic and level-headed.* -T/92. ♦ *... level-headed analysis ...* -T/92.

LIBERTY take liberties 1. usar sem cerimônia, abusivamente *You shouldn't try to take liberties with things that don't belong to you.* 2. proceder com liberdade indevida, portar-se com desrespeito *She's the kind of girl all men try to take liberties with.* 3. fazer alterações num texto, distorcer (fatos, dados etc.) *The translator took undue liberties with the Old English text and produced an unusual version of Beowulf.*

LICK a lick and a promise [col] trabalho malfeito, algo feito às pressas, que deixa a desejar *Our maid always gives the bathroom a lick and a promise.*

LICKETY-SPLIT [gir] velozmente *... all of a sudden here this young woman came down the hill, lickety-split.* -GES,133.

LID blow one's lid → **blow one's TOP**
blow the lid off [gir] revelar, divulgar, desmascarar (escândalo, fraude, negociata etc.) *Watergate blew the lid off the President's mismanagement and illegal deeds.*
keep a/the lid on [gir] ocultar, suprimir, não deixar escapar (segredo, informação etc.), não deixar fugir ao controle *They were able to keep the lid on the secret project for more than a year.*
put a/the lid on reprimir, conter, coibir, pôr fim a *... to put a lid on prices.* -T/78.

LIE give the lie to desmentir *His actions give the lie to his words.*
lie around 1. estar abandonado, não utilizado *Don't leave your toys lying around the kitchen floor.* 2. estar inativo, à toa, ficar matando o tempo *We were lying around waiting for something to happen.*
lie down deitar-se, reclinar-se *You'll feel better if you lie down for a while.*
lie low 1. esconder-se, ocultar-se *... there were ten of us [soldiers], lying low and dodging the enemy.* -T/72. 2. permanecer em inatividade, ficar na moita, aguardar os acontecimentos *Lie low until people forget about the trouble you have caused.*
white lie mentira inocente, inofensiva *You often have to tell a white lie when a young girl asks you if you think she is beautiful.*

LIEF would/had as lief preferiria *... I'd just as lief stay here and hold your hand ...* -WH,395.

LIFE bear/have/lead a charmed life ser imune ao mal, à má sorte etc., como se protegido por magia *Like Macbeth, he seems to bear a charmed life.* ♦ *... I'd begun to think that your brother had a charmed life, that no bullet could touch him.* -HJ,149.
(as) big/large as life em pessoa, em tamanho natural, como alguém é na realidade *When I opened the door, there he was – big as life.*

bigger than life → **larger than LIFE**

breathe new life into dar vida nova a *... Australian film makers ... are breathing new life into a once nearly moribund movie industry.* -T/78.

bring to life animar, dar vida, entusiasmo *Sue certainly knows how to bring a party to life.*

come to life 1. recobrar os sentidos *Blake lay unconscious for several minutes, then suddenly he came to life.* 2. animar-se, mostrar-se ativo, alerta, despertar da inatividade; parecer adquirir vida, aparentar ser real, vivo *[As Shakespeare's characters] ... move about [onstage] and start talking ... they come so completely to life that they seem to be real people ...* -CMSS,9.

for dear life para salvar a própria vida, com todas as forças, com ímpeto *Terry ran for dear life when the big bull charged at him.*

for life para o resto da vida, por toda a vida *As a result [of being shot] ... he is paralyzed for life from the neck down.* -T/78.

for the life of [col] [neg] como se disso dependesse a própria vida e, por mais que alguém tente, ser humanamente impossível para ... *whether her name was Julia or Judith he could not for the life of him have said.* -FV,18.

larger/bigger than life; larger-than-life; bigger-than-life maior ou mais importante, imponente etc. do que é na realidade; exagerado, hiperbólico, que vai além da realidade; fora do comum, épico, epopéico *[General Douglas MacArthur] ... was a realist who by the strength of his personality succeeded in making himself larger than life.* -T/64. ♦ *In U.S. folklore, nothing has been more romanticized than guns and the larger-than-life men who wielded them.* -T/68. ♦ *[Gregory Peck has] ... a bigger-than-life quality well suited to many of the heroic roles he's assumed.* -SS,315.

lay down one's life sacrificar-se, dar a própria vida *She laid down her life for a noble cause.*

lead a life viver, passar ou levar (vida) *Henry David Thoreau said that "the mass of men lead lives of quiet desperation".* ♦ *He led a quiet life in the country.*

the life of Riley [col] vida de abundância, conforto e prazer; boa vida *Since his uncle died and left him some money, he has been leading the life of Riley.*

life preserver bóia ou colete salva-vidas *The ancient life preservers sank when they were thrown to the people in the water.*

not on your life [col] de modo algum, absolutamente não *When I asked him if he would pass up the chance of visiting the Colorado Rockies he said, "Not on your life!"*

run for one's life correr para salvar-se, para fugir do perigo *There are too many [enemies] to fight! Run for your life!* -SLT,177.

still life natureza-morta *John paints still lifes. He's a still-life painter.*

take one's (own) life suicidar-se *... he was too optimistic and self-assured to take his own life.* -T/74.

take one's life in/into one's hands colocar-se em perigo de vida, arriscar-se *He took his life in his hands when he tried to capture the criminal single-handed.*

you (can) bet your life = **you BET** *You bet your life I'm going to hold you to your promise.*

LIFELIKE real, natural, que lembra ou imita fielmente a vida real *She painted a lifelike portrait of the famous scientist.*

LIFELONG que dura a vida inteira, vitalício *Movies and books have been Carlos' two lifelong passions.*

LIFT give a lift 1. dar carona *I picked him up right outside Boston and gave him a lift all the way to here.* -MG,442. 2. produzir sensação de bem-estar *A small drink right after I leave work gives me a lift.*

lift off levantar vôo (avião), ascender (foguete) ... *a plane ... finally lifts off from a Tehran runway ...* -T/81. ♦ *The camouflaged ... air transport ... lifted off late Sunday morning with four crewmen aboard ...* -T/86. ♦ *[The space shuttle]... Columbia lifts off with its first two astronauts ...* -T/81. ⇒ **liftoff** decolagem vertical (de foguete, míssil, helicóptero etc.) *The space shuttle* Challenger *exploded in midair after lift-off ...* -T/87.

LIGHT according to one's lights segundo seus princípios, crenças, opiniões, maneiras de ver as coisas etc. *I'm out to serve the community according to my lights and my ability.* -PRT,16.

bring to light tornar público, revelar, dar a conhecer ... *blunders and corruptions similar to those discovered in Laos were being brought to light in other countries.* -LW,19.

cast/shed/throw light on/upon elucidar, esclarecer ... *studies of Jewish culture in 1st century Palestine shed fresh light on the historical Jesus.* -T/88.

come to light aparecer, revelar-se, tornar-se público, vir à luz *No new evidence has come to light to suggest that he knew anything about the plan to overthrow the dictator.*

green light [col] permissão, autorização, luz verde ... *[President] Reagan had indeed given the plans a green light.* -T/87.

hide one's light under a bushel esconder suas habilidades, qualidades etc. por modéstia *Millican is not the kind of man who hides his light under a bushel.*

in a good/favorable//bad/unfavorable light de maneira favorável//desfavorável *[Those remarks] ... showed him in a bad light ...* -T/81.

in (the) light of considerando, tendo em vista *In light of the loss of prestige and the Watergate scandal, it is unbelievable that Nixon had so many loyal adherents.*

light into → **LAY into**

light up acender(-se), iluminar(-se) *Norma lit up a cigarette.* ♦ *Suddenly his face lit up with mirth.* -NEW,11.

one's own lights idéias, princípios, opiniões, padrões etc. de alguém *[He was] ... a renegade who followed his own lights.* -T/87.

out like a light [col] adormecido; desacordado, inconsciente *The doctor gave Joan some sleeping pills and she went out like a light.*

run a red light avançar sinal (semáforo) vermelho *[He] ... ran a red light in Washington and plowed into another car ...* -T/78.

see the light compreender, perceber *Time and again we warned him against keeping company with the wrong sort of people. Well, after the unfortunate occurrence the other night, we suspect he has begun to see the light.*

shed light on → **cast LIGHT on**
throw light on → **cast LIGHT on**

LIGHT-FINGERED que tem tendência para o furto, gatuno *Don't leave any money on your desk. There are too many light-fingered people who will pick it up.*

LIGHTHEARTED despreocupado, alegre, jovial, animado *Kathleen felt lighthearted that night.*

LIKE and the like e coisas assim, e assim por diante, e coisas desse tipo *[She] ... made a living collecting and selling old newspapers, rags and the like.* -WC,108.

if you like se quiser, se preferir, se for de seu agrado *[Edna Ferber's books] ... are authentic studies of the American scene at certain high dramatic moments ... They are also fantasies, if you like, or rhapsodies ...* -SV,55.

it's/that's (just) like him/her etc. é bem de, (isso) é típico de, é da natureza de *It is just like Elaine to be tolerant.* ♦ *That isn't like him at all.*

like anything [col] vigorosamente, extremamente *The boy ran like anything when the angry bull got loose.*

like best gostar mais, preferir (dentre todos/tudo) *Which Hemingway short story do you like best?*
like better gostar mais (de que outro) *I was convinced Mother had finally forsaken me. She liked my brother and sister much better.* -FLF,32.
like crazy/mad [col] furiosamente, impetuosamente, vigorosamente *Willie drives like mad when he goes to work in the morning.*
like it or lump it → **LUMP it**
that's more like it [col] assim é melhor, mais razoável, mais aceitável etc. *That's more like it. Now we're beginning to understand each other.*
the likes of [col] pessoas ou coisas semelhantes a; gente como, alguém como, coisas como *[She] ... worked with the likes of Louis Armstrong, Andy Kirk, Benny Goodman, Duke Ellington and Dizzy Gillespie ...* -T/81.
what is (somebody/something) like? como é alguém/algo? qual é sua opinião sobre? *Have you met Miss Jones? What's she like?*
what (something) is like como algo é na realidade *... by 1914 few could recall what war was like.* -SWLM,17.
LIKELY (as) likely as not provavelmente *... while an English householder is away on vacation, likely as not the bobbies [i. e., policemen] will keep an eye on his front door.* -T/63.
most likely muito provavelmente *I'll just go along now ... I'll be back for supper, most likely.* -SBW,14.
LIKE-MINDED da mesma opinião, gostos, interesses etc. *... a group of like-minded couples ...* -T/68.
LIKING take a liking to afeiçoar-se a, começar a gostar de *The children took an instant liking to the dog that they had found on the road.*
to one's liking do agrado de, ao gosto de *... this role of man of action was little to his liking ...* -YF,37.

LILY gild the lily tentar melhorar, tornar mais bonito etc. aquilo que já é perfeito *Some beautiful women use makeup when their natural beauty is enough and we say that they are gilding the lily.*
LIMB out on a limb [col] em situação difícil, em apuros *I went out on a limb for you this morning. I wont [sic] do it again.* -JJF,256. ♦ *Lil put herself out on a limb when she offered to help me.*
LIMELIGHT the limelight o centro das atenções *... in a brief blue gown ... [she] stole the limelight.* -T/63. ♦ *... Wright was eager for his moment in the limelight ...* -T/87.
LIMIT the limit [col] pessoa ou coisa intolerável ou notável; o máximo, o cúmulo *Carl is the limit. First he fell in the open sewer and then broke a window in the police car that came to get him out of the sewer.*
LINE all along the line de todas as maneiras; todo o tempo, a todas as horas; em toda parte *Jones has given me his full support all along the line. That's why I trust him.*
along those/similar/the same//different lines dessa//de outra maneira *Maybe a few more shocks like that will start him thinking along different lines.* -CN,81.
the bottom line [col] o fator decisivo, o ponto crucial, o fato essencial, a consideração mais importante, o resultado final, o desfecho *... the bottom line on both books is their extraordinary ability to engage the nation in a renewed dialogue on education ...* -T/87.
bring into line [col] exigir obediência, conformidade, fazer entrar na linha *... the old skeptical politicians [were] brought into line ...* -T/60.
down the line totalmente, inteiramente, completamente *... they have voted down the line for the New Frontier's [President John Kennedy's principles of government] programs.* -T/61. ⇒ **down-the-line** com-

pleto, total ... *he is a down-the-line supporter of current Israeli policies.* -T/80.
draw a/the line recusar-se a aceitar, a ir além de (determinado limite de tolerância) *[He] ... asks a group of young men where they draw the line at violence ...* -T/78. ♦ *Burke is a liberal but he draws the line at abortion.*
drop a line escrever bilhete ou carta *Don't forget to drop us a line when you get there.*
fall into line 1. submeter-se, pôr-se à mercê de, entrar na linha *Lee fell into line after he was told that the gangsters would harm his family.* 2. entrar em forma, alinhar-se *The regiments fell into line ...* -CB,63.
get a line on [col] informar-se a respeito de *See if you can get a line on his activities during the last three months.*
get into line fazer entrar em acordo; entrar em acordo, cooperar *The political leader had difficulty getting some of the liberals in the party into line.*
get/step out of line sair da linha, descontrolar-se, insubordinar-se *In the background ... there lurked the terror of the Gestapo and the fear of the concentration camp for those who got out of line ...* -SWLR,320. ♦ *... prices were getting out of line ...* -T/87.
hard line posição inflexível (relativa a uma política, atitude, dogma, crença, plano etc.), linha dura *Since 1980 [the Republican Platform Committee] ... has taken a hard line against abortion.* -T/92. ⇒ **hard-line** que prega uma posição inflexível; intransigente, radical *... a hard-line conservative ...* -T/69. ♦ *... hard-line Marxists ...* -T/87.
hold the line 1. manter as coisas como estão, manter uma posição firmemente, agüentar as pontas *Manufacturers will have to hold the line on prices.* -T/64. 2. não desligar o telefone, aguardar na linha *Please hold the line. Mr. Kendrick will speak to you in a minute.*

hot line linha telefônica de comunicação direta para ser usada em emergências, comunicações especiais etc. *... a New Jersey-based hot line that provides treatment [for drug addicts] ...* -T/86.
in line 1. em equilíbrio, em harmonia, sob controle *... a crusade to hold prices in line ...* -T/87. 2. → **stand in LINE**
in line for prestes a (ser atendido, chamado, obter algo etc.), no aguardo de *I was in line for [the vice presidency], but instead [another man got it] ...* -BS,35.
in (the) line of duty no cumprimento do dever *... an FBI agent had been killed in the line of duty.* -WD,102.
in line with em concordância com *... with computers, people can design their lives far more in line with their own wishes.* -T/78.
keep in line andar na linha, portar-se corretamente; manter na linha *If you keep in line you will have no trouble in the Army.* ♦ *If they're not kept in line there will be chaos in the party.*
lay/put on the line [col] 1. pagar, oferecer dinheiro *They had to lay $50,000 on the line for a corrupt politician in order to get the building contract.* 2. falar com franqueza, sem rebuços *You can believe McKibben. He always lays it on the line.* ♦ *He laid it on the line very clearly that he wouldn't tolerate such behavior.* 3. pôr em perigo, em risco (reputação, segurança etc.) *... he laid his political future on the line.* -T/63. ♦ *[He] ... put his political future on the line ...* -T/87.
line up 1. alinhar *... he lined up the prisoners.* -DK,192. 2. alinhar-se, enfileirar-se *The people were lining up outside the building.* 3. arranjar, conseguir, providenciar, organizar *[They] ... have lined up distributors [for their product] in 25 states ...* -T/86. ♦ *I can't line up a job for you. Go to the office in St. Louis.* -BRSR,24. ⇒
lineup 1. disposição em fileira de suspeitos ou criminosos para identificação *He*

was identified in the police lineup as the criminal by one of the victims. 2. time de futebol ou beisebol; escalação da equipe *His name is not in the lineup for today's game.*
on the dotted line na linha pontilhada *Just as soon as the Governor signs this proclamation on the dotted line, the new project will be begun.*
on the line [col] 1. em risco, em perigo *It's my life that's on the line, not yours!* -CG,142. 2. à vista (dinheiro, pagamento) *You must pay cash on the line.*
out of line 1. descabido, destoante, desproporcionado, incoerente, impróprio, inaceitável *Gary's behavior at the party was out of line.* 2. → **get out of LINE**
out of line with em desacordo com, inconsistente com *... the legal system ... is hopelessly out of line with reality.* -DDT,466.
read between the lines ler nas entrelinhas *Because her mother censored her letters, Cynthia wrote carefully in hopes that her boyfriend would read between the lines.*
somewhere along the line em determinada etapa do caminho, a certa altura dos acontecimentos *Somewhere along the line Carroll began to lose all interest in his job.*
stand in line ficar em fila, entrar na fila *He and Mrs. Hitchcock stood in line for a half-hour ...* -OF,11.
step out of line → **get out of LINE**
toe the line/mark [gir] seguir o regulamento à risca, obedecer sem replicar, comportar-se *Toe the line exactly as I say and no harm will come to you.*
walk the line → **walk the CHALK**
LINEN **wash one's dirty linen in public** lavar roupa suja em público *Edith has the bad taste to wash her dirty linen in public and embarrasses her listeners.*
LINGER **linger on** perdurar, persistir, prolongar-se, sobreviver *... the memories of the glories of the past linger on.* -SLE,144.

LINING **silver lining** perspectiva promissora, esperança consoladora, o lado bom de uma situação adversa *Always remember that each dark cloud or unfortunate incident has a silver lining.*
LION **beard the lion in his den** enfrentar alguém importante, poderoso etc. nos domínios dele *His wife wanted him to go to his boss and ask for a raise but he was afraid to beard the lion in his den.*
the lion's share a parte do leão, o maior quinhão *[The criminals] ... expanded cocaine production and grabbed the lion's share of the market.* -T/91.
LIP **hang on the lips of** = **hang on someone's WORDS** *They hung on the lips of the speaker as if he had been sent by heaven.*
keep a stiff upper lip [col] manter atitude de firmeza e determinação em face da adversidade, do perigo; não esmorecer, não perder a coragem *Even though the people trapped in the old mine were frightened, they kept a stiff upper lip until help came.*
lip service devoção verbal, louvores fingidos, palavras vazias [geralmente na expressão **pay/give lip service**] *[They] ... pay lip service to the economic readjustment, but refuse to carry it out in practice.* -T/81. ♦ *Many Christians give lip service only to their religion.*
smack one's lips estalar os lábios, ter ávida antecipação de um prazer *I smack my lips every time I think of a Virginia baked ham.*
LIQUOR **hard liquor** bebida com alto teor alcoólico, bebida forte *Beer, wine and hard liquor do not seem to differ in their impact on the fetus.* -T/89.
LISTEN **listen for** pôr-se à escuta, ficar atento para ouvir (determinado som) *He counted the seconds ticking off and listened for another sound, a sound of small-arms fire.* -SLS,273.
listen in escutar às escondidas, ouvir conversa alheia *On the old-fashioned party*

line telephone, all the neighbors could listen in on your conversation.
listen to ouvir, escutar, prestar atenção *I listened attentively to Ballard's arguments.*
LITTLE have little to do with → **HAVE anything to do with**
little by little aos poucos, pouco a pouco *Little by little the new coach restored the team's confidence.*
little does one imagine/know/realize/suspect/think etc. dificilmente se imagina/espera etc., quase não se pensa, mal se dá atenção etc. *Little did [he] ... realize that fairy tales, if examined carefully, contain the deepest truths about men.* -FLS,109. ♦ *Little did I know what I was getting into when I got involved with you.* -WCN,242. ♦ *When I met her, little did I imagine what I had let myself in for.*
little/young ones as crianças, os filhos pequenos *When my wife and I go on a trip we take the older children but the little ones stay with my mother.*
what little o pouco que *The government lost what little credibility it had ten years ago ...* -T/80.
LIVE live and let live ser tolerante, liberal, aceitar o modo de viver dos outros *[He] ... believed people should live and let live.* -EA,37.
live down redimir-se de erro, culpa, crime, escândalo etc. adotando vida nova e conduta correta *He found it difficult to live down the shame that his imprisonment had brought him.*
live fast levar vida desvairada, frenética, dissoluta, hedonista, entregar-se ao desregramento *Elvis Aron Presley always lived fast, and last week, at the age of 42, that was the way he died.* -T/77.
live high viver à tripa forra, na fartura *He lived high, and he lasted.* -T/87.
live in morar no local de trabalho, no emprego (empregada/o doméstica/o); morar na casa de outra pessoa *She works as a maid in a Beverly Hills mansion and lives in.* ⇒ **live-in** a. que vive no local de trabalho *... she worked for four years as a live-in maid ...* -T/72. ♦ *... a live-in housekeeper ...* -T/72. b. que vive com alguém (sem ser casado); relativo à coabitação *[He] ... has no plans to wed his live-in love ...* -T/87.
live it up [gír] viver à larga, entregar-se à boa vida *When he gets rich, he intends to live it up in Europe.*
live off viver de *[He] ... spent several years ... living off odd jobs ...* -T/73. ♦ *Sam lived off the charity of friends and relatives.* ♦ *Modern Americans visualize the frontiersman as a man who lived off the land.* -RR,7.
live on 1. alimentar-se de *Rachel lives on fruit and vegetables.* 2. viver de, custear sua vida (com salário, renda, caridade etc.) *Have you ever tried to live well on a small salary?* 3. continuar a existir *She died many years ago but her name lives on.*
live out sobreviver a, durar até o fim de, viver mais que *I don't think he will live out the night without a miracle.* 2. viver, passar (a vida) *... Tolstoy slipped out of the house with his physician, intending to live out his days in a monastery.* -T/88. 3. traduzir em ação, em experiência, vivenciar, viver (algo) na prática *He prefers to live out an American ideal, working with his family, building his own enterprise.* -T/78. 4. dormir fora do emprego (empregada/o doméstica/o) *We need a general cook, but she must live out.*
live through experimentar, atravessar; passar por (dificuldades, perigo etc.), sobreviver, resistir *[When reading fiction] ... the reader imaginatively lives through the presented experiences as though they were his own.* -CCC,97. ♦ *She lived through a night of terror when three thugs broke into her house.*
live up to mostrar-se à altura de, viver ou agir de acordo com (norma, ideal etc.)

... *any acceptable Republican candidate must live up to certain standards.* -T/63.

LIVED-IN que indica ser habitado, ocupado, utilizado (aposento, casa etc.) *He hardly ever used the living room or the study ... Only his bedroom had a "lived-in" look.* -RCT,48.

LIVING earn/make a/one's living ganhar a vida, o sustento *[He] ... was unable to earn a living ...* -T/76. ♦ *... an eccentric genius who made his living by tutoring the sons and daughters of English noblemen in natural philosophy ...* -GJ,36.

for a living para ganhar a vida, o sustento *What do you do for a living?* -DJ,85.

living standard → **STANDARD of living**

LOAD get a load of [gír] dar uma olhada em, atentar para; escutar, ouvir *Get a load of the fancy clothes our friend is wearing today.* ♦ *Get a load of this: The President has just resigned!*

get a/the load off one's chest → **get something off one's CHEST**

take a load off one's feet [gír] sentar-se, descansar *Get into the car and take a load off your feet.*

LOAN loan shark [col] agiota *He was shot in the head in his Hollywood Hills home ... for cheating Mafia loan sharks.* -T/77.

LOATH loath to avesso a, pouco inclinado a *... German workers are loath to accept any reduction in their comfortable standard of living.* -T/92.

LOCATION on location em local externo, onde se filmam as cenas externas de um filme *Many scenes of John Ford's movie* Stagecoach *were shot on location in Monument Valley, Arizona.*

LOCK lock away 1. fechar a sete chaves, pôr em lugar seguro *You had better lock away those jewels.* 2. prender, aprisionar, pôr na cadeia *When he was 21 he was locked away for several years...* -MJV, 6

lock in trancar dentro, prender *We kept them locked in for two days ...* -HM,116.

lock out fechar a porta a, deixar do lado de fora, deixar na rua; não permitir o acesso de operários a seu local de trabalho *The company locked out the workers and refused to negotiate with the labor union.* ⇒ **lockout** greve de patrões *A lockout is much less usual than a strike.*

lock, stock, and barrel [col] completamente, inteiramente, com tudo incluído *Smith was about to retire, so he sold his business lock, stock, and barrel for almost nothing.*

lock up 1. fechar à chave, trancar *Lock up the house when you leave.* 2. prender, encarcerar *... the FBI has locked up hundreds of top Mafia figures across the country.* -T/87. ⇒ **lockup** prisão, cadeia *He just got out of lockup.*

pick a lock abrir cadeado ou fechadura com gazua *The children used to pick the lock and enter the schoolyard to play basketball.*

under lock and key fechado a sete chaves, bem seguro *... into the flames went his private journal of 40 years, which he had kept under lock and key.* -T/67.

LOG sleep like a log → **sleep like a TOP**

LOGGERHEAD at loggerheads em desacordo, em disputa, em desavença *... the conflict in Yemen has kept Egypt and Saudi Arabia at loggerheads ...* -T/66.

LONG as/so long as 1. contanto que, desde que *We will take no invasive action so long as the hostages are not armed.* -T/87. 2. considerando que, já que *As long as you're up, get me a drink, please.* 3. durante, pelo tempo que *... police dogs have located remains that have been buried for as long as six years.* -T/86.

before long logo, em breve *Ginny will be here before long.*

be long demorar, tardar *Wait for me here. I won't be long.*

for long por muito tempo *... the radicals are unlikely to renounce violence for long ...* -T/87.

how long quanto tempo *How long has this been going on?* ♦ *How long will I have to wait?*

long ago há muito tempo *I met her long ago.*
the long and (the) short of a essência, o resumo, a síntese, tudo o que há para ser dito, aquilo que importa *I'm going, that's the long and the short of it.* -WH,156.
long before bem antes de *She left the office long before the others.*
long for desejar muito, ansiar por *Ricky longed for the sight of his old home.*
long on pródigo em, rico em, generoso, repleto de, bem suprido de, farto *... the critics were seldom long on praise for [Alan] Ladd's acting abilities ...* -HMT,14.
long since (desde) há muito tempo *Americans had long since grown used to a Soviet adversary ...* -T/87.
no longer; not any longer não mais, já não *Jim is no longer working for that New York corporation.* ♦ *... dogmas that no longer make sense ...* -T/68.
not long ago há pouco tempo, não faz muito tempo *The bus left not long ago.*
so long [col] até logo *Well, so long. I'll see you tomorrow.*
take long demorar, levar tempo *What I have to say won't take long.* ♦ *"What took you so long?", my husband said in exasperation when I returned two hours later.*
LONG-DISTANCE → long DISTANCE
LONG-DRAWN(-OUT) desnecessariamente longo, prolongado, enfadonho *... a long-drawn-out war.* -T/64. ♦ *... a long-drawn-out legal engagement ...* -T/60.
LONG-FACED → long FACE
LONG-RANGE//SHORT-RANGE 1. de longo//curto alcance; próprio para longas//curtas distâncias *The Air Force has developed a new long-range missile.* ♦ *Long-range investments are better for the economy of a developing country.* 2. a longo//curto prazo *This is a short-range plan.*
LONG-STANDING → of long STANDING

LONGTIME antigo, que existe há muito tempo *... a longtime political opponent ...* -T/87.
LONG-WINDED prolixo, enfadonho *He likes to give young couples long-winded advice on marriage.*
LOOK as to look → as to BE
dirty look olhar de desaprovação, olhar feio *The woman gave me a dirty look when I got in front of her in the line.*
good looks aparência atraente, beleza *At an early age he became conscious of his good looks.* -LI,10. ⇒ **good-looking** de aparência atraente, bonito, bem-apessoado *Dan was ... thirty-two, stubby and robustly good-looking ...* -SLS,22.
have/take a look dar uma olhada, passar os olhos, olhar *... he was glad for the chance to have a look at her.* -LM,125. ♦ *... you'd better have the doctor take a look at you ...* -WR,56.
it looks as if/though parece que *It looks as if it is going to rain.* ♦ *It looks as though the worst will happen.*
it looks like = **it LOOKS as if** *It looks like it might rain.*
look after cuidar de, tomar conta de *I just hoped he'd have sense enough to look after his own interests ...* -GJH,51.
look ahead pensar no futuro, fazer planos para o futuro *As Dan came down the stairs at 7:40 ... he was trying to look ahead to the complicated problems of the day at the office ...* -HJD,7.
look alive/lively [col] agir rápido, mexer-se, apressar-se, estar alerta [geralmente imperativo] *Look lively, men. We've no time to lose.* -SLT,133.
look at 1. olhar para, fitar, ver *Donna was lovely to look at.* 2. considerar, examinar *Have you tried to look at that problem from a different point of view?*
look back recordar, olhar para o passado *Looking back over the years, Henry did not know how they had survived so long ...* -LM,8.

look before one jumps/leaps medir a extensão do salto, tomar cautela, jogar seguro *Always look before you leap is indeed good advice.*
look down on/upon olhar com desprezo, menosprezar ... *the classical Greek tradition looks down on all forms of manual work as servile* ... -AM,114.
look for 1. procurar, buscar *I'm looking for my glasses.* 2. contar com, esperar *I look for promptness in my workers.*
look forward to aguardar com prazer, ansiar por *He looks forward to a better future.*
look good parecer bom, favorável, adequado etc., causar boa impressão, ser promissor *When a political candidate speaks on TV he has to look good.*
look high and low procurar por toda parte *Polly looked high and low for a new job.*
look in on fazer curta visita a *Fay was a nurse who looked in on the old people in her neighborhood when they were sick.*
look into examinar cuidadosamente, investigar ... *a Senate subcommittee ... looked into his dealings.* -T/87.
look it aparentar *He was only twenty and he looked it.* -RQ,115.
look like parecer-se com, ter aparência de *Don't you think that he looks like Fred Astaire?* ♦ *What does God look like to you?* v. **it LOOKS like**
look lively → **LOOK alive**
look on 1. observar, olhar, assistir, ser mero espectador *When she began peeling off her clothes, I just looked on in utter amazement.* ⇒ **looker-on** [col] espectador, observador ... *A crowd of lookers-on soon gathered at the scene of the fire.* 2. [ou] **look upon** considerar, reputar, encarar *I look on you as one of my most staunch supporters.* ♦ *Philosophers such as Socrates and the Stoics look upon philosophy as primarily a way of life rather than a purely speculative pursuit.* -AM,165.

look on with ler ou acompanhar a leitura juntamente com outra pessoa em um mesmo livro *If you have no book, the teacher will permit you to look on with me.*
look out 1. estar alerta, tomar cuidado, prestar atenção *Look out when you cross the street.* ⇒ **lookout** a. vigia, sentinela, guarda *He was the lookout for a teenage gang.* b. vigilância, espreita, observação *We better keep a lookout tonight ...* -LMT,29. c. → **on the LOOKOUT** 2. cuidado! *Look out! He's got a gun!*
look out for 1. tomar cuidado com, ficar atento para, estar preparado para *Look out for any dogs that seem to behave strangely.* 2. cuidar de, preocupar-se com ... *from his early youth he had to look out for himself.* -HHO,40.
look out on/upon fazer face para, dar para *My house looks out on the whole valley and the winding river.*
look over examinar, inspecionar, olhar de alto a baixo *Julia looked over the list of books and selected the ones she wanted to read.* ♦ *The Mexican looked him over but offered no comment.* -LN,11.
look sharp [col] ficar atento, alerta ... *a man has to look sharp or they'll eat him out of house and home.* -OE,6.
look through examinar, ler, passar os olhos em, folhear *He likes to look through the morning newspapers.*
look to 1. contar com, confiar em, depender de, colocar suas esperanças em *Don't look to me for help. I told you not to take on this job.* 2. dar atenção a, cuidar de *Journalists usually look to the validity of the information they are offered, and to its verifiability ...* -T/80.
look up 1. [col] melhorar, progredir, prosperar ... *the family's prospects were looking up after some grim years.* -T/60. 2. procurar (referência), consultar (dicionário, lista etc.) ... *look up every new word in a reliable dictionary and note carefully its spelling, pronunciation, and*

exact meaning. -PC,29. 3. [col] procurar (pessoa), visitar (alguém) *Look me up when you come to Boston and I'll be glad to show you around.*
look up and down olhar (alguém) de alto a baixo, examinar com os olhos *The old man ... looked him up and down with a swift flick of sardonic eyes.* -LD,27.
look upon → **LOOK on** 2
look up to admirar, venerar, respeitar *He looked up to you so; believed in you so.* -UJ,229.
take a look → **have a LOOK**
LOOK-ALIKE [col] 1. sósia, cópia exata, imagem fiel *... he is a stunning [James] Cagney look-alike ...* -T/87. 2. parecidíssimo, quase idêntico *Army fingerprints showed that the dead soldier was not Guinn but a look-alike Kentuckian ...* -T/67.
LOOKER-ON → **LOOK on** 1
LOOKOUT on the lookout atento, alerta, vigilante, de olho *Eileen is always on the lookout for good bargains.*
LOOM loom large mostrar-se de forma grande, exagerada, importante, ameaçadora, inevitável etc. *... Pierre Teilhard de Chardin looms large over the intellectual history of 20th century Catholicism.* -T/77.
LOOP knock/throw for a loop [gir] 1. vencer completamente, derrotar decisivamente *Ali [Cassius Clay] usually knocked his opponents for a loop.* 2. causar forte impressão, surpreender grandemente *The news of her death threw me for a loop.*
LOOSE on the loose 1. à solta, em liberdade *The escaped prisoner is still on the loose.* 2. [col] divertindo-se sem restrições, entregue ao desregramento *Benny acted like a man on the loose.*
LORD lord it over agir de maneira despótica e arrogante, dominar, dar ordens *Gus lorded it over the other kids because he was bigger, stronger and very ruthless.*
LOSE lose out [col] fracassar, ser malsucedido, perder *[He] ... lost out in his bid to become the new U.S. Ambassador to NATO.* -T/86.
LOSS at a loss 1. perplexo, embaraçado, sem saber o que fazer ou dizer *... he seemed at a loss for words ...* -T/74. ♦ *[We] ... are still at a loss as to what we did wrong.* -T/80. 2. com prejuízo, com perda, abaixo do custo *The store was selling electrical appliances at a loss to kill all competition.*
LOST be lost on/upon não ter efeito sobre, não influenciar, não ser percebido por *Russell's logic was lost upon his questioner.*
LOT cast/draw lots tirar a sorte, decidir por meio de sorteio *... it seemed that the two candidates might have to settle their contest by drawing lots.* -T/78.
cast/throw (in) one's lot with compartilhar a sorte de, unir-se ao destino de *[President George] Bush decided it was better to cast his lot with his party's conservative base ...* -T/92.
have a lot going for → **HAVE something going for**
lot/lots [col] uma porção, uma grande quantidade, um bocado *Bailey found out that he had a lot of friends.* ♦ *The widow has lots of money.*
see a lot of → **see a great DEAL of**
take a lot out of → **TAKE it out of**
thanks a lot muito obrigado *Thanks a lot for helping me.*
think a lot of → **think a great DEAL of**
LOUD loud and clear em voz alta, bem claro, alto e bom som *[His] ... voice came over Radio Uganda loud and clear ...* -T/79.
LOUDMOUTHED = bigmouthed *[He is] ... a loudmouthed vulgarian and an intellectual fraud with but a single saving grace, his love of music.* -T/61.
LOUSE louse up [gir] estragar, arruinar, atrapalhar *Don't let him louse up our plans.*
LOUSY lousy with [gir] bem suprido de, cheio de *She's lousy with secrets.* -SJD,25.

LOVE fall in love apaixonar-se *Zillah was a stunning brunette from Hot Springs and Lou fell madly in love with her.*
in love apaixonado, enamorado *... he was in love and he wanted to get married.* -BRS,22. ♦ *Betty's eyes were the eyes of a woman in love.*
love affair relação extraconjugal, caso *... his life was shattered, as it seemed to him, by the unhappy termination of a love affair.* -CS,271.
loved one ente querido, pessoa a quem se ama *[They] ... had lost loved ones in the war ...* -T/69.
make love 1. namorar, cortejar *Juliet was less than fourteen when Romeo made love to her.* -KAC,13. 2. acariciar (-se), abraçar(-se), beijar(-se) *In William Inge's play* Picnic, *Madge's mother asks her daughter if Alan, Madge's boyfriend, ever makes love to her.* ⇒ **lovemaking** namoro, beijos, abraços, carícias *... steady couples have a right to indulge in mild lovemaking – kisses, embraces ...* -EA,73. 3. fazer amor, ter relações sexuais *... he has come to her room to make love to her ...* -EA,22. ⇒ **lovemaking** relações sexuais *Their lovemaking went on for a long time.*
no love lost hostilidade, aversão, inimizade *There's no love lost between Henry and his sister-in-law.*
not for love or money de modo algum, nem por sombra, por preço nenhum *It was raining and you couldn't get a taxi for love or money.*
LOVE-IN → BE-in
LOVEMAKING → make LOVE
LOVER lovers' lane local ermo freqüentado por namorados *... a gunman in a grey Ford coupé equipped with a red spotlight prowled lovers' lanes in outlying sections of Los Angeles.* -T/60.
LOVESICK apaixonado, perdido de amor *Hank's lovesick expression caused all his school friends to tease him.*

LOWBROW [col] [implica freqüentemente sarcasmo ou menosprezo] 1. não-intelectual, simples, iletrado, inculto, vulgar *Joe prefers lowbrow pleasures like boxing and cowboy movies.* 2. pessoa iletrada, inculta, vulgar *Stan is just a lowbrow.* v. **highbrow; middlebrow**
LOWDOWN the lowdown [col] os fatos, a verdade, a informação correta *I wanted the lowdown on what had been happening since I went away.* -AIM,41. ⇒ **low-down** vil, baixo, detestável, desprezível *Shane called Wilson a low-down Yankee liar.*
LOW-KEY; LOW-KEYED discreto, comedido, reservado, recatado *... he is a very low-key but very alert guy.* -T/72. ♦ *... a low-keyed speech ...* -T/74.
LUCK as luck would have it por obra do acaso, quis o destino, por um capricho do destino *As luck would have it, I ran into her some ten years after we had last met.*
down on one's luck [col] sem sorte, azarado, na rua da amargura *Barbara had once been a famous movie star but was now down on her luck.*
hard luck má sorte, azar *Hard luck has followed Ben. Everything he has done has been a failure.*
in luck com sorte *You're in luck. We have just the right article for you.*
luck out [col] dar sorte, sair-se bem, ser bem-sucedido *... I lucked out. Had [i.e., wrote] a moderate best seller – a political biography.* -WI,211.
out of luck sem sorte *You're out of luck if you expect me to loan you my car.*
push one's luck abusar da sorte *You've done okay so far in the war. I don't believe in a guy pushin' his luck.* -SLS,231.
LUMP get/take one's lumps [col] levar pancada; receber castigo, crítica etc. *If I'd been a little slower getting there, Judy'd have got her lumps but good.* -CJC,66. ♦ *An economic adviser ... has to expect to take his lumps in terms of political reality.* -T/62.

in the lump no total, em geral, em conjunto *Individually, the bars in the area weren't much, but in the lump it was a good place to have fun.*
lump in one's throat nó na garganta *Robert Frost once said that "a poem begins with a lump in the throat ..."*
lump it [col] suportar contra a vontade, resignar-se a agüentar (algo desagradável) *If you don't like it, you can lump it.*
LUNCH free lunch algo pelo qual não se paga, coisa gratuita *No one likes increases in tax rates ... But it is time Congress quit fooling people. There is no free lunch.* -T/77.
LURCH leave in the lurch deixar na mão, abandonar (alguém em dificuldades) ... *Marconi left me in the lurch. I needed him and he failed me.* -PF,32.

MACKEREL holy mackerel → **holy COW**
MAD mad about 1. furioso, encolerizado a respeito de *Mr. Simpson was mad about the broken window when he saw it.* 2. arrebatado, emocionado por causa de, louco por *The girls were mad about the new singer.*
mad at irritado, furioso, indignado com *You don't have to get mad at me! I'm only doing my job.*
MADE made from feito de [algo que não aparece no produto final] *Wine is made from grapes.* ♦ *Paper is made from wood pulp.* v. **MADE of**
made of feito de [algo que ainda existe ou transparece no produto final] *This gate is made of iron.*
MADE-TO-MEASURE → **make to MEASURE**
MADE-TO-ORDER → **make to ORDER**
MAID old maid solteirona *She remained an old maid even though she had many proposals of marriage.*
MAIDEN 1. de solteira (nome) *Her maiden name was Macgillicuddy.* 2. inaugural, de estréia, inicial ... *the* Titanic ... *struck an iceberg and sank on its maiden voyage in 1912* ... -T/86. ♦ *a maiden flight* ♦ *a maiden speech*
MAIL ORDER reembolso postal *Norma buys books by mail order.*

MAIN in the main na maior parte, principalmente, de maneira geral, no todo ... *the Hindu masses in the main continued to follow the religious customs of their remote ancestors.* -RN,14.
MAINSTREAM 1. a corrente principal ou dominante, a tendência geral, a influência maior ... *the American South is entering more fully into the nation's political mainstream.* -T/76. 2. que segue a corrente principal ou dominante, da maioria *The President stands high in the opinion polls and the electoral polls because he stands for mainstream values.* -T/86. ♦ *... half the black youths in certain cities find themselves cut off from mainstream society.* -T/86.
MAJOR 1. matéria ou disciplina de especialização, de maior concentração (em curso universitário) ... *graduating from Harvard with a major in history and literature.* -T/86. v. **minor** 2. estudante que se especializa em determinada matéria ou disciplina *[She is] ... a science major at Smith College* ... -T/80. 3. especializar-se em determinada matéria ou disciplina *He majored in architecture, minored in physics* ... -T/63.
MAJORITY silent majority o segmento da população que não expressa publi-

camente suas opiniões ou preferências políticas *Nixon thought he had the silent majority behind him.*

MAKE 1. ingressar em, conquistar um cargo, uma posição, um lugar, reconhecimento etc. *... he made the varsity team despite his wiry physique.* -T/60. 2. ganhar *How do you make a living?* ♦ *Do you make much money?* 3. chegar a, alcançar, atingir *We made Black Rock by eleven a.m.* 4. chegar a tempo de pegar (trem, avião etc.) *You better get dressed if you're going to make that plane.* -MN,311. 5. ser mencionado em, aparecer em *That news really made headlines.* ♦ *The crime made the front page.* 6. vir a ser, tornar-se, dar *Ann will make an excellent nurse.* 7. servir para, proporcionar *[A book that] ... makes interesting and illuminating reading ...* -GD,305. 8. comparecer a, tomar parte em *He called his wife to tell her he'd be tied up at the office that evening and couldn't possibly make dinner at her mother's.*

make after perseguir, ir no encalço de *The thief ran but a crowd made after him and caught him.*

make as if/though fazer de conta que, fingir que *Dick made as if he were going to jump out the window.*

make away with fugir com, roubar *The thieves broke into the museum and made away with all the valuable paintings.*

make believe fazer de conta, fingir *We all like to make believe that we are wonderful, desirable and very intelligent.* ⇒

make-believe 1. fingimento, simulação, imaginação, fantasia *Walter Mitty lived in a world of make-believe.* 2. falso, fingido, fictício, inventado *The movies have given us a lot of make-believe worlds.*

make certain/sure certificar-se, assegurar-se, ter certeza *[He] ... made certain that the President would have a bouquet of good news for his hosts ...* -T/78. ♦ *Make sure the door is locked.*

make (it) clear/plain esclarecer, deixar claro, não deixar dúvida *... the letters make clear McFarlane's despair.* -T/87. ♦ *... we made it clear that we would not tolerate any breach of those terms.* -T/81. ♦ *... the rebels have made it plain that they will not agree to a cease-fire ...* -T/60.

make do fazer o melhor possível com aquilo que se tem, arranjar-se *People are making do with the equipment they have for yet another year.* -T/87.

make for 1. dirigir-se para, ir em direção a *When the fight began, he made for the door.* 2. favorecer, contribuir para, conduzir a *Johnson's activism has made for a turbulent personal life.* -T/77.

make free with 1. servir-se de (algo) sem cerimônia *"Make free with all the food and drink", he said to his guests.* 2. tratar com excessiva liberdade ou atrevimento *Archie tried to make free with Nan.*

make good 1. dar ou fazer algo em substituição, compensar, reembolsar, reparar danos *All damages to the cars in the parking lot will have to be made good.* 2. ser bem-sucedido, levar algo a cabo *Bob Hope often played roles in which his character was a coward who made good.* 3. cumprir (promessa etc.) *... he made good his promise.* -T/85.

make into converter, transformar *From Here to Eternity, a novel by James Jones, was published in 1951 and was made into a motion picture in 1953.*

make it 1. [col] ser bem-sucedido, sair-se bem, conseguir seu intento, superar dificuldades, triunfar *... women who try to make it in a man's world.* -T/92. 2. chegar (a um destino, lugar, encontro etc.) no horário, a tempo, cumprir um compromisso *He was supposed to take the 3:10 train to Yuma but he never made it.*

make it big [gir] fazer grande sucesso *[He was] ... trying to make it big in show biz ...* -T/81.

make it clear → **MAKE (it) clear**

make it difficult dificultar *[His] ... sensitive social conscience made it difficult for him to confront the immense poverty he saw.* -T/73.

make it easy on oneself tornar as coisas mais fáceis para *Why not make it easy on yourself and admit that you love her?*

make it plain → MAKE clear

make it snappy [gir] apressar-se, andar depressa *Make it snappy. I'm in a hurry.*

make it up to [col] compensar, reparar *I wanted so much to make it up to him for all he'd been through – to be a real wife to him at last.* -UJ,98.

make known tornar conhecido, público *He wanted it made known that he didn't approve of the way the committee spent the money so freely.*

make light of não dar importância a, minimizar *Miss Chapman is much too modest ... She makes light of her accomplishments.* -GR,45.

make like [gir] imitar, fingir-se de, simular *Make like you're crazy and the Indians will not harm you.*

make little of dar pouca importância a, depreciar *Hugh made little of the fact that he had been selected as the most successful salesman in his company.*

make merry divertir-se, brincar, festejar *[They] ... were making merry in the snow.* -EMW,9. ⇒ **merrymaking** divertimento, festança *... Christmas-time merrymaking ...* -T/69.

make of deduzir, compreender (o significado de) *I can never make anything out of what he says on his TV speeches.*

make off fugir apressadamente *When they saw the policeman approaching, the boys playing in the street made off.*

make off with fugir com, roubar *The terrorists made off with the stolen money in a black car.*

make oneself comfortable pôr-se à vontade, sentir-se em casa *When she had come in he said: "Make yourself comfortable".*

make or break consolidar ou destruir, fazer ter êxito ou fazer fracassar *Family connections can make or break a political career.* -T/92.

make out 1. preencher por extenso (formulário, cheque etc.), completar *Please make out a check for $1,000.* 2. compreender, entender o significado de, decifrar *I can't make out the signature on this note.* 3. fingir, fazer de conta *"Don't make out as though you don't know me", the angry girl said.* 4. afirmar (algo inverídico), representar como, fazer parecer *... they've made me out a villain.* -T/71. 5. ver ou ouvir com dificuldade, distinguir, avistar, identificar, reconhecer *... listening intently, he could make out the faint drone of airplane motors.* -SLS,267. ♦ *He squinted through the darkness and made out a figure approaching him.* -CHT,38. 6. [col] dar-se, sair-se, arranjar-se, ajeitar-se *How did you make out in the examination?*

make over 1. alterar, transformar, refazer, remodelar, renovar *... she was trying to make him over into a scholar.* LLN,7. 2. transferir, ceder, legar (propriedade) *Mr. Elliott made over his property to his children before he died.*

make ready preparar(-se), aprontar(-se), dispor(-se) *Donna made ready all the things that she thought might be needed for the party.* ♦ *... the ponderous ... prosecutor made ready to represent the state.* -T/66.

make sick → sick to one's STOMACH

make stick fazer pegar, fazer surtir efeito, fazer consolidar-se *The true scientist strives to make a theory stick by marshalling all the conceivable evidence against it.* -T/66.

make sure → MAKE certain

make tick [col] fazer funcionar, fazer agir de determinada maneira, motivar *As a psychologist, he understands people's behavior, what makes them tick.*

make up 1. compor, formar, constituir *Science tells us that animals and plants*

are made up of cells. ♦ *The committee is largely made up of married men.* ⇒ **makeup** composição, construção, contextura, estrutura; constituição (física, mental etc.), natureza, caráter, personalidade *The makeup of the government is along socialistic lines* ♦ *If there is an element of fear in his makeup, I have never seen it.* -MAT,34. 2. inventar, criar, imaginar, fabricar, tramar ... *he had told the FBI that he had made the whole story up.* -T/67. 3. arranjar, arrumar, pôr em ordem *The room had not yet been made up for the day and it was in some disorder.* -QE,43. 4. preparar, aprontar *We will try to make up a set of dishes exactly as you wish.* 5. completar, inteirar, suprir (o que está faltando) ... *strikers will get only half pay ... until lost production is made up.* -T/81. 6. v. **MAKE up for** 7. reconciliar-se, fazer as pazes *Mike and Jennifer decided to forget their old quarrels and make up.* 8. aplicar cosméticos, maquilar(-se) *Rose made up her face so carefully that she seemed twenty years younger.* ⇒ **makeup** cosméticos, maquilagem ... *without her makeup on, she was beginning to show the years a little.* -OC,2. 9. caracterizar-se para um papel (em peça, filme, televisão etc.) *[She was] ... made up in a satanic manner, wearing a long black Dracula cape ...* -BL,56.
make up for compensar, reparar, recuperar, recobrar *[He] ... seemed determined to make up for lost time.* -T/87. ♦ *... what he lacked in natural talent he made up for in perseverance.* -T/87.
make up to [col] bajular, agradar, tentar obter as boas graças de *Blake is always making up to the boss in a sickening way.*
on the make [col] 1. tentando melhorar sua condição social, econômica etc. *Johnson will stay with the important people at a party. He is on the make politically.* 2. à procura de aventuras sexuais *Watch Earl when a new attractive woman enters the room. He's always on the make.*

that makes two of us [col] sou da mesma opinião, estou com você, somos dois *When he told me he didn't trust Mr. Adams, I said: "That makes two of us".*
MAKE-BELIEVE → **MAKE believe**
MAKESHIFT improvisado, substituto, provisório ... *a small room that resembled a makeshift office.* -WI,300.
MAKING be the making of ser a causa do sucesso, do desenvolvimento de *The responsibility of a wife and family may be the making of him.*
in the making em curso, em produção, em processo de desenvolvimento, de vir a ser *This motion picture was two years in the making.* ♦ *... a plot in the making.* -T/81.
the makings 1. potencialidades, virtualidades, qualidades, capacidade *Businessmen today readily recognize that a good university executive may have the makings of a topflight corporation officer ...* -T/66. 2. fumo e papel para fazer os próprios cigarros *Hondo Lane took out the makings and built another cigarette.* -LL,6.
of one's own making causado por si próprio *Some of his troubles ... are hardly of his own making.* -T/87.
MAN as a/one man unanimemente *The crowd rose as one man to do homage to a great human being.*
best man padrinho do noivo *Jerry was Robert's best man when he got married to Emma.* -T/78.
dirty old man [gir] velho devasso, libertino, safado *For a great many years Freud's insights about human behavior were rejected simply because most people considered him little more than "a dirty old man".* -MJV,346.
every man for himself salve-se quem puder, cada um por si *When the ship began to sink, it was every man for himself.*
feel like a new man sentir-se muito bem disposto *Now that I've lost thirty pounds of excess weight, I feel like a new man.*

man about town; man-about-town homem de gostos requintados (geralmente de classe superior) que freqüenta clubes, restaurantes, festas, teatros etc., boa-vida, *playboy* In An Affair to Remember *Cary Grant played the role of Nicky Ferrante, a well-known man about town.*

man/girl Friday funcionário/a fiel, assistente eficiente de quem o patrão pode depender, braço direito *I became bodyguard and man Friday to my boss when we traveled to Latin America.* ♦ *... she's my girl Friday. She's giving me a hand in running this place.* -CGT,79.

the man in the street cidadão comum, homem do povo *The man in the street has very little idea of the complexities of political intrigue.*

a man of few words homem de poucas palavras *Yates was a man of few words but he certainly knew how to take action.*

a man of his word homem de palavra *You can trust McCrea because he's a man of his word.*

man of letters homem de letras, literato, escritor, crítico *Edmund Wilson, who died in 1972, was possibly the greatest American man of letters of the twentieth century.*

a man of the world homem experiente, conhecedor do mundo, homem vivido *Prince Aly Khan was a true man of the world.*

men's room sanitário masculino *The men's room is kept very clean.*

one's own man independente, capaz de pensar e agir por si mesmo, senhor de suas ações, dono de seu nariz *Jack [Kennedy] counted on his father for tactical opinions and financial support. But on the major decisions he was his own man.* -T/60.

right-hand man pessoa de confiança, braço direito *A left-handed compliment is not nice, but a right-hand man is indispensable.* -T/91.

to a man por unanimidade, todos, sem exceção *... the actors [in the movie* The Wild Bunch*] are faultless to a man ...* -T/69.

yes man → **YES-man**

man-made feito ou causado pelo homem, artificial, sintético *... man-made indignities ...* -SHO,2. ♦ *... a group of man-made chemicals called chlorofluorocarbons (CFCs) ...* -T/87.

MANNER all manner of todo tipo de, toda espécie de *[Marathon runners subject] ... their bodies to all manner of special exercises.* -T/80.

by no manner of means de nenhum modo, de maneira alguma *... she was by no manner of means short ...* -TRL,9.

in a manner of speaking de certa maneira, em certo sentido, por assim dizer *In a manner of speaking she is the real power behind the throne.*

(as/as if) to the manner born (como se) acostumado desde o berço, ou que tem uma aptidão natural para fazer algo, comportar-se de determinada maneira etc., nascido para *In the play* Pygmalion, *Eliza Doolittle, the Flower Girl, disguised as a lady plays her role as to the manner born.*

MAN-OF-WAR 1. navio de guerra *The Japanese man-of-war* Yamato *was sunk in a terrible battle.* 2. **Portuguese man-of-war** urtiga-do-mar, água-viva *The only protection against Portuguese men-of-war is to keep away from them.* -T/64.

MANY a good/great many muitos, um grande número de *For a good many years it has been obvious that not all Americans talk alike.* -AH,346. ♦ *A great many people were at the political meeting.*

as many o mesmo número de, outros tantos *[He visited] ... seven countries in as many days.* -T/69.

as many as tantos quantos *... as many as 1,400 had been slain in the attacks ...* -T/82.

how many quantos *How many times do I have to tell you not to do that?*

many a/an/another um grande número de, muitos, muitas (pessoas, coisas) *Many a girl would like to be in your place.* ♦ *Like many another television writer, he would like to retire some day to a farm to write plays.* -T/63.

many's the muitos são; há um grande número de *Many's the time that I had to give him money so that he could appear solvent.*

one too many um demais, um a mais; demais, em excesso, além do que é razoável, aceitável etc. *He'd had one too many drinks and fell on the floor when he got up to walk.*

so many 1. tantos *I had no idea there were so many taxies in New York.* 2. uns tantos, um número x (de), não mais que certo número (de), outros tantos, nada além de *There are only so many lies you can take, and now there has been one too many ...* -T/74.

MAP map out 1. fazer o mapa de, representar em um mapa *He will map out a route for you to take while you're visiting Europe.* 2. projetar, planejar em detalhe *... an [military] operation had been mapped out ...* -T/87.

MARBLE not have all one's marbles → **not have all one's BUTTONS**

MARCH on the march em marcha, em curso *... Soviet diplomacy is again on the march.* -T/87.

steal a march on antecipar-se a, sair na frente e chegar primeiro, ganhar terreno às escondidas, fazer (algo) antes que outro o faça *The French have apparently stolen a march on the British with an agreement negotiated by President Pompidou himself to supply 200 heavy tanks to Lybia ...* -T/69.

MARINE tell it/that to the marines [col] vá contar isso a outro, não venha com essa *You should tell that to the marines. No one here will ever believe it.*

MARK easy mark [col] 1. pessoa simplória, vítima ingênua, pato *Wesley was an easy mark for confidence men.* 2. alvo fácil, acessível *... the soldiers were an easy mark in the clearing.* -CHT,105.

leave one's mark influenciar, fazer sentir sua ação *[He] ... left his mark on U.S. politics.* -T/63.

make one's mark distinguir-se, ter sucesso, tornar-se conhecido e famoso *[He] ... had made his mark as a politician in the Republican convention of 1928 in Houston ...* -T/78.

mark down 1. reduzir o preço, remarcar *All the items on this list have been marked down for the special sale.* 2. tomar nota de, agendar *In her appointment book she had Mrs. Margullies marked down for a visit that afternoon.*

mark off/out demarcar, delimitar *He marked off the boundaries of his land with a stone wall.* ♦ *... the Fathers of the Church marked off woman's sexual needs completely.* -DDT,485.

mark out for escolher, destinar, assinalar *Clark has been marked out for promotion.*

mark up aumentar o preço *They unlawfully mark up the price of merchandise that is already on the shelves.*

off the mark → **wide of the MARK**
toe the mark → **toe the LINE**

wide of the mark; off the mark 1. longe do alvo *... the napalm and high explosives fell wide of the mark, exploding to the north and south of the knoll.* -T/87. 2. inexato, errôneo *... an image that is ... far off the mark.* -T/87.

MARKET corner the market monopolizar, açambarcar o mercado *... he has managed to create an image and a company that have nearly cornered a multinational market ...* -T/86.

in the market for querendo comprar, procurando (algo) para comprar *Mr. Mansfield is in the market for a new house.*

on the market à venda, disponível *There's a wide variety of compact cars on the market.*

MARRY marry into tornar-se membro de uma família ou grupo pelo casamento *The girls married into the best Jewish families in the city.* -MMA,44.
marry off promover o casamento de, achar casamento para (filha) *He had married off one of his daughters ... to a young man from São Paulo.* -WC,81.
MASS mass media os meios de comunicação de massa, a mídia *... the mass media are entirely one-way communication.* -PN,21.
MASTER past master perito, mestre, pessoa de grande habilidade *Daley is a past master at making plausible excuses for not being at work.*
MATCH be no match for não ser adversário à altura de, não ser páreo *[She] ... began to swim, dowstream, but she was no match for Hardie and he soon overtook her.* -GFT,45.
make a match promover casamento *Many nouveaux riches are eager to make a match between their daughters and some man with a title.*
meet one's match encontrar adversário à altura *He'll meet his match when he plays against Maxwell.*
strike a match riscar um fósforo *Cary struck a match and lighted the lamp.* -BF,23.
to match da mesma cor, tipo, qualidade etc., que se harmoniza, que combina (com) *Alice was wearing a lovely green dress and gloves to match.*
MATTER as a matter of fact na verdade, na realidade *No, I don't know that man. As a matter of fact I've never seen him before.*
be the matter ser o problema, a dificuldade, a irregularidade, algo que está errado *... I've made a great many mistakes, and ... a great many things are the matter with me.* -WSM,216. ♦ *The car won't start. What is the matter with it?*
for that matter com relação a isso, quanto a isso, na verdade *It isn't the first time he's been punished, or Ann either, for that matter.* -OJT,288.
is anything the matter? há alguma dificuldade?, algum problema? *You look pale. Is anything the matter?*
matter of course coisa de esperar, coisa natural, normal, rotineira *Two years ago I would have been amazed to hear a group of reputable scientists make such a startling statement. Now, however, I took it as a matter of course.* -RE,78. ⇒ **matter-of-course** de esperar, natural, lógico, rotineiro *It was a matter-of-course statement.*
matter of fact fato, coisa verídica, ocorrência *It is a matter of fact that Pierre Le Moyne d'Iberville was one of the founders of Louisiana.* ⇒ **matter-of-fact** prosaico, banal, sem emoção, trivial, literal *Audrey gave us a very matter-of-fact account of her trip to Monaco.*
no laughing matter assunto sério, coisa que não é motivo de riso *They all laughed when Harry missed the train, but to Harry, the prospect of facing an angry wife in the morning was no laughing matter.*
no matter sem importância, irrelevante *Don't worry about the performance today. It's no matter.*
no matter how/what/when/where/who seja como for/o que for/quando for/onde for/quem for; não importa como/o que/quando/onde/quem *No matter how old you are, you always feel better after a good night's sleep.* ♦ *... no matter what comes we'll go on.* -FV,16.
not mince matters/words falar francamente, não medir as palavras *Mr. O'Brien didn't mince matters when he told me to leave his house and never visit his daughter again.* ♦ *... I suggest you have a talk with Papa. He isn't one to mince words.* -HM,131.
nothing the matter nenhuma dificuldade, nenhum problema *There's nothing the matter with me. I'm all right.*

something the matter algum problema, transtorno, dificuldade *I knew there was something the matter with Ryan the moment I saw him.*
to make matters/things worse para piorar as coisas, para agravar a situação *The government's efforts to control subversion seem only to make matters worse.* -T/80. ♦ *To make things worse, Jim fell sick and had to be taken to a hospital.*
what's the matter? que é que há?; que se passa? *Eugene, what is the matter, tell me at once ...* -NEW,163. ♦ *What's the matter with that boy? Is he sick?*
MAY may/might as well → **as WELL**
MCCOY the (real) McCoy [gír] a coisa verdadeira, autêntica, genuína (algo que não é cópia ou imitação) *This whisky is the real McCoy.* ♦ *This is not a reproduction. It's the real McCoy.*
MEAL square meal [col] refeição substancial, satisfatória *He likes to eat three square meals a day.*
MEAN mean well ter boas intenções, ser amistoso *Ted means well but his manner is so brusque that he gives a bad impression.* ⇒ **well-meaning** bem-intencionado *Karen's mother was well-meaning but somehow they didn't like her.*
MEANS by all means 1. custe o que custar, a todo custo *We are determined to defend our land and our holy places by all means ...* -T/87. 2. sem dúvida, perfeitamente *By all means, we should try to get acquainted with the customs of the country.*
by means of através de, com o auxílio de, por meio de *Gus managed to capture the thief by means of a clever trick.*
by no means; not by any means de maneira alguma, absolutamente não *The dense tropical forest that covers most of the Amazon Valley is by no means a vast swampy jungle.* -WC,54. ♦ *... he was not by any means an easy master.* -DM,17.
means to an end modo de fazer ou obter algo, meios para um fim *Phil's marriage to Connie was a means to an end: her money.*
MEASURE for good measure como bonificação, como brinde, de inhapa, de quebra *As kids, when we went to the corner store the grocer always gave us extra bananas for good measure.*
have/take someone's measure julgar ou avaliar, conhecer os limites, a capacidade, o caráter de *Mr. Winslow is very intelligent. He has the measure of every man in his employ.*
in great/large measure em grande parte, amplamente *The U.S. air-traffic system is the safest in the world, and its success is due in large measure to its controllers.* -T/87.
in some measure até certo ponto *My financial aid to you will depend, in some measure, on your willingness to answer certain questions.*
make to measure fazer sob medida, sob encomenda *Rick's new suit has been made to measure.*
measure off marcar (determinado comprimento); medir e marcar, demarcar *When you measure off three feet of that rope, tie a rag on it and continue to measure off three-foot segments in the same manner.*
measure out 1. medir, demarcar, delimitar *Will you measure out two yards of that cloth for me?* 2. dar, conceder, ministrar, aplicar *He would measure out punishment to the soldiers who slept while on duty.*
measure up 1. ter as qualificações necessárias, ser capaz *Tom had some definite ideas of what a woman should be and he felt that his fiancée failed to measure up.* 2. atingir (determinado padrão), estar à altura de *The poor child could not measure up to the standards set for him by his father.*
take measures/steps tomar medidas, tomar providências *... East European authorities are taking measures to regulate*

the narcotics flow. -T/87. ♦ ... take steps to remedy the situation. -T/87.

take someone's measure → have someone's MEASURE

MEAT one's meat [gír] a especialidade, o interesse predileto, a ocupação ou atividade favorita de *Art history is his meat but he's also good at literature.*

MEDICINE give someone some/a dose/a taste of his own medicine → give someone a DOSE of his own medicine

take one's medicine receber o castigo merecido, sofrer as consequências *My father says I ought to plead guilty and take my medicine, that I deserve to be punished.* -MJV,2.

MEDIUM strike a happy medium chegar a um acordo satisfatório, a um consenso *Even though we were not in complete agreement on the new plan, we struck a happy medium with a few small concessions.*

MEET meet halfway fazer concessões mútuas, chegar a um acordo (com) *He made great efforts to meet the military halfway.*

meet with 1. [ou] **meet up with** topar com, deparar com, dar de cara com *They met up with a huge grizzly bear while hiking in Montana's Glacier National Park.* 2. encontrar-se com (alguém), reunir-se com *[The President] ... met with his top national security advisers last week ...* -T/91. 3. experimentar, receber, sofrer, enfrentar, ter, obter *At first Freud's theory of infantile sexuality met with strong opposition.* -FLS,109. ♦ *Their plans met with disaster.* ♦ *The show met with a resounding success.* 4. estar de acordo com, concordar com *If your plan meets with our needs, we will make a contract.*

MEETING call a meeting convocar uma reunião, uma assembléia *[He] ... called a special meeting of officials ...* -T/75.

MELT melt away 1. derreter(-se) *The warm sun had melted away the winter's snow ...* -WL,1. 2. desaparecer, dissipar-se *Judy Garland never seemed to overcome her personal problems, so that in real life her troubles didn't "melt away like lemon drops" as the* Over the Rainbow *lyrics promised.*

MEMORY in/within living memory na memória daqueles que ainda vivem *No other President in living memory has done so much to give credibility to his country.*

MEN → man

MEND on the mend restabelecendo-se, melhorando, em recuperação *My boss, who broke his leg and arm, is on the mend and is expected to be back at work next Monday.*

MENTION don't mention it de nada, não há de que *"Thank you for all your help." "Don't mention it."*

not to mention sem falar em, para não mencionar *They have factories in France, England and Germany, not to mention stores in all the principal cities.*

MERCY at the mercy of à mercê de *[In 1861] ... the United States troops were ordered out of the territory [of Arizona], leaving the pioneers at the mercy of Cochise and his Apache bands.* -MJ,291.

mercy killing eutanásia *... serious discussion of suicide and mercy killing for the incurably ill no longer provokes as much shock or indignation as in the past.* -T/80.

MESS mess around [col] vaguear, zanzar, vagabundear, ficar à toa, matar o tempo *Stop messing around and get to work.*

mess around with [col] 1. perder tempo com, ocupar-se com coisas sem importância ou improdutivas *He likes to mess around with old clocks and typewriters.* 2. namorar para passar tempo, manter namoro ou intimidade com *Stroud was messing around with other women and was caught by his wife.* 3. mexer com, molestar, importunar, destratar *Don't mess around with that guy. He's dangerous.* 4. manusear (algo) sem tomar cuidado, bulir (em algo) com descaso *I wish you'd stop messing around with my camera.*

mess up [col] 1. desarranjar, desarrumar, bagunçar, pôr em desordem, misturar *Dennis messed up his sister's hair until it looked like a mop.* 2. sujar *The children messed up the kitchen floor.* 3. estragar, arruinar, atrapalhar, pôr a perder *Jonas messed up the plan.* 4. maltratar, surrar, bater em *He was messed up by the rival gang.* 5. meter-se em encrenca, causar barulho *[Gang violence] will stay quiet until somebody else messes up.* -T/86.

MESSAGE get the message [col] compreender (insinuação, indireta etc.) entender o recado *[He] ... got the message that he is no longer above criticism ...* -T/92.

METE mete out impor (pena, castigo), aplicar (justiça) *... each prisoner waited now to see punishment meted out ...* -NE,197. ♦ *They mete out their own justice.*

METHOD method in one's madness imaginação, idéia ou conduta aparentemente maluca mas no fundo razoável *I thought his plan was completely crazy until I realized there was method in his madness.*

MID in one's mid-/middle twenties/thirties etc. mais ou menos aos 25/26, 35/36 anos etc. *A quiet, blue-eyed, serious-faced man in his mid-thirties.* -KD,16. ♦ *... leaders now in their middle or late 50s.* -T/76. v. **in one's EARLY twenties; in one's LATE twenties**

MIDDLE in the middle em situação difícil, entre dois fogos, sem saber o que fazer *When any decision is to be made Darren is always in the middle.*

the middle of nowhere lugar longínquo, remoto *... an ugly little town in the West stuck in the middle of nowhere ...* -LRT,71.

MIDDLE-AGED → **middle AGE**

MIDDLEBROW [col] [implica freqüentemente sarcasmo ou menosprezo] 1. de nível cultural médio, semi-intelectual *A few critics have called [J. D.] Salinger a "slick middlebrow writer ..."* -LAS,321. 2. pessoa de nível cultural médio *Anderson is a middlebrow. He is politically conservative, has conventional values and a moderate interest in intellectual and artistic matters.* v. **highbrow; lowbrow**

MIDDLE-OF-THE-ROAD moderado, nem liberal nem conservador *... the middle-of-the-road candidate.* -T/87. ♦ *... the [Democratic] party must appeal to the middle-of-the-road American if it wants to win.* -T/72.

MIGHT might as well → **MAY as well**

MILE go the extra mile fazer um esforço extra, ir além do que é habitual *[Nixon] ... also sought to prove to critics that the U.S. had "gone the extra mile" in seeking an agreement [of a cease-fire with the North Viet Nam government] ...* -T/72.

miles from nowhere em lugar extremamente longínquo, no fim do mundo *... we were God knows how many miles from nowhere with nothing under us but two miles of sky and a few more miles of water.* -RQ,25. ♦ *Carson lives on a ranch in Montana, miles from nowhere.*

MILK cry over spilled milk lastimar-se em vão, chorar a morte da bezerra *It's useless to cry over spilled milk.*

MILL through the mill [col] 1. experiente, traquejado, prático, conhecedor, que adquiriu eficiência de maneira árdua, que aprendeu sofrendo *That Roberts has been through the mill is evident by his acute awareness of a solution for our problems.* 2. que atravessou muitas dificuldades, que passou maus bocados *... a million living Americans have passed through the Marxist mill and have been brainwashed into silence.* -T/61.

MILLION feel like a million (dollars) [gír] sentir-se muito bem de corpo e alma *I felt like a million dollars when she gave me the good news.*

look like a million (dollars) [gír] aparentar saúde, bem-estar e alegria, ter ótima aparência *She always looks like a million.*

MINCEMEAT make mincemeat of [col] 1. fazer picadinho de, bater em, surrar *Leonard made mincemeat of his opponent in his first professional fight.* 2. reduzir a pó, arrasar, aniquilar (verbalmente) *Arnold made mincemeat of his rival's claim to being author of the plan.*

MIND be of a mind to estar inclinado a, tencionar, ter vontade de *... he was still of a mind to go on with the trapping expedition into the Rocky Mountains.* -MF,44.

be of one mind; be of the same mind estar de acordo, ser do mesmo parecer, ter a mesma opinião *Not all historians are of one mind concerning the causes of the fall of the Roman Empire.* ♦ *Palmer was of the same mind and attitude as before ...* -TW,31.

be of two minds estar indeciso, não saber que decisão tomar *[They] ... are of two minds about development.* -T/91.

bear/keep in mind lembrar-se, ter em mente, não esquecer *Always bear in mind that nothing's too good for a guest.* -TRL,10. ♦ *We must always keep in mind that words in themselves, and one by one, have little value.* -SN,432.

blow one's/someone's mind [col] 1. sofrer os efeitos produzidos por uma droga alucinógena, pirar/produzir efeito alucinógeno, fazer pirar *He blew his mind using LSD.* ♦ *LSD will blow your mind.* ⇒ **mind-blowing** psicodélico, que produz alucinações *mind-blowing chemicals* 2. experimentar intensa emoção, ter uma experiência profundamente marcante, ficar atônito, assombrado, muito entusiasmado; produzir intensa emoção em, deixar alguém profundamente agitado, estimulado, atônito, chocado etc. *General [theory of] relativity blows your mind.* -T/79. ⇒ **mind-blowing** que produz intenso arrebatamento, emoção, agitação, entusiasmo, estímulo etc. *... mind-blowing sensations ...* -T/72.

boggle the mind; the mind boggles [[col] ser inconcebível, inimaginável, demasiado fantástico, inaceitável à mente; ficar perplexo, aturdido, encher-se de espanto *... some statistics boggle the mind: the Beatles have sold, all over the world, upwards of 200 million records.* -T/80. ♦ *The mind boggles at the colossal amount of research that William L. Shirer had to do in order to write* The Rise and Fall of the Third Reich. ⇒ **mind-boggling** impressivo, impressionante, assombroso, inconcebível *... the mind-boggling complexities of relativity theory and the even more bizarre notions of quantum physics ...* -T/92.

bring/call to mind trazer à lembrança, fazer lembrar *That song brings to mind a girl I used to know.*

change one's mind mudar de idéia, de opinião *The purpose of argument is to make another person "change his mind".* -BCM,124.

come to mind vir à lembrança, ocorrer *The right answer didn't come to mind and I didn't know what to say.*

cross one's mind passar pela cabeça, vir ao pensamento, ocorrer *It never crossed my mind that I should have waited for her.*

get (someone/something) out of one's mind tirar do pensamento, esquecer *I can't get Nell out of my mind.* -HJH,23.

have a (good/great) mind to ter (grande) vontade de, estar (muito) inclinado a, propenso a *I have a mind to tell Sorensen what I think of him.* ♦ *He had a good mind to draw all his goddam money out of the bank.* -LRT,76.

have an open mind não ter preconceitos, ser receptivo a novas idéias *You can discuss any subjects with Chris because she has an open mind.* ⇒ **open-minded** liberal, receptivo, compreensivo, sem preconceitos *... an open-minded approach to a wide variety of money and banking problems.* -T/60.

have half a mind estar meio decidido, um tanto inclinado *I have half a mind to quit my job and try working in another city.*

have in mind tencionar, pretender, estar cogitando, ter em mente *That's not what I had in mind.*

in one's mind's eye na memória, na imaginação *It must be realized that fossils are not dead objects in the mind's eye of a paleontologist because he visualizes them as they existed in their environments.* -SR,7.

in one's right mind em seu juízo perfeito, de posse de suas faculdades mentais *Who in his right mind would have believed that the old man was really a Nazi war criminal?*

keep in mind → **bear in MIND**

know one's own mind saber o que quer *Edwina is the difficult type of woman to interest in buying because she knows her own mind.*

lose one's mind perder a razão, enlouquecer *In Somerset Maugham's novel The Razor's Edge, Sophie nearly loses her mind when her husband and little daughter are killed in a car crash.*

make up one's mind decidir-se, resolver-se *He listens to everybody's opinion and then makes up his mind.* -T/72.

mind you note bem, veja bem *I haven't done anything wrong, mind you.*

never mind não se incomode (com), não se preocupe (com); não tem importância, não faz mal, esqueça *Never mind about the last two letters. We can send them tomorrow.* ♦ *Never mind what the book says. Use your head to solve the problem.*

of sound mind são, racional, lúcido *He was of sound mind and in full possession of all his faculties when he shot the two men.*

one-track mind [col] mentalidade tacanha, limitada, sem visão *[He was regarded] ... as a clever, fanatic idealist with a one-track mind who thought ... that he alone was right ...* -TJ,181.

on one's mind no pensamento, na mente, preocupando *... a major general who had nothing in particular on his mind.* -CB,3. ♦ *What's on your mind, son?* -CEP,185.

out of one's mind louco, fora de si, aturdido, perturbado *You are out of your mind. Now, look here, be calm. Tell me what happened.* -WR,57.

prey on/upon one's/someone's mind atormentar, afligir *Axel's guilt preyed on his mind.*

put in mind fazer lembrar, trazer à lembrança *Standing there, she put Kern in mind of a fragile china doll that had to be handled very carefully.* -HWR,44.

put/set/turn one's mind to dar toda a atenção a, pôr todo o empenho em, dedicar-se inteiramente a *If you really put your mind to it you can finish it quickly.* ♦ *You are one man who I think could do anything you set your mind to.* -LRT,45.

put out of one's mind/head esquecer, tirar do pensamento, não pensar mais em *You must put those things out of your mind.* ♦ *Brian couldn't put Julia out of his head even after she married another man.*

set/put one's mind at rest/ease tranqüilizar-se, sossegar, despreocupar-se, descansar *You can set your mind at rest. We shall take care of any expenses you may have because of your injury.*

set one's mind on empenhar-se em, decidir-se a, dispor-se a, resolver-se a *It's difficult, but if you set your mind on doing it you will succeed.*

set one's mind to → **put one's MIND to**

slip one's mind fugir da memória de *I was supposed to pay that bill yesterday but it slipped my mind.*

speak one's mind falar francamente, dizer o que pensa *At times speaking my mind may make others uncomfortable, but oh what it does for me.* -T/78.

to one's mind na opinião de *Somebody once said that after death "the great mystery begins", but to my mind, the greatest mystery is existence itself.*

turn one's mind to → **put one's MIND to**
turn over in one's mind repassar na mente, pensar cuidadosamente, considerar (algo) sob todos os ângulos, estudar com cuidado ... *reading every sentence carefully and turning over in your mind what it says and what it means.* -MC,xii. ♦ *I'd like to turn over your offer in my mind a few days before I make a decision.*
weigh on one's mind preocupar, afligir, oprimir, acabrunhar *Lieutenant Rennick had to make a difficult decision before dawn and it weighed heavily on his mind.*
MIND-BENDER [col] droga alucinógena *Aztecs took ololiuqui (similar to LSD), peyote, marijuana and other mind benders.* -T/86. ⇒ **mind-bending** 1. psicodélico, que causa alucinações ... *the mind-bending potentialities of LSD.* -T/67. 2. que produz intenso arrebatamento, emoção, agitação, entusiasmo, estímulo etc. *[Stanley Kubrick's* 2001: A Space Odyssey*]* ... *uses some of the most mind-bending visual effects in motion-picture history.* -T/68.
MIND-BLOWING → **blow one's MIND**
MIND-BOGGLING → **boggle the MIND**
MIND-SET atitude, tendência, inclinação, maneira de pensar, condição ou disposição mental *Mothers' mind-sets have altered about their children, especially their daughters.* -T/76. ♦ *I don't think my critics know my mind-set.* -T/79.
MINOR 1. matéria ou disciplina de especialização universitária de concentração menor, menos importante ou de menor interesse *[He] ... was an Emory University senior ... with a major in psychology, a minor in business ...* -T/92. v. **major** 2. especializar-se (em determinada matéria, mas em concentração menor do que a principal [*major*]) ... *he majored in drama and minored in dance ...* -T/84.
MINT mint of money muito dinheiro *He made a mint of money when he invented a way to transmit pictures over great distances by radio.*

MINUTE by the minute cada vez mais, gradualmente, progressivamente *The sky's getting darker by the minute. We'll have wind before long and rain with it.* -SLT,137.
in two/ten etc. minutes/seconds flat [col] rapidamente, rapidíssimo *If you do that, the boss will fire you in one minute flat.*
just a minute/second espere aí, pare aí, alto lá, um momento *Now, just a minute. Where do you think you're going? You can't go in there!*
MIRACLE work miracles → **work WONDERS**
MISS a miss is as good as a mile erro é erro, tanto faz errar ou fracassar por 1 como por 1.000; safar-se (de alguém ou de algo) ainda que por um triz é tão eficaz quanto safar-se por ampla margem; vencer (ou ser derrotado) por uma pequena margem não deixa de ser uma vitória (ou uma derrota) *When the wall almost fell on him he gasped and smilingly said, "A miss is as good as a mile". Then he fainted.* ♦ *Never mind that they have lost the game by a narrow margin. Still, a miss is as good as a mile.*
miss out on perder (boa oportunidade, ocasião), deixar de usufruir, deixar passar *If you haven't seen* Gone With the Wind *you've missed out on one of the best movies of all time.*
MISTAKE and no mistake [col] sem dúvida alguma, com toda a certeza *Well, she's really a very smart girl and no mistake.*
make no mistake entenda bem, não se engane, não se iluda *Make no mistake: [he] ... just might be the President of the U.S. ...* -T/92.
MIX mixed up 1. [col] confuso, desorientado, perplexo, aturdido *Barbara got all mixed up and didn't know what to do.* ⇒ **mixed-up** ... *mixed-up human beings who happen to be deviates.* -T/68. 2. desordenado, misturado, bagunçado *I got my route numbers mixed up and lost my*

way. 3. [col] envolvido, implicado, ligado, relacionado *I understand your father is mixed up with lawless men ...* -LC,9. ♦ *I never had any idea of getting mixed up in politics ...* -AIM,66.

mix it up [gir] travar luta, envolver-se em disputa, competição *They began to mix it up just before the police arrived and put a stop to the riot.* ♦ *He has never lost his taste for mixing it up in the public economic debate.* -T/87. ⇒ **mix-up** 1. confusão *There was a mix-up with the names and Joe was given the wrong prize.* 2. luta, briga *After the game there was a big mix-up.*

mix with relacionar-se com *Joe was so good with people. He could mix with them and be friendly ...* -OJT,6.

MIXER good//bad mixer pessoa sociável//pouco sociável *Fraser is a good mixer and just the kind of person for a public relations job.*

MODERN-DAY dos dias atuais, do presente, contemporâneo *... he told reporters about his experience as a modern-day Robinson Crusoe.* -T/72.

MOM-AND-POP mom-and-pop business/store/shop pequeno negócio, empresa etc. *... the mom-and-pop shops that keep small rural towns alive.* -T/86.

MOMENT for the moment/present = for the TIME being *We will stay here for the moment.* ♦ *That will be all for the present.*

at a moment's notice = at/on short NOTICE *Audiences could see the hatred tighten every muscle [of actor James Cagney in a movie scene] at a moment's notice.* -BAJ,17.

MONEY for one's money [col] na opinião de, na preferência de, na escolha de *For my money, The Treasure of the Sierra Madre is John Huston's masterpiece.*

get one's money's worth receber o justo valor (na compra de algo) pelo dinheiro pago, adquirir algo que valha o que custou *You get your moneys'worth when you buy at our store.*

hard money moeda metálica *Paper money ... was practically worthless [during the American Revolution]. Businessmen insisted ruthlessly on "hard money" for every commodity and every army supply.* -SGF,349. v. **hard CASH**; **hard CURRENCY**

in the money [gir] 1. cheio da grana, endinheirado *[They] ... were in the money. DJ,20.* ♦ *[He] ... regards himself primarily as a writer, but it is his TV appearances that put him in the big money.* -T/87. 2. entre os três primeiros colocados (de corrida, disputa etc.) *... a colt named Jim French, which finished in the money at the Derby ...* -T/81.

launder money lavar dinheiro, i.e., transferir dinheiro proveniente de atividades ilegais para bancos ou investimentos estrangeiros a fim de disfarçar-lhe a origem e legitimá-lo *[The organization] ... was indicted and convicted for laundering drug money ...* -T/91.

made of money endinheirado, rico *What do you think I am, made of money? You're always asking me for something.*

make good money ganhar um bom salário *Glenn makes good money at his job and would hate to lose it.*

make money ganhar dinheiro, ter lucro, enriquecer *Ken could never make enough money to take care of his family.*

money to burn muito dinheiro, dinheiro para esbanjar *Michelle is young, beautiful, has money to burn and is looking for a husband.*

(right) on the money [col] exato, preciso, correto, impecável, irrepreensível *The [Columbia space] shuttle is "right on the money" and gives the U.S. a mighty lift.* -T/81. ♦ *Your guess was right on the money.*

put one's money on apostar em, depositar total confiança em *... [John Fitzgerald]*

Kennedy made his choice: to put his money on the new man [President Janio Quadros] in Brazil. -T/61.
ready money/cash dinheiro disponível *When I have the ready money I'll pay cash for a new car.*
spend money like water gastar dinheiro a rodo *Carl spent the money his father left him like water.*
MONKEY make a monkey (out) of [col] = **make a FOOL of** *He would make a monkey out of you if you tried to argue with him.*
monkey (around) with mexer com, brincar com, bulir em *Simon kept monkeying with the old clock.* ♦ *... the average housewife has no business monkeying around with a loaded revolver.* -T/67.
monkey business [gir] 1. criancice, travessura, comportamento tolo *The children are too quiet. They must be up to some monkey business.* 2. falcatrua, trapaça, logro, fraude, coisa suspeita, conduta imprópria (social, sexual etc.) *There is always monkey business going on in his transactions.* ♦ *... what, if any, monkey business transpired between her and [the] former Presidential Candidate ...* -T/87.
monkey on one's back [gir] 1. vício em drogas, toxicomania *When someone is strongly addicted to drugs we say he has a monkey on his back.* 2. problema grave, estorvo, empecilho, gravame, obsessão *[President Gerald Ford] ... decided to pardon Nixon "to get the monkey off my back one way or the other".* -T/79.
throw a monkey wrench in(to) the works/transmission/plan etc. frustrar, desestabilizar, fazer malograr (plano etc.) *The sudden death of the leader threw a monkey wrench into the works.*
MONSTER green-eyed monster ciúme *After less than a year's marriage to his beautiful wife, John became a victim of the green-eyed monster.* v. **green-eyed**
MONTH a month of Sundays [col] período excessivamente longo, muito tempo *We didn't expect this job to take a month of Sundays to finish.*
MOOD in the mood disposto, favoravelmente inclinado, propenso, de bom humor *... Marina was in no mood for a truce. She was still angry.* -MW,162. ♦ *Stop teasing me. I'm not in the mood.*
MOON once in a blue moon [col] muito raramente, quase nunca *They see each other once in a blue moon.*
MOONLIGHT [col] ter um segundo emprego, um trabalho extra *... university teachers moonlight on two or three different jobs to make ends meet.* -T/66.
MOP mop up 1. limpar, enxugar *Mop up the milk you spilled on the kitchen floor.* 2. eliminar todos os focos de resistência ainda remanescentes após uma batalha *The army moved forward mopping up all pockets of remaining resistance.*
MORE be no more não existir mais, ser falecido, estar morto *After thirty years of existence ... [he] was no more.* -BAS,20.
more and more cada vez mais *His wife became more and more demanding.*
more or less 1. um tanto, um pouco, até certo ponto *Rosie was more or less pleased to see me.* 2. aproximadamente, mais ou menos *The show was more or less a musical with a decent plot.*
no more não mais, já não é assim *In the past, working lunches at the Soviet mission had been well lubricated with Stolichnaya vodka and Armenian brandy. No more. Now the Soviet served their guests soda and fruit juice ...* -T/87.
there's more to someone/something than alguém ou alguma coisa não é tão simples assim, não é só isso, é mais complexo; o que foi dito não é tudo, explica apenas parcialmente *Contemporary psychology, as we have seen, has accustomed us to the fact that there is more to ourselves than we suspect.* -SHR,38. ♦ *There is a lot more to this man than his critics give him credit for ...* -T/76.

the more ... the less quanto mais ... tanto menos *The more I see of him the less I like him.* -SV,16.

the more ... the more quanto mais ... tanto mais *The more I think about it, the more I decide that you were in love with him.* -MN,287.

what's more além disso, além do mais, principalmente, sobretudo *Dawson is rich, young, and what's more, looking for a wife.*

MOSES holy Moses → holy COW

MOST **at (the) most** quando muito, no máximo, na melhor das hipóteses *You'll have to walk one mile at most.* ♦ *You'll get $1,200 at the most for that car.*

make the most of tirar o máximo proveito de, aproveitar (algo) ao máximo *Others are making the most of the situation ...* -T/87. ♦ *Make the most of the years you have left because life is short.*

most all/any/every/anyone/anywhere etc. quase todos/quase qualquer um/em quase toda parte etc. *He could be counted on to vote against most all Democratic legislation ...* -T/74. ♦ *I'd see her most every evening ...* -AIM,118. ♦ *He'd do most anything for a jug of whiskey.* -HJ,84.

MOTHBALL **in mothballs** fora de serviço ativo, desativado, em reserva (avião, navio etc.) ... *two World War II battleships now in mothballs.* -T/81.

MOTHER **every mother's son** todos sem exceção *Even though half of the people hated Joe, every mother's son of them came to his farewell party.*

mother tongue língua materna *Each mother tongue teaches its users a way of seeing and feeling the world, and of acting in the world, that is quite unique.* -MMU,83.

MOTHER-NAKED nu *Mother-naked, he was permitted to wrap himself in the wreck of his topcoat ...* -QE,135.

MOTION **go through the motions** [col] fazer algo só pelas aparências, sem sinceridade ou seriedade; simular, fingir, observar apenas as formalidades ... *if your heart isn't in what you are doing, if you are merely "going through the motions", you are doing it in a perfunctory way.* -NM,212. ♦ ... *Ford again went through the motions of performing his vice-presidential duties ...* -T/74.

motion picture = movie 1 ... *the [American newspaper] Daily News acclaimed it [Bonnie and Clyde] as one of the most significant motion pictures of the decade ...* -T/67.

put/set in motion iniciar, dar começo, pôr em movimento, desencadear *Sometimes the breeze from the sea would set the leaves into motion ...* -RQ,45. ♦ ... *[Thurgood] Marshall was a man resolved to continue the revolution he had helped to set in motion.* -T/91.

MOUNTAIN **make a mountain (out) of a molehill** fazer tempestade em copo de água *It wasn't that bad. You're making a mountain out of a molehill.*

MOUTH **down in/at the mouth** [col] cabisbaixo, desalentado, deprimido *You look so down in the mouth.*

from mouth to mouth de boca a boca, de pessoa a pessoa *The information, considered secret, spread from mouth to mouth and, finally, to the enemy.*

have a big mouth [gir] tagarelar, falar demais, falar o que não deve *Simpson's wife has such a big mouth that the whole neighborhood knew about his raise five minutes after he told her.* ⇒ **bigmouthed** loquaz, tagarela, boquirroto *You're a bigmouthed lout.*

keep one's mouth shut ficar de bico calado *A little boy who knew too much, but not enough to keep his mouth shut ...* -TW,5.

laugh on the other/wrong side of one's mouth; laugh out of the other/wrong side of the mouth [col] ficar com cara de bobo, ficar desapontado, lamentar-se, rir amarelo *He will laugh on the wrong side*

of his mouth when he finds out the gold I gave him is just as false as the dollars he paid for it.
make one's mouth water dar água na boca *When I see a picture of a baked Virginia ham, it makes my mouth water.*
mouth off falar em estilo empolado; falar com insolência, com impertinência *He has a bad habit of mouthing off at the wrong time and place.*
run off at the mouth [gir] falar demais, dizer tolices, coisas que não devem ser ditas *You must be going soft in the head in your old age to run off at the mouth like that.* -MG,38.
shoot off one's mouth/face [gir] falar demais, falar sem a devida cautela, ser indiscreto; contar vantagem *Don't shoot off your mouth about our plans to your wife.* ♦ *If you hadnt of [sic] gone and shot your mouth off to Houston none of this would ever happened.* -JJF,10. ♦ *Keep her out of his way. If she shoots off her face to him now, I think he might kill her.* -HJ,77.
shut one's mouth/face [gir] calar a boca *Shut your mouth if you know what's good for you.* ♦ *Shut your God damn stupid face ...* -OJ,6.
MOUTHFUL say a mouthful [gir] dizer uma verdade, dizer algo que tem muita propriedade, que faz muito sentido *You said a mouthful when you told her to mind her own business and let us run our jobs.*
MOVE get a move on [gir] 1. locomover-se, pôr-se a andar, circular *The policeman told the men who were loitering near the corner to get a move on.* 2. apressar-se *You'll have to get a move on if you expect to get to the game before it starts.*
make a move 1. fazer qualquer movimento, mexer-se *Don't make a move or the lion will rush to attack you. Keep still.* 2. dar um passo, agir, tomar medidas, providências *Murray never makes a move without consulting his lawyer.*
move away mudar-se *The Sullivans moved away without leaving any forwarding address.*
move in(to) 1. mudar-se (para nova residência) *Nixon moved into the White House at an extraordinary moment in American history.* -T/74. 2. introduzir-se, assumir o controle, tomar conta ... *The FBI moved into the case ...* -T/78. ♦ ... *Winter moves in with its backbone of ice and accoutrements of leafless trees and hard frozen ground.* -MG,7.
move in on [gir] aproximar-se de, convergir sobre, tentar assumir o controle de; atacar *When a gangster tries to move in on another's territory, there is generally a gang war.*
move in with ir viver com ... *he moved in with ... [her] in August 1986 ...* -T/92.
move on partir, ir-se *Just how long should adult children live with their parents before moving on?* -T/87.
move out mudar-se, deixar o local onde morava *After he moved out to Los Angeles in 1987 we never saw him again.*
move over mover-se para outro lugar ou posição, afastar-se *"Move over and let me sit down", he said to his son.*
on the move [col] em movimento, viajando, constantemente em atividade *Griffith was continually on the move and never stayed long in a place.* ♦ *Canada's New Democrats [are] on the move.* -T/87.
MOVIE [col] 1. filme cinematográfico *Movies have become the most popular form of entertainment in the world.* ♦ *Let's go see a movie.* 2. cinema, sala de espetáculos *Carlos went to a movie last night. He went to see* The Best Years of Our Lives.
movie star/actor/actress ator ou atriz de cinema *Some of my favorite movie stars in the 1950s were Bette Davis, Ingrid Bergman, John Wayne, Alan Ladd, William Holden, Burt Lancaster.*
movie theater/house cinema, sala de exibição *[He] ... entered a movie theater for the first time in his life as a six-year-old in England to see* Snow White. -T/73.

MOVIEGOER [col] freqüentador de cinema *Deborah Kerr's patrician good looks, gentle manners and beautiful English delighted moviegoers in the 1950s and 1960s.*

MOVIES go to the movies ir ao cinema, ir a uma sessão de cinema *In the 1950s I used to go to the movies on Wednesdays, Saturdays and Sundays.* ♦ *Today people go to see a movie; they no longer go to the movies.* -T/67.
the movies cinema (como arte, entretenimento, indústria, negócio, ocupação etc.) *... the movies, the liveliest of all the arts.* -KA,312. ♦ *He worked as a screenwriter in the movies for a few years.*

MOW mow down 1. ceifar *We picture time as carrying a scythe that mows all things down.* -MRMT,4. 2. matar de maneira súbita e violenta; matar em grandes números, dizimar, exterminar *When the soldiers came out of the woods, an enemy machine gun started shooting and mowed them down.* ♦ *In run-of-the-mill westerns, the hero always mows down the bad guys with his six-shooter.* 3. derrubar, prostrar; derrotar fragorosamente *He mowed down all opposition.*

MS. [rima com *his*] título dado a uma mulher, anteposto ao sobrenome ou nome completo e que, ao contrário de *Miss* ou *Mrs.*, não indica seu estado civil *The term Ms. ... devised as a female honorific that, like Mr., does not reveal marital status, is winning wider acceptance ...* -T/72. ♦ *Good morning, Ms. Thaxter.* ♦ *Have you met Ms. Clara Jones?*

MUCH as much tanto, outro tanto, a mesma coisa, o mesmo, a mesma quantidade, exatamente isso (algo que foi dito, que se subentende) *Motivation is as much an effect as a cause of learning.* -AD,430. ♦ *I paid $ 7,500 for the motorcycle and the car cost nearly twice as much.* ♦ *When the Secretary of State was asked whether a cease-fire was soon to be expected, he admitted as much.*

as much again outro tanto *Mrs. Chandler has $3,500. She'll need as much again to clear all her debts.*
as much as 1. tanto quanto *They enjoyed the movie as much as we did.* 2. praticamente, virtualmente *... he had as much as called her a liar ...* -LL,23.
how much quanto *How much did you pay for it?* ♦ *How much money must we give him?*
just so much → **so MUCH** 2 e 3
make much of dar grande importância a, tratar com muita consideração *In his speeches before minority groups he made much of the fact that his parents had been harassed immigrants.*
much as 1. por mais que *Much as I adore your company, there is still business to attend to.* -JJF,228. 2. de maneira bem semelhante, quase como *When I saw her again eighteen years later, she was still much as I'd remembered her.*
not much of a de pouco valor, ruim, ordinário, reles *She's not much of a singer.*
not much to look at sem atrativos, de aparência insignificante *The girl wasn't much to look at.* ♦ *The lake itself ... was nothing much to look at ...* -OC,4.
not to say much for ter pouca consideração por, não dar muito valor a *I can't say much for the singing in the new show, but the dialogue is wonderful.*
so much 1. tanto *I love you so much.* ♦ *She has so much to offer you.* 2. um punhado de, nada mais que, nada além de, não mais que, o equivalente de, unicamente, simplesmente *His new book is just so much nonsense.* ♦ *Larry learned to brush off his worries like so much water.* 3. um tanto, determinada quantidade, determinado limite *... she could be impressed just so much and no more.* -SEB,134.
so much as sequer *[He] ... was captured, and no enemy so much as touched an article of his belongings that first night.* -KM,413.

so much for vamos dar por concluído, vamos colocar um ponto final em, nada mais precisa ser dito ou feito com relação a, chega de, basta [diz-se também de alguém/algo que não tem credibilidade, que não merece respeito] *So much for empty promises. Let's forget her.* ♦ *So much for praising his many exploits. Let's talk about you, now.*

so much so a tal ponto, de tal maneira *Our knowledge of the human body is ever becoming wider and more complex – so much so as often to confuse the lay person ...* -SEE,xvii.

so much the better//worse tanto melhor// pior *If these [Goodwill] games aid the cause of world peace, so much the better.* -T/86. ♦ *If you fail to come at the appointed time, so much the worse for you.*

too much of a muito, por demais, demasiado, descomedido *... some European leaders ... think that he [the President of the U.S.] is too much of an amateur in statecraft.* -T/80.

MUCKRAKE investigar e denunciar corrupção, escândalo etc. real ou pretenso, principalmente na área política *Each time he is a candidate for political office, his enemies muckrake all the old stories.*

MUDDLE muddle through conseguir atingir o objetivo, sair-se bem em um empreendimento etc. apesar de trapalhadas, confusões, falta de planejamento etc. *For the time being, the system will continue to muddle through.* -T/84. ♦ *Although Hutchinson was extremely incompetent, he always managed to muddle through his problems.*

MUM mum's the word bico calado, pede-se silêncio, nem um pio, o silêncio é de ouro *The only common thread in all our beliefs and behaviors [about masturbation] is secrecy. Where masturbation is concerned, mum's the word.* -WCG,68.

MURDER get away with murder [col] escapar impunemente (a leis, regras, convenções etc.) *You and my brother think that you are so clever, that you can get away with murder always, that a woman can do nothing to stop you.* -HJ,41.

murder [col] coisa difícil, desagradável, arriscada etc. *The biology test was murder.*

murder will out um segredo, ato ilícito, crime ou criminoso sempre acaba sendo revelado *The police were unable to solve the mystery but some people said that murder will out.*

MUSCLE flex one's muscles exibir seus músculos, mostrar sua força (em sinal de advertência) *All right. So you've flexed your muscles and I'm impressed.* -CJC,103. ♦ *... we needed to teach these people a few lessons and to flex our muscles a little ...* -T/76.

muscle in [col] entrar à força, impor-se pela força *The Mafia men were trying to muscle in on a Brooklyn restaurant.*

MUSIC face the music [col] sofrer as conseqüências, arcar com a responsabilidade *Papa will make you face the music when he finds out you broke the window.*

set/put to music musicar, converter em gênero musical, pôr em música *Alan Jay Lerner and Frederick Loewe set George Bernard Shaw's play* Pygmalion *to music and as* My Fair Lady *it became one of the great musicals of all time.*

MUST a must [col] algo essencial, obrigatório, coisa indispensável, uma necessidade *... a highly educated and skilled work force is not a luxury but a must.* -T/91. ⇒ **must** essencial, necessário, obrigatório *[A book about the Vietnam war that] ... has become must reading for young officers.* -T/85.

MUSTARD cut the mustard [col] corresponder à expectativa, satisfazer às exigências, atingir a qualidade ou os requisitos necessários *... it is Actor [Jack] Lemmon [in* The Apartment*] ... who really cuts the mustard and carries the show.* -T/60.

MUSTER pass muster ser aceito, ser aprovado, passar, corresponder à expectativa • *That man would never pass muster if I were in charge of this group.*

NAIL (as) hard/tough as nails [col] insensível, impiedoso, implacável, duro; vigoroso, robusto *[Ernest] Hemingway, hard as nails on the outside, but soft as a baby impala on the inside ...* -T/67. ♦ *[Movie star] Randolph Scott was the quintessential cowboy hero: tall, gentlemanly, and tough as nails.* -SS,367.

hit the nail on the head exprimir-se com exatidão, dizer a pura verdade, acertar em cheio *When you said that our trouble was poor business management, you hit the nail on the head.*

nail down [col] 1. prender (alguém) a um compromisso, fazer (alguém) pronunciar-se claramente a respeito de *They couldn't nail him down to a promise to help their project.* 2. especificar com exatidão, fixar, estabelecer inequivocamente, chegar a uma decisão *The investigation committee is trying to nail down the blame on the guilty parties.*

NAME by name de nome *I knew your sister by sight but not by name.*

call (someone) names xingar, injuriar *He kept hitting her and calling her names.*

drop names [col] citar o nome de pessoas importantes ou famosas em uma conversa, dando a idéia de que se é íntimo delas *Samuels has the habit of dropping names as if he knew most of the important people in the country.* ⇒ **name-dropping** o ato de citar o nome de pessoas importantes ou famosas *Emily can't have a conversation without indulging in name-dropping.*

given/first/Christian name nome de batismo, prenome *His given name was Donald and we called him Don.*

go by the name of ser conhecido pelo nome (ou apelido) de, passar por *Sean Aloysius O'Feeney, who went by the name of John Ford, was the distinguished film director who gave us, among many others, masterpieces such as* Stagecoach, The Grapes of Wrath *and* The Searchers.

in the name of em nome de, em lugar de *The decoration of valor medal was received by Mrs. Jones in the name of her hero husband.*

maiden name → **maiden**

make a name for oneself adquirir renome, tornar-se bem conhecido, ficar famoso *You'll make a name for yourself one day.* -GA,10.

name after dar (a uma criança, coisa etc.) o mesmo nome de (outra pessoa, coisa etc.) *Flora was named after her mother.* ♦ *They named him Hector, after a famous hero in Homer's* Iliad.

name brand marca de alta qualidade, artigo ou produto muito conhecido *I only buy famous name brand products.*

name names identificar, citar especificamente os nomes de pessoas (que se está criticando ou elogiando), dar nomes aos bois ... *for the first time someone was naming names.* -TB,22.

the name of the game [col] o ponto crucial, o objetivo principal, a realidade da questão, o aspecto fundamental ... *in education, the scramble for funds is the name of the game.* -T/79. ♦ *Making a profit in any business undertaking is always the name of the game.*

to one's name de seu, que lhe pertença ... *you've got less than two bucks to your name.* -CJC,103.

you name it [col] o que você quiser, o que você disser, pode escolher *Ethnic tensions disturb and divide Sri Lanka, Burma, Indonesia, Iraq, Lebanon ... – you name it.* -T/91.

NAME-DROPPING → drop NAMES

NARROW narrow down reduzir(-se), diminuir, restringir(-se) ... *the choice of numbers had been narrowed down to three or four ...* -HJH,24.

NARROW-MINDED tacanho, preconceituoso, intolerante ... *narrow-minded views ...* -T/87. ♦ *... narrow-minded attitudes ...* -T/91. ♦ *a narrow-minded man*

NATIVE-BORN natural de um país, nativo *He was a native-born American who had lived in Brazil for many years.*

NATURE by nature por natureza, por índole *Rhoda was, by nature, a cold, calculating and unhappy woman.*

good nature bondade, afabilidade, boa índole *We all loved Mrs. Simpson because of her good nature.* ⇒ **good-natured** amistoso, amável, afável *a good-natured person* ♦ *... good-natured chuckles ...* -T/77.

second nature segunda natureza, hábito arraigado *Dancing is second nature to a child in Brazil.*

NEAR near by próximo, por perto ... *Soviet troops [are] on alert near by ...* -T/80.

NECESSITY of necessity necessariamente, inevitavelmente *Our trip to Paris must of necessity be postponed for a month or two.*

NECK break one's neck [col] fazer grande esforço, cansar-se, fadigar-se, matar-se *Jack almost broke his neck to be first in line when the movie star started to give autographs.*

get it in the neck [gir] levar na cabeça, sair perdendo, ser punido *Every time he tries to be kind and stop a quarrel between his neighbors, he gets it in the neck and usually finishes up with a black eye.*

neck and neck emparelhados, lado a lado, empatados, cabeça a cabeça ... *Japanese and American executives are neck and neck.* -T/92. ♦ *... a neck-and-neck race had been expected...* -T/92.

risk one's neck [col] arriscar-se, colocar-se em perigo de vida; arriscar a carreira, a reputação etc. ... *men didn't want to risk their necks without orders.* -GJI,49.

save one's neck [gir] salvar-se, livrar-se de um perigo, livrar a cara *I'm going to give you a chance to save your neck.* -WSM,219.

stick one's neck out [gir] arriscar-se, expor-se ao perigo, à crítica etc. *He has to be a courageous man, not afraid to stick his neck out ...* -MA,4.

up to one's neck → up to one's EARS

win//lose by a neck/nose vencer//perder por pequeníssima margem *He won the election by a neck.* ♦ *... John Major did win Britain's election "by a nose".* -T/92.

NEED if need be se necessário *If need be, the doctor will be ready to come to see your sick father at any hour.*

that's all I needed não me faltava mais nada, era só o que (me) faltava *And now the car won't start! That's all I needed!*

NEEDLE look for a needle in a haystack procurar agulha em palheiro *Looking for* *an honest politician is like looking for a needle in a haystack.*

NERVE **get on someone's nerves** [col] irritar, exasperar ... *some of her relatives are getting on her nerves as the wedding approaches.* -T/81.

get up the nerve = **screw up one's COURAGE** *He never got up the nerve to speak [in defense of the ideal of the law]* ... -FJH,35.

have a nerve [col] ser petulante, atrevido, descarado, cara-de-pau *You have one hell of a nerve, you know that?* -CG,109.

have the nerve to [col] 1. = **have the CRUST to** *Gloria looked at Nick and said: "I don't know how you have the nerve to talk to me!"* 2. ter coragem para, ter peito para *No one had the nerve to tell him the truth.*

hit/strike/touch a (raw) nerve tocar em um assunto delicado, em um ponto sensível, ferir a sensibilidade *[His] ... decision apparently struck a nerve.* -T/66. ♦ *Her silly remark hit a raw nerve.*

lose one's nerve perder a coragem, desanimar *Dan knew he had to jump out of the window before he lost his nerve.*

NERVE-RACKING/WRACKING/SHATTERING torturante, aflitivo, exasperante *Driving the clogged roadways around Los Angeles has always been nerve-racking.* -T/87. ♦ *Being lost in the bushveld [the South African open grassy country] is one of the most nerve-shattering experiences a man can have.* -LAK,29.

NEST **feather one's nest** [col] enriquecer (geralmente de maneira ilícita), aproveitando-se de oportunidades favoráveis *Jenkins is no fool and is quietly feathering his nest while being civil and courteous to everyone.*

nest egg fundo de reservas, economia *The few who accumulated small nest eggs in the U.S. are rapidly depleting them* ... -T/87.

NEVER **never ever** nunca jamais *He uses his full name ... only to sign checks and never ever the first initial H.* -T/92.

NEWFANGLED de invenção recente, de última moda, moderno (mas inaceitável para muitos por complexo e inútil) *When it was invented, people wanted to know to what use the newfangled thing called the automobile could be put.* ♦ *Michael is full of newfangled ideas.*

NEWFOUND; NEW-FOUND recém-encontrado, recém-conseguido *With his new-found Quakerism, [he] found a social conscience* ... -T/60. ♦ *A new-found confidence* ... -T/77.

NEWS **break the news** divulgar notícia (geralmente desagradável ou muito interessante, inesperada) *She was reluctant to break the news to her mother.* ♦ *Once upon a time, newspapers broke the news to the public. Then TV took over that role* ... -T/92.

news conference → **PRESS conference**

NEXT **next to** 1. vizinho a, junto a, pegado a, ao lado de *Who's the lovely girl next to you?* 2. (logo) depois de, em seguida a, subseqüentemente a, em segundo lugar, a seguir *Next to westerns, Carlos likes musical movies best.* 3. quase *What you're asking me to do is next to impossible.*

NEXT-DOOR → **next DOOR**

NICE **nice and** [col] agradavelmente, adequadamente, muito, bem ... *I get up nice and early before the sun and do the little things that need doin' around the house.* -OE,5. ♦ *My wife likes her coffee nice and hot.*

NICK **in the nick of time** na hora H, no momento crítico *The Seventh Cavalry arrived in the nick of time and saved the wagon train from the Indian attack.*

NIGHT **all night long** a noite inteira *They had to work all night long.*

at night à noite, de noite *People normally work during the day and sleep at night.*

a good night's rest/sleep uma boa noite de sono *I haven't had a good night's sleep in weeks.*

in the night na noite, dentro da noite, em algum momento durante a noite ...

you are the evil ones. You came in the night, and started killing us. -LM,196.
♦ The stranger had come like a thief in the night.

last night ontem à noite, a noite passada *Last night I dreamed I had gone back to the old house at Hard Rock where I used to live in as a boy.*

make a night of it [col] fazer uma boa noitada, divertir-se, festejar *They went to a nightclub and made a night of it.*

night shift turno da noite *The night shift at the General Motors plant in Wentzville, Mo. [Missouri]* ... -T/86.

NIGHTSPOT [col] boate *They went to a nightspot called The Red Cave.*

NITTY-GRITTY [gir] aquilo que realmente importa, o essencial, o principal; importante, essencial *Stop beating around the bush and get down to the nitty-gritty.* ♦ *... nitty-gritty details.* -T/81.

NO-ACCOUNT → **of no ACCOUNT**

NO-FRILLS sem complicações, simples, básico, sem enfeites, sem luxo, despido de superfluidades ... *the no-frills atmosphere [at a chain store organization] suits the predominantly blue-collar clientele just fine.* -T/87.

NO-HOLDS-BARRED → **no HOLDS barred**

NOISE noise about/around/abroad divulgar, propalar *Drake didn't want it noised about that he had invested in the new factory in town.*

NONE none the worse//better//wiser etc. de nenhum modo ou nem um pouco pior// melhor//mais ciente ou mais conhecedor etc. *I am none the worse for all the hostility she has shown toward me.* ♦ *Rose has read the instructions for making the sweater, but she's still none the wiser.*

none too nem um pouco, nada *As far as ... [they] were concerned, the action came none too soon.* -T/77.

NO-NONSENSE prático, pragmático, sensato, perspicaz, arguto, judicioso, de espírito lúcido *[He is]* ... *a no-nonsense administrator with an innate sense of justice.* -T/77.
♦ ... *the no-nonsense procedures of military justice* ... -T/87. ♦ ... *a no-nonsense woman* ... -T/86.

NON-U → **U**

NOOK every nook and cranny toda a parte, todos os recantos *[He]* ... *knows every nook and cranny of Broadway* ... -T/66. ♦ *[The fur trappers]* ... *explored every nook and cranny of the West* ... -BR,4.

NOON high noon 1. meio-dia, sol a pino *At high noon, U. S. marshall Will Kane shot it out with the four outlaws who had sworn to kill him.* 2. auge, apogeu ... *the high noon of Anglo dominance* ... -T/91.

NOSE blow one's nose assoar o nariz *He took a clean white handkerchief from his back trouser pocket and blew his nose gently.* -MG,16.

by a nose → **win by a NECK**

count noses → **count HEADS**

cut off one's nose to spite one's face fazer mal a si mesmo ou prejudicar-se por um acesso de raiva, por vingança, por inveja ou por despeito *The beautiful queen who turned into an ugly old witch to get revenge on Snow White is perhaps one of the most extreme instances of cutting off one's nose to spite one's face.*

follow one's nose seguir em linha reta, ir em frente *Follow your nose and you'll find the place easily. It's on this same road.*

keep one's nose clean [gir] não se meter em encrencas, andar na linha *You just keep your nose clean and you'll be all right.* -SJST,26.

keep/have/put one's nose to the grindstone trabalhar muito, trabalhar sem descanso, mourejar *Scott had to keep his nose to the grindstone to pay for his wife's foolish extravagances.*

lead by the nose dominar, ter total controle sobre *The say Ginny leads her husband by the nose.*

look down one's nose at [col] tratar com

superioridade, com desdém *[They] ... looked down their noses at these strangers and their strange customs.* -WC,78.
nose about/around bisbilhotar, xeretar, procurar *If he comes nosing around he won't find anything.*
nose out [col] 1. derrotar por pequena margem, superar *Julia nosed out all the other candidates for the job.* 2. descobrir (algo) por meio de busca meticulosa *Woodward and Bernstein nosed out some serious wrongdoings concerning the Watergate affair.*
on the nose [gir] 1. exato, correto; exatamente, precisamente, corretamente, no alvo *Our guess as to the number of people who would attend the meeting was right on the nose.* 2. pontualmente, na hora certa *At 3:30 A. M. on the nose ...* -QE,121.
pay through the nose pagar preço excessivo, pagar muito caro *... anyone who comes in to your office now must be prepared to pay through the nose.* -TR,20.
pick one's nose pôr o dedo no nariz *[The judge] ... was angered by the journalist picking his nose in court.* -T/77.
(as) plain as the nose on one's face [gir] óbvio, evidente, na cara *The solution is as plain as the nose on your face.*
poke/stick one's nose into [col] intrometer-se em, meter o nariz em *When I poked my nose into someone's affairs, my mother always said: "Mind your own business".* ♦ *Don't stick your nose into things that do not concern you.*
thumb one's nose 1. fazer fiau, levar o polegar ao nariz com os dedos estendidos [gesto grosseiro de menosprezo] *Bobby thumbed his nose at the smaller boy.* 2. mostrar menosprezo, tratar com indiferença *A whole generation thumbed its nose at everything that was held sacred in this country.* -T/81.
turn up one's nose at olhar com desprezo, desdenhar, torcer o nariz a *... consumers are finally starting to turn up their noses at the rising prices of foreign imports.* -T/87.
under one's (very) nose nas barbas de, sob as vistas de (geralmente sem ser percebido) *Came in and took their money from them, right under my nose, eh?* -TRW,52.

NOSEDIVE; NOSE DIVE queda vertical, mergulho, baixa súbita *... the [North Korean] economy had been on a slide since about 1973 and entered a nose dive in the mid-1980s.* -T/92. ⇒ **nose-dive** cair verticalmente ou acentuadamente *[He] ... watched the revenues from his print shop nose-dive 20% last year.* -T/92.

NO-SHOW [col] pessoa que solicita reserva de passagem (em empresa aérea etc.) e não comparece para a viagem, desistente; pessoa que está sendo esperada mas não comparece *There may be a few no-shows and you might get a seat on this flight.* ♦ *[He] ... was a no-show at the [Academy Award] ceremony.* -T/91.

NOTCH take down a notch → **take down a PEG**

NOTE compare notes comparar impressões, trocar idéias, discutir *... 700 members of the American Astronomical Society met in Vancouver to compare notes ...* -T/87.
make (a) note of anotar, registrar, tomar nota de *They made note of how many persons were physically unfit ...* -OH,11. ♦ *Barry made a note of the appointment so that he wouldn't forget it.*
note down anotar *Note the message down while it's still fresh in your mind.*
of note famoso, distinto, de renome, importante *His grandfather was a scientist of note who worked for Du Pont.*
strike a note expressar determinada idéia, impressão, qualidade, caráter etc. *The beautiful rugs in the living room struck a note of rich and satisfying color.*
strike/hit the right note dizer ou fazer a coisa apropriada à ocasião *[The President] ... hit all the right notes [in his*

speech]. -T/74. ♦ *Mr. Weatherby struck the right note when he suggested another date for the meeting.*
take note of observar, notar, reparar *Did you take note of the clever manner that the speaker used to gain the attention of his audience?*
NOTHING come to nothing dar em nada, não dar resultado algum *The hopes roused in him seemed likely now to come to nothing.* -CT,15.
for nothing 1. de graça *He got that beautiful book for nothing.* 2. inutilmente, em vão *You have done all that for nothing.* 3. sem motivo, sem uma boa razão, à toa *Orcas are not known as killer whales for nothing.*
in nothing flat [col] imediatamente, em um instante, em tempo recorde *We ... hope to get from nowhere to nowhere in nothing flat.* -BN,131.
make nothing of 1. não compreender *I can make nothing of his handwriting.* 2. não dar importância a, não fazer caso de, ter em pouca conta *Benny made nothing of the fact that he had been injured.*
next to nothing quase nada, muito pouco *... if an actor is offered a really good part, he'll do it for next to nothing.* T/87.
nothing but nada além (de), nada senão, apenas (isso) *He swore to tell the truth and nothing but.*
nothing doing [col] não, nada feito, impossível *When I tried to borrow his car he said: "Nothing doing".*
nothing less than completamente, inteiramente, nada menos que *Walter Huston's performance in The Treasure of the Sierra Madre was nothing less than extraordinary.*
nothing much quase nada, pouca coisa *... nothing much could happen unless the army took the lead ...* -GJI,47.
nothing short of nada menos que, somente algo como *Nothing short of an act of God will stop Hooper from continuing in his climb to the top of the company.*
nothing//something to write home about [col] sem importância, nada a comemorar, insignificante, medíocre, pouco interessante, nada de especial//excelente, importante, notável, admirável *His performance in that play was nothing to write home about.* ♦ *The parties that Jay Gatsby used to give at his Long Island mansion were something to write home about.*
stick/stop at nothing não ter escrúpulos (para conseguir algo), não se deter por nada *Julie sticks at nothing to get what she wants.* ♦ *You think I would stop at nothing where money is concerned.* -FC,13.
sweet nothings palavras açucaradas, juras de amor *Wade was whispering sweet nothings to his girlfriend.*
there's nothing to it é muito fácil, muito simples, não tem segredo *I can't understand why his wife makes such a fuss about housekeeping. There's nothing to it.*
NOTICE at/on short notice em pouco tempo, em prazo bem curto (após ter recebido aviso, comunicação, notificação, solicitação, ordem etc.) *That encounter ... was organized on short notice.* -T/80.
give notice dar aviso prévio *I'm expected to give two week's notice so I can be replaced.* -CT,16. ♦ *Some ... staff members have been given notice by telephone.* -T/87.
on notice de sobreaviso, prevenido, notificado *... that's private property you're dealing with ... I'm puttin' you on notice.* -BFW,32.
serve notice dar aviso, informar, participar *Nowadays [Marlon] Brando serves notice on producers and directors that he will work no longer than three weeks on a film.* -T/76.
sit up and take notice [col] ficar atento, alerta, prestar total atenção (devido ao inusitado de uma situação) *What he said really made me sit up and take notice.*
take notice//no notice of dar atenção, observar, reparar em, notar//não dar atenção

a, desconsiderar *I sat in the corner of the room and no one took notice of me.* ♦ *She took no notice of his arrival.*
until further notice até segunda ordem *This nightclub is closed until further notice.*
NOTION not have the faintest notion → **not have the faintest IDEA**
NOW as of now a partir de agora, deste momento em diante *You're fired as of now.* ♦ *The new plan of action is in operation as of now.*
by now a esta hora, a esta altura, neste momento ... *the clash of races is one of the great themes of 20ᵗʰ century fiction. Almost too familiar by now* ... -T/60.
from now on doravante, de agora em diante *From now on you must always lock the door when you leave.*
just now 1. agora, neste momento *Stephanie isn't at home just now.* 2. há pouco, há um instante *Mr. Shaw was here just now.*
now and again = NOW and then *I enjoy going to Hard Rock now and again to see old friends.*
(every) now and then uma vez ou outra, de vez em quando *Brad likes to go fishing with his father now and then.*
NOWHERE nowhere near 1. nada perto; distante, longe, afastado (no espaço ou no tempo) *The end of our task is nowhere near in sight.* 2. de maneira alguma, nem um pouco, nada *The official unemployment rate is nowhere near as severe as it was at the depth of the 1981-82 recession* ... -T/92.
out of nowhere (que acontece ou aparece) subitamente, como do nada *[They]* ... *appeared out of nowhere* ... -T/92.
NUDE in the nude nu, despido *She has appeared in the nude in some of her latest movies.*
NUKE [gir] qualquer arma nuclear *The demonstrators marched through the streets carrying placards and banners that read "No nukes".*
NUMBER a number of certo número de,

uma série de, diversos ... *he has been outspokenly critical of the Administration on a number of foreign policy questions.* -T/79.
any number of [col] grande quantidade de, muitos ... *there would be any number of restaurants where we could stop on our way.* -HEM,118. ♦ ... *the [kidnapping] case proved to have any number of sensational aspects.* -T/75.
back number 1. número atrasado de um periódico *Fay was searching for a story in a back number of* Time Magazine. 2. [col] pessoa ou coisa antiquada, bananeira que já deu cacho *She's an old maid but she doesn't like to be called a back number.*
get/have someone's number [gir] conhecer bem uma pessoa, descobrir seu verdadeiro caráter, intenções etc. *We've got your number* ... *we've got you under surveillance twenty-four hours a day.* -HJC,396.
have someone's number on it [gir] ter o nome (da pessoa que vai morrer) marcado (em uma bala ou qualquer outro agente que causa a morte) como se fosse pelo destino *I ignored the flashes of lightning all around me. They either had your number on them or they didn't.* -SJD,89.
in round numbers/figures em números redondos *There are about 250 million people in round numbers in the U.S.* ♦ *In round figures, he owes them $10,000.*
number among incluir, considerar como, contar como parte de, estar entre *[He]* ... *will be numbered among a handful of patients* ... *who have undergone at least a partly successful full-knee transplant.* -T/87.
number one [col] 1. a própria pessoa, si mesmo *Luke is the kind of person who thinks of number one first.* 2. a pessoa mais importante, influente etc. *When Sarah met Mike she really thought she had found number one.* ♦ 3. principal, número um, mais importante *Drugs are our number one problem today.*

one's//someone's number is up; one's//someone's number has come up [gir] alguém vai sofrer, será castigado, está perdido, vai morrer, sua hora chegou etc. *When the man came toward Nick with a gun in his hand, Nick thought his number was up.* ♦ *My life wasn't any more important than theirs [the life of other soldiers who had died in battle] and my number would no doubt come up, sooner or later, just as theirs had.* -CRST,94.

without number sem conta, em grande número *There are stars without number in the sky.*

NURSERY nursery school escola maternal *Before children enter regular first grade, they often attend a nursery school where they learn a little organization.*

NUT hard/tough nut to crack osso duro de roer, coisa dificílima de fazer, resolver, entender, superar etc. *The case of the twin brunettes was a tough nut to crack for the police.*

NUTS [gir] maluco, doido *... there's nothing I can do except be happy for you even if I still think you're nuts.* -SLS,231.

nuts about → **CRAZY about**

nuts and bolts os detalhes práticos (do funcionamento de uma máquina, empreendimento etc.), os elementos essenciais, o ABC *Harry spent a few months working in the construction industry and learned the nuts and bolts of building.*

off one's nut → **off one's HEAD**

NUTSHELL in a nutshell em síntese, em poucas palavras *Let me tell you, in a nutshell, what happened last night.*

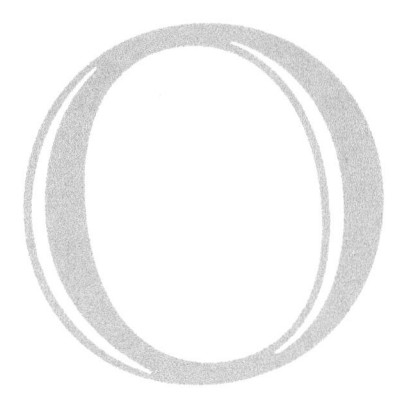

OAR **put one's oar in(to)** intrometer-se, interferir, meter a colher em *It seemed to him time to put his oar in ...* -DD,58. ♦ *Eric puts his oar into everyone's business.*
rest on one's oars cessar as atividades, tornar-se inativo, descansar, ficar inerte *[Western civilization] ... has maintained a high level of creative activity over a longer period of time than have previous societies, which rested on their oars after bursts of great achievement.* -MHJ,348.
OAT **feel one's oats** [gir] estar cheio de energia e vigor, sentir-se alegre e exuberante; sentir-se importante *Victor and Paul were feeling their oats and were playing tricks on the new boy at school.* ♦ *Jones seems to be feeling his oats this morning the way he's ordering the other employees around.*
sow (one's) wild oats cometer os excessos da mocidade; entregar-se à vida dissoluta e promíscua na juventude *I don't say that a man shouldn't sow a few wild oats now and then, but he has to keep it on the Q.T.* -LRT,75.
OCCASION **equal to the occasion** à altura da situação, capaz de enfrentar algo *No matter what happens, Owen is always equal to the occasion.*

have occasion ter motivo, razão, necessidade (de/para) *We've had very little occasion for punishments. Timothy is a good boy.* -SW,11. ♦ *We've had no further occasion for Conrad's services.*
on/upon occasion de vez em quando, de tempos a tempos *We still see each other on occasion.*
rise to the occasion mostrar-se à altura daquilo que a situação exige, saber lidar eficientemente com (problema, emergência etc.) *When the guest speaker failed to arrive, Mr. Smith rose to the occasion and gave a wonderful talk about helping our friends.*
take occasion aproveitar o ensejo, servir-se da oportunidade *I took occasion at dinner to tell my family that I had gotten a raise in salary.*
OCEANGOING; OCEAN-GOING; SEAGOING (navio) construído para navegar no mar *The Amazon River itself is navigable for ocean-going steamers up to some 2,300 miles from its mouth ...* -WC,55. ♦ *a seagoing schooner*
ODDS **at odds** em desacordo, em desavença, às turras *... he was at constant odds with colleagues ...* -T/87. ♦ *... Stalin and Churchill were bitterly at odds about who would rule Poland.* -T/85.

by all odds inquestionavelmente, sem dúvida *By all odds, George Orwell is the most unlikely culture hero to emerge in the '60s.* -T/68.

odds and ends sobras, restos, fragmentos, retalhos, miudezas, bugigangas, miscelânea *Snatches of stories he had heard crowded into his mind; fragments of ... songs, the tale of a pilgrim ... disconnected odds and ends of truth and legend, of fact and fancy.* -WL,27.

the odds are provavelmente, de acordo com as possibilidades *The odds are you'll never see her again.*

the odds are against as probabilidades são contrárias *... [Captain James T.] Kirk is an unusually good commander and the odds are against getting a better replacement.* -WS,228.

OFF 1. desligado, desconectado, desativado *The motor is off.* ♦ *The electricity is off.* 2. afastado (de), longe (de) (no espaço ou no tempo) *The village is six miles off.* ♦ *Sally's birthday is still two months off.* 3. não mais em contato (com), separado (de), fora (de), removido (de) *John's hat was off (his head).* 4. cancelado, encerrado, desfeito, não mais em vigor, sem efeito *The deal is off.* 5. a caminho, de partida, partindo, indo *Jackie is off to Denver in a couple of hours.* ♦ *[She] ... is off to a good start ... in her new career as a model.* -T/85. 6. de folga, de licença *Take the afternoon off.* ♦ *Smith has taken two days off.* 7. ao largo de, nas proximidades de *Kent lives on a small island off the coast of Florida.* 8. enganado, equivocado *Johnson was off in his calculations.* 9. excêntrico, doido, maluco *I think that guy's a little off, but not dangerous.* 10. estragado, deteriorado *This meat is a little off.* 11. [col] abstendo-se de, não mais usando *For the first time in years, she is off pills and getting a good night's rest.* -T/79.

off and on; on and off de quando em quando, a intervalos irregulares *Mary has had a pain in her breast off and on for the last two years.* ♦ *... it had been snowing on and off for a month ...* -EMW,1. ♦ *A light flashing on and off ...* -CN,29.

OFFBEAT [col] incomum, diferente, não-convencional *High Noon is an offbeat western about a U.S. marshall who has to face four revengeful outlaws singlehandedly.*

OFF-BROADWAY relativo a ou característico de teatros localizados fora da área da Broadway que encenam peças de caráter experimental e de baixo custo de produção *Off-Broadway theaters are located outside the famous main theatrical district of New York in buildings that were once used as stores, garages, offices and the like.* ♦ *[The play* Out! *is] ... an off-Broadway joy.* -T/86.

OFF-COLOR inconveniente, impróprio, indecente, de conotação sexual *... she ... used off-color language ...* -BC,133. ♦ *off-color jokes*

OFF-DUTY → **off DUTY**

OFFENSE take offense ofender-se, melindrar-se *Jesse made no comment. Billy had done nothing to which he could take offense ...* -CEB,39.

OFFHAND 1. de improviso, sem prévia reflexão ou preparo, de imediato *Offhand I would say that most people are in favor of democratic elections.* 2. [também **offhanded**] incerimonioso, brusco, seco, descuidado, indiferente, negligente, irresponsável *Joe treated her in an offhand manner.* 3. [também **offhanded**] impensado, extemporâneo, não-premeditado *Carl made an offhand statement and regretted it.*

OFFICE come into office = **take OFFICE** *He is widely blamed for many of the troubles that have beset the U.S. since he came into office.* -T/80.

in office empossado, no exercício do cargo, no poder *The mayor resigned after seven months in office.*

the Oval Office 1. o gabinete do Presidente dos EUA ... *the President of the U.S. will address the nation on radio and television from his Oval Office.* -T/74. 2. a sede do poder executivo dos EUA *Carter is in several ways the least experienced modern President in world affairs to occupy the Oval Office.* -T/77.
public office cargo público ... *competing candidates for public office* ... -T/87.
take office tomar posse, assumir cargo *Franklin Delano Roosevelt first took office in 1933.*

OFFING in the offing em futuro próximo, não muito distante ... *there is perhaps no happy future in the offing for this girl* ... -WF,35.

OFF-KEY 1. desafinado, desafinadamente *Some of the boys in the choir were singing off-key.* 2. irregular, inadequado, impróprio *Some of Marcia's comments sounded off-key.*

OFF-LIMITS; OFF LIMITS fora dos limites prescritos, interditado (local, área, assunto etc.) *Most of the more interesting places in Paris were off-limits to the American soldiers during the war.* ♦ *... there was a sort of gentleman's agreement that certain matters were off limits.* -T/87.

OFF-OFF-BROADWAY relativo a ou característico de movimento de vanguarda do teatro americano que dá ênfase à utilização de métodos inovadores e radicais. Suas peças são representadas em locais não-convencionais como pequenos salões, igrejas etc. [Che!, *a play*] ... *opened off-off-Broadway last March* ... -T/69. ♦ ... *an off-off-Broadway company lodged in a 16th-floor penthouse apartment on Manhattan's Upper West Side.* -T/80.

OFFSCREEN fora da tela, na vida real *Dan Duryea often played bad guy roles in movies but offscreen he was a likable family man.*

OFF-THE-CUFF → **off the CUFF**
OFF-THE-RECORD → **off the RECORD**
OFF-THE-SHELF → **off the SHELF**
OFF-THE-WALL → **off the WALL**

OFTEN all too often muito freqüentemente *Is racism so pervasive among police that the fight against crime all too often becomes a war on blacks?* -T/91.
as often as not → **OFTEN as not**
every so often de vez em quando *She drops in for a chat every so often.*
more often than not as mais das vezes *In real life when we come into conflict with our environment we complain but more often than not do nothing about it.* -MR,20.
(as) often as not metade das vezes, freqüentemente *As often as not Jean is home from work before seven.* ♦ *Often as not, the frontiersman was an antisocial misfit who helped create a climate of barbaric lawlessness.* -T/68.

OIL burn the midnight oil queimar as pestanas, estudar ou trabalhar até altas horas *Before the final tests all the students burned the midnight oil.*
pour oil on troubled waters apaziguar os ânimos, pôr água na fervura *There was much agitation among the Republicans but the President's speech poured oil on troubled waters.*

OLD of old de antigamente, de outrora *In days of old, when knights were bold, the peasant had a very difficult life.*

OLD-FASHIONED antiquado, fora de moda, obsoleto ... *he's an old-fashioned satirist.* -T/76.

OLD-TIMER pessoa velha, ancião, veterano *The old-timers had many stories to tell.*

OLIVE olive branch ramo de oliveira, oferta de paz, gesto de conciliação *In 1977 Egypt's President Anwar Sadat went to Jerusalem holding out the olive branch.*

ON be on to/onto [gir] estar ciente de, ter conhecimento de, ser conhecedor de, saber o que se passa *We are onto his tricks.* ♦ *[They] ... suspected that Helms was on to something.* -T/87.

on and off → OFF and on
on and on ininterruptamente, sem cessar *His speech went on and on as though it would never end.* ♦ *On and on he [Hitler] raged at the "clique of Prussian generals" who had tried to kill him ...* -CL,28.
ON-AGAIN, OFF-AGAIN ora sim, ora não; que pára e recomeça, que vai e vem *His on-again, off-again affair with a Gentile show girl ...* -T/85. ♦ *... on-again, off-again statements.* -T/73.
ON-CAMERA diante de uma câmera de televisão que está transmitindo ao vivo *... when she is on-camera, she holds the show in shape.* -T/60.
ONCE all at once 1. ao mesmo tempo, simultaneamente *He looked angry, yet satisfied and triumphant all at once.* -LM,203. 2. de repente, inesperadamente *All at once she started to shout.*
at once 1. imediatamente, de uma vez *When Pat looked at the suspect in the police lineup, she recognized at once the man that had attacked her.* 2. simultaneamente, ao mesmo tempo *The twin babies began to cry at once.*
for once pelo menos uma vez, por esta vez *My eyes were on Ragnar, and for once I saw him taken aback.* -MET,25.
once and for all de uma vez por todas *They used all their military might to crush the rebels once and for all.*
ONCE-OVER [col] espiada, olhada, lance d'olhos *[The neighbors] ... gave her a good once-over and they think she's going to have a baby.* -GES,143.
ONE at one da mesma opinião, de acordo, em harmonia *The doctors present were at one as to the method of controlling the spread of the epidemic.*
be one for/to ser de, ser dado a, ter propensão para *... [General Douglas] MacArthur [was not] one for personal revelations.* -T/64. ♦ *... he has never been one to press his luck too far.* -T/87.
for one quanto a (mim, você, ele, alguém etc.), por exemplo *I, for one, shall certainly cast my vote for the Democratic candidate.* -T/66.
one and all todos *Stewart was known to one and all as an able lawyer.*
(the) one and only o único *... you have the task of convincing the prospective employer that you are the one and only for the job.* -MNH,118.
one and the same o mesmo *... the Ultimate Reality [God] and the individual soul (atman) [in Hinduism], though seemingly apart, are, in actuality, one and the same substance.* -RN,20.
one by one um a um *One by one, the prisoners were brought before the general and were carefully questioned.*
one another = EACH other *... grammar-book writers often fail to agree with one another.* -MJL,24.
one up on [col] com uma vantagem sobre *[Her friend] ... was now cleverly one up on her.* -EJ,319. v. **one-up**
ONE-HORSE [col] de pouca importância, pequeno, de dimensões e recursos limitados *The first picture he [John Wayne] made for Monogram literally took place in a one-horse town ...* -T/69.
ONE-NIGHT STAND → **one-night STAND**
ONESELF be oneself 1. estar em seu estado normal de corpo e mente, estar são, saudável *What's the matter with you? You're not yourself this morning.* 2. ser natural, agir naturalmente, portar-se sem afetação *Don't try to imitate anyone. Just be yourself and everyone will like you better.*
(all) by oneself 1. só, sozinho, desacompanhado, isolado *Are you all by yourself? Nobody else with you?* -DP,21. 2. sem ajuda *He did it all by himself.*
ONE-SHOT [gir] que só acontece ou só é feito uma única vez; único, exclusivo, de cuja espécie não existe outro *... much of the 1987 reduction was due to one-shot ef-*

fects of the tax-reform law. -T/87. ♦ *... a one-shot deal ...* -T/87.

ONETIME; ONE-TIME antigo, ex-, de outrora, que já não é mais, que já não está em exercício ... *a onetime White House aid ...* -T/72. ♦ *one-time associates*

ONE-TRACK → **one-track MIND**

ONE-UP [col] ganhar ou ter uma vantagem sobre *He always tries to one-up his competitors.* v. **ONE up**

ONE-UPMANSHIP [col] a arte de manter-se à frente de outras pessoas; posição de liderança, supremacia *The game of nuclear one-upmanship is the outward manifestation of their [the U.S. and the U.S.S.R.] essentially political conflict.* -T/86. ♦ *She wants to make her daydreams of status and one-upmanship come true.*

ONE-WAY 1. de um só sentido, de mão única (rua) *Boston is the worst city in the U.S. for one-way streets.* 2. de ida, sem retorno (bilhete) *He bought a one-way ticket to Tomahawk Gap.*

ONION know one's onions [gir] = **know one's STUFF** *Hayden knows his onions and should succeed in his new business venture.*

ONLY only too muito, demais ... *as the astronomer knows only too well, repeated observations must be accepted as tantamount to proof.* -JM,13.

ON-SCREEN na tela, nos filmes, na televisão *On-screen, John Wayne was a blunt talker and straight shooter.* -T/87.

ON-THE-JOB → **on the job** 1

OPEN bring/drag (out) in(to) the open tornar público, dar a conhecer, revelar *[Psychoanalysis] ... brought sex out into the open ...* -DDT,482. ♦ *At the trial, all the facts were dragged out into the open.*
come out in the open revelar as intenções, vir a público, revelar-se, tornar-se patente *The depth and bitterness of [their rivalry] ... came out in the open in 1974 ...* -T/81.
(out) in the open às claras, em público *... the secret was out in the open and ac-* *cepted as a normal thing ...* -LRT,37. ♦ *... the program has been carried out in the open for everyone to see.* -PV,201.
open and aboveboard → **aboveboard**
open onto dar (acesso) a, ter abertura ou passagem para *The living room, exquisitely decorated, opened onto a small terrace full of beautiful, exotic plants.*
open up 1. abrir, desdobrar, expandir, desenvolver, tornar disponível, viável, acessível, oferecer; tornar-se disponível, oferecer-se, surgir *Space research has opened up many new fields in space biology and communications.* 2. expor à vista, mostrar, revelar *The Watergate trial opened up new evidence of corruption in the Nixon government.* 3.[col] tornar-se comunicativo, falar livremente, abrir-se *Never before had he spoken of himself, never opened up at all ...* -GA,11. 4. [col] começar a atirar, abrir fogo *[They] ... suddenly opened up with their guns.* -TB,12. 5. [col] aumentar a velocidade (de), acelerar, pisar na tábua *Frank opened up the Buick on the straight stretch of road and did about a hundred miles an hour for a time.*

OPEN-AND-SHUT simples, óbvio, sem dificuldade *It appeared to be a rare open-and-shut case, one of the few New York City homicides that result in a conviction and a long jail sentence.* -T/81.

OPEN-ENDED sem limites, restrições ou regras fixas, amplo, aberto, que permite modificações *I like to think of our "open-ended potential"...* -PJ,12. ♦ *... another open-ended international crisis ...* -T/91.

OPEN-HANDED; OPENHANDED generoso, mão-aberta, liberal, pródigo *... Russia cannot be openhanded toward East Germany without causing serious damages to its own economy.* -T/62.

OPEN-MINDED → **have an open MIND**

OPENER for openers [col] como primeiro passo, em primeiro lugar, primeiramente, para início de conversa, como preâmbulo *For openers, the chance that ... [his] en-*

emies can form a united front seems remote. -T/92.

ORDER bring/call to order chamar à ordem, impor silêncio para dar início a uma sessão, reunião etc .... *the chairman ... brought the meeting to order.* -T/60. ♦ *... Robert Kennedy ... climbed up on a chair to call the meeting to order.* -SJ,41.

in order//out of order 1. ordenado, organizado//desordenado, desorganizado *Cynthia's room is always in order.* ♦ *Her files were out of order and we were unable to find the information we were looking for.* 2. em bom estado, funcionando perfeitamente, em boas condições//desarranjado, enguiçado *Paul has checked his car and everything is in order.* ♦ *Our telephone is out of order.* 3. apropriado à ocasião, oportuno, propício, correto//inapropriado, inoportuno, incorreto, impróprio *It seems to me that a little Christian charity is in order here ...* -T/63. ♦ *A word of gratitude is in order here to Sebastian, Florinda and Mary for all their generous help.* ♦ *... it was out of order to make personal attacks on another chief of state ...* -T/60.

in order that para que, a fim de que *I must take the 7:45 train in order that I may arrive in Boston before noon.*

in order to a fim de, para *We have modified our environment so radically that we must now modify ourselves in order to exist in this new environment.* -WN,46.

in short order bem depressa, rapidamente *... marijuana is a gateway to harder drugs, the stuff like cocaine and heroin that can destroy people in very short order.* -T/87.

large/tall order [col] tarefa difícil *You want to fight the organization alone? That's a large order!* ♦ *[She] ... is used to filling tall orders ...* -T/86.

make to order fazer sob encomenda *Webb had his suits and shirts made to order.* ⇒ **made-to-order** feito sob encomenda *made-to-order shoes*

on the order of do tipo de, semelhante a; mais ou menos, aproximadamente *... a suspended swimming pool requiring "heavy construction on the order of the Maginot Line".* -T/87.

order about/around dar ordens arbitrariamente, bancar o mandão *He didn't like being ordered around, not even by three armed men.* -LN,8.

pecking order classificação social segundo ordem de agressividade, auto-importância etc., ordem das bicadas *Scientists now know that different organisms use pheromones to gather food, send out sexual cues, mark territory, maintain social pecking orders, sound alarms.* -T/79.

take orders 1. obedecer ordens *When the Nazi war criminals were brought to trial, they usually denied the charges saying that they had taken orders.* 2. aceitar encomendas, trabalhar sob encomenda *Turner takes orders for shaving equipment and collects the money when he delivers the material.*

tall order → **large ORDER**

ORDINARY out of the ordinary incomum, extraordinário, excepcional *Your request is a bit out of the ordinary but we will try to do as you ask.*

OTHER every other um sim outro não *They selected every other soldier as 'a hostage.*

other than 1. à exceção de, a não ser, exceto *They were given no choice other than work or go hungry.* 2. diferente, que não seja *People want their telephones to do something other than place calls and receive calls.* -T/87.

OTHER-DIRECTED que se pauta por valores e influências externas, conformista *[The sociologists David Riesman, Nathan Glazer and Revel Denney believe] ... the 20th century American ... to be "other-directed", seeking to get ahead by working within a "group" and attuning himself to the needs of others.* -HH,405. v. **INNER-directed**

OUT 1. fora, ausente (de casa, do escritório etc.) *Mr. Kendrick is out and we don't know when he will be back.* 2. publicado, em circulação *His second book ... will be out next week ...* -T/60. 3. fora de cogitação *That's out. I wouldn't accept the job under such conditions.* 4. incorreto, inexato *He was out in his calculations.* 5. [col] inconsciente, desacordado, adormecido *He was hit on the head and was out for a couple of minutes.* 6. apagado (fogo, cigarro etc.); desligada (luz) *The fire is out.* ♦ *By 10 o'clock p.m. all lights were out.* 7. [col] fora de moda *Long skirts are out again.* 8. descoberto, revelado, conhecido *Her secret was out and she was desperate.* 9. terminado *I'd like to get the tractor out of the damned mud before the day's out.* -SM,10. 10. [col] com prejuízo financeiro *We were out five hundred dollars when the rain ruined our picnic.* 11. fora do poder, fora do cargo, na oposição *The Communists are out.* 12. fora da estação, fora da época *Strawberries are out now.* 13. à vista, visível *There's a beautiful moon out tonight.*

on the outs [col] em desavença, às turras *... he and his sister were generally on the outs ...* -BS,32.

out and away = **by FAR** *Pelé was out and away the best soccer player in the world.*

out cold sem sentidos, desacordado *Something hit me back of my right ear. ... I was out cold, for a time at least.* -HRA,39. ♦ *He was knocked out cold in the second round.*

out for/to em busca de, à procura de, fazendo um esforço resoluto para (conseguir algo) *He was out for profit.* ♦ *She was just out for a good time.* ♦ *[He] ... is out to stop Soviet expansionism.* -T/81.

out from under → **GET out from under**

out loud alto, em voz alta *I'd had a strong desire for her, it had been in my thoughts often enough, but I had never said it out loud.* ♦ *He grinned and then laughed out loud.* -SRS,106.

out of 1. sem, desprovido de *Boyd was driving along a dark road on a lonely, rainy night and suddenly found he was out of gas.* ♦ *He's out of work.* 2. de, com (determinado material, artigo, substância etc.) *Julia's dress was made out of silk.* ♦ *They say you cannot get blood out of a stone.* 3. por (causa, motivo de) *Sometimes she weeps out of frustration.* 4. originário de, nascido de, saído de, tirado de, proveniente de *... persecution arising out of religious intolerance.* -HRW,10. ♦ *The mindless violence after the soccer match seemed straight out of a Sam Peckinpah movie.* 5. em, sediado em, que tem como base (determinado local) *... a wisecracking American-born British subject operating out of Alexandria, Va. ...* -T/87. ♦ *[He] ... and his secretary worked out of a small office ...* -LA,118. 6. a certa distância de *[They] ... once worked on one of North Carolina's grand plantations, Somerset, just ouf of Creswell on Phelps Lake.* -T/86. 7. dentre (um grupo etc.) *Of the women polled, seven out of ten voiced strong objections to the plan.*

out of it 1. fora de lugar, deslocado, isolado, perdido, de fora, sem participar de nenhum grupo *... the young man seemed hopelessly out of it ...* -T/86. 2. aturdido, atordoado, desorientado, desatento *He was completely out of it, completely withdrawn.* HA,299.

out there lá fora, a distância, acolá, em outro lugar que não aquele onde se está, fora de nossa esfera de contato etc. *If there is enough matter out there in space, gravity will slow and then finally reverse the expansion of the universe ...* -T/92. ♦ *People are realizing there's a major business opportunity out there [i.e., among the Spanish-speaking American communities].* -T/87. ♦ *What we see is a product of what we believe to be "out*

there". We see things not as they are, but as we are. -PN,97. ♦ ... there is another path to objectivity, that is, in the sense of greater perspicuity, of greater accuracy of perception of the reality out there outside ourselves, outside the observer. -MA,17.
out to → OUT for
OUT-AND-OUT completo, total, absoluto *Mr. Russell is an out-and-out skeptic.* ♦ *It can be persuasively argued that the [Viet Nam] war was an out-and-out mistake ...* -T/79.
OUTDOORS fora de casa, ao ar livre *The boys went outdoors when it stopped raining.*
the (great) outdoors o campo, regiões desabitadas longe das cidades, os grandes espaços abertos *... he wanted to ... live in the great big outdoors.* -GE,116.
OUTGOING 1. que está saindo, partindo; demissionário *The outgoing mayor left a huge debt for his successor to overcome.* 2. extrovertido, amistoso, sociável *The outgoing ways of the crown prince are better known than those of the King.*
OUT-OF-DATE → **out of DATE**
OUTSIDE at the outside no máximo *The builders estimate that, at the outside, my house will cost $75,000 without any landscaping.*
outside of [col] com exceção de, além de *Outside of Fran, none of the other girls was aware of what was going on.*
OVATION standing ovation ato de (uma platéia) aplaudir de pé (artista, espetáculo, discurso, personalidade etc.) com grande entusiasmo, aplausos calorosos *When Judy [Garland] strode onstage [at Carnegie Hall] she got a standing ovation that lasted almost five minutes.* -T/61. ♦ *Richard Burton's performance as Hamlet was greeted with a standing ovation.*
OVER 1. para o outro lado (de), a determinado lugar, além, à distância, ao longe *Somewhere, over the rainbow, there is an enchanted land.* ♦ *Jane went over to her friend's house.* 2. no decorrer de, enquanto se está ocupado com *They talked a lot over the weekend.* ♦ *Why don't we discuss this over lunch?* 3. terminado, acabado *The party is over.* ♦ *He loved her once but that's over.* 4. por causa de, a respeito de *Smith and Wilkins quarreled over politics* 5. outra vez, de novo, repetidamente *Do this exercise over.* ♦ *She played the record many times over.* 6. através (de uma região), por (determinado lugar) *Highwaymen had held up stagecoaches all over the early West ...* -HJ,1. 7. por um período, durante *... events which have taken place over long periods of years ...* -KAC,6. 8. através de, por (meio de comunicação) *I spoke to Mr. Clayton over the telephone last night.* ♦ *I've just heard the news over the radio.* 9. de uma beira, da beira de *Hank fell over the edge (of the cliff).*
all over 1. terminado, encerrado, acabado *Their romance was all over but he wouldn't admit it.* 2. por toda a parte, de ponta a ponta, de alto a baixo, completamente *Where have you been? We've been looking all over for you.* ♦ *Her words made me feel better all over.* 3. [col] sob todos os aspectos, essencialmente, característicamente, tipicamente, tal qual (alguém) é *She's always late, always in a hurry. That's Martha all over.*
(all) over again outra vez, novamente, mais uma vez *Those soldiers had better start learning discipline all over again.*
over against em contraste com, comparado com *The emergence of the rebel impulse that allows the adolescent to begin to define the self over against the authority of parents and society ... depends on the way rebellion is accepted.* -KS,75.
over and above além de *Over and above the cost of the new car are the registration and tax costs.*
over and over (again) repetidas vezes, outra e outra vez *The same mistakes, over*

and over. -BS,99. ♦ *... when he began to talk, he repeated the same sound or word over and over again.* -T/87.

over here//there aqui, cá//ali, lá *Hey, Nan, come over here!* ♦ *Put that chair over there by the window.*

over (and done) with → **GET (something/it) over (with)**

OVERAGE além do limite de idade *Since John was twenty-eight and overage for active service, he was rejected by the Army.*

OVERALL total, geral, global *An overall plan for the expansion of the school would be very helpful.*

OVERKILL a capacidade de destruir, por meio do emprego de armas nucleares, mais do que o número necessário de inimigos; volume ou quantidade (de algo) em excesso, mais do que é necessário ou suficiente *We should stop production of nuclear weapons. We have sufficient overkill now.* -T/62.

OVERSTAFFED com excesso de funcionários *The new manager thinks our office is overstaffed.*

OVER-THE-COUNTER → **over the COUNTER**

OWE owe it to oneself dever (algo) a si mesmo (por merecido) *Every American owes it to himself to read* Main Street *once.* -SV,51. ♦ *... I owe it to myself to enjoy myself.* -T/87.

OWING owing to por causa de, devido a *... the enthusiastic acceptance of the sexual theories of Freud was owing to a pseudo-scientific popularization that distorted his original concepts ...* -HRW,331.

OWN all one's own característico, próprio, todo seu *[Emily Dickinson's poetry] ... at its best has a quality all its own.* -HL,124. ♦ *[He] ... created an eccentric world all his own ...* -T/69.

for one's own para si, para ser de sua propriedade *Bobby would like to have that puppy for his own.*

of one's own seu, próprio, de sua propriedade *I want to settle down ... I want a home of our own.* -FP,74.

on one's own sozinho, independentemente, sem ajuda, por conta própria *[They] ... were simply left on their own, to fight on as best they could.* -T/89. ♦ *From now on you're on your own.*

own up [col] confessar, admitir *If the boys had owned up to the crime they might have escaped some of the punishment.* -SJE,68.

P mind/watch one's p's and q's agir com muita cautela, ter muito cuidado com o que diz ou faz, comportar-se, ser educado *You must always mind your p's and q's if you want to succeed socially.*

PACE keep pace acompanhar o ritmo, o passo, o andamento, o progresso ... *the process of reform cannot keep pace with public demands for more democracy.* -T/87.

put someone/something through his/its paces pôr à prova as habilidades de, fazer demonstrar capacidade, qualidades, conhecimento etc. *The animals were put through their paces every day until they were doing the tricks perfectly.*

set the pace estabelecer o ritmo, o andamento, regular a marcha, estabelecer um padrão a ser emulado *The boss set the pace at which he expected everyone to work.*

PACK packed with cheio de, repleto de *The big hall was packed with people.*

pack off enviar para, mandar embora, desfazer-se de *[He] ... was packed off to exile on a lonely island ...* -T/64. ♦ *When the kids were packed off to school she began to do her housework.*

pack up arrumar as malas, preparar(-se) para partir, dispor *In the summer of 1951, [film director George] Stevens packed up the entire cast and crew of Shane and moved them out to Jackson Hole, Wyoming, a spot that is almost mythical itself.* -HMT,182. ♦ *We'll pack up and drive to Yosemite for a week.* -SWS,32.

PAIN be at pains to esforçar-se grandemente para, enfrentar grandes dificuldades para *[The politicians] ... had been at pains to appear moderate ...* -T/87.

give a pain [gír] aborrecer, amolar, chatear *You and your silly prejudices. You really give me a pain.*

go to great/etc. pains to dar-se a um grande trabalho para *[Puccini] ... went to particular pains to give the work* [Madama Butterfly] *authentic local color, both dramatically and musically ...* -CMS,191.

growing pains 1. dores do crescimento *The repeated pains that Bob says he feels in his legs and back are really growing pains.* 2. dificuldades e problemas que ocorrem no início de um projeto, organização, empreendimento etc. *[Western society's] ... adventure in freedom is so recent that what appear to be our death rattles may be growing pains.* -MHJ,75.

in pain sentindo dores, com dores ... *if*

he was in pain, he gave no indication of it. -CJC,128.

on/under pain of sob pena de *For centuries, members of Italy's Mafia have sworn not to betray the organization's secrets on pain of death.* -T/92.

a pain (in the neck) [gir] 1. pessoa chata, desagradável *What a pain he is!* ♦ *That guy is a real pain the neck.* 2. coisa irritante, amolação, aborrecimento *It's a pain in the neck to have to talk to that woman.*

spare no pains não poupar esforços *They spared no pains to get the work finished on schedule.*

take (great) pains não poupar esforços, trabalho, atenção etc. *... the President took pains to show that his aim will be to encourage moderation.* -T/85.

PAIR pair off formar(-se) em pares, emparelhar(-se) *The teacher paired off the shy boys with a girl and forced them to dance.*

PALE beyond the pale além dos limites do decoro ou da aceitabilidade etc. (e portanto), inadmissível, inaceitável; em desgraça, excluído *Nixon went beyond the political pale and there was no return.*

PALM grease/oil the palm/hand subornar *If you grease enough palms with enough money you can get away with almost anything in this city.*

have an itching palm [col] ser ávido por dinheiro, vender-se, ser facilmente corrompível *He was accused of having an itching palm.*

have/hold in the palm of one's hand ter na palma da mão, dominar *Chuck had his girl in the palm of his hand until she found out that he had other girls as well.*

palm off [col] impingir, fazer passar uma coisa por outra *We expected the company would try to palm off the blame ... but ... [it] cannot escape responsibility.* -T/85.

PAN (jump) out of the frying pan into the fire (saltar) da frigideira para o fogo *When Joe quit his unpleasant job to join the army he didn't realize that he was jumping out of the frying pan into the fire.*

pan out [col] 1. resultar *And that plan of yours, how is it panning out?* -GA,153. 2. resultar bem, dar bom resultado *We got married too young. And the big things I'd planned didn't pan out.* -MAT,41.

PANIC-STRICKEN tomado de pânico, aterrorizado *[He] ... was panic-stricken at the idea of having to go out in the street.* -T/61.

PANT pant for ansiar ardentemente por *The audience was panting for more but the actors refused to do any more shows.*

PANTS catch with one's pants down [gir] surpreender; surpreender alguém em situação embaraçosa *We have been caught not only with our pants down, but with our pants off ...* -T/67.

a kick in the pants [col] revés humilhante, repúdio inesperado, menosprezo, pontapé no traseiro *Maybe he needed a kick in the pants.* -MN,29.

wear the pants/trousers [col] ser o senhor do lar, mandar na casa, cantar de galo *I wear the pants in my family.* -JJS,130. ♦ *Mrs. Jennings wears the trousers in that family. She always tells her husband what to do.*

PAPER on paper 1. consignado por escrito, impresso, anotado *... I had all the statistics down on paper.* -HMTO,10. 2. no papel, teoricamente, em teoria *... projects that appeared promising on paper sometimes proved disillusioning in reality ...* -T/87.

PAPERBACK livro brochado, brochura *First published in hardcover, his book is now available in paperback.*

PAPERWORK papelada (registros, relatórios, conjunto de documentos etc.) resultante das exigências burocráticas *... Government agencies were busy turning out reams of reports on how to eliminate unnecessary paperwork.* -T/64. ♦ *[The Soviet economy is] ... bogged down in a morass of bureaucratic paperwork.* -T/85.

PAR above//below/under par acima do normal, da média; bem-disposto//abaixo do normal, da média; indisposto *Jennifer's work is above par.* ♦ *I'm feeling below/under par this morning.*
  on a par equiparado, no mesmo nível ... *we will at last be on a par with our competitors.* -T/87.
  up to par 1. satisfatório, bom, dentro dos padrões aceitáveis *Anne's work has not been up to par lately.* 2. bem-disposto, bem de saúde, em forma *If you don't feel up to par you should see your doctor.*
PARCEL parcel out dividir, distribuir *A small reserve of government land may be parceled out to resolve some disputes ...* -T/92.
PARE pare down reduzir, diminuir, cortar *The President pared down the National Budget by eliminating unnecessary expenditures for the purchase of naval supplies.*
PARKING parking lot (área de) estacionamento *Elaine parked the station wagon in the empty parking lot.*
PAROLE on parole em liberdade condicional *Sent back to prison, he was released on parole four years later ...* -T/60.
PART act the part representar o papel (especificado) *The dancers tried to act the parts which the romantic tradition called for ...* -CB,2.
  the best/better part of a maior parte de, quase todo etc. *[He] ... returned to Washington, where he will stay for the better part of a month.* -T/92. ♦ *The [TV] networks have overheads of the better part of a billion dollars.* -T/87.
  do one's part fazer sua parte, cumprir sua obrigação *Everyone is expected to do his part in this company and you're no exception.*
  for one's part no que diz respeito a (alguém), quanto a *He was having difficulty breathing normally and Terens, for his part, was almost equally excited.* -AI,32.
  for the most part geralmente, de maneira geral, as mais das vezes ... *for the most part youths absorb from older youths a smattering of confusing sexual misinformation ...* -HEW,148.
  have/want no part; not want any part não querer tomar parte de, não querer saber de, recusar-se a participar de *I'll have no part in helping to convict him.* ♦ *Tell him for me I don't want any part of his daughter – or him, either.* -SM,17.
  in part em parte, parcialmente *The juvenile problem is due in part to the worldwide feeling of insecurity.*
  live the part desempenhar realisticamente o papel que está representando, identificar-se plenamente com a personagem *In* Julius Caesar, *he is not Marlon Brando playing Mark Anthony. He lives the part and is Anthony.*
  look the part ter a aparência adequada ou ser talhado para um trabalho, missão, função, papel etc. *[Movie star Alan] Ladd was incredibly handsome, and when he played juveniles, nice college boys, and spoiled heirs, he simply looked the part ...* -HMT,14.
  of parts talentoso, de habilidades *Kelly was a man of many parts.* -HJ,2.
  on the part of da parte de *We're not interested in help on the part of people who are not really concerned with our project.*
  part and parcel parte essencial, inseparável *The church cannot and will not tolerate any thoroughgoing study of man as part and parcel of nature.* -T/61.
  the parts of speech categorias gramaticais *The traditional parts of speech are: noun, pronoun, adjective, verb, adverb, preposition, conjunction and interjection.*
  part with separar-se de, desfazer-se de, dizer adeus a ... *there are wealthy people who just hate to part with a dollar or two for the better things of life.* -CEP,58.
  play a/the part desempenhar uma função, representar um papel *Money plays an important part in an election.* ♦ *Sir*

John Gielgud played the part of Cassius in Joseph Mankiewicz's Julius Caesar.
take in good part aceitar de bom humor, não levar a mal *They played many jokes on Howard, but he always took them in good part.*
take part in participar de, tomar parte em *[He] ... took part in five combat patrols against the Japanese in the Pacific.* -T/73.
take the part of 1. fazer o papel de, interpretar *She took the part of Mary, Queen of Scots in a play.* 2. [ou] **take somebody's part** ir em defesa de, apoiar, defender *Mothers generally take the part of their children when the father is angry with them.*
PARTIAL partial to afeiçoado a, apreciador de, que prefere (alguém ou algo) *She's partial to American musicals.* -T/87. ♦ *... American consumers partial to Toyota cars ...* -T/87.
PARTICULAR in particular especialmente *The entire group was good, in particular the young man who played the part of the beggar.*
PART-TIME de meio expediente, de meio período *... she has begun to think about a job, part-time now, full-time later.* -T/72. ♦ *He was a part-time reporter.* v. **full-time**
PARTY coming-out party festa de apresentação de uma jovem à sociedade *Betty's coming-out party will be held at their mansion.* v. **COME out** 7
crash the party → **crash the GATE**
party line 1. linha de telefone compartilhada *[Pillow Talk is a sex comedy that] ... has two stars [Doris Day and Rock Hudson] sharing a party line without knowing each other's identity.* -ML,445. 2. a linha do partido, a orientação política [principalmente do partido comunista]; os princípios, a orientação, a filosofia de uma organização, grupo etc. *Once in the Senate ... [he] voted the party line ...* -T/63. ♦ *He asked for an answer, and I gave him the party line [of the Catholic Church].* -KF,123.
party to partícipe, participante em, cúmplice de *I will not be a party to this deal.*
throw a party [col] dar uma festa *... he threw a splashy black-tie party for 650 of his friends at New York City's Plaza Hotel ...* -T/80.
PASS make a pass [gir] dar uma cantada *Daisy was angry at Charlie because he had made a pass at her.*
pass around passar a um e outro, distribuir *When a child has candy he doesn't like to pass it around to the other children.*
pass away 1. dissipar-se, extinguir-se, desaparecer, chegar ao fim *When the crises pass away, people forget their causes and don't try to take steps to prevent them from happening again.* 2. falecer *My father passed away on September 30, at 1:30 a.m.*
pass by 1. passar (por) *Where were you when the parade passed by?* ⇒ **passerby** transeunte, passante *Passersby were all staring at her.* 2. não dar atenção a, desconsiderar, não tomar conhecimento de *Dale passed me by and I felt very hurt.*
pass for passar por, ser tido como *... looking at what passes for normal life.* -T/87. ♦ *[He] ... is light-skinned enough to pass for white ...* -T/85.
pass off 1. não dar importância, menosprezar *The football coach passed off his losses as a mere period of bad luck.* 2. impingir *Many street vendors try to pass off articles that they claim are imported.* 3. passar-se por, fingir ser *Why did you pass yourself off as a Marine Corps captain?* -MN,272.
pass on 1. legar, transmitir como herança *The family jewels were passed on from mother to daughter and then to grandchild.* 2. entregar, passar adiante, passar às mãos de, transferir *In the mid-40s, when I was a teenager, my eldest brother used*

to subscribe to The Saturday Evening Post *and after he finished reading each copy of the magazine he would pass it on to me.* ♦ *Companies will be allowed to pass on to their customers all the increased costs of material, labor and overhead.* -T/73. 3. falecer *I was shocked to hear that your father has passed on.* -LB,15.

pass out 1. distribuir ... *the feminists are passing out leaflets on street corners protesting pornography* ... -JEP,82. 2. [col] desfalecer, perder os sentidos *Dean always passes out when he drinks too much.*

pass over 1. desprezar, desconsiderar, rejeitar, não dar atenção a, omitir *Some of those unpleasant facts were passed over in his report.* 2. preterir, deixar de promover *[Albert Einstein was]* ... *passed over for positions he considered desirable* ... -SC,25.

pass through passar (por), atravessar, experimentar ... *the freight train that passed through every morning just before noon.* -TW,8. ♦ *Joanna is passing through a very difficult period.*

pass up [col] recusar, rejeitar, deixar passar (oportunidade etc.) *The opportunity they had offered me was simply too good to pass up.*

a pretty/sorry pass situação desagradável, estado lamentável *Things have come to a pretty pass when our politicians care so little for things like honor, honesty and responsibility.*

PASSING in passing de passagem, incidentemente, por alto *He ... recollects, in passing, such spicy background scenes as the sailors' prison in San Francisco* ... -T/85.

PASSION fly into a passion → **fly into a RAGE**

PAT a pat on the back [col] estímulo, encorajamento ... *he received a ... pat on the back from a supporter.* -T/87. v. **pat someone on the BACK**

PATCH not a patch on [col] longe de ser igual ou comparável a, nem por sombra, nem de leve *Fred's ability to tell lies is not a patch on his brother Joe who won the Annual Liars Contest last year.*

patch together juntar, compor ou formar às pressas; reparar, consertar *The country will try to patch together another government.* ♦ ... *Nils and I [were] struggling to patch together the pieces of our marriage.* -UJ,98.

patch up 1. remendar, consertar, improvisar *[They] ... are trying to patch up old equipment that should have been junked years ago.* -T/79. 2. pôr fim a (conflito, diferenças etc.) ... *the pair patched up their differences.* -T/66.

PATH beat a path formar trilha ou caminho à força de tanto passar, pisotear, pisar etc. a vegetação, o mato, a grama *The boys had beaten a path through the grass.*

beat a path to someone's door ir correndo à procura de, ir atrás de *This is the age of the experts. When in doubt, don't guess, don't generalize. Beat a path to the door of the expert.* -FLS,18.

off the beaten path/track isolado, afastado, pouco conhecido; incomum, singular, original, longe do convencional, do corriqueiro ... *Majorca was a Mediterranean Bali Ha'i far off the beaten tourist track.* -T/61.

PAUSE give someone pause fazer parar e pensar, fazer hesitar *The strange reality of that situation gave pause to his enthusiasm.* ♦ ... *acts of aggression and mayhem that might give even hardened criminals pause.* -T/78.

PAY in the pay of a soldo de, a serviço de ... *there was the danger that Kelly [an outlaw] might have one of the telegraph agents in his pay.* -HJ,39.

pay back 1. pagar, restituir (empréstimo, dívida) *They paid the money back in ten months.* ♦ *When will you pay me back?* 2. vingar-se, desforrar-se *"It may take years* *but I'll pay you back for this", he shouted at the man who had betrayed him.*

pay down pagar de entrada (em compra a prestações) *He paid $50 down on his new television set.* ⇒ **down payment** pagamento inicial, entrada (em compra a prestações) *... with the money from his last films, he made the down payment on a $65,000, 290-acre ranch in Malibu Canyon.* -T/80.

pay off 1. pagar e demitir (empregado etc.) *Pay him off and send him out of here.* 2. saldar, liquidar (dívida) *Dalton has paid off all his debts.* 3. [col] subornar *The money has been used to pay off the conspirators.* ⇒ **payoff** suborno *[He] ... has taken payoffs from drug traffickers.* -T/87. 4. dar lucro, ser recompensador, produzir resultados profícuos *Their long carefull research finally paid off.* ⇒ **payoff** lucro, bom resultado *The long training and privations showed a payoff when the team began its game season.*

pay out 1. pagar, desembolsar *[FBI agents] ... paid out several thousand dollars for information.* -T/64. ⇒ **payout** pagamento, desembolso *... the payout on his contract, which reportedly is at least $300,000 a year.* -T/87. 2. afrouxar, dar (corda, cabo etc.), deixar passar pelas mãos *[The Captain] ... moved silently ... paying out the wires of the demolition charges.* -NE,449.

pay phone/station telefone público (geralmente acionado por inserção de moeda) *It is obvious that the kidnappers used a pay phone to contact the boy's family.*

pay up saldar, liquidar *The government insisted that he pay up all his back taxes or go to jail.*

strike/hit pay dirt [col] obter êxito, ser bem-sucedido; ganhar muito dinheiro *The investigation has been hitting pay dirt and the crooks are beginning to get worried.* ♦ *He really struck pay dirt when he invented the self-developing film and camera.*

PAYMENT down payment → **PAY down**

PEA as like as two peas (in a pod) praticamente iguais, virtualmente idênticos *Flora's twins, Victor and Paul, are as like as two peas.*

PEACE hold/keep one's peace manter silêncio, ficar calado *... awaiting his turn in the [barber] chair, [he] could hold his peace no more.* -T/87.

keep (the) peace manter a lei e a ordem, a harmonia *He was hired as sheriff to keep the peace in the lawless town.* ♦ *I finally agreed to ... have a talk with you just to keep peace in the family.* -GES,4.

peace pipe → **PIPE of peace**

PEAK at a/one's/its peak no auge, no apogeu *Tyrone Power was at his screen peak when he starred in* The Mark of Zorro.

PEARL cast (one's) pearls before swine lançar pérolas aos porcos *It is like casting pearls before swine to give them good whiskey when any cheap booze would make them content.*

PEBBLE not the only pebble on the beach não ser a única pessoa que existe, que merece atenção, que está disponível etc., não ser o único filho de Deus *Don't be so conceited. There are other people to be considered. You're not the only pebble on the beach.*

PEEL peel off 1. descascar-se *The beautiful plastic peeled off and left the ugly wood showing on our new bar.* 2. despir (-se) *The dancer started to peel off her clothes and the police raided the show.* 3. sair de formação, separar-se de grupo etc., desgarrar-se (avião ou automóvel) *The planes began to peel off and lose altitude to attack the ships far below.* ♦ *At rush hour, cars inch along Highway 101 ... and peel off into the parking lots ...* -T/78.

PEEVE pet peeve/annoyance/aversion/dislike etc. ojeriza especial, aversão particular, aquilo que mais irrita alguém, motivo de queixa, de aborrecimento ♦ *His pet peeve is people who talk in the* *movies about the end of the story.* ♦ *... a friendly letter should be light-hearted and avoid pet peeves and personal problems ...* -MNH,60. ♦ *That woman is my pet aversion.*

PEG **peg away** trabalhar com afinco, labutar, mourejar *We pegged away at the accumulated work and it seemed to be gradually disappearing.*

square peg in a round hole pessoa inadequada para o cargo que ocupa *Brown is a square peg in a round hole in this type of job and he should change to something that really suits him.*

take down a peg/notch humilhar, abater a vaidade de, a presunção de, reduzir o ego de *Andrews was taken down a peg when he was not reelected as mayor.*

PELL **pell mell** 1. de roldão, impetuosamente, desordenadamente *When the doors finally opened, the people rushed pell-mell into the theater.* 2. confuso, tumultuoso, desordenado *a pell-mell decision*

PEN **pen up** encurralar, engaiolar *... they were penned up like sheep in a small compound ...* -T/69.

PENNY **a pretty penny** [col] muito dinheiro *That beautiful Chinese vase must have cost you a pretty penny.*

turn an honest penny ganhar dinheiro honestamente *He refused to do anything illegal, but would only turn an honest penny.*

turn a pretty penny [col] ganhar bastante dinheiro, uma boa bolada *You can turn a pretty penny by playing the exchange if you have plenty of capital.*

PENNY-WISE **penny-wise and pound-foolish** econômico em ninharias e perdulário em coisas mais importantes, que faz economia de palitos *Many penny-wise and pound-foolish people save money on small items but throw away much more on unnecessary luxury items.*

PENT-UP confinado, enclausurado; reprimido, refreado, contido *She realized how pent-up she had been ...* -SEB,153. ♦ *Pent-up anger, unless it has some release, can cause neurosis.*

PEOPLE **of all people** → **of ALL (people/places/things etc.)**

PEPPER-AND-SALT → **salt-and-pepper**

PER **per se** em si, por si, como tal *Almost anything is harmless per se but when taken in excess, even water can be dangerous.*

PERCENTAGE **there's no percentage in** [col] não há vantagem, lucro, utilidade, proveito etc. em *There's no percentage in that for you.*

PERIL **at one's peril/(own) risk** por sua conta e risco, sob sua responsabilidade *... on issues like sexual freedom, those who ignore ... [tolerance] do so at their peril.* -T/86. ♦ *Remember, you're doing that at your own risk.*

PERIOD **cooling-off period** período de arrefecimento dos ânimos que visa permitir negociações entre dois grupos litigantes *They stopped the strike for a 30-day cooling-off period before signing a permanent pact.*

PERK **perk up** animar-se, recobrar-se, recuperar-se; erguer *The [robotics] industry is expected to perk up again ...* -T/897. ♦ *He perked up his ears when I told him that ...* -EA,11.

PETE **for Pete's sake** → **for Christ's SAKE**

PETER **peter out** [col] desaparecer gradualmente, exaurir-se, acabar-se, fracassar *[The organization] ... petered out late last fall but until then was meant to educate people ...* -T/92.

rob Peter to pay Paul despir um santo para vestir outro *Social Security is nothing more than a system of robbing Peter to pay Paul.* -T/81.

PHASE **phase out** desativar gradualmente (produção, operação, utilização etc.) *Sweden plans to phase out its twelve [nuclear power] plants before the year 2010.* -T/86.
⇒ **phaseout** desativação gradual *... agreements establishing timetables for the*

phaseout of ozone-destroying chlorofluorocarbons. -T/92.

PHONE on the phone → **on the TELEPHONE**

PHOTO FINISH 1. final de corrida de cavalos equilibradíssima cujo vencedor só pode ser decidido por foto ou imagem gravada *Battle Cry won the Kentucky Derby in a photo finish.* 2. disputa em que o vencedor tem margem ínfima *Will the first free election since 1971 end in a photo finish?* -T/87.

PICK pick and choose escolher cuidadosamente, ser exigente na escolha *... he was happy to be free to pick and choose a new job.* -T/66. ♦ *Building a vocabulary is a selective process. It's a matter of picking and choosing.* -GR,15.

pick apart = **pick to PIECES** *His performance was picked apart by the critics.*

pick off abater com arma de fogo *... pick off enemy soldiers.* -T/72. ♦ *... Skyhawks [jets] picked off five North Vietnamese PT boats ...* -T/66.

pick on 1. [col] irritar, apoquentar, atormentar, molestar, fazer de vítima *Why don't you pick on someone your own size?* -MG,16. 2. censurar, criticar, culpar *Craig's wife is always picking on him.* 3. escolher, selecionar *Gus was picked on to represent his school in the debate.*

pick out 1. distinguir, discernir, reconhecer *Can you pick out Bette Davis as a child from all these pictures of children?* 2. escolher, selecionar, separar *I'll go through all my books and pick out the ones I want to keep. The rest you can have.*

pick over examinar e selecionar os melhores espécimes *If you don't get to the special sale early, the bargains will have all been picked over by the women who know how to select the articles of value.*

pick up 1. erguer, apanhar do chão, levantar; pegar, apanhar; erguer-se, levantar-se (após uma queda) *Pick up the cards that you have thrown on the floor.* ♦ *The boy picked himself up after the fall.* 2. descobrir, ficar sabendo de *... fragmentary information picked up from contact with a relatively small number of friends ...* -KAC,23. 3. recuperar (saúde, forças), restaurar-se; reanimar, revigorar, estimular, fazer alguém sentir-se melhor *Drink this. It will pick you up.* ♦ *The boy's health soon picked up after his mother took him to his uncle's farm.* ⇒ **pick-me-up** [col] gole de bebida estimulante; qualquer estimulante, tônico, revigorante *Here. A little drink before dinner will be a good pick-me-up for you.* 4. obter, conseguir, adquirir, achar (pechincha etc.) por acaso *Kathleen picked up a nice dress on the bargain table at Macy's.* ♦ *[He] ... picked up a canvas [i.e., a painting] dated 1901 by a 26-year-old Spaniard named Pablo Picasso.* -T/78. 5. levar (pessoa ou coisa) em veículo; recolher passageiro; ir buscar (pessoa ou coisa), apanhar, dar carona; recolher, retirar (pessoa) do mar ou da água *The bus stopped at the corner to pick up passengers.* ♦ *He picked me up at my hotel.* ♦ *The rescue ship picked up many survivors from the sinking transatlantic liner.* ⇒ **pickup** a. recolhimento, coleta, ato de apanhar ou recolher algo *Garbage workers [on strike] skipped weekly pickups in some towns ...* -T/92. b. [ou] **pickup truck** caminhonete *He drives a beat-up old pickup.* 6. captar, receber, pegar (sinal de rádio, TV, estrelas etc.), avistar, ouvir, detectar, perceber, sentir (luz, sinal, som, odor etc.) *... a UFO was seen and simultaneously picked up on radar.* -RE,68. ♦ *The powerful telescope can pick up distant stars.* ♦ *... lizards and snakes do not pick up odors solely with their nostrils.* -SK,168. 7. acelerar, ganhar (velocidade), tornar-se mais rápido, mais vigoroso, mais ativo, mais intenso *This car picks up speed very quickly.* ♦ *The [political] campaign's momentum began to pick up last week ...* -T/84. ♦ *Now the* wind is picking up ... -T/76. ⇒ **pickup** aceleração *This car has good pickup.* 8. pôr em ordem, arrumar, arranjar *Let's pick up the room before she arrives.* 9. [col] progredir, desenvolver-se, melhorar *The economy is picking up.* ♦ *... it will probably be early next year before business again picks up ...* -T/80. ⇒ **pickup** progresso, restabelecimento, melhora (de negócios, atividades, saúde) etc. *There has been a pickup in business.* 10. [col] iniciar relacionamento informal e imediato com pessoa do sexo oposto (geralmente com conotação sexual) *He picked her up in a bar.* ♦ *One day he picked up a prostitute and spent the afternoon with her.* -LR,15. ⇒ **pickup** alguém a quem se conhece por acaso (na rua, em uma festa, no bar etc.) e que pode aceitar um relacionamento sexual imediato *Diane Keaton played a pickup in* Looking for Mr. Goodbar. 11. [gir] colocar sob custódia, deter, prender *He was picked up during a bank holdup.* ♦ *Joe was picked up for vagrancy.* 12. [gir] apanhar ou comprar (enquanto a caminho de) *Carla picked up some groceries on her way home.* 13. [col] pagar (a conta, a despesa) *Lee always picks up the bill for our noon lunch.* 14. retomar (atividade após interrupção), voltar a (assunto, tema), recomeçar, continuar *He was picking up his campaign right where he had left off – with attacks on the news media.* -T/87. 15. aprender, adquirir (habilidade, língua, técnica, hábito etc.) com facilidade, dominar; entender, compreender *Clint picks up ideas fast.* ♦ *Harriet picked up some of her husband's strange mannerisms.* 16. apanhar, juntar, reunir, recolher (coisas dispersas) *Hector and Octavius were told to pick up the many toys they had left all over the floor.* 17. localizar, encontrar, seguir (trilha, rastro) *The sheriff picked up the trail of the three outlaws somewhere near Apache Wells.* 18. adoecer de, pegar (doença) *... she'd picked up an intestinal virus ...* -QE,13. 19. fazer as malas *A few of the more impetuous among us cried out that we should pick up and go ...* -JJS,106. 20. ganhar, conseguir *Martin picked up two hundred dollars doing odd jobs here and there.*

pick up after (someone) pôr em ordem, limpar, arrumar lugar que alguém sujou, desarrumou, bagunçou *Muriel is always picking up after that lazy husband of hers.*

pick up with fazer amizade com, relacionar-se com *Glenda picked up with a weird crowd.*

PICK-ME-UP → **PICK up** 3

PICKLE in a (pretty) pickle [col] em apuros *You'll be in a pickle if you run out of gas on the way to Dry Butte.*

PICNIC no picnic [gir] coisa ou tarefa difícil, algo desagradável *Elroy found that it was no picnic to take care of the house while his wife was in the hospital.*

PICTURE the big picture visão global de uma situação, de uma questão etc. *Give me the big picture of our financial standing.*

come into/enter the picture entrar em cena, surgir, manifestar-se, interpor-se *The agreement was about to be completed when an unpredictable factor came into the picture.*

drop out of the picture desaparecer, deixar de ser visto *He was such a famous television personality that we were surprised when he dropped out of the picture.*

get the picture compreender, entender, ter uma visão geral da situação, dos fatos *Do you get the picture or do I have to explain it again?*

in//out of the picture em cogitação, fazendo parte de uma situação, muito relevante//fora de cogitação, relegado a posição sem importância *... company commanders should be put completely in the picture before we begin the last series of rehearsals with the navy.* -SLS,239. ♦

My chances for a trip to Europe this year are out of the picture.
the picture of health/happiness etc. a imagem perfeita da saúde/felicidade etc. *Diane looks the picture of health.* ♦ *[Mr. and Mrs. Wyeth] ... are the picture of relaxed domesticity ...* -T/86.
put someone in the picture pôr alguém a par da situação, dar-lhe todas as informações necessárias a respeito de um assunto *Will you put me in the picture before I go into the meeting and make a fool of myself because I don't know what they're talking about.*
take a good//bad picture ser//não ser fotogênico *Many good-looking people take a bad picture.*
PIE as easy as pie [col] extremamente fácil *I knew it'd be as easy as pie if you guys did just like I told you.* -CEP,88.
eat humble pie admitir o erro, pedir desculpas, humilhar-se *Brad had to eat humble pie when he realized how wrong he had been.*
pie in the sky doce esperança de ventura, bem-estar e felicidade no futuro ou em uma vida futura *There would be as much money as needed. I was promised the pie in the sky by and by. Expenses plus salary.* -BC,119.
PIECE cut to pieces cortar em pedaços; destroçar (um exército) *We dispatched an army to meet them [Charlemagne and his army], and it was cut to pieces.* -PM,14.
fall to pieces desintegrar-se, desmoronar, não se sustentar *The state was falling to pieces, but nobody would act ...* -GJI,49.
give someone a piece of one's mind [col] expressar francamente sua raiva ou indignação, dizer o que pensa *Julie gave the taxi driver a piece of her mind when he tried to overcharge her.*
go (all) to pieces perder o autodomínio, ter crise de nervos; descontrolar-se, chorar *I went all to pieces. I parked the car in at the curb and sat there and cried and shook and cried ...* -GES,98.
hack/pick/pull to pieces criticar severamente, achar defeitos *His theory to explain the disappearance of dinosaurs was picked to pieces by most paleontologists.* ♦ *The paper hacked the actor's performance to pieces.*
in one piece inteiro, incólume, são e salvo *Jack and Sheila were very lucky to get out of the burning car in one piece.*
in pieces em pedaços, esfacelado *The plane was found in pieces and scattered over a large area on the mountainside.*
(all) of a piece da mesma espécie, análogo, consistente, uniforme, coerente, concorde *... the kid's story ... doesn't seem to hang together all of a piece like it should ...* -HWW,4. ♦ *[Some of novelist John Cheever's critics argue that] ... his characters are too narrow and too much of a piece ...* -T/78.
pick to pieces → hack to PIECES
pick up the pieces salvar o que for possível de uma situação ou relação desastrosa, refazer a vida *After her marriage broke up, Joanna started to pick up the pieces and try to be happy again.*
piece by piece pedaço por pedaço, uma parte de cada vez *The police went over the automobile piece by piece looking for the cocaine they believed was hidden in it.*
a piece of advice conselho *Let me give you a piece of advice: don't do business with that man.*
a piece of cake [col] tarefa muito fácil *That job is no piece of cake. You'll find that out very soon.*
piece out prolongar, ampliar, emendar, completar (acrescentando pedaço, parte etc.) *When we built the deck for our camp, we had to piece out the finished boards with coarse hewn logs.*
piece together juntar, unir, reunir, compor *... a story pieced together from many sources ...* -CR,9. ♦ *The police pieced*

together obscure clues to arrive at the murderer.
pull to pieces → hack to PIECES
say one's piece → speak one's PIECE
shot to pieces → shot to HELL
smash to pieces = tear to pieces 1 ... *the Challenger [space shuttle] was smashed to pieces ...* -T/86.
speak/say one's piece [col] expressar sua opinião, dizer o que pensa ... *assert yourself, and ... speak your piece.* -CH,viii. ♦ *Say your piece ... Then get back to work.* -LLN,8.
take to pieces 1. desmontar, desmanchar *He likes to take old clocks to pieces.* 2. criticar severamente, atacar verbalmente *I've played along with you, hoping that you'd tell me the truth and I wouldn't have to take you to pieces in order to get the true story.* -GES,86.
tear to pieces/shreds 1. despedaçar, dilacerar *The little girl tore her doll to pieces.* ♦ *If you dare to look at any other woman I will tear you to pieces.* -EMW,31. 2. atacar verbalmente, demolir, aniquilar, reduzir a nada *The famous critic tore Glenda's performance to shreds.*

PIG buy a pig in a poke comprar nabos em saco *Never buy a pig in a poke is always sound advice.*

PIGEONHOLE 1. pôr de lado, arquivar *Most of the requests for aid sent to the Welfare department were pigeonholed and deliberately forgotten.* 2. classificar, rotular *Although he often takes liberal stands, his writings are not always easy to pigeonhole ideologically.* -T/86.

PIGGYBACK; PICKABACK 1. nas costas, nos ombros *He carried his little daughter up the hill piggyback.* ♦ *[He] ... had to be carried pickaback ...* -T/63. 2. em vagão-plataforma *The trains are carrying trucks piggyback on flatcars to save gas.*

PIGHEADED teimoso, turrão *[He] ... is a seething complex of contradictions: arrogant yet sensitive, pig-headed as well as lion-hearted.* -T/63.

PIGSKIN [col] bola de futebol americano *The American football is called a pigskin because pig bladders were originally used for playing.*

PILE make a/one's pile [col] enriquecer, fazer fortuna ... *he made a pile with his two aristocratic old-time saloons.* -BRSR,6.
pile in/into entrar desordenadamente, amontoar-se, apinhar-se (em veículo) ... *five of them piled into a blue Buick ...* -T/87.
pile up 1. acumular(-se), amontoar(-se) ... *problems that have piled up over the years.* -T/87. ♦ *He had piled up a fortune in Chicago real estate ...* -MMA,14. 2. destroçar, danificar, trombar (veículo) *On icy roads cars often pile up in horrible accidents.* ⇒ **pileup** [col] colisão de vários veículos, engavetamento ... *one of the worst pileups of the summer leaves a trail of shattered cars, trucks and trailers ...* -T/88.

PILL a bitter pill (to swallow) algo humilhante e desagradável *It will be a bitter pill to swallow if he loses his job.* ♦ *We will all have to swallow a bitter pill in order to curb the inflationary spiral.* -T/74.
on the pill [col] fazendo uso de contraceptivo oral *She has been on the pill ever since she came to the University.*

PILLAR from pillar to post de um lugar para outro, de uma situação difícil para outra, de Herodes a Pilatos, de tombo em tombo *Carstairs was driven from pillar to post and found no rest.*
pillar of the church/society etc. membro respeitado da igreja, da sociedade etc. *Mr. Smith had been a pillar of the church in his community.* ♦ ... *whether you are a member of the rabble in good standing or a pillar of society.* -SV,121.

PIN on pins and needles desassossegado, agitado, apreensivo *Michelle was on pins and needles waiting for my report.*

pin down 1. obrigar, sujeitar, prender (a acordo, contrato, compromisso, promessa, atitude etc.), fazer alguém definir-se, assumir uma posição ... *he immediately decided to try to pin the fading ex-President down to a TV contract.* -T/77. 2. impedir de mover-se, imobilizar, prender ... *rough hands seized her from behind and pinned her down.* -T/77. ♦ *Our men [soldiers] are pinned down on a slope.* -MAT,19. 3. definir com clareza e precisão, estabelecer com toda a certeza *I recognize the song but I can't pin down the name of it.* ♦ *[He] ... found it difficult to pin down facts about the princess ...* -T/80.

pin money 1. mesada dada a uma mulher dependente para gastos pessoais ... *she used pin money from relatives to buy her first machine-made piece of clothing, a short-sleeved dress in French blue.* -T/80. 2. dinheiro extraordinário para despesas eventuais *Karen earns pin money by giving private lessons.* 3. dinheiro miúdo, trocados, ninharia, migalhas *He works hard but his salary is pin money.*

pin (something) on someone [col] pôr a culpa em, responsabilizar, acusar *They tried to pin the robbery on Wade but luckily he could prove his innocence.*

pin up 1. prender com alfinete ou grampo *She pins up her hair when she begins to do her housework.* 2. fixar, pendurar *Pin up a notice about the basketball game on the bulletin board.* ⇒ **pinup** [col] a. fotografia ou pôster, geralmente de garota atraente e sensual, que pode ser pendurado na parede *He had lots of pinups on the walls of his apartment.* b. a garota de tal foto ou pôster ... *the pinups of the '40s – Betty Grable, Dorothy Lamour, Rita Hayworth ...* -T/77. c. relativo a ou designativo de foto ou pôster dessa natureza *[He redecorated] ... his room with a thousand pinup photos of [a TV singer] ...* -T/63.

PINCH in a pinch em uma emergência, em um apuro, em caso de necessidade *You're a real friend and I know I can always trust you in a pinch.*

PINCH-HIT pinch-hit for substituir, fazer as vezes de *I'm not a good public speaker but I'll pinch-hit for you while you're in the hospital.*

PINE pine away consumir-se, definhar *When his master died, the dog refused to eat and gradually pined away.*

pine for ansiar por ... *many Americans today are more than likely to pine for the impossible ...* -T/84.

PINK in the pink [col] em boas condições físicas, saudável, em ótima forma *Prizefighter Joe Pendleton kept repeating to Mr. Jordan and to Max Corkle that he was in the pink and eager to resume his boxing career.*

PINPOINT 1. indicar com precisão *They pinpointed the advantages of their plan.* 2. exato, preciso, detalhado *The Americans did pinpoint bombing in daylight raids over Nazi Germany.*

PIPE pipe back [col] retrucar *When he was rebuked by his father he always piped back with some unpleasant retort.*

pipe down [col] calar-se *They all began to talk at once and I told them to pipe down.*

pipe dream [col] esperança ilusória, idéia impraticável *The idea of a tunnel from England to France sounded like a pipe dream but it became a reality.*

pipe of peace; peace pipe cachimbo da paz *The union leaders and the company officials finally smoked the pipe of peace and the strike was ended.*

pipe up [col] começar a falar, manifestar-se (principalmente com voz estridente) *The speaker made a wrong statement and someone at the meeting piped up with an embarrassing question.*

put that in your pipe and smoke it goste ou não, você tem de aceitar isso *His wife told him that she intended to take the family car on her vacation and that he could put that in his pipe and smoke it.*

PIPELINE canal de informações (geral-

mente confidenciais) *Lovejoy had a direct pipeline to high political information.*
in the pipeline em preparo, em execução *The government has more big [criminal] cases in the pipeline.* -T/92.

PIPER pay the piper arcar com as conseqüências ou despesas, pagar caro por atos impensados *... his dutiful wife warned him that it was costing too much to pay the piper ...* -T/63.

PIT pit against opor(-se), colocar(-se) contra, competir contra *In* Predator, *a sci-fi movie, the hero is pitted against a formidable adversary from another planet.*

PITCH make a pitch [gir] tentar convencer com argumentos persuasivos, influenciar *... when [Ronald] Reagan went to Chicago ... for a meeting with top strategists, he made his pitch in person [to urge action on his presidential campaign].* -T/80.
pitch in [col] trabalhar com energia, pôr mãos à obra *... most residents gamely pitched in to bring Wichita Falls back to life [after it was severely hit by a tornado].* -T/79.
pitch into [col] 1. atacar física ou verbalmente *Evans pitched into the flaws in the other candidate's personality and fitness for the job.* ♦ *Rocky pitched into the big man with all his might.* 2. atacar (comida), comer com voracidade *The hobo pitched into the meal as if he hadn't eaten for days.*

PITCH-DARK/BLACK escuro como breu *The night was pitch-dark and Margie was afraid to go out alone.*

PITCHFORK rain pitchforks → **rain CATS and dogs**

PITY for pity's sake → **for Christ's SAKE**
take pity on apiedar-se de *Little children take pity on every stray animal or injured bird.*
what a pity que pena *What a pity her mother isn't alive to see how famous she has become.*

PLACE all over the place por todos os lados, espalhado, a torto e a direito *After the holdup, the police were swarming like flies all over the place.*
fall into place encaixar-se, fazer sentido, tornar-se claro *At first the instructions seemed rather complicated for Roger, but after a few minutes things fell into place.*
get no place → **GET nowhere**
give place to dar lugar a, ser sucedido por *The sense of peace gave place to a feeling of terror when a huge mushroom cloud appeared far in the western sky.*
go places [gir] ser bem-sucedido, ter futuro *[He] ... looked like a young fellow who would certainly go places.* -T/63.
in high places nas altas esferas, em lugares importantes, entre os poderosos *The testimony involved people in high places ...* -TB,15.
in//out of place 1. em seu lugar, no devido lugar//fora de lugar, deslocado *Even though there had been an explosion in the house, everything was strangely in place in the kitchen.* ♦ *[She seemed] ... strangely out of place in her black silk dress and white gloves.* -GE,32. 2. oportuno, apropriado//inadequado, impróprio, inconveniente *A florid or bookish style is never in place in business writing ...* -PC,182. ♦ *The hillbilly accent sounds out of place in Boston.*
in place of em vez de *I asked the waiter if I could have French fried potatoes in place of rice.*
in the first place primeiramente, para início de conversa, antes de mais nada *I think I'll go now. Maybe I shouldn't have come in the first place.*
jumping-off place 1. lugar remoto, isolado, o limite da civilização *How did you come to live in this jumping-off place?* 2. [ou] **jumping-off point** lugar utilizado como ponto de partida (de viagem, empreendimento etc.) *... [Esperança] will be our jumping-off place for the country beyond.* -UJ,13. ♦ *... the first fully manned satellite Space Station had been estab-*

lished as a 'jumping-off' place for exploration on the Solar system ... -SWJ, v.
know one's place conhecer o seu lugar, demonstrar submissão *He knows his place with the boss and is always polite and respectful.*
of all places → of ALL (people/things/places etc.)
one's place a residência de alguém ... *I'd appreciate it if you'd spend the night at our place.* -CTT,75.
out of place → in PLACE
a place in the sun um lugar ao sol, oportunidade de viver, de igualar-se aos outros *George Eastman just wanted a place in the sun, but his weak nature was his downfall.*
put someone in his place colocar alguém em seu lugar, fazê-lo saber qual é sua posição ... *it's about time someone put the "critics in their places ..."* -T/62.
take place acontecer, ocorrer, realizar-se, ter lugar *Ernest Hemingway's novel For Whom the Bell Tolls takes place in Spain at the time of the Civil War.*
PLAGUE   avoid like the plague evitar a todo custo, fugir de *You should avoid like the plague any discussion of politics with your boss.*
PLAIN-SPOKEN claro, franco, sincero ... *the plain-spoken President of Pakistan had demonstrated his old soldier's scorn for diplomatic niceties ...* -T/61.
PLAN   plan on planejar, ter em mente, tencionar *Don't plan on doing anything next week because my mother is coming to visit us.*
plan out planejar, projetar, idear ... *it is a good idea to plan out in advance of composing your message what you should say and how best to say it.* -PC,13.
PLANK   plank down [col] 1. pagar, contribuir *Each month he has to plank down twenty-five dollars for union dues and doesn't like it.* 2. pôr, colocar (geralmente com certa violência) no balcão, na mesa etc. *Joe planked down the money on the table.*
PLAY   at play brincando ... *a woman watching her four-year-old grandson at play ...* -T/75.
bring into play movimentar, pôr em ação, introduzir *When the battle seemed lost, the General brought new tanks into play and caused the enemy to fall back.*
come into play entrar em ação, passar a influir *Personal opinion often comes into play preventing a fair decision.*
fair play lealdade, jogo limpo *[He] ... had believed in democracy and fair play for the poor man.* -MMA,43.
foul play 1. crime, violência; assassinato *As is the case when any world figure dies unexpectedly, rumors of foul play inevitably circulated ...* -T/78. 2. deslealdade, trapaça, desonestidade *They suspect foul play in some of his financial dealings.*
make a play for [col] 1. tentar conseguir *They made a play for the rich widow's support.* 2. tentar atrair sexualmente *Did he seem to be drunk? Did he – did he make any kind of play for you?* -TR,102.
play along with cooperar com (em interesse próprio) *I knew she wasn't telling the truth but I played along with her just to see where it would lead.*
play around 1. divertir-se, brincar, tratar com displicência ... *they had better understand that we are not to be played around with.* -T/76. 2. ter relações amorosas com pessoa(s) do sexo oposto, manter relações sexuais extraconjugais *Human nature isn't monogamous. Both men and women like to play around.* -WCN,240.
play back → playback
play down fazer parecer menos importante, depreciar, menosprezar, apoucar, diminuir *They play down all the mistakes they have made and emphasize all their triumphs.*
played out cansadíssimo, exausto *The refugees were played out after a long day of questioning.*

play fair agir com lisura, jogar limpo *She didn't play fair at all ...* -WCN,288.

play fast and loose agir de maneira irresponsável, tratar sem consideração *[He] ... should not play fast and loose with the truth ...* -T/86.

play hard to get [col] fazer-se difícil, fingir desinteresse (por pessoa do sexo oposto) *Gina played hard to get, but Frank got her.* -T/60.

play it cool [gir] aparentar desinteresse, impassibilidade, frieza, não demonstrar entusiasmo ou emoção *Try to play it cool and not let our competitors learn about our plans ahead of time.*

play it safe → PLAY (it) safe

play it straight [col] jogar limpo, agir com sinceridade *... I'm going to play it straight with him, and we'll see how it goes.* -WSM,211.

play off jogar partida para desempatar, jogar partida decisiva *The High School team had to play off the tie before they could enter the second phase of the championship.* ⇒ **play-off** partida de desempate, partida decisiva *The championship will have to be decided by a play-off.*

play off one against the other colocar *a* contra *b* para obter vantagem própria *... he always played off both friends and enemies against one another ...* -T/77.

play on/upon fazer uso de, explorar, tirar proveito de *... devious and aggressive manipulators who would play upon our irrationalities and weaknesses in order to channel our behavior.* -PVH,227.

play out 1. representar, desempenhar (papel, função etc., também na vida real, até o fim) *Much of the American grief in Viet Nam was played out in the national imagination by way of movies and television.* -T/79. 2. tornar(-se) obsoleto ou gasto, gastar(-se), tornar(-se) ineficiente *We have played out all the old tricks to get money out of him and must think up some new trick.*

play (it) safe agir com cautela, ser prudente, não se arriscar *... there's no way of playing it safe in our business.* -AIM,96.
♦ *It is better to play safe and make a small but sure profit.*

play someone dirt → **do someone DIRT**

play someone false ludibriar, enganar, fraudar, trair *... he had a deep instinctive feeling for his work which rarely played him false.* -NEW,12.

play up [col] salientar, realçar, dar proeminência *The obvious tendency of modern romantic novels to play up the enjoyable promiscuity of their heroes and heroines ...* -EA,53.

play up to [col] adular, bajular *[The lieutenant colonel] ... frequently played up to his superiors.* -T/87.

PLAYBACK reprodução de música, diálogo, fala etc. logo após a gravação para verificar a qualidade *The playback showed that the recording of the song had been perfect.* ⇒ **play back** reproduzir qualquer som que acabou de ser gravado *... they played back a tape-recording of the last radio transmission ...* -T/64.

PLAY-BY-PLAY 1. detalhado, que pormenoriza cada ato ou incidente de um acontecimento *[The novels of Thomas Wolfe are] ... a play-by-play ... account of his loves and losses in a search for some transcendental meaning in the loneliness of life.* -SV,114. 2. narrativa detalhada *[He gives] ... a play by play of the Vice President's ... career ...* -T/72.

PLEASE as big as you please altivo, arrogante *In* The Gunfighter, *a western movie, a woman citizen complains that Jimmy Ringo, a notorious outlaw is in town, sitting in the local saloon "as big as you please".*

if you please 1. por favor, com sua permissão, se preferir *Close the window, if you please.* 2. você acredita?, dá para acreditar? *And this [movie* Bonnie and Clyde*], if you please, was the U.S. entry in this year's Montreal Film Festival.* -T/67.

PLEDGE take the pledge prometer solenemente abster-se de bebidas alcoólicas *After the accident he took the pledge and hasn't had a drink for over twelve years.*

PLUG plug along/at/away [col] trabalhar ou estudar com afinco, mourejar, esforçar-se muito *You may plug along fifty years before you get anywheres.* -BS,23. ♦ *Jordan plugged at being an actor until he was really successful.* ♦ *[He] ... has been living in ... Long Island, where he is plugging away on a novel.* -T/75.

plug in/into ligar (fio, cabo de aparelho em tomada de corrente elétrica ou em outro equipamento ou sistema) *Is the radio plugged in?* ♦ *... equipment that plugs into IBM systems.* -T/82.

pull the plug retirar o apoio, desmascarar, revelar a verdade *He'll pull the plug on us if he finds out you've been in prison.* ♦ *The Washington Post pulled the plug on the Watergate scandal.*

PLUME plume oneself on gabar-se de, orgulhar-se de *He plumes himself on the fact that he is descended from John and Priscilla Alden.*

PLUNGE plunge in/into lançar-se em, atirar-se em, mergulhar em *... when Jack [Kennedy] got into politics, the entire [Kennedy] clan plunged in with him as quickly as they would join a family game ...* -T/60. ♦ *... he plunged into anti-Fascist propaganda ...* -CS,512.

take the plunge aventurar-se a fazer algo ousado, arriscado etc. (após certa hesitação), decidir-se a afrontar (perigo, prova, desafio, situação etc.) *After months of indecision he finally decided to take the plunge and run for President.*

PLUNK plunk down pagar *[He] ... had plunked down $1 million on [an investor's] speculative endeavors ...* -T/86.

POCKET in one's pocket sob seu domínio, influência etc. *He had all the corrupt politicians in his pocket.*

line one's pockets aceitar suborno, locupletar-se desonestamente *Most old-time politicians lined their pockets while in office.*

out of pocket 1. sem dinheiro, de caixa baixa *After paying all his expenses, de found himself out of pocket.* 2. com prejuízo, com perda *I was out of pocket more than fifty dollars after taking my girlfriend to an expensive restaurant.*

pick someone's pocket bater a carteira de *The clever thief picked my pocket on the crowded street.*

pocket/spending money dinheiro para despesas miúdas *Fred's father gives him pocket money but nothing large enough to put a down payment on a car of his own.* ♦ *[He] ... was given a monthly allowance of one hundred twenty-five dollars, just for spending money.* -MMA,47.

POINT at one point em um determinado momento, de certa feita *... they appeared on a second-floor balcony at one point and tossed flowers to the crowd below.* -T/84.

at the point of a gun → **at GUNPOINT**

beside the point/question irrelevante, sem relação com o assunto em questão *All the argument about technology is beside the point. The problem is a political one.* -T/61.

boiling point → **BOILING point**
breaking point → **BREAKING point**
come/get to the point deixar-se de rodeios, ser objetivo *He confronted Jones and came straight to the point.* -BE,19. ♦ *How many times in your life have you been thoroughly irritated with a speaker or writer because "he never did get to the point"?* -SN,111.

get the point compreender o ponto essencial, o aspecto fundamental, a questão, o problema *You're beginning to get the point.*

have a point ter um argumento convincente, lógico, importante a seu favor, ter razão, estar certo *... atheists such as Freud*

have a point in viewing religion as something that in the past has hindered rather than helped man's self-development. -T/66.
♦ *When I gave him my opinion he said: "You have a point there".*
in point relevante, pertinente, apropriado *A few words concerning her character are in point here.*
jumping-off point → **jumping-off PLACE**
make a/the point propor uma idéia, opinião etc., demonstrar idéia, proposição, argumento etc. de maneira plena e clara ... *when he tried to put the story into words, it did not hang together and make a point, the way it did in thought.* -LD,21. ♦ *Your article makes the point that English dominates science, technology and popular culture, but it also prevails in education, diplomacy and publishing.* -T/87.
make a point of ter por princípio ou regra, fazer questão de, insistir em *Mr. Elliott makes a point of calling all the people who work for him by their first names.* ♦ *[He] ... made a point of taking his vacation in Bulgaria in July.* -T/66.
make it a point to = **make a POINT of** *Mindful of the germ theory of disease, Johnson always makes it a point to wash his hands carefully before he eats.* ♦ *... he made it a point to take an interest in the personal lives of his crew members.* -GE,26.
make one's point explicar com clareza a validade de sua idéia, opinião, sugestão, argumento etc. *Sometimes a writer or a speaker makes his point, or says what he has to say, magnificently, directly, and clearly, by breaking the rules.* -CH,vii.
miss the point não compreender o ponto essencial, não captar o significado, o aspecto fundamental *He completely missed the point of my argument.*
on the point of prestes a, a ponto de ... *she was on the point of getting the idea ...* -HJH,23.
the Point a Academia Militar de West Point *[He] Graduated from the Point in time to serve the last year of the War between the States ...* -LL,42.
point man pessoa na vanguarda dos acontecimentos, ponta de lança ... *[President] Reagan took time out to appoint a new U.S. trade representative, the point man in major negotiations dealing with international commerce.* -T/85.
point of view ponto de vista, modo de ver *From my point of view, his argument seems ideologically unsound.*
point out indicar, mostrar, apontar, chamar atenção para *It has been frequently pointed out that a primary purpose of communication is to transfer ideas.* -SN,431.
point up dar ênfase a, salientar ... *[Ernest] Hemingway selected his people and his incidents to point up something he had to say about life.* -SV,126. ♦ *... TIME Magazine not only concisely reports the news, it clarifies its complexities and points up its significance.* -T/80.
sticking point → **STICKING point**
stick to the point ater-se ao assunto em questão *Stick to the point. Don't get off the subject.*
stretch/strain a point fazer uma concessão, consentir em uma pequena quebra do regulamento, transigir, ir além do devido ou permitido *We wouldn't feel justified in giving you [$10,000 a year].... Nevertheless, we might stretch a point and give you nine thousand.* -WSM,58.
strong point forte, ponto forte *Public speaking has never been my strong point.*
talking point → **TALKING point**
there's no point não faz sentido, de nada adianta *Comets are of little interest to space travelers and there is no point in considering them ...* -GH,36.
to the point adequado à ocasião, ao momento, pertinente, relevante, objetivo *The six questions they had thought up in a collective manner were simple and to the point.* -HE,43.

to the point of até o ponto de (ser equivalente a, chegar a ser) *My beliefs were, and are, as simple – simple perhaps to the point of naïveté – as a non-intellectual's beliefs may be expected to be.* -KRI,570. ♦ *[They] ... were superstitious to the point of fatalism.* -T/84.
turning point → **TURNING point**
what's the point de que adianta, de que vale *What's the point in marrying just not to be lonely when you are old.* -T/72.
POINT-BLANK 1. muito próximo, contíguo *[He] ... was shot at point-blank range by unidentified gunmen ...* -T/87. 2. categórico, franco, direto *Carol gave him a point-blank answer.* 3. à queima-roupa, de muito perto *The mobster fired at him point-blank.* 4. categoricamente, francamente, sem rodeios *Karen refused Phil's offer point-blank.*
POKE poke about/around procurar, bisbilhotar *The inspectors will be poking around all the time.* -T/87.
POKER poker face [col] rosto inexpressivo, que nada comunica *I kept a poker face, so as to hide my true feelings.* ⇒ **poker-faced** inexpressivo *... the normally poker-faced Secretary ...* -T/87.
POLE one wouldn't touch someone/something with a ten-foot pole não querer saber de alguém/algo, não querer nada com, ter antipatia por *... I wouldn't touch you or your queer friends with a ten-foot pole.* -RW,146.
POLISH polish off [col] terminar rapidamente (trabalho, qualquer atividade), dar fim em (comida, bebida), derrotar, liquidar *... he likes to polish off a hard day's politicking with two or three dry martinis ...* -T/74. ♦ *Don can polish off a bottle of rum in a half hour and not get drunk.*
polish up [col] melhorar *... Moscow may be seeking to polish up its image before a possible U.S.-Soviet summit later this year.* -T/86.
PONY play the ponies → **play the HORSES**

POP pop in vir, chegar, aparecer, visitar inesperadamente *Every time we had lamb for Sunday dinner, my aunt was sure to pop in.*
pop off 1. morrer de repente *Reese popped off with heart trouble before he was fifty.* 2. partir às pressas, de repente *... Marcel Camus ... popped off to Brazil to make a film in color called* Black Orpheus. -T/63.
pop up aparecer de repente, surgir *... other challenges popped up.* -T/72.
PORE pore over ler, estudar ou examinar atentamente *Our antiquarians pore over the hints of dead languages they find engraved in stone.* -MM,19. ♦ *... the Committee has been poring over all the evidence on the shooting of President John F. Kennedy ...* -T/79.
PORT any port in a storm qualquer auxílio ou refúgio que possa aparecer em tempos difíceis, tábua de salvação *Prostitution to me meant a motley crew of battered old dames headed for the police lockup and bedraggled streetwalkers searching for any port in a storm.* -SJSN,15.
POSSUM play possum [col] fingir-se de morto, fingir que está dormindo *He played possum and the enemy soldiers passed by without noting that he was still alive.*
POST left at the post passado para trás, vencido, derrotado *Ford came out a year ahead of the other companies with the compact cars and its competitors were left at the post.*
POT go to pot [col] arruinar-se, deteriorar-se, ir para a cucuia, ir pro brejo *Some things could go to pot, but not his health, he thought.* -MRI,15.
keep the pot boiling 1. ganhar a vida, o sustento *We work hard to keep the pot boiling.* 2. manter a atividade, não parar o que se está fazendo *Everything is OK. Just keep the pot boiling.*
melting pot cadinho (também de raças) *São Paulo and New York are the biggest melting pots in the world.*

the pot calls the kettle black ri-se o roto do esfarrapado *With his admitted methods of investigation he is more like a pot calling the kettle black.* -T/72.

pot shot → **potshot**

POTATO hot potato [col] batata quente, pepino *The hot potato of terrorism is now in [President Ronald] Reagan's hands ...* -T/85.

small potatoes [col] 1. soma insignificante de dinheiro, ninharia, trocados, migalhas *Seven hundred and fifty a week is not small potatoes, eh?* 2. pessoa(s) ou coisa(s) de pouca importância *... he was only small potatoes in the mob.* -T/63.

POTBOILER [col] livro, peça, roteiro de filme etc. (geralmente de baixa qualidade) escrito com a finalidade exclusiva de lucro *Most potboilers are written with the potential of being made into a movie.*

POTLUCK take potluck aceitar como refeição o que houver sido preparado, comer do que houver *Why don't you come out to the house for dinner? We won't have nothin' special. But you can take potluck with us ...* -JJS,22.

POTSHOT; POT SHOT 1. tiro disparado contra alvo que não requer pontaria *He had gone mad and was taking potshots at the crowd.* 2. tirada mordaz *[The newspaper] ... got off some potshots at him [a political candidate] before he arrived.* -T/64.

POUND pound away 1. malhar, atacar *... as a professor of political science at the U.S. Army Intelligence Center ... he has been pounding away at Communism with archangelic zeal.* -T/66. 2. trabalhar com afinco *His father's still pounding away at his old job.*

pound out bater, martelar seguidamente (piano, máquina de escrever) *Author [Edna] Ferber ... tries to pound out 1,000 words every day of the week.* -T/63.

POUR pour down chover copiosamente; desabar, cair com força (chuva, temporal) *... all work ceases when the torrential seasonal rains pour down on the land.* -LAS,272.

pour in/into verter, derramar, despejar em abundância, fluir, invadir, afluir, adentrar continuamente, mover-se em torrentes ou em grande número *Congratulatory messages poured in from the world's capitals.* -T/61. ♦ *... the German hordes poured into his country ...* -SWLM,27. ♦ *American companies have poured in millions of dollars in industries in South America.*

pour out 1. manar, surgir continuamente, sair em abundância, em grande número *[In the opera Carmen] ... the crowd pours out of the arena singing phrases of the Toreador Song ...* -CMS,93. 2. pôr para fora, contar, desabafar *He poured out his life story to a group of student researchers.*

POVERTY LINE linha da pobreza [renda mínima, abaixo da qual, segundo o padrão de um país, uma família ou um indivíduo é caracterizado como pobre] *Poor families in the U.S. have an average of 4.5 children compared with three for those above the poverty line.* -T/69.

POVERTY-STRICKEN muito pobre, indigente *Buffalo Bill lost everything in bad investments and was poverty-stricken when he died in 1917.* -RR,616. ♦ *... poverty-stricken masses ...* -T/84.

POWER powder room banheiro de senhoras *I just happened to be on my way to the powder room.* -SEB,9.

take a powder [gír] desaparecer, sumir, fugir *... there's no law against taking a powder ...* -CRS,15. ♦ *Ray had taken a powder and no trace of him could be found.*

POWER come to power assumir o controle, a chefia, o governo *It was just a year ago that ... [he] came to power ...* -T/78.

in power no poder, no governo *The Democrats have been in power for seven years.*

more power to you boa sorte para você, tenha êxito *... in his innocence or wisdom*

he [Carl Sandburg] believes the American dream worth saving. More power to him! -SV,121.
power of attorney procuração ... *give me power of attorney to sell that damned ranch.* -SG,14. ♦ *... he had signed a power of attorney allowing Tamkin to speculate with his money ...* -BS,55.
the powers that be os poderes constituídos, as autoridades, aqueles que mandam *[They had] ... aligned themselves with the local powers that be.* -TB,12. ♦ *... she was "very definitely" chastised by the church's powers that be for her bold public action ...* -T/92.
PRACTICE in practice 1. na prática *In theory the plan had seemed perfect, but in practice it was rather disappointing.* 2. em forma, bem treinado *Marcia keeps in practice by swimming one hour everyday.*
make a practice of transformar em hábito, acostumar-se a *Don't make a practice of using our phone for personal calls.*
out of practice destreinado, fora de forma *I'm so out of practice that I won't be able to play a very good game of tennis with you.*
practice makes perfect a prática conduz à perfeição *There is no substitute for it [i.e., practice]. Practice really does make perfect.* -WCG,20.
practice on/upon adestrar-se em, exercitar-se em, treinar em *The medical students practiced upon the bodies of small animals before they attempted surgery with humans.*
practice what one preaches praticar aquilo que prega *Dr. Alfred Kinsey discovered that in sexual matters people do not always practice what they preach.*
put (something) in/into practice pôr em prática, executar, acionar *The plan must be put into practice immediately.*
PRAISE sing the praises of louvar, exaltar *Almost all books about ballet sing the praises of Anna Pavlova.*

PRECIOUS precious few/little pouquíssimo(s) *They have precious little time to rest ...* -T/91. ♦ *Precious few members of the committee turned up for the meeting.*
PRESENCE presence of mind presença de espírito *When the car overturned Al had the presence of mind to turn off the ignition and thereby prevent a possible fire.*
PRESENT at present na atualidade, atualmente, no momento, agora *They used to live on a farm but at present they're living in Portland, Oregon.*
for the present → for the MOMENT
PRESENT-DAY da atualidade, atual, moderno *... modern techniques of therapy practiced by present-day psychiatrists and psychologists.* -JS,25.
PRESS be pressed for ter muito pouco ou quase nada de, estar necessitado de *Most of us are pressed for time ...* -WCG,25. ♦ *Are you pressed for cash?*
go to press começar a ser impresso *Her new book is just going to press.*
press agent agente de publicidade *[He had been] ... a former press agent and a partisan Nixon speechwriter.* -T/87.
press/news conference entrevista coletiva *The President held a press conference at the White House.* ♦ *[He] ... called a news conference at [a] ... Denver hospital ...* -T/72.
press down 1. pressionar, apertar *[He] ... pressed down the PLAY button [on the tape recorder] ...* -WI,314. 2. oprimir, afligir, influir no ânimo *The jungle night pressed down like a black oiled tarpaulin.* -SSG,29.
press for solicitar com urgência, exigir, reclamar *... President Reagan decided to press for reductions of nuclear weapons.* -T/84.
press forward/on avançar impetuosamente, investir, arremeter *The crowd pressed forward onto the airfield to welcome the victorious team on their return home.* ♦ *[In the novel* The Grapes of

Wrath*]* *The Joads press on – across New Mexico and Arizona, to the edge of the California desert.* -LAS,270.
press run; pressrun; print run tiragem *The book ... [will have] a press run of 60,000.* -T/69. ♦ *[The new magazine's] ... print run for September ... is scheduled to reach 2,000,000.* -T/73.
yellow press → yellow JOURNALISM
PREVAIL prevail on/upon persuadir, convencer, induzir *Forced into exile for political reasons, Wagner at length sent the score [of his opera* Lohengrin*] to Franz Liszt at Weimar and prevailed on him to produce the opera.* -CMS,170.
PREY fall prey to 1. ser caçado e devorado (animal, ave etc.) por *The mouse fell prey to the hawk.* 2. tornar-se vítima, presa, alvo de, ser atormentado ou afligido por *... 6 million Jews and 5 million Polish Catholics and other victims ... fell prey to the Nazi horrors ...* -T/85. ♦ *In the novel* The Caine Mutiny*, Captain Queeg] ... couldn't take the strain of command any longer and he fell easy prey to the machinations of self-serving officers ...* -BA,125.
prey on/upon 1. caçar e devorar, alimentar-se de *... larger species [of crocodiles], which prey upon the smaller ones when they can.* -SK,47. 2. vitimar, explorar, atacar *Akira Kurosawa's* The Seven Samurai *tells the story of the inhabitants of a small village who are preyed upon by bandits.* 3. atormentar, afligir *His anxieties and fears constantly preyed on him.*
PRICE at any price a qualquer custo *We must win the game at any price.*
price tag custo, o preço de algo *[Automobile] ... price tags have risen an average 40% over the past five years ...* -T/77.
PRICK kick against the pricks dar murro em ponta de faca *It's no use kicking against the pricks.*
PRIDE pocket one's pride deixar o orgulho de lado, humilhar-se *During the Great Depression many people had to pocket their pride and ask for charity.*
pride oneself on/upon orgulhar-se, ufanar-se de *Today we pride ourselves on being the most idealistic nation in the world ...* -HRW,5. ♦ *... the West has long prided itself on its technological lead ...* -T/87.
take pride in sentir orgulho em *... we take ... pride in our astounding material success.* -HRW,5.
PRIME in one's prime na plenitude da mocidade, em seu período de maior pujança, de maior atividade, no auge *Thoreau was in his prime when he built his cabin near Walden Pond.*
past one's prime não mais na flor dos anos, já além da primavera da vida *Jane is still a lovely woman but she's past her prime.*
the prime of life a flor da idade, o vigor dos anos, a mocidade *Whenever my father wanted to convey the idea that someone was young, vigorous and active he'd say that the man or woman in question was "in the prime of life".*
prime time horário nobre (em rádio e televisão) *... critics from the New Right who complain about sex and violence on prime time ...* -T/81. ⇒ **prime-time** de ou relativo ao horário nobre *... a prime-time network program ...* -PN,20. ♦ *... prime-time shows ...* -T/87.
PRIMROSE primrose path 1. vida de prazeres e sensualidade, hedonismo *The primrose path looks very inviting to young people.* 2. maneira de agir ou linha de ação aparentemente fácil e sedutora, mas na realidade temerária ou desastrosa *[He was] Angry at having been "led down the primrose path" by Nixon ...* -T/74.
PRINT in print 1. disponível, existente, que não está esgotado (diz-se de livro, material impresso) *She [Edna Ferber] is justly proud that all of her bestsellers are still in print ...* -T/63. 2. impresso (em jornal, livro etc.), publicado *[He] ... is fearful of reprisals if his name is seen in print.* -T/87.

out of print esgotado (livro) *Most of Luke Short's western novels have been out of print for many years.*
print out imprimir (dados armazenados em computador) *... he told the ... computer to print out a program for plotting complex aerospace data in graph form.* -T/72.
⇒ **printout** listagem, impressão de dados *The company sent us a printout of our account which listed all unpaid items.*
print run → **PRESS run**
PRIVY privy to conhecedor de, a par de, inteirado de, ciente de *He was privy to some of the Government's top secrets.*
PRIZE prize fighter; prizefighter boxeador *[Ernest Hemingway's* Fifty Grand *is a short story]... about a prize fighter who is bribed to allow himself to be defeated.* -HMJ,336.
PRO the pros and cons os prós e os contras *I'm not here to discuss the pros and cons of various national health insurance proposals ...* -T/79.
PROFILE keep/maintain a high//low profile procurar sobressair-se, mostrar-se, chamar atenção, aparecer, fazer alarde// esquivar-se à publicidade, usar discrição, não fazer alarde *Each pair [of patrolmen on the beat] was given ... instructions to ... keep as high a profile as possible.* -T/72.
♦ *If you keep a low profile, you won't lay yourself open to criticism.*
PROFIT profit by/from aproveitar-se de, beneficiar-se de, lucrar com *Tom has greatly profited by his aunt's advice.* ♦ *I could never profit from experience ...* -FLF,48.
turn a profit auferir lucro *... the Houston Post [a newspaper] turned a profit last year ...* -T/87.
PROGRESS in progress em andamento, em curso *... many investigations [of the political scandal] are now in progress ...* -T/86.
PROMISE as good as one's promise → **as good as one's WORD**
break one's promise → **break one's WORD**

show promise dar sinais de progresso, dar esperanças de bom futuro, prometer *As a young artist he showed promise but never developed into a first-rate performer.*
PROOF proof against à prova de, refratário, imune, resistente *The new paint made our cellar proof against water and mildew.*
the proof of the pudding is in the eating só a experiência o dirá *Don't ask me what it tastes like. The proof of the pudding is in the eating.*
PROPERTY real property → **real ESTATE**
PROWL on the prowl 1. rondando, vagueando, à procura de presa *... the fear that any community feels when a murderer is on the prowl.* -T/66. 2. em busca de parceiro sexual *... Paul was what he was, a deceiver of women, constantly on the prowl ...* -WPI,26.
PSYCH psych out [gír] amedrontar(-se), (fazer) perder a coragem, assustar(-se), pressionar psicologicamente, intimidar, perturbar, deixar ou ficar nervoso *Alfred Hitchcock's* Psycho *really psyched me out.*
♦ *Don't psych out. It's not a bad job.*
psych up [gír] aprestar-se psicologicamente, ficar pronto, preparado (para uma competição, prova, momento difícil etc.) *He psyched himself up for the important task ahead.*
PSYCHO [col] indivíduo psicótico, psicopata *When Arbogast met Norman Bates, he had no idea that Bates was a psycho.*
PUBLIC public-address system → **public-address SYSTEM**
PUFF UP 1. inchar, intumescer(-se) *His face was all puffed up when he had food poisoning.* 2. envaidecer-se, ficar cheio de si *Mrs. Bennett is all puffed up now that her husband has become a vice-president of the company.*
PULL pull a fast one [gír] tapear, enganar *[He was] ... always trying to pull a fast one of some kind.* -AIM,95.

pull apart = TAKE apart 3 *His arguments were easily pulled apart by his political adversaries.*

pull back recuar, fazer recuar, retirar (-se) *Hitler's top generals urged him to pull back from Normandy ...* -T/84. ♦ *The [United Nations] Security Council ordered each of the combatants [Iran and Iraq] to pull back its forces to its own territory.* -T/87. ⇒ **pullback** retirada militar bem organizada, bem planejada *a pullback of troops*

pull down 1. demolir, destruir *Many old buildings were pulled down to make a place for the United Nations building.* 2. reduzir, diminuir, baixar ... *an economic slowdown in the next month or two will pull down the cost of borrowing money.* -T/81. 3. deprimir, abater, debilitar *Mr. Goddard's many problems have pulled him down lately.* 4. [col] ganhar, receber (dinheiro, salário etc.) *[Elvis] Presley, then 18, was pulling down $35 a week as a truck driver ...* -T/77. ♦ *[He] ... pulls down $45,000 per year ...* -T/72.

pull in 1. apertar *He pulled in his belt.* 2. [também **pull into**] chegar, chegar ao destino; parar (veículo) em determinado lugar, fazer uma parada *The train pulled in at nine p. m.* ♦ *We will pull in at the next roadside restaurant and have a bite to eat and use the restrooms.* 3. [gír] prender, capturar *The police pulled in all the known sex criminals in their search for the child's murderer.* 4. puxar para dentro, recolher *The insect pulled in its antennae when I touched it.*

pull off 1. tirar, despir (roupa); descalçar (sapato, bota) *Gina pulled off her sweater.* ♦ *It's very difficult to pull off tight boots.* 2. [col] executar, levar a cabo, conseguir realizar (tarefa, plano etc.) apesar de dificuldades *[He] ... pulled off another neat political trick that keeps him marching toward the White House.* -T/92.

pull (something) on (someone) 1. aprontar (algo) contra (alguém), fraudar, enganar *Chuck had pulled a dirty trick on Jim.* 2. puxar, sacar (revólver, faca) contra *The thief pulled a knife on me.*

pull oneself together refazer-se, recompor-se, controlar-se, dominar as emoções *Helen dried her tears, powdered her face and generally pulled herself together before her guests arrived.*

pull out 1. partir *We arrived just as the bus was pulling out.* 2. retirar-se *When the foreign troops pulled out, the local troops lost ground to the rebels.* ⇒ **pullout** = **pullback** ... *a possible pullout of Soviet troops.* -T/87. 3. [col] retirar-se de um acordo, compromisso etc., safar-se de uma dificuldade ... *Socialist political bosses threatened to pull out of their coalition with the conservative People's Party.* -T/63. 4. sacar, tirar, mostrar *[A man] ... pulled out a Bowie knife and stabbed him in the back ...* -SH,20. ♦ *Martin pulled out a ten-dollar bill and gave it to the man.* 5. extrair, arrancar *She has just had a tooth pulled out.*

pull over encostar veículo à guia da calçada, à beira da estrada etc. *Pull over to the curb and park in front of the Post Office.*

pull through [col] 1. sair de um aperto, atravessar com êxito uma crise ou situação difícil; tirar de aperto ou dificuldade *We have just pulled through a serious, critical business slump.* ♦ 2. curar-se, recuperar-se *It seems that the old lady will not pull through.*

pull together 1. cooperar, trabalhar em conjunto, em harmonia *Do you believe the Democratic Party is ever going to pull together to elect a President?* -T/92. 2. reerguer, reabilitar, reconstituir, reconduzir à normalidade *Presidente Duarte is pullling his country together and enjoys wide support from the people.* -T/85. 3. v. **PULL oneself together**

pull up 1. arrancar *The child pulled up all the markers that his father had placed in the garden.* 2. parar, fazer parar, deter

(-se), estacar *A car pulled up in front of the old house.* ♦ *We were pulled up by the highway police who were searching all the cars for the escaped prisoners.* 3. trazer para perto *He pulled up a chair and sat down.* -CEP,183. 4. emparelhar com, ficar lado a lado de *[A fast driver] ... angered by a car that did not move from the fast lane pulled up alongside the offending vehicle and fatally shot a passenger in the front seat.* -T/87. 5. censurar, repreender, chamar a atenção de *Hughie was pulled up for using bad language.*

pull up short parar ou deter-se abruptamente *When someone shouted "Liar", he pulled up short and for a time seemed unable to continue his speech.*

PUNCH beat to the punch → **beat to the DRAW**

pack a punch [col] produzir grande efeito, impacto, ter força, vigor, ímpeto *[The Decline of the American Empire, a movie] ... a cinematic phenomenon that packs a punch completely out of proportion to its size.* -T/86.

pull (one's) punches [col] 1. desferir socos deliberadamente ineficazes, bater de leve, sem ferir *He pulls his punches when he plays with friends.* 2. criticar de maneira deliberadamente leniente, falar com moderação, comedir-se *[General George S. Patton] An intelligent, quick-witted man who does not pull punches either in battle or in private life.* -BRF,16. ♦ *In her autobiography she bares a lot of secrets and pulls no punches.*

punch in//out → **CLOCK in//out**

punch line o ponto no qual reside a parte mais importante de um discurso, o clímax de uma história, a graça de uma piada etc. *His speech was vapid and boring until he delivered his punch line.* ♦ *The punch line of a joke is often the only thing worth hearing.*

PURPOSE answer/serve the/one's purpose servir a um objetivo *I don't think your plan will serve our purpose.*

on purpose de propósito, intencionalmente *He broke the chair on purpose.*

to no/little purpose em vão, inutilmente *Vickie was told that Ron would cause her grief but our advice was to no purpose.*

for (all) practical purposes na realidade, a bem dizer, virtualmente, praticamente *The layer of air around the earth, for all practical purposes, is approximately 100 miles thick ...* -FI,13.

PURSUANT pursuant to de acordo com, de conformidade com *Pursuant to Mr. Wingate's instructions I am now giving you the rest of the money.*

PUSH be pushing [col] estar beirando (determinada idade, tantos anos de vida) *Polly admitted she's pushing forty.*

push ahead/forward/on avançar, prosseguir, continuar *Despite his public activities, Einstein managed to push ahead with his scientific work.* -T/79. ♦ *We were cold and tired but we knew we had to push on to help the people in the snowbound train.*

push around [col] impor-se de forma arbitrária, tratar de maneira rude, bancar o mandão, intimidar *I'm not going to let you push him around, you hear me?* ♦ *... it is difficult to separate him [Clark Gable] from the screen image of the man who pushed women around.* -JR,19.

push for tentar conseguir ou realizar algo exercendo pressão *The new President is pushing hard for many social reforms.*

push off [col] partir, ir embora *The soldiers pushed off at daybreak.*

push on → **PUSH ahead**

push open abrir *She pushed open the front door of her house and went into the living room ...* -MG,30.

push through fazer passar, fazer aprovar (projeto, lei) por meio de pressão *[The Prime Minister] ... pushed through major transportation and telecommunications projects ...* -T/92.

PUSHOVER [gir] 1. tarefa fácil, canja,

moleza *Heavy work is a push-over for construction machinery powered by Waukesha engines.* -T/64. 2. pessoa facilmente persuadida, influenciada ou manipulada, pessoa facilmente receptiva a qualquer coisa ou a outra pessoa; adversário fácil de ser derrrotado ... *he is no pushover for either Moscow or the White House.* -T/87. ♦ *Mike's a pushover for big blondes.* 3. mulher que se entrega facilmente *He got tired of having sex with pushovers and found happiness and satisfaction with his second wife.*

PUSSYFOOT [col] evitar comprometer-se, agir com grande cautela *Clint pussyfoots around and never makes a concrete statement.*

PUT hard put → **(hard) PUT to it**

not put it past (someone) acreditar que (alguém) seja capaz de (tomar uma atitude, praticar um ato geralmente censurável, leviano, maldoso, ilegal etc.), não se surpreender (com tal atitude) *I wouldn't put it past Crosby to disobey orders and call a retreat.* -CN,311. ♦ *I wouldn't put it past him to inform on us to the secret police.*

put about virar de bordo, mudar de rumo *The small sailboat put about and raced for the safety of the harbor.*

put across [col] 1. = **PUT over** 2 *The professor had a hard time trying to put across Einstein's Theory of Relativity to his students.* 2. = **PUT over** 3 *... if [the Italian Premier] ... cannot put the economic plan across, then no politician can.* -T/78.

put aside 1. pôr de lado, descartar, rejeitar *He put aside his first wife and married a much younger woman.* 2. economizar, guardar *I thank God that I've put aside some money in my lifetime.* -HJT,49.

put away 1. guardar, repor no devido lugar *[She] ... finished wiping the silverware and put it away.* -MG,387. 2. economizar, poupar *He has enough money put away to last him the rest of his life.* 3. deixar de lado *Put your troubles away and come dance with me.* 4. [col] confinar (na cadeia ou em hospital para doentes mentais) *Many of Nixon's advisors were put away.* ♦ *Ezra Pound was put away in an institution for the insane but was later freed.* 5. [col] comer ou beber (muito) *For a little girl, she can put away a great amount of food.* ♦ *My father used to put it away, ... but he was a quiet drinker.* -BAJ,18. ♦ *[He can] ... put away as many as four bottles [of beer] within an hour.* -T/92. 6. [col] matar; executar, sacrificar (animal) *Arthur was put away by an accidental gunshot.* ♦ *[He] ... had his favorite dogs put away ...* -T/60.

put back repor no lugar, devolver *Put this book back in the shelf.*

put by pôr de lado, guardar, economizar *You should put by a small sum each month for your children's education.*

put down 1. pôr de lado, largar, deixar *Once you start reading his new book it is absolutely impossible to put it down.* ♦ *Put that gun down!* 2. reprimir, esmagar, sufocar, debelar *The regular Army Troopers soon put down the attempted rebellion.* 3. escrever, anotar *His words were carefully put down on paper.* 4. [gir] humilhar, menosprezar, depreciar, criticar *Say anything you like, but don't put him down.* -T/81. ⇒ **put-down** réplica esmagadora, resposta que obriga a meter a viola no saco, observação ou ato humilhante *Bernie's harsh remark was a put-down that Lesley will never forget.* 5. atribuir *Mason's failure was put down to inexperience.* 6. classificar, estabelecer a identidade, nacionalidade, profissão etc., caracterizar *I would put you down for a German, not a Yankee.* ♦ *Looking at him I'd put him down as a university professor.* 7. aterrissar, pousar (avião) *[The plane] ... put down at Rockland in rough weather.* -T/62. 8. colocar o nome de alguém em uma lista (de contribuição etc.) *You can put me down for twenty dollars for the fund to help the sick janitor.*

put forth 1. propor, apresentar, oferecer *Dr. Burke put forth some provocative ideas in his speech.* 2. tornar manifesto, publicar *A message was put forth in all the land that the king was to arrive.* 3. lançar *Plants won't put forth new leaves if they have no sun.*
put forward propor, formular, apresentar *... a peace plan [was] ... put forward by [the opposition leader] ...* -T/85.
put in 1. chegar ao porto, aportar, fundear *... U.S. Navy warships ... regularly put in to this liberty port.* -T/87. ♦ *The ship put in at the nearest port for repairs.* 2. inserir, interpolar, acrescentar (algo à conversa) *"Now, wait a minute", Hayes put in, "I never said that!"* 3. passar, empregar (tempo, energia, esforços etc. segundo a maneira indicada, em alguma ocupação) *[The Prime Minister] ... puts in a busy [daily] schedule.* -T/76. ♦ *... he put in some hectic years as a rancher ...* -RJ,15. 4. fazer (ligação telefônica) *Skinner put in an urgent person-to-person call to Smith in Hawaii.* 5. apresentar (queixa, pedido etc.); fazer formalmente (oferta) *Actor Jack Nicholson put in a successful bid of $7,728 for a [Italian painter] Tiepolo chalk sketch.* -T/78.
put in for requerer, solicitar *... he put in for space-flight training.* -T/61.
put it expressar, declarar, dizer *Let's put it this way: what she doesn't know won't hurt her.* ♦ *[He] ... was, to put it bluntly, in big trouble.* -T/66. ♦ *... sweeping new programs, to put it mildly, are not ... [the Administration's] forte.* -T/87.
put off 1. adiar, protelar *Never put off till tomorrow what you can do today.* 2. fazer esperar, livrar-se (de alguém) com evasivas ou subterfúgios, esquivar-se de, despistar *Norman keeps putting me off when I ask him to return the money that he borrowed.* 3. perturbar, desagradar, embaraçar *I was really put off by his rude remark.* 4. intimidar, coibir, dissuadir, fazer desistir *Don't let one failure put you off from working on your invention.* 5. deixar descer (de veículo), desembarcar *Ask the driver to put you off at the public library.*
put on 1. vestir, calçar, pôr; aplicar (à pele) *He put on his coat and left.* ♦ *Put your shoes on.* ♦ *Madge is putting on lipstick.* 2. simular, fingir *His sickness is only put on to gain sympathy.* ⇒ **put-on** falso, fingido *Don't pay any attention to his put-on face. He's really guilty.* 3. acrescentar; ganhar (peso) *During Christmas, the stores put on extra help to take care of the increase in business.* ♦ *In three weeks ... I put on six pounds ...* -T/60. ♦ *He's putting on weight.* 4. encenar; organizar (espetáculo, show etc.) *They're going to put on a new show on Broadway.* 5. aplicar (freios, força, pressão, velocidade etc.) *He put on the brakes and the car stopped.* 6. [gír] zombar (de alguém) fingindo ar de seriedade, pregar uma peça, enganar, iludir *Did he really say that? I don't believe it. You're putting me on.* ⇒ **put-on** peça, brincadeira, gozação, caçoada, logro *They believed her story but it was just a put-on.*
put out 1. extinguir, apagar (fogo, luz, cigarro) *Make sure you put out the lights when you leave the house.* ♦ *Put out that cigarette.* 2. pôr para fora, expulsar *They were put out of the game for fighting with the referee.* 3. desconcertar, embaraçar, perturbar *She was put out by the unpleasant incident at the club.* 4. causar inconveniência, incomodar, amolar *Are you sure it won't put you out if I stay here overnight?* 5. aborrecer, irritar, deixar zangado *Jill gets very put out if her husband doesn't notice her new clothes.* 6. publicar, divulgar *Time Magazine is put out once a week.* 7. produzir, fornecer *Arrow Shirt Company puts out the best shirts in the U.S.* 8. envidar, aplicar, exercer; esforçar-se, empenhar-se *Clearly he had put himself out to be agreeable to her ...*

-JJS,197.   9. fazer-se ao mar, zarpar *The ship had put out from San Francisco.*
put over   1. adiar, transferir *The staff meeting has been put over to next Wednesday.*   2. [col] comunicar com clareza, transmitir eficazmente, fazer entender, tentar convencer, persuadir *I'm trying to put over the fact that you can be a new star if you cooperate with me.*   3. [col] fazer ser aceito, bem-recebido, fazer ter êxito, transformar em sucesso, levar a cabo eficazmente *Critics today, ... speak of the way I use my hands to put over a song.* -RLI,19.
put right   consertar, corrigir, pôr em ordem *If your TV is not working well, Harry can put it right for you.*
put something over on   [col] impingir (algo desonesto, ilícito, contrário à ética), levar a acreditar iludindo *You thought you were putting something over on me, didn't you?* -UJ,211.
put through   1. levar a cabo, executar com êxito *The new management has put through several changes in the organization.*   2. fazer ligação telefônica; pôr em contato por telefone *Tania put through a call to her mother in Toronto.*   3. fazer atravessar (dificuldade, momento difícil, situação desagradável, provação etc.) *You have put your wife through a lot of suffering.*   4. pagar para fazer freqüentar (escola, curso etc.) *Young Anton Chekhov, at 19, began writing stories for cheap magazines to put himself through medical school and support the family.* -T/62.
put together   1. construir, montar, formar (um todo juntando partes), organizar, preparar *Doug likes to put together model cars and airplanes.*   ♦ *... the United Nations is trying to put together the world's first space treaty ...* -T/66.   2. unir, reunir, juntar, somar, adicionar   *... Jupiter, a planet that contains more matter than all the other planets in the solar system put together.* -T/77.   3. [gír] [também **well put together**] (mulher) escultural, bem-feita de corpo, de formas bem proporcionadas *She's certainly well put together.*   ♦ *[In the movie* Never So Few, *Frank Sinatra tells Gina Lollobrigida] " ... you're put together like a Christmas package."* -T/60.
(hard) put to it; hard put   em situação difícil, em apuro, encrencado *Campbell is hard put to finish his novel within the contractual time.*   ♦ *Calhoun was hard put to it to raise the necessary money to pay all his debts.*
put two and two together   concluir (algo) pela evidência dos fatos, chegar à conclusão que os fatos justificam *I can put two and two together. I have a pretty good idea of what's going on here. You don't have to tell me!*
put up   1. erigir, edificar, construir *The East Germans put up the Berlin Wall in 1961.*   2. pendurar, suspender, afixar no alto, em uma parede etc. *Police last week temporarily detained about 20 union members for putting up wall posters.* -T/81.   3. contribuir, suprir, pôr, apostar (dinheiro) *Each player puts up twenty dollars before the game begins.*   4. [col] alojar(-se), hospedar(-se) *My wife and I like to put up at the same hotel in Hot Springs where we spent our honeymoon.*   ♦ *Could you put me up for the night?*   5. propor como candidato, indicar (para eleição, cargo etc.) *He was put up as a possible presidential choice by his state.*   6. oferecer, apresentar, propor (para consideração, discussão, decisão etc.) *Your proposal will be put to the committee next week.*   7. oferecer, colocar à venda, em leilão etc.) *[He] ... put a country house that he bought two years ago up for sale ...* -T/74.   8. opor, intentar (luta, resistência etc.) *[General] Eisenhower was convinced "the Germans would put up a strong fight for Paris".* -CL,10.   9. pôr em conserva (legumes, frutas) *American women put up fresh fruit in jars for winter eating when the fruit is hard to get.*   10.

[col] persuadir, incitar, instigar *He was always putting little kids up to ringing the doorbells of the old eccentrics in our neighborhood.*

put up with suportar, tolerar, agüentar *... we have to put up with things we don't agree with ...* -T/91. ♦ *I can't put up with that woman any longer.*

put wise [gir] informar, alertar, avisar, advertir, cientificar, esclarecer *He put us wise to the fact that the boss could watch the workers through a hidden peephole.* ♦ *Nora was put wise to the nasty things they had been saying behind her back.*

PUT-UPON importunado, abusado, incomodado, ludibriado *I felt no special inclination to be put-upon and told her so frankly.* ♦ *... a put-upon parent ...* -T/87.

Q. on the q. t. = **on the QUIET**
QUALM have qualms preocupar-se, ter dúvidas, apreensões, escrúpulos *Frank had qualms about having lied to his wife.* ♦ *U.S. officials had no qualms about the swift use of force in the incident.* -T/87.
QUARRELL pick a quarrel → **pick a FIGHT**
QUARTER ask//give no quarter não pedir// dar quartel, clemência *The Wehrmacht [German armed forces] soldiers were ordinary guys ... but the SS troops were something else. They gave no quarter.* -T/84.
at close quarters muito próximo, de perto, contíguo *His aim is to study friction between the sexes and to determine how human beings from diverse cultures and classes behave when they live at close quarters.* -T/73.
QUEER queer oneself prejudicar-se, colocar-se em situação embaraçosa *Howard makes a wonderful appearance but queers himself by talking too much with prospective employers.*
QUEST in quest of em busca de *Jason and the Argonauts set off in quest of the Golden Fleece.*
QUESTION beg the question admitir como verdadeiro algo que tem de ser provado *To say that we have a soul and the rest [of all other animals] do not begs the question and is at least debatable.* -BN,13.
beside the question → **beside the POINT**
beyond question 1. certo, inconteste, indisputável *... his integrity was believed to be beyond question.* -GJI,47. 2. inquestionavelmente, sem dúvida *Burr is, beyond question, the best candidate that we have interviewed so far.*
bring/call in/into question questionar, pôr em dúvida *For the first time probably in his career, his integrity has been brought into question.* -T/87. ♦ *Leigh's mistake called into question his ability to handle a difficult situation.*
burning question → **burning ISSUE**
in question 1. em questão, em discussão *The man in question is not to be trusted.* 2. em dúvida, sob suspeita *His integrity is in question.*
leading question pergunta capciosa, que induz a determinada resposta *... he had skilfully framed leading questions, trying ... to make Crosbie drop a hint of their assignment.* -SBW,6.
open question questão em discussão, algo ainda sem resposta *Since Galileo we have decided open questions in science by ob-*

servation and experimentation. -HHO,26.

out of the question inadmissível, impossível *The President said that the possibility of invasion is now completely out of the question.*

pop the question [col] propor casamento ... *in 1967, Elvis [Presley] popped the question, even though, according to Priscilla, "we were perfectly content the way we were".* -T/73.

put a question to fazer uma pergunta a ... *he knew that he had no reason to put questions to her.* -HWR,81.

raise a question fazer uma pergunta, levantar uma questão *Many questions were raised at the meeting but only a few were answered.*

shoot questions at crivar de perguntas *It must be difficult for the President when the reporters begin to shoot questions at him so rapidly.*

without question = beyond QUESTION 2 *Freud is, without question, the founder of modern psychiatry.* -DR,176.

QUICK cut/hurt/touch to the quick magoar profundamente, ofender *Waldo can make such mean comments that someone is always touched to the quick.* ♦ *Shirley's harsh words cut him to the quick.*

the quick and the dead os vivos e os mortos *It is far easier in fiction than in life to distinguish between the quick and the dead.* -T/73.

a quick one [col] pequena dose de bebida, trago, gole *Let's have a quick one at the new bar before we go home.*

QUICK-TEMPERED → **have a hot TEMPER**

QUICK-WITTED perspicaz, esperto, sagaz *Jacobs was a clever, quick-witted man.*

QUIET on the quiet; on the q. t. [gír] em segredo, confidencialmente, em surdina *She left town on the quiet one night.* -SG,38. ♦ *His mother has been drinking on the q. t. for years.*

quiet down acalmar(-se), aquietar(-se) *The murmuring voices quieted down ...* -EW,43. ♦ *It took him a long time to quiet down the noisy crowd that had come to hear him speak.*

QUITE quite a incomum, invulgar, formidável, excepcional, excelente; e tanto *His father is quite a man.* ♦ *quite a party* ♦ *quite a surprise*

QUITS cry quits desistir, dar-se por vencido ou satisfeito *Business had been so slow that we were almost ready to cry quits and close our store forever.*

R the three R's os três fundamentos da educação *[Reading, (w)Riting, (a)Rithmetic] Many parents are demanding that more attention be placed on the three R's and less on play activity.*

RACE throw a race → **throw a FIGHT**

RACK rack and ruin estado de completa destruição, ruína etc. *The old mansion went to rack and ruin after the last Longfellow died and no heirs could be found.*

rack up [gir] acumular, ganhar, marcar (pontos, vantagem etc.) *Last year the business racked up close to $15 million in sales.* -T/87. ♦ *Mark Spitz racked up many victories in the Olympic Games.*

RACKET make/raise a racket [gir] fazer muito barulho, algazarra *The people in the next apartment raise a racket at about 11 every night.*

RAG chew the rag → **chew the FAT**

from rags to riches da miséria à riqueza *Callahan went from rags to riches in a few years.* ⇒ **rags-to-riches** que passou da miséria à riqueza *... Cliff's rise was a rags-to-riches saga in the best American tradition ...* -GM,278.

RAGE fly into a rage/passion encolerizar-se *He flew into a rage when his wife smashed his car.* ♦ *... she flew into a passion when relatives suggested the story [that her son had murdered a boy] might be true.* -MMA,51.

in a rage furioso, enfurecido, colérico *Nick was in a rage, yelling obscenities at me.*

(all) the rage a grande moda, a paixão atual, a mania do momento *Psychoanalysis was the rage [following the First World War], and its influence was felt in every theater of life.* -HC,17.

RAIN be rained out ser interrompido ou cancelado pela chuva (partida, competição, evento etc.) *The game they had so eagerly waited for was rained out.*

it never rains but it pours uma desgraça nunca vem só *First the radio went on the blink, then the refrigerator refused to work and now the water has stopped. It seems as if it never rains but it pours.*

not know enough to come in out of the rain ser ignorante, estúpido, burro *Sometimes he does such foolish things that you would think he doesn't know enough to come in out of the rain.*

rain check 1. canhoto de ingresso (ou senha etc.) que dá direito a assistir à partida, luta etc. no futuro se a original for cancelada ou interrompida pelo mau tempo *The fight promoters had to issue rain checks when the outdoor fight was called off because of the bad weather.* 2. convite válido para outra ocasião por ser impossível aceitá-lo no momento *I'm busy this week but if you'll give me a rain check for next week, I positively will be able to visit your new home.*

rain down fazer cair abundantemente, derrubar em profusão; cair em abundância *Thousands of bombs were rained down upon Europe in World War II.* ♦ *... craters ... produced by the impact of meteorites raining down on the moon ...* -JRR,91.

(come) rain or (come) shine chova ou faça sol, aconteça o que acontecer *I'll be there next Saturday, rain or shine.*

RAINBOW chase rainbows voar nas asas da fantasia, embalar ilusões, procurar algo inutilmente *Please, tell me doctor, am I chasing rainbows?*

RAISE get a raise receber aumento de salário *In my company everybody gets a raise at the first of the year.*

RAKE rake in arrecadar, acumular, ganhar rapidamente *[James Stewart] ... quietly and steadily made movies that raked in millions ...* -TH,10.

rake up tornar público, divulgar *Some newspapers are always raking up some new scandal about public officials.*

RAKE-OFF [gir] comissão ilícita, quinhão, suborno *The police must be getting a rake-off to allow such an indecent show to continue week after week.*

RANDOM at random ao acaso, a esmo *Pick up a book at random, open to a page at random ...* -LCT,147.

RANK break ranks 1. retirar o apoio ao grupo, partido etc., tornar-se dissidente, romper (com) *[The West German Chancellor] ... pledged not to break ranks with the allies ...* -T/80. 2. sair de forma, romper formação *The soldiers broke ranks and fled into the woods.*

close ranks cerrar fileiras, dar apoio *... in times of crisis ... we will close ranks and fight to the death for each other.* -RJ,14.

of the first rank de primeira qualidade *Fitzgerald, Hemingway and Faulkner are novelists of the first rank.*

pull (one's) rank [gir] usar seu posto, posição social etc. para exigir obediência, cumprimento de ordens etc. *Now, don't try to pull your rank on me, captain. My father is a general.* ♦ *If Carson can't convince you to do it, he'll pull rank and force you to do it.*

the rank and file 1. soldados rasos em geral *... the army now became convinced that, no matter what [Jango] Goulart did, the rank and file of the forces would no longer respond to discipline.* -GJI,48. ⇒ **rank-and-file** relativo aos soldados rasos *... rank-and-file troops ...* -T/78. 2. gente comum, o povo; as classes subordinadas (em contraposição aos líderes) *The rank and file often are not in agreement with the union leaders.* ⇒ **rank-and-file** do povo, comum, da camada social humilde *... rank-and-file union workers ...* -T/85.

rise from/through the ranks 1. chegar de praça a oficial, subir na hierarquia militar *It's much easier to rise through the ranks in the American Army than in the British Army.* 2. fazer-se por si, progredir por esforço próprio *Hal B. Wallis ... rose from the ranks at Warner Brothers to become one of Hollywood's most durable, successful producers ...* -T/86.

RAP beat the rap [gir] ser absolvido do crime que cometeu, safar-se da pena *Even though he was guilty of the crime, his clever lawyer helped him beat the rap.*

not care/give a rap [gir] = **not care a DAMN** *She doesn't care a rap if she loses her job because she has an independent income.*

take the rap [gir] assumir a culpa de outra pessoa, ser condenado por crime praticado por outra pessoa *A gang member often* takes the rap for his boss and serves a year or two in prison.

RASPBERRY the raspberry = the BRONX cheer *Because he had been accused of collaboration with the Germans, he was given the raspberry each time he appeared on the ABC stage.*

RAT the rat race [gir] a luta extremamente intensa, agitada, rotineira e contínua das pessoas para passarem umas à frente das outras nos negócios, na profissão e na vida social *... some consumers are already showing signs of disillusionment with the rat race of materialism.* -T/87.

smell a rat suspeitar de trapaça, desconfiar de algo *They smelled a rat when the enemy troops offered to call a temporary truce.*

RATE at any rate em todo caso, de qualquer maneira, seja como for *Never mind if they didn't pay you for your work. At any rate you have gained a valuable experience.*

at this//that rate desta//daquela maneira, velocidade etc. *At this rate of construction this building will not be ready for at least five years.*

RATTLE rattle/reel off dizer ou recitar rápida e facilmente *[In the 1941 Broadway musical* Lady in the Dark, *Danny Kaye] ... in 39 seconds, rattled off the names of Russian composers Malichevsky, Rubinstein, Arensky, Tchaikovsky, and some 50 others ...* -RD,98. ♦ *Ted can reel off the names of all the players who have been on the baseball teams for the last twenty years.*

RAVE [col] 1. elogio extraordinário, crítica ou recensão extravagantemente favorável *Carnal Knowledge ... won an Oscar nomination for the actress [Ann-Margret] and raves from many critics ...* -T/73. 2. extravagantemente lisonjeiro ou favorável *... The Apartment [a movie] ... opened in Manhattan to rave reviews ...* -T/60. ♦ *... a clarinet player getting rave notices while playing in Benny Goodman's band.* -T/65.

rave about/over falar de ou escrever sobre (alguém ou algo) com grande entusiasmo, elogiar muito *The whole world raved about* Black Orpheus *but it was not too well received in Brazil.* ♦ *The critics raved over Elizabeth Taylor's performance in* Who's Afraid of Virginia Woolf?

RAW in the raw 1. em estado natural, bruto, não-refinado *On the island, we had a chance to observe life in the raw.* 2. [gir] nu, despido *... in Europe this summer, Teutonic tourists in the raw have been all too well observed ...* -T/62.

RAZOR-SHARP 1. afiado como navalha *James Bowie's famous knife had a guarded hilt and a 10-inch long razor-sharp blade.* 2. agudo, aguçado, fino, penetrante, intenso, pungente *... razor-sharp social observation.* -T/69.

RAZZLE-DAZZLE [gir] alvoroço, algazarra, confusão *There was so much razzle-dazzle to the presidential campaign that few people noted the inept qualities of the candidates.*

REACH reach back recuar no tempo, remontar (a uma época, ao passado) *The Kurds' ethnic roots reach back thousands of years to the dawn of Mesopotamia.* -T/91.

reach down estender (mão, braço, pé) para baixo, abaixar-se para tentar alcançar *... Hugh cautiously reached down to rub his right thigh and knee.* -MF,4.

reach for estender, esticar (mão, braço, pé) para tentar alcançar, tocar ou pegar *He reached for a magazine on the coffee table.*

reach in/into pôr a mão dentro de *Liza opened her purse, reached in, and took out a ten-dollar bill.* ♦ *The man reached into his pocket, pulled out several envelopes ...* -HJT,34.

reach out 1. estender (a mão, o braço), esticar-se, tentar alcançar *His ego is so apparent that it almost reaches out and grabs you by the throat.* -T/60. ♦ *He*

reached out a hand to help the girl. 2. tentar comunicar-se (com), tentar fazer contato (com) *It's very hard to reach out to that boy.*
reach over estender a mão, o braço *Al reached over and picked up something from the kitchen table.*
READ read (someone) ouvir e compreender (geralmente em intercomunicação via rádio) *"How do you read me?" "I read you loud and clear."*
read into atribuir determinado significado a *Many people read into Shakespeare ideas and meanings which the Bard of Avon never intended to convey.*
read off ler completamente, por inteiro (lista, relação, texto etc.) *[He] ... got to his feet and ... read off a six-page speech.* -T/60.
read out ler em voz alta *He picked up the letter and read it out to his wife and son.*
read out of expulsar de (grupo, partido, sociedade etc.) lendo publicamente as razões da expulsão *Most of the Saints [i.e., Mormon believers] turned furiously against their prophet [Joseph Smith], who responded by reading them out of the church ...* -BR,536.
read over/through ler um texto todo, ler do princípio ao fim, ler inteiramente *The President-elect arose at eight, read over the text of his inaugural address ...* -SJ,15. ♦ *Studying well means much more than simply reading through an assignment.* -CCC,vii.
read up on informar-se a respeito de (alguém ou algo) pela leitura, estudar (algo) cuidadosamente *Before each meeting he has read up on his guest.* -T/77. ♦ *... the student of literature who attempts to "read up on" primitive languages is struck very early by their great diversity.* -SWL,42.
READY at the ready 1. de prontidão, preparado, pronto para entrar em ação *... royal guards in gold-threaded tunics and pantaloons stood at the ready ...* -T/66.
2. pronto para ser usado *[The soldier], ... his rifle at the ready, stalked through the darkness, like a soft-footing panther.* -CRST,86.
READY-MADE 1. já pronto, feito à máquina, pronto para vestir ou consumir, pronto para uso imediato *Most men buy ready-made suits these days for obvious reasons.* 2. comum, sem originalidade, banal *... efforts to avoid ready-made solutions ...* -T/86. 3. conveniente, adequado *All he needed was a ready-made excuse.*
REAL for real [gir] 1. sério, sincero; verdadeiro, real, genuíno *... Gorbachev "may be for real ..."* -T/87. ♦ *Is your hair for real or are you wearing a wig for a joke?* 2. seriamente, de verdade *The two boys were fighting for real.*
REALIZE little does one realize → **LITTLE does one imagine**
REALLY really and truly de verdade, verdadeiramente *... now for the first time, he really and truly looked worried.* -WCN,247.
REAPER the grim reaper; Grim Reaper o ceifeiro implacável [a personificação da morte: esqueleto envolto em mortalha empunhando uma gadanha] *We had counselled them to be ready for the Grim Reaper ...* -EF,20.
REAR bring up the rear vir à retaguarda de uma fileira, de um grupo, de uma competição etc., vir em último lugar, fechar a marcha *... I was the youngest [soldier] and brought up the rear.* -FS,9.
REASON bring to reason fazer (alguém) ver a luz da razão, fazer agir com sensatez *We tried everything to bring him to reason.*
for/with good reason justificadamente, com razão *Abnormal behavior has for good reason been designated the country's number-one health problem.* -CJ,5. ♦ *Of all malignancies, breast cancer is perhaps the one most feared by women, and with good reason.* -T/87.
in/within reason razoável, dentro dos limites *Lois has promised to do everything*

in reason to help you. ♦ *If your request is within reason, we will try to grant it.*
it stands to reason é lógico, é claro, é evidente *It stands to reason that neither Jackson nor Brooks spoke the truth.*
listen to reason ouvir a voz da razão *Hugh has an independent mind and will listen to reason.*
reason out procurar solucionar (problema), achar uma resposta *He had a way of reasoning out things to make them look real simple.* -UL,2.
with good reason → **for good REASON**
within reason → **in REASON**
RECALL beyond/past recall impossível de ser recuperado, revogado, lembrado etc.; irreversível(mente), irremediável(mente). *Some of the words in the note were blotted beyond recall.*
RECEIPT on/upon receipt ao receber, no ato do recebimento (de algo) *On receipt of your signed approval we will begin the construction of your summer home.*
RECENTLY as recently as = **as LATE as** *As recently as 1980, Poland was the only East bloc nation in which drug abuse was openly discussed.* -T/87.
RECEPTION warm reception 1. recepção cordial, acolhida calorosa *When Yuri Gagarin returned from his round-the-world space flight he got a warm reception.* 2. severo contra-ataque, investida violenta, ação ofensiva *When the rival gang came into our territory we gave them a warm reception.*
RECKON reckon with//without contar com, levar em conta//não contar com, não considerar, não levar em conta *When you consider buying a car you must reckon with future repair and parts replacement bills.* ♦ *When planning their annual picnic, they reckoned without the possibility of rain.*
RECORD break the record bater o recorde *... in the U.S. it [the movie* The Lovers*] has broken box-office records ...* -T/60.
(just) for the record (só) para constar, para ser registrado, para ser conhecido ou lembrado *For the record, he was a five-star General of the Army, and his first name was Douglas.* -T/64.
go on record expressar-se de público, manifestar-se *... the man who helped develop the Soviet H-bomb went on record opposing atmospheric testing of a 100-megaton weapon.* -T/87.
off the record; off-the-record confidencial, não-oficial, que não deve ser citado ou publicado *... the story [of German surrender in World War II] was off the record until the Allied governments announced it.* -T/85. ♦ *... 80 Representatives and Senators gathered for an off-the-record briefing by President Carter ...* -T/78. ♦ *an off-the-record remark*
on (the) record 1. conhecido, registrado, de que se tem notícia *... he was only twelve years old – the youngest child on record to die from heroin in the city.* -T/69. 2. expresso de público, manifesto, declarado oficialmente *[Napoleon] ... is on record for saying that "Three hostile newspapers are more to be feared than a thousand bayonets".* -MMU,28. ♦ *... she was willing to speak on the record.* -T/92.
set the record straight dar/citar os fatos corretamente, corrigir o erro, colocar as coisas em seu devido lugar *So much misinformation has been published about the event that we would like to set the record straight with the factual information.*
RED in/into the red em débito, no vermelho; deficitariamente *... the company is still running in the red ...* -T/87. ♦ *... $220 million in the red ...* -T/87.
RED-BAITING perseguição a comunistas *I ... denounced red-baiting, and appealed [to the college students] for their support ...* -KRI,572.
RED-BLOODED vigoroso, forte, saudável, cheio de energia *In any gathering where ... red-blooded men and women come to exchange ideas, the subject of sex is often the chief topic of conversation.* -HEW,9.

RED-CARPET → roll out the red CARPET

RED-EYE 1. [gír] uísque forte e de péssima qualidade *Give me some of that red-eye.* 2. vôo (viagem aérea) noturno *He had taken the red-eye special and arrived at Miami International Airport on schedule.* -WI,164.

RED-HANDED em flagrante *... he had been caught red-handed before witnesses.* -DJ,33.

RED-HOT 1. extremamente quente *Didn't you know you left the coffeepot on the fire? All the water boiled out and it was red hot.* -WR,56. 2. muito entusiasmado, emocionado, agitado, irrequieto, intenso, violento *... I found out that he's a red-hot Indian hater.* -CHT,30.

RED-LETTER → red-letter DAY

RED-LIGHT → red-light DISTRICT

REEL reel off → RATTLE off

right off the reel → right off the BAT

REFER refer to 1. referir-se a, aludir a, reportar-se a, mencionar, citar *In his letter of October 28, he referred to an unpleasant incident that had taken place on that same day.* 2. dizer respeito a, ter relação com, ser relevante ou pertinente a *Her remark, I found out later, referred to all of us.* 3. recorrer a, consultar (alguém ou algo) para obter informação, auxílio etc. *Refer to a dictionary when you don't know the meaning of a word.* 4. remeter a, encaminhar a, indicar a (alguém) para obter informação, auxílio, apreciação, decisão etc. *My doctor referred me to a lung specialist.* ♦ *They referred the question to the President.* 5. atribuir a, imputar a *Greg referred his team's failure to sheer bad luck.*

REGARD as regards = in/with REGARD to *I'm sorry to say I have no information whatever as regards Miss Falkenburg's whereabouts.*

in/with regard to quanto a, com relação a, no que diz respeito a *I have nothing new to tell you in regard to that matter.*

REGARDLESS regardless of indiferente a, sem dar atenção a, independentemente de *Biggs decided to go ahead with his plan regardless of consequences.*

REIN give (free/full) rein dar rédea (larga), dar (plena) liberdade *Chapman placed the whole project in my hands and gave me free rein in developing it.* ♦ *[He] ... gave rein to his worst fears ...* -T/64.

keep a (tight) rein on manter controle sobre, restringir, trazer a rédeas curtas *I'll have to keep a rein on these regular [war] correspondents ...* -CN,74.

keep in rein manter sob domínio *He could never keep his emotions in rein when he got excited.*

rein in/up 1. deter, refrear *You learned to rein in your emotions.* -T/78. ♦ *... Congress has reined in some of the Attorney General's power.* -T/87. 2. fazer parar (o cavalo), puxar as rédeas (a) *... he reined up and sat swaying in the saddle.* -LLN,8.

take the reins assumir o comando, tomar as rédeas *The new President will take the reins on January 20.*

RELATIVE relative to com relação a, relativamente a *Wheeler gave us no information relative to his family background and education.*

RELIEF on relief recebendo algum tipo de pensão ou auxílio do governo *Thousands of out-of-work people are on relief for the first time in their lives.*

REMARK pass a remark fazer uma observação, um comentário *When the girl went by the group of men one of them passed a vulgar remark.*

REMIND remind one of lembrar, fazer recordar de (alguém ou algo), trazer à lembrança *She reminds me of a girl I met in my youth.* ♦ *Strachey's song* These Foolish Things *reminds me of you.*

RESCUE to the/someone's rescue em socorro, em auxílio de *Andrew came to the rescue of the little boy who was drowning in the lake.* ♦ *[They] ... came to his* *rescue during these moments of [political] attacks by outsiders.* -T/92.

RESORT **last resort** último recurso, última instância *He is not exactly the man we want for the job but as a last resort we may have to hire him.*

RESPECT **pay one's last respects** prestar a última homenagem (a falecido) comparecendo à cerimônia fúnebre *... more than 1,000,000 people shuffled by the body [of Pope John XXIII] to pay their last respects.* -T/63.

pay one's respects apresentar seus respeitos, prestar suas homenagens, fazer visita de cortesia *We are going to pay our respects to the newly elected mayor.*

with respect to com relação a *What do you intend to do with respect to the missing jewel?*

REST **at rest** 1. parado, imóvel, inativo *In explaining his views, Einstein makes abundant use of the observer who may be at rest or may be moving.* -WN,20. ♦ *The ocean waves are never at rest.* 2. em repouso (descansando ou dormindo; morto, sepultado) *She lies at rest in the village cemetery.* 3. sossegado, em paz, em estado de tranqüilidade *You can set your mind at rest now. All your troubles are over.*

lay to rest 1. sepultar *The dog was laid to rest by the children as if he were a human being.* 2. dar fim, fazer cessar, pôr termo *The President's forceful speech laid all doubts to rest.*

put to rest = **lay to REST** 2 *The President ... may have put some of the more obvious questions to rest.* -T/87.

rest room banheiro público (principalmente quando localizado em hotel, restaurante, teatro etc.) *Smoking is now permitted only in certain hallways and rest rooms ...* -T/87.

RETREAT **beat a (hasty) retreat** retirar-se (às pressas) *Bud beat a hasty retreat when he saw a policeman.* ♦ *... one*

Hawker Hunter [jet fighter] was shot down, the others beat a retreat. -T/66.

REVERSE **in/into reverse** 1. em recuo, em retrocesso *... the hardest winter in a century, throwing the economy into reverse ...* -T/86. 2. em marcha a ré *I couldn't turn the car around in the narrow street so I had to put it in reverse and back out.*

RHYME **neither rhyme nor reason; without/no rhyme or reason** sem lógica, sem sentido, sem pé nem cabeça *This test has neither rhyme nor reason. You must study and retake it.*

RIB **stick to one's/the ribs** [col] ser substancial, nutritivo, satisfatório (alimento, refeição) *You eat that bread ... It'll stick to your ribs.* -LMT,32.

RICH **that's rich** [col] isso é engraçado, divertido, esquisito, ridículo; essa é boa *That's rich. You in love with her? That's really rich.* -HJC,296.

RIDDANCE **good riddance** bons ventos o levem, já vai tarde *When Matt told his wife he was leaving for good she said: "Good riddance!"*

RIDE **along for the ride** participando (de alguma atividade, brincadeira etc.) apenas por diversão *... The Man Who Shot Liberty Valance, a good movie with [James] Stewart more or less along for the ride in a reasonable performance ...* -TH,112.

go for a ride dar uma volta, fazer um passeio *Would you like to go for a ride in my new car?*

ride out 1. resistir, agüentar (tempestade) *The sea was rough but the ship managed to ride out the storm.* 2. sobrepujar, sobreviver a, superar *... the President had convinced his family that he would ride out the crisis.* -T/74. ♦ *... would he try to ride out the scandal?* -T/87.

ride roughshod over tratar mal, tiranizar *He rode roughshod over his employees.*

riding high feliz e otimista, confiante, triunfante, bem-sucedido *... despite his enemies ... [he] was riding high ...* -T/63.

take for a ride [gir] 1. raptar e assassinar *He had apparently been taken for a ride and his body had been dumped into a wooded section along the road.* 2. zombar de, brincar com *Don't pay any attention to Floyd. He's always taking someone for a ride.* 3. enganar, lesar, tapear *Friend, you've been taken for a ride.*

thumb a ride [col] pedir carona (levantando o polegar) *Don travelled all over the New England states by thumbing rides.*

RIG rig out 1. equipar (embarcação) *Flynn rigged out his boat with all the newest equipment.* 2. [gir] vestir, prover de roupas *It takes all a man's salary to rig out his children for each new school year.*

rig up improvisar, erigir às pressas, armar rapidamente *The schools were rigged up as temporary homes for the flood victims.* ♦ *They had an army tent rigged up at the edge of the grove ... -HW,3.*

RIGHT by right(s) de direito, por justiça *By rights Jacobs should have been promoted to major instead of Captain Jones.*

dead to rights sem possibilidade de fugir à culpa, apanhado em flagrante *... I've got him dead to rights with the evidence to convict. -QE,124.*

in one's/its own right por si mesmo, por sua própria capacidade, méritos, condição etc. *Whereas [Gerald] Ford became President after Richard Nixon resigned, [George] Bush was elected in his own right. -T/92.* ♦ *... French and Italian directors simply assume that cinema is an important art in its own right. -T/63.*

in the right com a razão, do lado da verdade, da lei, da justiça *Before The Devil's Doorway and Broken Arrow western movies always had Indians doing the wrong things and white people always in the right.*

put/set to rights [col] arrumar, pôr em ordem, corrigir *She can put her house to rights by nine o'clock in the morning.* ♦ *[When Ulysses returns from Troy he] ... restores his son to honor and sets his little kingdom to rights. -T/61.*

right and left a torto e a direito, indiscriminadamente, por toda a parte *The government is not arresting officers right and left. -T/61.*

right away/off imediatamente, sem demora *... I want to see him right away. -FC,17.* ♦ *We're getting a doctor. He'll be here right off. -SJE,98.*

right here bem aqui, exatamente neste lugar *Right here is where the famous cow kicked over the lantern and started the Chicago Fire in 1871.*

right now já, agora mesmo, neste instante *You're going to tell me what happened last night. Right here and right now.*

right off → **RIGHT away**

right on [gir] 1. é isso aí!, falou!, tá certo! *"The police is looking for you, Joe. You'd better get out of here." "Right on, Bud!"* 2. correto, certo, exato *[his] ... comment is right on. -T/92.*

right there ali mesmo, bem ali *Put that box right there.*

right up there entre os melhores, tão bom ou tão importante quanto *Judy Garland was right up there with the great people in show business.*

set to rights → **put to RIGHTS**

stand on one's rights fazer valer seus direitos *As a property owner, I will stand on my rights and refuse to move until the state government pays for appropriating my land.*

tell/know right from wrong distinguir o certo do errado *They said that Ruby Gentry couldn't tell right from wrong.*

RIGHT-HAND → **right-hand MAN**

RIGHT-WING → **LEFT-wing**

RING give someone a ring/buzz [col] dar um telefonema a *When he arrived at the airport he gave his sister a ring and she drove over and picked him up.*

ring out ecoar, soar *... his final words rang out like a shot ... -T/80.* ♦ *A shot*

rang out and someone started running.
ring true//false//hollow parecer verdadeiro// falso *His story didn't ring true, so they began to investigate it.* ♦ *Terms like Sikh, Hindu, Jew, Christian and Muslim ring hollow when they are used to sanctify acts of violence.* -T/84.
ring up 1. telefonar para *Ring me up when you come to Boston.* 2. registrar ... *the company rang up profits of $260 million last year...* -T/87. 3. conseguir, alcançar, conquistar ... *her rare appearances on television ring up records.* -T/66.
ring with ressoar com, ecoar com *... his words ring with conviction and sincerity ...* -SRE,27. ♦ *The place rang with laughter ...* -SSG,18.
run rings/circles around [col] superar (alguém) por larga margem (em alguma atividade, habilidade etc.) *Pelé could run rings around any other player.*
RINGER (dead) ringer for [gir] sósia, imagem, cópia de *He's a dead ringer for his father.*
RINGSIDE ringside seat 1. cadeira de primeira fileira (junto ao ringue, palco, picadeiro etc.) *If you sit in a ringside seat, one of the wrestlers may fall on top of you.* 2. lugar ou posição privilegiada, que permite uma visão íntima de ... *I have a ringside seat at the tragedy that is unfolding here.* -T/75.
RIOT read the riot act advertir severamente com ameaça de castigo, repreender energicamente *Ricky's father reads the riot act to him every time he arrives home late from a party and has had the family car.*
run riot 1. fazer baderna, desordem; descontrolar-se, exceder-se, exorbitar ... *the [Chinese] Red Guards were running riot.* -T/66. 2. fugir ao controle, sair da realidade *In his paintings, his imagination seems to have run riot.* 3. crescer profusamente, vicejar, alastrar-se *Inflation is running riot again.* ♦ *Weeds are running riot among the flowers in our garden.*

RIP rip/tear into [col] 1. atacar (física ou verbalmente) *Ted ripped into the other boy with fury.* ♦ *... a wave of cops tore into the crowd ...* -T/91. ♦ *Mr. Andrews ripped into his son for staying out until 2 a.m.* 2. dar começo a, iniciar com ímpeto, atacar *The band ripped right into* Long Tall Sally. ♦ *... Bruce [Springsteen] and the E Street Band tore into Springsteen's own anthem,* Born to Run ... -T/80.
rip off 1. arrancar ... *winds ranging up to 100 m.p.h. ripped off the roof [of the church] ...* -T/77. 2. [gir] roubar, furtar, lesar *Why did he decide to rip off his employer?* -T/87. ⇒ **rip-off** roubo, furto, estelionato *To cut down the rising incidence of automated rip-offs, companies that own computers are installing more and more gadgetry to improve security.* -T/72.
rip out [col] esbravejar, vociferar, gritar com ira *He became angry and ripped out a few curses.*
RIPE ripe for pronto para, propício, oportuno, preparado, no ponto de *The whole country was ripe for revolution.*
RISE get a rise out of [gir] irritar *His mother could always get a rise out of his vain father by calling him "old man".*
give rise to suscitar, dar origem a *In the 18th century the Enlightenment ... gave rise to the idea that all human beings are born equal ...* -T/92.
on the rise em aumento progressivo, crescendo, em ascensão *The number of old people is on the rise ...* -KR,2. ♦ *... violence is still on the rise.* -T/86.
rise to mostrar-se à altura de, esforçar-se para enfrentar *Conway sensed the challenge in Carter's voice and rose to it.*
rise up rebelar-se *Hundreds of thousands of young Chinese rose up against their government in 1989.* -T/91.
RISK at one's own risk → **at one's PERIL**
at risk com risco, com grande perigo *This is a person who deeply loves others ... and*

who takes action, often at great personal risk, to help others. -JS,11.

run a/the risk correr o risco, arriscar-se, expor-se ao perigo *If you invest in that type of business, you run the risk of losing all your money.*

take a risk arriscar-se *There are people who take risks for their beliefs ...* -HG,73.

RIVER   sell down the river trair, enganar, abandonar *Holmes was sold down the river by a man he considered a friend.*

ROAD   hit the road [gír] 1. partir, ir-se, pôr-se a caminho; dar o fora *Let's hit the road before it gets too dark and foggy.* 2. viajar *Once he was sworn in as Vice President, Ford hit the road as a traveling salesman for the presidency and the Republican Party.* -T/74.

one for the road [gír] a última bebida, o último trago antes de partir *Before you go, let's have one for the road.*

on the road 1. viajando, percorrendo determinado território (vendedor) *Loman has been on the road for many years and prefers it to an office job.* 2. excursionando, em turnê (artista, companhia de atores) *Like Willie Nelson, I'm going on the road again.* -T/81.

road hog [gír] motorista que dirige seu veículo pelo meio da pista *A road hog is a car driver who keeps to the middle of the road and won't let anyone pass.*

royal road caminho ou maneira fácil *It has often been said that there is no royal road to success.*

take to the road viajar, pegar a estrada *The 1986 fall in the cost of gasoline encouraged many Americans to take to the road more often.* -T/87.

ROCK   between a/the rock and a/the hard place entre a cruz e a caldeirinha, sem escolha *[The heroes played by movie star John Wayne] ... were not like Hemingway's. They ... had ... a stubbornness – foolish, willful and glorious – when they were caught between the rock and the hard place.* -T/79. ♦ *... the EPA [Environmental Protection Agency] is between a rock and a hard place, with an enormous task to confront ...* -T/80.

go on the rocks [col] 1. fracassar, ser malsucedido *Most Hollywood marriages go on the rocks because of the differences in careers.* 2. falir, quebrar *His business has gone on the rocks.*

have rocks in one's/the head [gír] ser maluco, não ter bom senso *Do you think I have rocks in my head?* ♦ *"Could you loan me fifty dollars?" "You got rocks in the head?"*

on the rocks [gír] 1. falido, sem dinheiro, arruinado, fracassado *Their marriage is on the rocks.* ♦ *... a corporation is financially on the rocks ...* -T/77. 2. com cubos de gelo (bebida) *He prefers his Scotch on the rocks.*

rock bottom o ponto ou o nível mais baixo, o fundo (do poço) *The ex-queen of the silver screen, after a ten-year exile in the gutters of the world had finally hit rock bottom.* -BM,210. ⇒ **rock-bottom** o mínimo, o mais baixo *... rock-bottom wages ...* -T/92. ♦ *... widespread corruption and rock-bottom morale.* -T/92.

Rock of Ages Jesus Cristo; a fé cristã *His mind was brilliant and his character founded on the Rock of Ages ...* -T/65.

ROCKER   off one's rocker → **off one's HEAD**

ROCKIES   the Rockies as (Montanhas) Rochosas *He lives on a small ranch in the Colorado Rockies near Denver.*

ROD   hot rod [gír] automóvel (geralmente velho) com motor superalimentado ou substituído por outro de maior potência *... high school kids who had competed in running hot rods across the desert ...* -MN,9.

ROGER [col] 1. [em comunicação de radiotelefonia] mensagem recebida e compreendida *"OK. Roger and out", said the flier.* 2. certo, sim, entendido *When I asked him to help me he said, "Roger".*

ROLE play a/the role desempenhar determinado papel, cumprir uma função *Charles King played the role of the bad guy in B films for many years.* ♦ *Abraham Lincoln played a major role in American history.*
ROLL call the roll fazer a chamada *The teacher calls the roll every morning.* ⇒ **roll call**
roll call chamada (para verificação de presença), lista de chamada *Willie was late for roll call, as usual.*
roll around retornar, reaparecer, chegar novamente *By the time July rolled around I had settled all my debts.*
roll back 1. reduzir, fazer voltar (preço) a nível anterior *We hope that the Senate will roll back some prices of essential materials.* ⇒ **rollback** redução (de preço), queda, diminuição *During the recession the large industries had a rollback in their price.* 2. rechaçar, fazer recuar *... the U.S. will ... try to roll back the spread of Soviet-aided Communism.* -T/87. ⇒ **rollback** rechaço, recuo, retrocesso *... a rollback of proabortion laws ...* -T/87.
roll call → **call the ROLL**
rolled into one simultaneamente; unido em um todo; em uma só pessoa ou coisa ao mesmo tempo *[Death Comes for the Archbishop, a novel by Willa Cather] is also a better "western" than all the novels of Zane Grey and all the horse operas of Hollywood rolled into one.* -SV,84.
roll in chegar, entrar, aparecer (em grandes quantidades, em abundância) *There is plenty of money rolling in now.* ♦ *... UFO [Unidentified Flying Object] reports were rolling in at the rate of several per day ...* -RE,50.
roll off copiar, duplicar (em máquina impressora) *Before the month is out, printing presses will have to roll off about 50 billion new cruzeiros ...* -T/63.
roll out [gir] pular da cama, levantar-se *We had to roll out at five.*
roll over virar-se para o outro lado (principalmente na cama) *Roll over and let me sleep.* ♦ *If government cannot provide protection, what is the answer? Roll over and let the criminal element do whatever it chooses?* -T/80.
roll up 1. enrolar, arregaçar *She had taken off her shoes and stockings and rolled up her sleeves.* -DP,7. 2. acumular *... the Big Three [GM, Ford, Chrysler] rolled up financial losses that analysts predict could exceed $6 billion.* -T/92. 3. [col] chegar (em veículo) *Dick rolled up in his sports car at ten a.m.*
ROOF hit the roof → **hit the CEILING**
raise the roof [gir] ficar furioso, protestar violentamente, armar barulho *He raised the roof when he saw the bill for repairs to his car.* 2. aplaudir, ovacionar, fazer grande algazarra, festejar *When the wage increase was announced to the waiting strikers, they raised the roof with yells and applause.*
the roof fell in quando menos se esperava algo desagradável aconteceu *He thought that he had planned the robbery carefully but the roof fell in on him.*
ROOM make room for criar espaço para, conseguir lugar para *... somebody shouted, "Make room for this idiot!" and people got out of his way.* -OFW,36.
room and board casa e comida (pensão) *When he first came to Brazil he had room and board in a family house.*
room at the top oportunidade para ocupar posição de comando, de destaque, um lugar nas altas esferas (entre os melhores na profissão ou os mais ambiciosos) *[He] ... was the epitome of the autocratic tycoon who believed there was room at the top for only one.* -T/60. ♦ *[American frontiersman Kit Carson] ... discovered that in New Mexico there was room at the top even for a rough, superstitious, illiterate mountain man.* -BD,23.
room for oportunidade, possibilidade, ocasião, espaço para *... he always allowed room for argument ...* -T/78. ♦ *If your*

writing cannot be misunderstood, it leaves no room for ambiguity. -PC,27.

room service serviço de quarto (em hotel) *We called for room service to send us sandwiches and a bottle of beer.*

ROOST rule the roost mandar, dominar, imperar, exercer a autoridade ... *the same old [political] parties that have ruled the roost for years still seemed in control.* -T/62.

ROOT at the root of na origem, na base, no fundamento ... *malnutrition is at the root of most of America's health, emotional and social problems ...* -T/72.

pull up roots mudar-se, deixar um local, um ambiente onde se vive há muito tempo *Another ... family pulling up roots because of the husband's career.* -T/81.

put down roots lançar raízes, fixar-se permanentemente *[He] ... was born in Australia ... and put down his roots in that rough-and-ready land.* -T/64.

root for torcer por, simpatizar com, desejar bom êxito a *He roots for the Red Socks.* ♦ *Most of the Hollywood community is publicly rooting for the newcomer.* -T/87.

root of all evil a raiz de todos os males (o amor ao dinheiro) *St. Paul does not say that money is the root of all evil. He says that it is the love of money which leads men to their moral destruction.* -AM,65.

root out 1. extirpar, eliminar, erradicar *The American Revolution had no medieval legal institutions to discard or to root out ...* -MMU,29. 2. descobrir, desenterrar *They knew their group had a double agent and they did everything to root him out.*

root up desenraizar, arrancar pelas raízes *... 200 million coffee trees have been deliberately rooted up in Brazil ...* -T/63.

take root criar raízes, firmar-se, consolidar-se *The idea for the invasion [of Cuba] had taken root during the early summer of 1960.* -T/61.

ROPE give someone enough rope to hang himself dar a alguém liberdade de ação até exceder-se e sofrer as conseqüências *We've got to give them enough rope to hang themselves now ...* -NE,364.

give someone some rope dar liberdade de ação, deixar agir como lhe aprouver, deixar à vontade, dar corda a *He'd obviously given Morbius as much rope as he was going to.* -SWJ,42.

know the ropes [col] entender do riscado, estar totalmente familiarizado com determinado assunto *Siegel has been in this business longer than any of us and he knows the ropes.*

on the ropes [gír] em dificuldades, encrencado, próximo à ruína *They thought he was on the ropes but he recovered.* ♦ *Fascism is on the ropes – again.* -T/73.

rope in/into [gír] 1. enganar, lograr, fraudar, atrair, engodar *Although Sam is not naive, he was roped into the nefarious scheme by his trust in his friends.* 2. persuadir (alguém) a se oferecer para um serviço etc., arranjar (alguém) como assistente etc. *Gray was roped in as a committee member.*

rope off isolar ou cercar (rua, área etc.) com cordas *The building was on fire and the police roped off the adjacent area.*

ROSE coming up roses [col] indo às mil maravilhas *... it was clear that things were coming up roses.* -T/87. ♦ *... for a while, everyhting was coming up roses.* -BM,203.

ROTE by rote de cor, de memória, mecanicamente *Learning something by rote, memorizing it on the surface of your mind is not the surest way to remember it.* -NM,18.

ROUGH be rough on ser desagradável, penoso, ruim, prejudicial para *The hot sand is rough on bathers who don't wear sandals at the beach.*

roughing it ficar privado do conforto da civilização, viver rusticamente (como em uma excursão, expedição etc.) *They are roughing it in the Rocky Mountains this summer.*

rough out delinear, esboçar *He usually roughed out his story in a few days and then carefully constructed each chapter in a leisurely manner.*

rough up atacar, surrar, maltratar *You could've roughed him up a little. You didn't have to kill him.* -TD,216.

ROUGH-AND-READY 1. cru, rude, tosco, improvisado (mas eficiente) *The barn party was just a rough-and-ready gathering of frontier cattle people ...* -LM,129. 2. vigoroso, despachado, ativo, resoluto *Tunstall had a number of employees and a rough-and-ready foreman ...* -CEB,41.

ROUGH-AND-TUMBLE 1. briga desordenada; dissensão, rivalidade, luta entre membros de uma organização, partido etc. *A rough-and-tumble broke out between the two factions last night.* ♦ *[He has had] ... long years of experience in the rough-and-tumble of elections and boardrooms ...* -T/91. 2. desordenado, violento, tumultuoso, anárquico *The western pioneers enjoyed a rough-and-tumble fight as much as we do a football game.* ♦ *... rough-and-tumble techniques ...* -T/85.

ROUGHHOUSE [gir] brincadeira desordenada e anárquica, algazarra, bagunça *"Now, children, don't have a roughhouse while I'm at the store", the tired mother said.*

ROUGHNECK [gir] 1. indivíduo valentão, desordeiro, grosseirão *A group of roughnecks entered the store and threw all the merchandise on the floor and beat up the owner.* 2. indivíduo que opera equipamento de perfuração de poço de petróleo *[He is] ... a roughneck who makes $1,300 a week installing oil-rigging equipment.* -T/80.

ROUND **go the rounds** circular de pessoa a pessoa (notícia, boato, piada etc.) *Have you heard the latest joke going the rounds about the President?*

make the rounds 1. visitar lugares um após outro, ir de um lugar para outro, visitar os lugares costumeiros ou rotineiros *While in New York we made the rounds of all the famous nightclubs.* 2. = **go the ROUNDS** *What political gossip is making the rounds in the U.S. today?*

round off 1. dar forma arredondada a, tornear *I cut out the table top into a square by machine but rounded it off by hand.* 2. rematar, finalizar, burilar, completar, aperfeiçoar *Holt was thirty years old and most of the sharp edges of his character were being rounded off in the mill of time and experience.* -SG,9.

round out 1. completar, perfazer *Rounding out the senior staff are two lawyers with extensive Capitol Hill [i.e., legislative] experience.* -T/87. 2. ampliar, aumentar *Would you like to round out your income with an extra job?*

round up 1. arrebanhar *Cowboys work hard when they round up cattle.* ⇒ **roundup** ato de arrebanhar o gado, rodeio *Cowboys work hard at roundup time when all the cattle are gathered and branded.* 2. [col] reunir, juntar *I think we should be able to round up the money he needs.* -GD,301. ⇒ **roundup** resumo, sumário *Just give me a roundup of the latest news.* 3. capturar, prender (suspeitos, malandros, indivíduos envolvidos em um crime etc.) *Scores of suspects have been rounded up and interrogated ...* -T/72. ♦ *In the movie* Casablanca, *after Major Strasser is shot, Captain Louis Renault orders the police to "round up the usual suspects".* ⇒ **roundup** prisão de suspeitos, malandros, fugitivos etc. *... a roundup of fugitive soldiers by government forces.* -T/87.

ROUND-THE-CLOCK → **around the CLOCK**

ROUND-TRIP → **round TRIP**

ROUTE **en route** 1. a caminho, em trânsito *[The two reporters] ... were en route to another assignment in South America ...* -T/78. 2. ao longo do caminho *They were going on a long journey by car but were unaware of the problems they would meet en route.*

ROW¹ [rima com **go**] **a hard/long/tough row to hoe** osso duro de roer, tarefa difícil ... *the country will have a tough row to hoe for the remainder of the year [after harsh anti-inflation steps are taken].* -T/78.
in a row sucessivamente, em seqüência ... *he sometimes wears the same suit several days in a row* ... -T/78. ♦ *For the second year in a row* ... -T/78.
ROW² [rima com **cow**] **kick up/raise a row** [col] protestar violentamente, armar barulho *Dexter kicked up a row when he found out that someone had been using his summer cottage for clandestine parties.*
RUB rub it in [gir] enfatizar ou repetir constantemente um incidente desagradável, repisar um assunto (com a intenção de irritar ou caçoar) *"I know I lost. You don't need to rub it in", the badly defeated boxer said.*
rub off remover esfregando (mancha, sujeira etc.) *[The rifle was] ... so new that the grease had not all been rubbed off.* -BF,11.
rub off on passar de uma coisa para outra, de um lugar para outro, de uma pessoa para outra (por contato, proximidade etc.) *I hope that some of my enthusiasm for psychology rubs off on you by the time you finish the book...* -MJV,9 ♦ *... his worries have rubbed off on her.* -T/67.
rub out 1. apagar *Rub out the first few names and put our friend's name at the head of the list.* 2. [gir] assassinar *They say he was rubbed out by the Mob.* ⇒ **rubout** assassinato ... *a classic Mafia rubout.* -T/75.
rub up polir, lustrar *Rub up the chrome on this car and we can sell it at a higher price.*
rub up against ter contato com, achar, encontrar ... *country children ... rub up against life more than city children do.* -GD,158.
RUBBER rulbber stamp [col] cópia, estereótipo, pessoa sem originalidade *Many Hollywood stars are just rubber stamps of the current idol.* ⇒ **rubber-stamp** 1. aprovar, apoiar ou endossar automaticamente, mecanicamente, sem reflexão *They have rubber-stamped his decision.* 2. que aprova automaticamente (resoluções, decisões etc.) *[The dictator] Pushed a resolution through his rubber-stamp National Assembly ...* -T/67.
RUBBERNECK [gir] 1. pessoa curiosa, que tudo quer ver; turista *A bunch of rubbernecks had gathered at the scene of the accident.* 2. olhar à volta com curiosidade ou admiração ... *rubbernecking around at the Louvre [Museum].* -T/60.
RUG pull the rug (out) from under [gir] retirar o apoio, dar uma rasteira ... *the opportunity to pull the rug out from under ... [the German chancellor] came in late October* ... -T/66. ♦ *He'll never pull the rug from under you.* -FH,90.
sweep (something) under the rug tentar ocultar (algo vergonhoso, problemático etc.) *Many politicians try to sweep the problems under the rug rather than solve them.*
RULE as a rule geralmente, por via de regra ... *for the most part orphans live solitary lives and are, as a rule, cool of heart.* -WF,36.
rule of thumb regra prática baseada na experiência *In the everyday business of living we do indeed establish convenient rules of thumb* ... -WP,30.
rule out 1. eliminar, descartar, rejeitar, recusar, inviabilizar *The police ruled out suicide as the cause of death.* ♦ *Military intervention [in Iran] was ... ruled out because of the delicacy of Persian gulf oil politics* ... -T/81. 2. desclassificar, excluir *He was ruled out of the game by the umpire.*
RUN dry run teste simulado, ensaio *They went through several dry runs with the big guns before they really fired them.*
get the run of entender o jeito de (fazer algo) *At first the work seemed difficult, but*

after Bill got the run of things it seemed less difficult.

give someone a run for his money fazer uma disputa acirrada contra, não facilitar a competição, luta etc. para alguém, dar uma canseira em alguém *In the 1960 presidential election Nixon gave Kennedy a run for his money.*

have a long//short run ter longa//curta permanência em cartaz *My Fair Lady had a very long run on Broadway.*

have the run of ter livre acesso a, permissão para usar *He figured that ... he'd have the run of the place, but I let him know who was boss right off ...* -CHT,31.

in the long run com o passar do tempo, como resultado final *The architect must speak a language the public can understand, else in the long run he will perish.* -WJ,386.

in the short run a curto prazo, em curto prazo *In the short run, Nixon's politics of polarisation are paying off.* -T/69.

make a run for it tentar fugir, tentar escapar de um perigo, correr para salvar-se *We had to run for it when the wild bull charged at us.*

on the run 1. em grande atividade *He is kept on the run trying to please his many bosses.* 2. apressadamente, sem fazer pausa *Walt eats his meals on the run.* 3. em fuga *There is a feeling among the Indians all over the Territories that they have the white man on the run.* -CHT,45.

run across = **COME across** 1 *Anita ran across an old friend yesterday.*

run/fall afoul/foul of entrar em conflito com ... *a federal jurist runs afoul of Congress.* -T/88. ♦ *He ran foul of the law in the East and fled to the West Coast where he was unknown.*

run after perseguir, buscar, procurar; ir atrás de, buscar a companhia de *Guy will run after anyone who is wearing a skirt.*

run against competir contra (em uma eleição) *In the 1960 presidential election Kennedy ran against Nixon.*

run along ir embora *Well, it's getting late. I'd better be running along.*

run amok/amuck ser possuído de furor, investir furiosamente contra; descontrolar-se *He ran amuck in the crowded street firing his rifle at anyone in his way.*

run around andar sem destino, passear ociosamente, vadiar, zanzar *I don't want you running around, and that's final.* -RP,23. ⇒ **runaround**, the [col] evasivas, desculpas, respostas incompletas *The detective felt he had been given the runaround when he tried to get information from the suspect.*

run around with 1. andar em companhia de, estar freqüentemente com *Wanda used to run around with a hippie crowd in the late 1960s.* 2. ter relações extraconjugais com *It was rumored that he was running around with his wife's best friend.*

run away 1. fugir, escapar *Several prisoners have run away.* ⇒ **runaway** fugitivo *We know what Huck Finn went through trying to decide what to do with the runaway slave ...* -LAS,xvi. 2. fugir de casa, abandonar o lar *Most young boys want to run away at least once in their lives.* 3. ficar fora de controle ... *the [atomic] reactor that had so nearly run away was safe.* -T/79. ⇒ **runaway** a. desequilibrado, fora de controle, desgovernado ... *the potential menace of runaway nuclear accidents.* -T/79. ♦ ... *runaway inflation neared the 800% mark ...* -T/87. b. que ocorreu rápida ou facilmente, de grande sucesso, disparado ... *a runaway best-seller.* -T/87. ♦ ... *one of the industry's runaway successes.* -T/87.

run away with 1. fazer perder o controle (de emoções, sentimentos) *Conrad would never let his emotions run away with his sense of right and wrong.* 2. fugir com (namorada, amante etc.) *Kathleen ran away with the handsome chauffeur.* 3. roubar e fugir com (o produto do roubo) *Barry ran away with all the funds in the*

club treasury. 4. vencer por larga margem *Our candidate ran away with the presidential election.*
run counter to opor-se a, contradizer *The theory of evolution developed by Charles Darwin run counter to the biblical account of creation in Genesis.*
run deep ter raízes profundas *The Judaeo-Christian tradition and its offshoot, puritanism, run very deep in Western culture.* -T/72.
run down 1. deixar de funcionar, perder a força motriz, parar *The [second] law [of thermodynamics] ... says that the universe is running down, dispersing its energy.* -T/81. ♦ *... an alarm clock went off ... and slowly ran down.* -T/66. 2. atropelar, chocar-se contra e derrubar ou fazer afundar *A taxicab ran the man down and killed him.* 3. procurar, seguir a pista de, perseguir e capturar ou matar *[The cowboys] ... learned that the best way to capture the [wild] horses was to run them down.* -MJ,67. 4. buscar (a origem), localizar *There is nothing more difficult than running down a rumor of political origin.* 5. examinar, investigar, verificar, conferir (itens etc.) seguindo uma lista, ordem etc. *I ran down three pages of Smiths in the telephone directory before I found the Smith I wanted.* ⇒ **rundown** resumo, sumário, relatório, descrição detalhada *Give me a quick rundown on our out-of-town stores.* 6. difamar, menosprezar; criticar severamente *Gilmore is always running down anyone who gets ahead of him in his company.* 7. perder o vigor físico, definhar, declinar (a saúde), deteriorar-se, degringolar *Helen has been feeling run down lately.* ⇒ **run-down** exausto, extenuado; debilitado, enfraquecido, adoentado; desmantelado, em ruínas, deteriorado *You look a little run-down yourself. This [a prescription] is for vitamins.* -SRS,35 ♦ *... a slightly run-down section of Paris ...* -T/87. ♦ *... the existing machinery was dismayingly run-down.* -T/60.

run dry secar, esgotar-se *In Los Angeles, small rivers run dry in the summer.* ♦ *[There isn't] ... much chance of the black gold [oil] running dry.* -T/66.
run for candidatar-se a (cargo eletivo) *Smith's going to run for President.* ♦ *[He] ... was running for re-election.* -T/60. ♦ *He ran for the Senate in 1948 ...* -T/63.
run for it = **make a RUN for it** *Ned ran for it when he saw the police coming after him.*
run foul of → **RUN afoul of**
run high elevar-se, exaltar-se, atingir alto grau de intensidade *... all during 1948 the interest in UFO's (Unidentified Flying Objects] was running high.* -RE,49. ♦ *... skepticism is running very high.* -T/87.
run in 1. [col] fazer breve visita *He ran in to see his cousin Horace who had had a severe stroke.* 2. [gír] prender *The police ran in the people who were near the scene of the crime.*
run into 1. chocar-se com *The bus ran into a car and four people were killed.* 2. encontrar inesperadamente ou acidentalmente, topar com; encontrar, experimentar (problemas, perigo etc.) *I ran into an old friend the other day.* ♦ *... as many as two-thirds of the marriages ...run into serious disagreement over sexual relationships.* -KAC,12. ♦ *... run into difficulties ...* -T/80. 3. atingir, alcançar (número, cifra etc.), chegar a *The cost of the programs in the National Plan of Action might well run into billions of dollars.* -T/77.
run low 1. escassear, estar no fim *... a mother who sometimes had to take in sewing when the money ran low.* -LI, 10. 2. estar ficando desprovido de *The soldiers were running low on ammunition.*
a run of luck maré de sorte, sucessão de acontecimentos auspiciosos *They had a wonderful run of luck and sold all their household goods before they left for the U.S.*
run off 1. fugir; sair correndo, sair às pressas, ir-se *The thief ran off when he*

saw the policeman coming. ♦ *Hector and Octavius ran off to play in the park.* ♦ *[He] ... ran off from his studies at Yale [during the American Revolution] to join the army* ... -SGF,104. 2. expulsar, afugentar *Brennan ran off the two men who had trespassed on his property.* 3. imprimir, copiar, reproduzir, duplicar *Let's run off about two hundred copies of that story.* 4. drenar, escorrer *Rainwater runs off quickly in this area.* 5. escrever às pressas, rabiscar, compor, esboçar rapidamente (artigo, poema, discurso etc.) *He can run off a magazine article in a day.* 6. decidir, desempatar *The final race will be run off tomorrow.* ⇒ **runoff** competição ou eleição de desempate ... *Johnson and Coleman will face each other in an August 27 runoff.* -T/63.
run off with 1. fugir com (namorado, amante etc.) *... one of his workers ran off with another's wife ...* -WC,81. 2. roubar *Hayes ran off with the rich widow's jewels.*
run on continuar, prosseguir; continuar a falar, tagarelar *His speech kept running on until half of those present had fallen asleep.* ♦ *Donna ran on, while her friend tried to signal her to shut up.*
run out 1. acabar, terminar, esgotar-se, expirar *Time was running out. Dan Fowler had only twelve hours to find the killer.* ♦ *Food and medicine began to run out.* -T/89. 2. expulsar *He told of the sheriff trying to run him out of town ...* -LD,21.
run out of ficar sem, não ter mais, esgotar o suprimento de *The rich widow has run out of money.* ♦ *[He] ... ran out of ideas ...* -T/66.
run out on [col] abandonar *Ken ran out on his wife several years ago.*
run over 1. recapitular, ensaiar, rever *The ballet group ran over two of the most difficult pieces before the first performance.* 2. exceder, ultrapassar *The price for my furniture ran well over what I had expected to pay.* 3. atropelar *A truck driver ran over and killed a pedestrian.* 4. visitar, ir a (determinado lugar) *Run over to our house before you go back to the States.*
run ragged [col] levar à exaustão, causar cansaço a *[You're] Always running yourself ragged trying to do something you can't do ...* -WPT,28. ♦ *The customers ran me ragged in the store today.*
run short 1. não ter o suficiente, ficar sem, privado de *[She] ... ran short on adjectives.* -T/68. ♦ *The Soviets have run short of cement ...* -T/86. 2. estar esgotando-se, escassear *... patience was running short.* -T/80. v. **SHORT of**
run through 1. rever, recapitular, examinar, ensaiar *I'll run through these bills and give you an estimate later.* ⇒ **run-through** a. ensaio, exercitação, treino, prática *After listening to [Leonard] Bernstein's brief run-through [of Stravinsky's* Sonata for Two Pianos*], the students tried again ...* -T/72. b. sumário, resumo *I'll give you a run-through of the essential points discussed at the meeting.* 2. dar fim a, consumir, desperdiçar, esbanjar *Eric ran through the money that he had inherited from his father in less than two years.* 3. trespassar, atravessar (com espada etc.) *In* The Mark of Zorro, *in one of the best duels ever staged for the screen, the hero runs the vicious Captain Pasquale through with his sword.* 4. permear, impregnar, estar presente em *Do real differences exist ... [between the two sexes and will] such differences run through all of men's and all of women's behavior?* -MM,17.
run to 1. montar a, chegar a, totalizar *... the total cost [of the project] will run to millions of dollars.* -T/62. 2. tender para, ter tendência a produzir ou ter determinada qualidade, característica, forma etc. *American women run to thin legs.* ♦ *Henry's tastes run to the simple things in life.*
run up acumular, aumentar, elevar *Elliott ran up bills because he had run out*

of money. ♦ *[He] ... has run up a $65 million fortune in real estate ...* -T/60. ♦ *... the gasoline began to run out and the prices to run up ...* -T/79.

run up against deparar com, topar com *Mason said that the case of the red scarf was the most baffling one he had ever run up against.*

run up to correr para perto de, aproximar-se de (pessoa ou lugar) *Little Tony ran up to his mother and began to tug insistently at her sleeve.*

run wild 1. dar largas aos seus impulsos, viver desregradamente *Many young boys as soldiers, and away from home, ran wild for the first time in their lives.* 2. não ter restrição, freio, limite ou moderação; tornar-se indócil, indisciplinado, turbulento; rebelar-se, fugir ao controle *... a few rascals like [him] ... have let greed run wild ...* -T/87. ♦ *... rumors of possible resignation [of the President] were running wild ...* - T/74.

RUNDOWN → **RUN down**

RUN-IN [col] desentendimento, discussão, briga *... his first serious run-in with the law came when he was arrested at 16 on a charge of auto theft.* -T/60.

RUNNER front runner → **FRONT-runner**

RUNNER-UP o segundo colocado em qualquer competição ou eleição *Holland, the brilliant runner-up in a magnificent final [soccer] game against Germany in '74.* -T/78.

RUNNING consecutivamente, sem interrupção [posposto a um adjetivo] *... for five years running, the Brooklyn Dodgers [a baseball team] were something less than spectacular.* -SRS,1.

in the running//out of the running concorrendo, competindo, no páreo, com possibilidade de vencer, de ter êxito// fora de competição, fora do páreo, sem possibilidade de vencer *He's still in the running, remember.* ♦ *Sooner or later a rival [gangster] will try to put him out of the running, permanently.* -T/78.

RUN-OF-THE-MILL típico, comum, habitual, sem nada de especial *The Indian Fighter was the usual run-of-the-mill western and the moviegoers didn't like it.* ♦ *In high school he was a run-of-the-mill student.*

RUSH rush hour a hora do tráfego mais intenso, de maior movimento de veículos e de pessoas nas ruas *It was morning rush hour and traffic was particularly heavy.*

SACK get//give the sack [gir] ser demitido//demitir *You'll get the sack if you don't pay more attention to your work.* ♦ *The boss gave him the sack yesterday.*
hit the sack/hay [gir] deitar-se, ir para a cama *After a hard day's work, it's a pleasure to hit the sack.* ♦ *I've got to hit the hay early tonight.*
SADDLE in the saddle no comando, na direção, com as rédeas nas mãos *The dictator had been in the saddle for many years and only death got him out of power.*
saddle shoe sapato esporte branco com um largo contraforte preto ou marrom sobre o peito do pé *Saddle shoes have gone in and out of style so often that you would think they had riders.*
saddle with sobrecarregar (alguém) com, impor grande responsabilidade sobre (alguém), dar tarefa desagradável a *Before 1900, women were saddled with large numbers of unwanted children.* -SE,285. ♦ *Beatrice was saddled with the responsibility of caring for the children.*
SAFE safe and sound são e salvo *In spite of all the difficulties he had on his trip, Jordan arrived home safe and sound.*
SAIL sail into [col] 1. atacar, enfrentar (problema, tarefa etc.) *Benny sailed into the work with so much energy that the other workers were amazed.* 2. entrar majestosa e graciosamente em, andar com passo firme e confiante *The movie star sailed into the room like Queen Mary, followed by her eager fans.* 3. criticar duramente, censurar *The speaker sailed into his opponents on the civil rights issue.* 4. atacar fisicamente *The new boy at school sailed into the bully with such force that the big boy was knocked down.*
sail through passar facilmente por, atravessar com facilidade *Most people sail through life without ever having a great emotional crisis.*
set sail zarpar, empreender uma viagem *Columbus set sail from Palos, Spain on August 3, 1492.*
trim one's sails gastar menos, podar excessos; restringir atividades, gastos etc. *Many big business companies have had to trim their sails and operate on a lower budget during the recession.*
under sail com as velas desfraldadas, velejando, navegando *When I got there the ships were already under sail.* -SGF,153.
SAILING clear/plain/smooth sailing campo livre, caminho desimpedido, facilidade de ação, trajetória sem obstáculos *From now*

on everything will be clear sailing for us. ♦ *It was not always smooth sailing for Mr. Edwards. He did have his problems.* -SJE,80.
SAKE for Christ's/God's/goodness/heaven's sake pelo amor de Deus, por caridade, por compaixão [exprime irritação, impaciência, surpresa] *For Christ's sake, why don't you shut up!* ♦ *For God's sake, isn't there any way I can convince you?* -WCN,235. ♦ *For heaven's sake, stop that noise!*
for the sake of por causa de, no interesse de, em consideração a, em atenção a, em benefício de, a bem de *She sacrificed her career for the sake of her family.* ♦ *I know how you feel about this, but please do it for your sister's sake.*
SALAD salad days 1. anos da mocidade, período de inexperiência *Life had been wonderful for Nick in his salad days, but recently he has had too many difficulties.* 2. apogeu, auge, predomínio *In the salad days of the New Deal [i.e., President Roosevelt's Administration] Jack [Kennedy] grew up, absorbing his father's ambiguous politics ...* -T/60.
SALE no sale [col] nada feito, nada disso, impossível *When I tried to borrow his car he said, "No sale".*
on sale à venda *Tickets for the Olympic Winter Games went on sale on September 27.*
SALT back to the salt mines [col] de volta ao batente *... [I've got to] get back to the old salt mines tomorrow.* -GE,52.
salt away [col] economizar, guardar *... salting away money for his three-month-old daughter's college education ...* -T/87. ♦ *... a sizable chunk of the money [from a sham transaction] may remain salted away in Swiss bank accounts.* -T/80.
the salt of the earth o sal da terra, pessoa(s) simples, comum(ns) mas honesta(s), sincera(s), decente(s) *According to Matthew [5:13], Jesus said to his disciples: "Ye are the salt of the earth".*

worth one's salt capaz, competente, digno do nome, da profissão etc. *... no police commander worth his salt would admit he couldn't control crime ...* -T/81.
SALT-AND-PEPPER; PEPPER-AND-SALT salpicado de branco e preto, cinzento (tecido), grisalho (cabelo) *... [Paul McCartney's] stylish long hair has gone salt-and-pepper.* -T/92.
SAME all/just the same não obstante, contudo, ainda assim, de qualquer modo, apesar de tudo, apesar disso [i.e., algo já mencionado] *The two gangsters hadn't threatened him in a physical way, but he was scared all the same.* ♦ *The atmosphere of the earth and the conditions beneath it must have changed enormously during its long history, but life went on just the same.* -LJ,156.
all the same; all one igual, indiferente, a mesma coisa, tanto faz *Do as you wish. It's all the same to me.* ♦ *It's all one to me whether Cynthia goes or stays.*
much the same quase o mesmo, quase a mesma coisa *... the major ocean basins and the major continental land masses are today much the same as they have been since a very early period of the earth's history.* -CR,11.
SATURDAY Saturday night special [gir] revólver pequeno e de cano curto *... "Saturday night specials", the cheap, easily concealed pistols that have been flooding American cities and turning thousands of quarrels and robberies into murders.* -T/75.
SAUCE hit the sauce → hit the BOTTLE
SAVE save up economizar, juntar dinheiro *Bert has saved up enough money to buy a car.*
SAY be said to diz-se (de alguém) que, segundo se diz, segundo dizem (de alguém) *Irving Berlin, the famous American songwriter and composer, is said to have composed 1500 songs.*

easier said than done falar é fácil, difícil é fazer *"Why don't you tell that to the boss yourself?" "That's easier said than done."*
have a say//no say in ter//não ter direito de opinar, de participar de uma decisão *[He] ... will have a powerful say in the makeup of any future Labor government.* -T/80. ♦ *Guy had no say in the matter.*
have one's say expressar sua opinião *The father let the boy have his say ...* -BCS,12. ♦ *[He] ... has had his say on everything, from motorcycling to gun control in the U.S.* -T/92.
never say die não se entregar nunca, não desanimar *"We never know when we're beaten", he says of himself and his staff. "We never say die."* -T/61.
that is to say isto é, em outras palavras, ou por outra *As a boy, he used to say he'd like to be a paleontologist, that is to say, someone who studies prehistoric forms of life on earth.*
to say nothing of para não mencionar, sem falar em *Terry was seriously hurt in the car accident, to say nothing of the three injured people in the other car.*
what do you say que acha de?, que tal? *What do you say we go upstairs and have a cup of coffee?* -SSG,12. ♦ *What do you say to a cold beer now?*
you can say that again [col] você disse uma verdade, você está absolutamente certo *When Wes said it would be months before we finished the job I replied: "You can say that again!".*
you don't say so não diga! que surpresa! *"That's the man who refused to marry the countess." "You don't say so!"*
you said it [gir] você tem toda a razão, você está absolutamente certo *When the plane finally landed safely after a near accident, the lady next to me said, "God was certainly riding with us," and I replied, "You said it!"*

SAYING **there's no saying/telling** é impossível dizer ou prever, não se sabe *... there was no saying who would win the runoff election ...* -T/78. ♦ *... there's no telling when the unexpected is liable to happen ...* -SWS,37.
SAY-SO [col] 1. a palavra (de alguém), asserção, afirmação *... the police had only ... [his] say-so that all those other incidents had ever really happened.* -T/63. 2. ordem, poder de decisão, autorização, recomendação, autoridade *... that ought to give me the right to have a say-so about what I do.* -CEP,89.
SCALE **scale back** reduzir, diminuir *He [President Ronald Reagan] is certain to resist any attempts to scale back the U.S. presence in the [Persian] gulf.* -T/87.
scale down//up reduzir//aumentar *All aid both military and financial will be scaled down by Congress this year.*
tip/turn the scale(s) [col] 1. pesar, ter o peso de *A big man, Paul tips the scale at 250 pounds.* 2. ser o fator decisivo, fazer pender a balança *His speech at the convention tipped the scales in favor of the conservatives.*
SCAM [gir] maracutaia, trapaça, fraude, estelionato *Kickbacks, bribes and currency scams became fairly common business practices.* -T/92.
SCAPEGOAT bode expiatório *... in Germany [in the 1930s], Jews were being made the scapegoats for loss of the war and Einstein's pacifism was bitterly remembered.* -T/79.
SCARCELY scarcely any = hardly ANY
SCARE **scare away** afugentar, espantar *Gail was the best-looking girl in town but her father was so strict that he scared away any possible suitors.*
scare off afugentar *Investors have been scared off because of recent company scandals.*
scared stiff [col] morto de medo *Norman was scared stiff when the stranger pulled out a knife and came toward him.*
scare up [col] juntar com dificuldade, conseguir com esforço, arranjar às pressas ...

the Army recruiter who went out to scare up some new boys during World War II. -T/86. ♦ Tim managed to scare up the money he needed.

SCENE **behind the scenes** nos bastidores, em particular, secretamente *There is a perfectly legitimate public curiosity about what goes on behind the scenes.* -T/67. ⇒ **behind-the-scenes** encoberto, velado, confidencial *I have tried to give the reader a behind-the-scenes glimpse into all areas of television activity ...* -WS,13. ♦ *... behind-the-scenes negotiations ...* -T/81.

come on the scene surgir *What, exactly, is our [i.e., of mankind] position with regard to the world? How is it that before man came on the scene the landscape was more static?* -WCB,162.

make a scene dar escândalo, provocar incidente desagradável *When Joan has had a few drinks she often makes a scene in the bar.*

make the scene [gir] chegar, surgir *The Cubans finally made the scene aboard a Puerto Rican tugboat ...* -T/66.

on the scene no local, presente *... Soviet merchant ships that had arrived on the scene.* -T/86. ♦ *The miners [of all pioneers who went West] were first on the scene.* -BR,617.

steal the scene → **steal the SHOW**

SCENT **throw off the scent** despistar, desnortear *When the police investigated the crime they were thrown off the scent by the diary they found.*

SCHEDULE **behind schedule** atrasado, com atraso, fora de prazo *... the program is two years behind schedule.* -T/87.

on schedule dentro do prazo, no horário *... the vast majority of repayments are right on schedule ...* -T/64. ♦ *Liz arrived at the International Airport on schedule.*

scheduled for/to escalado para, designado para, programado para *[He] ... is scheduled to visit the Chinese capital later this month ...* -T/75. ♦ *[He] ... was scheduled for a five-month stint as flight engineer aboard the Mir space station ...* -T/92.

SCHOOL **high school** escola secundária, curso secundário *Some courses [in sex education] start in elementary school and continue through high school ...* -RC,35.

old school método ou modo antiquado ou conservador de encarar ou fazer as coisas *... a negotiator of the old school.* -T/87.

school of hard knocks escola da vida, experiência *This is something I learned in the school of hard knocks.*

SCI-FI ficção científica *Among the stars of the sci-fi firmament, Arthur C. Clark ... is one of the very brightest.* -T/84.

SCORE **even a/the score** = **pay off a (an old) SCORE** *He will try to even the score with Hugh if he has a chance.*

have a score/scores to settle ter contas a acertar *Wyatt Earp and his brothers had a score to settle with the Clanton boys.*

know the score; know what the score is [col] conhecer os fatos (da vida), de uma situação, conhecer a realidade, saber das coisas *Ruth looked like a quiet, sheltered young woman but she really knew the score.* ♦ *Teresa knew what the score was.* -AIM,95.

on the score of; on this/that score a esse respeito, quanto a isso *... the President would not concede error on that score.* -T/87.

pay off/wipe out/settle a (an old) score vingar-se, saldar (antigas) ofensas, ajustar contas *The movie* Winchester 73 *tells the story of a man who trails a renegade to settle an old score.*

SCOT-FREE impune, livre de condenação *He was let off scot-free at the only trial he ever had ...* -GD,206. ♦ *[Five defendants] ... got off scot-free ...* -T/60.

SCOTT **Great Scott** Caramba! Santo Deus! *Great Scott! Look who's here!*

SCOUT **scout around** procurar, buscar *I scouted around and found a clean snack bar where I could eat something.*

SCRAP [col] briga, desavença *Two of his enlisted men got into a scrap with some GIs [enlisted men in the U.S. Army] in a cheap brothel here.* -FH,12.
not a scrap nem um pouco, nem um fragmento, nada *There isn't a scrap of truth in the story Neil told us.*
SCRAPE enrascada, encrenca, situação difícil *In Hitchcock's* Strangers on a Train, *Bruno Anthony's mother says that "Bruno's been in some very awkward scrapes".* ♦ *He got into a serious scrape and wound up in jail.*
scrape along/by arranjar-se, sair-se bem (apesar de problema, dificuldade etc.), conseguir viver (financeiramente), sobreviver *... he was an only child whose parents scraped along on odd jobs until the family moved to Memphis when Elvis [Presley] was 13.* -T/77.
scrape through conseguir (passar, escapar, contornar etc.) com dificuldade *[He] ... scraped through with another narrow victory.* -T/80.
scrape together/up economizar, juntar, conseguir com dificuldade *I could probably scrape together a few dollars in the next two months.* ♦ *... scraping together a livelihood as best he could.* -GJ,13. ♦ *[Tokyo Rose] ... used to bring food, medicine, cigarettes – whatever she could scrape up for the prisoners.* -TJ,978.
SCRATCH from scratch do início, do zero *... [the Bolsheviks] set themselves to build a new society from scratch ...* -OH,16. ♦ *They went into bankruptcy and had to start from scratch with a new product.*
scratch out conseguir (ganhar a vida) com grande esforço, com dificuldade *Most of the unemployed Mexicans are landless peasants, and they ... scratch out a bare living ...* -T/79.
scratch pad bloco para rascunho, bloco de anotações *He wrote down the address on a scratch pad.*
up to scratch/snuff [col] satisfatório, adequado, de acordo com as expectativas, consoante os padrões exigidos, em boas condições físicas *The recently produced electrical appliances have not been up to scratch.* ♦ *Chapman's work has not been up to snuff lately and we think that he should see a doctor.*
without a scratch ileso, incólume, sem um arranhão *We thought Steve had been killed in the car accident but he came through without a scratch.*
SCREEN the big screen o cinema *After a few minor movies in the early 1950s, he [Robert Preston] all but disappeared from the big screen ...* -SS,328.
screen out impedir a passagem ou a entrada de; classificar, selecionar ou separar por meio de exame meticuloso *It has been claimed that our minds screen out far more than we accept, else we would live in a world of chaos.* -PJ,11. ♦ *... rules that screen out many women from certain job categories.* -T/72.
the small screen [col] a telinha, a televisão *Some 3 billion viewers in 100 countries watched the 1987 Olympic Games on the small screen.*
SCREENPLAY roteiro (história e diálogos) de um filme *A multitalented writer, [Alan Jay] Lerner won a 1951 Oscar for his screenplay for* An American in Paris. -T/86.
SCREW have a screw loose [gir] ser excêntrico, ter um parafuso de menos *He has always acted as if he had a screw loose, but still has a way of making people like him.*
put the screws on/to [col] exercer pressão sobre, intimidar, coagir *The boss is going to put the screws on all those who have been slack and slow with their work.*
(all) screwed up [gir] 1. arruinado, fracassado, errado *... he was stuttering and I knew then something was badly screwed up.* -T/81. 2. confuso, embaraçado, atrapalhado; emocionalmente instável *Mike is a poor, unfortunate screwed up kid.*

screw up 1. torcer(-se), contorcer(-se) (as feições, o rosto) *His face reddened and screwed up.* -AI,20. ♦ *[He] ... screwed up his face in distaste.* -SRS,5. 2. → **screw up one's COURAGE** 3. [gir] estragar, arruinar, pôr a perder *I'm afraid if I look too far ahead, I'll screw up the work I'm doing now ...* -T/91. 4. [gir] cometer erro, fazer trapalhada, dar mancada *[He kept telling his men that they] must be prepared for anything [in combat]. "If you screw up, you die", he told them.* T/87. ⇒ **screwup** erro grosseiro, disparate, mancada *The plan did not work out well. It was a typical military screwup when more people came than they had planned for.*

SCROUNGE scrounge around [col] escarafunchar, esgaravatar, vasculhar, procurar, caçar *[I had only $900] ... and had to scrounge around to make up the difference of $300 ...* -BL,95.

SEA at sea 1. no mar, em uma viagem marítima, navegando *The ship is at sea.* ♦ *Life at sea can be very rough.* ♦ *Many sailors have been buried at sea.* 2. [ou] **all at sea** desorientado, confuso, perplexo *The police were all at sea over the bank robbery.*
follow the sea trabalhar como marinheiro *For some twenty years he [Joseph Conrad] followed the sea, chiefly in the English merchant service ...* -SV,61.
go to sea tornar-se marinheiro *He had gone to sea at 17 ...* -T/63.
put (out) to sea zarpar, fazer-se ao mar *The three small boats put to sea and were never heard of after that.*
sea change mudança profunda, transformação *... momentous sea changes of modern times ...* -T/64.
sea dog lobo-do-mar, marinheiro tarimbado *Long John Silver was an old sea dog.*

SEAGOING → **OCEANGOING**

SEAL seal off fechar, vedar *[The police] ... sealed off all roads leading out of the city ...* -T/72. ♦ *... Iran sealed off the French embassy in Teheran.* -T/87.

SEAM come apart at the seams [gir] 1. romper-se, desmanchar-se, fazer-se em pedaços *How much political and economic freedom can Yugoslavia give to its six republics and two autonomous provinces without coming apart at the seams?* -T/72. 2. perder o controle emocional *When Ella goes to a funeral she comes apart at the seams.*

SEARCH (you can) search me [gir] sei lá *"Where's Joe?" "Search me!"*
search warrant mandado de busca *If they want to look inside our house, let them get a search warrant!* -SRS,145.

SEASON in season 1. na época ou na estação, na temporada (de caça, pesca, frutas) *... he and his little friends fished in and out of season in the northern lakes.* -MMA,47. ♦ *Strawberries are now in season* 2. no cio *... Missy [a female dog] was in season ...* -SEB,139.
out of season fora de época, de temporada (de caça, pesca, frutas etc.) *[They] ... could be arrested for shooting a squirrel out of season.* -T/72.

SEAT be seated queira sentar-se, sente-se *Please be seated.*
by the seat of one's pants [gir] por instinto, intuição, prática, experiência *World War I pilots flew by the seat of their pants.*
hot seat [gir] 1. cadeira elétrica *He's going to get the hot seat for murdering his wife.* 2. situação difícil, incômoda, constrangedora *The cool Secretary [of State is] in the hot seat.* -T/87.
take a back seat → **take a BACKSEAT**
take a seat sentar-se *He came in, took a seat, and we began to talk.*

SECOND in two/ten/etc. seconds flat → **in two/ten/etc. MINUTES flat**
just a second → **just a MINUTE**
second to none inferior a nenhum/ninguém, insuperável *... America is second to none in strength ...* -T/78.

split second fração de segundo *It happened in a split second but the damage was tremendous.*

SECONDHAND → **at second HAND**

SECOND-RATE inferior, de segunda classe, de menor importância ... *many of his paintings were second-rate.* -T/69.

SECRECY swear to secrecy fazer alguém jurar segredo *All members of the FBI are sworn to secrecy and made to promise that they will not write any articles for newspapers about their activities.*

SECRET make no secret of não fazer segredo de, não ocultar *Henry makes no secret of the fact that he married Lady Fairwell for her money and social position.*
open secret segredo de polichinelo *It is an open secret that he has been buying votes in the rural areas.*
top secret; top-secret ultra-secreto, de máximo sigilo, altamente confidencial *top-secret papers* ♦ *top-secret information* ♦ *a top-secret weapon*

SECURITY security blanket 1. pequeno cobertor ou qualquer pedaço de tecido macio que uma criança segura e que lhe dá proteção, confiança, tranqüilidade e bem-estar *Linus in "Peanuts" is rarely without his security blanket.* 2. pessoa ou coisa que constitui amparo ou proteção psicológica para alguém ... *a serious search for values that are more than security blankets.* -BL,144.

SEE I'll be seeing you a gente se vê, até qualquer dia, até a vista *So long, kid. I'll be seeing you.*
see about 1. tratar de, cuidar de, tomar providências sobre *We will see about getting some fans and better lights for the office.* 2. considerar, examinar, estudar *I can't give you an answer right now but I'll see about it.*
see after = **LOOK after** *I will take care of the food and you see after the transportation for our picnic.*

see fit achar adequado, julgar conveniente *[He] ... can run things as he sees fit ...* -T/81.
seeing that considerando que, visto que *Seeing that it would snow for hours and block the roads, we called the bus company and canceled our trip.*
see into 1. investigar, examinar, averiguar *If you can wait a minute I will see into that matter for you.* 2. perceber, compreender *Mrs. Crane saw into her daughter's odd behavior at once.*
see off acompanhar alguém até o local de embarque ou partida *The whole village gathered to see us off.* -RQ,67.
see out 1. levar a cabo, completar *Alec was given a difficult task but he saw it out.* 2. acompanhar alguém até a porta, até a saída *I'll see you out to the door when you are ready to leave.*
see red [col] enfurecer-se *Vicky saw red when Guy said he couldn't take her to the dance.*
see through 1. perceber, detectar, não se deixar enganar por ... *I know enough now to see through your lies.* -HJ,42. ♦ *I knew that you saw through me. But what am I to do?* -DD,61. 2. levar (algo) a cabo, ir até o fim, até que (algo) esteja terminado *You must see this job through if you begin it or not start it at all.* 3. auxiliar nas despesas, suprir necessidades; ajudar (alguém) durante período de dificuldades, doença etc., dar assistência *We have enough cash to see us through until the end of the year.* ♦ ... *she was consulting cancer doctors who saw her through breast surgery for a malignant tumor.* -T/92.
see to encarregar-se de, tratar de, certificar-se de que, cuidar para que *Will you see to this matter at once?* ♦ *Our parents were able to see to it that we were exposed to the best education money could buy ...* -RJ,13.
see you (around) = **I'll be SEEING you** *See you, kid.* ♦ *See you around, Billy.*
see you later até logo, até mais tarde *See you later, Al.*

SEED go/run to seed estragar-se, arruinar-se, deteriorar-se; perder o vigor, definhar, decair *The house had gone to seed from lack of care.* ♦ *Once a very clever professor, Mr. Sorensen has now gone to seed.*

SEEK not far to seek fácil de perceber, óbvio, claro *The reasons for his failure are not far to seek.*
seek out procurar, buscar, tentar encontrar *... seek out the facts behind a twelve-year-old crime.* -T/63. ♦ *They explored ... the West seeking out passes through mountain barriers ...* -BR,4.

SEEM as to seem → as to BE

SEE-THROUGH transparente *Lorene was wearing a see-through blouse and Wade was amazed at the size of her areolae and erect nipples.*

SEIZE seize on/upon apoderar-se de, agarrar, aproveitar-se de (idéia, oportunidade etc.) *[He] ... seized upon the offer ...* -T/87. ♦ *Moore seized upon the unexpected opportunity.*

SELF one's old/former/normal/usual/etc. self a sua verdadeira personalidade; seu comportamento normal, costumeiro; o estado normal de uma pessoa *Sue has emerged from her black despair and is her old self again.* ♦ *... though Adams was his usual impassive self, Jerry Farman was growing more and more impatient.* -SWJ,37.

SELF-CONSCIOUS constrangido, embaraçado, inibido *Now, when you get on the stage don't be self-conscious. All of the people are your friends and want you to become a success.*

SELF-DEFEATING que contraria suas próprias intenções, que atua contra si próprio *Banning books and prosecuting theater owners can actually be self-defeating, since they lend false glamour to the forbidden and the illicit.* -T/69.

SELF-EFFACING reservado, modesto, discreto, recatado *... a self-effacing ... civil servant who supervises the files, mail and other administrative functions ...* -T/66.

SELF-MADE vitorioso por esforço próprio, que venceu por si mesmo *Many a self-made man had the help of a hardworking wife.*

SELF-POSSESSED calmo, tranqüilo, senhor de si *Money, a good social position and beauty help give her a self-possessed manner.*

SELF-RIGHTEOUS farisaico, hipócrita *Mrs. Hamilton's self-righteous attitudes always annoy me.*

SELF-SEEKING egoísta, que cuida exclusivamente de seus interesses *[His] ... ideas and attitudes are the tactics of a self-seeking careerist ...* -T/92.

SELF-SERVING egoístico, que visa aos próprios interesses *[His argument was only] ... a self-serving excuse to hide the truth.* -T/73.

SELF-STYLED pretenso, suposto, que se intitula *... Scott Joplin, the self-styled King of Ragtime ...* -T/72. ♦ *... self-styled critics ...* -T/85.

SELF-TAUGHT autodidata, autodidático, instruído por si mesmo, sem auxílio de professores *Mr. James was a self-taught trumpeter.*

SELL hard//soft sell técnica agressiva// suave e discreta de vender ou de fazer publicidade *The hard sell is considered extremely impolite in Japan ...* -T/63. ♦ *The soft sell is replacing the unpleasant hard sell in some TV advertisements.*
sell for custar (determinada quantia), ser vendido por (tanto) *... a Porsche [automobile], which currently sells for an average price of $42,000 ...* -T/87.
sell off liquidar, vender a preço especial *To raise badly needed cash, the firm is trying to sell off unprofitable businesses.* -T/85.
sell (someone) on convencer (do valor, da conveniência etc. de algo), persuadir (a aceitar algo) *[The then Secretary of the Department of Health, Education and Welfare] ... sold Nixon, though not*

Congress, on a national health insurance plan. ⇒ **sold on** persuadido, convencido (do valor, da qualidade, das possibilidades etc. de algo) *[General Douglas MacArthur] ... was one of the first Army generals to be sold on the potential of strategic air power.* -T/64.
sell out 1. vender (todo o estoque de); liquidar (negócio) *The store has sold out its whole stock of washing machines.* ♦ *They sold out the company.* 2. ser totalmente vendido, liquidado *... the magazines quickly sold out on newsstands across the U.S.* -T/67. ♦ *The [tickets to the football] game had sold out months ago in just a few days ...* -T/86. ⇒ **sellout** a. algo de grande vendagem, sucesso de vendas *Record stores all over the country reported sellouts on the new Lennon-Ono album.* -T/80. b. evento (artístico, esportivo etc.) para o qual todos os ingressos foram vendidos *The show was a sellout.* 3. [col] trair (amigos, causa, princípios etc.); vender-se, corromper-se *[They] ... accused him of selling out to the enemy.* -T/76. ♦ *I take it you are willing to sell out your employer for a price?* -OFW,43.
sell short subestimar, depreciar, desmerecer *You've got what it takes, Tony. Don't sell yourself short.* -DK,120.
soft sell → **hard SELL**
SEND send away for encomendar (algo) pelo correio *Once we sent away for a book of French lessons.* -CTT,20.
send for mandar buscar, mandar chamar, pedir para vir; encomendar *Send for the doctor in a hurry! This man is dying!* ♦ *Mills has sent for a hardcover copy of Thomas Mann's* The Magic Mountain.
send off expedir, despachar *Please send this letter off immediately.* ⇒ **send-off** [col] bota-fora, despedida *The new Secretary of State received a rousing send-off for his maiden diplomatic mission ...* -T/80.
send out enviar, emitir, despachar *They had read every message that the spy sent out.*

send out for mandar buscar, encomendar *He got hold of a catalog from a Western supply house in the States and sent out for books, a cowboy hat, chaps, and pistols with holsters.* -LRT, 43.
send packing mandar embora, despedir sumariamente *... the Cuban ambassador was sent packing by the new Prime Minister ...* -T/81.
send up [col] sentenciar a uma pena, mandar para a cadeia *He was sent up for a short stretch in a state prison.* -T/72.
SENSE argue/beat/drive/knock/talk etc. (some) sense into pôr (um pouco de) juízo na cabeça de *We tried to argue some sense into her, but it was no use.* ♦ *Thanks for knocking some sense into my head.* -GE,283.
come to one's senses 1. recuperar os sentidos *When Chris came to his senses he found that he had been drugged and kidnapped.* 2. recobrar o juízo, a razão, cair em si *Vivian clung to the hope that her husband would come to his senses.*
in a sense de certa maneira, em certo sentido *In a sense, many movies could be called really historical while others have distorted history completely.*
make sense fazer sentido, ser compreensível *The story she told us makes no sense.*
make sense (out) of compreender, achar significado em *... a man desperately trying to make sense out of what has happened to him.* -T/63.
out of one's senses fora de si, de seu juízo, disparatado *Owen must have been out of his senses when he said that.*
talk/speak sense falar com sensatez, dizer coisa que faça sentido, ser sensato *Talk sense, Johnny. You know we can't do what you propose.* ♦ *... we ought to be ... able to know when we are speaking sense and when we are just vaporizing.* -WP,32.
there is no sense (in) não é sensato, não faz sentido *Well, there is no sense in asking for trouble.* -SRU,75.

SENTENCE **serve a sentence** cumprir pena na prisão *Alger Hiss did not serve all of his sentence but got out early because of good behavior.*

SERVE **serve someone right** é bem-feito, é bem merecido (o infortúnio, o castiço) *He ought to be put in jail for the rest of his life. It would serve him just right.*

serve up oferecer, apresentar, proporcionar *The military band served up a good rendition of John Philip Sousa's Stars and Stripes Forever.*

SERVICE **at someone's service** às ordens de, à disposição de *We are at your service day and night.*

be of service ser útil, prestativo *Can I be of service to you in any way?*

in the service nas forças armadas, prestando serviço militar *Collins was in the service for 3 years, 3 months and 18 days.*

press into service colocar em serviço, em uso, pôr para trabalhar *In the harvest weeks ahead, more volunteers and soldiers will be pressed into service.* -T/60. ♦ *When rescue workers ran out of ambulances, they pressed pickup trucks into service ...* -T/86.

see service 1. ter utilidade, ter préstimo, prestar serviços *She went to the closet and took out her hat which was seeing service for the seventh autumn in a row.* -MG,18. 2. prestar serviço militar *Some of the men had seen Army service.* -FV,24.

service station → **GAS station**

SERVICEMAN membro das forças armadas, soldado *William Wyler's The Best Years of Our Lives tells the story of three servicemen coming home after World War II and the problems they face in adjusting to civilian life.*

SESAME **open sesame** abre-te sésamo, chave mágica (para conseguir acesso a alguma coisa, atingir um resultado etc.) *She thought that her beauty would be an open sesame to Hollywood stardom.*

SET **be (dead) set against** ser terminantemente contrário a *[They were] ... dead set against the use of force.* -T/66. ♦ *She was so set against smoking and drinking.*

set about começar a, aplicar-se a, pôr-se a *Returning to Brazil, Portinari set about painting the life and spirit of his own country ...* -CS,561.

set afire/aflame 1. = **set on FIRE** *His car was riddled and set afire by a fusillade from a Communist ambush.* -T/60. 2. agitar, abalar, alvoroçar, inflamar *... the father of relativity [Albert Einstein] remains a moving figure, a 20th century Newton who set physics aflame ...* -T/79.

set apart 1. diferenciar, distinguir *Before Darwin, man was set apart from the rest of the animal kingdom by virtue of his having a soul.* -HC,11. 2. reservar, pôr de lado, separar *Set these plates apart from the others.*

set aside 1. pôr de lado, separar, reservar, economizar *... set aside some time for idleness.* -T/66. ♦ *Each week he sets aside a few dollars for his Christmas Club bank account.* 2. descartar, rejeitar, anular *... evidence which we cannot set aside or brush away.* -HGI,24.

set back 1. atrasar (os ponteiros, o relógio) *set one's watch back* ♦ *set back the clock* 2. impedir (o progresso, a marcha), atrasar, fazer retroceder *[He] ... has set back the chances for peace in the Middle East.* -T/78. ⇒ **setback** revés, vicissitude, contratempo *His plan had a setback just when he thought everything was going along smoothly.* 3. [gír] custar (dinheiro a alguém) *How much will the new car set me back?*

set down 1. tomar nota de, colocar por escrito, registrar (também pictoricamente) *[They] ... set down plenty of facts and observations ...* -GD,199. ♦ *... some [of the pictures painted on the walls of prehistoric caves] may have been left behind by unknown early Van Goghs and Cézannes who wanted to set down some of the beauty they saw in the world around them.*

-SWM,10. 2. colocar em uma superfície ou no chão *Joan set down her drink on the small table.* 3. deixar descer (passageiro de um veículo), parar para desembarcar *The bus set down four passengers near Central Station.* 4. aterrissar (avião) ... *the plane set down on the airstrip at Shannon, Ireland ...* -SWLM,24. 5. estabelecer, dispor (regras, princípios etc.) *The rules are clearly set down.* 6. considerar, ter na conta de *He has often been described as a psychic, but we set him down as a fake.* 7. atribuir *Miss Clooney sets down her success to perseverance, hard work and a fine singing voice.*

set forth 1. expressar em palavras, expor, relatar, apresentar ... *it is difficult to shape a definitive statement clearly setting forth the origins of our Amerind [American Indian] ...* -BCMT,10. 2. partir, iniciar viagem *He set forth on a dangerous voyage.*

set free libertar *When Will saw the caged birds he bought them only to set them free.*

set in manifestar-se, aparecer, alojar-se *She was ready to leave the hospital when pneumonia set in and she died suddenly.* ♦ *Boredom starts to set in.* -WCG,13. ♦ *A heavy fog set in early that afternoon.*

set loose soltar, libertar, dar rédeas soltas a *When we came near his land he set loose a pack of snarling, savage dogs.*

set off 1. fazer explodir, detonar ... *mysterious terrorists who were setting off bombs in public buildings ...* -T/63. 2. ativar, fazer funcionar (mecanismo) *A cleaning woman accidentally set off the alarm in the bank.* 3. realçar, acentuar, dar relevo a, contrastar *Zillah's dark hair falling around her shoulders set off her cool, classic beauty.* 4. iniciar uma viagem, partir *Lando, his boys Pepe, Paul and Hamilton and I set off on our trip up the White Rock at midnight so that we would be able to watch the dawn from the summit.* 5. dar início; iniciar-se *The fall of one Swiss bank set off a panic in international banking.*

set on/upon 1. atacar, agredir ... *he was set upon by a pit bull.* -T/86. ♦ ... *the army's rear guard was set upon by the Christian Basques ...* -PM,316. 2. fazer atacar, atiçar, açular *The old man set his dogs on the intruders.* 3. decidido a, disposto a *I know you are going to do what you are set on doing.* -HO,130. ♦ *If you are set on hiring him, give him double pay ...* -HG,40.

set out 1. iniciar uma viagem, pôr-se a caminho, partir *In 1925, upon graduation from college, I had set out for Europe ...* -SWLM,vii. 2. empreender, intentar, propor-se, tomar a seu cargo ... *he set out to assure the world that the Egyptian government would honor existing treaties ...* -T/81. 3. exibir, dispor, expor *We set out our equipment for a weekly inspection.* 4. declarar, definir, descrever *She has set out her opinion on the subject very clearly.* 5. plantar *We set out our tomato plants when we thought the danger of frost was over.*

set right esclarecer, corrigir, colocar nos devidos termos *[They] ... saw no way to set matters right.* -OH,16. ♦ *Let me set you right about your duties in this company.*

set straight corrigir, orientar corretamente, dar a informação certa a *Mr. Fowler will set you straight on the plan to follow.*

set to 1. começar energicamente (a fazer algo), pôr-se a *Whatever he attempts to do he sets to with a determined effort to finish in record time.* 2. começar a lutar, brigar *The two girls set to in a scratching and hairpulling contest.* ⇒ **set-to** desavença, disputa, briga *[General] MacArthur had a memorable set-to with [President] Franklin Roosevelt ...* -T/64.

set up 1. erguer, levantar *Let's set up the flag.* 2. erigir, construir, armar, montar *Set up the tent.* 3. inaugurar, instituir, estabelecer(-se), instalar(-se), fundar, dar início a *Some of us doubt whether the system that has been set up can work.* -T/81. ♦ *Benjamin Franklin set himself up as a printer in Philadelphia.* ♦ *[She] ... set up a law firm with her husband ...* -T/76. 4. colocar no poder *The Soviets set up a puppet regime in Afghanistan.* 5. prover, dar os meios necessários (dinheiro, condições etc.) para, equipar *Philip's rich aunt set him up in a luxurious antique shop.* ♦ *Bill's father set him up in business.* 6. arranjar (bebida, comida, divertimento, dinheiro ou qualquer outra coisa gratuitamente ou como obséquio) para *He was a fawning sycophant with cops, setting them up with free booze and dates with his girls ...* -T/67. 7. arranjar, ajustar, organizar, preparar, planejar em detalhes *Everett set up a meeting between the two men.* ⇒ **setup** organização, estrutura, plano, arranjo, disposição *The setup of General Motors is a marvel of efficient organization.* 8. apresentar-se como, pretender ser *And who are you ... to set yourself up as a judge and jury?* -HWW,36. 9. propor, apresentar (teoria, plano etc.) *He sets up ... hypotheses, and concludes that Kinsey's findings [presented in Kinsey's books on sexual behavior in men and women] contribute little so far to the integrity of the family.* -GD,15. 10. proferir, soltar (grito, clamor) *Someone set up the cry that the British were landing and the Bostonians ran to fortify Breed's Hill.* 11. causar, provocar *His troubled childhood set up serious inner conflicts.* 12. restabelecer, refazer, reanimar, restaurar as forças *A good night's sleep will set me up.* 13. colocar em posição perigosa, preparar cilada ou armação contra *So you've been stealing money from your bank, and you set me up as the fall guy to cover your operations.* HJ,136. ⇒ **setup** [col] a. trama, conspiração, cilada *Winslow didn't realize it until too late that it had been a setup.* b. luta arranjada, marmelada, qualquer tipo de conchavo *The fight was a setup.*

the smart set a grã-finagem, a alta sociedade *The term smart set ... seems sadly unsmart today.* -T/69.

SETTLE settle back acomodar-se num assento; instalar-se confortavelmente *... the passengers settle back for a five-hour flight across the spectacular cloudscapes of the South Pacific.* -T/86. ♦ *[John] Lennon ... settled back with [Yoko] Ono in the Dakota [an apartment building in N.Y. City] to raise their son Sean ...* -T/80. ♦ *[He] ... had comfortably settled back into his lucrative Houston law practice ...* -T/77.

settle down 1. estabelecer-se (em um emprego, profissão etc.); fixar residência *[In The Razor's Edge, Isabel Bradley] ... is unable to convince [Larry Darrell] ... to settle down to the job she asks him to accept.* -BDF,141. ♦ *They setted down in a small town in New Hampshire.* 2. estabelecer vida regular e rotineira *Walt seems to be the type that will never settle down.* 3. acalmar-se, sossegar, aquietar-se, acomodar-se; assentar-se, sentar-se *... quietness returns as the exhausted men [soldiers in battle] on both sides settle down for the night, content for the moment to live and let live.* -MAT,283. ♦ *[He] ... settles down in a reclining first-class seat ...* -T/87. 4. aplicar-se seriamente a *... they were just getting settled down to work after the New Year's holiday ...* -RE,50. 5. baixar, descer, cair (a noite) *Darkness slowly settled down ...* -SL,7.

settle for aceitar (algo de menor valor, importância etc.) em lugar daquilo que se desejava *Mrs. Winthrop had hoped to get a Mercedes-Benz but she settled for a new Volvo.*

settle in/into fixar-se, estabelecer-se em um novo local, nova residência, emprego etc. *... she has settled in at the University of New Mexico as a teacher of American and women's studies.* -T/86.

settle on/upon   decidir-se por, escolher, resolver-se a   *Have they settled on the day for the picnic yet?*
SEW   (all) sewed up [col] 1. sob domínio absoluto, garantido, assegurado, no papo   *He thinks he has the election all sewed up.*   2. contratado, comprometido   *When David Selznick offered Clark Gable the role of Rhet Buttler in* Gone With the Wind, *Gable told him that he was sewed up by his M-G-M contract.* -BRSP,49.
SEX   the fair sex   o belo sexo   *The fair sex is also the most resistant to disease.*
have sex   ter relações sexuais   *He went over to her apartment and had sex with her.*
sex appeal   atração sobre o sexo oposto   *Movie stars in the thirties were chosen mainly for their sex appeal, not acting ability.*
SHACK   shack up with [gir] dormir ou morar junto com (parceiro sexual)   *... he spends his time shacking up with "can't-say-no girls" ...* -T/60.   ♦ *Who's his wife shacking up with? ...* -FJH,35.
SHADOW   beyond the shadow of a doubt   sem sombra de dúvida   *... Jack Kennedy has demonstrated beyond any shadow of a doubt that he is the young political master.* -T/60.
cast a shadow   1. toldar, sombrear, desolar, deprimir, consternar, desencorajar, abater o ânimo   *Chernobyl is certain to cast a shadow across the Soviet Union and the world for a long time to come.* -T/86.   ♦ *The assassination of [Rajiv] Gandhi has cast the darkest shadow over Indian politics.* -T/91.   2. deixar forte marca, exercer influência   *[His father had been] ... prominent in the state, and he had cast a long shadow.* -MG,392.
a shadow of one's former self   pálida imagem daquilo que (alguém) foi ou era, uma sombra do que foi ou era   *Victims [of violent crime] who do not receive appropriate understanding and treatment often ... become reclusive shadows of their former selves.* -T/81.
SHAGGY   shaggy-dog story → **shaggy-dog STORY**
SHAKE   a fair shake [gir] tratamento justo, bom acolhimento, lisura   *We promise to give you a fair shake if you join our group.*
give the shake [gir] eludir, esquivar-se a, fugir de, livrar-se de   *We tried to give the police the shake but didn't succeed.*
in a shake [col] em um momento, em um instante   *I'll be with you in a shake.*
in the shake of a lamb's tail; in two shakes of a lamb's tail   em um átimo, em um instante, rapidamente   *I'll be ready in two shakes of a lamb's tail.*
no great shakes [col] não-importante, nada de extraordinário, comum   *Dannel [sic] Boone was no great shakes to look at, being but middle-heighted and getting on in years now.* -GJH,15.
shake [col] livrar-se de, eludir   *Perkins tried to shake the reporter who was tailing him.*
shake down [col] 1. extorquir dinheiro de   *... the lousy flatfoot [i.e., a policeman] who was always waiting for me on Friday to shake me down.* AIM,16.   ⇒ **shakedown**   extorsão   *Biggs tried to pull a shakedown on a society woman with whom he had had intimacies.*   2. revistar (pessoa ou lugar)   *... shaking you down to find out the girl's identity and her address.* -GES,91.   ⇒ **shakedown**   busca, procura, revista   *The police gave the place a good shakedown.*
shake loose   desprender, soltar, libertar   *The [Vietnam] war, and the protest against it, shook loose forces in American life and gave them a style and prestige they might not otherwise have had.* -T/85.
shake off   livrar-se de, desembaraçar-se de, repelir, escapar de   *... [he] had shaken off his nervousness of the week before ...* -T/72.   ♦ *He couldn't shake off the two enemy agents who were pursuing him.*

the shakes [gir] = **the CREEPS** *Virginia's got the shakes. She looks like she's just seen Dracula.*
shake up 1. mexer, misturar, bater, preparar *My wife always shakes up cocktails before dinner.* 2. sacudir, abalar, perturbar, desagradar, afligir *The terrible news shook me up.* 3. [col] agitar, despertar, espertar, avivar *These workers look lazy. Let's shake them up a little.* 4. reorganizar, redistribuir *The Thatcher government shakes up the school system with a bill that radically changes the way Britain teaches its young.* -T/88. ⇒ **shake-up** reorganização, reforma, mudança drástica *... he can ... give the organization the shake-up it so badly needs.* -T/92.
SHAME a crying shame uma grande vergonha, uma ignomínia *It's a crying shame the way some gangsters are allowed to remain unmolested by the police.*
it's a shame 1. é uma vergonha *It's a shame to do a thing like that.* 2. é uma pena, uma lástima *It's a shame that her career as a talented soprano has come to an end.*
put to shame 1. envergonhar *Tommy's dishonest behavior has put his parents to shame.* 2. superar de longe, pôr no chinelo *His encyclopedic knowledge of History put many of us to shame.*
shame on you você deveria envergonhar-se *How could you do such a thing? Shame on you!*
what a shame que pena *What a shame you can't stay for lunch.*
SHANTYTOWN favela *Urban areas [in Latin America] are rapidly expanding, and with them the poverty-stricken shantytowns of the continent ...* -T/69.
SHAPE in poor shape despreparado, em más condições, em estado precário *The British Army at the moment [1940] was in poor shape.* -SWLR,1004.
in shape 1. em forma, em boas condições físicas *He is getting in shape for his upcoming fight with the ex-champion.* 2. em boa ordem *The whole house was in shape when we returned from our trip.*
lick into shape [col] 1. moldar, dar forma a *He was called in to lick the proposed plan into shape.* 2. disciplinar, tornar proficiente (por meio de trabalho ou treinamento intensivo) *The tough Marine sergeant licked the clumsy recruits into shape in two months of hard drill.*
out of shape 1. deformado, torto *Timmy had sat on uncle Fred's hat and the hat was now out of shape.* 2. fora de forma, destreinado *Ryker had not fought for two years and now had to train earnestly because he was out of shape.*
shape into dar (determinada) forma a *The colonel shaped his army unit into an efficient instrument.*
shape up [col] 1. comportar-se bem, agir de acordo com as expectativas *If Nick doesn't shape up he'll be in trouble with the police.* 2. tomar forma; desenvolver-se, progredir, melhorar, assumir aspecto favorável *... the way things were shaping up spelled bad news.* -AIM,117. ♦ *Our plan is shaping up very well.*
take shape tomar forma, concretizar-se *During Egypt's early years, a complicated religion gradually took shape.* -SJV,16.
whip into shape [col] 1. = **lick into shape** 2 *The army units had been whipped into shape by a competent commander.* 2. obrigar a se comportar adequadamente, fazer andar na linha *Men do get out of hand, and when they do, you have to whip them back into shape.* -SEB,88.
SHAVE close shave → **close CALL**
SHEET three sheets in/to the wind [gir] embriagado *Barney went to a party last night and got three sheets to the wind.*
SHELF off the shelf diretamente do estoque, da loja, não-encomendado nem feito sob medida *[You can't] ... acquire ideological direction off the shelf just like a business buying a state-of-the-art*

computer system. -T/92. ⇒ **off-the-shelf** disponível em estoque, que se pode adquirir imediatamente *off-the-shelf software components*
on the shelf em inatividade, na reserva, aposentado, fora de circulação, de uso *Miss Wyman had been on the shelf for ten years but was recalled to her old teaching job.* ♦ *... put [this thing] ... on the shelf for later use.* -T/92.

SHELL shell game embuste, trapaça, vigarice *Don't try to play a shell game with me. I'm not a fool from the country.*
shell out [col] pagar, desembolsar *You don't have to shell out too much money for the new digital watches.*

SHIFT shift for oneself → **FEND for oneself**

SHILLY-SHALLY vacilar, hesitar, perder tempo *I'm a blunt man. I don't believe in shilly-shallyin' around about business.* -TRW,35.

SHINE shine up to [gir] tentar agradar, bajular *He was so busy shining up to her, I doubt if he knows what she thinks ...* -SL,34.
take a shine to [gir] começar a gostar de, afeiçoar-se a *Joe took a shine to a girl he met at a party.* ♦ *... more corporate customers are taking a shine to the newest machines at the core of Apple's line ...* -T/87.

SHINGLE hang out one's shingle [col] começar a exercer uma profissão liberal (medicina, advocacia etc.), abrir consultório, escritório etc. *After Army service in the war, he hung out his lawyer's shingle ...* -T/72.

SHIP give up the ship desistir de lutar, de esforçar-se para conseguir algo, abandonar as esperanças [geralmente neg] *You can't give up the ship now! Keep going!*
run a taut ship 1. manter o navio bem arrumado, em boas condições, bem-disciplinado e eficiente *Utterly efficient, he*

[Commodore Perry] ran a taut but not too happy ship, stressing maximum standards of hygiene and minimum shore liberty. -T/67. 2. administrar (algo) eficientemente, conduzir com pulso firme *In the 1960 campaign, Bobby [Kennedy] is running a taut ship.* -T/60.
ship off 1. despachar, enviar *Please ship the goods off immediately.* 2. [col] mandar (para determinado lugar), mandar embora às pressas, livrar-se de *Both children were shipped off to a school in Switzerland.* 3. embarcar em navio, partir *After graduating from Ohio State, she shipped off aboard a Norwegian freighter as a dishwasher ...* -T/72.
ship out 1. partir ou viajar de navio; embarcar ou ser transportado sob ordens militares *He shipped out to Bombay as an officer in the East India Company.* -T/67. 2. enviar por navio *... shipping out ... 3 ½ tons of gold.* -T/85.
when my ship comes in/home quando eu tiver (ou herdar) dinheiro, quando eu ganhar a sorte grande *When my ship comes in, I'll give you everything you want.*

SHIRT keep one's shirt on [gir] não se exaltar, manter-se calmo *Flint can keep his shirt on in the most heated arguments.*
lose one's shirt [gir] perder tudo, ir à bancarrota *Jordan lost his shirt at the races in a three-month period.*
stuffed shirt [gir] pessoa presunçosa e maçante *He was nothing but a stuffed shirt.*

SHIRTSLEEVES in one's shirtsleeves; in shirtsleeves em mangas de camisa *In this crazy old newspaper business, I work in my shirt-sleeves, you know.* -OJT,5. ⇒ **shirt-sleeve; shirt-sleeves; shirt-sleeved** informal, simples, direto *... three days of shirt-sleeve discussions ...* -T/64.

SHOE fill someone's shoes; step into someone's shoes substituir uma pessoa e demonstrar competência equivalente *Her* *colleagues feel that no single individual will be able to fill her shoes.* -T/78. ♦ *It is time ... to think about the man who must stand ready to step into the President's shoes.* -T/64.

in someone's shoes no lugar ou nas circunstâncias de *Put yourself in his shoes. What would you do?*

the shoe is on the other foot a situação inverteu-se, as coisas mudaram *When you had money you laughed at poor people, but now that you have lost all your inheritance, the shoe is on the other foot.*

step into someone's shoes → **fill someone's SHOES**

where the shoe pinches onde está o problema, onde o sapato aperta *You'll find out where the shoe pinches once you've taken over your father's business.*

SHOESTRING **on a shoestring** [col] com um capital mínimo, com pequeníssimo capital *Many firms were started on a shoestring.* ♦ *Most [schools] operate on shoestring budgets ...* -T/84.

SHOO **shoo away** enxotar, afugentar *After Tuttle had planted his garden he had to spend most of the day shooing away the birds that came to eat the seeds.*

SHOOT **shoot ahead** disparar na dianteira *Brazil has shot ahead of the rest of Latin America in industrial production.*

shoot down 1. matar a tiros *... there were always a dozen men ready to shoot him down from a darkened alley ...* -HW,6. 2. abater, derrubar (avião) *... [Boris] Yeltsin confirmed that in the 1950s the Soviet Union shot down nine U.S. aircraft ...* -T/92. 3. invalidar, pôr fim a, frustrar; derrotar, recusar, desacreditar *... a planned $600 million tourist resort that was shot down by the Egyptian legislature because of concern about damage to the nearby pyramids.* -T/87.

shoot it out travar duelo a bala, resolver questão a tiros *In High Noon Gary Cooper plays a U.S. marshall who has to shoot it out single-handed with four gunmen.* ⇒ **shoot-out** tiroteio, confronto decisivo resolvido a tiros *[The battle of the Little Bighorn is] ... perhaps the least documented shoot-out in U.S. history.* -T/84.

shoot off fazer explodir (fogos de artifício), detonar (arma de fogo) *... every kid for miles around was shooting off firecrackers.* -DJ,viii.

shoot out 1. mover-se rapidamente, disparar, correr, lançar-se, arremessar-se, projetar-se *[He] ... shot out through the main door.* -DD,63. 2. → **SHOOT it out**

shoot straight/square [col] falar com sinceridade, ser franco e honesto, agir decentemente, tratar com justiça *[J. Edgar] Hoover had slurred Puerto Ricans and Mexicans, insisting people of those two nationalities couldn't shoot straight.* -WI,65. ⇒ **straight/square shooter** pessoa honesta, sincera, digna de confiança *... nobody ever said you aren't a straight shooter, or don't believe in justice ...* -BCM, 127.

shoot up 1. crescer com rapidez, aumentar, subir, elevar-se subitamente *Boys generally shoot up when they are about thirteen years old.* ♦ *... by the end of that year [1959, Doris Day] ... had shot up to number one at the box office.* -HA,227. ♦ *... the [flying] saucer shot up from the ground and disappeared into the clouds.* HD,15. 2. promover algazarra, confusão e terror disparando tiros a torto e a direito *Texas Jack and his outlaw band rode into town and shot up the place.* 3. alvejar, atirar em *He was seriously shot up in the war.* 4. [gir] injetar (droga) na veia *... children buying drugs or shooting up ...* T/87. ⇒ **shoot-em-up** filme em que predominam cenas de tiroteio e matança, principalmente *western He likes to watch old shoot-em-ups on TV.*

SHOOTER **straight/square shooter** → **SHOOT straight**

SHOP **closed shop** indústria, fábrica, em-

presa, negócio etc. que emprega somente trabalhadores sindicalizados *The closed shop is a stain on a democratic society.*
close up shop → **shut up SHOP**
open shop estabelecimento que emprega trabalhadores sindicalizados e não-sindicalizados *The open shop, with both union and non-union workers, has been a topic in labor relations for many years.*
set up shop montar um negócio, estabelecer-se comercialmente ... *he bought some steam-cleaning equipment and set up shop in his family's garage.* -T/87.
shop around (for) pesquisar as melhores condições de aquisição de um artigo (preço, qualidade etc.); procurar o que melhor lhe convém (determinado artigo, serviço etc., dentre o que está disponível) ... *shopping around for just the right investment plan ...* -T/81. ♦ ... *we must now go out and shop around for a medical expert ...* -TR,77.
shop for procurar, ir em busca de ... *shopping for an investment banker ...* -T/85.
shut/close up shop fechar as portas, encerrar as atividades *During Carnival almost everyone shuts up shop in Rio.* ♦ *The Reagan Administration ... ordered Libya's diplomatic mission in Washington to close up shop and leave the U.S.* -T/81.
talk shop falar de assuntos ligados ao seu trabalho ou profissão *Laura and Betty went into the kitchen while their husbands talked shop.*

SHOPLIFT roubar (artigo exposto em loja) *He was arrested for shoplifting.*
SHOPPING go shopping/fishing/swimming etc. ir às compras/ir pescar/ir nadar etc. *My wife and I are going shopping.* ♦ *The boys like to go fishing and swimming in the summer.*
shopping list lista de compras; lista de itens diversos *High on the Chinese shopping list [of military equipment they need badly] are communications equipment, radar, artillery, helicopters ...* -T/78.
SHOPTALK jargão de uma profissão, ocupação, negócios etc. *[She began to speak in] ... the somewhat prosy shoptalk of a college-educated actress ...* -T/81.
SHOPWORN 1. deteriorado, sujo, desbotado, manchado etc. por haver permanecido longamente exposto em loja *The articles that are shopworn in big stores are generally sold for a lower price.* 2. desgastado, rotineiro, banal, corriqueiro ... *the movie [Meatballs] is a series of shopworn jokes, executed with no discernible flair.* -T/79.
SHORE shore up estear, escorar, apoiar *They had excavated next to the high building and had to shore up the adjacent wall.* ♦ *The U.S. seeks to shore up security in the Persian Gulf.* -T/80.
SHORT for short de forma abreviada, abreviadamente *Her name is Deborah but we call her Debbie for short.*
in short em suma, em poucas palavras *The director, in short, should exercise absolute control over the movements in his film.* -FJ,124. ♦ *She's rich, young and beautiful. In short, the ideal girl for you to marry.*
short and sweet breve e objetivo, não-enfadonho ou desagradável *Don't tell such a complicated story. Make it short and sweet.*
short for apelido de, forma abreviada de *Dick is short for Richard and Connie is short for Constance.*
short of 1. necessitado de, com falta de, carente de, malprovido de *We are always short of trained workers.* ♦ *[He is] ... short of everything from money to time ...* -T/80. 2. antes de, aquém de, a menos de, faltando determinada distância para chegar a um local, objetivo, nível, padrão etc. *[The ferry boat] ... was just 10 km short of its destination ...* -T/91. 3. exceto, senão, a não ser *Short of cutting off your head, you couldn't get rid of it [one's memory] even if you wanted to.* -PL,115.
short on parco, parcimonioso, insuficiente, com menos do que o necessário *[A*

novel] ... short on narrative technique but long on expertise. -T/87. ♦ *Short on cash ...* -T/87. ♦ *... people who are short on time ...* -T/72.

SHORTCHANGE 1. dar troco a menos *You must be careful when you buy movie tickets with a large bill or you may be shortchanged.* 2. [col] privar de algo devido; enganar, ludibriar *[Walter] Hunt [an American inventor] has been shortchanged historically because he never persisted with any single invention long enough for it to bring him fame and fortune.* -T/60.

SHORTCUT atalho, caminho mais curto; maneira ou método mais rápido e direto *We took a shortcut across the frozen lake and arrived at school fifteen minutes before our friends.* ♦ *... a shortcut to first principles ...* -WP,30.

SHORT-FUSED → have a short FUSE

SHORTHANDED com deficiência de pessoal, carente de funcionários, de mão-de-obra *They are shorthanded now and orders are piling up.*

SHORT-RANGE → LONG-RANGE

SHORT-SPOKEN lacônico, breve e ríspido *Fran was short-spoken, even rude, when she answered my question.*

SHORT-TEMPERED → have a hot TEMPER

SHOT big shot [gir] pessoa importante e de influência; manda-chuva, figurão, chefão *... I'm a private secretary to a big, big shot in the Hawaii sugar trade.* -JJF,251.

call one's shot predizer, prever, prognosticar, antever *When you said he'd be elected, you really called your shot.*

call the shots/tune [col] dar as ordens, mandar, decidir o que deve ser feito *It's clear that ... [he is] calling the shots.* -T/86. ♦ *I'm the boss and I call the tune.*

(crack/dead/good) shot atirador (exímio) *He was the best shot with a rifle I have ever seen ...* -LC,6. ♦ *Annie Oakley was the most famous crack shot in American History.*

half shot [gir] meio embriagado *When he arrives home on payday he's usually half shot.*

have/take a shot at [col] fazer uma tentativa, experimentar fazer (determinada coisa) *Now he'll have a shot at getting it [a big part of his support] back.* -T/87. ♦ *I didn't know much about the work but I took a shot at it anyhow.*

like a shot rapidamente, sem hesitar, subitamente *I got out of there like a shot ...* -SH,22.

long shot possibilidade remota, algo que tem poucas probabilidades de ocorrer; aposta, risco *This whole venture is a long shot and no one knows where it will lead.*

not by a long shot [col] de maneira alguma, nem de longe *[Is he] ... the ideal man to negotiate release of the American hostages [in Beirut]? Not by a long shot.* -T/85.

parting shot observação, comentário, ato etc. inamistoso, desagradável, hostil etc. que alguém faz no momento de despedida *[His] ... parting shot on the eve of his ... retirement stunned the nation.* -T/92.

a shot in the arm [col] estímulo, incentivo *The economy needs a shot in the arm ...* -T/92. ♦ *... the Twenty-third Psalm gave me a shot in the arm.* -RQ,91.

a shot in the dark tentativa, adivinhação, palpite às escuras *His answer to the question was a lucky shot in the dark and he was passed to the next class.*

shot through with entremeado de, entressachado de, mesclado de, cheio de *... their faith was ... shot through with pagan superstitions ...* -MHJ,19.

SHOTGUN shotgun wedding casamento forçado pelo pai da noiva *Seven Brides for Seven Brothers ends with a shotgun wedding.*

SHOULDER give/turn a/the cold shoulder to [col] tratar com desprezo ou indiferença; esnobar *... He was given the cold* *shoulder by Indonesian leaders.* -T/92. ♦ *Most people turn a cold shoulder to the sufferings and hardships of the less fortunate.* ⇒ **cold-shoulder** = **give a cold shoulder to** *[He was] ... cold-shouldered by most of his Yale colleagues.* -T/64.

put one's shoulder to the wheel esforçar-se, empenhar-se, meter ombros a uma tarefa *We put our shoulders to the wheel and found out that we were able to finish the job in half the time that we had estimated.*

rub shoulders with → **rub ELBOWS with**

straight from the shoulder sem rodeios, diretamente, com toda a franqueza *In politics, and in every kind of relationship ... [he] believed in dealing straight from the shoulder whenever possible.* -T/73.

SHOUTING be all over but the shouting já estar (algo) praticamente decidido, resolvido, terminado, liquidado etc. só restando cumprir as formalidades finais *On election night, the Kennedy group said that it was all over but the shouting.*

shouting distance → **within hailing DISTANCE**

SHOVE shove around tratar com rudeza, intimidar, maltratar *Tommy was small and had been shoved around by bigger boys.*

shove off [gír] ir embora, dar o fora *... I guess I'd better be shoving off. I've got a lot of work to do.* -BH,12.

SHOW get/put the show on the road [gír] dar início (a uma atividade, empreendimento etc.), pôr em ação, em movimento *Let's get this show on the road, Major. Tell [them] ... I'm ready.* -KJ,14.

give//get a fair show [col] dar//receber boa oportunidade (de agir, defender-se etc.) *The American likes to give his opponents a fair show to prove their abilities.*

give the show away [col] deixar escapar um segredo, falar demais *Vince gave the show away when he told Nancy he'd seen Carl at the club the day before.*

put on a show fingir, simular, fazer de conta, representar uma farsa *I suspected too that he might be putting on a show for me.* -MJV,4.

run the show [col] mandar, exercer o poder, dar as ordens *He's not happy unless he's running the whole show.*

show around conduzir, guiar, levar para ver, servir de cicerone *Look me up when you come to Kalamazoo and I'll be pleased to show you around.*

show biz [col]; **show business** a indústria do entretenimento, o mundo dos espetáculos (teatro, cinema, televisão etc.) *Irving Berlin used to say, "There's no business like show business".* ♦ *[The Band Wagon is a] Top musical of Broadway show biz.* -ML,32.

show in pedir (a alguém) que entre, conduzir (alguém) para dentro de um local *"Don't keep Mr. Ross waiting outside. Show him in", the boss said to his secretary.*

show off 1. exibir, mostrar, expor, ostentar *[She] ... was so proud of her new watch that she rushed to her grandparents' house ... to show it off.* -T/79. 2. exibir-se, mostrar-se, empavonar-se *... the female theory that all men are little boys at heart; they only like to show off.* -T/67. ⇒ **show-off** indivíduo exibido, fanfarrão *... he was always the class cutup and show-off.* -T/61. 3. realçar, acentuar *The green grass and the beautiful trees show off the lines of the white colonial style house.*

a show of hands levantar de mãos (em sinal de votação ou resposta) *... he called for a show of hands by those who had friends fighting in Angola or Ethiopia ...* -T/78.

show out mostrar a saída, acompanhar até a porta *"Will you please show this lady out", he said to his secretary.*

show through transparecer, manifestar-se, revelar-se *... Petrarch's love was real, and it shows through in his poems.* -DDT,200. ♦ *[His] ... doubts showed through.* -T/65.

show up 1. aparecer, estar presente, comparecer; manifestar-se *He showed up for a local television interview ...* -T/80. ♦ *Many diseases take a long time to show up.* -T/80. 2. mostrar, revelar, indicar *The election of an unknown candidate showed up the need for more careful campaigning by the other parties.* 3. denunciar, desmascarar *The journalist showed up the experts and now they won't forgive him.* 4. constranger, causar vergonha a *He was damned if he was going to be shown up by a couple of women!* -SLT,178.

steal the show/scene receber mais aplausos e atenção que os atores principais, conquistar a platéia; transformar-se no centro das atenções, ter melhor receptividade que os outros *[Lawrence] Kasdan cast [Kevin] Costner as the goofy, gunslinging Jake in* Silverado, *and he stole the show.* -T/87. *Independent filmmakers are stealing the scene in Hollywood.* -T/87.

stop the show ser ovacionado (ator) pela platéia a tal ponto que o espetáculo é impedido de prosseguir *The new dancer stopped the show with her fantastic twirls and became a star overnight.*

SHOWCASE local, oportunidade, evento, meio etc. de exibir de maneira favorável, atraente, interessante etc. alguém ou alguma coisa *His house was a showcase of good taste and refinement.* ♦ *... New York City's Carnegie Hall, built in 1891 and perhaps the nation's most famous musical showcase ...* -T/86.

SHOWDOWN discussão, encontro, luta etc. para resolver uma pendência, um impasse etc.; confronto decisivo *Linden had a showdown with his boss and decided to leave.* ♦ *... a face-to-face showdown with the Russians.* -T/64.

SHOWING make a good//poor showing causar boa//má impressão, fazer boa//má figura *You may not be our best runner, but you can make a good showing if you try a little harder.*

SHRED not a shred of nem vestígio de, nem sombra de *There isn't a shred of evidence his father is still alive.*
tear to shreds → **tear to PIECES**

SHRIFT give//get short shrift dar// receber pouca atenção, quase nenhuma consideração; dar//receber tratamento ríspido e lacônico *The father of eight children, he gave them short shrift.* -T/91. ♦ *One of the shortcomings of the rebuilding program is that design was given short shrift.* -T/86. ♦ *... his crackpot ideas were given short shrift ...* -SWLR,998.

SHRUGG shrugg off 1. desprezar, não dar atenção a *Nolan was always shrugging off his responsibilities.* ♦ *He shruggs off threats to his personal safety.* -T/92. 2. despir (peça de roupa) *She shrugged off her fur coat and sat down.*

SHUT shut down cessar operações, atividades, deixar de funcionar, fechar temporariamente (fábrica etc.) *... the government's reform progam has shut down.* -T/87. ♦ *... three newspapers had been shut down.* -T/87. ♦ *... a city shut down by snow ...* -T/87. ⇒ **shutdown** paralisação temporária de atividades; cessação do trabalho *Detroit has had many shutdowns.*

shut off 1. interromper, impedir a passagem de, fechar (água, eletricidade, tráfego etc.) *If you don't pay your bill, the company will shut off your electricity.* 2. fazer cessar o funcionamento de, desligar; desligar-se, deixar de funcionar *... a pilot accidentally shut off the plane's engines.* -T/87. ♦ *Dewey parked the car near the corner and shut off its lights.* ♦ *My washing machine shuts off automatically.* 3. isolar, separar *[After the suicide of his wife Rosa, Paul (played by Marlon Brando in* Last Tango in Paris*)] ... seeks to shut himself off from the world.* -BRF,62.

shut out 1. excluir, deixar de fora, impedir, bloquear (entrada, som, visão etc.) *The mind, perhaps, can shut out feeling, but the body keeps reminding us.* -GS,101.

2. vencer o adversário impedindo-o de marcar pontos, deixá-lo a zero *In the first two games Brazil shut out Spain and Italy.* ⇒ **shutout** partida na qual uma das equipes não consegue marcar nenhum ponto *You often get a shutout in baseball but I never heard of a shutout in basketball.*

shut up 1. prender, confinar *She had been shut up in her bedroom.* 2. fechar, trancar (estabelecimento, casa, cômodo) *The gambling casino has been shut up since the governor came into power.* ♦ *Let's shut up the house before it begins to rain.* 3. [col] parar de falar, calar-se; fazer (alguém) calar-se, mandar calar a boca [geralmente considerado indelicado] *Why don't you shut up?* ♦ *He wanted to insult her and shut her up once for all ...* -SGT,72.

SHY shy away afastar-se, esquivar-se, evitar, recuar *A man shies away from an overly aggressive female ...* -T/76. ♦ *In our society, we tend to shy away from casual public discussion of certain topics...* -HR,20.

shy of [col] 1. necessitado de, com falta de *I'd like to buy a car but I'm a little shy of cash right now.* 2. aquém de (determinado número, valor, quantidade, distância etc.) *She is some months shy of her 20th birthday.* -T/87.

SICK sick (and tired) of cansado de, aborrecido com, cheio de, farto de, entediado com ... *I'm sick and tired of being an instrument or an idea. I want to be a woman before it's too late.* -GE,268.

SIDE be on the safe side acautelar-se, prevenir-se, precaver-se contra um possível perigo, agir com prudência *Be here at eight-thirty sharp or you won't be taken. In fact, you'd better be here by eight, just to be on the safe side.* -WCN,279.

bright side o lado agradável, bom, positivo, otimista de algo inauspicioso sob outros aspectos *[He] ... believed in looking on the bright side.* -T/60. ♦ *[They were] ... persistently looking on the bright side of things.* -PVH,199.

get on the good side of agradar, adular *Moscow wasted no time in trying to get on the good side of the new government.* -T/80.

get up on the wrong side of the bed acordar de mau humor, ficar irritadiço *If you get up on the wrong side of the bed, you are grumpy.* -T/91.

know on which side one's bread is buttered; know which side one's bread is buttered on saber onde estão seus interesses, saber o que melhor lhe convém *He looks stupid but believe me, he knows on which side his bread is buttered.*

on all sides por todos os lados, de toda parte *Congratulations came on all sides when he was elected President.*

on the far side of além de, com mais (de determinada idade) *Mr. Rutherford is on the far side of sixty.*

on the side 1. como bico, como ocupação secundária *[He was] ... earning a bit of money on the side.* -DD,97. ♦ *He founded his own orchestra ... while appearing in nightclubs on the side.* -T/60. 2. como prato extra *I want a grilled steak and baked potatoes on the side.*

on the wrong side of the blanket de filiação ilegítima ... *a former governor of a Southern state who was accused of fathering a child on the wrong side of the blanket.* -CE,241.

seamy side o lado desagradável, miserável, sórdido da vida *When you do social work among the poor, you see the seamy side of life.*

side by side lado a lado, juntos *We are all aware of some of our illogical dreams in which two completely opposite statements can exist side by side ...* -KR,3.

side with tomar o partido de, apoiar *[They] ... criticize him for siding with Iran in its war against Iraq.* -T/81.

split one's sides rebentar de rir *Danny Kaye could not only make me split my*

sides but tears ran out of my eyes at the same time. ⇒ **sidesplitting** engraçadíssimo, impagável *sidesplitting jokes*
take sides tomar partido *Never take sides in a family dispute unless you want to lose a friend.*
this side of aquém de, antes de, que não chega a (local, objetivo, nível, padrão etc.), a pouquíssima distância de, quase (até, em) *... the mountain lion, or puma, a species just this side of extinction.* -T/73. ♦ *I am committed to support the President this side of treason or madness.* -T/65.
the wrong side of the tracks o setor mais pobre e socialmente inferior de uma comunidade *... he was born in a shack down on the wrong side of the tracks in Wichita Kansas.* -JJF,629.
SIDEKICK [gír] amigo íntimo, companheiro constante, chapa; assistente *Matthew is an intelligent man but his sidekick is a rough, arrogant chap from Tennessee.*
SIDESTEP evitar, esquivar-se (a), fugir (a), tirar o corpo fora *... he repeatedly sidestepped questions on abortion [and other topics] ...* -T/86.
SIDETRACK desviar, afastar (do assunto, propósito, objetivo etc.) *He cleverly managed to sidetrack any attempt to carry the plan into effect.*
SIGHT at first sight/glance à primeira vista *It had been a simple discovery at first sight ...* -LJS,7. ♦ *At first glance nothing seemed to be wrong.*
at/on sight 1. imediatamente ao ver, ao pôr os olhos em, ao reconhecer *Mr. Cacoyannis can translate Greek at sight.* ♦ *I could never read music at sight when I was in school.* ♦ *The police were told to arrest Culpeper on sight.* 2. à vista, contra apresentação *A bill payable at sight.*
catch sight of avistar, enxergar *[She] ... caught sight of the [flying] saucer as it moved across a field ...* -HD,15.
come into sight → **come into VIEW**
in sight//out of sight à vista, próximo// fora do alcance da vista, distante, afastado, sumido *The war was just finishing its third year, the end of it was nowhere in sight ...* -CB,2. ♦ *He was out of sight before the soldiers could shoot at him.* ♦ *She's dropped completely out of sight, and yet he knows she isn't dead.* -CRS,16.
keep in sight; keep sight of trazer na lembrança, não esquecer *Keep in sight the fact that you're no longer young.*
know by sight conhecer de vista *I know that woman by sight.*
lose sight of perder de vista, esquecer *What people lose sight of is that we've got to educate everybody – even the 35 IQs [i.e., schoolchildren with an intelligence quotient of 35] – and we've got them in school.* -T/87.
on sight → **at SIGHT**
out of sight → **in SIGHT**
raise//lower one's sights aumentar// diminuir suas expectativas, objetivos, ambições etc. *Unchallenged for re-election in 1948, Nixon raised his sights in 1950 and ran for the Senate ...* -T/74. ♦ *With growing opposition to U.S. involvement in Nicaragua [President Ronald] Reagan lowers his sights.* -T/85.
second sight capacidade de prever o futuro, clarividência *Some people believe that there are gifted persons who have second sight and can foretell the future.*
see the sights ver as atrações turísticas de um lugar *Mr. Tarasoff went to New York and naturally wanted to see the sights.* ⇒ **sight-seeing** 1. visita aos pontos turísticos de um lugar *... the President of France had one final bit of sight-seeing on his agenda ...* -T/66. 2. próprio para visitar os pontos turísticos *A sight-seeing bus tour through the Rocky Mountains ...* -T/87.
set one's sights pretender alcançar ou conseguir, ter em mira, empenhar-se em, ambicionar *Besides setting its sights on the U.S., Japan has invested heavily in the economies of its Asian neighbors.* -T/85. ♦ *[She] ... set her sights on a doctoral*

degree in clinical psychology ... -T/92.
a sight [col] algo chocante ou aflitivo, coisa horrível, ridícula *You look a sight in that awful dress!*
a (damn/damned) sight better/more etc. muito melhor, mais etc. *I don't have all the answers now. But I know a damned sight more that I did when I was in [his] ... shoes.* -T/66. ♦ *I'm a damn sight smarter than you give me credit for being.* -GES,146.
a sight for sore eyes [col] uma beleza para os olhos, pessoa ou coisa que se vê com prazer *She was neither short nor tall, but exactly the perfect height to match the perfect lines of her body ... a sight for sore eyes ...* -SWJ,48.
sight unseen sem examinar, sem investigar, às cegas *... we had made the deal sight unseen ...* -LN,4.
SIGHT-READ tocar ou cantar música escrita à primeira vista, isto é, sem prévio estudo ou ensaio *Many jazz musicians cannot sight-read. Some of them cannot even read music at all.*
SIGHT-SEEING → see the **SIGHTS**
SIGN high sign [gír] sinal ou gesto convencionado, aviso, advertência *When the robber entered the room, the policeman gave the high sign to his coworker.*
sign in//out assinar o nome num livro de registro, livro de ponto etc. indicando a hora de chegada//saída *When the doctors arrive at the hospital they sign in. They sign out when leaving and give a destination and a telephone number.*
sign off anunciar fim de transmissão radiofônica, sair do ar *Fliers often signed off by saying, "Roger and out".*
sign on contratar, empregar; empregar-se, alistar-se *The company is going to sign on more workers.* ♦ *[He] ... signed on as professor of architecture at the University of Southern California ...* -T/63. ♦ *He signed on as the group's manager in 1961.* -T/80. ♦ *[He] ... had signed on as a captain with the 2nd New Hampshire Regiment.* -T/86.

sign out 1. assinar o nome em um livro de ponto, lista etc. ao sair de um lugar *You're supposed to sign out before leaving.* 2. assinar, registrar ou autorizar o empréstimo ou a saída de (algo) *... Bernstein signed out a company car and drove to McLean ...* -BC,82.
sign over transferir (a propriedade de) algo *[They] ... signed over 80 acres of land ... as a site for the new ... Eisenhower Medical Center ...* -T/66.
sign up 1. contratar, empregar; empregar-se *They signed him up for the new job.* 2. matricular-se, inscrever-se, alistar-se *[He] ... joined the Marines in 1959 when he was 18, later signed up at the University of Texas ...* -T/66.
SILICON Silicon Valley Vale do Silício *Some people still call it Santa Clara County, Calif., but more and more it is referred to as Silicon Valley, the place the miracle-chip industry calls home.* -T/78. ♦ *... Silicon Valley, the heartland of American technology ...* -T/87.
SILVER silver bullet solução miraculosa *[He] ... admits that these programs are "not a silver bullet that will take care of everything".* -T/87. v. **magic BULLET**
silver lining → every **CLOUD has a silver lining**
silver wedding bodas de prata *They celebrated their silver wedding on January 24, 1984.*
SIMPLEMINDED simples, ingênuo, crédulo; tolo *simpleminded advice* ♦ *a simpleminded man*
SIN ugly as sin muito feio *She was as ugly as sin but had a wonderful personality.*
SINGLE single out escolher, selecionar *The commission singled out four critical areas for immediate investigation ...* -T/87.
SINGLE-HANDED só, sem ajuda, sem qualquer auxílio *Already he [Wild Bill Hickok] was known throughout the West for the McCanles affair, in which he killed three desperadoes single-handed.* -SH,42.

SINGLE-MINDED decidido, determinado, firme, férreo, tenaz *[They] ... spend their whole career training with single-minded dedication ...* -T/87.

SINK sink in penetrar, entranhar-se, ser absorvido pela mente, calar no espírito *It took quite some time for the idea to sink in ...* -T/64. ♦ *She told them the bad news and paused to let the words sink in.*
sink or swim ser bem-sucedido ou fracassar por conta própria *[The firms are] ... condemned to sink or swim in the market.* -T/91.

SIPHON siphon off 1. transvasar, trasfegar, verter (líquido) de um lugar para outro *Throughout the 1,400-mile meandering of the mighty Colorado [river] ... water is siphoned off to Wyoming, Utah, Nevada, Colorado, Arizona, New Mexico and ... California.* -T/80. 2. [col] utilizar para outra finalidade, transferir (dinheiro) desonesta ou ilegalmente, roubar *Funds for Education were siphoned off and used by the Road Construction group.*

SISTER weak sister [gír] pessoa covarde, fraca, pusilânime, indigna de confiança [geralmente um homem] *[The colonel] ... put away the document, rubbed his hands briskly, and glanced around at his captains as if to see if there were any weak sisters.* -SLS,241.

SIT sit around ficar inativo, na ociosidade, ficar à toa *We can't just sit around and do nothing.* -T/92.
sit back 1. sentar-se confortavelmente, reclinar-se, recostar-se, pôr-se à vontade *... the two boys sat back and stared into the fire.* -YF,34. 2. repousar, sossegar, espairecer, permanecer passivo, inativo, indiferente *Don't just sit back and pretend that nothing has happened.*
sit bolt upright estar sentado em posição ereta ou endireitar-se (em assento, cadeira etc.) com postura rígida *I sat bolt upright on the sofa when I heard a strange noise outside the living room.*

sit by ser mero espectador, observar e permanecer passivo *We can't just sit by and let this happen. We've got to do something about it.*
sit down sentar-se; sentar-se (com outras pessoas para participar de uma reunião, conferência etc.) *Murphy sat down at the table and ate his meal.* ♦ *[He] ... proposed that the rebels sit down with his government on September 15 to discuss a cease-fire and amnesty.* -T/87. ⇒ **sit-down** 1. servido (jantar, refeição etc.) a pessoas sentadas (em restaurante etc.) *... it's a sit-down dinner here in the Lanai Room of the hotel.* -HA,3. 2. **sit-down; sit-down strike** greve na qual os participantes permanecem no local de trabalho recusando-se a trabalhar ou a sair até conseguirem um acordo *There's a sit-down strike at the factory.*
sit in on participar, estar presente (como observador) *He doesn't welcome us to sit in on his talks when he meets with other nations.* -T/87. ⇒ **sit-in** ato de protesto organizado no qual os participantes se sentam no chão ou nos assentos de determinado lugar e recusam-se a ser desalojados *[They] ... have held numerous sit-ins to protest low wages and poor working conditions.* -T/79.
sit on 1. fazer parte de (comissão, grupo de discussão, júri etc.) *Craig has sat on many charity group committees for the last ten years.* 2. [col] reprimir, conter, fazer calar *Kissinger could sit on hecklers with a few clever, unoffensive phrases.*
sit out 1. assistir (a espetáculo) até o fim *The show was boring but I managed to sit it out.* 2. não tomar parte em, deixar de participar de, ficar de fora, esperar (inativo) até que algo termine *[he] ... decided to sit out the 1992 campaign.* -T/92. ♦ *Stevens sat out his movie contract to its end.* 3. sentar-se ao ar livre *At the first sign of spring all the old people sit out in the park.*

sit through assistir (a espetáculo, filme etc.) até o final *[He] ... had the patience as well as the endurance ... to sit through the entire performance [of the three-hour lecture].* -KA,v.

sit tight [col] aguardar os acontecimentos, esperar pacientemente, não tomar nenhuma atitude *You have nothing to fear. So sit tight and relax, OK?*

sitting pretty [gir] em situação privilegiada, em situação de fartura, prosperidade, vivendo confortavelmente *We'll be sitting pretty when we come into all that money.*

sit up 1. soerguer-se, sentar-se (pessoa que estava deitada) *Ruth was able to sit up two days after her very serious operation.* 2. endireitar-se (na cadeira), sentar-se em postura ereta *The teacher told all the children to sit up tall in their seats.* 3. não se recolher, não ir para a cama, velar *I sit up nights trying to figure out how to save your career ...* -MN,237. 4. [col] ficar subitamente alerta, surpreso, interessado, chocado etc. *The news made me sit up.*

sit up for esperar (acordado) pela volta de uma pessoa à noite *Mrs. Jones still sits up for her children to come home, even though they're over 21.*

sit up with fazer companhia a, permanecer com (principalmente pessoa doente etc.) durante a noite *She sat up with a sick friend last night.* ♦ *[The reporter] ... sat up with ... [the Senator] until 2 a.m. one night [to interview him] ...* -T/63.

sit well agradar, quadrar, ser conveniente, convir, fazer bem *It would not sit well with American veterans for the President to lay a wreath at the graves of Nazi soldiers.* -T/85. ♦ *... the meal did not sit well.* -T/64.

SITCOM sitcom; situation comedy série cômica de TV ou rádio que retrata situações ridículas ou absurdas vividas por personagens permanentes, geralmente de uma ou mais famílias, amigos, colegas de trabalho etc. *... groundbreaking sitcoms like All in the Family and MASH demon-strated more than a decade ago that TV comedy is not incompatible with social commentary.* -T/87.

SIX at sixes and sevens [col] confuso, desorganizado *Everything was at sixes and sevens at the office.*

it's six of one and half a dozen of the other é a mesma coisa, tanto faz, dá na mesma *Whether or not he becomes mayor of our town is six of one and half a dozen of the other to me.*

SIX-GUN; SIX-SHOOTER [col] revólver de seis tiros *[The western town] ... was arid, bleak, lawless, dominated by the cattlemen, and the law was the six-gun.* -OFW,1. ♦ *... every man was armed with six-shooters and many of them had Winchesters.* -CEB,45.

SIZE cut down to size [col] reduzir (alguém) a seu verdadeiro valor, importância, prestígio etc., colocar (alguém) em seu lugar *He was cut down to size by the Supreme Court decision.*

size up [col] avaliar, fazer uma estimativa, formar uma opinião de, tirar uma conclusão de *He sized her up as a naïve woman ...* -WR,124. ♦ *[He] ... was possessed of ... an amazing capacity to size up people and situations ...* -SWLR,21.

that's (about) the size of it [col] isso descreve muito bem a situação, o caso etc., está correto, é isso mesmo *... if you hadn't been caught, you'd go right on smoking every day, I don't know how many times a day. Is that about the size of it?* -OJT,286.

SKELETON skeleton in the closet segredo, escândalo, coisa vergonhosa ocorrida no passado e que deve ser ocultada *... he is haunted by the fear of rattling skeletons in the family closet ...* -MR,9.

SKID hit the skids [gir] entrar em declínio, decair, arruinar-se *Joe hit the skids after his wife and kids left him.*

on the skids [gir] em declínio, em decadência *This economy is not on the skids.* -T/85. ♦ *... as a [film] director on*

the skids, he was hired to write a screenplay ... -BA,127.
put the skids on/to/under [gir] arruinar, destruir, provocar o fracasso, a queda de; fazer perder reputação, fama etc. *Faulty management put the skids to the business.*
skid row; Skid Row área velha de uma cidade grande onde se congrega a escória da sociedade, baixo mundo, boca do lixo *... after making the rounds of Skid Row bars, ... [he] holed up in a 90¢-a-night flophouse ...* -T/66.

SKIN by the skin of one's teeth por um triz, por um fio, por uma margem insignificante *Bruce took the entrance examinations for Harvard and got in by the skin of his teeth.*
get under someone's skin [col] 1. irritar, exasperar, incomodar *It was not so much what he said but the way he said it that got under my skin.* 2. impressionar, afetar, tocar os sentimentos de, abalar *[He] ... does something to me, and it gets under my skin, and I get all tingly all over when he walks in and gives me that up and down look of his.* -CEP,139. v. **under the SKIN**
have a thick//thin skin ser insensível//sensível a críticas, injúrias etc. *You could insult him with the most vile curses and they would all fall off his thick skin.* ⇒ **thick-skinned** insensível, duro, empedernido, impérvio, imperturbável *Reese is so thick-skinned that nothing seems to bother him.* ♦ *[He] ... has a notably thin skin ...* -T/61. ⇒ **thin-skinned** sensível, suscetível, melindroso *O'Brien is rather thin-skinned and can't take criticism.*
it's no skin off my nose [col] não é de minha conta, não me diz respeito, não é meu problema *You can go on disobeying orders for all I care. It's no skin off my nose anyway.*
jump out of one's skin [col] surpreender-se, assustar-se, ter um sobressalto, ter uma emoção repentina e violenta *I almost jumped out of my skin when I heard an eerie cry in the still of the night.*

save one's skin [col] salvar a pele, escapar ileso *[They] ... worked with the Nazis to save their own skin.* -T/61.
skin game [col] burla, fraude, trapaça *Even with all the police supervision and the exposés in the newspapers, skin games are able to flourish.*
skin magazine [col] revista masculina, revista de nus femininos *... the skin magazines appeal to the same basic audience: more than 60% of* Penthouse *readers, for example, also read* Playboy. -T/73.
soaked to the skin → **WET through**
under the skin no fundo, no íntimo, fundamentalmente *... under the skin they feel individual responsibility again.* -T/86. ♦ *The only reason that I was not killed was because my Chinese friends knew me under my skin and risked their lives for me.* -T/73.
wet to the skin → **WET through**
SKIN-DEEP superficial *The classic saying is: "Beauty is only skin-deep".*
SKIP skip it [col] deixe pra lá, esqueça, não se incomode *"Let me thank you for all your help." "Oh, skip it."*
skip out [col] fugir, escapar *The new bank clerk skipped out with the money involved in the day's business and fled to Mexico.*
skip over passar por cima de, omitir *Don't skip over any names on the list. We want to be sure that we send a notice to everyone.*
SKULL skull practice/session [gir] reunião (de equipe esportiva, de empresários, de políticos etc.) na qual se analisam táticas e erros passados, se trocam idéias e se traçam estratégias futuras *Generally, the first meeting after a big game is devoted to skull practice.* ♦ *... he summoned 37 Cabinet members for an all-day skull session to determine what the government should aim to do in the coming year.* -T/87.
SKY out of a clear (blue) sky subitamente, inesperadamente, de repente, de supetão,

do nada ... *he calls me into his office out of a clear blue sky and asks if I can handle the job* ... -GM,282. v. **out of the BLUE to the skies** muito, amplamente, grandemente *The President's foreign policy has been praised to the skies.*

SKY-HIGH 1. altíssimo, elevadíssimo, exorbitante, excessivo *The sky-high cost of housing keeps climbing across the U.S.* -T/79. ♦ *... sky-high interest rates ...* -T/87. 2. às alturas, às nuvens *... the anxiety went sky-high ...* -WCG,72.

SKYJACK [col] seqüestrar (avião durante o vôo) *Terrorists have skyjacked another plane.*

SKYROCKET 1. foguete, rojão *On the fourth of July the air is full of bursting skyrockets.* 2. aumentar abruptamente, subir rapidamente, disparar (preços etc.) *[The company's] ... stock has skyrocketed almost nonstop since ... 1970.* -T/87. ♦ *Unemployment skyrocketed.* -T/87. ♦ *... Oswald Spengler ... skyrocketed to fame with his book* The Decline of the West ... -SWLR,95.

SLAM-BANG [col] 1. violento, rude, abrupto, estrondoso; violentamente, rudemente, com estrondo *Bob and Carol had a slam-bang argument last night and Bob has left home.* 2. completo, total, vigoroso, rigoroso; completamente, totalmente, com vigor, com rigor *He's doing a slam-bang job as mayor.* 3. direto, retilíneo; diretamente, em linha reta *He ran slam-bang into the cop on the corner.*

SLAP slap down reprimir, repelir, rejeitar rudemente, fazer (alguém) calar-se *[He] ... was slapped down first by the Secretary of State ...* T/91.

a slap in the face insulto, ofensa *[He] ... has called Hoffman's proposal a "slap in the face to the people of our country".* -T/87.

a slap on the wrist repreensão muito branda, punição leve *[He] ... found it simply inconceivable that an Air Force officer could betray strategic weapons secrets and get away with just a slap on the wrist.* -T/81. v. **slap on the WRIST**

SLATE be slated for/to proposto para, indicado para, designado para, escolhido para; programado para, planejado para *... Lin Piao, a veteran of the Long March, was slated to succeed Mao Tse-tung.* -T/66. ♦ *[He] ... was slated to arrive in October.* -T/92. ♦ *Wheeler is slated for the vice-presidency.* ♦ *The meeting has been slated for next Thursday.*

a clean slate ficha limpa, boa reputação *How would you like to start your life all over again with a clean slate?*

wipe the slate clean apagar os erros do passado, começar vida nova, passar uma esponja sobre *We hope they wipe the slate clean and start all over again.*

SLAVE slave away mourejar, trabalhar sem cessar *... [Charles] Darwin slaved away [trying to understand evolution] for two decades before opening his mouth [i.e., before he published* The Origin of Species*] ...* -WCB,145.

slave driver chefe ou capataz muito severo *That slave driver Charlie – he's been working us all day.* -SJG,298.

SLEDDING hard/rough/tough sledding = hard GOING *It was hard sledding the first few years but after they had established a reputation for style and quality, their business was a success.*

SLEEP drop off to sleep → **DROP off** 4

get some sleep dormir, dormir um pouco *Get some sleep and you'll feel better.*

go to sleep 1. pegar no sono, adormecer, deitar-se, recolher-se *You look very tired. Why don't you go to sleep?* 2. [col] ficar entorpecido, dormente (pé, mão) *My left foot has gone to sleep.*

put to sleep sacrificar (animal com droga, tóxico etc.) *The dog was sick and had to be put to sleep.*

sleep off restabelecer-se (de fadiga, bebedeira etc.) pelo sono, curar a bebedeira

[He was drunk] ... and went home to sleep it off. -T/63. ♦ ... to sleep off a hangover ... -T/64.

sleep on/upon [col] refletir cuidadosamente sobre algo antes de se decidir, consultar o travesseiro *I don't want to accept your offer right now. I'll sleep on it and give you an answer tomorrow.*

SLEEVE   hang on the sleeve of adular, bajular, cortejar, não largar de *Leigh is the type of snob that hangs on the sleeve of any celebrity who comes to town.*

have something up one's sleeve ter algo escondido, ter algo de reserva, ter alguma surpresa preparada *... she had a whopping big secret up her sleeve ...* -CEP,186. ♦ *... you always have one or two surprises up your sleeve.* -OJT,76.

laugh in/up one's sleeve rir à socapa *He told us a story about his early struggles but we were laughing up our sleeves because we knew he had married the boss's daughter to achieve success.*

roll up one's sleeves preparar-se para agir, arregaçar as mangas *[He] ... rolled up his sleeves ... and plowed into his work ...* -T/64.

SLICK   slick up [col] arrumar-se, alinhar-se, adornar-se *The cowboys got all slicked up before they went into town on Saturday nights.*

SLIP   give someone the slip livrar-se de alguém, eludir, fugir de, passar por alguém sem ser notado *So you thought you could give me the slip?* -HJ,55.

pink slip [col] aviso de demissão, bilhete azul *[He got] ... a pink slip from the hardware factory where he had worked [for years] ...* -T/91.

slip away escapulir, fugir *... the supposed subversives had quietly slipped away from the town by night ...* -T/69. ♦ *... the values of the [American] Revolution are slipping away.* -T/76.

slip of the tongue *"lapsus linguae"*, erro involuntário na conversação, lapso *When he used a dirty word it was a slip of the tongue but a very costly one.*

slip on//off vestir//tirar (roupa) rapidamente *She slipped on her new flimsy red dress and went to the hoedown.* ♦ *[He] ... slipped off his coat and sat down in the chair.* -HW,17.

slip over [col] sobrepujar alguém mediante fraude, impingir algo fraudulentamente *She is always trying to slip something over on her clever mother without success.*

slip up cometer um erro, dar mancada *Julia slipped up when she gave you that information.* ♦ *I slipped up on a chance to invest in a company that has made a fortune.* ⇒ **slipup** [col] erro, mancada *If there are any slipups you will be held responsible.*

SLOUGH   slough off desfazer-se de, livrar-se de, abandonar, largar *You must slough off your worries.*

SLOW   slow down/up 1. reduzir a velocidade, diminuir a marcha, afrouxar o passo *... the train suddenly slowed down ...* -BE,16. ♦ *He began to run and then he slowed down, for he was afraid.* -BRT,82. ♦ *Slow up when you come to the intersection.* 2. tornar(-se) mais lento, mais vagaroso; diminuir, abrandar(-se), declinar *The war between the two countries shows no sign of slowing down.* ⇒ **slowdown** diminuição, redução, queda *... a slowdown in sales ...* -T/92. 3. retardar o progresso, o andamento, o ritmo de *The recent floods in that area have slowed down all outdoor activities.* 4. levar vida mais calma, mais lenta, moderar a atividade *When she learned last year that she had a generally fatal form of cancer, she refused to let it slow her down.* -T/78.

SLUG   slug it out [col] = **FIGHT it out** *The two men stepped out into an alley to slug it out.* ♦ *In 1943 ... First Armored Corps struggled across [the north coast of Africa] ... slugging it out with Marshal Rommel and his Afrika Korps.* -HG,5.

SLUSH   slush fund [gir] dinheiro usado para manobras políticas, suborno, corrupção etc. *[Nixon] was accused of having an improper $18,000 slush fund set up for him by California businessmen.* -T/81.

SLY on the sly em surdina, às escondidas, sorrateiramente *She's been drinking on the sly.* ♦ *The way he looks at me on the sly ...* -BS,65.

SMACK smack of saber a, ter gosto de, ter visos, traços ou sugestão de, cheirar a ... *he wrote only what he believed smacked of the truth.* -MWL,221. *His insinuations smack of treason.*

SMALL small of the back a parte inferior das costas *She felt a sharp pain in the small of her back.*

SMALL-TIME [col] insignificante, inferior, pouco conhecido, de pouca importância *[He] ... began his career in crime as a small-time hoodlum ...* -T/78. ♦ *... a small-time gambler ...* -T/77.

SMART-ALECK → **smart ALECK**

SMARTEN smarten up ficar esperto, alerta, não se deixar surpreender *Joey smartened up as he grew older.*

SMASH smash hit [col] grande sucesso, êxito de bilheteria *My Fair Lady was a smash hit on Broadway for more than six years.*

SMEAR smear campaign campanha difamatória *It was a smear campaign to cause trouble for the governmental candidate.*

SMELL smell out perceber, descobrir pelo olfato *Experiments have revealed that sharks can smell out one part of human blood in 10 million parts of water ...* -T/75.

SMILE wipe the smile off one's face → **wipe the GRIN off one's face**

SMOKE go up in smoke 1. = **go up in FLAMES** *Fort Buchanan went up in smoke when the Apaches raided it.* 2. dar em nada, fracassar completamente *All his hopes went up in smoke when the new government took over.*

holy smoke → **holy COW**

smoke out 1. fazer sair da toca, do esconderijo, por meio de fumaça, desentocar *The outlaws were hiding in a cave and the sheriff had to smoke them out.* 2. desmascarar, descobrir *I'll smoke out the reason for this power failure if I have to spend a month at it.*

smoke screen cortina de fumaça, dissimulação, disfarce *... ideological quarrels have often been a kind of smoke screen hiding personal animosity.* -T/77.

SMOOTH smooth over paliar, atenuar, suavizar, minorar, acalmar, aplanar *A Southern woman is obliged to smooth over all social irritations with good manners and a smile.* -T/76.

SNAG hit/strike a snag esbarrar contra um obstáculo, topar com uma dificuldade ... *the cease-fire agreement hit a snag.* -T/73. ♦ *His career has hit a few snags.*

SNAIL a snail's pace passo de cágado *He was driving at a snail's pace.* ⇒ **snail-paced** muito vagaroso, extremamente lento *... technical reasons are to blame for the snail-paced progress.* -T/86. ♦ *... snail-paced speed limit.* -T/87.

SNAKE snake in the grass amigo falso, pessoa traiçoeira *He turned out to be a snake in the grass and betrayed his friends to the Gestapo.*

SNAP cold snap onda de frio *A cold snap could kill off the crawling worms that denude the conifers in early spring.*

not care/give a/the snap of one's fingers não dar a mínima importância, não fazer caso de *He doesn't care a snap of his fingers whether he wins or loses thousands of dollars at cards.*

snap into it [gír] apressar-se, pôr mais energia no que está fazendo *Snap into it, man! We haven't got all day!*

snap it up [gír] mostrar mais ação, trabalhar com mais energia, apressar (algo), apressar-se *"All right, men", the big sergeant shouted. "Let's get moving, and snap it up!"* v. **SNAP up**

snap out falar com impertinência, com brusquidão, proferir com hostilidade *"I don't have to tell you anything!", he snapped out when I asked him a question.*

snap out of (it) [col] tornar-se alerta, atento, ativo; sair de um estado de desatenção, torpor, tristeza etc. *He was in a half conscious state but snapped out of it when the guns began to roar.*

snap up apossar-se de, agarrar, pegar, tomar para si, deitar as mãos em (ávida ou repentinamente), aceitar ou adquirir imediatamente *... consumers have snapped up 30 million copies [of a board game] ...* -T/87. ♦ *... 9,000 printed copies of the Soviet leader's speech were quickly snapped up at the newsstands [in West Germany].* -T/87. ♦ *... students snapped it up [Margaret Mead's book* Coming of Age in Samoa*], partly because its ideas interested them ...* -T/78.

soft snap [gír] tarefa fácil *This new job is really a soft snap.*

SNATCH in/by snatches por intervalos, por curtos períodos, a espaços, aqui e ali, descontinuamente *I always learn songs in snatches, and rarely learn the whole song correctly.*

SNEAK sneak away/off/out escapulir sem ser percebido, sair ou ir furtivamente *The police caught him just as he was sneaking away.* ♦ *The thief managed to sneak out of the hotel through the service entrance.*

sneak into entrar sem ser percebido, introduzir-se furtivamente em *Brian sneaked into the house through the back door.* ♦ *The boy snuck into class without being noticed.*

sneak up on/to aproximar-se sorrateiramente de, avançar gradualmente em direção a, chegar-se pouco a pouco a *[Crocodiles] ... seldom attack openly but sneak up on you under water ...* -LAK,87. ♦ *He sneaked up to the woman's house and looked through the window.*

SNEEZE sneeze at [col] desprezar, desdenhar [geralmente neg] *I have never believed that victory and money were the only things in life, although ... these things are not to be sneezed at.* -T/60.

SNOW snowed in retido pela neve *Snowed in, surrounded by howling wolves, Will waited twenty-nine days before Harrington returned to rescue him.* -SH,37.

snowed under 1. sobrecarregado *Rosie was so snowed under with work that she was unable to leave the office before eight p.m.* 2. engolfado, oprimido, encoberto *... a child ... snowed under by his fears and troubles ...* -HJH,215.

SNUFF snuff out 1. apagar, extinguir (vela, chama, cigarro etc.) *Carla snuffed out her cigarette in the ashtray.* 2. suprimir, destruir, pôr fim a *An atom bomb can snuff out many lives in very few seconds.* ♦ *... his life had almost been snuffed out a few hours before ...* -SWLR,1370.

up to snuff → **up to SCRATCH**

SO and so on/forth e outros, e assim por diante, etcétera *Bobby went to a farm and saw horses, cows, sheep and so on.* ♦ *She bought potatoes, onions, carrots, tomatoes and so forth.*

just so 1. em perfeita ordem, arranjado com precisão, em boas condições *He always likes his desk arranjed just so.* 2. desde que, contanto que *For our part it matters very little how the novelist manages his camera-eye just so he puts in focus for us a world that is both plausible and lasting.* -LAS, xviii.

or so aproximadamente, mais ou menos, ou coisa que o valha *We walked very slowly and I had to rest every hundred yards or so.* -RQ,32.

so as to a fim de, para *Check all your work carefully so as to insure that our machines will leave the factory in perfect condition.*

so that de modo que, de maneira que, a fim de que, para que *The basic reason why anyone studies composition is so that he may learn to communicate with maximum effectiveness.* -VC,1.

so what? [col] e daí? que importa? *So you've lost your girl. So what?*
SOAKING soaking wet → **WET through**
SO-AND-SO [col] 1. sujeito, fulano, camarada *I feel sorry for the so-and-so who is going to take my place.* -T/67. 2. indivíduo canalha, patife *Tell that so-and-so to get out of here.*
SOAP **soap opera** [col] telenovela ou radionovela (caracterizada por sentimentalismo e melodrama) *In the 1996 edition of his* Movie and Video Guide, *Leonard Maltin says that "Jorge Amado's novel [Gabriela] ... was developed into a top soap opera on Brazilian television".*
soft soap [col] lisonja, adulação, bajulação *My boss flattered me in every way, but despite the soft soap he told me the company was firing me.* ⇒ **soft-soap** lisonjear, adular, bajular *Don't let him try to soft-soap you, Lieutenant. Be tough with him.* -CHT,90.
SOB **sob story** [col] narrativa sentimental, relato de desgraça, problemas pessoais etc. que objetiva despertar compaixão, solidariedade *She told them a fictitious but wonderful sob story of her early life and the people began to give her money.*
SOBER **sober down** moderar-se, acalmar-se, aquietar-se, tornar-se ajuizado, ponderado *I'd say she'd sober down in twenty years or so.* -DD,53.
sober up desembriagar-se, ficar sóbrio *Get out of the sun and off the street till you sober up.* -BT,27.
SO-CALLED assim chamado, popularmente ou impropriamente denominado *... the so-called laws of nature ...* -FI,1. ♦ *In the so-called "post-war" period since 1945, at least 20 million people have died in over 100 conflicts.* -T/91.
SOCK **knock someone's socks off** [col] pasmar, assombrar, causar espanto a, deixar atônito, causar grande surpresa a *Believe me, what she had to tell me really knocked my socks off.*

sock away economizar, guardar (dinheiro) *[You might] ... consider socking away a little more of your income.* -T/87.
socked in interditado (aeroporto, área etc.) por causa de neve, chuva, neblina, poluição etc. *Toledo [Ohio] airport was socked in solid with fog.* -T/60. ♦ *Pollution has socked in Burbank ...* -T/73.
SOFT-CORE não totalmente explícito [diz-se de filmes, livros, revistas etc. pornográficos] *The Supreme Court upheld the conviction of ... a purveyor of soft-core magazines and books, but drew a distinction between sexual and obscene material.* -T/76. v. **HARD-CORE** 2
SOFTEN **soften up** 1. amolecer, atenuar (-se), suavizar(-se), abrandar(-se), comover(-se) *The material we have been using has softened up.* ♦ *She was strict with her children, but her grandchildren have softened her up a bit.* 2. enfraquecer a resistência de inimigo bombardeando-o ou atacando-o com artilharia *[The Allies] repeatedly bombed and shelled the Calais area as though to soften it up for an invasion.* -T/84.
SOFTHEARTED sensível, compassivo, terno, bondoso *She's a softhearted woman.*
SOFT-PEDAL [col] atenuar, moderar, suavizar, apoucar *A clever politician advertises all the small favors he has done for the public but carefully soft-pedals all the unfulfilled promises.*
SOFT-SOAP → soft **SOAP**
SOFT-SPOKEN afável, de fala mansa *Doctor Maxwell was a man of about fifty, soft-spoken and unassuming.* -KJS,21. ♦ *... a soft-spoken executive.* -T/62.
SOLD **sold on** → **SELL (someone) on**
sold out → **SELL out**
SOLDIER **soldier on** prosseguir obstinadamente numa atividade apesar de dificuldades, perseverar, não esmorecer *Despite many difficulties, Paul soldiered on.*
SOLID **(in) solid with** [col] em boas relações com *Jessup is in solid with the new*

President and may be able to help us get a government contract.
SOME and then some [col] e mais do que isso, e mais ainda *We espouse all the views of the Moral Majority and then some.* -T/81.
SOMEHOW somehow or other de uma/alguma maneira ou de outra ... *somehow or other, the natives had always known that salt was necessary to maintain their good health.* -RQ,105.
SOMETHING or something [col] ou coisa assim, ou coisa parecida, ou algo parecido, ou coisa que o valha *She must have been crazy or something when she did that.*
something awful/fierce/terrible [col] extremamente, excessivamente, demais *The Apaches mutilated ... [a family of settlers] something awful.* -CHT,49. ♦ *Terror was building up in me something fierce.* -AK,133.
something else 1. coisa diversa, diferente, outra coisa *This car won't serve our purpose. We need something else.* 2. [gír] pessoa ou coisa especial, sensacional, extraordinária *Loreta was a lovely girl, but Donna was something else. She was a knockout!*
something else again coisa ou assunto totalmente diferente do que está sendo discutido, outra história, outros quinhentos *They have been praising his work lately. Now, whether they really mean it is something else again.*
something has got to give algo tem de ceder; alguma mudança, ajuste etc. tem de ocorrer ou ser efetuada/o *The Johnny Mercer song* [Something's Gotta Give] *says: "When an irresistible force such as you meets an old, immovable object such as me, ... something's gotta give".*
something like that algo assim, coisa parecida, mais ou menos isso *"You're trying to tell me that I'm sick only in the mind?" "Something like that ... Your pains, Mr. Bedeker, are imaginary."* -SRS,33.
something of a/an um pouco de, algo de *[Bret] Harte, an Easterner by birth and education, was something of an infant prodigy with a yearning to write.* -RR,612. ♦ *[He was] ... a competent artist and something of a poet.* -T/67.
something or other alguma coisa, algo, uma coisa ou outra *Be careful with Harlan. He's always angling for something or other.*
something to write home about → **NOTHING to write home about**
SOMETIME 1. antigo, ex- *her sometime boyfriend* 2. em algum momento, em determinado ponto, ocasião etc. *He had fallen off the third floor roof sometime during the night.* -T/72.
SON favorite son homem escolhido pelos líderes políticos de um dos partidos de seu estado para disputar a candidatura à presidência da república na convenção nacional do partido *[He is] ... the favorite son among evangelical Christians for the Republican nomination ...* -T/86.
SONG for a song por uma ninharia *Those five old houses ... They were sold for a song.* -EJ,120.
song and dance 1. número de espetáculo teatral no qual artistas cantam e dançam *[Gene Kelly] ... projected an easy grace and wit that made him the most sought-after song-and-dance man in Hollywood.* -T/67. 2. [col] conversa, explicação (exagerada ou falsa); conversa mole, lero-lero, desculpa esfarrapada *When I ask the man why he hasn't come to fix my TV set, he gives me the usual song and dance about too much work.*
SOON as soon as logo que, assim que *He went on with his plans; he would strike as soon as possible.* -FS,14.
had/would sooner → **HAD rather**
no sooner ... than no mesmo momento em que *She had no sooner hung up than the telephone rang again.*
sooner or later mais cedo ou mais tarde *Sooner or later all things must come to an end.*

would/had (just) as soon preferivelmente, de preferência, preferiria ... *he would as soon be defeated as return without fighting.* -FS,11. ♦ ... *I'd just as soon he forgot about it [the incident] for good.* -OJT,321.

SORT of sorts; of a sort comum, regular, sofrível, inferior *Dorothea was a former personality who had been an actress of sorts ...* -MN,11.

out of sorts [col] mal-humorado, irritado; indisposto ... *why was [he] ... so out of sorts?* -T/66.

sort of [col] = **KIND of** *He was sort of angry [because] you didn't say good-by.* -UL,6.

sort out separar, selecionar, organizar *We sort out the interesting news from the commonplace.*

SO-SO mediano, médio, regular, passável; medianamente, mais ou menos, assim-assim *Herbert is only a so-so golfer.* ♦ *He plays chess only so-so.*

SOUGHT-AFTER procurado, solicitado, requestado, desejado, popular ... *he was popular, well liked and much sought-after.* -MMA,49. ♦ *[Marlon Brando is] ... one of the most sought-after stars in the business.* -BRF,65.

SOUL bare one's soul desnudar a alma, fazer confissões, revelar seus sentimentos, segredos etc., desabafar-se *Though she bared her soul in the [Washington] Post [magazine] article, she modestly declined an offer from Playboy to bare anything else.* -T/80.

living soul pessoa, indivíduo *If you ever so much as breathe a word of this to a living soul ...* -CEP,67.

search one's soul examinar a consciência, analisar suas motivações, sentimentos etc. *Frankly, my dear, you ought to search your soul and find out what you've done wrong.* ⇒ **soul-searching** exame de consciência *After a great deal of thought and soul-searching he arrived at a painful decision.*

soul [col] negro; característico de ou referente aos negros americanos ou à sua cultura ... *many Negro jazzmen honestly feel that white jazzmen cannot "feel" the "soul" music that the "soul brothers" and "soul sisters" are producing these days.* -T/62.

soul food pratos típicos da cozinha negra do Sul dos EUA *[The] ... anniversary ... was celebrated with the traditional music and soul food ...* -T/75.

soul of honor pessoa íntegra, honrada *You can trust Frank. He's the soul of honor.*

SOUND sound bites gravação de um trecho de discurso, declaração, comentário etc., principalmente de uma figura pública, transmitido em um telejornal ... *American voters are giving every sign of being sick of sound bites and slogans ...* -T/92. ♦ *Gorbachev was always too demonstrative and emotional a politician to be easily packaged in television sound bites ...* -T/92.

sound off [gir] criticar, expressar livremente sua opinião, insatisfação, queixa etc. *They sound off pugnaciously on politics ...* -T/84.

sound out sondar, investigar, inquirir *The women in the poorer neighborhoods were sounded out about their views on abortion and the results were most surprising.*

sound track trilha sonora (de filme) *The sound track was not well synchronized with the lip movements of the actors and the movie became laughable.*

sound truck caminhão provido de alto-falantes (para propaganda etc.), caminhão de som *The sound trucks went through the street screaming the merits of the Democratic candidates.*

SOUP in the soup [gir] = **in hot WATER** *You'll be in the soup if they find out what you've done.*

SOUTH the Deep South as regiões mais tipicamente sulistas e conservadoras do

Sul dos EUA, os estados que confinam com o Golfo do México ... *she witnessed up close the black-white struggle in the Deep South* ... -T/76.

SPACE spaced out [gir] sob o efeito de droga, drogado *[The 1960s] ... made drugs widely acceptable, and it soon seemed to be taken for granted that a large segment of the populace would be permanently spaced out.* -T/80.

wide-open spaces espaços abertos livres e ilimitados, o sertão, o campo ... *the wide-open spaces of the West* ... -T/87. ♦ *[They] ... go on fossil-hunting trips in the healthy atmosphere of the wide-open spaces* ... -SR,2.

SPADE call a spade a spade falar sem rodeios, dar nomes aos bois, não ter papas na língua *The nation has been looking for a leader who is sure of himself, who calls a spade a spade – even if it isn't.* -T/85.

in spades [col] extremamente, em alto grau, amplamente, duplicadamente, em dobro *Some day ... that bastard will get his. In spades. He'll get his comeuppance so good that he'll never forget it.* -MG,400.

SPARE to spare de sobra, restante *[His] ... life had interest and turbulence to spare.* -T/92. ♦ *... the plane landed with just three minutes of fuel to spare.* -T/71.

SPARK spark plug 1. vela de ignição *[The function of spark plugs] ... is to ignite the fuel mixture by introducing a spark into the engine.* -FI,241. 2. [col] pessoa ou coisa que inspira, estimula, anima, impulsiona etc. *Lucy is the spark plug of the team.* ♦ *Ralph Nader's [book]* Unsafe at Any Speed *was the spark plug that started major safety reforms in the automobile industry.* -T/66.

SPEAK not to speak of sem falar de, sem precisar mencionar; afora, além de *Hollister was president of his class at the university, not to speak of his being the best football player and the fastest man on the track team.*

roughly speaking grosso modo, mais ou menos, falando de maneira geral *Roughly speaking, I'd say that your assessment of the situation is correct.*

so to speak por assim dizer *I could only know much later that his world died with him, so to speak* ... -SWLM,18.

speak for falar por, falar em nome de ou em defesa de *She spoke for all of us.*

speak for itself ser evidente, não necessitar de explicações ... *the facts speak for themselves.* -T/64.

speak for oneself falar por si, externar sua opinião *[They] ... are unable to speak for themselves.* -HMTO,13. ♦ *I'm only speaking for myself, of course. I don't know how the other members of the committee feel about this.*

speak for yourself você não fala por todos (o que você acabou de dizer é a sua opinião, não é a opinião geral) *Speak for yourself, Mickey. I don't consider myself an alcoholic.*

speak highly/well of falar muito bem de, ter em alto conceito *People who have worked with Mr. Stanley speak highly of him.*

speak out/up 1. falar em voz alta *Speak up. I can't hear you well.* 2. dizer o que pensa, manifestar-se com franqueza *[Margaret Mead] ... spoke out frequently on social and political problems that many of her colleagues preferred to avoid.* -T/78. ♦ *He [Albert Einstein] spoke out courageously against social injustice.* -T/79. ♦ *The real heroes are people who speak up to their President, make their views known* ... -T/87.

speak to falar com, conversar com, dirigir a palavra a *Have you spoken to Miss Winters yet?* ♦ *... today, defying everything our industrial society lives by, ... [Henry David Thoreau's book* Walden*] speaks to us more urgently than ever.* -FCT,157.

speak up for defender, apoiar, recomendar, falar a favor de *Len had no one to* *speak up for him and he felt alone and sad.*

speak well for mostrar o valor ou a capacidade de, recomendar, ser favorável a *The speed with which the city was cleaned up after the storm speaks well for the organization of the public services.*

speak well of → **SPEAK highly of**

to speak of digno de menção, relevante, significativo, importante *There had now been no rain to speak of for almost two months ...* -UJ,230. ♦ *He had no screen career to speak of ...* -T/63.

SPEED put on speed aumentar a velocidade, acelerar *The train seemed to put on speed the last few miles of the journey.*

speed up acelerar(-se) *The warm temperatures of the tropics speed up the processes of reproduction and growth ...* -CR,23. ⇒ **speedup; speed-up** aceleração, apressamento *... a speed-up of the pace of individual life ...* -TA,47. ♦ *[He] ... promised a rapid speedup of U.S. arms deliveries to Thailand.* -T/80.

SPEEDING speeding ticket multa por excesso de velocidade *The sophisticated way to beat speeding tickets is to use a miniaturized radar-emission detector.* -T/77.

SPELL cast a spell encantar, fascinar, maravilhar *... you'd think Mr. Gratton had cast a spell over you.* -TRW,33. ♦ *... Hollywood casts a spell on U.S. moviegoers.* -T/84.

spell out 1. soletrar, escrever por extenso, sem abreviaturas *The written word spells out in sequence what is quick and implicit in the spoken word.* -MMU,82. 2. explicar detalhada e cuidadosamente, deixar bem claro *... he has begun to spell out his own plans for diplomacy and defense ...* -T/88.

under a/someone's spell enfeitiçado, encantado, fascinado, maravilhado *Even Frank Sinatra fell under the spell of Tom Jobim's music and recorded many of his songs.*

SPENDING spending money → **POCKET money**

SPICK-AND-SPAN em boa ordem e imaculadamente limpo *Mother's kitchen was always kept spick-and-span.*

SPIN go for a spin [col] dar uma volta (de automóvel) *How would you like to go for a spin in my new car?*

spin out prolongar, aumentar, esticar (a extensão ou a duração de história, caso etc.) *[Writer James Agee] ... went on spinning out great ideas for the future ...* -T/84. ♦ *[He] ... spun out his story with a dazzling display of charm, ...* -T/87.

SPIN-OFF 1. produto derivado, derivação, desdobramento, coisa oriunda de outra, filhote, subproduto *... technological spin-offs from space [research] like ... miniature computers.* -T/72. 2. série de televisão calcada em personagens e situações de produção ou filme anterior *ABC [TV network] has annnounced plans to introduce a spin-off of* Dynasty *[a TV soap opera] next fall ...* -T/85.

SPIRIT get into the spirit of things/the thing deixar-se levar pela mesma disposição de espírito, animação, atitude etc. das pessoas presentes ou do evento de que se participa *As Christmas draws near, we all get into the spirit of things.*

in good/great/high//low/poor spirits alegre, animado, feliz, eufórico//triste, deprimido *Though she showed remarkably good spirits, she once lost her temper ...* -T/73. ♦ *Marie was in high spirits when she learned that she had won the lottery.* ⇒ **high-spirited** animado, alegre, jovial, entusiasmado *[They] ... celebrate Independence Day in typically high-spirited style ...* -T/84.

kindred spirit pessoa cujos gostos, crenças, atitudes, sentimentos etc. têm grande afinidade com os nossos, alma gêmea *To tell you the truth, I still miss the conversation of such kindred spirits as yourself ...* -SWJ,61.

spirit away/off/out levar secretamente para algum lugar, fazer desaparecer, raptar *A group of grave robbers ... had spirited away the coffin containing the body of Marshal Philippe Pétain ...* -T/73. *[He] ... spirited himself off into the woods ...* -KM,8. ♦ *They spirited out some 4,000 items [from the company's files], photocopied them, returned the originals.* -T/66.

that's the spirit é assim que se fala, é assim que se faz *"That's the spirit, Henry", he told the boy approvingly.* -CEP,186.

SPIT spit and image; spitting image [col] retrato escarrado, semelhança perfeita *Jeremy is the spitting image of his father.*

spit it out [col] desembuche, diga logo *Say all you want to say. Spit it out!*

spit out emitir, proferir, dizer com veemência, com raiva etc. *Sally's mother spat out angry words at me.*

SPITE in spite of apesar de, a despeito de *In spite of our differences, we're still good friends.*

SPLASH make a splash [col] causar sensação, chamar atenção *When he first came into political prominence he made quite a splash.*

SPLIT split up 1. separar, separar em partes, dividir, rachar *Let's split up the money.* 2. separar-se, dividir-se, divorciar-se *The Glenn Miller orchestra split up after the bandleader's plane disappeared during the war.* ♦ *In 1945 his parents split up ...* -T/78. ⇒ **split-up** separação, rompimento, divisão *There has been a split-up in the partnership.*

SPOIL be spoiling for [col] estar ansioso por, estar doido por, estar querendo muito *Hardee was always spoiling for a fight.* -FS,11.

SPONGE sponge on/off [col] viver à custa de *Garfield went from relative to relative and managed to live by sponging on their good nature.* ♦ *He's always sponging off his uncle.*

throw in the sponge/towel [col] reconhecer a derrota, dar-se por vencido, desistir da luta, esforço etc. *Frank always throws in the sponge and leaves the game if he is not the star.* ♦ *McGee was taking such a beating that his manager threw in the towel and the referee stopped the fight.*

SPOON be born with a silver spoon in one's mouth nascer em berço de ouro, nascer muito rico *Hagen was born with a silver spoon in his mouth and never did an honest day's work in his life.*

SPOT hit the high spots [col] cobrir os tópicos principais; discutir, mencionar, ver os pontos, partes ou lugares mais importantes *... the summary [of each chapter in the book] ... obviously cannot cover everything that is in the chapter, but it does hit the high spots.* -MC,xi.

hit the spot [col] agradar, satisfazer plenamente *That meal really hit the spot.*

hot spot [gir] 1. área de tensão, zona perigosa *... hot spots like the Middle East.* -T/92. 2. boate, clube noturno *Frank visited some of the hot spots when he was in Paris.*

in a (bad/tight/tough) spot [gir] em apuros, em dificuldade, em posição perigosa *He'll be in a tight spot if he doesn't get some money quick.* ♦ *They found themselves in a tough spot.*

on the spot 1. no mesmo instante, no ato, na hora, imediatamente *The chief engineer was fired on the spot.* -T/81. 2. no local em questão *If you call us when your car is not working well, we can be on the spot in thirty minutes.* 3. [gir] em situação difícil, embaraçosa ou perigosa *You'll be on the spot if you do that.*

soft spot 1. sensibilidade, ternura, afeição, fraqueza sentimental *Carlos has a soft spot for every stray cat.* 2. ponto vulnerável, calcanhar-de-aquiles *... a political leader who had no soft spot ...* -T/81.

spot check controle, fiscalização ou verificação realizada por amostragem; conferência aleatória ... *making a spot check one recent night, private guards at a Memphis nightclub found 32 patrons carrying guns.* -T/81. ⇒ **spot-check** verificar ou controlar por amostragem, fazer verificação aleatória em ... *he felt that the present system of spot-checking was all that was feasible, or necessary.* -T/79.

SPOTLIGHT the spotlight notoriedade pública, plena atenção da mídia, posição de proeminência ... *the two leaders reveled in the spotlight* ... -T/85. ♦ *[She] ... found living in the spotlight uncomfortable.* -T/78. ⇒ **spotlight** salientar, pôr em foco, atrair a atenção para ... *the losses have spotlighted serious declines in the party's popularity.* -T/87.

SPREAD spread oneself thin [col] tentar fazer muitas coisas ao mesmo tempo *[She] ... was spreading herself thin and she knew it.* -T/87.

SPRING no spring chicken [gir] (pessoa) que já não é jovem *Eloise ... you are no spring chicken ...* -FJH,45.

spring fever sensação de indolência, languidez, preguiça etc. atribuída ao início da primavera *The first warm days of May bring spring fever and make it hard to concentrate on your work.*

spring something on revelar ou mostrar subitamente (algo), causar surpresa a *He may spring any surprise on us any time.* ♦ *[He] ... sprang another surprise ...* -T/81.

spring up surgir, brotar, crescer etc. rapidamente *The first concentration camps [in Nazi Germany] sprang up like mushrooms during Hitler's first year of power.* -SWLR,374. ♦ *A wind sprang up from the sea that afternoon.*

SPRUCE spruce up 1. arranjar, pôr em ordem, dar boa aparência a *Offices are being spruced up with fresh paint.* -T/87. 2. vestir-se com apuro, enfeitar-se, embonecar-se *We had to get all spruced up to go to church on Sundays.*

SPUR on the spur of the moment sob o arroubo do momento, impulsivamente, sem refletir *On the spur of the moment Charlie made a promise that would be hard to keep.*

win one's spurs consagrar-se, fazer sua reputação, distinguir-se, ganhar fama, tornar-se perito em sua atividade *He will never win his spurs in the scientific community, which stands aghast at his unscientific methodology.* -T/66.

SQUARE back to square one de volta ao ponto inicial, ao ponto de partida (de uma tarefa, de um empreendimento etc.) sem ter feito nenhum avanço *The detective realized that he had been following a false clue and was back to square one.*

on the square [col] honesto, justo, sincero; honestamente, sinceramente, com justiça *He's so completely on the square that he would arrest his own mother for parking overtime in front of a church.* ♦ *Sam has always treated me on the square.*

square away 1. [col] aprestar, aprontar, pôr em ordem, preparar com prontidão ... *an assortment of advisers seemed unable to square away the final details [of the anti-inflation program].* -T/78. 2. = **SQUARE off** *When he hears a bell, he squares away and thinks he is in the ring again.*

square off colocar-se em posição de ataque ou defesa, levantar os punhos (no boxe); preparar-se para lutar *[Both men] ... squared off for a direct and bruising battle.* -T/66. ♦ *... when the U.S. and the Soviet Union were squared off against each other.* -T/92.

square oneself [col] desculpar-se, retratar-se, pedir perdão, conciliar-se *He's angry with me and I don't know how I can square myself with him.*

square up pagar, liquidar, acertar (conta) *I have to square up my outstanding debts before I can think of traveling to Europe.*

SQUEEZE put the squeeze on [gir] exercer pressão sobre, pressionar fortemente a fim de praticar extorsão, obter alguma coisa, resultado, vantagem etc., forçar a agir de determinada maneira, pôr contra a parede *They put the squeeze on all the merchants on Market Street.*

squeeze in/into introduzir, inserir, encaixar; forçar para dentro, enfiar à força; entrar à força *... she made the same sort of trip to Japan and managed to squeeze in a side visit to the Olympics.* -T/72. ♦ *Despite a tight schedule, Janet managed to squeeze in time to pay a visit to her sister.* ♦ *The four girls squeezed into the back seat of John's car.* ♦ *Marvin squeezed in before anyone was able to stop him.*

squeeze off disparar (arma de fogo), desfechar (tiro) *Squeezing off a quick shot as he hurried down the trail ...* -SF,35. ♦ *... the intruder squeezed off five shots with a handgun ...* -T/80.

squeeze out forçar para fora, fazer sair, extrair à força *... the new policy might enable biotechnology companies to take control of the livestock industry, squeezing out small-time breeders ...* -T/87.

SQUIRREL **squirrel away** esconder, guardar, amontoar, acumular (para uso futuro) *... the organization has squirreled away an estimated $400 million in bank accounts in Liechtenstein, Switzerland and Cyprus.* -T/91.

STAB **make/take a stab at** fazer uma tentativa para, com o objetivo de *[He] ... had made several stabs at starting a career ...* -T/86.

stab in the back [col] ato traiçoeiro, deslealdade, perfídia *It was a stab in the back when his so-called friends refused to support him in his bid for election.* v. **stab in the BACK**

STABLE **lock the stable door after the horse is stolen** pôr trancas à porta depois de roubado *"Why lock the stable door after the horse is stolen?", the bank manager said to the police who placed a guard around the bank.*

STACK **blow one's stack** → **blow one's TOP**

stacked against contrário a, adverso a, antagônico a *The odds were stacked against him and he knew it.*

stacked in favor favorável a *The income tax laws are stacked in favor of the rich.*

stack up [col] 1. comparar-se a, contrastar com *How do American women stack up against the women of Brazil?* 2. resultar, surdir, mostrar-se *... I waited for everything to stack up right.* -CJC,138. ♦ *If everything stacks up right our plan will be successful.*

STAG **go stag** [col] ir a festa, baile etc. sem companhia feminina *So many men went stag to the dance that men outnumbered girls by fifteen to one.*

stag party/dinner etc. festa, jantar etc. só para homens *It was a stag party for the husband to-be.*

STAGE **at this stage of the game** a esta altura do campeonato, a esta altura dos acontecimentos, neste momento *At this stage of the game it would be unwise to reject their offer.*

set the stage preparar o cenário, o terreno, lançar os alicerces, tornar possível *This preliminary study ... will set the stage for further researches ...* -EA,18. ♦ *[He] ... set the stage for the power struggle now under way.* -T/77.

stage fright nervosismo de ator ou orador diante da platéia *When Claire found herself in front of the large audience she was taken with stage fright and couldn't say a word.*

stage whisper aparte, cochicho audível (em peça teatral) *He was famous for his clever stage whispers.*

STAGESTRUCK; STAGE-STRUCK apaixonado pela arte dramática, desejoso de tornar-se ator *My parents were hopelessly stagestruck ...* -RLI,7.

STAKE **at stake** em jogo, em risco, em perigo *... our vital interests and national security are at stake ...* -T/81.

have a stake in ter um interesse, parte, participação em *Gilmore has a stake in that company.*
pull up stakes [col] mudar-se, partir ... *pulling up stakes in Boston, where he had lived all his life, and moving up to a tobacco farm ...* -SM,4.
stake out 1. demarcar, marcar com estacas; delimitar, delinear ... *staking out the territory.* -T/66. ♦ *Half of the urban area of Los Angeles is staked out by street gangs.* -T/84. 2. [col] vigiar continuamente, manter sob vigilância (criminoso, suspeito, lugar etc.), campanar *A team of journalists staked out a man's home to discover who was spending the night there.* -T/87. ⇒ **stakeout** vigilância contínua (de um criminoso, suspeito, lugar etc.), campana ... *taxis make excellent camouflage for stakeouts and street patrol ...* -T/75.
stake someone on/to [col] dar dinheiro ou recursos a, prover alguém do necessário (principalmente dinheiro), pagar, ajudar, oferecer, presentear, brindar *"Hey, Mister, could you stake a fellow American on a meal?" [Fred C.Dobbs addressing a man in a white suit in* The Treasure of the Sierra Madre.*]* ♦ *[His] ... gold medal in Montreal started him off as a full-blown celebrity and staked him to a professional career of main events only.* -T/84.
STAMP stamp out 1. apagar (fogo, cigarro etc.) com pisadas *Stamp out the fire.* 2. suprimir, eliminar, debelar *[The big company] ... has ruthlessly stamped out smaller competitors ...* -T/72. 3. moldar, modelar, dar forma a, estampar *One of the most brilliant soldiers of all time, MacArthur stamped out his character and achievement on a full half-century of history.* -T/64.
STAND make a stand opor resistência, fazer frente, resistir *The British troops tried to make a stand at Dunkirk but it was impossible to hold off the enemy.*
one-night stand 1. apresentação única de um grupo, espetáculo, ator, orquestra etc. em determinada cidade (freqüentemente como parte de uma turnê) *Harry James's orchestra played one-night stands all over the country before he became famous.* 2. [col] relacionamento sexual por uma noite apenas *[She] ... has done a one-night stand with Wagner in a London Hotel ...* -T/78.
stand behind apoiar ... *both conservatives and liberals in the party are ready to stand behind the President.* -T/73.
stand by 1. permanecer leal a, dar apoio a, ajudar, defender ... *if he couldn't stand by his friends in a crisis he didn't deserve to have any friends.* -JJF,230. ⇒ **standby** pessoa ou coisa na qual se pode confiar, que é sempre eficiente etc., especialmente em uma emergência; escolha favorita *Peanut butter is a standby in American homes for the children of the family.* ♦ *A country band is playing old standbys ...* -T/78. 2. cumprir (promessa etc.), respeitar, acatar, confirmar, sustentar, manter, ater-se a *He stands by his story.* 3. aguardar, ficar à espera, ficar em alerta, estar presente, a postos, estar preparado *Stand by for instructions.* ⇒ **standby** pronto para usar em uma emergência, necessidade etc. *The hospital clinic has a standby oxygen tank.* ⇒ **on standby** de prontidão *[The police department] ... did not have enough officers on standby for riot duty as needed ...* -T/92. 4. assistir sem participar, sem interferir, ser mero espectador *We buried Scott in a deep grave. All of us stood by silent while Hester read from her small Bible.* -SHE,47.
stand fast/firm manter-se firme, inabalável, não ceder, não recuar, não mudar de opinião ... *those who [in the future] ... live here in this land ... can forever be thankful to the ones that stood fast then and would not abandon the country.* -GJH,1.
stand for 1. simbolizar, significar, representar *The initials YMCA stand for Young Men's Christian Association.* 2. ser a fa-

vor de, apoiar, defender *Freud stood for a philosophy of life that is based on science rather than on metaphysics or religion.* -HC,20. 3. [col] [geralmente neg] aceitar, tolerar *I won't stand for such nonsense.* ♦ *The teacher refused to stand for the discourtesies in her class.*
stand good ser válido, estar em vigor *My offer still stands good.*
stand high ocupar lugar importante, ter influência, ser bem-visto *[He] ... stands high on the national board of governors of the [organized crime] Syndicate.* -TB,11.
stand in for substituir, fazer as vezes de *... he hired his attorney to stand in for him.* -T/92. ⇒ **stand-in** 1. *doublé*, pessoa que assume o lugar de ator/atriz enquanto se preparam as câmeras e se acendem as luzes para uma cena *The stand-in should not be confused with a double, a stuntman who replaces the star in scenes that require a dangerous activity.* -SS,400. 2. substituto *The last female state Governor was Lurleen Wallace in Alabama, a stand-in for her husband George, forbidden by the state constitution to succeed himself.* -T/72.
stand in (well) with [col] manter boas relações com, estar nas boas graças de *It is good to stand in well with the boss.*
stand (someone/something) tolerar, suportar, agüentar, resistir, sofrer, permitir *I can't stand that woman.* ♦ *How can you stand such nonsense?* ♦ *I can't stand the damp cold weather anymore.*
stand off 1. manter a distância, afastar, repelir *You think you can ... stand us off.* -BAS,53. ⇒ **standoff** empate, entrave, batalha indecisa, neutralização, impasse *... the continuing diplomatic standoff between France and Iran.* -T/87. ♦ *... a military standoff ...* -T/66. 2. manter-se a distância, retrair-se *... enemies, who chanced upon one another suddenly in the darkness and then uneasily stood off, watching each other.* -TW,3. ⇒ **standoff-**

ish retraído, reservado, arredio, frio *Luke appears standoffish but he's really only shy.* 3. fazer esperar, livrar-se (de alguém) com evasivas, esquivar-se a *He's always trying to stand off his many creditors.*
stand out 1. sobressair, ser visível, ser facilmente notado *The stars stood out quite clearly in the moonless night.* 2. ser proeminente, notável, distinguir-se *In spite of everything, the Kinsey Report still stands out as a major contribution to the study of human sexual behavior.* ⇒ **standout** [col] pessoa ou coisa admirável, excepcional, notável, de marcada superioridade *[In* The Caine Mutiny, *Humphrey] Bogart is a standout as Captain Queeg, the skipper of the* Caine. -SSH,146. 3. **stand out against** não ceder, resistir, ser inflexível *The Romans stood out against the onslaught of barbarian tribes for many years.*
stand pat não ceder, resistir, não mudar de opinião, atitude, decisão *I'm going to stand pat and not change my mind in this discussion.*
stand still imobilizar-se, parar, deter-se, não se mexer *In* The Day the Earth Stood Still, *Klaatu, the visitor from outer space, neutralizes the electricity all over the world for thirty minutes, and brings human technology to a standstill.* ⇒ **standstill** parada, cessação, imobilização *... all building activity gradually came to a standstill.* -WJ,379.
stand tall sentir-se altivo e seguro para enfrentar qualquer situação *He stood tall in defense of his protégée.*
stand to estar sujeito a (ganhar ou perder) *No doubt ... [he] and his family stand to gain from his adventure.* -T/88. ♦ *[He] ... stands to share in the profits, which could be large ...* -T/87.
stand up 1. ficar em pé, levantar-se *He finished his whiskey and stood up.* -BF,33. ⇒ **stand-up** a. tomado em pé (lanche, refeição) *a stand-up lunch* b. que exige

que se fique em pé, em que não existem assentos *a stand-up bar* c. que atua sozinho (geralmente em pé) no palco ou defronte de uma câmera de TV *[Bob Hope and Phyllis Diller] ... a pair of fine stand-up comedians ...* -T/66. d. realizado no palco ou diante de uma câmera de TV *... he was starting in stand-up comedy 31 years ago.* -T/91. 2. ser convincente, válido, consistente, coerente ... *a legitimate charge based on evidence that will stand up in court.* -T/92. 3. durar, resistir, agüentar ... *I met many men who had stood up marvelously against exceedingly tough blows and who had survived honorably.* -HE,17. 4. [gir] não comparecer a um encontro marcado, deixar na mão, dar o bolo *He needs a woman and the only one he ever loved stood him up at the church ...* -FJH,44.
stand up and be counted dizer claramente o que pensa, assumir posição clara e firme, ainda que perigosa ou que contrarie interesses *It was time ... for men of honor to stand up and be counted.* -MG,396.
stand up for apoiar, defender ... *we must stand up for what is right.* -T/85.
stand up for oneself não se deixar intimidar, proteger-se, defender-se *If you don't stand up for yourself, no one else will.*
stand up to enfrentar corajosamente; resistir a, permanecer em boas condições *I can stand up to you any time.* -LB,10. ♦ *Good leather will stand up to all kinds of wear and weather.*
take a stand tomar uma decisão, assumir uma posição definida, declarar-se a favor ou contra ... *the Administration's fervent public efforts to take a strong stand against terrorism ...* -T/86.
take the stand sentar-se no banco das testemunhas para depor ... *he took the stand in his own defense ...* -T/66. ♦ *[He] ... took the witness stand before the House Un-American Activities Committee and made a series of accusations ...* -T/61.
STANDARD double standard norma, padrão, critério social etc. que admite maior liberdade e maiores direitos a um grupo do que a outro(s), especialmente o código de comportamento sexual aplicado com maior rigor às mulheres do que aos homens; dois pesos e duas medidas ... *our double standard of morality allows much greater sex freedom to males than to females.* -EA,251. ♦ *... a shocking double standard in pay scales and promotion opportunities [for men and women] ...* -T/72.
standard of living; living standard padrão de vida *The one thing above all others that America prides itself upon is the high standard of living of its people.* -KRI,565. ♦ *... men engaged in seeking a high living standard ...* -WPT,64.
up to standard de acordo com o padrão, critério, qualidade etc. exigido *Your work, I'm sorry to say, hasn't been up to standard, Mr. Fox.*
STAND-IN → **STAND in**
STANDING (good/high) standing reputação, distinção, respeito, posição de prestígio, de relevo *Mr. Wilkins was a man of standing in our community.* ♦ *These are all men of high standing.* ♦ *[He] ... remained in good standing in official circles.* -T/69.
of long standing de longa data, de há muito *William, Ayrton, Milton, John and Lou are friends of long standing.* ⇒ **longstanding** de longa duração, antigo, que existe há muito tempo ... *many Americans have been laid off from long-standing jobs ...* -T/92.
standing room espaço para pessoas permanecerem em pé (quando não há mais assentos disponíveis em teatro, estádio, trem etc.) *Even before they leave the first station, trains often have standing room only.* -T/79.
STAR see stars [col] ver estrelas, sentir atordoamento em consequência de pancada na cabeça *I saw stars when my sister hit me on the head with her unbreakable doll.* ♦

stars in one's eyes sentimento de euforia, júbilo, felicidade, otimismo *There were stars in his eyes when he talked about his new girlfriend.* → **starry-eyed** excessivamente romântico, idealista, visionário, fantasioso *... a statesman must never be viewed as starry-eyed.* -T/81.
thank one's (lucky) stars agradecer a sua boa estrela *You can thank your lucky stars that you were not killed in that accident.*
STARCH take the starch out of [col] tirar a vitalidade, a energia, a determinação, a coragem de, deixar cansado, debilitado, enfraquecido *... the sight of him took the starch out of Judy's knees.* -CJC,93.
STAR-CROSSED infeliz, malfadado, infausto *Our lives are star-crossed and filled with all kinds of surprises ...* -SF,17. ♦ *Abelard and Heloise were star-crossed lovers.*
STARRY-EYED → **STARS in one's eyes**
START false start tentativa malograda, início infrutífero *After 14 months of frustration and false starts, the U. S. and Iran reach a breakthrough on general terms for freeing the 52 American hostages ...* -T/81.
fresh start novo começo, nova oportunidade, vida nova *America, the land of fresh starts and clean slates ...* -T/91.
from the start desde o início, desde o começo *From the start he had trouble dealing with abstract questions.* -T/79.
get/be off to a flying/good/fast etc.// bad/slow etc. start começar bem//mal *They settled all the details and the plan was off to a good start.* ♦ *The current round of talks got off to an encouraging start last month.* -T/87. ♦ *The meeting got off to a bad start and at the end nothing had been resolved.*
start back começar a voltar *As he started back for the house a big dog came around from the rear and stood near the door.* -BT,50.
start for ir para *Suddenly Ernie got up and started for the door.* ♦ *They started for home early in the morning.*

start off sair, partir, pôr-se em marcha, começar, dar início a *A large expedition starts off, laden with supplies.* -GH,64. ♦ *They started off in the big truck.*
start out começar, empreender (viagem, tarefa, relacionamento etc.), dar os primeiros passos *After starting out as an actor, he founded the Group Theater ...* -T/80. ♦ *We started out at dawn on October 30th.* -RQ,100.
start over recomeçar *... at the age of thirty-four, ... as an ex-inmate of a mental institution, I was released to start my life over again.* -RLI,7. ♦ *Nothing stops the real criminals from starting over.* -T/87.
start up 1. dar início a, começar, principiar *... he was able to work part time in a grocery store and start up a social life.* -T/92. ♦ *... huge outlays [are] necessary for starting up or expanding production of buses, subway cars and trolleys.* -T/79. ⇒ **start-up** a. ato de dar início, de pôr em funcionamento, em movimento *... demonstrators gathered ... to protest the scheduled start-up [of a new French nuclear-power plant] this fall.* -T/86. b. inicial *Start-up expenses are high ...* -T/92. 2. fazer funcionar, dar partida a (motor, máquina) *Ron started up the car and drove away.* 3. funcionar, pegar (motor, máquina, carro) *The motor started up.* 4. levantar-se subitamente *Bobby started up from his seat when the teacher called his name.*
start with para começar, em primeiro lugar, inicialmente *... the futility of addressing audiences that were, to start with, in thorough agreement with all that I might say.* -KRI,571.
STARTER for starters [col] em primeiro lugar, para início de conversa *For starters, both his leadership skills and his character have been questioned.* -T/87.
STASH stash away [col] guardar, esconder, economizar *Rawlings stashed away millions of dollars in Swiss banks.* ♦ *... he*

had $327 million ... stashed away for a rainy day ... -T/60. ♦ [She] ... still has [her husband's] 248 letters to her numbered and stashed away in her house ... -T/73.
STATE in/into a state [col] emocionalmente agitado, nervoso ... every time ... [she] appears in a state her husband's popularity rises ... -T/92.
in state com grande pompa, fausto, magnificência [The] ... Emir of Zaragoza sat in state on a throne of blue marble in the cool garden of his palace. -PM,13.
lie in state estar exposto (corpo) em câmara ardente [He] ... lay in state in Washington's National Cathedral ... -T/65.
state of the art estágio de desenvolvimento, grau de evolução ou progresso que uma ciência, uma técnica, uma atividade etc. apresenta em um determinado momento The state of the art [in high-tech copiers] is the laser printer, which mimics handwriting. -T/86. ⇒ **state-of-the-art** atualíssimo, avançadíssimo, de última geração, de ponta ... the android called the T-1000 ... is a state-of-the-art killing machine sent from the future to do battle with Arnold Schwarzenegger. -T/91. ♦ ... a state-of-the-art computer system. -T/92.
the States [col] os EUA Don went back to the States in 1975.
STATESIDE stateside; Stateside [col] 1. dos EUA, vindo dos EUA, feito ou ocorrido nos EUA ... stateside magazines ... -FH,8. 2. nos EUA, para os EUA I'll come back over now and then. I'm not going Stateside. -JJF,17. ♦ ... he was a military expert, having served Stateside in the Marines during World War I. -T/78.
STATION filling station → **GAS station** **station house** posto policial, delegacia de polícia We got out of the car in front of the station house. -CJC,130.
station wagon perua, caminhonete [He] ... drives a worn 1969 red Ford station wagon ... -T/80.

STATUS status seeker pessoa que busca prestígio, posição social elevada, importância, eminência etc. Status seekers are careful to wear the correct clothes, be seen in the right places with the right people. -KS,60.
STAVE stave off evitar, afastar, impedir, protelar, manter a distância The dam has staved off droughts in agricultural areas. ♦ ... stave off a future energy crisis ... -T/87.
STAY stay clear of → **KEEP clear of**
stay in//out permanecer em casa, não sair//ficar fora de casa, não voltar para casa The elderly stay in a lot, and when they do go out they tend to be in group situations ... -T/81. ♦ "Now, don't stay out too late, dear", Nan's mother said as her daughter left for the party.
stay put [col] permanecer no mesmo local ou na mesma posição We Americans, it is said, like to stay put, especially if we are comfortably off. -SWLM,vii. ♦ I told him to stay put but he kept on walking.
stay up permanecer acordado, não se deitar, não ir para a cama We all stayed up until after midnight.
STAYING staying power vigor constitucional, capacidade de resistência He was riding a horse of fine staying power. ♦ ... an army that has repeatedly shown staying power ... -T/86.
STEAD stand in good stead ser de grande auxílio, ser vantajoso, ser útil (principalmente em uma necessidade) ... his leadership qualities will stand all Americans in good stead ... -T/69.
STEAL steal away/in/out/past/through etc. mover-se furtivamente, às escondidas, esgueirar-se, entrar ou sair sorrateiramente The two suspects stole away in the night. ♦ They stole forward in the shadow of the trees. -SLT,96. ♦ [Enemy soldiers] ... had stolen into their midst under cover of darkness ... -T/80.
steal up on aproximar-se sorrateiramente

de *We tried to steal up on the lone Indian who was guarding the captives.*

STEAM blow/let off steam [col] desabafar-se, exprimir a raiva, descarregar sentimentos reprimidos *Though both men were armed, ... they were only letting off steam ...* -LB,10. ♦ *He played tennis after he finished working to let off steam.*

(all) steamed up [col] zangado, irado, agitado, nervoso *Be careful not to get him all steamed up.*

on/under one's own steam [col] pelos próprios esforços, por sua própria opção, voluntariamente, sozinho, sem ajuda *It was a long and difficult journey, but she managed to get there under her own steam.*

STEEL-TRAP penetrante, agudo, rápido, vivo, esperto, sagaz ... *Perry Mason, whose steel-trap mind is always ahead of everybody else's ...* -T/73.

STEEPED steeped in imerso em, saturado de, impregnado de, cheio de *[Mark Twain] ... was steeped in the life and traditions of the [Mississippi] river, and as a young man worked for some years as a steamboat pilot.* -RR,611. ♦ *Some of the movies she made in the early fifties are steeped in nostalgia.*

STEER steer clear of → **KEEP clear of**

STEM stem from originar-se de, provir de, resultar de *Nick's troubles stemmed from his early poverty.*

STEP dog someone's steps/heels seguir os passos de, perseguir ... *to say that the family was poor would be an understatement. Poverty dogged our every step.* -MAT,8.

fall into step with 1. acompanhar o passo de, seguir ao lado de *[He] ... fell into step beside her and took her suitcase from her hand.* -SJST,26. 2. agir da mesma forma que, fazer o mesmo que, seguir o exemplo de *Smith started out to be honest and independent but soon fell into step with the rest of his political colleagues.*

in step//out of step 1. com o passo certo, em cadência//com o passo errado, fora de cadência *Jim marched in step with the other soldiers.* ♦ *He was out of step with all the other soldiers in the parade.* 2. em harmonia, ajustado, em sintonia//em desarmonia, em desacordo ... *the South of the future should be better prepared for a role of leadership ... more in step with the rest of the country.* -T/76. ♦ *Lilian Smith's [novel] Strange Fruit was unfashionably out of step with its time and place.* -T/66. ♦ *[He] ... is out of step with the times.* -T/72.

keep step acompanhar o passo, o ritmo, o andamento *The large nations all try to keep step with each other in the production of commercial goods and armaments.*

one step ahead of → **one JUMP ahead of**

step aside sair do caminho, afastar-se, demitir-se, renunciar *He told the big man to step aside and let him pass.* ♦ *... the Shah's only hope of calming the unrest [of the Iranian people] is to step aside in favor of his son.* -T/78.

step by step passo a passo, gradualmente, lentamente *Step by step the Redstone [rocket] had been readied for launch.* -T/61. ⇒ **step-by-step** gradual, progressivo, realizado por etapas *He wants a step-by-step setup of negotiations between the two countries.*

step down demitir-se, renunciar (cargo, posição etc.) *Six weeks ago he stepped down as PTL president ...* -T/87.

step forward 1. passo à frente, progresso, melhoria *This is a great step forward. You can be proud of it.* 2. apresentar-se para prestar auxílio, informação, ser útil etc. *[They] ... should now step forward and tell us the whole truth.* -T/86.

step in intervir *As tension mounted, the Federal Government mercifully stepped in.* -T/66.

step in the right direction medida acertada na consecução de um objetivo *The creation of many new primary schools is a*

step in the right direction toward general education in the country.
step into 1. entrar em *She stepped into the living room.* ♦ *It was Heraclitus who said: "You cannot step twice into the same river".* 2. chegar, entrar (em uma situação, condição etc.), assumir ou empreender de repente ... *stepping into a job that requires him to pay the bills himself.* -T/81.
step lively apressar-se, ser rápido, ativo, ligeiro *Step lively! We have to finish this before five o'clock.*
step on it [col] dirigir mais depressa, acelerar; apressar-se *You'll have to step on it if you want to get there before the show starts.*
step out 1. sair; sair por um momento *[He] ... opened the door. I stepped out into the sunshine.* -CG,62. ♦ *... the minute he stepped out on the sidewalk he met the sheriff again ...* -LD,21. 2. sair (para passear, divertir-se, ir a uma festa etc.) *I'm all dressed up to step out and I can't leave because of the rain.*
step out on [col] ser infiel a, trair *I didn't know ... [he] was even married ... Married to a young gal and she steps out on him.* -FJH,35.
step (all) over → **WALK (all) over**
step up 1. aumentar, ampliar, intensificar, acelerar ... *the U.S. began stepping up military aid to the Aquino government in September ...* -T/87. ⇒ **step-up** aumento, acréscimo, avanço, progresso *The step-up of American arms shipments to Jordan [led to severe criticism by the official Soviet news agency] ...* -T/80. 2. aproximar-se, chegar-se *"Step up and sign the petition", the man said.* 3. galgar cargo, posição etc. mais alto, mais importante, receber uma promoção *[He] ... had just stepped up from the chancellorship to the presidency ...* -T/60.
take steps → **take MEASURES**
watch one's step 1. olhar onde pisa, andar com atenção *Watch your step when you go down the stairs.* 2. tomar cuidado, acautelar-se, prestar atenção *[He] ... warned the opposition to watch their step.* -T/87.
STEW in a stew [col] preocupado, agitado, nervoso, ansioso, confuso *[She] ... was in a stew this morning ...* -LMC,9.
STICK more (of something) than you can/could shake a stick at [col] muitos, mais do que se pode contar *There were more people at the Vanderbilts' party than you could shake a stick at.*
not hold a stick to → **not hold a CANDLE to**
stick around [gír] permanecer no local, ficar por perto, esperar, não ir embora *I can't stick around much longer. I've got to go now.*
stick by permanecer leal a, apoiar *If you get in trouble we will stick by you.*
stick (it) out [gír] tolerar, resistir até o fim, agüentar o rojão ... *I stuck with you when things were rough, and again when they were smooth, so I'll stick it out to the bitter end ...* -WL,231.
stick out 1. sobressair, projetar-se *A lot of money was sticking out of his pocket.* 2. ser óbvio, ser aparente ... *you love me. You know you do. It sticks out all over your face ...* -JJ,499. 3. esticar, estender, espichar *When he came into the town with food, hands were stuck out toward him in supplication.* 4. manter-se firme, inabalável, persistente *I stuck out for the price I had asked in cash for my apartment.*
stick to 1. manter-se fiel a, não abandonar *You had better stick to your word.* 2. ater-se a, não divergir, não se desviar de, perseverar, persistir, aferrar-se a, não abrir mão de *He never sticks to the facts when we argue with him.* ♦ *He has always stuck to his principles.*
stick together [col] permanecer unido, não se separar *We're all together and we'll stick together. ... We can't let anything happen to each other.* -HET,37. ♦ *He won the 1954 Nobel Prize for his explanation of*

the chemical forces that make atoms stick together ... -T/60.
stick up 1. sobressair, ressaltar, projetar-se para cima *Bobby's hair has a funny way of sticking up at the back.* 2. [gir] assaltar à mão armada *[She] ... stuck up a Wells Fargo bank in San Francisco ...* -T/63. ⇒ **stick 'em up** mãos ao alto *"Stick 'em up", said the masked rider to the people in the stage coach.* ⇒ **stickup** assalto à mão armada *[He is] ... facing trial for a grocery stickup in Philadelphia ...* -T/64.
stick up for [col] apoiar, defender, tomar o partido de *Stick up for your rights!* ♦ *... a tough boss who will stick up for his department.* -T/80.
stick with [col] 1. permanecer com, não se separar de, apoiar *If you stick with me I won't let you down.* 2. continuar fazendo, não desistir *They have stuck with the original plan.* 3. vender algo inferior, falso etc. a, impingir *The man tried to stick me with a fake Rolex watch.* 4. [geralmente pas] ficar com algo do qual é difícil ou impossível livrar-se, ficar preso a, arcar com um estrepe, um abacaxi *Firms have been stuck with unsold machines ...* -T/87. ♦ *When Jake married Alice he didn't know he was going to be stuck with supporting her parents and two lazy brothers.*
take a stick to surrar, açoitar com vara *I'll take a stick to you if you don't do what you're told.*
STICKING sticking point questão delicada, dificuldade que leva a um impasse *There are many sticking points, but the biggest is European agriculture, which is still heavily subsidized and highly protectionist.* -T/92.
STICK-IN-THE-MUD [col] pessoa de idéias antiquadas, indivíduo retrógrado *After more than 50 years ... I remain an up-to-date, stick-in-the-mud optimist.* -T/87.
STICKLER a stickler for indivíduo extremamente escrupuloso na observação de regras, regulamentos etc., fanático por *A stickler for just the right detail, he [a cartoonist] frequently consults his favorite reference, the Sears, Roebuck catalogue ...* -T/61.
STINK raise a stink [gir] queixar-se com veemência, protestar, ficar furioso *The rest of the staff raised a stink when they discovered that John was the only one who had received a raise.*
STIR cause/make a stir causar agitação, comoção *The murder of Patrice Lumumba in the early 60s made quite a stir in the international political circles.*
stir up incitar, provocar *The Sacco-Vanzetti case stirred up a lot of political and social trouble.*
STITCH in stitches morrendo de rir, rindo incontrolavelmente *[He is] A natural born entertainer ... He keeps us all in stitches.* -BRSR,29. ♦ *Danny Kaye had me in stitches when he played a buffoon who is mistaken for a bureaucrat in* The Inspector General.
not a stitch on sem roupa, despido, nu *... the shy blonde hasn't a stitch on ...* -T/66.
a stitch in time saves nine uma precaução tomada a tempo evita muitos problemas [usa-se também abreviadamente] **a stitch in time** precaução útil, medida cautelosa *The construction of a dam on the Colorado river was a stitch in time against the threat of floods.*
STOCK in stock// out of stock disponível, em estoque, à venda//em falta *The salesclerk told me that the book I'm looking for is currently out of stock.*
put/take stock in [col] dar crédito a, dar importância a, depositar confiança em, fiar-se em *... taking little stock in miracles ...* -LCT,13. ♦ *He felt she didn't take any stock in what he was saying.* -LM,71.
stock in trade recursos, habilidades, qualidades, particularidades, maneira de ser ou de fazer algo que uma pessoa utiliza no desempenho de sua ocupação ou funções *Fred Astaire's dancing ability was*

his stock in trade. ♦ *... sanctimony is often his stock in trade ...* -T/92. ♦ *Beauty, charm and talent were Audrey Hepburn's stock in trade.*
stock up estocar, abastecer-se *Appliance dealers in Atlanta could not meet demand for freezers from consumers wanting to stock up on meat.* -T/73.
take stock 1. fazer balanço, contar o estoque *They took stock of all the goods in the store.* 2. fazer uma avaliação, uma estimativa, examinar cuidadosamente *Willy Loman [the main character in* Death of a Salesman*] experiences a profound sense of failure ... and takes stock of his accomplishments.* -HMJ,243.
take stock in → **put STOCK in**
STOCK-STILL imóvel, estático *The man stopped stock-still for a moment ...* -CJC,36.
STOMACH have no stomach for não ter desejo, disposição ou inclinação para, não tolerar *... the nation has no stomach for real reform ...* -T/87. ♦ *He never had much stomach, or much head, for politics ...* -T/61.
sick to one's stomach desgostoso, enojado, ultrajado *It made me sick to my stomach that she was so used to his mistreatment.* -GJH,86.
stomach [geralmente neg] suportar, tolerar, agüentar *I couldn't stomach his insults and left the meeting.*
turn one's stomach embrulhar o estômago de, causar náusea a *... this kind of business, Major, turns my stomach.* -FH,7.
STONE leave no stone unturned mover céus e terras, envidar todos os esforços *The investigator left no stone unturned until he found out the cause of the plane accident.*
run into a stone wall → **run into a BRICK wall**
stoned [col] 1. embriagado *Boris got stoned on vodka last night.* 2. drogado *... in the old days, it was rare for someone to come to work stoned on drugs ...* -T/86.

a stone's throw curta distância, distância muito pequena *[The school was] ... a stone's throw from the beach.* -FLF,31.
STONE-BROKE → **broke**
STONE-DEAF surdo como uma pedra *The old man is stone-deaf and won't hear us.*
STOP bring to a stop fazer parar, deter, parar *I brought the car to a stop right in front [of the hotel] ...* -SSG,18.
come to a stop deter-se, parar *... the train suddenly slowed down and almost immediately came to a complete stop.* -BE,16.
pull out (all) the stops empregar todos os esforços, recursos etc. (para alcançar um objetivo) *[In Billy Wilder's film* One, Two, Three, James*] Cagney pulled out the stops in a performance whose pace equals his most frenetic work of the thirties.* -BAJ,137.
pull to a stop parar, deter-se *A big truck pulled to a stop fifty yards away from where he stood.*
put a stop to → **put an END to**
stop by fazer breve visita a (quando a caminho de outro destino, lugar etc.), passar por *[She] ... was so concerned about her father that she stopped by his house several times a week ...* -T/77.
stop off fazer breve parada em algum lugar quando a caminho de outro destino *On their way home, the Johnson's stopped off in Geneva and in Paris ...* -T/61.
stop over fazer breve estada em um lugar durante o curso de uma viagem *I did not stop over in London, for I intended to return here after the Continent [of Europe] had been visited.* -SWLM,25. ⇒ **stopover** parada, escala *... all the passengers were told to leave the plane during a Denver [Colorado] stopover.* -T/86.
stop short parar de repente, deter-se bruscamente, estacar *The man came running up the path but stopped short when he saw us.*
stop short of parar a pouca distância de, não chegar a *... she stops short of drawing conclusions of any sort.* -T/74.

stop up obstruir, tapar, entupir *Somebody had deliberately stopped up the toilet.*
STORE in store reservado, destinado, à espera ... *I'm sure that a lot of good things are in store for you.* -OJT,48.
mind the store cuidar dos negócios, estar de serviço, estar encarregado de *Who is going to mind the store now that the boss is dead?*
set/lay/put store by dar importância a, valorizar *[I've] never laid much store by ghosts ...* -SLT,137. ♦ *Farm people set much store by many simple home remedies that have been used for generations.*
store up armazenar, estocar, acumular *If we could store up generated electricity economically, we would have a limitless source of power.*
STORM storm in a teacup → **TEMPEST in a teapot**
take by storm 1. tomar de assalto *The citadel was taken by storm during a dark, foggy night.* 2. conquistar, cativar, impressionar agradavelmente, fazer grande sucesso ... *in 1972, [Marlon] Brando once again took the world by storm with his portrayal of Vito Corleone in the hugely successful* The Godfather ... -BRF,64.
weather the storm vencer a tempestade, sair ileso de uma crise etc., sobreviver a uma dificuldade *Unable to weather the storm following the Watergate affair, Nixon resigned.* ♦ *... they weathered the storm of criticism ...* -GD,163.
STORY as/so the story goes; the story goes segundo dizem, ao que consta, consta que *As the story goes, Zillah Snow, a stunning brunette, came from Hot Springs in the fall of 1953.* ♦ *[Lieutenant Colonel George Armstrong] Custer illegally invaded the [Black] Hills [of South Dakota] in the summer of 1874, the story goes, looking for gold.* -T/66. ♦ *... so the story goes, once started a conference by lighting a stogie and announcing: "This may be a phallus, but, gentlemen,*

let us remember it is also a cigar". -T/66.
shaggy-dog story história longa e inconseqüente com final irrelevante, sem graça, frustrante etc. *... a shaggy-dog story is a tale without any real ending ...* -T/84.
tall story/tale [col] história fantástica, exagerada, difícil de acreditar *In* The Reivers, *William Faulkner ... revels in his role as a teller of tall tales, at which only Mark Twain is his equal.* -T/62. ♦ *He was always singing and telling tall stories.* -SJS,59.
to cut a long story short para encurtar a história, para resumir *To cut a long story short: they met, fell in love and married three months later.*
STRAIGHT straight away/off imediatamente, sem demora, sem hesitação *When Ruth heard that her child had been in an accident, she came straight away.* ♦ *Naomi told Jeff straight off how she felt.*
straight out abertamente, diretamente, sem rebuços *... she'd asked him straight out if they were still sleeping together ...* -EA,23.
STRAIGHT-ARROW → **straight ARROW**
STRAIGHTEN straighten out arrumar, endireitar, acertar, pôr em ordem, corrigir *I think he's going to make a genuine effort to straighten things out.* -GFT,14. ♦ *... he was hired last February to straighten out the campaign organization.* -T/80.
straighten up 1. endireitar-se, ficar ereto *Tom straightened up and apparently said something to her ...* -WSM,287. 2. corrigir-se, emendar-se, regenerar-se *You had better straighten up before it's too late.* 3. = **STRAIGHTEN out** *Be sure to straighten up your room before you leave.*
STRAIGHT-FACED → **straight FACE**
STRAIGHT-SHOOTER → **SHOOT straight**
STRAIT in dire/serious etc. straits em situação difícil, em sérias dificuldades, em grande aperto *[He]... found his brother*

in Connecticut helpless, alone and in dire medical straits. -T/64. ♦ The people are in such desperate straits that they might even support a dictatorship. -T/92.

STRANGLE strangle hold; stranglehold gravata (golpe de luta livre); qualquer força ou ação que restringe ou reprime, domínio total, controle pleno *Less than five months after the worst winter in memory finally relaxed its strangle hold, the eastern two-thirds of the nation was racked by a heat storm ...* -T/77. ♦ *The war will certainly put a stranglehold on the economy.*

STRAPPED strapped for cash/money [col] necessitado de grana, sem dinheiro *... his father knew ... how badly he was strapped for money ...* -BS,38. ♦ *I happen to be strapped for cash at the moment.*

STRAW catch/clutch/grasp at a straw/straws agarrar-se a qualquer coisa (em uma situação de desespero) que ofereça a mínima esperança de tentar salvar-se, provar um argumento etc. *Lem clutched at straws.* -PRT,68. ♦ *You're grasping at straws if you think you can count on his support.*

the last/final straw a gota d'água, o último ato, acontecimento etc. que torna uma situação insustentável *When Fred's wife was brought home drunk at 2 a.m. it was the last straw and he told her so after she had sobered up.*

a straw in the wind rumor ou indicação de que algo vai acontecer *There were straws in the wind concerning a cessation of hostilities.*

straw vote/ballot prévia eleitoral, votação experimental *The straw vote is generally considered a fair indication of the actual election.* ♦ *... to win a straw ballot at the November 7 dinner, just as Jimmy Carter's supporters did twelve years ago.* -T/87.

STREAK a streak of luck maré de sorte *Our team had a streak of good luck even though our players were not too wonderful.*

talk a blue streak [col] falar pelos cotovelos *Around most people I'm silent as a clam, but somehow you seem interested, and I find myself talking a blue streak.* -HJE,105.

a winning//losing streak [col] maré de sorte//azar *Our team has been on a winning streak.*

yellow streak (down one's back) [col] traço de covardia no caráter de uma pessoa *Drake is a good man with a Colt [six-gun] but he's got a yella [sic] streak ...* -SG,26.

STREAM stream of consciousness fluxo de consciência; os processos de pensamento consciente considerados como um fluir incessante e caótico e não como eventos separados *[James] Joyce's brilliant use of stream of consciousness [in his novels* Ulysses *and* Finnegans Wake*] produced a host of imitators ...* -HMJ,1096. ⇒ **stream-of-consciousness** relativo à técnica narrativa que consiste em revelar ao leitor os processos do fluxo de consciência de uma personagem de ficção *[James Joyce's]* Ulysses *had stunned the literary world with its brilliant stream-of-consciousness technique.* -T/66.

swim against the stream → **swim against the CURRENT**

STREET down/up one's street → **down/up one's ALLEY**

on Easy Street/easy street [col] financeiramente independente, rico *If I win the first prize of two hundred thousand dollars I'll be on easy street.*

run the streets vadiar pelas ruas *Many poor children who run the streets finally turn to a life of crime.*

street smarts [col] habilidade para lidar com a violência das ruas e situações difíceis de uma cidade grande *... [I] realized that I had no street smarts ...* -T/86. ⇒ **street-smart = streetwise** *[She's] ... a street-smart 14-year-old from New York ...* -T/92. ♦ *An aggressive, street-smart prosecutor ...* -T/87.

take to the streets sair à(s) rua(s) para protestar, fazer passeata ... *students took to the streets to press for greater democratization ...* -T/87. ♦ *... several thousand people took to the street to chant freedom slogans and sing patriotic songs.* -T/87.
a two-way street relacionamento, situação etc. que requer tato, concessões mútuas, tolerância etc. *McAllister insisted that the agreement must be a two-way street.*
walk/work the streets ser prostituta de rua *[She] ... once worked the streets.* -T/79. ⇒ **streetwalker** prostituta de rua *She was indignant at being taken for a streetwalker ...* -SJSN,50.
STREET-SMART → **STREET smarts**
STREETWISE [col] conhecedor da violência das ruas e apto a lidar com ela *Streetwise cops have no difficulty sizing up the psychology of their enemies.* -T/81.
STRENGTH on the strength of valendo-se de, com base em, fundamentado em, estribado em, fiando-se em *I hire people on the strength of my ability to judge human nature.* -CJC,35. ♦ *[The company] ... will produce an estimated $1.6 billion in revenues this year, mainly on the strength of exports to the U.S. ...* -T/87.
STRESS lay stress on salientar, dar importância, relevo ou ênfase a *Ginny laid stress on the fact that her father had been a general.*
STRETCH at a stretch de uma só vez, de um fôlego, sem interrupção *[He] ... sits, sometimes for three or four hours at a stretch, in his small private study ...* -T/80.
stretch of the imagination esforço de imaginação *By no stretch of the imagination could I picture Elizabeth as the future movie star she was to become.*
STRIDE get into one's stride; hit one's stride [col] alcançar velocidade, atuação, eficiência normal ou esperada; atingir sua competência, capacidade, desempenho, rendimento etc. pleno *A good athlete never hits his stride until he has been in intensive training for some months.* ♦ *Although Hemingway distinguished himself in the novel, many of his critics are of the opinion that it was in his short stories that he hit his stride.*
make strides avançar, fazer progresso *There is no question that women in the legal profession have made great strides.* -T/76.
take in (one's) stride lidar facilmente com problema, dificuldade etc., enfrentar algo calmamente, sem se preocupar ou se atrapalhar *[He] ... takes criticisms of his contradictory manner in stride.* -T/80. ♦ *... it is the mark of true strength to take both defeat and victory in one's stride.* -T/61.
STRIKE have two strikes against/on one [col] estar em desvantagem, em posição desfavorável ou crítica *... the would-be princess had two strikes against her: she was a Roman Catholic and a divorcée.* -T/85. ♦ *[He] ... had two strikes against him at birth.* -DJ,3.
how does that/the idea etc. strike you? que lhe parece?, que acha disso? *How does that idea strike you?*
on strike em greve *... thousands of truck drivers ... went on strike for higher pay ...* -T/87. ♦ *Television and radio workers were on strike ...* -T/84.
strike back revidar, retaliar *... U.S. employers have decided to strik back at the drug plague.* -T/86. ♦ *He struck back at the press which had vilified him.*
strike down 1. abater, derrubar *MacLaughlin had died at the corral, struck down by three arrows.* -LL,48. ♦ *[John Lennon was] ... struck down by the gun of a crazed fan in 1980 ...* -T/92. 2. afligir subitamente, prostrar; vitimar [diz-se de doença] *... Franklin Roosevelt was struck down, at the age of 39, by infantile paralysis ...* -T/60. ♦ *Spanish influenza struck down more soldiers than the enemy guns in World War I.* 3. anular, cancelar, invali-

dar ... *the Supreme Court struck it [death penalty for espionage] down 15 years ago* ... -T/87.

strike for lutar por, combater por (um objetivo), fazer greve por (determinada reivindicação) *The workers are striking for higher wages and better working conditions.*

strike home → **HIT home**

strike it rich [col] 1. descobrir petróleo, minério precioso etc. *When Snyder found precious gems in the rocks on his land, he thought he had finally struck it rich.* 2. enriquecer súbita ou inesperadamente *He struck it rich when an old relative died and left him a fortune.*

strike one as ocorrer a, vir ao pensamento de, parecer a, afigurar-se (a alguém) como *[This] ... advice may strike you as insultingly simple-minded* ... -AJ,31. ♦ *... the Christian and particularly the Anglo-Saxon, cultures are preoccupied with sexuality in ways that strike outsiders as peculiarly odd ...* -WA,11.

strike one that ocorrer (a alguém) que *It has just struck me that Doris might not be telling us the whole truth.* ♦ *It struck Sullivan that Flynn might be the right actor for the part of the king.*

strike out 1. cancelar, riscar, eliminar, excluir *She struck out the first three names on the list.* 2. pôr-se a caminho de ou nadar em direção a (com vigor, determinação) *When Warren's boat sank, he struck out for shore.* ♦ *... he was forever striking out across unknown expanses devoid of food or water ...* -VE,209. 3. = **HIT out** 1 *Henry struck out wildly, trying to hit the other boy.* 4. seguir um novo caminho, iniciar algo novo, uma ação, uma atividade *At 18, he struck out on his own, taking jobs as a house painter ...* -T/81. 5. eliminar o batedor (no beisebol) *If a pitcher struck out all the batters in a game, it would be a sensation.* 6. fracassar, ser malsucedido, não conseguir *Ted tried his best to take Susan out last night but he struck out.*

strike up começar a tocar, cantar, soar etc. *... the band struck up rock tunes designed to appeal to the younger generation ...* -T/84. ♦ *... the band strikes up.* -T/84. 2. mandar tocar, cantar, soar etc. *George Gershwin's* Strike Up the Band *is a very popular American song.* 3. dar início a, começar (amizade, relacionamento, conversa, correspondência etc.) *... he was in the habit of striking up friendships with students ...* -T/67. ♦ *The two young men struck up a conversation with the two girls.*

wildcat strike greve ilegal, não autorizada pelo sindicato *Electrical workers went on a wildcat strike ...* -T/63.

STRIKING striking distance → **within striking DISTANCE**

STRING have two strings to one's bow; have a second string to one's bow ter mais de uma maneira de conseguir algo, ter alguém ou uma alternativa a que recorrer *Jones has two strings to his bow. If he loses his job as a teacher he can always find work as a translator or interpreter.*

hold all the strings [col] ter domínio total de uma situação *The U.S. was accused of trying to hold all the strings in Middle East policy making.*

on a/the string [col] sob controle, sob domínio, em sujeição, na palma da mão *Have you ever heard the song* I've Got the World on a String? ♦ *Bill Griffin always has two or three girls on the string.*

pull strings/wires usar influência pessoal, mexer os pauzinhos *... Dad has pulled strings to get his daughter into a dance company ...* -T/87. ♦ *Hollister has influential friends in Washington and can pull wires if necessary.*

string along [col] 1. seguir, acompanhar, apoiar, colaborar, concordar *Whatever you do, baby, I'll always string along.* ♦ *Frankly, I think my chances are better to string along with him.* -HJ,57. 2. enganar, iludir, pregar uma peça em *He had been* stringing along many women and getting money from all of them with false promises.

strings attached condições, reservas, restrições, limitações *You were offered a fair share of all we had, and with no strings attached.* -RK,205. ♦ *... Moscow's ... proposal had a number of familiar strings attached.* -T/87.

string out dispor em fila, em linha, em série, enfileirar *... the eight states [Montana, Idaho, Wyoming, Nevada, Utah, Colorado, Arizona, New Mexico] strung out along the Rocky Mountains are collectively the nation's most thinly settled ...* -T/80.

string up [col] enforcar *In* The Ox-Bow Incident, *a movie based on Walter Van Tilburg Clark's novel, an angry mob catches three supposed cattle rustlers [thieves] and strings them up.*

STRIP comic strip = **comics** 1 *When I was a kid my favorite comic strips were Buck Rogers, Superman, Dick Tracy, Li'l Abner and many others.*

strip away eliminar, livrar-se de, desfazer-se de, excluir, remover *... to strip away all that is fake and artificial.* -HA,178.

strip down despir-se *The doctor asked John to strip down to his undeshorts for a medical examination.*

strip of despojar de, privar de, esbulhar, roubar *... they were stripped of their political rights ...* -T/64. ♦ *He was stripped of almost all his money.*

strip off 1. despir(-se) *[He] ... stripped off his shirt and went back to digging.* -LLN,25. ♦ *The two boys stripped off their clothes and dived into the lake.* 2. tirar, arrancar *The nurse stripped off her gloves.*

STRIPE of different/many/various etc. stripes de diferentes/muitos/vários etc. tipos, espécies *... pacifists, Trotskyites, clergymen, socialists of various stripes ...* -T/69. ♦ *Extremists of many stripes ... believe that violence is the only way to achieve their goals ...* -T/85.

STROKE at a stroke → **at a BLOW**

a stroke of luck um golpe de sorte, um acaso feliz *What a stroke of luck finding you here!*

STRONG strong on muito bom em, eficiente em, eficaz em, entendido em *Wheaton [College], though short of Ph.D.s in some departments, is strong on dedicated teaching.* -T/80.

STRONG-ARM → **put the (strong) ARM on**

STRUNG strung out [gír] 1. apreensivo, nervoso, agitado *I wouldn't get too strung out over this thing if I were you.* 2. viciado em drogas; debilitado devido ao uso de drogas; drogado *Some of the guys I went to high school with are in jail now. Some have been strung out on drugs.* -T/86.

STUCK [col] 1. preso, entalado, tolhido, imobilizado, encalhado *Bud was so fat that he got stuck when he tried to go under the fence.* 2. em dificuldades, em uma enrascada, impossibilitado de agir ou prosseguir; atrapalhado, confuso *I got stuck on the fifth question on the exam.* ♦ *... they may get stuck supporting the contras [Nicaraguan rebels] without U.S. help.* -T/86. 3. enganado, ludibriado, burlado *Mabel got stuck by the salesman.*

stuck for [col] impossibilitado de prosseguir (atividade, tarefa etc.) por falta de *They were unable to continue the construction because they were stuck for cement.*

stuck on [gír] apaixonado por, gamado por *Lou was stuck on Zee from the moment he first saw her.*

stuck on oneself [col] convencido, cheio de si *Why are you so stuck on yourself?*

stuck with → **STICK with**

STUCK-UP [col] = **STUCK on oneself** *Some people think she is stuck-up but she's really shy and afraid to make new friends.*

STUFF big stuff [gír] coisa ou pessoa importante *He has a reputation for knowing*

what is big stuff in the international art world.
do/show/strut one's stuff [gir] mostrar sua habilidade especial, mostrar o que sabe fazer *Can you sing? Well, get up on that stage and do your stuff.*
know one's stuff [col] conhecer seu assunto, ser competente em seu serviço, entender do riscado *Anthony is an electrical engineer who knows his stuff and will certainly succeed in his new job.*
right stuff essência, caráter, capacidade, conhecimento, habilidade etc. que tornam alguém apto para uma tarefa, missão, emprego etc. *Does [he] ... have the right stuff to be President at a time of domestic upheaval, economic unease and global uncertainty?* -T/92.
strut one's stuff → **do one's STUFF**
stuff up tapar, obstruir *The boy stuffed up the exhaust pipes and the room filled with smoke.*
STUFFING knock the stuffing out of [col] dar uma surra em *Terry tried to knock the stuffing out of John Stark but John was stronger and Terry lost the fight.*
STUMBLE stumble across/on/upon topar com, encontrar por acaso *He stumbled upon a spy ring.* ♦ *... investigators kept stumbling across his name in the statements of other witnesses.* -T/61.
STUMBLING stumbling block obstáculo, empecilho, dificuldade *... human rights will continue to be a major stumbling block in the U.S.-Soviet relations.* -T/87.
STUMP go on the stump [col] falar em comício *The politicians willl go on the stump months before the coming election.* ♦ *[He] ... went on the stump for Nixon ...* -T/73.
stump for [col] falar em comício a favor de *He [John Wayne] stumped for his friends Barry Goldwater and Ronald Reagan.* -T/69.
up a stump [col] perplexo, confuso *We did everything to find some way to solve our problem but always ended up a stump.*

STUNT stuntman; stunt man pessoa que assume o lugar de ator/atriz em cenas de perigo ou que requerem grande habilidade física, acrobacias etc. *[Stuntmen are] The men and women who perform dangerous physical feats in motion pictures (usually doubling for actors).* -SS,412.
SUBJECT subject matter tema, assunto *Does knowledge of subject matter suffice in teaching a given subject effectively?* -AD,5.
SUBSCRIBE subscribe to 1. aprovar, apoiar, dar endosso a *They subscribe to a wide variety of political and religious beliefs ...* -MJ,4. 2. ser assinante de *When I was in my teens, my eldest brother used to subscribe to* The Saturday Evening Post *and after he finished reading each copy he would pass it on to me.*
SUBSTITUTE substitute for colocar ou utilizar (alguém/algo) em substituição, pôr em lugar de *Pearl was sick, so Maggie substituted for her.* ♦ *Mother substituted margarine for butter.* ♦ *[Some people] ... fear that science will undermine the mystical concepts that they have substituted for reality.* -KAC,13.
SUCCESS nothing succeeds like success o sucesso leva a maiores sucessos *After he was awarded the Nobel Prize for Literature, he began to receive invitations to speak at several universities both here and abroad. Nothing succeeds like success.*
SUCH as such como tal, assim, nessa condição, em si *Many problems we will face are simply not soluble – and we have got to accept them as such.* -T/91.
such and such tal e tal *She told me to meet her there at such and such a time.*
such as tal como *A day such as this will always be remembered.* ♦ *People such as Tom and Harry are not to be trusted.*
SUCKER be a sucker for [col] gostar muito de, ser incapaz de resistir a, ser fã de, ser vidrado em *I'm a sucker for a party.* -EJ,98.

SUDDEN (all) of a sudden de repente, inesperadamente *Of a sudden it came to him that Morton ... had no right to do that.* -PJW,88. ♦ *All of sudden she began to cry.*

SUIT bring/file suit iniciar ação judicial, instaurar processo *He brought suit against a restaurant that had served him spoiled shrimp.* ♦ *She is planning to file suit against the police ...* -T/86.
follow suit seguir o exemplo de, fazer o mesmo, imitar *Dad was always singing about the house. I followed suit.* -RLI,19.
long/strong suit ponto forte, especialidade *Criticism was his long suit.* -T/63. ♦ *Foreign affairs has not been [President] Carter's long suit ...* -T/80. ♦ *Bad taste has always been Brooks' strong suit ...* -T/81.
suit oneself fazer o que bem entender, fazer como achar melhor *All right, we won't talk about the subject then. Suit yourself. But don't say I didn't try to warn you.*

SUM a lump sum importância paga de uma só vez, quantia global *When Brad is twenty-one he will receive his inheritance in a lump sum.*
sum up sumariar, resumir, sintetizar, recapitular *The humanism of the early modern centuries is not an attitude that can be summed up clearly.* -BCS,42. ♦ *Freud's own philosophy of life can be summed up in a phrase: "Knowledge through science".* -HC,20.

SUMMER Indian summer veranico, período de dias mais quentes que se segue ao primeiro frio do fim do outono *The afternoon was beautiful with the lazy, blue beauty of Indian summer.* -MG,19.

SUN under the sun sob o sol, no mundo, em existência *Ecclesiastes says: "There is nothing new under the sun".* ♦ *The reference shelves of the library brim with facts and expert opinion about everything under the sun.* -PL,15.

SUNBELT the Sunbelt o Sul dos EUA (onde predominam bom tempo e luz solar intensa durante a maioria dos dias do ano) *Many companies have moved to the Sunbelt in recent years.* ♦ *During a decade of tremendous growth, Sunbelt cities attracted millions of people from the depressed urban centers of the North.* -T/86.

SUNDAY Sunday best [col] as melhores roupas que uma pessoa tem *[They are] ... dressed in their Sunday best.* -T/74.

SUPPLY in short supply escasso, insuficiente *... long-range policies are in short supply in this Administration.* -T/86.

SUPPOSED be supposed to [pas] 1. julgar-se que, presumir-se que, considerar-se que, esperar-se que, acreditar-se que, supor-se que *Heflin is supposed to arrive on the 3 o'clock train from Yuma.* ♦ *This herb is thought to have great medicinal properties and is supposed to keep people young and healthy.* 2. dever, ter de, ter obrigação de, ser exigido ou esperado (de alguém) *Like everyone else, you're supposed to obey the law.* ♦ *Where's Susan? She was supposed to be here at nine.* 3. [neg] não ter permissão de ou para, não poder *The students are not supposed to smoke in the classroom.* ♦ *I'm not supposed to give you that information.* 4. servir para, destinar-se a *What's that small gadget supposed to do?*

SURE for sure certo; com certeza, sem dúvida *One thing is for sure: Clyde will never show his face around here again.* ♦ *I'll pay you the money on Friday for sure.*
sure enough [col] de fato, com efeito, sem dúvida, como era de esperar *He said he'd come at ten, and sure enough he did.*
to be sure efetivamente, com efeito, sem dúvida, na verdade *There were, to be sure, some dissenting voices at the meeting.*

SUREFIRE; SURE-FIRE [col] infalível, certeiro, garantido *If he were a candidate in our elections, he'd be a surefire winner.* -T/87. ♦ *This is a sure-fire business investment.*

SUREFOOTED; SURE-FOOTED que tem passo firme, que não escorrega, não tropeça, que não erra; certeiro, firme, seguro *What keeps him [film director Billy Wilder] sure-footed may well be an obsession with the craft of story-telling.* -T/60.

SURFACE **on the surface** sob todas as aparências exteriores, superficialmente *On the surface Lincoln [a town] looked like a sleepy Mexican town.* -GFT,7.

scratch the surface tratar de maneira superficial, não se aprofundar em ... *the reporter's own stories [on the Watergate affair] had only scratched the surface ...* -BC,276.

SURPRISE **take by surprise** apanhar de surpresa *We were taken by surprise when my sister announced that she had just married Joe.*

SWALLOW **swallow whole** 1. engolir sem mastigar *Children must be taught to take small bites because they have a tendency to swallow whole large pieces of food.* 2. acreditar piamente, engolir *We told them an unbelievable story and they swallowed it whole.*

swallow up absorver, sorver, fazer desaparecer, consumir *All my father's savings were swallowed up during the Great Depression of the 1930's.*

SWAN **swan song** canto de cisne, último ato, despedida *The Harder They Fall (1956), [Humphrey Bogart's] ... 75th film, was his swan song ...* -RD,20.

SWAY **hold/have sway** exercer domínio, autoridade, poder, influência; imperar, predominar ... *[President] Reagan is finding that he has little sway over Central America's agenda.* -T/87. ♦ ... *[the Celts] held sway over Central Europe for 700 years ...* -T/78.

SWEAR **swear by** ter grande fé ou confiança em *Since silicone breast implants were introduced internationally 30 years ago, millions of women have sworn by their results.* -T/92.

swear in ajuramentar, fazer (alguém) prestar juramento ao ser investido em cargo *John F. Kennedy was sworn in on January 20, 1961.* ♦ ... *[Tancredo] Neves was to be sworn in on March 15 [1985] as Brazil's first civilian President after 21 years of military rule ...* -T/85.

swear off [col] decidir-se a renunciar, abster-se de (bebida, fumo, vício etc.) *Americans who swear off smoking can expect to gain weight ...* -T/91.

swear out → **swear out a WARRANT**

SWEAT **no sweat** [gir] 1. fácil, simples, descomplicado *Robert's new job as assistant manager is no sweat and he's very happy about it.* ♦ 2. facilmente, sem problema, sem dificuldade, não há problema, tudo bem *When I asked him if I could count on his cooperation, he replied: "Sure, no sweat".*

sweat (it) out [gir] aguardar com ansiedade e impaciência *You'll have to sweat it out until they find the real culprit.*

SWEEP **a clean sweep** 1. limpeza geral, remoção de coisas ou pessoas não mais necessárias *When we organized the factory we made a clean sweep of the machine department and brought in all new equipment.* 2. vitória ampla, rapa *They were certain he'd win the election by a clean sweep.*

sweep all/everything before one/it → **CARRY all/everything before one/it**

sweep out of sair majestosamente de *Sweeping out of last week's press conference like Errol Flynn in a gray suit ...* -T/85.

sweep the city/country/nation/world chamar grande atenção, causar muita sensação *A wave of terrorism is sweeping the world.*

SWEET **sweet on** [col] enamorado de, apaixonado por *He is sweet on the girl who came to work in his office.*

SWEET-TALK → **sweet TALK**

SWIM **in the swim** [col] sintonizado com a atualidade, com a moda etc., imerso em atividades sociais etc. ... *a maneuver to*

keep [a possible candidate] ... from getting into the political swim ... -T/63.
SWIMMING go swimming → **go SHOPPING**
SWING get in/into the swing of things [col] adaptar-se (a uma nova situação etc.), participar ativamente *Jake had a new job but it didn't take him long to get into the swing of things.*
in full swing [col] em plena atividade ou andamento, no auge *... the Christmas shopping season went into full swing last week... -T/87.*
swing [col] ser enforcado *You will swing if they catch you stealing again.*
swing open abrir(-se) (porta) *Mary swung the door open, making way for the man. -OJT,5.* ♦ *The door swung open.*
SWITCH be/fall asleep at the switch [col] estar/ficar desatento, dormir no ponto, bobear *When Carl's great opportunity came he was asleep at the switch.*
switched on [col] 1. atualizado com a moda, atitudes, idéias novas etc. *Jennifer is switched on to all the new fads in current music.* 2. drogado *A small dose of heroin and he is switched on for hours.*
switch on//off ligar//desligar (interruptor, corrente elétrica, luz, aparelho elétrico etc.) *He switched on the air conditioner.* ♦ *Switch off the light.* ♦ *She switched off the ignition.*
SWOOP at/in one fell swoop de um só golpe, de uma só vez, ao mesmo tempo *The police caught the gang at one fell swoop.* ♦ *In one fell swoop, he [Charles de Gaulle] disposed of France's colonies in Black Africa... -T/66.*
SWORD cross swords with 1. duelar com espadas, esgrimir contra *Captain Esteban Pasquale had never crossed swords with anyone as skillful as Zorro and when they met, the masked avenger quickly dispatched the nasty vilain.* 2. travar debate com *I hope I'll never have to cross swords with him.*
put to the sword passar a fio de espada *[The captured enemies] ... were all put to the sword. -PM,17.*
SYNC(H) in//out of sync(h) [col] de acordo, concorde, em harmonia//em desacordo, em divergência *Father and son were hopelessly out of sync.* ♦ *We're in synch on that subject ... -T/91.*
SYSTEM all systems (are) go [col] tudo está funcionando bem, podemos prosseguir *"All systems are go, Apollo 8", the controller reported. -T/69.*
get something out of one's system [col] livrar-se de pensamento, influência, lembrança, desejo etc. desagradável; desabafar-se, pôr para fora *You still haven't got that girl out of your system, have you?*
one's system o corpo humano, o organismo *They will ... be tested for the presence of drugs in their systems. -T/86.*
public-address system; p. a. system sistema de alto-falantes para comunicações ao público em reuniões, eventos esportivos, logradouros etc. *[The man's] ... death was announced over the school's public-address system ... -T/72.* ♦ *... when the guy came over the p. a. system he was stuttering. -T/81.*
the system; System a estrutura da sociedade, a organização da política, dos negócios etc. considerada sob seus aspectos negativos, restritivos etc. *... the indomitable little guy preposterously pitted against the tyranny of circumstances and the system. -T/64.* ♦ *... he was strong enough to attack the System and its institutions ... -JRE,48.*

T to a T precisamente, perfeitamente, com exatidão, com perfeição *The meal was cooked to a T.* ♦ *The agreement suited her to a T.*

TAB keep tabs on [col] vigiar, controlar, ficar de olho em *[He wants] ... to keep tabs on his stock transactions.* -T/63. ♦ *... an undercover agent hired from a nationwide detective agency ... to keep tabs on the performance of key subordinates.* -PV,3.

pick up the tab [col] pagar a conta, arcar com as despesas *Order what you like and I'll pick up the tab.* -WPT,41.

TABLE at table à mesa, durante uma refeição *She always had good manners at table.*

clear the table tirar a mesa *His wife cleared the table right after dinner.*

keep a good table servir refeições boas e fartas em sua casa *The Irish are noted for always keeping a good table.*

set/spread the table pôr a mesa *His mother set the table in the dining room.* ♦ *The table had been spread for a large family meal.*

turn the tables on inverter as posições, mudar a situação *The school basketball team unexpectedly turned the tables on their much stronger rivals to win the tournament.*

under the table [col] em segredo, furtivamente, às escondidas *[They] ... have long been taking money under the table from sponsors.* -T/72. ⇒ **under-the-table** secreto, clandestino, ilícito *... under-the-table transactions.* -T/82.

wait at/on table(s); wait table servir à mesa, trabalhar como garçom *Jerry had to wait on tables to supplement the family income.* -T/74. ♦ *... doing things like waiting tables.* -T/92.

TABLE-HOP [col] ir a várias mesas em um restaurante, boate etc. para conversar com pessoas ali sentadas *... he table-hopped informally, just chatting with the 200 loyal Democrats [at a political dinner].* -T/63.

TACK abordagem, linha de ação, método, sistema *... the Russians were off on a new tack ...* -PVH,198. ♦ *... proposed that the Church take a new tack in its theology of marriage ...* -T/66. ♦ *If that doesn't solve the problem, take a different tack.*

tack on (to) acrescentar, adicionar, anexar como suplemento *The Senate ... [tacked on] an amendment to the bill extending ... the President's authority to enforce wage-price controls.* -T/73.

the wrong tack linha de ação errada; política, atitude ou posição incorreta, equivocada ... *the policymakers were taking the wrong tack.* -T/87.

TAG **tag along** [col] seguir de perto, acompanhar, ir atrás de *When I went fishing, my youngest sister always tagged along to watch me.*

tag/tail end 1. fim, ponta, extremidade *Fred is always at the tail end of his group.* 2. parte final, conclusão *Tillie appears only at the tag end of* The Cat's Pajamas *[a novel] ...* -T/68. ♦ *The Waltons, a successful TV series, deals with the daily routine of a Virginia family during the tail end of the Depression years.*

TAIL **on one's tail** [col] na cola de *The FBI has put an agent on the terrorist's tail.*

tail end → **TAG end**

turn tail 1. fugir, evadir-se ... *two Libyan MIG-25s [jet fighters] ventured out beyond the twelve-mile limit and then turned tail ...* -T/86. 2. virar as costas (para fugir), rodar sobre os calcanhares *He got panicky, turned tail and ran for the wagons ...* -CHT,40.

with one's tail between one's legs com o rabo entre as pernas, amedrontado, humilhado *He made fifty or sixty men run with their tails between their legs.* -HO,104.

TAILLIGHT luz de lanterna traseira (de veículo) *Lucy's eyes were fixed on the taillights of the car ahead.*

TAILOR **tailored for** feito para, adequado para, talhado para *An application letter and résumé should be tailored to the viewpoint of the reader ...* -MNH,114. ♦ *The part of Dardo in* The Flame and the Arrow *was tailored for Burt Lancaster.*

TAILOR-MADE feito sob medida, sob encomenda *a tailor-made suit* ♦ *This car has been tailor-made for the family's needs.*

TAILSPIN declínio, queda, colapso *The company went into a tailspin because of the oil crisis.* ♦ *... the Polish economy [is] in a tailspin ...* -T/80.

TAKE **be taken** [col] ser ludibriado, cair no conto do vigário *He was taken by a clever confidence man for about 5 grand.*

be taken ill → **TAKE sick**

it takes é necessário, é preciso, requer, exige ... *it takes more than assurance and confidence to make a good speaker.* -SN,425. ♦ *It took me a few seconds to understand her.* ♦ *It takes a lot of nerve to do what he did.*

it takes two to tango [col] duas pessoas são igualmente responsáveis por algo que requer a participação de ambas; quando um não quer, dois não brigam etc. *It takes two to tango, talk or love.*

on the take [gir] recebendo suborno *City officials and police ... on the take.* -T/69. ♦ *... alleged "lawmen" are on the take ...* -BM,12.

take after assemelhar-se a, parecer-se com, sair a (em aparência ou temperamento) *Which do you take after in temperament, your father or your mother?* -CT,10. ♦ *[General] MacArthur was said to take after his father ...* -T/64.

take amiss levar a mal, ofender-se com, interpretar mal *I'm sorry if my words have been taken amiss. I assure you I didn't mean to offend you in any way.*

take apart 1. desmontar, desmanchar, separar *I remember my brother Mario always taking apart engines of old cars.* 2. destruir, desmantelar, demolir, arrasar, despedaçar ... *the Communist artillery began taking the city apart ...* -T/72. 3. criticar severamente ou maliciosamente, enxovalhar; investir contra, atacar com violência *They took apart his story until it was completely unbelievable.*

take away tirar, levar, retirar *The joy one gets helping others cannot be taken away.* -T/66.

take back 1. devolver, levar de volta *He took the jewel back to its rightful owner.* 2. aceitar em devolução *The store refused to take back the bathing suit I had bought*

there. 3. retirar, retratar-se, desdizer-se *I'm sorry that I said that. I take it back.* 4. fazer voltar ao passado (em pensamento) *The movie I saw last night took me back to my youth.*
take down 1. desmontar, arriar, baixar *When the party was over they reluctantly took down the decorations.* 2. demolir, pôr abaixo *The old building was taken down.* 3. tomar nota de, anotar, escrever *My conversations with don Juan, ... were taken down as they ocurred ...* -CCT,24. 4. humilhar, abater *He was taken down a lot when the truth about his infamous past became known.*
take for tomar por, considerar (erroneamente) *He is not the crackpot that many people here take him for.* ♦ *"What do you take me for, a fool?", the bystander said to Prof. Higgins.*
take for granted 1. pressupor verdadeiro, aceitar como um fato que não necessita ser confirmado, aceitar naturalmente, sem questionar, sem pensar *I had always taken it for granted that I couldn't draw or paint.* -T/87. ♦ *... ideas that take violence for granted.* -T/66. ♦ *The authority of Science is very much taken for granted these days.* 2. supor que alguém ou algo é como é, aceitá-lo com indiferença, sem apreciar seu valor, sem dar-lhe atenção ou consideração *Most children take their parents for granted and only miss them when they die.*
take in 1. receber, admitir, acolher *West Point [the U.S. Military Academy] will take in about 100 women cadets ...* -T/76. 2. ajustar, diminuir, encurtar (roupa) *Louise lost so much weight while she was sick that she had to take her dresses in a couple of inches.* 3. abranger, incluir *Metropolitan Boston takes in many fairly large cities on its city boundaries.* 4. entender, compreender, assimilar, perceber, captar *The human mind has a capacity beyond our conscious understanding to take in and imitate what it sees.* -GS,108. 5. assistir, comparecer a, visitar *Let's have dinner and take in a show, huh?* 6. [col] iludir, enganar, fraudar *... I was taken in by a man that was a little smarter than I was.* -T/62. 7. receber pensionista, hóspede *Mrs. Miller had a big house and no family so she took in skiers during the height of the winter carnival.* 8. levar a uma delegacia como prisioneiro *We['ve] got to take him in, that's all. That's [sic] the orders.* -CN,30. 9. pegar (trabalho) para fazer em casa *... a mother who sometimes had to take in sewing when the money ran low.* -LI,10.
take it 1. [gír] agüentar pancada, dor, castigo etc. (sem protestar), ser forte *You can't take it and you'll never be a good boxer.* 2. [gír] suportar crítica, revés, desaforo, brincadeira, gracejo etc. *Unlike most people, he [George Orwell] could take [it] but he could not dish it out.* -T/68. 3. presumir, supor, ser levado a entender, julgar *If you don't call for this suit by Saturday I will take it that you're no longer interested in buying it.*
take it easy [col] 1. acalmar-se, não se exaltar, agir com calma *Take it easy, baby ... I won't hurt you.* -JJF,802. 2. descontrair-se, sossegar, espairecer, não se apressar, deixar o barco correr *You sit in the shade and take it easy and I will cut the grass with the power mower.*
take it from me [col] vá por mim, pode crer *Take it from me, there's no future in this kind of a life, nothing but regrets.* -DJ,43.
take it hard ficar desapontado, sentir-se magoado *Don't take it hard. I promise you that you'll have the money to visit Europe next year.*
take it or leave it pegar ou largar, aceitar ou desistir *[He made her an offer] ... letting her know she could take it or leave it.* -FC,17.
take it out of; take a lot out of [col] can-

sar, fatigar *A fast game of tennis will take it out of you if you're not in good condition.* ♦ *The three days on the raft had taken a lot out of Owen ...* -RQ,116.
take it out on → **TAKE out on**
take kindly to gostar de, aceitar de bom grado [geralmente neg] *[They] ... have not taken kindly to such cynicism.* -T/63. ♦ *He does not take kindly to criticism of his monetary policies.*
take lying down [col] aceitar complacentemente, sem protestar [geralmente neg] *You can rest assured we are not going to take this lying down.*
taken aback surpreso, perplexo *My eyes were on Ragnar, and for once I saw him taken aback.* -MET,25.
taken by/with atraído por, cativado por, interessado em *Will was very much taken by Daisy's good looks.* ♦ *She was taken with the charm of Mel's personality.*
take off 1. tirar (peça de roupa, sapato etc.) *She had taken off her shoes and stockings ...* -DP,7. ♦ *Gary took off his glasses.* 2. remover, limpar *This cleaning fluid will take off the most resistant spots.* 3. ir-se, retirar-se; fugir *He and his brother ... took off for Boston ...* -T/64. 4. folgar, tirar folga *... he had planned to take the following week off to attend a medical convention ...* -KJS,194. 5. deduzir, subtrair, descontar *He took off two hundred dollars on the price of the old car.* 6. decolar (avião) *What time did the plane take off?* ⇒ **takeoff** decolagem *... they waited 40 minutes for takeoff.* -T/86. 7. [col] imitar grotescamente, parodiar, arremedar *You should see Jack take off Klaus when Klaus is being scolded by his father.* → **takeoff** imitação satírica, mímica, arremedo, paródia, caricatura *Fran's boss walked in when she was doing a takeoff of him for the benefit of the office force.* 8. deslanchar, começar a crescer, desenvolver-se, progredir, tornar-se conhecido, popular *... her career in sales was taking off.* -T/85. ⇒ **takeoff** deslanche, desenvolvimento *... an economic takeoff.* -T/87.

take on 1. empregar, contratar *They are not taking on any more scientists in the space program.* 2. empreender, incumbir-se de, tomar a seu cargo *He took on the Foreign Ministry post in November ...* -T/82. 3. assumir (aparência, qualidade, característica etc.), adotar, adquirir, alcançar, atingir *... [John] Lennon's contributions [i.e., his songs] to The Beatles have taken on mythic proportions.* -T/92. 4. lutar contra, enfrentar *I'm afraid to take him on. He's too big and fast for me.* 5. [col] ser tomado de grande emoção, especialmente de ira ou aflição *She takes on when she goes to a wedding or a funeral.* ♦ *As a child, Doris used to take on when she couldn't have what she wanted.* 6. receber, aceitar (cliente, paciente etc.) *[A lawyer] ... taking on an occasional underdog client.* -T/87.
take it on/upon oneself 1. tomar sobre si, assumir o encargo, ficar responsável *[He] ... took it upon himself to draft a speech for the President ...* -T/87. 2. arrogar-se o direito *He took it on himself to pry into the personal life of the famous singer.*
take someone wrong entender mal, interpretar mal *Don't take me wrong. I'm not in favor of this decision.*
take out 1. extrair, arrancar, tirar, sacar *The dentist took out the tooth that was hurting me.* 2. remover, limpar, fazer desaparecer *This solution takes out stains from any material but it also takes out the color.* 3. tirar, requerer, adquirir, obter (documento etc. emitido por órgão oficial ou empresa) *[He] ... took out naturalization papers ...* -HMJ,612. ♦ *... she had taken out some $160,000 in insurance policies on her husband's life ...* -T/74. ♦ *The two took out a marriage license in Manhattan ...* -T/75. 4. [col] acompanhar, levar a passeio *He took her out to dinner*

last night. 5. ir-se, retirar-se, partir para *The boys took out for home when it began to rain.*
take out in aceitar (bem, mercadoria etc.) como pagamento em lugar de dinheiro *Since it seemed very unlikely to get the rest of my money back, I agreed to take it out in goods.* ♦ *During the Depression, school fees were taken out in trade, as farmers gave food instead of money to pay for tuition for their children.*
take out on [col] descarregar seus ressentimentos em *She hates her husband, and she takes it out on the world.* -WH,285. ♦ *... she took out her frustrations on her two children by beating them ...* -T/77.
take over assumir o comando de, a direção de, tomar conta de *... the military took over the country.* -T/78. ♦ *... a new city administration was about to take over Birmingham.* -T/63. ⇒ **takeover** tomada de poder, de comando, de direção, encampação *The prospect of a government takeover of oil companies has worried the big industries.*
take seriously levar a sério, dar importância *... she never took her writing very seriously.* -BRS,46.
take sick/ill adoecer *When Frances took sick I had to call in a doctor.* ♦ *I've just had a call that my father has taken ill.*
take to 1. dirigir-se para, retirar-se para, ir para (geralmente para refugiar-se, esconder-se, descansar etc.) *They took to the hills.* 2. acostumar-se a, habituar-se a, adaptar-se a, adotar (hábito, *hobby*, passatempo etc.) *He took to drink when his wife was killed in an auto crash.* ♦ *He took to carrying a Bible ...* -T/78. 3. aplicar-se a, dedicar-se a, devotar-se a *She took to the work.* -T/87. ♦ *He took to biology as a bird to flying.* 4. começar a gostar de, afeiçoar-se a, sentir-se atraído por *He took to the girl at once.*
take up 1. ocupar-se com, começar a interessar-se por, devotar-se a, dedicar-se a (estudo, profissão, ocupação, *hobby* etc.) *David enjoys a martini or two before dinner, but has never taken up smoking.* -T/62. ♦ *... she took up the game [tennis] a year ago.* -T/78. ♦ *Dennis has decided to take up another profession.* 2. levantar, apanhar, pegar *Some things that we eat with our fingers are much more messy than others that we would always take up with knife and fork.* -HR,14. 3. considerar, discutir (assunto, tópico etc.) *My Senator promised the voters that he would take up the school bussing question at the next session.* 4. assumir (cargo, função, emprego, trabalho, responsabilidade etc.); adotar (atitude, posição etc.) *He takes up office in January.* ♦ *[He] ... had taken up a new life in exile.* -T/77. 5. ocupar, tomar, encher (tempo, espaço) *Housework takes up most of a woman's time.* ♦ *One shelf was taken up with* National Geographic *magazines ...* -LRT,46. 6. continuar, retomar (algo interrompido) *... in a moment he took up the conversation again.* -VR,32. 7. advogar, apoiar, esposar (causa) *[He] ... took up the cause of Indian rights.* -T/87. 8. reagir favoravelmente a, aceitar (oferta, convite, aposta, desafio etc.) *[Elvis Presley] ... used his music as an open invitation to release, and kids took him up on it.* -T/77. 9. encurtar, apertar (roupa) *She took up the hem of the dress.* 10. estabelecer-se em, fixar-se em, assentar-se em, tomar (acomodação, alojamento) *She took up residence in a hotel ...* -T/67.
take up with 1. falar com (alguém) sobre determinado assunto, discutir (algo) com, debater idéias com *You will have to take it up with the manager if you want a definite opinion.* 2. [col] fazer amizade com, começar a andar com *[He] ... never seemed to make friends with nice boys, and he finally took up with some bad ones.* -T/60.
TAKING for the taking para quem quiser, à espera de quem quiser tomar posse de *The oil is there for the taking, of course,*

but it is simply too expensive to get out of the ground.
TALE **spin a tale** → **spin a YARN**
tall tale → **tall STORY**
tell tales revelar segredos, mexericos, intrigas ... *he was dismissed because of evidence that he had been telling tales to the ... [former secret police] for years.* -T/92. ⇒ **telltale** denunciador, revelador ... *scientists have found practically no telltale fossils from the crucial period between 8 million and 5 million years ago ...* -T/77.
tell tales out of school revelar informação confidencial, dar com a língua nos dentes *Now that our secret has been revealed, the boss wants to find out who's been telling tales out of school.*
TALENT **talent scout** caça-talentos, pessoa que procura novos valores para o cinema, teatro, esportes etc. *Young hopeful movie stars are always waiting for some talent scout to find them.*
TALK **back talk** → **TALK back**
make something talk [col] tocar um instrumento com grande perícia *You make that piano talk, Mr. West.* -HW,23.
now you're talking assim sim, é assim que se fala *Go to a soccer game? Now you're talking!*
small talk bate-papo, conversa amigável, conversa fiada *They engaged only in small talk at table ...* -BFW,23. ♦ *The two men made small talk while Ann served coffee.*
sweet talk [col] lisonja, palavras doces, lábia *In spite of John's sweet talk, Ruth didn't fall for him.* ⇒ **sweet-talk** levar na conversa, engabelar *He sweet-talked the girl into having sex with him.*
talk about falar de, falar sobre, discutir *They were talking about politics and economics.* ⇒ **talked-about** discutido, comentado *The most talked-about ethical problem ...* -T/60.
talk about flowers/ethics/money/bad language/movies/new fads etc. [exclamação de surpresa, admiração, repulsa etc.] (e) por

falar em, falando de, já que estamos falando de, que dizer de *Talk about ethics! He's the most unscrupulous businessman I've ever met.* ♦ *Talk about the high expectations of new parents.* -T/86.
talk/answer back [col] replicar rudemente, retrucar *"Don't talk back to me", her father said angrily.* ♦ *As children we never answered back our parents.* ⇒ **back talk** resposta grosseira, retruque *Do as you're told and no back talk.*
talk big [col] contar vantagem, gargantear *He talks big but his actions are never as big as his talk.*
talk down 1. fazer calar (uma pessoa) em uma conversa falando mais, mais alto ou empregando melhores argumentos (que ela) *Welles is a large man with a powerful voice and easily talks down anyone in an argument.* 2. dar pouca importância a, apoucar, diminuir, menosprezar *Try to talk down the fact that our cars use much gas and oil.*
talk down to falar a alguém de maneira condescendente, tratar seu interlocutor ou ouvinte como uma pessoa de pouca cultura ou inteligência *Mr. Templeton always talks down to people who have not been to university.* ♦ *[Ralph Waldo Emerson] ... did not talk down to his audiences ...* -HL,148.
talk into//talk out of [col] convencer a, persuadir a, induzir a//dissuadir, fazer mudar de opinião *[The] ...mother tried to talk the boy into becoming a lawyer ...* -T/81. ♦ *When I told him I was leaving, he tried to talk me out of it.*
the talk of the town o assunto do momento, pessoa ou coisa sobre a qual todos estão falando *Meryl Streep became the talk of the town after her impressive performance in* The French Lieutenant's Woman.
talk out discutir (assunto, questão, problema etc.) visando ao esclarecimento ou à solução *Gray is never willing to talk things out with his wife.* ♦ *[The soldiers*

had] ... a chance to talk out their experiences and begin to absorb them. -T/79.
talk out of → **TALK into**
talk over 1. conversar sobre, debater, discutir After [they] ... talk over their differences ... -T/81. ♦ ... you and I are going to have a lot of business to talk over. -LN,113. 2. persuadir, convencer Maybe we can talk her over to our side.
talk show programa de TV ou de rádio no qual pessoas famosas debatem temas ou são entrevistadas [Margaret] Mead ... appeared on television talk shows to endorse everything from greater international cooperation to women's liberation ... -T/78.
talk to falar com, conversar com Sue and Carol talked to each other for almost an hour. ⇒ **talking-to** [col] repreensão, descompostura I'm going to have your father give you a talking-to. -OJ,5.
talk up 1. falar a favor de, apoiar, promover, elogiar Detroit ... [is] talking up its electric car research ... -T/67. 2. falar alto e claro, dizer o que pensa A once silent witness talks up and denounces [the wife of a famous politician] ... -T/91.
tall talk [col] fanfarronice, bravata, conversa fiada He was famous for his tall talk and eventually became the subject of a musical comedy.
TALKIE [col] filme sonoro The Jazz Singer (1927) is considered to be the first feature-length talkie. ♦ The talkies ushered in a new era in moviemaking.
TALKING talking point fato, dado, elemento etc. persuasivo que deve ser salientado em uma discussão; tópico, assunto With ... updated talking points, [President] Reagan went back ... for his afternoon session with [First Secretary of Communist Party] Gorbachev. -T/86.
TALKING-TO → **TALK to**
TANDEM in tandem 1. um atrás do outro, em fila, em série All his wagons had the horses in tandem. 2. em sociedade He always works in tandem with his wife.

TANGENT fly/go off at a tangent mudar subitamente de uma atitude, orientação, trajetória etc. para outra He had all the reason and logic of the French, whereas I often contradicted myself and flew off at tangents. -MH,8.
TANGLE tangle up enredar-se, envolver-se This unfortunate boy just got tangled up with the wrong guys and they left him holding the bag. -AIM,139.
TANK tank up [col] 1. encher o tanque de um automóvel Let's tank up before we start out for the White Mountains. 2. encher a cara, o caco, embriagar-se Dean got all tanked up at the party last night.
TANTRUM throw a tantrum → **have/throw a FIT**
TAP blow taps dar o toque de silêncio (no quartel) The scene in which private Robert E. Lee Prewitt blows taps in the movie From Here to Eternity is a most touching one.
on tap 1. de barril (chope) My father had marvelous German beer on tap ... -HA,207. 2. [col] à mão, disponível, pronto para uso The soccer teams do not have enough players of star quality on tap.
tap → **wiretap**
TAPE red tape burocracia, formalidades oficiais excessivas He was a man of action frustrated by red tape. -T/87.
TAPER taper down diminuir, decrescer We're very busy now but we think that business will taper down by the end of the month.
taper off diminuir, afilar-se, cessar gradualmente Gregg had been drinking a lot but has tapered off lately.
TARGET (right) on target dentro das expectativas, na meta, correto ou preciso na interpretação ou previsão de algo Not all the planning has been invariably on target. -T/87. ♦ ... his advice seems to be right on target. -T/77.
TASK task force 1. força-tarefa On June 6, 1944 the mightiest task force the world has ever seen was launched across the

English Channel to set in motion the invasion of Normandy. 2. grupo tático, grupo de trabalho *[President John] Kennedy assembled a task force of advisers.* -T/82.

take to task chamar às contas, recriminar, repreender, reprovar *Parents are always taking their children to task for something or other.*

TASTE give someone a taste of his own medicine → **give someone a DOSE of his own medicine**

have a//no taste for ter gosto ou preferência por//não gostar de, não apreciar *Mr. Wagner has a taste for classical music.* ♦ *As a young officer he saw combat in Korea and Viet Nam, but it is said he has no taste for bloodletting.* -T/86.

in bad/poor//good taste de mau//bom gosto *Her suggestion was in bad taste.* ♦ *His article was in poor taste and was strongly criticized by the other papers.*

leave a bad taste in someone's mouth produzir desagrado, aversão, raiva, vergonha em *The way she talked back to her mother left a bad taste in my mouth.*

a taste of 1. pequena porção de comida ou bebida, prova *I've just had a taste of that Italian salami and I must say it is simply delicious.* 2. primeiro contato ou experiência com *The boy visited a cattle ranch in Montana and had a taste of life in the wide open spaces.*

taste of ter gosto de, saber a *This soup tastes of garlic.*

there's no accounting for taste(s); there's no disputing colors and taste gosto não se discute *Jay likes to sport loud ties and flashy clothes. Well, there's no accounting for tastes.* ♦ *An old proverb says: "There's no disputing colors and taste".*

to someone's taste para o gosto de, da maneira que alguém gosta de ou prefere algo *The paintings I saw at the annual exhibition of modern art were not to my taste.*

TAX (income) tax return declaração de imposto de renda *Everybody is supposedly eager to cheat the Government on his tax return.* -T/66. ♦ *... my business manager was lost in sessions with accountants to review my income tax returns.* -MN,37.

TEACH teach someone to corrigir, punir, tirar o mau hábito de *This will teach you to behave politely the next time you're spoken to.*

TEACHER teacher's pet o/a aluno/a preferido/a do/a professor/a *Tommy was such a teacher's pet that the other children hated him.*

TEAM team up associar-se, unir-se (em um esforço cooperativo) *In 1967 Francis A. Sinatra and Antonio C. Jobim teamed up to produce wonderful recordings of some of Jobim's great bossa nova songs.*

TEAR[1] [rima com *bear*] **go on a tear** [gir] cair na farra, na gandaia *He's generally well behaved but feels that he must go on a tear once a year.*

tear apart 1. = **TAKE apart** 1 *Analysis is tearing apart, and synthesis is seeing whole. Most of us cannot see the whole until we have seen the parts.* -CCC,xi. 2. = **TAKE apart** 2 *... the centrifugal forces that have already torn apart the U.S.S.R. are now at work in Russia and Ukraine.* -T/92. 3. = **TAKE apart** 3 *She is not happy unless she's tearing someone apart.*

tear around mover-se rapidamente, correr para lá e para cá *The two of them were tearing around the neighborhood last night looking for Paulie.* -LMC,9.

tear at 1. atacar ou puxar violentamente, tentar arrancar, cortar ou rasgar puxando *In helpless, futile anguish, she tore at the pillow that night.* -T/66. ♦ *[They were] ... rolling on the floor, tearing at each other's clothes ...* -T/87. 2. causar angústia, afligir *Clearly, that problem tears at her.* -T/87.

tear away mover-se rapidamente, sair ou partir em grande velocidade *Brad tore away in his new car.*

tear down 1. derrubar, demolir *The Berlin Wall was finally torn down in 1989.* 2. desaprovar, condenar, criticar negativamente, difamar *Thelma is always tearing down other people.*

tear into → **RIP into**

tear off 1. rasgar, arrancar (pedaço, parte) *[In May, 1945] Berlin lay ravaged with its roofs torn off ...* -T/85. 2. tirar (peça de roupa), despir com grande pressa *He walked forward, tearing off his clothes as he went.* -BRT,83. 3. sair correndo, sair precipitadamente *... he turned and tore off down the street.* -OF,40.

tear oneself away retirar-se ou sair a contragosto, afastar-se contra a vontade *Joseph tore himself away from her embraces.* -DDT,9.

tear up 1. despedaçar, destruir *... the larger ones [crocodiles] have a gruesomely efficient means of tearing up a good-sized animal.* -SK,44. 2. rasgar em pedaços, reduzir a pequenos fragmentos *Maggie tore up the letter into little pieces.*

TEAR² [rima com *dear*] **burst into tears** desfazer-se em lágrimas *Lesley burst into tears when they told her the bad news.*

in tears a chorar *She was in tears when I left.*

TEARJERKER [col] história, filme etc. ridiculamente sentimental *The movie* Imitation of Life *was a real tearjerker.*

TEE tee off 1. dar a tacada inicial (no golfe) *You tee off first. I'm not a good golfer.* 2. começar, principiar *The campaign teed off with a big banquet.* ⇒ **teed off** [gir] irritado, zangado *Bud was teed off because he had to wait fifteen minutes for his girl.*

TEEM teeming with cheio de, repleto de *[A speech] ... teeming with platitudes and somewhat short of substance ...* -T/87.

TEENS in one's teens na adolescência, entre 13 e 19 anos de idade *I was in my teens when I first heard that story.*

TEENAGER adolescente *Teenagers like the same songs, the same clothes and the same movie stars.*

TEENY-WEENY [col] pequenininho, miudinho, minúsculo *Remember the teeny-weeny, polka-dot bikini?*

TEETH → **tooth**

TELEPHONE on the (tele)phone ao telefone *Mr. Parkinson is on the telephone right now. Can I take a message?* ♦ *Tell Miss Payton she's wanted on the telephone.*

TELL I'm telling you [col] estou lhe dizendo, esteja certo de que o que digo é verdade *I'm telling you, he can't be trusted to finish the job on time.*

tell apart; tell (something) from (something) diferenciar, distinguir (um do outro) *... those who knew them [twin brothers] well could tell them apart by their expressions ...* -EMW,19. ♦ *If you cannot tell the good guys from the bad guys in the western, your reactions will be all wrong ...* -CCC,11.

tell it like it is [gir] falar com toda a franqueza, revelar todos os fatos *[George Orwell's] ... posthumous honor is a tribute to his passion for truth; ... he told it like it was.* -T/68.

tell of falar de, discorrer sobre, contar, narrar *Good supervisors encourage employees to tell them of minor occurrences and conditions which may eventually impair their productivity.*

tell off [col] censurar, descompor, dizer umas verdades a alguém *He told off his critics in a TV speech and lost many conservative votes.*

tell on 1. causar efeito, impressão, fazer-se sentir *The growing dishonesty of his relationship with his wife had begun to tell on his work.* 2. denunciar, delatar *I'm afraid of what Garth might do to us. If he tells on us the police will have us arrested.*

tell someone where to get off [col] repreender severamente, dizer algumas verdades a *Yvonne told George where to get off when he tried to kiss her.*

(I'll) tell you what [col] tenho uma idéia, tenho uma sugestão, eis o que podemos fazer *Tell you what. Why don't we ask her to meet us there?*
you never can tell nunca se sabe *I hope we won't need all the equipment we're taking with us on this trip, but you never can tell.*
you're telling me [col] já sei disso, não precisa me dizer, disso sei eu *"He's a heel!" "You're telling me! I was married to him once, remember?"*
TELLING there's no telling → there's no SAYING
TELLTALE → tell TALES
TEMPER have a hot/quick/short temper zangar-se facilmente, ter pavio curto *[He] ... does not deny that he has a hot temper ...* -T/78. ♦ *In those days I had a very bad, quick temper ...* -HEM,115. ⇒ hot-tempered; quick-tempered; short-tempered irascível, genioso *... for days a rancor burned in him, making him short-tempered with Hitch ...* -LD,21. ♦ *He was touchy and hot-tempered.* -LAK,70.
hold/keep//lose one's temper manter//perder a calma *Major, I'm trying to keep my temper.* -SGT,65. ♦ *... next time don't lose your temper. If you have trouble come to me.* -LRT,51.
in a temper de mau humor *Connie went to bed in a temper after she quarreled with her husband.*
temper tantrum explosão de mau humor, irritação súbita *[He] ... has long been famed for ... his temper tantrums ...* -T/79.
TEMPERATURE run a temperature → run a FEVER
TEMPEST tempest in a teapot; storm in a teacup tempestade em copo d'água *Don't worry about that. It's only a tempest in a teapot.* ♦ *The whole affair was just a storm in a teacup.*
TEN ten to one muito provavelmente, quase certo *Ten to one he'll win the race.*
TENTERHOOKS on tenterhooks muito nervoso, ansioso, aflito *If you had taken my advice you wouldn't be on tenterhooks now.*
TERM bring to terms impor condições *He thought he could bring his opposition to terms by underselling them and ruining their business.*
come to terms 1. chegar a um acordo, a um entendimento *They argued for a long time but finally came to terms.* 2. aceitar (fato ou situação desagradável etc.), conformar-se com, admitir *... successive American Presidents have used inflation, foreign borrowing and other devices to avoid coming to terms with some fundamental problems in the nation's economy ...* -T/87.
in no uncertain terms com toda a clareza e sem papas na língua, sem deixar (margem a) dúvidas, sem rebuços, com todas as letras *[He] ... chewed the mayor out in no uncertain terms.* -T/66. ♦ *[In 1959] ... he told Visitor Nikita Khrushchev off in no uncertain terms.* -T/61.
in terms of em relação a, sob o aspecto de *... attempts were made to explain nature's phenomena in terms of her daily operations.* -GJ,23.
on good//bad terms with em boas//más relações com *To be on good terms with the world, you must have a good and clear conscience.* -T/86.
on speaking terms de bem, em relações amistosas com *... the two men are barely on speaking terms.* -T/80.
term paper trabalho escrito (ensaio, dissertação, relatório etc.) que um aluno é solicitado a apresentar ao fim de um período trimestral ou semestral para avaliação de seu aprendizado *... the experience of writing the term paper has tremendous value for any student.* -PL,165.
TERMINAL 1. próximo à morte, nos últimos estágios de uma doença fatal *... a terminal patient approaching the end.* -T/73. 2. que leva à morte, fatal *terminal cancer* v. terminally ILL

TERROR **holy terror** criança terrível, endiabrada ... *the second and last son ... a holy terror ...* -T/87.

TEST **put to the test** pôr à prova *Broken physically ... and shaken mentally, he nevertheless ... put to the test the doctrine of unselfish love and self-immolation.* -CS,270.

THANK **I will thank you** você estará me prestando um favor, eu ficarei agradecido [usado ironicamente] *I will thank you to mind your own business and get away from here.*

no thanks to apesar de *Everything's OK again now, no thanks to you.*

thanks a lot → **thanks a LOT**

thanks to graças a, por causa de [às vezes em tom irônico] *Thanks to you we now have a new basketball.* ♦ *Thanks to you we are now in deeper trouble than we ever were.*

THAT **at that** [col] 1. sem mais delongas, nesse ponto, como tal, assim como está *Let's not argue about this, Ray. It's better to let it go at that.* 2. mesmo assim, ainda assim, apesar disso *Laurie didn't seem to love Owen when they married, but at that they managed to be happy.* 3. além disso, ademais, ainda por cima, também ... *Buffalo Bill was not a phony – or just a legend like Paul Bunyan – but a real man, and an intelligent and able one at that.* -T/61.

in that visto que, porque, porquanto, em razão de que *They had lost contact with Martin in that Martin had become very involved with his work.*

is that it? não é isso? não é assim? *You are afraid I might go to the police and tell them what I know. Is that it?*

is that so? não diga! é mesmo? verdade? *When Pete said he was doing his best to help me, I said: "Is that so?"*

(just) like that sem mais nem menos, sem mais preâmbulos *I was furious when I found out what Oscar had done. I could kill him just like that.*

that far/large/long etc. tão longe assim/ grande assim/comprido assim etc. *Did you go that far?* ♦ *Is it that long?*

that is isto é, quer dizer *Carlos likes classical music and westerns, good westerns, that is.* ♦ *Come to see me tomorrow at 10 a.m., that is, if you can make it.*

that much/many tanto assim/tantos assim *Do you hate me that much?* -WR,57. ♦ *I didn't think he had that many cars.*

that's a good one! essa é boa! *He calls me a liar. That's a good one!*

that's all é só, é tudo, só isso *I just wanted to talk to her, that's all.* ♦ *You think I love you, but I don't. I'm only attracted to you, that's all ...* -WCN,235.

that's/it's all right 1. não se incomode, não precisa desculpar-se, está tudo bem *When he said he was sorry for all the inconvenience he had caused, I replied: "That's all right".* 2. não há de que, não precisa agradecer *She thanked me and I said: "That's all right".*

that's all there is to it/that e isso é tudo, e é só isso *You can't walk out now. You made a deal and you have to honor it and that's all there is to it.* ♦ *Well, you're going to college. That's all there is to that.* -TM,82.

that's/there's ... for you assim é que (alguém/algo) é, isso é que é; isso é típico de *My ammunition [though old] was still good. That's American equipment for you.* -RQ,102.

that's it 1. é isso (mesmo), essa é a verdade, está correto *That's it. I understand it now. You were really in love with him.* -MN,287. 2. pronto, é isso aí, ponto final *... once he makes a decision, that's it – no dissent – either go out and do it or get off the team ...* -T/92.

(and) that's that e ponto final, e pronto, e acabou-se *You can't just come and tell me you had a child in Italy, and that's that.* -WSM,274. ♦ *... the Administration has made up its mind, and that's that.* -T/78.

THEME theme park parque de diversões no qual os entretenimentos obedecem a uma idéia/tema ou grupos de idéias ou temas, parque temático ... *Heritage is the third most popular theme park in the country (after the two Disney operations).* -T/87. ♦ ... *[Steven] Spielberg's Jurassic Park [is about] ... dinosaurs roaming through a modern theme park.* -T/92.

THEN from then on desde então, desde essa ocasião, a partir daí *I last saw her in 1954. From then on we went our separate ways.*

(but) then again; but then (mas) por outro lado, (mas) ao mesmo tempo, (mas) também é verdade que *This might be the answer to our problems. Then again, it might not.* ♦ *The building would have been big even for a town three times the population of Lincoln, but then the county itself was a large one ...* -GFT,7.

THERE not all there [col] amalucado, abilolado, destrambelhado *After Joe came back from Vietnam, he seemed at times not all there.*

THICK in the thick of na parte mais densa, intensa ou renhida de; no auge, na culminância *The soldiers were in the thick of the battle now.* ♦ ... *[they] ... were in the thick of the bargaining.* -T/64. ♦ *She liked to be in the thick of things, whenever there was singing, storytelling, or laughter.* -MHH,20.

thick with 1. carregado de, cheio de, apinhado de *The spring sky was thick with stars.* ♦ *A garden thick with flowers.* 2. [col] muito amigo de, íntimo de *Cole is thick with all the local politicians.*

through thick and thin em quaisquer condições ou situações, apesar de todas as dificuldades ... *Eisenhower has stayed popular through thick and thin ...* -T/60.

THICKHEADED estúpido, imbecil, obtuso *Howard's such a thickheaded guy.*

THICK-SKINNED → **have a thick SKIN**

THIEF (as) thick as thieves íntimos, muito amigos, unha e carne *The women in the club were as thick as thieves during the meeting.*

THIN thin down emagrecer, afinar, adelgaçar-se *Olivia is trying to thin down.* ♦ ... *the Queen's younger sister, a newly thinned-down Princess Margaret ...* -T/78.

thin out diminuir, rarear, tornar(-se) menos denso *There was much talk among the troopers, but as the sun rose higher and the heat pressed down, it thinned out and died.* -SL,125. ♦ ... *jungles had thinned out ...* -T/77.

THING all things considered levando tudo em conta, considerando todos os aspectos (de algo) *All things considered, the restrictions against smoking today hardly seem dire at all.* -T/86.

be all things to all men/people tentar agradar a todos ... *the massive drive to produce items that will be all things to all men.* -PV,188. ♦ ... *American colleges and universities sought to be all things to all people.* -T/92.

a close/near thing = **close CALL** *The [1960 presidential] election was a near thing. Kennedy won by only 113,000 votes out of 68.8 million.* -T/74.

do one's (own) thing [gir] fazer aquilo que mais lhe agrada ou que se tem vontade de fazer, seguir seus interesses e inclinações, sua especialidade, seu forte, ficar na sua ... *the attitude of a growing number of Americans today: do your own thing no matter what it is or who it affects.* -T/73.

do the right thing fazer a coisa certa, agir decentemente *She was such a selfless mother that she was willing to sacrifice anything in order to do the right thing by her children.*

first thing (in the morning) em primeiro lugar (logo de manhãzinha) *[He] ... told me to come around to see him first thing in the morning ...* -CG,135.

first thing off the bat [col] imediatamente, sem perda de tempo *Tomorrow morning, first thing off the bat, I'm going* to the bank to get some money and then buy my ticket for Europe.

first things first as coisas mais importantes, principais etc. (devem vir, ser feitas etc.) em primeiro lugar *"First things first" has always been good advice for those who would put the cart before the horse.*

(the) first/next thing one knows [col] quando menos se espera, logo, da noite para o dia, no instante seguinte *The boat struck a huge wave and the first thing I knew I had been thrown into the water.* ♦ *You've got to do as I say or the next thing you know you'll be in trouble with the law.*

for one thing para citar um exemplo, por um (dos) motivo(s), uma das razões é que, em primeiro lugar **(and) for another (thing)** (e) por outro motivo, em segundo lugar *I'm rather skeptical about his plan. For one thing, it isn't practical. For another (thing), it will demand a number of huge investments.*

get things done → **get (something) DONE**

get things off one's chest → **get (something) off one's CHEST**

get things/one thing/it/something straight deixar bem claro, não dar margem a dúvidas, entender bem *I've been trying to find out what exactly happened last night, but it's hard to get things straight.* ♦ *Let's get something straight ... I don't love you. I never will.* -MWL,64.

have a thing about → **the/a THING**

have a thing going for → **HAVE something going for one**

it's a good thing ainda bem que *It's a good thing Johnny is a strong swimmer.*

just one of those things → **(just) one of those THINGS**

just the thing aquilo que é mais adequado, mais conveniente, mais importante *After a tiring day at the office, a good movie on TV is just the thing for relaxation.*

know a thing or two ter muita experiência ou conhecimento, saber das coisas, entender do assunto *Vincent knows a thing or two about modern art because he studied in Montparnasse.*

let things go (at that) → **LET it go (at that)**

make a big thing about/(out) of dar demasiada importância a, fazer um cavalo de batalha *This country makes such a big thing about age, particularly if you're a woman ...* -T/87. ♦ *Look, it was only a misunderstanding. Let's not make a big thing out of it.*

make things hum fazer com que as coisas se ativem, injetar eficiência, ânimo, provocar agitação, rebuliço etc. *When the new owner takes over the factory, he'll make things hum.*

much the same thing praticamente a mesma coisa, coisa bem semelhante *What you're saying is nothing new. Your brother told me much the same thing a few days ago.*

a near thing → **a close/near THING**

the next thing one knows → **the first THING one knows**

not know the first thing/a thing about não saber nada de, desconhecer totalmente *I don't know a thing about Egyptian art. I'm just a magazine illustrator.* ♦ *[He] ... doesn't know the first thing about cars ...* -T/69.

not the thing procedimento desaconselhável, inadequado *This is not the thing to do in this situation.*

of all things → **of ALL (people/things/places etc.)**

(just) one of those things uma dessas coisas que acontecem, uma dessas coisas da vida *I'm afraid of shots. I hate needles. It's just one of those things.* -SW,10.

other things being equal se as outras circunstâncias forem as mesmas, desde que o resto permaneça inalterado *... in the highly verbal, highly intellectual civilization in which we now live, the man with a better vocabulary has a better chance of success, other things being equal ...* -LNW,10.

poor (little/old/young etc.) thing coitadinho, pobrezinho *The poor little thing imagined that her boyfriend was going to marry her.*

see things [col] ver coisas, ter alucinações *Are you really Anna Livia or am I seeing things?*

start things humming = make THINGS hum *He started things humming when he exposed corruption in government.*

start things off iniciar, dar começo, pôr em ação *He held my hand and said I was very beautiful. That was what started things off between us.*

sure thing [col] 1. certeza, coisa certa, que ocorrerá sem dúvida *Don't be afraid to bet on that horse. It's a sure thing.* 2. é claro, certamente *"Can I count on your discretion?" "Sure thing."*

sweet/cute (lovely/little/young etc.) thing pessoa encantadora; gracinha; belezinha, coisinha louca *Doris is just the sweetest thing in the world.* ♦ *She was about the sweetest thing in skirts.* -TRL,112. ♦ *She was such a sweet-looking thing...* -BRSR,29. ♦ *Who's that cute little thing?*

take off one's things tirar sobretudo, paletó, chapéu etc. *Take off your things and have a drink with us before we leave for the game.*

take things easy = TAKE it easy 2 *[He told me] ... to take things easy.* -AIM,42.

teach a thing or two ensinar algumas coisas (a), dilatar os horizontes (de) *... allow [him] to teach them a thing or two about how the world runs.* -T/87.

tell someone a thing or two dizer algumas verdades a alguém *I told Mr. Simpson a thing or two and made it quite clear that he would no longer get my support.*

the thing 1. a coisa da atualidade, aquilo que está na moda, o estilo predominante *It is quite the thing now to be able to converse in more than one language.* 2. o importante, o essencial, o objetivo, a meta *The thing is not to let them know we're here.* ♦ *The thing to do is to let them think she's in Ireland.*

the/a thing [gir] singularidade, atitude excêntrica ou neurótica, sentimento irracional, obsessão, atração, gosto, fobia, aversão etc. *I still had this very big thing for Robert Mitchum.* -AK,24. ♦ *He had always had a thing for her ever since high school days.* ♦ *[He] ... has this thing about money; he refuses to spend it, on himself or anyone else.* -T/69. ♦ *[She] ... had the dopiest thing about always making sure the door was locked.* -BL,93. ♦ *... individuals with a thing about weapons ...* -T/67.

the thing is a questão é, a verdade é que *The thing is, are you willing to risk all your money on an investment like that?* ♦ *The only thing is, I didn't poison him.* -QE,129.

to make things worse → **to make MATTERS worse**

THINK little does one think → **LITTLE does one imagine**

think back recordar *I often think back with nostalgia to the time when we first met.*

think better of refletir, reconsiderar, optar por um meio mais sensato *We wanted to go fishing, but then thought better of it. There were alligators around ...* -RQ,136.

think fit julgar conveniente, apropriado *After due consideration he thought fit to accept the contract.*

think highly/much of ter em alto conceito, admirar, respeitar *I thought too much of him and he'd been too good to me ...* -GJH,16. ♦ *... she had been Peter's teacher in the past, and he thought highly of her opinion.* -SW,7.

think little/nothing of 1. considerar (algo) normal, fácil, simples etc., não ver nada de extraordinário em *Many girls in show business think nothing of baring their breasts these days.* 2. não dar valor

a, dar pouca ou nenhuma importância a *I think little of the government's plan to fight drugs.*
think nothing of it não há de que, não foi nada, não precisa agradecer *When he thanked me I said: "Think nothing of it".*
think of 1. lembrar-se de *I would rather live in America than anywhere else I could think of ...* -T/78. ♦ *Funny, I can't think of her name.* 2. achar, julgar, opinar *What do you think of Tennessee Williams' A Streetcar Named Desire in comparison to his other plays?* 3. pretender, tencionar *When are you thinking of going to the U.S.?* 4. pensar em, cogitar, imaginar, conceber *No one would think of disturbing the boss when he is in conference.* 5. considerar, dar atenção a *First of all, I've got my wife and kids to think of.*
think out refletir em, pensar bastante sobre; elaborar mentalmente, conceber, idear *Dianne had thought things out and knew exactly what she wished to say.* ⇒ **thought-out** cuidadosamente considerado, bem-planejado e organizado, criteriosamente elaborado *[James Joyce's Ulysses] ... is probably the most completely organized, thought-out work of literature since The Divine Comedy.* -FCT,96.
think over considerar cuidadosamente, refletir sobre, estudar *I'll think over your offer and let you have my decision tomorrow morning, OK? I'll think it over.*
think tank [gír] grupo de pesquisa intensa ou de pensadores, centro de investigação *The George C. Marshall Institute, a Washington think tank ...* -T/87. ♦ *... the Stanford Research Institute is one of America's largest and best-known think tanks.* -T/73.
think through refletir cuidadosamente em, ponderar sobre, analisar *... I have had to think through my own feelings with a thoroughness that has not been demanded before ...* -T/87.
think twice pensar melhor, considerar com mais cuidado *You had better think twice before you do that.*

think up idear, inventar, imaginar, planejar *... [Freud] retreated into his own private world to think up psychoanalysis all by himself.* -T/79.
THINKING put on one's thinking cap estudar cuidadosamente um problema a fim de solucioná-lo, pensar bastante sobre algo *Alan felt he must put on his thinking cap before he answered Mr. Anderson's question.*
wishful thinking crença naquilo que se deseja crer, crença baseada em desejos e não em fatos *[A New Delhi newspaper has said that India's new educational policy is] ... "steeped in wishful thinking rather than hardheaded realities".* -T/86. ♦ *A lot of this stuff [space travel] is wishful thinking, juvenile or adult.* -LJ,7.
THIN-SKINNED → **have a thick//thin SKIN**
THIS this is it chegou a hora, é agora, este é o momento *Well, this is it! You can't turn back now.*
THORN a thorn in one's side/flesh espinha atravessada na garganta *He'd been a constant thorn in the side of my predecessors ...* -TR,23.
THOROUGHGOING completo, perfeito, rematado, consumado, meticuloso *... unlike [H. L.] Mencken he [Edmund Wilson] is a thorough-going and consistent liberal.* -HDR,557.
THOUGHT give thought to considerar cuidadosamente, dar atenção a *[They] ... already had given the problem some thought. ...* -SWLR,1045. ♦ *I've never given it much thought.*
never give someone/something another/a second thought não pensar mais em, não mais dar atenção a *He never regretted what he had done or gave it a second thought.*
on second thought pensando bem, reconsiderando *At first I agreed with Ryle's plan, but on second thought I began to see many weaknesses in it.*

second thoughts mudança de idéia ou opinião após reconsideração *When she said that, I began to have second thoughts about our relationship.*
THOUGHT-OUT → **THINK out**
THOUGHT-PROVOKING estimulante, provocante, interessante *[Sex researchers William] Masters and [Virginia] Johnson have produced a tought-provoking inquiry into the sexual life of homosexuals.* -T/79.
THRALL in thrall sob o fascínio ou a influência (de), em estado de submissão; cativo, absorto *The orchestra was playing Gershwin's* An American in Paris *and the melody held me in thrall.*
THRASH thrash/thresh out/over discutir (problema, questão, assunto etc.) detalhadamente com vistas a uma conclusão, decisão etc. *... the Joint Chiefs of Staff meet regularly to thrash out their problems ...* -T/92. ♦ *... they wanted time to thresh out in private conferences the agenda for the summit.* -T/69.
THREAD hang by a thread estar por um fio, em condição crítica *After three days in the hospital, his life is still hanging by just a thread.*
THRESH thresh out/over → **THRASH out/over**
THRESHOLD on the threshold of no limiar de *... on the threshold of fundamental and far-reaching decisions ...* -T/66.
THROAT clear one's throat pigarrear, tossir para livrar-se de pigarro *He cleared his throat and hastened to change the subject.* -WPI,43.
cram/jam/ram/shove something down someone's throat [col] forçar alguém a aceitar (engolir) algo desagradável, indesejado etc., enfiar goela abaixo *Oppressed people have so many things jammed down their throats.*
fly at someone's throat atacar súbita e furiosamente *[They] ... were staunch friends as long as I can remember. Now they were flying at each other's throat.* -LB,16.

jump down someone's throat [col] retrucar violentamene, dar resposta malcriada *Every time I've opened my mouth today you've jumped down my throat.* -HWL,43.
stick in one's throat ser difícil ou desagradável dizer, não conseguir dizer *I tried to tell Rita how sorry I was but the words stuck in my throat.*
THROES in the throes of às voltas com, diante de ou no meio de (problema, dificuldade, agonia, decisão etc.) *... the company was in the throes of serious losses.* -T/66. ♦ *... in the throes of mid-life.* -T/87. ♦ *Carole was in the throes of a new romance.*
THROTTLE at full throttle a todo o vapor *... this elaborate and complex research program will continue at full throttle.* -T/87.
THROUGH all through durante (todo o período de) *All through his business career he proved to be highly competent in his work.*
be through ter concluído, encerrado (trabalho, atividade, hábito etc.) *I'm usually through at six, but today I have to work until seven.* ♦ *When you're through with that book, put it back on the shelf.*
be through with estar terminado, acabado, chegado ao fim (relacionamento, amizade etc.) *Gladys will be through with Al in another month or so, I'm telling you.* ♦ *I'm glad I'm through with you.*
through and through completamente, inteiramente, profundamente, de cabo a rabo *... he knows ... [C. M.] to be an honest man through and through.* -T/62. ♦ *Johnny had been walking in the rain and was wet through and through.*
THROW throw away jogar fora, descartar, desperdiçar *Don't throw away a good book like that.* ♦ *... carelessly and recklessly and for no good reason, Lieutenant Couzens had thrown away his life.* -FP,2.
⇒ **throwaway** descartável *Disposable razors are one thing, but will anyone buy a throwaway camera?* -T/87.

throw in 1. [col] associar-se, unir-se *Once you throw in with Joel Kelly you will never be independent again.* -HJ,25. 2. incluir (algo) como brinde, bônus etc. (em uma venda, negócio etc.), dar de quebra *If you buy a new car, they'll throw in thirty gallons of gas.* 3. encaixar, interpor, intercalar *He threw in a varied assortment of technical facts that gave the article a distinct, authoritative flavor.* -RE,93.

throw off 1. livrar-se de, lançar fora, rejeitar *The Declaration of Independence states, among other things, ... that the people retain the right to throw off a government which attempts to use arbitrary power in defiance of their will.* -SRE,26. ♦ *throw off a cold* 2. enganar, desorientar, iludir, frustrar, desviar a atenção de, fugir a, desconcertar *Don't be thrown off by his false promises.* 3. [col] fazer, produzir, escrever, compor etc. (algo) com rapidez e facilidade ou rotineiramente *It was really a poem, not something Sylvia had simply thrown off. It was a fine piece of writing, full of feeling, imagination, symbolism and meaning.*

throw on vestir (roupa) às pressas, jogar no corpo *Mark threw on his coat and hurried off to the airport.*

throw oneself at (someone/someone's head) tentar conseguir a afeição ou o amor de (um homem), tentar conquistar, oferecer-se a *We disapproved of the way Helen was throwing herself at Stephanie's brother at the party.*

throw out 1. descartar, atirar fora *He threw out many old books and magazines when he moved to a small apartment.* 2. rejeitar, recusar-se a aceitar *... the courts threw out the law as unconstitutional.* -RR,586. 3. fazer sair, expulsar, mandar embora *The police threw out the agitators who were annoying the speaker.* 4. sugerir, propor, expressar *She threw out a hint as to what we might do in this case.*

throw over abandonar, rejeitar *He ... has thrown over his girl of two years standing ...* -GD,163.

throw overboard livrar-se de, desfazer-se de, jogar fora *... [I would not] throw it [a rule] overboard every time it forced a tough choice on me.* -MD,60. ♦ *Glenn learned to throw his troubles overboard and accept life as it is.*

throw together 1. construir, fazer (algo) às pressas e a esmo *... homes thrown together anyhow to keep out the wet and cold.* -WA,155. ♦ *... my hastily thrown together shelter.* -RQ,48. 2. juntar, reunir, pôr (pessoas) em contato (geralmente por acaso) *... both father and son were thrown together in a desperate situation ...* -WS,228.

throw up 1. [col] vomitar *Each time Sean gets on a boat he feels that he's going to throw up.* 2. construir apressadamente, erigir às pressas *He passed a row of nine identical shacks thrown up by the railroad for construction workers ...* -OFW,37. 3. mencionar repetidamente (algo a alguém), jogar na cara *Don't keep throwing up old stories to me when you're angry with me.* 4. abandonar, desistir de, renunciar a *Without warning he [Janio Quadros] threw up the presidency in a tantrum and walked out.* -GJI,41. 5. apresentar, produzir, dar a conhecer *... Chou En-lai – a man as brilliant and ruthless as any the Communist movement has thrown up in this century ...* -T/78.

THROWBACK retrocesso, regressão; reversão ao passado *Williams said that the methods of news information being given to the press was a throwback to old times.* ♦ *[One of the new Mafia dons] ... is a throwback to the gun-crazy gangland bosses of the past ...* -T/92.

THRUST thrust on/upon impor, forçar *... we also recommend legislation to protect persons from having sexual materials thrust upon them without their consent ...* -RC,57.

THUMB all thumbs desajeitado, canhestro *She knew that she was shy and all thumbs ... -MG,21.* ♦ *He was all thumbs when he had to fix something around the house.*
green thumb habilidade especial para o cultivo de plantas *Mr. Passos' green thumb was famous in reference to orchids.*
stick out like a sore thumb [col] ficar muito evidente, ser muito óbvio *There's a flaw in your plan and it sticks out like a sore thumb.*
thumbs down//up; thumbs-down//-up rejeição, recusa, desaprovação//aceitação, aprovação *... the staff voted thumbs down. -T/86.* ♦ *... major-league baseball owners gave a thumbs-up to the $125 million sale of the Seattle Mariners [to a Japanese investment group] ... -T/92.*
thumb through folhear (revista, livro etc.) *She thumbed through the afternoon newspaper.*
turn thumbs down on recusar, rejeitar, desaprovar *Voters turn thumbs down on a referendum for economic reform. -T/87.*
under someone's thumb sob o domínio, autoridade, influência de *The director of the school likes to keep everyone under his thumb.*
twiddle one's thumb ficar inativo, à toa, cruzar os braços *While Gwen waited for Fred, she just sat on the sofa and twiddled her thumbs.*
THUMBNAIL muito pequeno, curto, breve, conciso *Jordan gave me a thumbnail description of the man they were looking for.*
THUNDER steal someone's thunder apropriar-se de (ou adaptar para seus propósitos) idéia, plano, argumento, invenção, método de ação etc. de adversário, concorrente, rival etc. antes que este o utilize, privando-o de seu devido mérito; fazer ou dizer algo que outra pessoa pretendia fazer ou dizer *He had planned to create a sensation by talking about the new plans for war, but the speaker before him stole his thunder.*

TICK on tick [col] a crédito, fiado *This store sells nothing on tick. All sales are cash.*
tick away/by passar, escoar-se (segundos, minutos, o tempo) *The minutes ticked by as he pondered the situation.* ♦ *... they stood around ... as the moments ticked away. -UL,6.*
tick off 1. enumerar, ticar, marcar com um tique, assinalar *He can tick off an impressive list of philosophers ... who he says have influenced his thought. -T/81.* 2. [gir] irritar, aborrecer *His silly remark really ticked me off.* 3. suceder-se, passar (segundo, minuto, o tempo) *He counted the seconds ticking off ... -SLS,273.* ♦ *... the days ticked off. -T/75.*
TICKET split//straight ticket em uma eleição geral, voto dividido, isto é, para candidatos de mais de um partido//voto exclusivo para os candidatos do mesmo partido *Brady is a loyal party member and always votes a straight Republican ticket.* ♦ *Yates is an independent voter and frequently votes a split ticket.*
the ticket [gir] a coisa certa, apropriada, necessária, desejada etc., o mais indicado *To keep the good life rolling in high gear, an annual income of $600,000 from trust funds totaling $30 million should be just the ticket. -T/67.* ♦ *You look great, Gloria. I can see you're keeping your weight down. That's the ticket!*
write one's own ticket impor condições, ditar, exigir, escolher o que mais lhe convém *You'll see someday why I want to be an engineer so badly ... They do all kinds of jobs ... A good civil engineer writes his ticket. -UL,13.* ♦ *... as in any contract, every point is up for negotiation. A publisher simply can't write its own ticket. -T/86.*
TICKLED tickled pink → **tickled to DEATH**
TIDE stem the tide deter a maré, opor resistência, refrear *Many scientists are trying to stem the tide of the AIDS epidemic.*
tide over ajudar a vencer ou transpor

(dificuldade, má situação financeira etc.), tirar de um aperto ... *there will be enough money to tide the company over until February ...* -T/84. ♦ *He was luckier in his two marriages to rich women, who helped to tide him over in tough times.* -T/73. ♦ *... she needed a snack to tide her over between lunch and dinner ...* -T/87.

turn the tide mudar o curso dos acontecimentos *The Battle of Bunker Hill turned the tide against the English in the American Revolution.*

TIDY tidy up arranjar(-se), pôr(-se) em ordem, (fazer) ficar arranjado, bonitinho *Let's tidy up before we leave.* ♦ *Let's tidy up the room.*

TIE tie down prender, restringir, sujeitar *Dailey feels somewhat tied down now that he has a wife and two children.* ♦ *... I'm an intern, and I'm pretty well tied down to the hospital.* -T/66.

tie in 1. ter ligação, relacionar-se, ligar-se, unir-se *He was suspected of being tied in with the gang.* ♦ *... sex is a pretty serious subject and one that ties in closely with our lives.* -T/86. ⇒ **tie-in** [col] relação, conexão *He is believed to have a tie-in with the Mafia.* 2. coadunar-se, condizer, corresponder, encaixar-se, coincidir *The information he gave us does not tie in with the facts.*

tie into [col] atacar furiosamente, partir para cima de *The small boy tied into the bigger one with gusto.*

tie one on → **HANG one on**

tie together unir, prender *The force that ties the solar system together is gravity.* -GH,37.

tie up 1. atar, amarrar, prender *She tied up the package.* ♦ *... the horses were tied up in the inner circle.* -CHT,38. 2. obstruir, impedir, bloquear, deter, reter *Meg was tied up for hours in the traffic jam.* ⇒ **tie-up** interrupção, parada, suspensão, obstrução temporária *... advising drivers on where ... and when ... to expect the worst tie-ups ...* -T/86. 3. manter ocupado, atarefado, tomar todo o tempo de *Mr. Ross will be tied up for the evening.* 4. associar(-se) a, unir(-se) intimamente a, relacionar(-se) com *He was a fool to tie up with that crooked lawyer.* ♦ *Hunt was tied up with a gang of international thieves.* ⇒ **tie-up** conexão, relação, envolvimento *Is there any tie-up between exercise and disease?* -T/66. 5. vincular, empatar, tornar inalienável (dinheiro, bens, propriedades) *All my money is tied up in investments.* ♦ *... most of ... [his] property was already tied up ...* -T/78.

TIGHTFISTED → **closefisted**

TIGHT-KNIT; TIGHTKNIT; TIGHTLY-KNIT; TIGHTLY KNIT 1. bem-organizado, bem-ordenado *a tightly knit company* ♦ *a tight-knit group* 2. bem-integrado e unido por laços afetivos *... tightly-knit family circles.* -TD,29. ♦ *... [a] tightly knit family ...* -T/74.

TIGHT-LIPPED taciturno, lacônico, pouco comunicativo *He was always a tight-lipped man.* ♦ *Quigley smiled in a tight-lipped way.* -DK,111.

TIGHTWAD [gír] pão-duro, avarento *Because Joe earned a good salary and never spent much money, everyone thought that he was a tightwad.*

TILT (at) full tilt a toda velocidade, com toda a força *... they heard the pounding of a horse running full tilt.* -SL,5. ♦ *... he said that he was going to work "at full tilt all the way".* -T/73.

TIME against time → **against the CLOCK**

ahead of time adiantadamente, antecipadamente, antes da hora *... he knew about the impending invasion ahead of time.* -T/78.

all the time continuamente, sem parar, a todo momento, sempre *... she talks all the time.* -T/61. ♦ *My head is sore; it hurts all the time.* -BRT,70.

at all times sempre, continuamente, constantemente *She must be under observation at all times.*

at a time de cada vez ... *I cannot talk of more than one thing at a time, with words threaded like beads on a string* ... -BN,14.

at one time em determinada ocasião, em certa época, antigamente *The simplest truths about common, ordinary, everyday things which nearly everyone knows today, each represented great discoveries at one time.* -FI,4.

at some other time → **(at) some other TIME**

at the same time 1. simultaneamente, ao mesmo tempo *Both letters arrived at the same time.* 2. contudo, todavia, não obstante *This thing can be very useful to us. At the same time, we've got to be extremely careful in dealing with it because it may also be dangerous.*

at the time nessa ocasião, oportunidade, naquele momento *I was working in New York at the time.*

at times às vezes *At times I think he's nuts.*

be a long time coming demorar muito para chegar *The money was a long time coming.* -T/78. ♦ *[In Thailand] Democracy could be a long time coming.* -T/92.

beat time marcar o compasso *[He was] ... beating time to the military marches with his cane* ... -SWLR,19.

before one's time anteriormente ao nascimento de uma pessoa; antes de alguém começar a viver, trabalhar etc. em algum lugar, antes da época de *World War II ended in 1945, long before my time.* ♦ *Angela worked for the company from 1987 to 1990, but that was before my time.*

behind the times antiquado, atrasado, fora de época, de moda ... *people who never seem to grasp the situation and are always behind the times.* -HGI,viii. ♦ ... *he is a generation or so behind the times* ... -T/63.

bide one's time aguardar uma oportunidade favorável *He merely bided his time and awaited his opportunity to take action.* -JJS,106. ♦ *[They]* ... *bided their time until orders came from Washington.* -T/87.

the big time [gír] o mais alto nível em qualquer profissão, ocupação, posto, cargo, atividade etc. ... *Joe Kennedy moved out of Boston into the big time of Wall Street* ... -T/60. ♦ *Hollywood was fame and fortune. Hollywood was "the big time".* -KA,107. ♦ *In 1971 he broke into the big time* ... -T/81. ⇒ **big-time** grande, importante, excelente, de primeira, de alto nível *At 22* ... *[Emerson Fittipaldi] left Brazil for Britain to break into big-time European racing.* -T/72. ♦ ... *the big-time financial world* ... -T/87. ♦ ... *big-time crime* ... -T/63.

by the time quando, no momento em que *By the time the skies cleared [after the tornado had passed], at least 59 people had been killed* ... -T/79. ♦ *By the time he was seventeen he had been in and out of jail several times...* -MJV, 6

do time [col] 1. cumprir pena na prisão *He did time in jail and in mental wards.* -T/77. 2. cumprir determinado tempo (como aprendiz, interno etc.) *A solid, working New York actor who did time with Joseph Papp's New York Shakespeare Festival and the Lincoln Center Repertory* ... -T/75.

fall on/upon bad/evil/hard times cair na pobreza, na rua da amargura, sofrer revés, infortúnio *[She was]* ... *the daughter of a socially impeccable Maryland family that had lately fallen on hard times* ... -T/66. ♦ *The movie musical has indeed fallen on hard times* ... -SLE,144. ♦ ... *companies temporarily fallen on bad times.* -GM,279.

(the) first//second etc. time around a primeira//segunda etc. vez (em que se tenta ou se empreende algo) *Tricks [i.e., special effects] that were hard first time around [in the movie* Star Wars*] were*

easy the second time [i.e., in The Empire Strikes Back*]* ... -T/80.
for some time to come por muito tempo ainda (futuramente) *... there will undoubtedly be unpleasant repercussions for some time to come.* -T/91.
for the time being por ora, por enquanto *All I can say for the time being ... is that you will have to go with us.* -WL,99.
from/since time immemorial → **TIME immemorial**
from time to time a intervalos, de tempo a tempo, de quando em quando *Although it has been a long time since we finished college, we still see each other from time to time.*
full time em tempo integral, durante horário integral *Marcia works full time at that job.* ♦ *... a serious nationwide effort to get women involved full time in politics.* -T/72. ⇒ **full-time** de horário ou tempo integral *a full-time job* ♦ *Those who cannot find regular full-time employment take whatever part-time or temporary jobs they can get.* -T/87. v. **PART-time**
hard times tempos difíceis, período penoso *Fear of hard times may be a growing incentive to save ...* -T/87.
have a bad/hard/rough/tough etc. time (of it) passar maus bocados, sofrer dissabores *You're giving me a very bad time, Mr. Agnew. I'm only trying to help you.* -GE,193. ♦ *... American women are having a harder time today than they were a few years ago.* -T/72. ♦ *He had a rough time of it in the army.*
have a good/high/wonderful time divertir-se, passar bons momentos *The boys and girls were laughing and having a good time.* ♦ *... he has a wonderful time getting what he wants.* -T/78.
have a time [col] 1. passar maus pedaços, ter dificuldades *She had a time trying to find out where his mother lives.* 2. passar bons momentos, divertir-se *The kids went on a picnic and had themselves a time.*

have the time of one's life [col] divertir-se imensamente *Hector, Victor, Paul and Octavius were playing hide-and-seek and were having the time of their lives.*
if I've told you once I've told you a hundred/thousand etc. times já lhe disse (isso) umas cem/mil etc. vezes *If I've told you that once, I must have told you that a hundred times. Never put off till tomorrow what you can do today!*
in good time a seu tempo, no momento adequado *... there were things he would have to tell Lem in good time ...* -PRT,28.
in less than no time; in next to no time = **in no TIME** *In next to no time Hercule Poirot had discovered the murderer.*
in no time (at all/flat) em um instante, rapidamente, mais que depressa *If you say the things we want to hear, you'll be out [of prison] in no time.* -T/86. ♦ *In no time at all I fell in love with her.* ♦ *In no time flat we became bitter enemies.*
in one's time no tempo de, na época de *I've seen a lot of good westerns in my time, but* Shane *and* The Searchers *were superb.*
in time 1. a tempo, em tempo, antes que seja tarde demais *I like to arrive in time to see the curtain go up on a stage play.* 2. com o passar do tempo, no futuro *In time he learned to speak German very well.* ♦ *Einstein had unshaken faith...that his Unified Field Theory would in time produce an explanation of the "atomic character of energy", and demonstrate the existence of a well-ordered universe.* -DR,192. 3. no ritmo, dentro do compasso *[He] ... paddled [the canoe] without effort ... and we [the other paddlers] kept in time with him.* -RQ,68. ♦ *They began to dance, whirling and shaking their hands in time to the music.*
it is about/high time já não é sem tempo, já é (era) hora, até que enfim *"It's about time you got here", he told his wife when she arrived.* ♦ *It's high time that the*

people stop crying depression and do something constructive to stop it.
keep (good) time 1. funcionar com precisão (relógio), mostrar a hora certa *My watch always keeps good time.* ♦ *A quartz clock keeps time with great accuracy.* 2. manter o ritmo, o compasso (ao cantar ou dançar) *[She] ... kept time to the music with a little tambourine.* -T/62.
keep up with the times modernizar-se, adaptar-se à época em que se vive *He keeps up with the times by reading* Time Magazine.
kill time matar o tempo, preencher o tempo, fazer hora *... he was just fooling around to kill time ...* -HG,58.
live on borrowed time ter ultrapassado a expectativa de vida, viver além do que se espera *Allan Quartermain said that as a hunter and safari guide in Africa for fifteen years, he had been living on borrowed time.*
long time no see [col] há quanto tempo (não nos vemos)! *"Long time no see", he said to his old army buddy who indeed he hadn't seen in many years.*
lose no time não perder tempo *[They] ... lost no time in enjoying their new riches.* -T/73.
make good/excellent etc. time viajar depressa, deslocar-se de um lugar para outro com rapidez *They would leave at seven sharp and they should make good time.* -RCT,20.
make time 1. ir ou viajar depressa *You'll have to make time to get there by six o'clock.* 2. [gir] convencer mulher a ter intimidade com, cantar *Joe's trying to make time with his new secretary.*
many a time → MANY a/an/another
many's the time → MANY's the
many times over muitas vezes, repetidamente *He is a millionaire many times over ...* -T/78. ♦ *The story of what happened that night would be told many times over in the years that followed.*

mark time 1. marcar passo *The soldiers marked time while the car passed by them.* 2. aguardar os acontecimentos, ficar na expectativa *We had to mark time while the director of the program searched for his notes.*
most of the time na maioria das vezes, quase sempre, freqüentemente *Most of the time now she just sits in the garden reading poetry.*
not any time soon não tão cedo, não dentro de pouco tempo *Waldo is not likely to be visiting us any time soon.*
not give someone the time of day [col] não dar a mínima atenção a, desconsiderar, desprezar *A couple of guys came around to see me ... but I didn't give them the time of day.* -AIM,74. v. **TIME of day**
once upon a time certa vez, era uma vez *Once upon a time there was a girl named Dorothy who dreamed she had gone to the wonderful land of Oz.*
on time 1. na hora exata, na hora indicada, no horário, pontualmente *Dunne was right on time for his appointment with the bank manager.* 2. a crédito *... many middle-class families buy on time ...* -WC,113.
pass the time of day trocar cumprimentos, saudar alguém *[He] ... was at his best, as he always was on Saturday evening, passing the time of day with the ranch women ...* -SG,7.
play for time ganhar tempo, tentar protelar (algo desagradável, inevitável etc.) *In the opinion of many political scientists the dictator's days are numbered and he is only playing for time.*
serve time = **do TIME** 1 *... Cole has served time for robbery and cocaine dealing.* -T/86. ♦ *... persons serving time in penal institutions as sex offenders.* -KAC,19.
(at) some other time em outra ocasião/hora *"I want to talk to you, McNally." "Some other time. It's late and I've got to go now."*

stall for time ganhar tempo *Lindon kept stalling for time and hoping that the police would arrive in time to save him from the gangsters.*

take one's time não se apressar, agir com calma *He took his time to answer, trying to guess at what was in the big man's mind.* -HJ,112.

take time 1. dar atenção, dedicar tempo *Few [travelers], if any, take time to appreciate the people [of East Africa].* -T/87. 2. levar tempo, demorar *Decisions and economic measures take time.* -T/91.

take time off ausentar-se do trabalho, folgar *[He] ... had taken time off from work to make the trip.* -T/87.

take time out fazer um intervalo, interromper suas atividades a fim de descansar, dedicar-se a outra coisa etc. *Perhaps she is too busy in New York to take time out for experiences.* -MG,379. ♦ *[He] ... took time out to go fishing ...* -T/73.

tell time saber (dizer) as horas *Some people have difficulty telling time when their watch has no numbers.*

this time around desta vez (em contraste com as anteriores) *This time around I'll pay for the drinks.*

time after time = TIME **and again** *Time after time my mother told me to stay off the lake when the ice was thin.*

time and (time) again muitíssimas vezes, repetidamente *Time and again he has expressed his dedication to the cause of world peace ...* -T/68. ♦ *... stumbling time and time again to the precipice of disaster ...* -T/87.

time and tide wait for no man o tempo e a maré não esperam por ninguém *You should never hesitate to grasp an opportunity that comes your way. Remember that time and tide wait for no man.*

time hangs heavy o tempo passa vagarosamente (principalmente quando não se tem nada a fazer) *... time hung heavy on his hands and he undertook to make some experiments ...* -UM,60.

time immemorial tempos remotos, tempos imemoriais, tempo antiqüíssimo *Since time immemorial poets and novelists have celebrated the diversity of woman ...* -T/72. ♦ *Wine has been a favorite drink from time immemorial.*

the time is ripe é chegada a hora *... felt the time was ripe on all sides for a sincere diplomatic push ...* -T/87.

the time is up o prazo (tempo concedido) está esgotado *He was done for. His time was up.* -MF,103.

time of day hora do dia *I didn't know what time of day it was because heavy clouds obscured the sky.* v. **not give the TIME of day**

time off folga, descanso *I have some time off tomorrow and I'm going fishing.*

time (hanging) on one's hands tempo disponível, tempo de sobra, ociosidade, período de indolência *I had time on my hands and her in my arms that night.* ♦ *... people have too much time on their hands – too much leisure.* -T/69.

time out intervalo, interrupção, suspensão, descanso *[Breakthrough, a movie, is a] Run-of-the-mill glory-drenched war story with time out for occasional romance.* -SSH,127. ♦ *We take time out for a short period at ten o'clock to have coffee.*

time out of mind = TIME **immemorial** *... a specifically "traditional" way of life that existed in Europe since "time out of mind" ...* -SE,xiii.

time was foi-se o tempo em que, bons tempos eram aqueles, era uma vez *Time was when I was quite a tennis enthusiast.* -CBC,25.

waste no time não perder tempo, agir rapidamente *When the bombs began to fall, they wasted no time getting out of the area.*

what time is it? que horas são? *"Do you know what time it is?" "No, what time is it?"*

when it came time quando chegou a hora *When it came time for college ... [he] filled* *out just one application – to Harvard.* -T/92.

TIME-HONORED de longa tradição, tradicional, venerado *It is a time-honored custom to have turkey for dinner on Thanksgiving Day in the U.S.*

TIME-OLD antiqüíssimo *... the time-old nightmare struggle for a daily existence.* -SV,8.

TINKER not give a tinker's damn/dam *I don't give a tinker's damn whether you go or stay.*
not worth a tinker's damn/dam sem nenhum valor, inútil *Your suggestion isn't worth a tinker's damn.*
tinker with ocupar-se com, mexer com, tentar consertar de maneira fútil, amadorística, inábil etc. *He likes to tinker with old clocks.* ♦ *Stop tinkering with that engine.*

TIP on/at the tip of one's tongue 1. na ponta da língua, a ponto de ser dito *It was on the tip of my tongue to tell Martha what I thought of her.* ♦ 2. a ponto de lembrar-se *The answer was on the tip of my tongue but I couldn't put it into words.*
tip off [col] avisar, informar *... the victim's father tipped off the cops ...* -LMC,25. ♦ *He tipped me off to something I hadn't noticed.* ⇒ **tip-off** aviso, informação *The FBI agents acted on a tip-off and arrested the spies.*
the tip of the iceberg a ponta do *iceberg*; a parte visível – geralmente pequena – de algo cuja extensão ou implicação total se desconhece *Increasingly, it appears that the AIDS cases so far reported around the world are only the tip of the iceberg.* -T/86.

TIRE flat tire pneu furado *I had two flat tires on my trip to Black Rock.*

TIRED tired out exausto *Don't make so much noise, children. Your father's tired out from a hard day's work.*

TO to and fro para cá e para lá, de um lado para o outro *... the terrible Minotaur [of Greek mythology], pacing to and fro in the labyrinth built to cage him.* -CJM,20.

TO-BE futuro, que logo será, que está por vir ou acontecer [posposto ao substantivo] *Sean's bride to-be is a lovely lass from the Scottish Highlands.*

TO-DO [col] rebuliço, alvoroço *There was a great to-do at the meeting last night.*

TOE on one's toes [col] pronto para a ação, atento, alerta *Gene Kelly once said that "you have to be on your toes when you dance with Fred Astaire".*
step/tread on someone's toes desagradar alguém, pisar nos calos de *Don't step on his toes. He's very influential and may help us if we approach him in the right manner.* ♦ *I don't like to tread on people's toes but I'll do what has to be done.*
turn up one's toes [gir] esticar as canelas, morrer *We had expected him to die last week, but he finally turned up his toes this Friday.*

TOEHOLD ponto de apoio, base, escora, esteio *[By the afternoon of June 6, 1944, the day the invasion of France began in World War II] ... the Americans had a toehold on two beaches [in Normandy] and the British on a third ...* -SWLR,1348.

TOKEN by the same token pela mesma razão, da mesma forma, conseqüentemente *As far as my work was concerned, she was my most honest and intelligent critic. By the same token, she was the most helpful.* -CBC,16.

TOLL take a/its toll causar perda, dano, sofrimento etc., exigir alto tributo, fazer pagar caro *Epidemics have taken a great toll of lives in past generations.* -KR,1. ♦ *... the years in exile have clearly taken their toll on Sakharov's health ...* -T/87.

TOM peeping Tom *voyeur* *The peeping Tom sneaked up to the woman's house and watched her through the bathroom window as she took a bath.*
Tom Collins bebida preparada com gim, ou vodca, uísque etc., soda, suco de limão

ou lima e açúcar *Mitch ordered a whisky and soda and I ordered a Tom Collins.*

(every) Tom, Dick and Harry qualquer um, todo o mundo, fulano, sicrano e beltrano *Do you want to look like every Tom, Dick and Harry with those sloppy blue jeans?*

TOMORROW like there is/was no tomorrow sem se preocupar, sem pensar no futuro *That night they made love like there was no tomorrow.*

tomorrow is another day amanhã é outro dia, novas oportunidades surgirão *Don't give up hope. Remember that tomorrow is another day.*

TONE set the tone estabelecer padrão, moda, estilo, atitude, espírito, tendência geral *... certain classes of our society ... which are socially dominant and which set the tone for others.* -HR,13. ♦ *... groups that set the tone of aristocratic life ...* -BCS,38.

tone down suavizar, abrandar, moderar *Tone down your voice when you speak on the telephone.* ♦ *He refused to tone down his criticisms.*

TONGUE bite one's tongue esforçar-se ao máximo para não dizer o que pensa, conter-se *His remark was so rude that I had to bite my tongue to refrain from telling him what I thought of him.*

bite one's tongue off [precedido de *could*] arrepender-se de ter dito algo *I could have bitten off my tongue as soon as the words came out of my mouth.*

find one's tongue recobrar a fala *Elvira found her tongue and managed to tell us all that had happened.*

hold one's tongue parar de falar, calar-se *Voices of the past rang clear, ordering me to hold my tongue.* -FLF,46. ♦ *Hold your tongue. Don't say another word.*

keep a civil tongue in one's head falar com educação, com respeito, dobrar a língua *"You keep a civil tongue in your head", said Ouida angrily.* -TM,87.

lose one's tongue ficar acanhado, embaraçado, não saber o que dizer *Have you lost your tongue now? Come, answer me.* -VR,31.

on everyone's tongue; on every tongue na boca do povo *[In the 1930s and 1940s] ... formless clichés concerning his [Sigmund Freud's] defects as man and scientist were on every tongue.* -NB,9.

speak with forked tongue mentir, ser de duas caras *He speaks with forked tongue and cannot be trusted.*

stick one's tongue out mostrar a língua *... Linda still sticks her tongue out at grownups.* -T/77.

(with) (one's) tongue in (one's) cheek (com) ironia, zombaria ou insinceridade *He had tongue in cheek when he said that.* ♦ *When he said he had quit drinking for ever, he had his tongue in his cheek.* ♦ *Some [of the magazine articles on UFO's] were written with tongue in cheek ...* –RE,47. ⇒ **tongue-in-cheek** irônico, zombeteiro *... Superman II, a stylish ... tongue-in-cheek movie ...* -T/81.

tongue twister palavra ou frase difícil de pronunciar *One of my brother's favorite tongue twisters was: "She sells sea-shells on the seashore".*

watch one's tongue tomar cuidado com o que diz *You'd better watch your tongue.*

TONGUE-IN-CHEEK → **(with) (one's) TONGUE in (one's) cheek**

TONGUE-LASH [col] repreender severamente, desancar *... his younger brothers ... tongue-lashed him last year in private family council.* -T/60. ⇒ **tongue-lashing** recriminação, descompostura *... she'd given him a tongue-lashing over the death of her uncle.* -HWR,135.

TONGUE-TIED incapaz de falar devido a acanhamento, timidez etc., mudo, sem fala *When he was invited to join a convivial group at a table or bar he was tongue-tied and embarrassed.* -DJ,85.

TOOL tools of one's/the trade qualquer coisa necessária ao exercício da profissão ou atividade de *Dictionaries and thesauri are the tools of his trade.*

TOOTH armed to the teeth armado até os dentes ... *twelve or thirteen men armed to the teeth ...* -CEB,48.
buck teeth dentes ressaídos, dentuça *Horace Tillinghast has a large mouth and buck teeth.*
cut one's teeth on → **cut one's EYE-TEETH on**
cut teeth começar a ter dentes, nascerem os dentes a *The baby is cutting teeth and cries most of the time.*
false teeth dentadura postiça *Mr. Gibson wears false teeth.*
fly in the teeth of → **fly in the FACE of**
get/sink one's teeth into [col] ocupar-se plenamente com, concentrar-se totalmente em algo que constitua um desafio real, entregar-se a uma tarefa etc. com vigor e entusiasmo *Actors are always saying how much they like sinking their teeth into a role.* -T/92. ♦ *This is a challenging job, something Sawyer can really get his teeth into.*
in the teeth of 1. frontalmente contra, enfrentando, fazendo face a *They kept sailing in the teeth of the storm.* 2. a despeito de, em oposição direta a, em desafio a, contrariando ... *to defend traditional values in the teeth of outraged demonstrations.* -T/91.
kick in the teeth [col] 1. desacolher, repudiar, desamparar, negar apoio *Whenever a man gets sentimental and schmaltzy about a girl, she kicks him in the teeth.* -WCN,288. 2. desprezo, repúdio, rejeição, insulto *Instead of praise, she got a kick in the teeth.*
lie in/through one's teeth mentir descaradamente *For the first time their eyes met, really met, and it struck Lou that Anita was lying through her teeth.* -EJ,317.
long in the tooth já maduro, entrado em anos, velho *I'm getting a little long in the tooth to be an ingénue ...* -T/78.
pick one's teeth palitar os dentes *He's the kind of man who picks his teeth in public.*

pull someone's teeth tirar o poder de, deixar ineficaz, impotente *The reactionaries may pull their [of liberal-line reformist governments] teeth ...* -GJI,605.
set one's teeth cerrar os dentes, preparar-se para enfrentar algo difícil, desagradável etc. *Arthur set his teeth against the intense pain.*
set someone's teeth on edge irritar, exasperar, incomodar, causar arrepio ... *the heavy smell of decay [was] setting his teeth on edge ...* -MRI,20. ♦ *When someone rubs his fingers over a balloon, it sets my teeth on edge.*
show one's teeth mostrar hostilidade, irritação, zangar-se *Many a timid dog seems fierce by showing his teeth to strangers.*
sweet tooth [col] predileção por doces, por açúcar *Brazilians have a sweet tooth and a habit of drinking frequent cups of coffee half-filled with sugar ...* -WC,30.
teeth força cominatória, meios eficazes de impor, de dar força (a uma lei) ... *police have increased radar patrols to give the rules some teeth.* -T/92.
tooth and nail com unhas e dentes, desesperadamente, de todas as maneiras possíveis *A mother will fight tooth and nail to help her children become successful.* ♦ *We are going to go after them tooth and nail.* -T/87.
TOP at the top of one's voice/lungs à plena voz, com toda a força dos pulmões *One afternoon I was singing at the top of my voice ...* -RLI,19. ♦ *She was shouting at the top of her lungs.*
blow one's top/lid/stack [gir] ficar furioso, zangar-se extremamente *Oliver blew his top when they told him what had happened.* ♦ *Don't blow your stack when I give you the bad news.*
come out on top [col] sair-se bem, vitorioso *A lot of Egyptian politicians have fallen by the wayside during the Sadat era, but Mubarak has come out on top.* -T/81.
from top to bottom de alto a baixo, inteiramente *The police searched the apart-*

ment from top to bottom for clues that might lead to the murderer.

from top to toe da cabeça aos pés *Joe looked at the girl from top to toe.*

off the top [gir] da renda bruta, do total *When they made that deal Greene's lawyer got 10 percent off the top.*

off the top of one's head [col] de improviso, sem pensar muito, sem preparação prévia *[He] ... must be talking off the top of his head.* -T/63.

on top of 1. sobre, no ponto mais alto de *She put the new book on top of the others.* 2. [col] além de *On top of the many accusations that had been made against him, it was later disclosed that he was also involved with the Mafia.* 3. [col] muito próximo de, contíguo a *The car was picking up speed and was almost on top of the two boys.* 4. exercendo domínio total sobre (algo, situação etc.) no controle de *Vaughn always seems to be on top of his job.*

on top of the world eufórico, experimentando sensação de perfeito bem-estar, felicíssimo *... he is ... feeling on top of the world ...* -T/87. ♦ *He's on top of the world now and doesn't need your support.*

sleep like a top/log dormir como uma pedra *Even though bombs were dropping all around him, he slept like a top.* ♦ *The snow stopped, the wind dropped, the tent was warm, and we must have slept like logs ...* -RK,246.

top off completar, rematar, dar um toque final, encerrar com chave de ouro *The conductor topped off the musical program with a superb rendition of Stravinsky's The Fire-Bird.* ♦ *Mrs. Macgillicuddy prepared her husband's dinner and topped it off with his favorite dessert.*

top out atingir a altura máxima, parar de crescer *... the aspiring basketball star topped out at 5 ft 7 in.* -T/77. ♦ *... the corn is already seven feet high in spots and not close to topping out.* -T/86.

TOP-DRAWER do mais alto nível, de primeira classe, excelente, importantíssimo *Simone Signoret gave a top-drawer performance in the movie* Room at the Top. ♦ *No cocktail party can be considered top-drawer without at least one reference to the "myth of the vaginal orgasm"...* -T/72.

TOPFLIGHT [col] da melhor qualidade, excelente, superior *... a topflight scientist ...* -T/60. ♦ *... a topflight job.* -T/60. ♦ *... topflight weapons ...* -T/87.

TOP-LEVEL [col] do mais alto nível, da categoria mais elevada *[Many of our employees] ... are not reaching top-level jobs ... because they cannot write brief, well-constructed, and understandable reports.* -SN,5. ♦ *... top-level law school graduates ...* -T/79.

TOP-NOTCH; TOPNOTCH [col] de primeira linha, de grande conceito, excelente *M.I.T. [Massachusetts Institute of Technology] is the top-notch engineering school in the U.S.* ♦ *He is a topnotch businessman ...* -T/76.

TOP-RANK; TOP-RANKING do mais alto nível ou importância *He [Norbert Wiener] was a top-rank mathematician who fathered a new branch of science [cybernetics] ...* -T/64.

TOPSY-TURVY confuso, atrapalhado, em desordem, de pernas para o ar *Topsy-turvy times ...* -T/87. ♦ *... topsy-turvy politics ...* -T/78. ♦ *The world is topsy-turvy nowadays.*

TORCH carry a/the torch 1. empreender uma cruzada *He once carried the torch for industrial reform in the U.S.* 2. amar (principalmente sem ser correspondido) *... the author confesses to carrying a torch for the novel's heroine ...* -T/86.

torch song [gir] canção sentimental de amor não-correspondido *In the early thirties, Libby Holman used to sing* Body and Soul, *the big torch song of the era.* ⇒ **torch singer** cantor de canções sentimentais, de *blues* *In* Love Me or Leave Me *Doris Day played Ruth Etting, the torch singer of the 1920s.*

TORN be torn between (A and B) ter de fazer uma escolha difícil *Gus was torn between his love for his wife and the passion for the girl he had met at Waikiki Beach.*
torn by dilacerado, despedaçado etc.; torturado, atormentado, dividido etc. *The country had been torn by tribal violence.*
♦ *He was torn by conflicting impulses.*

TOSS toss off 1. fazer, escrever, compor, proferir etc. rápida e facilmente *... at 15 ... [Frederick Loewe] tossed off ... a popular song called* Kathrin ... -T/60. ♦ *... he tossed off a bawdy joke.* -T/87. 2. beber rapidamente, beber de um gole *[He] ... tossed off the rest [of the whiskey] in his glass and set it down.* -SJS,64.

TOSS-UP; TOSSUP caso de probabilidades idênticas; incerteza, questão duvidosa *In pre-Hitlerian Germany it was often a tossup whether a restless youth would join the Communists or the Nazis.* -HETB,25.

TOTE tote bag sacola de lona, plástico, pano etc. aberta na parte superior, usada para transportar compras, pacotes, roupas, sapatos etc. *They had suitcases, attaché cases, plastic tote bags. They looked almost like tourists.* -T/87.

TOUCH be/get in touch with estar/entrar em contato com, comunicar-se com *[The Etruscans] ... were highly civilized and were always in close touch with Greece, both commercially and culturally.* -WJ,38.
keep in touch manter-se em contato *Although she moved to Australia many years ago, Antoinette has always kept in touch with her relatives and friends in Brazil.*
lose one's touch perder a habilidade, perder o jeito, decair *What's the matter? Are you losing your touch?*
lose touch perder contato *The psychiatrist said that the patient was losing touch with reality.*

make a touch [gir] pedir dinheiro emprestado, dar uma facada *I try to avoid meeting him because he always makes a touch for twenty dollars and never repays it.*
not touch someone/something não querer ter nada a ver com, não querer saber de, não querer meter-se em *... to invest in business that other banks often would not touch ...* -T/62.
out of touch sem contato, sem comunicação *Many politicians are out of touch with the people they are supposed to be serving.*
♦ *... he seems to be still out of touch with the most basic kind of emotional reality.* -T/73.
soft touch [gir] pessoa facilmente persuadida, especialmente a dar ou emprestar dinheiro *Let's ask Harry for some money. He's a soft touch.*
touch and go situação crítica, perigosa, incerta, na qual o menor abalo pode provocar comoção, desastre etc. *Nicole had been in an automobile accident and for months it was touch and go but finally she had a complete recovery.*
touch down pousar, descer, aterrissar, tocar o solo (avião, espaçonave) *... a 727 ... touched down in Great Falls, Montana because of a pressurization problem ...* -T/87. ♦ *On the momentous day when [American astronauts] Armstrong and Aldrin touched down on the moon, all the world seemed to stand in awe.* -T/79.
⇒ **touchdown** aterrissagem, pouso *The touchdown was a bit rough ...* -T/85.
touch off 1. provocar, causar, desencadear, iniciar *The discovery of gold in the Pike's Peak [Colorado] country touched off the inevitable conflict [between white men and the Cheyenne and Arapaho Indians].* -BR,656. 2. fazer explodir, detonar *... the Japanese touched off the powder magazine at Pearl Harbor.* -TB,15.
touch on/upon aludir a, referir-se a, mencionar ligeiramente *[He] ... had delivered a speech ... that touched on the three is-

sues he believes are of paramount importance ... -T/81.

touch up   retocar, reconstituir, corrigir *Sheila touched up her makeup before she went out on the street.* ♦ *With a little touching up on the outside the house will look a hundred percent better.*

TOUGH   tough out [col] suportar estoicamente ... *[President] Reagan and his top aides try to tough out the scandal ...* -T/87.

TOUGH-MINDED   realista, prático, astuto, sagaz, obstinado, que não se deixa influenciar facilmente, insensível, férreo *... candidates and parties must come up with specific, tough-minded solutions to well-perceived problems.* -T/87. ♦ *He is a tough-minded, chillingly efficient young man ...* -T/73.

TOW   in tow   1. (conduzindo) atrás de si, (trazendo) em sua companhia *The old hen came along the road with her chicks in tow.* ♦ *[He came] ... without his wife in tow.* -T/87. 2. a reboque, rebocado *The truck came by with my father's car in tow.*

TOWEL   throw in the towel → **throw in the SPONGE**
towel off   enxugar-se com uma toalha *... I came naked out of the bathroom, toweled off and powdered.* -CG,133.

TOWER   tower above/over   elevar-se sobre, estar sobranceiro, salientar-se, destacar-se, sobressair a *Danny towers above all the other kids in his class.* ♦ *[He] ... towered over the commissars as the most influential figure in Poland ...* -T/81.

TOWN   hit town   chegar à cidade *He always hits town just before Carnival begins.*
(out) on the town   [gir] divertindo-se com os entretenimentos noturnos – teatros, boates, bares etc. – que uma cidade grande tem para oferecer *[They were] ... out for a night on the town.* ♦ *... in New York he ... went on the town with [a friend] ...* -T/61.
paint the town (red) [gir] pintar o sete, divertir-se, fazer uma farra *If my candidate wins, I'm going to paint the town.* ♦ *When Hank was released from the army, he painted the town red.*

TOY   toy with   entreter-se com (idéia etc.), considerar sumariamente; brincar com, distrair-se com, ocupar-se com *They had been toying with the idea of opening a branch office in Rome.* ♦ *As a boy, he toyed with suicide ...* -T/91. ♦ *Harriet sat on the sofa toying with her bracelet.*

TRACE   kick over the traces   indisciplinar-se, rebelar-se, abandonar a compostura, o comedimento etc. *When in the army and in a foreign land, most soldiers kick over the traces.*
trace back   seguir o rastro, a pista, a trilha de; descobrir as origens (de alguém/algo) investigando o passado; atribuir *... all energy or power with which we come in contact can be traced back to the sun.* -FI,8. ♦ *Lew's stuttering problem, his parents suspect, can be traced back to a childhood incident.*

TRACK   fast track   [col] conduta, comportamento ou trajetória que leva ao sucesso rápido *[He] ... roared onto the fast track as a future presidential candidate.* -T/92. ♦ *He's ... no novice on the celebrity circuits, both the Hollywood and social fast tracks.* -T/87.
in one's tracks   no lugar exato onde alguém se encontra; imediatamente, abruptamente, de repente *Joe stopped in his tracks and looked squarely at his brother.* -CHT,38. ♦ *... the stark terror on the child's face stopped Welles in his tracks.* -SW,10.
inside track   [col] posição ou situação vantajosa; precedência, primazia *[He] ... seemed to have the inside track to the presidency.* -T/60.
keep//lose track of   não perder de vista, acompanhar o desenvolvimento ou o curso de//perder de vista, perder informação sobre, perder consciência ou noção de, perder contato com *ATIC [Air Technical Intelligence Center] is responsible for*

keeping track of all foreign aircraft and guided missiles. -RE,20. ♦ *Keeping track of the changes that are transforming the American economy isn't easy.* -T/92. ♦ *He had lost track of time.* ♦ *I lost track of him once for a couple of years ...* -LRT,47.

make tracks [col] ir-se embora, sair apressadamente, fugir *When the storm began we made tracks for home.*

off the beaten track → **off the beaten PATH**

off the track fora do assunto, da questão *You're getting off the track. That's not what we're talking about.*

on the right//wrong track certo, correto//errado, em erro; no rumo certo//errado *With the confidence of a man who knows that he is on the right track, Freud continued to explore man's mind by the method of psychoanalysis.* -HC,16. ♦ *You're on the wrong track if you think I'm going to do that.*

on the track of seguindo, perseguindo, no encalço de *Two FBI agents were on the track of the spy.*

on track nos trilhos, no rumo certo, correto, sem erro *... the Administration's diplomacy was on track ...* -T/78. ♦ *... officials have shied away from predicting when the [space] program would get back on track ...* -T/87.

throw off the track despistar *We made a false trail so that anyone that might be following us would be thrown off the track.*

track down 1. procurar até encontrar *The TV man is trying to track down the defect in my new set.* 2. perseguir até prender, capturar *In Elia Kazan's movie* Panic in the Streets, *Richard Widmark tracks down the murderers of a man suffering from pneumonic plague.*

track up deixar pegadas, sujar o chão *The children came in the kitchen and tracked up the floor with their muddy shoes.*

TRADE by trade de profissão, de ofício (com referência a trabalho que requer habilidade, arte mecânica etc.) *Sebastian was a carpenter by trade.* ♦ *... a professional dancer by trade ...* -T/72.

ply one's trade trabalhar em, ocupar-se de, exercer (ocupação, ofício) *[He] ... plies his trade in a restaurant ...* -T/80.

trade in dar o automóvel, eletrodoméstico etc. usado como parte do pagamento do novo que está sendo adquirido *Keith trades in his old car as part payment on a new model every two years.* ⇒ **trade-in** automóvel, eletrodoméstico etc.. usado entregue como parte do pagamento na aquisição de um modelo novo *He always uses his old car as a trade-in for a new one.*

trade off dar, ceder algo em troca de outra coisa *... an eventual "grand compromise" that would trade off defense for offense ...* -T/86. ⇒ **trade-off** cessão ou troca de uma coisa por outra *France and the U.S. made some trade-offs at their summit meeting.*

trade on aproveitar-se de, explorar, tirar partido de *Adrian traded on my friendship to get money out of my personal friends.*

TRAFFIC traffic jam congestionamento de trânsito *[They were] ... snarled in a huge traffic jam on their way home.* -T/78.

TRAIL blaze a/the trail/way desbravar, abrir caminho, explorar, descobrir, ser pioneiro *Negroes helped blaze trails in America, sometimes as slaves but often as scouts ...* -T/63. ♦ *John Fitzgerald Kennedy hoped to blaze a trail to new glory for his country.* ⇒ **trailblazer** desbravador, pioneiro *Daniel Boone was one of the first trailblazers.* ⇒ **trailblazing** inovador, precursor, vanguardeiro *[William Faulkner's novels* The Sound and the Fury *and* As I Lay Dying*] ... are certainly among his most violent in theme and trailblazing in technique.* -FCT,207.

(hot) on the trail of seguindo (de perto), no encalço de, na pista de *[In* Edge of Eternity, *Cornel Wilde plays] ... a deputy* *sheriff hot on the trail of a murderer ...* -SSH,304.

trail hand vaqueiro *In the old days, a trail hand was a cowboy hired to help drive cattle over the long trails leading from Texas.*

trail off diminuir, decrescer, cessar gradualmente *"Would you excuse me if I" – Her voice trailed off, and she turned away.* -UJ,33.

TRAILER trailer park/camp/court área de estacionamento para *trailers* provida de água, eletricidade etc. *We found many trailer parks on our trip to the Colorado Rockies.*

TRAIN catch/take a train pegar um trem *Hurry up! I have to catch a train at 12:40.*

through train trem direto, que não requer baldeação *This is a through train from Boston to New York and doesn't stop at New Haven.*

train of thought encadeamento de pensamentos, seqüência de raciocínios *... what Stan had just said started a train of thought ...* -CJC,120. ♦ *The doorbell rang and interrupted my train of thought.*

TRASH white trash [pej] pessoa branca e pobre do sul dos EUA; os brancos pobres do sul dos EUA *After the Civil War, much of the white trash became powerful politically in the South.*

TRAVEL travel light viajar com o mínimo de bagagem *Arlene was traveling light and her bag contained everything she would need.* ♦ *He travels light and takes one small suitcase from coast to coast.* -T/78.

TREASURE (treasure) trove descoberta valiosa, achado precioso *Archaeologists uncover a treasure trove of Mayan history.* -T/92. ♦ *... the commission has come across a treasure trove of material that gives its report the potential for being truly explosive ...* -T/87. ♦ *... a trove of information ...* -T/92.

TREAT Dutch treat [col] costume de cada pessoa pagar por si (refeição, festim, bebida, divertimento etc.) *He said to his friend, "I'm sorry but this will have to be a Dutch treat. I'm broke".*

my treat eu pago, a despesa é por minha conta *What do you say to some hot dogs and root beer? My treat.* -CGT,11.

stand treat pagar a despesa *Who's going to stand treat at the ice cream bar?*

the treat is on me eu pago as despesas *Let's go to a good restaurant. The treat's on me.*

treat someone to 1. convidar para (comer, beber e/ou divertir-se); pagar a despesa de; obsequiar, oferecer, presentear (algo a alguém) *Bruce treated Ann to dinner at a first-class restaurant.* ♦ *Our parents treated us to exciting vacations in Atlantic City ...* -FLF,26. ♦ *He treated himself to a cold beer.* 2. oferecer ou proporcionar algo agradável, satisfação, prazer, [às vezes com ironia] etc. *[He] ... treated us to a brief lesson in morality.*

TREE bark up the wrong tree bater em porta errada, empregar mal seus esforços *He was barking up the wrong tree when he thought Mitch would help him.*

up a tree [col] em dificuldades, no mato sem cachorro, sem saber o que fazer *Boyd was up a tree when the police found him at the scene of the crime.*

TRIAL bring to trial levar a julgamento, colocar no banco dos réus *To bring the Emperor [Hiroito] to trial [after the Japanese surrender in World War II] would provoke guerrilla warfare throughout the nation and perpetuate a military government.* -TJ,989.

on trial 1. em experiência, (sendo) submetido a prova, teste etc. *This new TV set has been bought on trial so that I can return it if I don't like it.* 2. em julgamento *He testified in German courts on behalf of academics on trial for their political views.* -SC,31. ♦ *Searched and fingerprinted as a common criminal ... he was subsequently put on trial.* -KRI,589.

stand trial ser submetido a julgamento ... *it is more or less certain that the boy, Chavez, will stand trial.* -MD,66.
trial and error ensaio e erro, método das tentativas *[He] could not learn by observing the masters. He learned by trial and error.* -DJ,4.
TRICE in a trice em um instante, em um abrir e fechar de olhos *In a trice the boy was gone.*
TRICK dirty trick ursada, ato traiçoeiro, deslealdade, sujeira, falseta *Unlike the Greek and Elizabethan heroes, the Hemingway hero does not understand his fate. It's simply a dirty trick.* -T/61. ♦ *He played a dirty trick on his friend.*
do the trick → do the JOB
every trick in the book todas as artimanhas, estratagemas etc. (para conseguir algo) *Dinah used every trick in the book to get what she wanted.* ♦ *Beware of that guy because he knows every trick in the book.*
not miss a trick [col] estar sempre atento, perceber tudo, aproveitar as oportunidades *Clyde never misses a trick when it comes to thinking up new ways to trap tourists.*
play a trick pregar uma peça *Events had played a very bad trick on people ...* -GJKT,184.
the tricks of the trade 1. os macetes da profissão, técnica, habilidade *To succeed in any profession you've got to know the tricks of the trade.* 2. maneira astuta, ardilosa, trapaceira, fraudulenta etc. de agir para conseguir algo ... *former agents of the Central Intelligence Agency and private U.S. companies that have long supplied the CIA with such tricks of the trade as gun silencers, concealable explosives [etc.] ...* -T/81.
turn the trick = do the JOB
TRIED-AND-TRUE testado e aprovado, comprovado, válido ... *tried-and-true merchandising strategies.* -PVH,200. ♦ *... O'Brien applied all his tried and true*

organizational techniques to *[John] Kennedy's winning campaign against Republican Richard Nixon.* -T/61.
TRIGGER quick on the trigger → quick on the DRAW
trigger off provocar, iniciar, causar, ativar, desencadear *The speaker's harsh words triggered off an immediate reaction from the audience.*
TRIGGER-HAPPY [col] 1. que usa armas de fogo de maneira irresponsável, que aperta o gatilho à mínima provocação ou sem pensar duas vezes *Be careful of him if he's carrying a gun. He's very trigger-happy.* ♦ *... a trigger-happy gunman.* -T/86. 2. agitado, exaltado, agressivo *Eddie gets trigger-happy when there is any unusual excitement.*
TRIGGERMAN; TRIGGER MAN [col] pistoleiro, matador ... *a trigger man ... entered the restaurant ... and began sizing up what he took to be his victims.* -T/72.
TRIM in trim em forma, em boas condições físicas *The President keeps in trim by swimming and doing gymnastics each morning.*
TRIP bad trip [gír] experiência negativa de pânico, alucinação, depressão etc. causada por ingestão de droga; qualquer experiência negativa ou infeliz *Tim has never been the same since his bad trip with LSD.* ♦ *For many college students, LSD became a bad trip.* -T/86.
go on a trip viajar *I'm going on a trip to Paris this summer.*
round trip viagem de ida e volta *The round trip will cost you $237.* ♦ ⇒
round-trip de ida e volta ... *round-trip tickets ...* -T/89.
take a trip viajar *He took a long, leisurely trip to La Jolla ...* -SJST,16.
trip up 1. (fazer) tropeçar *Joe tripped up on the rug and nearly fell.* ♦ *A loose board on the floor tripped him up.* 2. urdir armadilha, fazer cair ou pegar no laço, enredar com perguntas hábeis *I had no*

fear of being tripped up in cross-examination. -T/73.
TROLLEY off one's trolley [gír] maluco *Are you off your trolley?*
TROOP troop in/off/out mover-se, entrar, sair etc. (em bando) *He turned back into the house. The others trooped in after him.* -BT,196. ♦ *... the more energetic and ambitious girls trooped off to the cities, many of them to the North.* -DDT,431.
TROOPER swear like a trooper xingar, proferir obscenidades *She looked like a perfect lady but on occasion could swear like a trooper.*
TROT trot out [col] exibir, mostrar, apresentar, submeter à apreciação *[Movie] Director Tony Richardson is trotting out a fifth version [of* The Charge of the Light Brigade*].* -T/67.
TROUBLE ask/look for trouble = ASK for it *Well, there's no sense in asking for trouble.* -SRU,75.
borrow trouble preocupar-se desnecessariamente ou prematuramente *Let things take care of themselves. It's silly to borrow trouble.*
get in/into trouble encrencar-se, meter-se em dificuldades, em apuros *... when impulsive behavior gets the person into trouble ... he learns how dangerous the instincts are.* -HC,67.
go to the trouble; take the trouble dar-se ao trabalho, inconveniência, aborrecimento etc. *That robust literary charlatan Frank Harris went to the trouble of inventing all kinds of elaborate sexual adventures to confess ...* -T/81. ♦ *He took the trouble to find out where the girl worked.*
in trouble 1. aflito, em dificuldades, em apuros *... Sophocles and Tolstoy told of tragedies and of people in trouble.* -CMSS,7. 2. grávida (jovem solteira) *Just don't go getting any nice girl in trouble.* -TM,104.
look for trouble → ask for TROUBLE
make/cause trouble causar problemas, desordem, distúrbio, provocar briga *If you make any trouble I'll call the police.* ⇒ **troublemaker** indivíduo encrenqueiro, brigão, desordeiro *Carl is a troublemaker. Avoid him.*
put to the trouble causar aborrecimento, incômodo, inconveniência, trabalho etc. *I don't want to put you to that trouble.* -NE,29.
save someone the trouble poupar o trabalho, a inconveniência, o incômodo a *You don't have to quit your job. I'll save you the trouble. You're fired.*
take the trouble → go to the TROUBLE
(the) trouble is o problema é que, a dificuldade está no fato de que *Our mayor is doing the best he can to run this town. Trouble is, his best isn't good enough.*
the trouble with o mal de, o problema de *... the trouble with her is that she's just utterly irrational about her own feelings.* -WCN,293.
TROUBLEMAKER → make TROUBLE
TROUBLESHOOTER perito em eficiência, eliminador de dificuldades, contratempos etc., quebra-galho; reparador *... during World War II he was a top Roosevelt troubleshooter for refugee and relief problems in North Africa ...* -T/85. ⇒ **troubleshoot** localizar e resolver problemas (de qualquer natureza) *... NASA struggles to troubleshoot its new craft ...* -T/84. ♦ *He sent his best man to troubleshoot the problem in his new factory.*
TROUSERS wear the trousers → wear the PANTS
TROVE → (TREASURE) trove
TRUCK have no truck with [col] evitar qualquer relacionamento ou negócios com *He has never had any truck with that man.*
TRUE true to fiel a *Russell was always true to his principles.*
TRUE-BLUE sincero, verdadeiro, leal *... true-blue loyalist ...* -T/87. ♦ *... his true-*

blue compatriot Harry Truman ... -T/92.
♦ *a true-blue friend*
TRUMP hold all the trumps → **hold all the ACES**
trump card recurso infalível, trunfo *[He] ... holds another trump card for a future power play: he has threatened to cut off petroleum exports to the U.S. ...* -T/80.
trump up forjar, tramar, inventar (acusação, história, desculpa etc.) *They trumped up charges against him and had him arrested.* ⇒ **trumped-up** falso, falsificado, forjado *... during the French Revolution, he [Lavoisier] was arrested on the trumped-up charge that he had mixed water into the tobacco of the soldiers.* -HHO,36.
TRUMPET blow one's own trumpet → **blow one's own HORN**
TRUST on trust 1. a crédito *They have supplied their merchandise on trust.* 2. em confiança, cegamente, sem prova *We had to take his story on trust.*
trust to confiar em, deixar a cargo de *I didn't have a reservation for a Rio hotel during Carnival, but I trusted to luck and got an excellent room at the Copacabana Palace.*
TRUTH in truth de fato, na verdade *Buddhists feel that there is in truth no death, though every form must die.* -T/63.
TRY give (something) a try fazer uma tentativa, um esforço; tentar, experimentar *You'll never find out your true possibilities as a salesman unless you give this job a good try.*
try and [col] = **TRY to** *Try and get Mrs. Kirby on the phone and tell her I want to get in touch with her husband.* -GES,17.
try for tentar obter, tentar conseguir *He tried for a job with an oil company but was turned down for lack of experience.*
try hard esforçar-se ao máximo *It seemed that he was trying hard to be patient with me.* -CCT,23.
try on experimentar, provar (roupa etc.) *Try this dress on and tell me if you like it.*

try out 1. usar experimentalmente, submeter a teste ou experiência *I always try out the latest model cars before I make any decision about buying.* 2. procurar conseguir (posição, classificação, lugar, emprego etc.), testar sua capacidade, habilidade, aptidão etc. para *He was waiting for summer vacation to end so he could enter the University of Connecticut and try out for the freshman team.* -T/74.
♦ *Nancy is trying out for the lead in the school play.* ⇒ **tryout** [col] oportunidade para alguém demonstrar sua capacidade, aptidão etc. *He was given a tryout for the lead in* Partners in Crime.
try to tentar, procurar, fazer uma tentativa, um esforço, esforçar-se por *Try to get your work done before six o'clock.*
TUBE go down the tube(s) [col] fracassar, falhar, ir para a cucuia, ir por água abaixo, entrar pelo cano *There is absolutely no way the rest of the world, particularly Europe, can survive if America goes down the tube.* -T/87. ♦ *I didn't invest 42 years of my life to go down the tubes over an incident that I had nothing to do with.* -T/91.
the tube [col] a televisão *Let's see what's on the tube at this late hour.*
TUCK tuck away ocultar, esconder, pôr em lugar isolado *... they have more than $7.5 trillion tucked away in banks ...* -T/92. ♦ *Many valuable papers had been found tucked away in an old family bible.*
tuck in 1. prender (lençol, coberta) sob o colchão; enfiar para dentro (orla, fralda etc.) *Carolyn tucked in the blankets of the little girl's bed.* ♦ *Cary tucked in his shirttail.* 2. aconchegar (alguém) sob as cobertas *Mostly everyone can fondly remember his mother tucking him in bed and kissing him good-night.*
TUCKER tuckered out cansado, exausto *Earl was all tuckered out before the football game was over.*
TUG tug of war; tug-of-war 1. cabo de guerra, competição atlética na qual duas

equipes puxam, cada uma para seu lado, as pontas de uma corda *The tug-of-war went on and on but the blue team finally proved to be the better team.* 2. luta pela supremacia, pelo poder; conflito entre duas forças antagônicas ... *a tug of war for economic and psychological advantage.* -T/88.

TUMBLE **tumble to** [col] compreender subitamente, perceber, entender (idéia, situação etc.), sacar *It was the kind of idea that is a natural – so simple you wonder why nobody ever tumbled to it before.* -AIM,106.

TUNE **call the tune** → **call the SHOTS**

change one's tune [col] mudar de atitude, de comportamento, de opinião *Wynn was always pleasant with me until he found out that we were both after the same promotion and then he changed his tune.*

in//out of tune afinado, em harmonia// desafinado, em desarmonia, em divergência, em discordância *His father was never in tune with the times.* ♦ *... his foreign policy was out of tune with public opinion.* -T/81.

sing a different tune mudar de tom, de atitude, de comportamento *Newman began to sing a different tune when I threatened to sue him for damages.*

to the tune of [col] na importância de, no total de *The U.S. is aiding the [Afghan] ... rebels to the tune of many millions of dollars a year.* -T/85.

tune in sintonizar *Stay tuned in for the next episode.* -T/73. ♦ *... some 32 million Americans tuned in on the CBS television adaptation of Charles Dickens'* A Tale of Two Cities. -T/80.

tune out [gir] perder o interesse por, desinteressar-se de, deixar de dar atenção a, desligar-se *[In Ingmar Bergman's film* The Silence*] ... God seems to have tuned out on the human race, and vice versa.* -T/64.

tune up 1. afinar(-se), afinar os instrumentos de uma orquestra *The orchestra was tuning up for the performance.* 2. ajustar, regular, pôr em boas condições (motor) *I had my motor tuned up this week.*

TURF **one's (own) turf** [col] os domínios de, o território de, a área de atividade ou influência de *... the U.S. must have the ability to combat the Soviets and their proxies on their own turf ...* -T/85.

TURKEY **cold turkey** [gir] 1. de chofre, de um só golpe, de repente, de maneira total e abrupta [diz-se da retirada de drogas em um tipo de tratamento a viciados] *He kicked his habit cold turkey.* ♦ *Judd went off heroin cold turkey.* 2. de improviso, sem ensaiar, sem prévia reflexão *You said that you and Kirby went to see Dr. Babb cold turkey, that you didn't telephone or have an appointment.* -GES,56. 3. de maneira absolutamente franca, brusca, abrupta *They talked cold turkey about their differences.*

talk turkey [col] falar a sério, falar francamente, às claras *The principal really talked turkey to the students who had caused the explosion in the chemistry laboratory.*

TURN **at every turn** a cada passo, em todas as situações, continuamente *... Secret Service men protected the Prince at every turn ...* -T/81.

by turns alternadamente, sucessivamente *He was by turns boastful, rudely humorous and overbearing.* -HET,14.

a good//bad turn boa//má ação *When a politician does a good turn, he makes sure that it has been widely publicized.*

in turn à sua vez, por seu turno *Zeus, wrote Homer, gives all of us in turn good luck and bad.* -T/92.

one good turn deserves another amor com amor se paga *Kay was very kind and helpful to me once. Now it's my turn to help her. As they say, one good turn deserves another.*

serve someone's turn servir aos seus propósitos, convir aos seus objetivos, ser

eficiente para o que se pretende *That car will serve my turn for the time being.*
speak/talk out of turn falar inoportunamente, ser indiscreto, dizer o que não deve *When you mentioned his wife you didn't realize that you had spoken out of turn.*
take a turn dar um passeio, uma volta *Let's take a turn through the park.*
take a turn for the better//worse melhorar//piorar *Things have taken a turn for the better.* ♦ *... his health had taken a serious turn for the worse.* -T/86.
take a wrong turn/turning transviar-se, afastar-se do bom caminho, desnortear-se *His life took a wrong turn ...* -T/92. ♦ *They [Macbeth and his wife] were violent human beings who took a wrong turning ...* -CMSS,180.
take turns revezar-se *Ab and I will take turns staying awake tonight.* -SG,69.
talk out of turn → **speak out of TURN**
to a turn ao ponto exato, à perfeição (alimento assado/cozido) *I like my meat cooked to a turn, not overcooked.* ♦ *... we'll have this fat duck done to a turn ...* -YF,33.
turn against rebelar-se contra, opor-se a *Many people turned against the dictator when he began to persecute the Church.*
turn around 1. virar-se, dar meia-volta *When I heard the noise I turned around and saw a masked man pointing a gun at me.* ⇒ **turnaround/turnabout** reviravolta, virada; mudança de opinião, atitude etc. *... an economic turnaround ...* -T/81. ♦ *The hoped-for turnaround cannot come too soon ...* -T/87. 2. fazer voltar, dar meia-volta em *The driver turned the old Buick around and tried to chase me.* 3. modificar(-se) radicalmente, mudar para melhor *... their boss began to turn the situation around ...* -T/88. ♦ *... important painful experiences, such as disgrace, failure, death of loved ones ... which the person has been able to "turn around" and make into significant learning or growth experiences.* -JS,11. 4. agir de maneira abrupta, inesperada etc. *Bob and Carol had been married for two years when Bob suddenly turned around and left home.*
turn away 1. mandar embora, mandar sair, despedir *I cannot simply turn her away. I owe her an explanation.* 2. recusar, rejeitar *[He] ... has turned away most requests for interviews ...* -T/86. 3. não permitir o ingresso de, não aceitar *Those who had no tickets for the show were turned away.* 4. ir-se, afastar-se, sair, dar as costas a *Scholars turned away from the study of diplomatic and military affairs ...* -T/80.
turn back 1. voltar, recuar, regressar *She had left home and couldn't turn back now.* 2. fazer voltar, mandar recuar *The police turned back all the curious people who tried to reach the scene of the terrible fire.* 3. repelir, impedir o avanço de *... the elite troops had initially turned back the rebels in Santo Domingo ...* -T/66.
turn down 1. reduzir, diminuir (som, intensidade, volume etc.); declinar, reduzir-se *... turn the radio down again.* -CN,35. ♦ *First there is the question of why economic activity turned down in 1929.* -GJKT,174. 2. recusar, rejeitar *... Ford turned down offers to play professional football.* -T/74. ♦ *He was offered a good job but turned it down.* ⇒ **turndown** rejeição, recusa, repulsa, mau acolhimento *After several turndowns, the movie star finally agreed to talk to the press.*
turn down cold [gír] recusar completamente, rejeitar sumariamente *When Oliver asked for a raise, his boss turned him down cold.*
turn in 1. entregar, apresentar, passar às mãos de *The president of the company turned in his resignation.* 2. delatar, trair *Young Nazi children often turned in their no-Nazi parents to the Gestapo.* ♦ *The boy will get kicked out of school if you turn him in.* 3. v. **TURN oneself in** 4.

desempenhar, dar, oferecer (atuação, representação, trabalho etc.) *Judy Garland turned in a superb performance in* A Star is Born. 5. [col] recolher-se, ir para a cama *[They] ... had turned in for the night.* -HWR,155. 6. = **TRADE in** ... *people who earn their livelihood by persuading us to turn in last year's car for this year's model ...* -JW,20.
turn into transformar(-se) em *They say he can turn lead into gold.* ♦ *... both the French and the Russian revolutions turned into nationalist movements ...* -HETB,14.
turn loose = **LET loose** 1 ... *Davis turned the horses loose ...* -PJW,89. ♦ *He turned the dogs loose on me to frighten me.*
turn off 1. desligar (luz, aparelho elétrico etc.); fechar (torneira); interromper (fluxo de água, gás etc.) *Turn off the radio.* ♦ *He turned off the living-room lamp ...* -MRI,15. ♦ *Please turn the water off.* 2. sair de, deixar (rua, estrada, trilha etc. e entrar em outro caminho) *When you come to a group of tall pines, turn off the main road and follow the winding road near the pines.* 3. [gir] deixar desinteressado, entediado, deprimido etc. *Many newspaper readers are turned off by the constant bad news.* 4. [gir] repelir, desestimular (sexualmente), fazer perder o desejo *Even though she smiled at me, there was something in her appearance that turned me off.*
turn of phrase fraseado, torneio, modo de dizer ... *especially happy turns of phrase can evoke admiration or amusement.* -SWL,95.
turn of the century virada do século, começo do século *The Art Nouveau had a brief vogue about the turn of the [twentieth] century ...* -WJ,373.
turn on 1. ligar (luz, aparelho elétrico, motor etc.); abrir (torneira); deixar fluir (água, gás etc.) *turn on the lights* ♦ *turn on the radio* 2. [col] mostrar, exibir subitamente *When Sharon turns her charm on,*

she's irresistible. 3. [gir] deixar interessado, entusiasmado etc., causar prazer a *He was always turned on by the sight of marching men and flags flying.* 4. [gir] deixar drogado, dopado, produzir euforia *He had been taking drugs and we could see he was turned on.* 5. [gir] estimular sexualmente, excitar *I know what turns men on and have known since I was fifteen.* -HS,340
turn on/upon 1. atacar (física ou verbalmente); mostrar hostilidade para com, insurgir-se contra, opor-se a *He turned on her with such a blaze in his eyes that she moved back half a step.* -LM,168. ♦ *The tame bear in the Russian circus turned on his master and almost killed him.* 2. depender de ... *the case seemed to turn solely on the word of a confessed Communist agent determined to destroy a man ...* -T/61. 3. ter como tema principal, concentrar atenção em, girar em torno de, apoiar-se em, centralizar-se em *The plot [of the novel] turns on an invasion from the troubled north by strange blacks equipped with European weapons ...* -T/72.
turn on to fazer gostar de, fazer apreciar, fazer interessar-se por *Famous players have turned the public on to golf.*
turn oneself in entregar-se à polícia ... *he did not turn himself in or confess.* -T/87.
turn out 1. expulsar, mandar embora, pôr na rua ... *he had been turned out of his studio ...* -CS,500. 2. apagar, desligar (luz) *Turn out the light before you go to bed.* 3. produzir, fabricar *They turn out plastic bags and cartons for the milk industry.* ♦ *He turned out a couple of books about famous English crimes.* 4. [col] comparecer, apresentar-se, ir a determinado local, participar *A large crowd turned out to meet the famous movie star at the airport.* ⇒
turnout número de pessoas que comparece a algum local, afluência *The turnout at ... the hearing was unusually large ...* -T/87. 5. vir a ser, tornar-se, resultar, ter-

minar em, dar em *[He] ... may turn out to be just the right man for the job.* -T/92.
♦ *Everything turned out all right in the end.* 6. vir a saber-se, transpirar *It turned out that his mother herself had written the mysterious letter.* 7. [col] levantar-se (da cama) *I had to turn out quite early this morning.*
turn over 1. girar, revolver, virar (para outra posição, outro lado) *The girl turned over in her sleep.* ⇒ **turnover** rotatividade de pessoal, índice de substituição de funcionários em determinado período *The turnover in this office is so great that we never get to know our coworkers very well.* 2. virar de cabeça para baixo, capotar *Our sled turned over and we all fell in the snow.* 3. entregar, passar às mãos de, transferir *Arrested by British forces in 1945 ... [the Nazi war criminal] was turned over to Italian authorities in 1947...* -T/77. 4. movimentar (dinheiro em negócio) *He's turning over $3,000 a week in his new business venture.* ⇒ **turnover** quantidade de dinheiro movimentada por uma firma em determinado período; cifra de negócio, grau de atividade econômica *The annual turnover in this company is spectacular.* 5. comprar e vender (mercadoria) *That store turns over its stock rather rapidly.* ⇒ **turnover** rotatividade de mercadorias em determinado período; movimento de compras e vendas *We need a big turnover to make money.* 6. v. **turn over in one's MIND**
turn pale empalidecer *Cora turned pale when the husband she thought dead suddenly appeared at her new husband's home.*
turn to 1. voltar-se para, recorrer a, buscar o auxílio de ... *[Julian] Huxley turned to the fossil evidence of man's early history.* -GJ,307. 2. mudar de uma ocupação ou profissão para outra *He has turned to one job or another so often that his list of past occupations looks like a vocabulary list of jobs.* 3. (fazer) mudar de uma coisa ou estado para outro, transformar(-se) *... the pleasure trip turned to disaster.* -T/86.
♦ *... the look of her [the Medusa's] eyes turned men to stone ...* -CJM,25. 4. abrir um livro na página ou capítulo indicado *Turn to page 49 and read the first paragraph.* 5. pôr-se a trabalhar com energia, pôr mãos à obra *They all turned to and had the work finished very soon.*
turn up 1. desenterrar, revelar, achar, descobrir *The police turned up enough evidence to incriminate him.* 2. aumentar, intensificar (volume, som) *Turn up the volume of the radio a little so I can hear the words of the songs better.* 3. vir, chegar, comparecer, apresentar-se *Some of the people who were invited to his party failed to turn up.* 4. aparecer inesperada ou subitamente, surgir, vir à luz, ser encontrado ou recuperado *The missing letter eventually turned up in one of our old files.*
turn upon → **TURN on**
TURNCOAT vira-casaca ... *the country's intellectuals argued endlessly about betrayal, turncoats, witch hunts and political innocence.* -T/61.
TURNING POINT reviravolta, momento crítico, mudança decisiva *The overthrow of the Shah in 1979 was the turning point in the long struggle against monarchism in Iran.*
TURTLE turn turtle virar de pernas para o ar, emborcar, capotar *[His] ... small foreign car veered off the road and turned turtle ...* -T/60.
TURTLENECK gola olímpica; (de) gola olímpica (suéter ou camiseta) *[He is] ... wearing a turtleneck sweater.* -T/76.
TV TV dinner refeição ou prato pré-preparado para ser comido enquanto se assiste à TV *... people eating TV dinners on trays ...* -T/66. ♦ *Sue was heating up a TV dinner.*
TWENTIES the Roaring Twenties a década de 1920, caracterizada por pros-

peridade e otimismo, estilo de vida agitado e extravagante, e grandes mudanças sociais *F.Scott Fitzgerald depicted the lively period of the Roaring Twenties in his novel The Great Gatsby.*

TWICE-TOLD batido, sabido, conhecido, já contado ... *twice-told tales about familiar figures.* -T/87.

TWINKLING in the twinkling of an eye em um átimo, em um abrir e fechar de olhos *It happened in the twinkling of an eye on a bright sunshiny afternoon.* -EF,9.

TWO-BIT → **two BITS**

TWO-EDGED → **DOUBLE-edged**

TWO-FACED de duas caras, falso, fingido, hipócrita *[He is] ... able to project double images without getting accused of being two-faced.* -T/60.

TWO-FISTED [col] viril, másculo, vigoroso, impetuoso *He was always the two-fisted good guy in silent movies.* ♦ *... the Republican Party ... adopted a two-fisted policy of its own ...* -T/66.

TWO-TIME 1. [gír] enganar, trair, ser infiel *"I just don't like to be two-timed!" "Well, who's two-timing you?"* -TM,173. 2. que já fez, ganhou, sofreu etc. algo por duas vezes ... *a two-time burglary victim.* -T/81. ♦ *[He is] ... a two-time Pulitzer prizewinner ...* -T/92.

TWO-WAY 1. de duas mãos ou direções, bidirecional *This is a two-way street. Be careful.* v. **a two-way STREET** 2. de transmissão e recepção *With two-way radio, [train] engineers and conductors can talk back and forth with dispatchers while trains are speeding across the country.* -BE,14.

TYPE type; typecast selecionar ator/atriz para o papel de personagem que tenha seu tipo físico, personalidade etc., ou repetidamente para o mesmo tipo de papel *Though he was typed as a gangster, [James] Cagney excelled in many other parts.* -SS,68. ♦ *If a girl is typecast as a comedienne, she can seldom get a dramatic part.*

U

U/NON-U característico das classes superiores, aristocrático, elitista, de escol, culto//não-característico das classes superiores, não-aristocrático, não-elitista, inculto [diz-se geralmente da maneira de falar, vestir-se, comportar-se etc.] *Nancy Mitford ... was best known for her scalding portrait of British society and its linguistic divisions, "U" (upper class) and "non-U".* -T/73. ♦ *His voice is flat and distinctly non-U.* -T/77. ♦ *[James Bond was] ... always teddibly [i.e., terribly] English and utterly U (though Connery was a working class Scot).* -T/87.

UMBRAGE take umbrage at ofender-se com, ressentir-se de, melindrar-se com *Lang took umbrage at Walton's comment.*

UMBRELLA que abrange vários ou muitos indivíduos, tipos, grupos etc. *Evangelicals. An umbrella term for U.S. Protestants who stress conservative doctrine and morality ...* -T/87. ♦ *... the Menninger Foundation, an umbrella organization for a multitude of psychiatric services.* -T/73. ♦ *... the National Democratic Front, an umbrella group for various guerrilla factions ...* -T/86.

UNBEKNOWN unbeknown/unbeknownst to sem o conhecimento de, sem que (alguém) soubesse *... unbeknownst to the spies, the scheduled strategy meeting at the camps had been postponed.* -T/73.

UNCALLED-FOR desnecessário e inoportuno, impertinente *Dunne sued the newspaper for the many uncalled-for remarks it had printed about him.*

UNCLE Dutch uncle mentor severo, pessoa que critica e repreende energicamente mas com brandura *Lin Piao is the [Red] Guards commander, but their Dutch uncle seems to be Premier Chou En-lai.* -T/66. ♦ *He talks to his kid brother like a Dutch uncle.*

say/cry uncle [col] desistir, render-se, admitir a derrota, pedir água *Although Bobby was taking a beating from the other boy, he wouldn't say uncle.*

UNDERAGE de menor idade, menor *You're still underage.* ♦ *... all intercourse with a girl underage is rape ...* -MD,49.

UNDERCOVER secreto, furtivo, disfarçado *He was an undercover agent.* ♦ *... another undercover operation ...* -T/84. v. **GO undercover; under COVER**

UNDERDOG perdedor, derrotado; oprimido, desventurado, digno de dó, desgraçado, vítima de injustiça social *In America ... people pull for underdogs ...* -T/85. ♦ *He held a dislike for the strong and sympathy for the underdog.* -T/91.

UNDERSTAFFED com pessoal insuficiente, com deficiência de funcionários *The office is understaffed and work is piling up.*

UNDER-THE-COUNTER → **under the COUNTER**

UNDOING be someone's undoing ser a causa da desgraça, ruína, queda de, ser o fim de *Was it bad luck or bad faith that was my undoing?* -T/61.

UNDREAMED undreamed of insuspeito, impensado, não-imaginado *The microelectronic revolution promises to ease, enhance and simplify life in what was undreamed of even by the utopians.* -T/78.

UNHEARD-OF novo, desconhecido, sem precedente, inaudito *A hurricane in New England was unheard-of before 1938 but is now a common occurrence.*

UNLOOKED-FOR inesperado, imprevisto *unlooked-for praise* ♦ *unlooked-for difficulties*

UNTHOUGHT-OF não-imaginado, inesperado, imprevisto *... the desire continually burning within for the new, the wild, the unthought-of...* -RP,71.

UP be all up estar tudo acabado, estar no fim, sem esperanças etc. *When the unfavorable election results came in, he decided that it was all up with his chances as mayor.*

on the up and up; on the up-and-up [gír] honesto, legítimo, franco, confiável *Gilmore is always on the up and up in his business dealings.* ♦ *I wanted everything strictly on the up-and-up.* -AIM,98.

up against [col] enfrentando, fazendo face a *He was clawing for a way to make her see what he was up against.* -LM,167. ♦ *[They're] ... up against a task they had hoped to avoid ...* -T/91.

up against it [col] em dificuldades financeiras, em apuros *... I was up against it now – I no longer had the soothing assurance of support from home ...* -NEW,74.

up and about/around restabelecido, bem; de pé novamente e com saúde após ter-se recuperado de doença *... I had offered to take over his chores for him until he was able to be up and around again ...* -JJS,211.

up and down para cima e para baixo, para cá e para lá, de um lado para outro *He was pacing up and down in his office waiting for an important phone call.*

up close de perto, próximo *Up close the man seemed more fearsome.*

up for em oferta, considerado para (vender, alugar etc.) *... the yacht is up for sale at a mere $35 million.* -T/87.

ups and downs altos e baixos, as vicissitudes da vida *... China has had her ups and downs.* -LW,32. ♦ *... auto [i.e., the automobile industry] profits ... closely follow the economy's ups and downs.* -T/91.

up to 1. à altura de, capaz de (fazer, executar algo), em condições de *... he may not be up to the job.* -T/87. 2. até o limite de, até (determinado número, valor, momento, data etc.) *A few dollars will purchase for you a copy of a dictionary that may have cost up to a million dollars to produce.* -AH,276. ♦ *Little about the organization has been changed up to now.* -TB,7. 3. (ser) da incumbência de, (estar) na dependência de *The boss said to the workers: "It's up to you whether or not you go on strike".* 4. ocupado em, fazendo, planejando secretamente, tramando *When children become very quiet, they're up to something.* ♦ *He's up to no good. Be careful.*

up to here [col] farto, saturado, aborrecido, cheio *I'm up to here with Joan's complaints and whining.*

UP-AND-COMING [col] diligente, ativo, ambicioso, que mostra vontade de progredir, de vencer *[He was] ... an up-and-coming real estate operator.* -T/61. ♦ *... up-and-coming Southern cities ...* -T/60.

UP-AND-UP → **on the UP and up**

UPBEAT otimista, animado, alegre, jovial *[She] ... spoke in terms that were generally upbeat, but critical of some particulars.* -T/77. ♦ *... a meeting described by one*

participant as "unusually upbeat"... -T/81.
on the upbeat melhorando, progredindo, prosperando *Recession is over and business is on the upbeat.*
UP-FRONT [col] desinibido, totalmente sincero, aberto, franco, honesto *She was so up-front about her sexual preferences that I felt embarrassed as I listened to her.* ♦ *... an up-front answer.* -T/87. v. **up FRONT**
UPGRADE melhorar a qualidade de; elevar o nível, a posição, a importância, a estima, o valor de *The auto industry ... struggles to upgrade the quality of cars ...* -T/80.
on the upgrade melhorando, progredindo, em ascensão *Our business was slow at first but now it is on the upgrade.*
UPPER on one's uppers [col] em dificuldades financeiras, na penúria *She turned out to be on her uppers.* -BT,69.
UPSIDE upside down 1. de cabeça para baixo *She turned the glasses upside down on the kitchen table.* 2. em confusão, em desordem *The evil world of Nazism turned all values upside down.* -T/85.
UPTIGHT [gir] 1. tenso, nervoso, ansioso, constrangido, embaraçado *We still get uptight when we have to talk about sexual matters with our children.* 2. zangado, irado, irritado *I don't see what you're getting so uptight about.* 3. em dificuldades financeiras *The country's economy is in an uptight situation.*
UP-TO-DATE → **up to DATE**
UP-TO-THE-MINUTE recentíssimo, atualizado, que inclui as últimas descobertas, pesquisas, informações etc. *... an up-to-the-minute book based on recent scientific findings ...* -SEE,xvii. ♦ *... up-to-the-minute information ...* -SJJ,xii.
UPWARD upward(s) of mais de, acima de *They still owe me upwards of $5,000.* ♦ *... the big gymnasium was crowded with upwards of two thousand students.* -KRI,572.
USE be of use//no use ter utilidade, ser útil, servir//não ajudar, não adiantar, não resolver, não ter utilidade *... a chap does what he can when he feels he's of some use.* -SLS,287. ♦ *This old tool is of no use to me.*
be used to estar acostumado a, ter por hábito *[He] ... is used to speaking bluntly and forcefully.* -T/77. ♦ *Floyd had been used to a very active life.* v. **USED to**
have no use for 1. não ter necessidade de ou oportunidade para (utilizar algo) *They had no use for the extra car.* 2. não querer saber de, não tolerar, não gostar de *... hard-right conservatives who had never had much use for the Secretary of State.* -T/87. ♦ *Braga was a grossly fat man ... Cary had no use for him.* -BF,18.
I can/could use (something) eu gostaria muito (de), (isso) me faria bem, seria ótimo, benéfico etc. *I think I can use a drink ...* -WI,26. ♦ *I could use a shower right now.*
it's no use não adianta, é inútil *I talked to him but it was no use.* -TM,79.
make use of usar, utilizar, fazer uso de *Nicole made good use of the opportunity she was offered.*
put in/into use utilizar, fazer uso de, pôr em ação *In this type of job you can put into use all your mechanical ability as well as your knowledge of the subject.*
put to use usar, utilizar, empregar, fazer uso de *[Man's] ... curiosity resulted in his learning things that he could put to use to make his life simpler, easier, and more comfortable.* -FI,4.
used to costumava, tinha por hábito *Alec used to smoke three packs of cigarettes a day.* ♦ *She used to live in Hot Springs.* v. **be USED to**
use up consumir, gastar tudo, esgotar *[He was] ... using up most of his available cash.* -HWR,104.
what's the use (of)? de que adianta? *What's the use of talking? Edith will never agree to our suggestion.*
USHER usher in introduzir, anunciar, marcar o início de *The development of the re-*

combinant DNA technique ushered in a new era of genetic engineering ... -T/77. ♦ *... the late Nikos Kazantzakis knew that progress is often ushered in by violence.* -T/64.

UTMOST do one's utmost fazer o máximo possível, fazer tudo o que se pode fazer *Yugoslavia's separatist problem has become worse at the very time when [President] Tito is doing his utmost to solve it.* -T/72.

UTTERANCE give utterance to expressar, pôr em palavras *Eve gave full utterance to her feelings.*

U-TURN volta ou conversão de 180 graus (de um veículo) *[He] ... made a U-turn in the intersection at Seventh Street.* -WJT, 139.

V

VACATION **on vacation** de férias *Mr. Hubbard is on vacation. You'll have to speak with his assistant.*

VAIN **in vain** em vão, inútil, inutilmente *All his efforts have been in vain.* ♦ *We tried in vain to get Emily to play in our basketball team.*

VANISHING **vanishing point** 1. ponto de fuga (de uma perspectiva) *... the great [air] field with its long, smooth concrete runways stretching almost to the vanishing point ...* -GE,41. 2. ponto, estágio etc. de cessação, extinção, desaparecimento etc. *One of the greatest fears was that the [psychoanalytic] therapy would reduce my sexual desires to the vanishing point.* -KJS,129.

vantage point posição vantajosa, ponto de observação, ponto de vista *[They] ... watched from their hillside vantage point ...* -T/86. ♦ *... he searched for a fresh vantage point from which to look down on American presidential politics.* -T/92.

VARIANCE **at variance** em desacordo, em divergência, em conflito *... the law ... was at complete variance with human practices.* -GD,200. ♦ *Gibson's appraisal of the problem is at variance with the known facts.* ♦ *Gwen and Cora are at variance with each other.*

VENGEANCE **take vengeance on/upon** vingar-se de *[She is] ... grown up and ready to take vengeance on her father's tormentors.* -T/87.

with a vengeance [col] para valer, com vontade, com força, em grau extremo *The two men set to work with a vengeance.*

VENT **give vent to** dar vazão, desabafar, descarregar *Angela gave vent to her anger when they called her a liar.*

VENTURE **joint venture** associação ou empreendimento entre empresas ou pessoas que visa realizar um programa comercial ou industrial *... the firm was interested only in developing some sort of joint venture.* -T/87.

VERGE **on the verge of** à beira de, a ponto de *The Catcher in the Rye, a novel dealing with two days in the life of Holden Caulfield, an adolescent boy on the verge of a nervous breakdown ...* -HMJ,989.

verge on/upon estar a ponto de, estar próximo de, tocar as raias de *The things Adele told me verge on the ridiculous.*

VIEW **come into view/sight** surgir à vista, aparecer *As our bus went around a bend in the mountain road, a small town came into view.*

in view of em vista de, por causa de,

devido a *In view of recent developments many changes will be introduced.*
on view em exibição, em exposição, aberto ao público *A selection of Norman Rockwell's covers and illustrations for The Saturday Evening Post are currently on view at the Museum of Modern Art.*
take a dim view of não ver com bons olhos, ser cético quanto a, encarar com pessimismo *... they ... took a dim view of the state of American life.* -SWLM,21.
with a view to com a intenção de, a fim de *He bought apartments in the center of the city with a view to selling them when they increased in value.*

VILLAGE global village aldeia global *A generation ago, social theorist Marshall McLuhan proclaimed the advent of a "global village", a sort of borderless world in which communications media would transcend the boundaries of nations.* -T/92.

VINE die/wither on the vine fracassar (no início de um empreendimento etc.) por falta de apoio, interesse etc. *The plan for reorganizing the town library died on the vine.*

VIRTUE by/in virtue of em virtude de, devido a, por causa de, por meio de, mediante *By virtue of its intrinsic nature ... the Kinsey Report ... is an event of great importance in our culture.* -GD,213.
make a virtue of necessity fazer de boa vontade aquilo que é desagradável mas não pode deixar de ser feito *Carl's new job was not exactly what he wanted but he made a virtue of necessity and accepted it cheerfully.*

VISIT pay a visit → **pay a CALL**
return a visit retribuir uma visita *Let's return a visit to that young couple with whom we spent our vacation last year.*
visit with [col] conversar, papear com *She spent most of the afternoon visiting with a friend.*

VOICE give voice exprimir, expressar, declarar publicamente *Jerome gave voice to what he really felt.*
have a voice in ter o direito de opinar, ter voz ativa em *She had no voice in the decision.*
raise one's voice levantar a voz, gritar *I can hear you perfectly well. You don't have to raise your voice.*
still small voice a voz da consciência *That still small voice kept telling me not to go ahead with my intended plan.*
(a) voice crying in the wilderness pregação inútil, esforços baldados *General Billy Mitchell, who warned America against war in the air, was a voice crying in the wilderness.*
with one voice a uma voz, por unanimidade *With one voice all the members of the committee approved the proposal to build the new factory.*

VOICE-OVER voz do narrador, narração (em comercial de TV ou filme) *... in recent years, he [actor Howard Duff] has done, and enjoyed doing, voiceovers for television commercials ...* -RD,53.

VOLUME speak volumes for revelar muito sobre, ser muito significativo, dizer muito de *... those 40 [bestselling novels that will appear on the bestseller charts every year] can speak volumes about their readers.* -T/81.

VOTE put to a/the vote submeter a votação, decidir pelo voto *... a meeting that night put it [a decision] to a vote.* -JJS,107.
vote down eliminar pelo voto, rejeitar por escrutínio *The bill was finally passed by the Senate this year, but was voted down in the House [of Representatives].* -T/80.
vote for votar em, dar o voto a *He voted for Clinton in 1992 and again in 1996.*
vote out destituir pelo voto *[He] ... was voted out of office last week.* -T/80.

VOUCH vouch for responder por, garantir, assegurar, atestar *I've known him for several years, sir, and I can vouch for him.* -HWR,54.

WADE wade in/into [col] 1. atacar (tarefa etc.) com energia, agir com vigor *There's much to be done. Let's wade in and get it over with.* ♦ *They waded into the task.* 2. comer vorazmente, devorar *The boys waded into the food their mother had put on the table.* 3. atacar, investir contra *Danny waded into the boy who had called him a liar.*

wade through caminhar, avançar (pela água, lama, neve etc. com lentidão, esforço e dificuldade) *Nathan and I had to wade knee-deep through the freezing water.* 2. avançar vagarosamente e com dificuldade (em uma tarefa maçante) ... *readers too busy to wade through columns of testimony in those newspapers ...* -T/63. ♦ *The boy waded through a dull and tiresome lesson.*

WAGON fix someone's wagon [gír] punir, castigar; arruinar, vingar-se de *I'll fix his wagon if it's the last thing I do.*

hitch one's wagon to a star ter grandes ambições, esperanças, sonhar alto demais *Don't hitch your wagon to a star, but work and plan your career intelligently.*

on//off the wagon [gír] abstendo-se de bebidas alcoólicas//bebendo novamente *Hank has been on the wagon since his accident.* ♦ *[He] ... plans to go off the wagon soon ...* -T/60.

WAIT lie in wait ficar de emboscada ... *a band of Comanche hunters lying in wait for the approach of buffalo.* -VE,228.

wait on/upon servir a, atender a (cliente) *A little but very efficient girl waited on us in the store.* v. **wait on TABLE**

wait out aguardar pacientemente (o término de um período, um resultado, uma decisão etc.) *You'll just have to wait out the week until the list of approved students is published.* ♦ *The army deserters are waiting out a new decision on amnesty.*

wait up não se deitar, à noite, aguardando o regresso de alguém ou algum acontecimento *Don't wait up for me, mom, because I won't be home until very late tonight.*

WAITING waiting game suspensão temporária de ação para aguardar oportunidade propícia; compasso de espera *[He] ... played a coy waiting game, but the betting was that he would eventually accept the bid [to run for mayor] ...* -T/73.

waiting room sala de espera *The waiting room at the train station was full of young people all going to the mountains for winter sports.*

WAKE in the wake of na esteira de, atrás de, depois de, como resultado, em conseqüência de *World War II ... had left in its wake more problems than it had solved.* -TJ,990. ♦ *Nixon had problems with blood clots in the wake of his surgery.*

wake up despertar, acordar *Suzy usually wakes up at seven every morning.* ♦ *Clem's mother woke him up at six.*

WALK go for a walk ir passear, ir dar uma volta *She had gone for a walk when I arrived.*

take a walk dar uma volta, dar um passeio, andar um pouco *Let's take a walk in the woods.*

walk away/off with 1. roubar, levar consigo *The thieves walked away with all the wedding presents.* 2. vencer ou conquistar facilmente (prêmio etc.), desbancar os competidores *His school walked away with all the State science prizes last year.* ♦ *[Kevin Costner's* Dances With Wolves*] ... walked off with seven Oscars ...* -T/91. ⇒ **a walkaway** vitória fácil *The contest was a walkaway for him.*

walk back voltar a pé *I didn't have enough money for a taxi so I had to walk back.*

walk in chegar, entrar *In a well-known song, lyricist Ira Gershwin says: "One look and I had found a world completely new/When love walked in with you".*

walk of life condição social, esfera de atividade etc. *... the disaffected are found in all walks of life ...* -HETB,30. ♦ *As a social worker, Edith has come in contact with people from all walks of life.*

walk off ir-se, partir *Bailey simply turned on his heel and walked off.* ♦ *[He] ... walked off his job as Cuba's intelligence chief in Prague ...* -T/87.

walk off with → **WALK away with**

walk out 1. retirar-se, ir embora subitamente *In the middle of the meeting he stood up and walked out.* 2. fazer greve *Employees at major banks ... walked out, demanding that they be given protective security.* -T/78. ⇒ **walkout** greve *The oilworkers' walkout climaxed two months of labor unrest ...* -T/78.

walk out on [col] abandonar, desertar *Did Rhett [Buttler] really leave Scarlett [O'Hara] forever, as apparently he intended, when he walked out on her in the final pages of the book [*Gone With the Wind*]?* -SV,91.

walk/step (all) over [col] tratar sem consideração, maltratar, impor sua vontade sobre, subjugar *He walks over his employees so much that few stay in his employ very long.* ♦ *Max had married a nice girl but he stepped all over her.*

walk tall manter a cabeça erguida, não ter de que se envergonhar *... women are walking ... tall since she [Mary Robinson, first woman President of Ireland] was elected.* -T/92.

walk up to aproximar-se de, chegar-se a *A strange guy walked up to me and mumbled something I couldn't understand.*

WALKING walking distance → **within walking DISTANCE**

walking papers/ticket [col] bilhete azul, aviso de demissão *Howie was given his walking papers by the new boss.*

WALK-ON 1. pequeno papel no qual o ator ou a atriz aparece por alguns instantes e tem poucas falas ou nenhuma; figurante que faz esse papel *... Raquel [Welch] ... played a few movie walk-ons ...* -T/66. 2. pequeno, insignificante, sem falas (papel em peça ou filme); de pequeno papel, de ponta (ator) *He started with walk-on and bit parts ...* -WS,219. ♦ *The Player [a movie, has an] ... imposing cast of walk-on stars.* -T/92.

WALKOVER vitória fácil, "passeio" *The game with Greece was a walkover for Brazil.*

WALK-UP 1. prédio de apartamentos ou escritórios sem elevador *... a six-floor walk-up ...* -HA,295. 2. apartamento ou escritório acima do andar térreo em prédio sem elevador *The apartment was a walk-up, on the fifth floor of a downtown Seattle slum.* -AK,239. 3. localizado acima do andar térreo (apartamento ou escritório) em prédio sem elevador *... his third-floor walk-up apartment ...* -T/60.

WALL **climb the wall** [gir] ficar muito tenso, ansioso, emocionado, exaltado *I was ready to climb the wall before the policemen decided to let me go.*

drive/force/press/push etc. to the wall deixar num beco sem saída, colocar em situação difícil ou desesperadora *The government ... has been driven to the wall.* -T/87. ♦ *The loss of the coffee crop pushed many small farmers to the wall.*

go to the wall fracassar, ser derrotado, falir *Cavanagh went to the wall when his friends gave him no financial help.*

off the wall; off-the-wall [col] incomum, inusitado, surpreendente *Some of his remarks were really off the wall.* ♦ *[President] Reagan's economic policy is an off-the-wall approach.* -T/87.

up the wall [gir] em estado de tensão, ansiedade, agitação, frustração *... the remarks [he made] drove my family up the wall.* -T/77.

wall in fechar com tijolos, murar *Their garden is walled in.*

wall off separar com parede, isolar, delimitar *The passageway had been walled off.* ♦ *Walled off from real satisfaction [in prison], he [the Marquis de Sade] created a world of imaginary sexual delights of his own ...* -GD,196.

wall up emparedar, fechar com parede(s) *In Edgar Allan Poe's short story "The Cask of Amontilado", an insulted man chains his enemy in an underground niche and walls up its entrance.*

WALLFLOWER [col] pessoa tímida, especialmente uma moça, que em um baile ou uma festa permanece sentada por não ter par *At fifteen she was overgrown and a wallflower at parties.* ♦ *At a party he was a wallflower ...* -LRT,76

WALLOP **pack a wallop** [gir] 1. conter grande dose de álcool, ser forte (bebida) *Vodka with vermouth packs a wallop.* 2. ter grande força psicológica, produzir grande emoção, causar impacto *When an Indianapolis jury found [Mike] Tyson guilty of rape ... the verdict packed a wallop.* -T/92.

WALL-TO-WALL 1. que cobre completamente o piso, o chão (de uma sala, de um quarto etc.) *... the furniture in his office was also expensive, with wall-to-wall carpeting, oil paintings, modernistic lamps and many magazines.* -WCN,273. 2. que ocupa determinado espaço ou tempo por inteiro; de fora a fora, completo *[He] ... was raised in a 17-room Park Avenue apartment with a paneled library and wall-to-wall antiques.* -T/60.

WANE **on the wane** em declínio, em decadência *... the [U.S.] space program is on the wane because of insufficient funding.* -T/80.

WANNA-BE **wanna-be; wannabe** [col] indivíduo que quer ser ou aspira a ser outra pessoa, ou tenta parecer ou agir como outra pessoa *[It has been said that the CIA provides] ... top-secret training for James Bond wannabes.* -T/91.

WANT **for want of** por falta de *Many of ... [Shakespeare's] plays abound with excursions into what I may call, for want of better words, the realm of the supernatural.* -EM,31.

in want em privação, na penúria, carente *The social worker found many families in want in the slum area.*

you want to [col] você deve/devia/deveria (fazer algo, agir de determinada maneira) *If we're going to pull together [i.e., work together], you want to look before you leap.* -LP, 83 ♦ *You want to be extremely careful with your money.* ♦ *He's a vindictive man. You don't want to get on his* *hit list [a list of persons to be eliminated, murdered etc.].* -T/87.

want ad [col] anúncio classificado (do tipo "precisa-se") *He went through the want ads in the newspaper.*

want for ter necessidade ou falta de, precisar de, carecer de ... *it was wonderful to ... find a hot meal waiting for him, to have her hovering around, anxious to see that he wanted for nothing ...* -LRT,65. ♦ *He comes from a rich family so he doesn't want for money, clothes or a good meal, or whatever.*

want in//out querer entrar//sair; querer entrar//sair de uma sociedade; assumir// libertar-se de (um compromisso etc.) *The Negro [as a race] does not want out. He wants in ...* -T/67. ♦ *[They] ... desperately want out of Viet Nam ...* -T/69.

WAR at war em guerra *After months of border clashes, Iraq and Iran were at war ...* -T/80. ♦ *Homer told of adventure and men at war [in* The Iliad and The Odyssey*] ...* -CMSS,7.

hot/shooting war guerra de verdade (o oposto de guerra fria) ... *it was inevitable that the economic war would degenerate into a shooting war.* -BAS,12. ♦ *... another hot war was about to start in the Middle East.* -T/80.

WARD ward off repelir, rechaçar, desviar, afastar, evitar *[She] ... was slashed on her arms and hands when she tried to ward off the blows ...* -T/72. ♦ *... our men ... warded off the enemy.* -DM,44.

WARM warm to/toward 1. tornar-se amistoso com, simpatizar com, afeiçoar-se por *Slowly Warren warmed toward the little boy.* 2. tornar-se interessado, entusiasmado por, mostrar-se receptivo a *He was warming to the task he had been assigned.*

warm up 1. aquecer(-se) *Jack and I built a fire at the edge of the lake to get warmed up when we had finished skating.* ♦ *Here, this drink will warm you up.* 2. requentar, tornar a aquecer (alimento já preparado) *There's some food in the refrigerator. Warm it up for your supper.* 3. fazer aquecimento preliminar momentos antes de participar de jogo, competição etc., ficar preparado *The runners began to warm up for the race.* ⇒ **warm-up** atividade preparatória, aquecimento *Both teams have a five-minute warm-up before the game begins.* 4. tomar gosto, tomar interesse *Newman warmed up to his speech in the middle of it and really swayed his listeners.* 5. tornar-se mais amistoso, começar a simpatizar (com) *He warmed up to us after the strangeness of the first few hours in a new school.* ♦ *Assad [Syria's President] may hope to keep Tehran and Moscow off balance by warming up to the West ...* -T/87. ♦ 6. animar, entusiasmar *Danny warmed up the audience with a couple of jokes.*

WARM-BLOODED 1. de sangue quente *The feathered creatures called birds are warm-blooded animals.* -GET,10. 2. ardente, impetuoso *While traveling in Iberia, Kiley fell in love with a warm-blooded Spanish brunette.*

WARMED-OVER 1. requentado *warmed-over food* 2. antiquado, surrado. repetido, batido, trivial, corriqueiro *warmed-over Republicanism ...* -T/92.

WARMHEARTED afetuoso, bondoso, generoso, cordial *Her mother is a warm-hearted woman.*

WARPATH on the warpath 1. preparado para a guerra, em pé de guerra *The Cheyenne and the Sioux led by chiefs Sitting Bull and Crazy Horse went on the warpath and wiped out Lieutenant Colonel George Armstrong Custer and some 260 cavalrymen in the Battle of the Little Bighorn.* 2. indignado, furioso, pronto para brigar *Leslie went on the warpath when she realized what they were trying to do to her son.*

WARRANT swear out a warrant obter mandado de prisão contra uma pessoa acusando-a sob juramento *She swore out a warrant for Goddard's arrest.*

WARTS-AND-ALL [col] sem retoques, com todos os defeitos, sem omitir nada ... *a warts-and-all biography [of movie star William Holden] ... was published after the actor's death.* -RD,86.

WASH be washed out = **be RAINED out** *Because of the rain the game was washed out.*

come out in the wash [gir] ser revelado ou explicado mais cedo ou mais tarde, acabar tudo bem *He refused to go into details about the case, but I'm sure it'll all come out in the wash.*

wash away levar, carregar, arrastar, remover (a ação da água em movimento ou figurativamente) *... we had several really bad local storms. Over 60% of the [beach] sand was washed away.* -T/87. ♦ *I pray to God to wash away all my sins.*

wash down 1. limpar lavando *Jimmy is washing down his car.* ♦ *Don't forget to wash down the walls.* 2. acompanhar com bebida (o que se come) *[He] ... consumed mammoth meals, washed down by heroic quantities of aquavit and Danish beer.* -T/73.

wash off remover(-se) por lavagem *The stains on her dress won't wash off.* ♦ *Wash those marks off the wall.*

wash out 1. remover(-se) por lavagem *The stain on Margie's dress won't wash out.* ♦ *She washed the stain out of John's shirt.* 2. desbotar *This material has fast colors. They will not wash out.* ♦ *Grace was wearing an old blue dress that had long since washed out its color.* ⇒ **washed-out** a. desbotado *a washed-out dress* b. [col] pálido, descorado, abatido, esgotado *Chuck always looks washed-out when he has a cold.* 3. [gir] falhar, fracassar, eliminar, ser eliminado, ser rejeitado *He washed out at aviation school.* ⇒ **wash-out** fracasso, fiasco; pessoa que fracassa *The new play was a washout.* ♦ *Nora was beautiful, but as a main character in a Shakespeare play she was a washout.* 4. v. **be WASHED out** 5. destruir ou danificar pela força da água *The heavy spring floods washed out bridges and roads in the American Northeast.*

wash up 1. lavar o rosto e as mãos, lavar-se *[He] ... headed as usual to the bathroom to wash up.* -WR,59. 2. levar à praia; dar à praia *... the tides eventually wash up the bodies of those who drown.* -T/74. ♦ *... three pilot whales ... had washed up on a Cape Cod beach.* -T/87.

washed-up; washed up 1. [col] cansado, exausto *I feel washed up today.* 2. [gir] liquidado, arruinado, no fim *... almost every commentator wrote [in 1962] that Nixon was politically washed up.* -T/74. ♦ *He's a washed-up actor.*

WASTE waste away definhar-se, debilitar-se *... a father wasting away in jail.* -T/73. ♦ *... his muscles wasted away ...* -T/87.

WATCH keep watch; keep (a) careful/close watch vigiar atentamente, manter sob vigilância, ficar de olho *... the FBI [is keeping] ... a close watch on the operation.* -T/87. ♦ *[He] ... kept close watch on the fund-raising efforts ...* -T/87. ♦ *keep a careful watch on that radar screen.* -DK,452.

on the watch alerta, vigilante *The police are on the watch for cocaine pushers in that area.*

stand watch ficar de vigia *The captains decided to take turns standing watch.* -FV,23.

watch it [col] cuidado! fique atento! preste atenção! *Watch it, Mike. You nearly stepped on a loose stone.*

watch oneself tomar cuidado, ser prudente, discreto *You'd better watch yourself. You may be heading for trouble.*

watch out tomar cuidado; ficar atento, alerta *Watch out! Here comes another bomb!* ♦ *Watch out for good business opportunities.*

watch over guardar, cuidar de, tomar conta de, proteger, ser responsável por ... *hearing the sounds of the night relaxed me and I felt like I was watching the whole world.* -JS,8.

WATER fish in troubled waters pescar em águas turvas, tirar proveito de uma situação confusa ou de problemas alheios *Those who fish in troubled waters may soon be in trouble themselves.*

hold water ser válido, lógico, consistente, resistir a críticas *Few of the statements contained in his testimony hold water.*

in deep water [col] em dificuldades, às voltas com problemas *Owen will be in deep water when the auditors come to check the accounts.*

in hot water [col] enrascado, em apuros *Jack is in hot water with the police.*

like water off a duck's back sem causar grande efeito, impressão, reação etc. *Troubles that might be unbearable to weaker people rolled off him like water off a duck's back.*

of the first water de primeira água, da melhor qualidade *Jackson Pollock is considered an artist of the first water by lovers of abstract art.*

throw cold water on jogar um balde de água fria em, desencorajar, arrefecer o entusiasmo de *[She] ... threw cold water on that proposal.* -T/73.

tread water 1. manter-se à tona da água com o corpo ereto fazendo movimentos com as pernas e os braços, flutuar *When my boat sank, I started to swim toward the shore. I took rests, treading water slowly.* 2. não progredir, estacionar, marcar passo *... many of the [highschool] graduates tend to be unchallenged by high school and ... just tread water for two or three years until they go off to Harvard or Caltech.* -T/85.

water down 1. diluir, acrescentar água a, batizar *This wine has been watered down.* ⇒ **watered-down** diluído, batizado *watered-down whisky* 2. atenuar, amenizar, moderar, tornar mais fraco *The report he presented to the board of directors had been watered down.* ⇒ **watered-down** atenuado, amenizado, suavizado, moderado *... too many of our insights are based not on Freud but on the watered-down psychology of TV cop shows.* -T/87.

water over the dam águas passadas *We had a serious argument a few years ago, but that's water over the dam. It's forgotten now.*

water under the bridge = **WATER over the dam** *Forget the failure you had. It's water under the bridge now.*

WAVE make waves [col] causar agitação, alvoroço, criar comoção, perturbar a calma *... while he has left political life, O'Neill is still capable of making waves.* -T/87. ♦ *... follow the rules, do your job, don't make waves.* -T/86.

WAY all the way 1. de/desde (... até) *All the way from Idaho to New Mexico the cattle business boomed ...* -RR,585. 2. o caminho todo, a extensão toda, até onde for possível *She drove all the way to San Francisco.* 3. [col] sem reserva, sem limites, inteiramente *You're right about this. I'm with you all the way.*

blaze the way → **blaze a TRAIL**

by the way a propósito, por falar nisso *By the way, John, have you seen Mary this morning?*

by way of 1. via, por, passando através de *The intruder ... had entered the 17-room mansion by way of a flagstone patio on the lake side of the house ...* -T/66. 2. à guisa de, como forma de *He said that by way of an apology.*

change one's ways → **mend one's WAYS**

clear the way abrir caminho, retirar obstruções, desimpedir *... the White House has cleared the way for fresh negotiations between the two countries.* -T/86.

come someone's way vir na direção de, vir ao encontro de, apresentar-se a, acontecer a *[Other people are]* ... *envious of all the fame and good fortune that has come his way* ... -T/92.

cut both /two/many ways ter prós e contras, ter efeito favorável e desfavorável, ter mais de um efeito *It is an issue that cuts many ways.* -T/79. ♦ *His argument cuts both ways.*

elbow one's way abrir caminho à força, às coteveladas *Reese elbowed his way through the crowd.*

every which way [col] 1. em todas as direções, por todos os lados *Cars screech to a halt, and people leap out, running every which way* ... -T/87. 2. em desordem, irregularmente *The children had left their toys scattered in confusion on the living room floor every which way.*

feel one's way agir com cautela, explorar o terreno *Howells is feeling his way in his new business but hopes to be able to work well in a few months.*

fight one's way abrir caminho com esforço, com luta, com dificuldade *All Americans like to see someone who has been defeated fight his way back to the top.* -T/87. ♦ *They fought their way out of the trap* ... -T/66.

find its way chegar ... *very little [of the provisions] found its way to the starving army.* -SGF,349. ♦ ... *during* ... *[Shakespeare's] lifetime about half of [his plays]* ... *found their way into print.* -CMSS,8.

find one's way achar o caminho, saber ir para (determinado lugar) *D'you think you can find your way to Central Station?*

from way back (desde) há muito tempo *I know him from way back.* -CEB,45. ♦ *The 71-year-old cardinal, a reformer from way back* ... -T/62.

get/stand in the way impedir, estorvar, obstruir, bloquear, tolher o passo a *He [a character in a film] simply kills anyone who gets in his way.* -WM,192. ♦ *If you really want to marry her, I won't stand in your way.*

get/have one's (own) way fazer o que quer, o que bem entender, fazer prevalecer sua vontade ... *the Soviets realized they could not "get their way" in Afghanistan.* -T/87. ♦ *If censors had their way, they'd tell people what to see, and read and think.*

get under way iniciar-se, começar (a acontecer), pôr-se em movimento, a caminho ... *the election campaign got under way* ... -T/81. v. **under WAY**

give way 1. quebrar(-se), ceder, romper-se, desmoronar *The bridge gave way when the ice-choked water smashed against it.* 2. recuar, ceder terreno, sair da frente *The angry mob sullenly gave way when the tanks came into the city square.* 3. fazer concessões, transigir, permitir *They tried to reason with her and get her to change her mind but she never gave way.*

give way to 1. sucumbir a, entregar-se a *She never gave way to despair.* 2. dar lugar a, ser substituído por *Her faint smile gave way to laughter.* 3. fazer concessões, transigir, permitir *Why should I give way to her unreasonable demands?*

go all the way [col] 1. concordar inteiramente *I can't go all the way with you in your thinking, I have some reservations.* v. **all the WAY** 2. ter relações sexuais *Many young girls go all the way in this permissive age of the pill.*

go a long way to/toward auxiliar grandemente (na realização de algo) *AIDS is on the increase, but common, everyday measures of hygiene can go a long way toward controlling the disease.*

go one's different/separate ways separar-se, seguir caminhos individuais, terminar um relacionamento *Nancy and Burt decided to go their separate ways.*

go one's own way agir independentemente, não depender de ninguém ... *do business with them if it is essential, and then go your own way* ... -KJS,192.

go out of one's/the way esforçar-se (para fazer algo, favor etc.) *Randall often goes*

out of his way to be friendly to people. ♦ *[Thomas Wolfe]...went out of his way, in* The Web and the Rock, *to create believable characters out of whole cloth.* -HDR,168
go someone's way 1. ir na mesma direção de alguém *Are you going my way?* 2. [col] ser favorável, sair tudo bem para *Everything seems to be going my way.*
the hard way da maneira mais difícil, árdua ou inconveniente *He learned his lesson the hard way.* ♦ *We all learn the hard way.* -DK,5.
have a long way to go ter muito que se desenvolver, evoluir, aprender etc.; estar longe, faltar muito para *India's effort [in the war against AIDS] still has a long way to go.* -T/86.
have a way of ter uma propensão para, um hábito, mania etc., teimar em *Real people have a way of keeping themselves to themselves; characters in books open their hearts.* -LAS,xvi.
have a way with ter jeito, saber lidar com, saber persuadir, influenciar etc. *Mr. Collins used to say that the Irish have a way with words.* ♦ *She's got a way with the child.* -CHT,35.
have come a long way ter feito grande progresso, ter mudado muito *Certainly English has come a long way from its Anglo-Saxon stage ...* -AH,336. ♦ *Telephones have come a long way ... since Alexander Graham Bell made the first call on his invention ...* -T/87.
have it both ways desfrutar duas vantagens ou opções ao mesmo tempo, querer duas coisas opostas, incompatíveis *You either dress well and go hungry or wear old clothes and have a full stomach. You can't have it both ways.*
have it one's (own) way fazer como quiser, como preferir *All right, all right. Have it your own way. I don't care.*
have one's (own) way → **get one's (own) WAY**
in a bad way muito doente, mal *Nat's breathing with difficulty. I think he's in a bad way.*
in a big way [col] com muito entusiasmo; grandemente, muito ... *if you're really serious about increasing your vocabulary in a big way, you'll find it pays to stop to think of individual words.* -NM,24.
in a way de certo modo, até certo ponto *In a way, I'm glad she's gone.*
inch one's/its way avançar vagarosamente, mover-se ou deslocar-se gradualmente *The soldiers carefully inched their way through the minefield.* ♦ *... the [Reagan] Administration may be inching its way back to a role in the Middle East negotiations.* -T/85.
in more ways than one de várias maneiras; em mais de um sentido *... our world is in crisis in more ways than one.* -BN,163. ♦ *In more ways than one American attitudes toward illegitimacy are peculiarly topsy-turvy.* -EA,89.
in no way de maneira alguma *Frank was in no way to blame for what happened later.*
in one's/the way no caminho, atrapalhando, estorvando *You're in my way.*
in the way of no tocante a, no que diz respeito a; do tipo de, na qualidade de, no gênero de *All I had in the way of a firearm was an old worn-out .45 Colt ...* -LAK,46.
in the worst way [gír] muitíssimo, grandemente, extremamente *He wanted her in the worst way.*
know one's way around estar familiarizado (com locais, hábitos, normas etc.), estar bem informado; sair-se bem em qualquer situação *The heroines of current films know their way around too well ...* -WM,21. ♦ *He enjoys cooking gourmet dinners and knows his way around French wines.* -T/69.
lead the way 1. ir à frente (de um grupo), indicar o caminho *With fur traders and missionaries leading the way, the French*

pushed their dominion rapidly westward across the northern third of the [American] continent ... -VE,18. 2. estar na vanguarda, liderar *They're leading the way in laser technology.*

look the other way fazer vista grossa a, olhar para o outro lado *Most colleges officially frown on student sex on campus but handle the matter by looking the other way.* -T/76.

make one's way dirigir-se, encaminhar-se, ir; progredir, fazer carreira ou progresso, impor-se *[He] ... had made his way across the desert and through mountain passes ...* -MJ,41.

make one's way in the world conquistar seu lugar ao sol *[He had] ... a voracious appetite to make his way in the world.* -T/76.

make way abrir espaço, abrir alas, afastar-se, deixar passar *The bodyguards found it very difficult to make way for their boss in the hostile crowd.*

mend/change one's ways emendar-se, corrigir-se *You must mend your ways or you'll be put in jail by the police.*

more than one way to skin a cat outras maneiras ou possibilidades de realizar uma tarefa, atingir um objetivo etc. *The bright child likes to experiment, to try things out. He lives by the maxim that there is more than one way to skin a cat.* -HJH,206.

not know which way to turn/jump não saber o que fazer, não saber para onde se voltar *When Simon lost his job and ran out of money, he didn't know which way to turn.* ♦ *He was so confused he didn't know which way to jump.*

on one's/the way 1. a caminho (de algum lugar) *If you'll excuse me, I've got to be on my way now.* ♦ *Rosie was on her way to San Francisco Airport.* 2. progredindo (rumo a um objetivo) *... [Catherine] Deneuve is well on her way to becoming a serious star ...* -T/68.

on the way em gestação, que vai nascer (bebê) *He has three kids and one on the way.* -T/87.

on one's/the way out saindo de moda, em declínio, em desuso, no ocaso *... agoraphobia [fear of open spaces] is on its way out as a cocktail-party topic.* -T/77.

the other way (around/round) ao contrário, inversamente, o oposto *What is sense to you may be nonsense to another, or the other way around.* -BN,126. ♦ *[Gorbachev] ... is living proof that it is people who make history, not the other way around.*

out of the way 1. fora do caminho, fora do alcance, onde não estorve *Get those things out of the way.* ⇒ **out-of-the-way** afastado, remoto, pouco freqüentado; de difícil acesso *Neal took Karen to a small, out-of-the-way restaurant.* ♦ *... an out-of-the-way town in southeastern Virginia.* -DP,23. 2. incomum, inusitado, invulgar *Something extremely out of the way happened to me ...* -SJD,163. 3. impróprio, errado, inconveniente *Heywood said something out of the way and his wife didn't like it.*

a/the parting of the ways separação, ruptura, despedida, adeus *... the two friends came to a mysterious and bitter parting of the ways ...* -T/61.

pave the way preparar o terreno, o caminho *[In 1971] ... National Security Adviser Henry Kissinger secretly arrived in Beijing [Peking] to pave the way for a presidential visit by Nixon.* -T/91.

pay one's/its (own) way pagar sua parte das despesas, ser auto-suficiente financeiramente *... he paid his own way to the University of Houston ...* -T/84. ♦ *The newly organized railroads can be paying their own way in a few years.*

pick one's way andar cuidadosamente, escolhendo o caminho e vendo onde pisa *... the horsemen picked their way cautiously through the darkness.* -YF,37. ♦ *We had to pick our way along the edge of the canyon.*

push one's way abrir caminho à força *He had to push his way through the reporters to get to the door.*

put out of the way 1. deixar de lado, abandonar *Put out of the way all other projects and concentrate on the new compact cars.* 2. matar, eliminar *Fred was put out of the way by members of a rival gang.*

rub the wrong way desagradar, irritar *There's something about him, something around the eyes, that rubs me the wrong way.* -MG,48.

see one's way (clear) achar que é possível, conveniente, razoável etc. (fazer algo) *Apparently ... [he] had not yet seen his way through to a clear position on this basic question.* -SJH,45. ♦ *George couldn't see his way clear to accepting her offer.*

see which way the cat jumps ver o que acontece, aguardar o desenrolar dos acontecimentos *Let's wait and see which way the cat jumps before we take any action.*

set in one's ways/habits obstinado, intransigente, arraigado em seus hábitos, atitudes etc. *Connors was now an old man and very set in his ways.* ♦ *Large companies prefer to hire younger men who have not become set in their habits.*

shoot one's way out abrir caminho a fogo, a bala *When the agent and the Turkish police got the drop on the crooks, they tried to shoot their way out.* -T/64.

stand in the way of atrapalhar, prejudicar, estorvar ... *stubborn obstacles still stand in the way of an ... agreement.* -T/87.

that's the way it goes assim é a vida, assim são as coisas, assim é que é *It was expensive to bribe the authorities, but that's the way it goes.*

that's the way the ball bounces [gir] = **that's the WAY it goes** *It's rough but that's the way the ball bounces.*

that's the way the cookie crumbles [gir] = **that's the WAY it goes** *When he realized he had lost his money in investments he said: "That's the way the cookie crumbles".*

that way 1. dessa maneira, desse jeito, assim *Oh, what a horrible thing – to destroy our literary creations that way!* -BRT,132. 2. por ali, naquela direção *You're looking for Callaway? He went that way!*

there are no two ways about it não há alternativa, não há outra saída, não há escolha *Cindy would have to leave the following morning and there were no two ways about it.*

to someone's way of thinking na opinião de *To my way of thinking, he shouldn't have said that.*

under way em andamento, em curso, em progresso ... *a broad movement was under way to make government more directly responsible to the people.* -OH,10.

way [col] bem, muito, bastante, longe ... *the project is way behind schedule ...* -T/84. ♦ *It's way too early to tell if there are going to be any complications ...* -T/87.

way back há muito tempo; bem longe, lá atrás *That happened way back in 1960.*

way of life modo de vida, costumes sociais ... *everyone has a view of life as part of his way of life.* -BCS,12.

way off distante *Space travel, complete with spacemen, still seems a long way off.* -GH,144.

way out saída, solução [de dificuldade, de problema] *The President seized on this proposal as a way out of a very difficult position.* -T/86. ♦ *In the end, as a way out, she commits suicide.* -DDT,455. ♦ *Lydecker had been caught in a trap and there was no way out.*

(which) way the wind blows/is blowing; how the wind blows tendências, probabilidades, circunstâncias; para onde o vento sopra, aquilo que é suscetível de ocorrer *Whichever way the economic winds blow ... [he] intends to profit from them.* -T/87. ♦ *... someone who changes his mind according to which way the wind is blowing.* -T/87.

work one's way penetrar, introduzir-se ou avançar pouco a pouco ou com esforço e dificuldade *The snake venom worked its way through the blood stream but Jim was still alive when we reached the hospital.* ♦ *[They] ... were working their way toward the peak of Everest ...* -EF,13.

work one's way through college etc. trabalhar e ganhar seu sustento enquanto estuda *[She] ... worked her way through the University of Florida ...* -T/81.

work one's way up progredir pelo trabalho, pelos próprios esforços *[He] ... worked his way up from a small-town bank teller to become a vice president ...* -T/81.

worm one's way in(to) introduzir-se, insinuar-se astuciosamente *... a narcotics agent ... wormed his way into the confidence of a band of international traffickers ...* -T/64.

worm one's way through abrir caminho, avançar lentamente e com dificuldade, serpear *She wormed her way through the dense crowd around the injured child to bring him some water.*

WAY-OUT moderno, vanguardeiro, avançado *... today's way-out generation ...* -EM,230.

WAYSIDE fall/go by the wayside ser negligenciado, deixar de ser considerado, ficar ou ser posto de lado, cair em desuso, ser descartado *A lot of Egyptian politicians have fallen by the wayside during the Sadat era ...* -T/81. ♦ *... a few myths have fallen by the wayside.* -T/72.

WEAR wear and tear uso, desgaste etc., deterioração causada pelo uso *... the furniture ... showed some, but not much evidence of wear and tear ...* -HJD,6.

wear away gastar pelo uso, desgastar pelo atrito *The wind and the rain wore away bits of the solid rock ...* -SJV,1.

wear down 1. gastar ou danificar pelo uso, atrito etc., desgastar-se *The air and water that make our planet livable have worn down the oldest rocks ...* -JRR,91. 2. exaurir, enfraquecer, debilitar, abalar a saúde, nervos etc. *The constant competition and nervous strain of the advertising agency wore him down.* 3. vencer a resistência (de alguém) pela persistência *Hugh wore down his girl's opposition to marriage by constant gifts and attentions.*

wear off diminuir gradualmente até desaparecer, passar, dissipar-se *She gave me a sedative but the effect soon wore off.* ♦ *During 1948 the novelty of UFO's had worn off for the press ...* -RE,49.

wear on 1. produzir irritação em *The stresses of the big city wear on people more than those things that bother people in small towns.* 2. passar vagarosa e tediosamente (o tempo) *As the days wore on, the fires in the city filled the skies with smoke.* -SSG,13.

wear out 1. desgastar-se até perder a utilidade, gastar(-se) pelo uso *... they wore out several batteries listening to Vatican Radio ...* -T/63. ⇒ **worn-out** gasto, usado, estragado pelo uso, cediço *worn-out clothing* ♦ *worn-out arguments* 2. cansar(-se), exaurir(-se) *The troops marched through the redrock country [of northern New Mexico] until they wore out their horses ...* -BD,18. ⇒ **worn-out** cansado, exausto *Glen looked worn-out after a tiring day at the office.*

wear thin 1. chegar ao fim, estar prestes a romper-se, adelgaçar-se, desgastar-se *[A quilt] ... was worn thin from age.* -T/77. ♦ *... I could see that his temper was wearing thin.* -UJ,167. 2. tornar-se cediço, batido *I had heard that joke several times and it was beginning to wear thin.*

wear through gastar pelo uso, desgastar pelo atrito *... Thai soldiers were wearing through their U.S.-made boots within six months ...* -T/66.

WEATHER keep a weather eye open estar alerta, ficar atento *While we were stealing the corn Billy kept a weather eye open for the farmer.*

under the weather [col] 1. doente, desanimado, abatido *His wife has been under the weather.* 2. embriagado *Shawn's a little under the weather.*

WEDLOCK out of wedlock de pais solteiros *[Tom, the protagonist in the novel Tom Jones represents] ... as a group all young men born out of wedlock and searching for their true identity ...* -MR,11.

WEED weed out eliminar, suprimir (algo supérfluo, indesejável, ineficiente etc.) *He used to talk about war as an efficient way to weed out the weak members of society ...* -T/92.

WEEK a week of Sundays [col] um longo período, muito tempo *I haven't seen her in a week of Sundays.*

WEIGH weigh down 1. fazer vergar com o peso, sobrecarregar *... knights and soldiers weighed themselves down with heavy, cumbersome suits of steel.* -VA,38. ♦ *[Kinsey's Sexual Behavior in the Human Male] ... was described by a portion of the press as a dry and dull tome weighed down with forbidding statistical tables and charts ...* -KAC,11. 2. oprimir, acabrunhar, angustiar *Ted looked weighed down when I last saw him.*

weigh on/upon 1. pesar sobre, ser um fardo *The albatross in Coleridge's "The Ancient Mariner" weighed upon the man's shoulders like a guilty burden.* 2. preocupar, afligir *Lucy's many responsibilities weighed on her.*

WEIGHT carry weight ter importância, influência, valor, prestígio *He is so close to the President that his advice carries extraordinary weight.* ♦ *Such explanations carried little weight ...* -T/80.

pull one's (own) weight fazer sua parte, dar sua contribuição *If you pull your own weight, do a competent job, you're accepted.* -T/76.

put on weight ganhar peso, engordar *Say, ain't [aren't] you putting on a little weight, honey?* -BRSR,116.

throw one's weight around ser mandão, agir com arrogância *... don't throw your weight around too much. There are other good men around here.* -SG,32.

weight down sobrecarregar; oprimir, pesar sobre *He was weighted down with guns and ammunition.* -LMT,42. ♦ *... Tom ... began to think of himself as weighted down with "loneliness and terror"...* -NEW,27.

WELCOME wear out one's welcome; overstay one's welcome permanecer como visita mais tempo do que o razoável, conveniente ou apropriado, abusar da hospitalidade; visitar alguém com muita freqüência *By the time he resigned [as American ambassador to England] in 1940, [he] had worn out his welcome in England ...* -T/64. ♦ *... he's overstayed his welcome.* -JJF,246.

you're welcome não há de quê; de nada (em resposta a um agradecimento) *When I thanked her for all her help she replied: "You're welcome".*

WELFARE on welfare recebendo auxílio da Previdência Social *... the woman has been on welfare since her five-year-old was born.* -T/77.

WELL as well também, igualmente *[His] ... handwritten notes have become more thoughtful than usual, and longer as well.* -T/91. ♦ *Doris is not only a singer but a dancer as well.*

(just) as well 1. com igual razão, sem inconveniente, com o mesmo efeito, com a mesma justificativa, igualmente, sem nenhum prejuízo *We might just as well stay home as go to a movie or something.* ♦ *Linus might as well go first as last.* 2. conveniente, preferível, melhor, desejável, apropriado, prudente, sensato, aconselhável, vantajoso *It is as well that things have happened this way.* ♦ *It is just as well to learn the practical side of things, no matter what you do.* ♦ *"We may as well sit outside", she said. "It'll be cool-*

er." -SEB,48. ♦ *This life is so hopelessly insecure you might as well be dead and get it over with.* -WCN,247.

as well as assim como, bem como, e também, e não apenas *You know as well as I do that the average girl doesn't like a man to humble himself before her.* -WCN,288. ♦ *Her new book will interest linguists as well as anyone concerned with literary theory.*

well and good muito bem, que assim seja *... if a man wants to retell his story, well and good. It is a way of passing the time.* -MAT,38.

well up 1. brotar, verter, transbordar, inundar *I can still remember the tears welling up in my mother's eyes the night my father died in her arms.* 2. crescer, avolumar-se *... such horror welling up within him.* -SCD,42. ♦ *Great joy welled up inside Glenda.*

WELL-ADVISED prudente, sensato *... prospective entrants are well-advised to read the fine print before signing any of the numerous contracts available.* -T/87. ♦ *a well-advised gesture*

WELL-BEING bem-estar, conforto *... the mother has an overwhelming importance to its [her baby's] well-being.* -WF,ix.

WELL-BUILT grande, musculoso e forte *Clint is a tall, well-built man.*

WELL-FIXED [col] próspero, abastado *He was better than well-fixed – he was rich ...* -SJE,80.

WELL-GROOMED 1. asseado, limpo, bem-penteado, bem-vestido etc., de boa aparência *Ted Carter is a well-groomed young man.* 2. bem-cuidado, bem-arranjado, bem-tratado *That is a well-groomed lawn.*

WELL-GROUNDED 1. bem-preparado, instruído *He was well-grounded in classical literature.* 2. bem-fundado, assentado ou fundamentado em bases sólidas, em fatos *His fears were well-grounded and he lost his job a few days after the incident.*

WELL-HEELED [gír] abastado, próspero *He was fairly well-heeled and could afford to give away a million dollars for the charity fund.* ♦ *... Palos Verdes, California, a well-heeled suburb of Los Angeles.* -T/81.

WELL-MEANING → MEAN well

WELL-NIGH quase *... his mission seemed well-nigh impossible.* -T/86.

WELL-OFF 1. abastado, bem de vida, próspero *[She] ... came from a well-off, but by no means rich lawyer's family ...* -T/78. 2. livre de preocupações, responsabilidades etc., em boa situação *Children don't realize they're well-off until they try to go to work for a living.*

WELL-PUT bem explicitado, inequívoco, expressivo *The arguments in his speech were well-put and made a success with the audience*

WELL-READ muito lido, instruído, culto *... he was a well-read, articulate businessman capable of great charm ...* -T/60.

WELL-ROUNDED de ampla educação, cultura etc. amplo, abrangente, completo, bem-desenvolvido *Snyder has a well-rounded background in American literature.* ♦ *We were taught to be well-rounded in everything ...* -T/73.

WELL-TAILORED bem-vestido *The court sentenced the five well-tailored ex-Nixon men to various jail sentences.*

WELL-TIMED oportuno *... a well-timed, well-expressed greeting can improve relations between a company and its patrons.* -PC,8.

WELL-TO-DO próspero, abastado, rico *[He married] ... the daughter of a well-to-do Dallas businessman ...* -T/91.

WELL-WISHER → WISH someone well

WET all wet [gír] enganado, equivocado, errado *You're all wet if you think you can get away with that.*

dripping wet → WET through

wet through; wet/soaked to the skin; dripping/soaking/wringing wet completamente molhado, encharcado, ensopado *It was raining hard now and he was wet through.* ♦ *Howie was wet to the skin* *when he was caught in the rain.* ♦ *[He] ... clumped back to his chair and found it dripping wet.* -SCD,11.

WHACK **out of whack** [col] defeituoso, avariado, com defeito, funcionando mal; desordenado, desarranjado *The motor has been out of whack and we haven't been able to find the trouble yet.* ♦ *... the chronological order [was] all out of whack.* -AK,35.

WHALE **a whale of a** [col] coisa de bom tamanho, algo excepcionalmente grande, ótimo etc. *... they were having a whale of a good time ...* -HJC,356.

WHAT **what about** → **HOW about**
what if e se? *What if he finds out what you've done?*
what is (someone/something) like? como é alguém/algo?, qual é sua opinião de? *Have you met Miss Jones? What's she like?*
what (something) is like como algo é na realidade *... by 1914 few could recall what war was like.* -SWLM,17.
(and) whatnot; what not e não sei que mais, e outras coisas do gênero etc. *... that marvelous agglomeration of nerves, nuclei, and whatnot which we call the brain ...* -LCT,14.
what of e com referência a, que dizer de *What of the lawyers who deliberately aid and abet their clients in flouting the ethics and morals of society?* -T/73.
what of it? = **SO what?** *All right, so I'm late. What of it?*
what's more principalmente, mais importante *Della is rich, young and pretty, and what's more, she's looking for a husband.*
what's up? que é que há? que se passa? *"What's up?", he said when he saw the room in disorder.*
what with por causa de, devido a (uma ou mais razões) *What with inflation and the high cost of living you are always looking for ways to supplement your income.*

WHEEL **at the wheel** na direção (de veículo), ao volante *With Jubin at the wheel,*

a black Renault sped off into the night. -T/72.
big wheel [gir] = **big SHOT** *Brady is a big wheel in that club.*
wheel and deal [gir] negociar ou fazer acordos com astúcia, com esperteza, sem dar muita atenção à ética *... party leaders wheeling and dealing ...* -T/87. ♦ *[He] ... has wheeled and dealed all over the world.* -T/87. ⇒ **wheeler-dealer** indivíduo sagaz, astuto, ardiloso *[He] ... was a wheeler-dealer with a hand in ... many U.S. activities ...* -T/66.

WHEELHORSE; wheel horse pessoa que trabalha com muita eficiência, principalmente em uma organização política ou partido *[He] ... was a reliable party wheel horse ...* -T/60.

WHERE **where it's at** [col] = **where the ACTION is** *Easy Rider is a major movie that follows two youths on their search for where it's at.* -T/69. ♦ *[People] ... over 30 who don't know where it's at ...* -T/69.

WHILE **after/in a while** depois de algum tempo, pouco depois, logo *He had gone on a business call but came back after a while.*
all the while = **all the TIME** *... all the while, he doubted his own worth and was painfully conscious of living in the shadow of his father.* -T/62.
once in a while de vez em quando *I enjoy seeing an American like you, once in a while – somebody from home who realizes what we face here.* -WPT,308.
while away passar (o tempo, as horas, os dias etc.) de maneira agradável *... diversions to while away the hours.* -T/72. ♦ *Ian likes to while away summers just lying in the sun on the beach.*
worth someone's while valer a pena, valer o tempo empregado por, compensar o esforço de *It is well worth your while to improve your vocabulary.* ⇒ **worthwhile** que vale a pena, proveitoso, vantajoso *Most things that are worthwhile in life cost you something.* -HLW,40.

WHIP crack the whip [col] exercer sua autoridade de maneira tirânica ou ameaçadora ... *he can crack the whip without stinging the ego.* -T/67.
have/hold the whip hand = **get the upper HAND** *The mama in the American family often has the whip hand but she uses it cleverly.*
whip out puxar ou tirar súbita e vigorosamente, sacar *Whipping out a pistol, he shot one councilman ...* -T/86.
whip up [col] 1. preparar ou aprontar (algo) rapidamente *Mrs. Walton could whip up a meal for twenty people on very short notice.* 2. instigar, incitar, provocar, estimular *[He] ... enlisted his own wife to whip up support for him.* -T/66. ♦ *[The dictator has been] Whipping up popular sentiment against the American and British military presence ...* -T/69.
WHISPERING whispering campaign boatos maledicentes, insinuações maldosas que visam desacreditar um candidato a cargo público, um grupo etc. ... *in spite of the whispering campaign against him in 1960, Kennedy never gave the slightest support to McCarthyism.* -SJ,24.
WHISTLE blow the whistle [gír] 1. trair, denunciar, dedar, botar a boca no trombone *The* Washington Post *blew the whistle on the Watergate break-in.* 2. fazer parar, interromper, pôr um paradeiro, dar um ultimato *The Supreme Court blew the whistle on Nixon when he tried to withhold tapes.*
clean as a whistle [col] limpo, asseado, bem arrumado, em perfeita ordem *That luncheonette is clean as a whistle.*
wet one's whistle [col] tomar um trago, molhar a goela *On his way home from work, he always stops at the neighborhood bar to wet his whistle.*
whistle for tentar conseguir em vão, ficar querendo *If he thinks he'll get money from me, he can whistle for it.*
WHISTLE-STOP cidadezinha, vilarejo etc. onde o trem normalmente só pára quando há embarque ou desembarque *At 9:45 a.m. the express train from L. A. was passing through a whistle-stop in Arizona called Black Rock.*
WHITE poor white [pej] pessoa branca e pobre do sul dos EUA; brancos sem eira nem beira; ralé, gentalha *[In his short stories, Erskine Caldwell] ... has chosen to portray the poor whites and share-croppers of the Deep South ...* -HRW,242.
WHITE-COLLAR 1. de função administrativa, burocrática; de escritório ... *managers and other white-collar workers.* -T/92. 2. relativo a ou próprio de pessoas ou para pessoas dessa classe ou de tal nível socioeconômico ... *a pleasant, white-collar neighborhood of small apartments ...* -T/66.
WHITEWASH encobrir, ocultar, coonestar (erros, irregularidades, faltas etc.) *They tried to whitewash the scandal.*
WHIZ whiz kid [col] pessoa (geralmente jovem) muito inteligente, criativa, bem-sucedida etc. ... *Wall Street's whiz kids ...* -T/87. ♦ *[He] ... was a whiz kid who finished college at 19 ...* -T/73.
WHODUNIT [col] história ou filme policial de mistério *Whodunits are the favorite reading material of all social classes in America.*
WHOLE as a whole em bloco, em conjunto, como um todo *Skyscrapered Manhattan, taken as a whole, is one of man's most fascinating architectural conglomerations.* -T/64.
on the whole de maneira geral, considerando todos os aspectos ... *on the whole, children suffer when their parents get divorced.* -T/80.
WHOLEHEARTED sincero, sério; totalmente devotado, entusiasmado etc.; sem hesitações, sem restrições ... *he deserves wholehearted support.* -T/64. ♦ *... wholehearted cooperation ...* -KAC,93.
WHOOP whoop it up [gír] fazer grande algazarra, gritaria, alarido *The prisoners*

of war whooped it up when they heard that the war was over.

WHOOPEE make whoopee [gir] cair na gandaia, na farra, divertir-se a valer, foliar *Grayson accused his wife of making whoopee while he was in jail.*

WHY why(s) and wherefore(s) razão(ões), causa(s), motivo(s), porquê(s) ... *science does not attempt to tell us the why and wherefore of things* ... -AM,16 ♦ ... *the whys and wherefores of the case clearly did not intrigue the Russians.* -T/64.

WIDE wide of muito afastado de, muito longe de *The bullet hit wide of the target.* ♦ *His statement was wide of the truth.* v. **wide of the MARK**

wide open 1. bem aberto, escancarado *[She was] ... lying on her back with her eyes wide open.* -ST,19. v. **wide-open SPACES** 2. vulnerável, sem defesa, sem proteção *You left yourself wide open when you asked him that question.*

WIDE-AWAKE desperto, alerta, vigilante, arguto, atento, atilado, esperto *We need wide-awake young people in our business.*

WIDE-EYED de olhos arregalados por motivo de surpresa, espanto, admiração ou falta de refinamento, ingenuidade etc. ... *wide-eyed customers inspecting the new models in an auto showroom.* -T/78. ♦ ... *Luke [Skywalker], the wide-eyed farmboy [of* Starwars*] who was always yearning for bigger things ...* -T/80.

WIFE old wives' tale fantasia, ficção, superstição, crenças sem fundamento *Olivier had placed little credence in the legend of a nebulous avenger, believing it ... [was nothing but] an old wives' tale.* -WL,68.

WILDCAT 1. arriscado, duvidoso, inseguro financeiramente ... *to gamble and speculate in wildcat stocks ...* -T/60. 2. irregular, ilegítimo, não-autorizado ... *wildcat strikes have reduced coal production and hours worked ...* -T/77.

WILDFIRE like wildfire rapidamente, como um rastilho de pólvora *The news [of an American GI murdering an English soldier] ran through the British Armed Forces like wildfire ...* -FH,13. ♦ ... *the new custom spread almost like wildfire ...* -BN,109.

WILD-GOOSE wild-goose chase busca, tentativa, esforço etc. fútil, inútil ou infrutífero, coisa que não leva a nada *The police officer was sent on a wild-goose chase when he was told that the mysterious killer was in the stadium.*

WILL at will à vontade, à sua escolha, quando quiser *The soldiers were told to fire at will when the enemy began to attack.* ♦ ... *guerrillas are free to roam much of the country at will.* -T/87.

if you will se for de seu desejo, se assim o quiser, se prefere usar esse(s) termo(s) *In an historic sense, we are witnessing the unraveling, if you will, of the greatest challenge to the world peace today, and that is the Marxist-Leninist movement.* -T/81.

with a will com disposição e entusiasmo, energicamente ... *Janie went to the task with a will.* -ST,71.

WILLIES the willies [gir] = **the CREEPS** ... *I want to get out of here, this place is giving me the willies.* -WCN,162.

WILLY-NILLY quer queira, quer não, compulsoriamente *The doctor prescribes the drug, for which the patient must pay, willy-nilly.* -T/69.

WIN win out/through sair-se vitorioso, triunfar (apesar de dificuldades), alcançar o sucesso (afinal) ... *the desire for peace once again wins out.* -T/87. ♦ ... *the film [*The Grapes of Wrath *ended] ... on a strong declaration of faith in the ability of the American people to win through.* -KA,242.

win over converter (alguém) à sua causa, a seu partido etc., persuadir, convencer *[People who]'... show an untiring zeal in winning others over to their way of thinking.* -PC,254.

WIND[1] [rima com *grinned*] **get one's second wind** → **second WIND**

get one's wind tomar fôlego, recuperar a respiração, descansar *We need just a little rest and we can get our wind and start again.*
get the wind up → **have the WIND up**
get wind of ficar sabendo de, inteirar-se de *The plot [to kidnap the Premier] was thwarted when loyal officers got wind of it ...* -T/78.
gone with the wind desaparecido, sumido, passado, levado pelo tempo *"The politics of race has gone wih the wind", proclaimed Georgia's Governor George Busbee in his 1975 inaugural address.* -T/76.
have/get the wind up assustar-se, amedrontar-se, alarmar-se *Christ help me! I've never been afraid to die! ... How can I ... with four Canadian war decorations be the only one to get the wind up?* -GE,275.
how the wind blows → **(which) WAY the wind blows**
in the wind na iminência (real ou aparente) de acontecer, em cogitação *Fuller knew something was in the wind and decided to get away before the police arrested him.*
sail close to the wind chegar muito próximo daquilo que é impróprio, ilegal, desonesto etc. *Many a businessman sails as close to the wind as possible in an effort to keep down production expenses.*
second wind 1. recuperação do ritmo relativamente normal da respiração (após a exaustão inicial durante um exercício, esforço etc.) *My breathing became more difficult as I ran, but I soon got my second wind and finished sixth in the race.* 2. energia renovada, recuperação de forças para a continuação de uma tarefa, empreendimento etc. *The politicians must rest to get their second wind before the final campaign rush.*
take the wind out of someone's sails destruir a autoconfiança de, abater o orgulho de, frustrar a expectativa de, causar desapontamento a *The fact that he wasn't elected governor took the wind out of his sails.*
winds of change sinais, indicações, tendências de mudanças (sociais, econômicas, políticas) *... the winds of change are with us now ...* -T/92.

WIND² [rima com *find*] **wind down** 1. diminuir gradualmente (até acabar, chegar ao fim) *The civil war ... shows no sign of winding down.* -T/87. 2. desenrolar-se, afrouxar-se (corda de relógio, mecanismo, brinquedo etc.) *My watch wound down and stopped.* 3. descontrair-se, espairecer o espírito *You're so tense. Take the day off. Try to wind down a bit.*
wind up 1. dar corda a, retesar a mola de (relógio, mecanismo, brinquedo etc.) *She forgot to wind up the clock.* 2. acabar, terminar, concluir *What time did the meeting wind up?* ⇒ **windup** fim, final, conclusão, desfecho *... the windup of it [violation of the law] was that I got sentenced to a year ...* -AIM,35. 3. acabar (em), terminar (como), ir parar (em) *You'll wind up in jail some day.* 4. pôr em ordem, arranjar, arrumar, organizar, regularizar *He wound up his affairs before leaving for Boston.* 5. deixar preocupado, ansioso, nervoso, tenso [geralmente pas] *... she became so wound up that she had to take sleeping pills before going to bed ...* -T/77.
WINDBAG [col] fanfarrão, falastrão *Most politicians are windbags and people rarely believe what they say.*
WINDFALL achado, coisa providencial, favor do céu, bafejo da fortuna (geralmente dinheiro) *The discovery of two thousand dollars hidden in an old trunk in the attic was a welcome windfall for my father.*
WINDOW out the window [col] descartado, não mais cogitado, sem efeito *The agreements ... have been thrown out the window.* -T/92. ♦ *... his job had gone out the window.* -GES,178.
window dressing deturpação de fatos com a finalidade de produzir impressão

favorável, falsa impressão, aparência enganosa *Some of the President's recent moves may be just window dressing.*
WING   clip someone's wings limitar os meios, os recursos, o poder de, cortar as asas de ... *Gorbachev's opponents tried to clip his wings a bit.* -T/87.
in the wings perto, à mão, nos bastidores e preparado para agir, assumir o lugar de outro etc. *[He] ... has stood patiently in the wings ...* -T/67. ♦ *There is always someone standing in the wings ready for your position.*
under one's wing sob a proteção de, sob os cuidados de *Under the wing of his brother ... his career developed quickly ...* -T/61.
wing it improvisar, fazer algo sem preparação *[President George H. W.] Bush is best when he wings it in his own words.* -T/91.
WINK   forty winks [col] uma soneca *I always try to get in forty winks on afternoons when there is nothing to do.* -DK,12. ♦ *... he slept forty winks ...* -SEB,58.
not sleep a wink; not get a wink of sleep não dormir, não pregar o olho *She didn't sleep a wink last night.* ♦ *I didn't get a wink of sleep all night.* -OJ,26.
wink at fingir que não vê (algo ilícito, ilegal, impróprio etc., como se em conivência) *We can't just wink at this. Something has to be done about it.*
WIPE   wipe away enxugar, limpar esfregando *She ... wiped away her tears ...* -T/61.
wipe off limpar, apagar, tirar, retirar, eliminar ou fazer desaparecer esfregando *Mother told Sue to wipe off the spilled milk.* ♦ *wipe off the table* ♦ *wipe off the dust*
wipe out 1. limpar esfregando o interior de *Wipe out that bucket.* 2. cancelar, apagar *Larson has wiped out his debt.* ♦ *The teacher told Joey to wipe out what he had written on the blackboard.* 3. destruir, aniquilar, dizimar, eliminar, erradicar, reduzir a nada *The first settlers in Virginia were wiped out by Indians and swamp fever.* ♦ *The village of Lidice in Czechoslovakia was wiped out by the Nazis in reprisal.* ♦ *All her bitterness could not wipe out the love she felt for Mark.* 4. [col] matar, assassinar *He was wiped out by a rival gang.*

WIRE   down to the wire 1. próximo do prazo final, no fim ... *the election campaign came down to the wire ...* -T/78. 2. [col] sem dinheiro, a nenhum, na última lona *By the end of the month Len is down to the wire.*
live wire 1. fio eletrizado *During the hurricane, the danger from live wires strewn all over the roads was a great problem for the rescue workers.* 2. [col] pessoa ativa, enérgica, empreendedora *McKibben is known as a live wire in his company.*
pull wires → **pull STRINGS**
under the wire no último momento, no limite, na linha de chegada *My great-grandfather just got in under the wire when the claims were being filed for the free lands in the Oregon Territory. The next day no more claims were allowed.*
WIRETAP   wiretap; tap 1. ouvir ou gravar secretamente conversa telefônica de outras pessoas, grampear telefone *I think our phone has been tapped.* 2. [ou] **wiretapping** espionagem telefônica, escuta clandestina de telefone ... *the FBI started a series of wiretaps that ultimately monitored the telephones of 13 Government officials ...* -T/76. ♦ *He was accused ... of having approved the Watergate wiretapping plans ...* -T/73.
WISE   wise to [gir] ciente de, a par de, informado de (situação, motivo, razão, verdade etc.) *She was wise to all his tricks.*
wise up [gir] 1. inteirar-se, ficar sabendo, perceber, aprender *Holt's wife suddenly wised up to the fact that he was running around with other women.* 2. informar, pôr ao corrente *He is so naive that someone should wise him up to the facts of life.*

WISECRACK [col] observação mordaz, sarcasmo, gracejo *Bob Hope was the best with the fast, subtle wisecrack.*

WISELY not wisely but too well não com racionalidade, com a cabeça, mas com a emoção (o que poderá trazer conseqüências desagradáveis) *It was said that the queen of Scotland loved her country not wisely but too well.*

WISH wish on/upon exprimir um desejo ou um pedido servindo-se de algo (estrela etc.) como talismã *He wished upon a star that someday he would see her again.*

wish (off) on impingir, livrar-se de (tarefa, pessoa etc. geralmente desagradável, passando-a a outro) *Poor Joe, somebody was always wishing some dirty job on him.* ♦ *Just because you don't like your girl friend any more, don't try to wish her off on me.*

wish someone well desejar felicidades ou bom êxito a, desejar tudo de bom a *There is reason to wish him well, but also reason for skepticism.* -T/87. ♦ *"I know you wish us well", he said. "I wish all of you well."* -RK,186. ⇒ **well-wisher** pessoa que deseja felicidade ou êxito a alguém, simpatizante *The new President received messages from well-wishers in the international world.*

WIT at one's wit's/wits' end desorientado, sem saber que fazer *All her attempts to solve her problem had failed and she was now at her wit's end.*

frighten/scare someone out of his wits dar um grande susto em, apavorar *... the woman ... [was] trembling as she seemed to look for something, scared out of her wits.* -BFW,25. ♦ *The children were frightened out of their wits when they saw their mother during an epileptic seizure.*

have/keep one's wits about one estar/ficar atento, prevenido, esperto, equilibrado, em seu juízo *Olivier told himself that no matter what occurred he must keep his wits about him.* -WL,49. ♦ *Prayer gave me the strength to keep my wits about me ...* -HE,252.

to wit a saber, isto é *... all [species of the cuckoo bird] indulge in a highly organized form of nesting behavior, to wit: they lay their eggs in the nest of other birds ...* -GET,207.

WITCH witch hunt; witch-hunt caça às bruxas, investigação de supostas atividades políticas subversivas, de deslealdade, de opiniões impopulares etc. *[The Crucible, a play by Arthur Miller] ... an allegory built around the New England witch trials of the seventeenth century, drew an ironic parallel to the anti-Red "witch hunts" of the Fifties.* -HDR,402. ⇒ **witch-hunter** investigador de atividades subversivas, de pessoas que têm opiniões impopulares, heterodoxas etc., perseguidor de comunistas *... that ultimate American witch-hunter, the late Joe McCarthy.* -T/81.

WITH with it [gír] ciente da situação, informado, alerta, por dentro, atualizado, na moda *The Kennedys are bright and new; they're with it.* -T/66. ♦ *If you're not in favor of abortion, people say that you're not with it.*

with someone [col] 1. do lado de, a favor de, apoiando, da mesma opinião *I agree with Senator Walker's analysis of the situation. I'm with him.* 2. acompanhando o raciocínio de, entendendo *Do as you're told or you will no longer work for this company. Are you with me?*

WITNESS bear witness dar testemunho, depor, testificar *[He] ... was hard pressed to explain the failure of history to record the changes which nature seemed to bear witness to.* -GJ,59.

WIVES old wives' tale → **WIFE**

WOLF cry wolf dar alarme falso *The boy in Aesop's fable had cried wolf so many times that no one believed him anymore.*

keep the wolf from the door ter apenas o necessário para se manter, evitar a miséria, a fome *During the Great Depres-*

sion in the early thirties many people had difficulty keeping the wolf from the door.
lone wolf [col] pessoa solitária, independente *In those days, John ... [was] already regarded ... as pretty much of a lone wolf ... -OE,5.*
wolf down engolir, devorar, comer vorazmente *Big John wolfed down two sandwiches and left hurriedly.*
wolf in sheep's clothing lobo em pele de cordeiro *He turned out to be a wolf in sheep's clothing.*
WOMB from womb to tomb = **from the CRADLE to the grave** *... the uninhibited, innocent sexuality ... according to Freud, controls man's actions from womb to tomb. -T/66.*
WONDER do/work wonders/miracles fazer milagres, produzir efeitos prodigiosos *Though he certainly cannot claim to have worked any miracles, [Bill] Clinton can point to some solid accomplishments. -T/92.* ♦ *The new medicine has worked wonders for him.*
for a wonder excepcionalmente, surpreendentemente, estranhamente *For a wonder, she arrived on time for her appointment.*
it's a wonder é surpreendente *It's a wonder that Mr. Norris has refused to accept your generous offer.*
(it's) little/no/small wonder não admira, não causa surpresa *It is small wonder ... that the abstract vocabulary of culturally disadvantaged children is deficient in range and precision ... -AD,217.* ♦ *Most of us have preconceived and prejudiced notions about almost everything. Is it any wonder then, that our problems are so difficult to be solved?* ♦ *No wonder he got the job. He's the owner's son.*
work wonders → **do WONDERS**
WOOD not see the woods for the trees → **not see the FOREST for the trees**
out of the woods [col] fora de perigo, não mais em dificuldades *I don't think we're out of the woods yet. -T/87.* ♦ *... Brazil is by no means out of the financial woods as yet. -GJI,70.*
take to the woods [col] fugir, dar no pé *When the heat of August hits New York, the people take to the woods.*
WOOL pull the wool over someone's eyes [col] enganar, iludir, ludibriar *... he'll make use of your friendship to pull the wool over your eyes. -CHT,83.*
WORD as good as one's word/promise fiel à sua palavra, fidedigno, confiável *The old truth, that a man is as good as his word, still holds. -T/81.* ♦ *When Grayson said he would give us the money on Friday, he was as good as his promise.*
break one's word/promise faltar à palavra, quebrar uma promessa *You promised me you would keep quiet about this but you seem to have broken your word.*
breathe a word [geralmente neg] falar, tagarelar, ser indiscreto, abrir a boca *Don't breathe a word of this to anybody.*
by word of mouth de viva voz, oralmente *Since West Africa had no literature, customs and rituals were always memorized and handed down by example and word of mouth. -SMS,20.*
dying words últimas palavras *In Shakespeare's Julius Caesar Brutus's dying words are: "Caesar now be still; I kill'd not thee with half so good a will".* ♦ *"Rosebud" was Charles Foster Kane's dying word.*
eat one's words desdizer-se, retratar-se, desculpar-se *Swanson had to eat his words when he was proved wrong.*
fighting words observação insultuosa, provocação, desacato, desaforo *There have always been fighting words which will arouse Irishmen or Southerners to blind fury. -CH,14.*
four-letter word vulgarismo sexual e escatológico, palavra obscena, palavrão *She speaks out, at times in four-letter words, on Women's Lib or birth control. -T/72.*

from the word go [col] desde o início, desde o princípio *Their marriage was doomed from the word go.*

get a word in (edgewise/edgeways) ter oportunidade de falar, de interromper ou de entrar em uma conversa *Each of the six Senators present seemed to want to get in a few words ...* -T/79. ♦ *I always find it difficult, I mean* really *difficult, to get a word in edgewise when my wife and her sister are talking.*

get word ser informado *[She] ... soon got word that the proslavery men knew where he [her husband] was and were planning to kill him.* -SH,22.

give one's word dar sua palavra, prometer *I've given you my word and can't go back on it now.*

give the word dar o sinal, indicar *Just give the word and we'll start building the house.*

go back on one's word faltar à palavra, roer a corda *The colonel went back on his word and allowed the massacre of the enemy soldiers who had surrendered.*

hang on someone's words; hang on someone's every word ouvir atentamente as palavras de *The crowd hung on the speaker's words.* ♦ *... the captain [was] hanging on his every word ...* -TW,31. ♦ *... nations hang on a President's every word.* -T/74.

have a word with conversar com, ter uma palavra com (por um instante ou em particular) *May I have a word with you?*

have words discutir, bater boca *The new teacher had words with one of the office staff and left the school.*

household word/name palavra ou nome familiar, comum, muito conhecido, famoso *Xerox has become a household word.*

in a word em uma palavra, em síntese, em resumo *He's a liar and a thief. In a word, he's not to be trusted.*

in other words em outras palavras *Dick was handsome, young and rich. In other words, the ideal husband for any girl.*

in so many words 1. sem mudar uma palavra, literalmente, à letra *He wanted to marry her and told her that in so many words.* 2. francamente, sem rodeios, com toda a clareza *Brad told Mac in so many words what he thought of him.*

in words of one syllable em linguagem clara, franca, direta *In words of one syllable, I think he's a pain (in the neck).*

keep one's word manter a palavra *You can trust her. She has always been known to keep her word.*

the last word 1. a última palavra, a resolução definitiva, a decisão final *He has always enjoyed having the last word ...* -T/87. 2. [col] o que há de mais moderno, a última moda, a última palavra *This is the last word in vacuum cleaners.*

leave word deixar recado *Ring his office and leave word that I want him to call just as soon as he comes in.* -GES,17.

mark my words atente para minhas palavras, ouça o que estou dizendo *"Mark my words", the old man cried. "No good will come if you try to travel to another planet."*

not a word silêncio, bico calado, nem um pio *Remember, not a word to her about this!*

not mince words → **not mince MATTERS**

put in a (good) word for; say a (good) word for recomendar, interceder por *I'll put in a good word for you. That's all I can do.* -DK,191.

put in/into words expressar verbalmente, enunciar, dizer *... the actual content [of the experience the Buddha had under the Bo Tree] ... was never and could never be put into words.* -WAW,54.

put words in/into someone's mouth dar a entender ou afirmar que alguém disse algo que realmente não disse *I never said that! Don't try to put words in my mouth.*

say a (good) word for = put in a (good) WORD for

say the word dar a ordem, aprovar, autorizar *You'll want to be sure you can trust me. But I'll be glad to help, any time you say the word.* -SW,15.

send word mandar dizer, notificar, informar, avisar *[The President] ... sent word for the Cabinet to assemble next morning.* -T/74.

take someone's word for it aceitar a palavra de, acreditar em *It can't be done. Take my word for it.* ♦ *OK, I'll take your word for it if you say so.*

take someone at his word confiar em (alguém) e aceitar sua palavra *... the Soviet leader was sincere in his desire to rebuild détente and should be taken at his word.* -T/88.

take the words out of someone's mouth tirar as palavras da boca de *You took the words out of my mouth when you said that he's not to be trusted.*

true to one's word cumpridor de sua palavra, fiel à sua promessa *Judge Sullivan, true to his word, began giving Nellie English lessons ...* -MWL,62.

weigh one's words pesar as palavras, atentar bem no que diz *[He was] ... a man who weighed every word carefully and would vouch for his opinions with his life.* -MH,15.

word for word palavra por palavra, literalmente, exatamente *... true undestanding of a foreign tongue demands more than the ability to translate word for word.* -MJL,126.

word is out já não é segredo, a notícia se espalhou *The word is out that he's leaving next week.*

words fail me não tenho palavras, não sei o que dizer *Words fail me. I really don't know what to say.*

a word to the wise conselho aos que sabem ouvir; a bom entendedor meia palavra basta *A word to the wise should be sufficient, so watch out how you conduct yourself in the next few months.*

WORD-OF-MOUTH → **by WORD of mouth**

WORK at work 1. no trabalho, trabalhando, ocupado *At 7:30 in the morning he is usually hard at work.* ♦ *The bulldozers are at work as never before, because our population is increasing.* -WCB,167. 2. agindo, em operação, em ação, em atividade *... the centrifugal forces that have already torn apart the U.S.S.R. are now at work in Russia and Ukraine.* -T/92.

gum up the works [gir] frustrar, estragar, emperrar, fazer malograr (plano, objetivo etc.) *He always gums up the works when he tries to help us.*

have one's work cut out for ter um trabalho ou uma tarefa difícil a cumprir, ter muito que fazer *Whoever takes over that job will certainly have his work cut out for him.*

in the works [col] em preparo, em andamento, em curso *... a policy change is in the works ...* -T/91. ♦ *She has a new book in the works.*

make short/quick work of lidar com ou livrar-se de (alguém ou algo) com rapidez e eficiência *The Sioux [Indians] ... made short work of Custer and the 212 cavalrymen whom he led [in the Battle of the Little Bighorn].* -T/66.

out of work desempregado *He's been out of work since last May.*

shoot the works [gir] 1. arriscar tudo em uma jogada ou aposta *We were so sure that Lightning would win the Derby that we decided to shoot the works.* 2. gastar tudo o que se tem, não poupar despesas *I'm going to shoot the works on a trip to Europe.* 3. fazer uma tentativa ou um esforço supremo, dar tudo o que se tem *This is your last chance to make a new high jump record. So, shoot the works.*

work in/into introduzir, encaixar, inserir, incluir *In your next political cartoon, try to work in some humorous situation concerning the Royal Family.* ♦ *The* *musicians worked new numbers into their repertoire.*

work off 1. livrar-se de, dissipar, descarregar, eliminar (por esforço ou atividade) *Jack is so overweight that he should try to work off about forty pounds.* ♦ *... I need a hobby in which destructiveness and aggressiveness can be worked off.* -T/72. 2. pagar (um débito) com trabalho *Kendall has worked off his debt.*

work on 1. ocupar-se com, labutar em, trabalhar em, aplicar seus esforços a *She's been working on a new novel.* 2. influenciar, tentar persuadir, atuar sobre *I'll try to work on my father to get him to let me take the car tonight.*

work out 1. solucionar, resolver pelo raciocínio *He worked out the difficult problem in just a few seconds.* 2. calcular *I'll work out an estimate and call you later when I have it ready.* 3. [seguido de *at* ou *to*] montar a, importar em, chegar a *The bill for repairs to your car works out to one hundred dollars.* 4. elaborar, planejar, idear, preparar, desenvolver, expor *When Henry Adams studied the glorious medieval cathedrals he was inspired to work out his "dynamic theory of history" ...* -MHJ,11. ♦ *We have worked out a way to save on fuel costs.* 5. resultar, redundar, acontecer (de determinada maneira) *Nothing has worked out as we had planned or hoped.* 6. mostrar ser eficiente, funcionar, dar resultado *I'm afraid the plan didn't work out.* 7. exaurir, esgotar (mina, veio etc.) [geralmente pas] *That silver mine was worked out many years ago.* 8. praticar exercício físico, fazer ginástica, manter a boa forma atlética *Most of the sports-club members work out in a gym at least once a week.* -T/73. ⇒ **workout** exercício físico, treino *... he begins the day with a vigorous two-hour workout.* -T/87.

work over [col] surrar, espancar *Never give an armed robber the excuse he is looking for to work you over.* -T/81.

the works [gír] 1. tudo, o serviço completo, a operação completa, todos os itens ou ingredientes etc. *When I eat a banana split, I like it with the works: marshmallow, fruit sauces and nuts with a cherry on top.* ♦ *... medium-range missiles, long-range strategic weapons, space defenses – the works.* -T/86. 2. injúrias, maus-tratos; surra, sova; assassinato *He was afraid the gang would give him the works.*

work up 1. subir ou aumentar gradualmente, avançar aos poucos, progredir *He wanted his son to begin with the lowest job and work up into an executive job to really know the business.* 2. formar, compor, preparar, elaborar, desenvolver, causar, idear *We're working up a plan to convert fresh water from ocean water.* 3. excitar, provocar, instigar, incitar *She worked up the audience with evangelical fervor as she preached ...* -T/72. 4. despertar, gerar (interesse, entusiasmo etc.) *Edwards was unable to work up enough enthusiasm for the new plan.* 5. adquirir, juntar, criar (coragem) *Bronson was trying to work up enough courage to ask his boss for a raise.* 6. ficar ou deixar nervoso, irritado, irado *You're getting yourself all worked up.* -ST,163.

work up to avançar gradualmente para; chegar a (ponto principal, clímax etc.) *Many of O. Henry's short stories work up to a surprising end.*

WORKAHOLIC indivíduo viciado em trabalho *... he is a workaholic who shuns receptions and cocktail parties.* -T/80.

WORLD all over the world em todo o mundo, no mundo inteiro, universalmente *[He] ... has a wide range of friends and contacts all over the world.* -T/92.

around/round the world no mundo inteiro, em todo o mundo *... genuine currents of democratic change have brought new political freedoms to dozens of nations around the world.* -T/87.

bring into the world dar à luz, trazer ao mundo *Mother wants the little boy she*

suffered such agonies to bring into the world to be a great artist ... -TM,12.
come down//up in the world arruinar-se, empobrecer etc.//ascender socialmente, prosperar, enriquecer etc. *Once a famous and wealthy woman, Karen had come down in the world.*
come into the world vir ao mundo, nascer *Coming into the world with one parent is a handicap, no matter how mature and moneyed the mother may be.* -T/92.
dead to the world profundamente adormecido *Elmer was dead to the world five minutes after he went to bed.*
for all the world 1. por nada deste mundo [geralmente neg] *She loved her husband the way he was and wouldn't have him look different for all the world.* 2. sob todos os aspectos, em tudo, exatamente *She looked for all the world like a famous movie star of the 1940s.*
for the world; for worlds [neg] = **for all the WORLD** 1 *I'd never hurt you for the world.* ♦ *He managed to master his surprise [at the conversation he overheard in the hotel lobby] ... He would not have left now for worlds.* -HJ,5.
from around the world de todo o mundo *... leaders from around the world signed a declaration promising to reduce infant mortality by one-third by the year 2000.* -T/91.
get on in the world progredir, fazer carreira, subir na vida *Many American feminists assume that a woman's libido must be denied if she wants to get on in the world.* -T/71.
give the world to dar tudo para, ser capaz de fazer qualquer coisa para *I'd give the world to see the thief's face when he opens my suitcase and finds not the money he thinks he stole but my dirty laundry.*
how in the world → **how on EARTH**
not long for this world com pouco tempo de vida, com os dias contados *Toward the end of August it seemed that she was not long for this world and, unfortunately, on September 7 she died.*
out of this world [gir] magnífico, fabuloso, espetacular, maravilhoso, superlativo *Walter Huston's performance as the old prospector in* The Treasure of the Sierra Madre *was superb, out of this world.*
set the world on fire alcançar grande fama e sucesso; produzir grande efeito, realizar algo que chame atenção *He'll never set the world on fire with his plays for children.* ♦ *[Perez Prado] ... proceeded to set the musical world of Latin America on fire with recordings of excellent fidelity ...* -SMS,181.
think the world of ter muita afeição ou grande admiração por *She thinks the world of her children.*
what/where/who/why in the world → **how/what/where etc. on EARTH**
the world is one's oyster o mundo oferece tudo de bom, prazeroso etc. para; o mundo foi feito para; alguém pode fazer da vida tudo o que quiser *When Oliver graduated from Princeton, he felt the world was his oyster.*
a world of muito, um mundo de, grande quantidade de *Drink this. It will do you a world of good.*
the world over = **all over the WORLD** *The world over, charms of all kinds tend to be rather chanted than spoken.* -SWL,103.
worlds apart totalmente diferente *... my scientific investigation was forgotten or was at least redirected into channels that were worlds apart from my original intention.* -CCT,14.
WORLD-CLASS da mais alta qualidade, classe etc., dos melhores do mundo *[He] ... promises to get "world-class experts" together to solve a national problem ...* -T/92.
WORLDWIDE geral, universal, que engloba o mundo inteiro *... the influence of Western art has been world-wide ...* -CEO,ix.

WORM the worm may turn até os mais humildes podem se rebelar (quando pressionados) *The worm may turn some day and quiet Mr. Smith may go wild and really raise hell with his domineering wife.*
worm in/into penetrar pouco a pouco em, introduzir-se manhosamente em *Sheldon wormed his way into Laura's confidence.*
worm out extrair, arrancar (segredo, informações etc.) *The spy tried to worm out secrets out of her.*
WORN-OUT → **WEAR out**
WORRY worry along/through conseguir viver, arranjar-se (apesar de problema, dificuldade etc.) *Despite the stress of modern life, most people still manage to "muddle through", worrying along and solving their problems after a fashion.* -CJ,5.
WORSE for the worse → **for the BETTER**
worse off em situação pior que a anterior (mais pobre, mais infeliz etc.) *... the younger generation is worse off than its parents.* -T/92. ♦ *... U.S. carmakers [are] worse off than they've been in decades.* -T/91.
WORST at one's/its worst na pior situação possível, no que tem de pior, sob os piores aspectos, nos piores momentos *[The Treasure of the Sierra Madre is an] Excellent film of gold-prospecting, greed and human nature at its worst ...* -ML,605.
at (the) worst na pior das hipóteses *At the worst, you will only lose your time and it may be a profitable experience.*
do one's worst causar o maior dano possível, todo o mal que puder, agir da maneira mais desagradável *He does his worst to make his family uncomfortable when they have company.*
get/have the worst of levar a pior, ser derrotado, perder (luta, discussão, debate etc.) *The two men were fighting and the fat one was getting the worst of it.*
if (the) worst comes to (the) worst se acontecer o pior *If worst comes to worst, we can always sell our car and use the money to solve our difficulties.*

WORTH be worth it valer a pena *Greg's yacht cost a lot of money, but it was worth it.*
be worth seeing/considering/reading/having etc. valer a pena ver, considerar, ler, ter etc. *If these things [security, good pay, reasonable leisure for the enjoyment of life] are worth having, they are worth fighting for.* -KRI,565.
for all one is worth com todas as forças, com a máxima energia, com todo seu potencial, com denodo, ao máximo *The policemen were chasing the burglar and he was running for all he was worth.*
for what something/it is worth pelo que (algo) possa representar, pelo valor ou utilidade que (algo) possa ter *... we had the statements of witnesses, for what they were worth.* -TB,16. ♦ *Let me tell you my opinion for what it's worth.*
WORTHWHILE → **worth someone's WHILE**
WOULD would rather → **had rather** [sob *have*]
WOULD-BE que se diz ser, que aspira a ser; pretenso, suposto, pseudo *[Tyrone] Power and would-be expatriate, Orson Welles, were the only Americans in the cast [of* The Black Rose*].* -BDF,162. ♦ *... a would-be writer ...* -T/87.
WOUND¹ [rima com *found*] **wound up** → **WIND up 5**
WOUND² [rima com *crooned*] **lick one's wounds** recuperar as forças após uma derrota, refazer-se de um fracasso etc., retemperar-se *The battalion retired to a rear area to lick their wounds.* ♦ *Today the radicals are licking their wounds.* -T/73.
WRAP under wraps em segredo; encoberto *... the company may have known about safety problems for years and kept them under wraps.* -T/92. ♦ *Negotiations for the swap [of prisoners] had been carried out under tight security wraps.* -T/76.
wrapped up in totalmente devotado a, inteiramente absorvido em, com toda a

atenção concentrada em *Mr. Taylor is so wrapped up in his business that he has no time for his family.*
wrapped up in oneself preocupado apenas consigo mesmo *He's so wrapped up in himself he couldn't see anything about anything ...* -HET,315.
wrap up 1. agasalhar-se *Wrap up well before you go out.* 2. [col] concluir, finalizar, resolver, liquidar, levar a um final (geralmente feliz) *I've got some business to wrap up and then I'll see you.* -FC,16. ♦ *The arms-control group worked through the night, finally wrapping up its session at 6.30 a. m. on Sunday.* -T/86. 3. sintetizar, sumariar, fazer um resumo de *For millions of well informed men and women,* TIME Magazine *each week wraps up the whole world's news.* -T/80. ⇒ **wrap-up** sumário, resumo *Each week* TIME *Magazine ... [presents] a complete wrap-up of the affairs of the world.* -T/81.
WRECK a nervous wreck pessoa com os nervos em frangalhos *She was held captive by the terrorists for six days and when she was finally rescued she was a nervous wreck.*
WRINKLE a new wrinkle [col] inovação, novidade, novo enfoque, última moda *The newest wrinkle is the organic food supermarket ...* -T/71.
WRIST slap on the wrist; slap the wrist of; slap someone's wrist repreender com brandura, ser leniente *She slapped Carlson's wrists for telling lies.* v. **a SLAP on the wrist**
WRIT writ/written large de maneira ressaltada, acentuada; mostrado de modo mais claro, maior, ampliado, bastante óbvio *In theatrical tradition, the fortunes of king and queen were the human situation writ large.* -T/68. ♦ *The shock and concern of official Washington [over the assassination of Egypt's President Anwar Sadat] were also written large on the faces of scores of dignitaries ...* -T/81.

WRITE write down anotar, registrar por escrito *The Greeks ... were addicted to writing things down, and it is only through their literature that we know anything at all of the Phoenicians.* -BCMT,25. ♦ *Write down every dime you spend.* -MD,60.
write off 1. cancelar (débito etc.), deduzir *We can write off these expenses on our income tax.* ♦ *... the Soviets have written off some $4 billion in economic loans to Damascus ...* -T/87. ⇒ **write-off** eliminação de um item dos livros contábeis, cancelamento; redução, depreciação *He got a tax write-off on his business loss.* 2. considerar como sem valor, insignificante, inútil; dar por perdido, desconsiderar, esquecer, rejeitar, pôr de lado *[Phil's death] ... was written off as a hunting accident, but everyone in the family knew the truth.* -KJS,18. ♦ *[Poet Ezra Pound] ... cannot be written off and must, more and more, be written about.* -T/60.
write out escrever, pôr no papel; escrever por extenso, escrever com todos os detalhes *"Writing things out", ... is simply a more rigorous way of talking things out.* -BCM,7. ♦ *Write out carefully all the things you want me to bring back from the States.* ♦ *Mr. Parkinson wrote out a check for $5,000.*
write up descrever, narrar; compor, escrever (relatório, relato, reportagem, artigo, narrativa etc.), desenvolver por escrito *He wrote up an account of his 12-day tour of New Hampshire.* ♦ *Nichols wrote up a special report to the president of the company.* ⇒ **write-up** reportagem, história, artigo (freqüentemente elogioso, em jornal, revista etc.) *Our school's basketball team got a wonderful write-up in* LIFE *Magazine.*
written all over transparecendo claramente, manifestamente; expressando com toda a clareza, sem disfarce *Contempt was written all over Greta's face.* ♦ *He was,a*

man who had enjoyment of life written all over him.

WRITING   put in writing pôr o preto no branco, pôr no papel *I wish to have our verbal contract put in writing and signed by all parties concerned.*
writing on the wall → the HANDWRITING on the wall
WRITTEN → write
WRONG   do wrong fazer mal, cometer erros, falhar *[They] ... had prosecuted him and somehow done him wrong.* -NE,328.
♦ *John was deeply in love with Mary and, in his eyes, she could do no wrong.*
⇒ **wrongdoing** erro, dano, injustiça, má ação, comportamento impróprio, transgressão *None [of those people] were accused of any wrongdoing.* -T/87.
get in wrong with [col] incorrer no desagrado de, pôr-se mal com *He got in wrong with the school officials and was expelled.*
in the wrong errado, em erro, em equívoco, sem razão *... you shouldn't have humbled yourself to her like that, even if it looked like you were in the wrong.* -WCN,288.
two wrongs don't make a right um erro não justifica outro *If you're planning to take revenge on him, remember that two wrongs don't make a right.*
what's wrong (que é) que há? que se passa? que está acontecendo *What's wrong, Darlene? You look so sad.*
what's wrong with 1. qual é o problema, a falha, o defeito etc. de *What's wrong with this machine?* 2. que mal há nisso, qual é o inconveniente disso? *What's wrong with letting me have the car this evening?*
WRONGDOING → do WRONG

X   x out   cancelar, eliminar, anular, riscar com um x   *X out the first paragraph you wrote.*

XMAS (CHRISTMAS)   Natal   *We wish you a Merry Xmas.*

X-RATED   para adultos, impróprio para menores (filme etc.)   *... VCRs [videocassette recorders] bring X-rated films into the home ...* -T/87. ♦ *... an erotic X-rated ballet.* -T/87.

X-RATING   interdição para menores (em filmes etc.)   *The film [Last Tango in Paris] will carry an X-rating, which bars admission to viewers under 18.* -T/73.

YARN spin a yarn/tale [col] contar uma história, principalmente fantástica, exagerada, difícil de acreditar *Old sailors liked to gather a group of young children and spin yarns about sea monsters and mermaids.*

YEAR advanced in years idoso, de idade avançada ... *Williams' parents ... are advanced in years.* -T/81.

for years há muitos anos, há muito tempo *In his ironic way, Henry Higgins said that "in America [people] haven't used English for years".*

get along/on in years envelhecer ... *Dannel [i.e., Daniel] Boone was ... getting on in years now.* -GJH,15. ♦ *[She] ... was getting pretty well along in years ...* -KRI,591.

lean years anos de dificuldade, de escassez, de improdutividade, de vacas magras ... *a lean year for the U.S. economy ...* -T/92. ♦ *After two punishingly lean years, [Billy] Wilder at last got a screenwriting job at Paramount.* -T/60.

over the years através dos anos *My relations with him ... have been warm and friendly over the years.* -KJS,190.

YEAR-ROUND (que funciona, está em atividade ou ocorre) durante o ano inteiro *Hundreds of volunteers devote time and energy year-round to the church.* -T/91.

YELLOW-BELLIED [gir] [pej] medroso, covarde *You yellow-bellied little jerk!*

YELLOW-BELLY; YELLOWBELLY [gir] [pej] pessoa covarde *You're nothing but a yellowbelly.*

YEOMAN yeoman('s) service/work bons e leais serviços, grande auxílio, ajuda eficaz *[He was] ... a North Carolinian who had done yeoman service for Candidate Kennedy in ... [his] native state during the 1960 campaign.* -T/61.

YES-MAN; YES MAN [gir] homem servil, vaquinha de presépio *[He] ... had worked for Hoffa in various union posts since 1934 and was considered little more than a yes man.* -T/81.

YOU you're welcome não há de que *She thanked me and I said: "You're welcome".*

YOUNG with young prenhe [fêmea de animal] *Our old cow is with young.*

young ones → **LITTLE** ones

YUP [*Young Urban Professional*]; **YUPPIE** [col] jovem de formação universitária com emprego de alta remuneração e gostos refinados que vive numa cidade grande ... *a Porsche [automobile] ... became such a ... status symbol that ... yuppies cheerfully endured price increases as steep as 20% in the past year.* -T/87. ♦ *... a group of yuppie women ...* -T/87.

ZAP [gir] 1. mover(-se), atacar, agredir, alvejar, destruir, matar etc. com súbita força e violência *He was zapped when he went down the lonely street in the dark* 2. derrotar fragorosamente *The visiting team got zapped in the game last night.* 3. energia, vigor, vivacidade, ímpeto *Watch that kid. He's full of zap.*

ZERO **zero hour** hora em que algo está marcado para começar, o momento crucial, a hora H *... the zero hour for the synchronized attack [against the enemy position] ...* -SLS,273.
zero in on 1. ajustar a mira em, determinar a posição correta do alvo; mirar, fazer pontaria em (alvo); focalizar (câmera) em *Our guns were zeroed in on the enemy installations.* ♦ *Onstage, television cameras zeroed in on their target.* -T/61. 2. dar toda a atenção a, concentrar-se em (objetivo, resolução de problema etc.) *The Democrats also zeroed in on the issues and themes they will stress in the campaign.* -T/84. ♦ *Researchers zero in on the genetic causes of colon cancer.* -T/87.

ZILCH [gir] nada, zero; pessoa insignificante, joão-ninguém *He was an old zilch who thought he was an Einstein.*

ZING [gir] vigor, animação, vitalidade, energia, entusiasmo, qualidade estimulante *Can't you put some more zing in your singing?*

ZIP 1. [col] mover-se rapidamente, deslocar-se com rapidez *It's easy to zip from New York to Paris for a weekend by jet.* 2. zunido, silvo *We heard a shot and the zip of a bullet.* 3. [col] energia, vigor, vitalidade, força, ânimo *She used to be so full of zip in those days.*
zip code código de zona postal *What is your zip code?*

ZONK **zonked (out)** [gir] bêbado; drogado *Is he zonked on drink or on drugs?*

ZOOM **zoom away/past/up etc.** passar velozmente, zumbindo, mover-se com grande velocidade (veículo, aeronave etc.) *The sports car zoomed past us.* ♦ *Several planes zoomed overhead.*
zoom in on aproximar-se de uma pessoa ou objeto (a câmara de cinema ou de televisão) mantendo-o sempre em foco *In this scene, the camera slowly zooms in on the young lovers as they kiss.*

Bibliografia de Abonações

AD Ausubel, David P. et al. *Educational Psychology – A Cognitive View*. Nova York: Holt, Rinehart and Winston, 1978.

AH Allen, Harold B. et al. *New Dimensions in English.* Cincinatti, Ohio: McCormick-Mathers Publishing Co., Inc., 1966.

AI Asimov, Isaac. *The Currents of Space*. Nova York: Signet Books, 1953. (Ed. orig. Doubleday and Company, Inc.)

AIM Anonymous. *I, Mobster*. Nova York: Gold Medal Books, 1951.

AJ Appelbaum, J., e Evans, N. *How to Get Happily Published*. Nova York: Harper and Row, 1978.

AK Andersen, Kristin *The Wholesome Hooker*. Nova York: Leisure Books (Nordon Publications), 1973.

AM Adler, Mortimer J. *Great Ideas from the Great Books*. Nova York: Washington Square Press, Inc., 1961.

AT Anderson, Thomas. *Your Own Beloved Sons.* Nova York: Bantam Books, 1957. (Ed. orig. Random House, Inc.)

BA Barbour, Alan G. *Humphrey Bogart*. Nova York: Galahad Books, 1973.

BAJ Bergman, Andrew. *James Cagney*. Nova York: Galahad Books, 1973.

BAS Bester, Alfred. *The Stars My Destination*. Nova York: Signet Books, 1957. (Ed. orig. Galaxy Publishing Corporation.)

BC Bernstein, Carl e Bob Woodward. *All the President's Men*. Nova York: Warner Books, Inc., 1975. (Ed. orig. Simon and Schuster.)

BCM Brooks, Cleanth e Robert Penn Warren. *Modern Rhetoric*, 2. ed. Nova York: Harcourt, Brace and Company, 1958.

BCMT Boland, Charles Michael. *They All Discovered America.* Nova York: Perma Books, 1963. (Ed. orig. Doubleday and Company, Inc.)

BCS Brinton, Crane. *The Shaping of the Modern Mind*. Nova York: Mentor Books, 1953. (Ed. orig. Prentice-Hall, Inc.)

BD Brown, Dee. *Bury My Heart at Wounded Knee*. Nova York: Bantam Books, 1972. (Ed. orig. Holt, Rinehart and Winston.)

BDF Belafonte, Dennis e Alvin H. Marill. *The Films of Tyrone Power*. Secaucus, Nova Jersey: The Citadel Press, 1979.

BE Block, Eugene B. *Great Train Robberies of the West*. Nova York: Avon Books, 1959 (Ed. orig. Coward-McCann.)

BF Bonham, Frank. *Bold Passage*. Nova York: Pocket Books, 1952. (Ed. orig. Simon and Schuster.)

BFW Blake, Forrester. *Wilderness Passage*. Nova York: Bantam Books, 1958. (Ed. orig. Random House, Inc.)

BH Basso, Hamilton. *The View from Pompey's Head*. Nova York: Pocket Books, 1956. (Ed. orig. Doubleday and Company, Inc.)

BJ Bardwick, Judith M. *Danger in the Comfort Zone*. Nova York: Amacom (American Management Association), 1991.

BL Bruce, Leni. *How to Talk Dirty and Influence People*. Chicago: Playboy Press, 1967; Nova York: Pocket Books, 1967. (Ed. orig. HMH Publishing Co.)

BM Bruno, Mike e David B. Weiss. *Prostitution, U.S.A*. Los Angeles: Holloway House Publishing Company, 1965.

BN Berrill, N. J. *Man's Emerging Mind*. Nova York: Premier Books, 1957. (Ed. orig. Dodd, Mead and Company.)

BR Billington, Ray A. *Westward Expansion*, 2. ed. Nova York: The Macmillan Company, 1960.

BRF Bookbinder, Robert. *The Films of the Seventies*. Secaucus, Nova Jersey: Citadel Press (Carol Publishing Group), 1990.

BRS Baker, Rachel. *Sigmund Freud for Everybody*. Nova York: Popular Library, 1955. (Ed. orig. Julian Messner, Inc.)

BRSP Bowers, Ronald. *The Selznick Players*. Nova Jersey: A. S. Barnes and Company, 1976.

BRSR Bissell, Richard. *A Stretch on the River*. Nova York: Signet Books, 1951. (Ed. orig. Little, Brown and Company.)

BRT Bradbury, Ray. *The Illustrated Man*. Nova York: Bantam Books, 1952. (Ed. orig. Doubleday and Company, Inc.)

BS Bellow, Saul. *Seize the Day*. Nova York: Popular Library, 1958. (Ed. orig. The Viking Press.)

BT Blackburn, Thomas Wakefield. *Sierra Baron*. Nova York: Bantam Books, 1958. (Ed. orig. Random House, Inc.)

BW Burnett, W. A. *Adobe Walls*. Nova York: Bantam Books, 1956. (Ed. orig. Alfred Knopf, Inc.)

CB Catton, Bruce. *A Stillness at Appomatox*. Nova York: Pocket Books, 1958. (Ed. orig. Doubleday and Company, Inc.)

CBC Crosby, Bing. *Call Me Lucky*. Nova York: Pocket Books, 1954. (Ed. orig. Simon and Schuster, Inc.)

CCC Colwell, C. C. *A Student's Guide to Literature*. Nova York: Washington Square Press, 1968.

CCT Castaneda, Carlos. *The Teachings of Don Juan*. Harmondsworth, Inglaterra: Penguin Books, 1973. (Ed. orig. The University of California Press.)

CD Chidsey, Donald Barr. *Captain Adam*. Nova York: Avon Books. 1953.

CE Cray, Ed, org. *Bawdy Ballads*. Londres: Anthony Blond, Ltd., 1970.

CEB Corle, Edwin. *Billy the Kid*. Nova York: Bantam Books, 1954. (Ed. orig. Little, Brown and Company in association with Duell, Sloan and Pearce.)

CEO Christensen, Erwin O. *The History of Western Art*. Nova York: Mentor Books, 1959.

CEP Caldwell, Erskine. *Place Called Estherville*. Nova York: Signet Books, 1952. (Ed. orig. Duell, Sloan and Pearce, Inc.)

CG Chase, Glen. *Crack Shot*. Nova York: Leisure Books, 1973.

CGT Chase, Glen. *The Jersey Bounce*. Nova York: Leisure Books, 1974.

CGU Chase, Glen. *Up Your Ante*. Nova York: Leisure Books, 1973.

CH Coon, Horace. *Speak Better – Write Better English*. Nova York: Signet Key Books, 1954.

CHT Conrad, Harold. *The Battle at Apache Pass*. Nova York: Avon Publishing Co., 1952.

CJ Coleman, James C. *Abnormal Psychology and Modern Life*. 5. ed. Glenview, Illinois: Scott, Foresman and Company, 1976.

CJC Craig, Jonathan. *Case of the Silent Stranger*. Nova York: Belmont Tower Books, 1973. (Ed. orig. Fawcett Publications, Inc.)

CJM Campbell, Joseph. *The Masks of God: Occidental Mythology*. Londres: Souvenir Press, 1974. (Ed. orig. The Viking Press.)

CL Collins, Larry e Dominique Lapierre. *Is Paris Burning?* Nova York: Pocket Books, Inc., 1965. (Ed. orig. Simon and Schuster, Inc.)

CMS Cross, Milton. *Stories of the Great Operas*. Nova York: Perma Books, 1955. (Ed. orig. Doubleday and Company, Inc.)

CMSS Chute, Marchette. *Stories from Shakespeare*. Nova York: Mentor Books, 1959. (Ed. orig. The World Publishing Company.)

CN Calmer, Ned. *The Strange Land*. Nova York: Signet Books, 1952. (Ed. orig. Charles Scribner's Sons.)

CR Carson, Rachel L. *The Sea Around Us*. Nova York: Mentor Books, 1954. (Ed. orig. Oxford University Press.)

CRS Carr, Robert Spencer. *Beyond Infinity*. Nova York: Dell Books, 1951. (Ed. orig. Fantasy Press.)

CRST Carter, Ross S. *Those Devils in Baggy Pants*. Nova York: Signet Books, 1952. (Ed. orig. Appleton Century Crofts, Inc.)

CS Cheney, Sheldon. *The Story of Modern Art*. Nova York: The Viking Press, 1956.

CT Costain, Thomas B. *Below the Salt*. Nova York: Perma Books, 1963. (Ed. orig. Doubleday and Company, Inc.)

CTT Capote, Truman. *The Grass Harp*. Nova York: Signet Books, 1953. (Ed. orig. Random House, Inc.)

DD Divine, David. *Boy on a Dolphin*. Nova York: Avon Publications, Inc., 1957. (Ed. orig. The Macmillan Company.)

DDT Day, Donald. *The Evolution of Love*. Nova York: The Dial Press, 1954.

DJ Dinneen, Joseph F. *Underworld U.S.A*. Nova York: Perma Books, 1957. (Ed. orig. Farrar, Straus and Cudahy, Inc.)

DK Dodson, Kenneth. *Away All Boats*. Nova York: Bantam Books, 1956. (Ed. orig. Little, Brown and Company.)

DM Dolan, Mary. *Hannibal*. Nova York: Avon Publications, 1958. (Ed. orig. The Macmillan Company.)

DP Dick, Philip K. *The Cosmic Puppets*. Nova York: Ace Books, 1957.

DR Downs, Robert B. *Books That Changed the World*. Nova York: Mentor Books, 1956.

EA Ellis, Albert. *The Folklore of Sex*. ed. rev. Nova York: Grove Press, Inc., 1961.

EF Edwards, Frank. *Stranger Than Science*. Nova York: Ace Books, 1959. (Ed. orig. Lyle Stuart.)

EJ Elbert, Joyce. *The Crazy Ladies*. Nova York: Signet Books, 1969.

EM Ebon, Martin. *They Knew the Unknown*. Nova York: Signet Books, 1972. (Ed. orig. The World Publishing Company.)

EMW Elwood, Muriel. *Web of Destiny.* Nova York: Bantam Books, 1952. (Ed. orig. The Bobbs-Merrill Company, Inc.)

EW Ellis, William Donohue. *The Bounty Lands*. Nova York: Dell Books, 1958. (Ed. orig. The World Publishing Company.)

FC Fisher, Clay. *The Big Pasture*. Nova York: Pocket Books, 1956. (Ed. orig. Houghton Mifflin Company.)

FCT Fadiman, Clifton. *The Lifetime Reading Plan*. Nova York: Avon Book Division, The Hearst Corporation, 1960. (Ed. orig. The World Publishing Company.)

FH Fast, Howard. *The Winston Affair*. Nova York: Bantam Books, 1959. (Ed. orig. Crown Publishers, Inc.)

FI Frazee, Irving e Earl L. Bedell. *Automotive Fundamentals*. Chicago: American Technical Society, 1953.

FJ Feldman, Joseph e Harry Feldman. *Dynamics of the Film*. Nova York: Hermitage House, 1952.

FJH Ford, Jesse Hill. *The Liberation of Lord Byron Jones*. Nova York: Signet Books, 1967. (Ed. orig. Little, Brown and Company.)

FL Forster, Logan A. *Proud Land.* Nova York: Bantam Books, 1958. (Ed. orig. Random House, Inc.)

FLF Freeman, Lucy. *Fight Against Fears*. Nova York: Pocket Books, Inc., 1953.

FLS Freeman, Lucy e Marvin Small. *The Story of Psychoanalysis*. Nova York: Pocket Books, 1960.

FP Frank, Pat. *Hold Back the Night*. Nova York: Bantam Books, 1956. (Ed. orig. J. B. Lippincott Company.)

FS Foote, Shelby. *Shiloh*. Nova York: Signet Books, 1954. (Ed. orig. The Dial Press, Inc.)

FV Fisher, Vardis. *Tale of Valor*. Nova York: Pocket Books, 1960. (Ed. orig. Doubleday and Company.)

GA Guthrie, Jr., A. B. *These Thousand Hills*. Nova York: Pocket Books, 1957. (Ed. orig. Houghton Mifflin Company.)

GD Geddes, Donald P. org. *An Analysis of the Kinsey Reports*. Nova York: Mentor Books, 1954. (Ed. orig. E. P. Dutton and Company.)

GE Gann, Ernest K. *The High and the Mighty*. Nova York: Perma Books, 1954. (Ed. orig. William Sloane Associates, Inc.)

GES Gardner, Earle Stanley. *The Case of the Screaming Woman*. Nova York: Pocket Books, 1959. (Ed. orig. William Morrow.)

GET Gilliard, E. Thomas. *Living Birds of the World*. Londres: Hamish Hamilton Ltd., 1958. (Ed. orig. Chanticleer Press, Inc.)

GF Gwaltney, Francis Irby. *Between Heaven and Hell*. Nova York: Popular Library, 1956. (Ed. orig. Rinehart and Company, Inc.)

GFT Gruber, Frank. *Tales of Wells Fargo*. Nova York: Bantam Books, Inc. 1958.

GH Goodwin, Harold Leland. *The Science Book of Space Travel*. Nova York: Pocket Books, Inc., 1956. (Ed. orig. Franklin Watts.)

GJ Greene, John C. *The Death of Adam*. Nova York: Mentor Books, 1961. (Ed. orig. Iowa State University Press.)

GJH Giles, Janice Holt. *The Kentuckians*. Nova York: Bantam Books, 1955. (Ed. orig. Houghton Mifflin Company.)

GJI Gunther, John. *Inside South America*. Nova York: Pocket Books, 1968. (Ed. orig. Harper and Row.)

GJK Galbraith, John Kenneth. *A View from the Stands*. Boston: Houghton Mifflin Company, 1986.

GJKT Galbraith, John Kenneth. *The Great Crash, 1929*. 50th. Anniversary ed. Boston: Houghton Mifflin Company, 1979.

GM Griffith, Maxwell. *The Gadget Maker*. Nova York: Pocket Books, 1956. (Ed. orig. J. B. Lippincott Company.)

GR Goodman, Roger B. e David Lewin. *New Ways to Greater Word Power*. Nova York: Dell Publishing Company, Inc., 1955.

GS Griffin, Susan. *Pornography and Silence*. Nova York: Harper and Row Publishers, Inc., 1981.

HA Hotchner, A. E. *Doris Day: Her Own Story*. Nova York: Bantam Books, 1976. (Ed. orig. William Morrow and Company.)

HC   Hall, Calvin S. *A Primer of Freudian Psychology.* Nova York: Mentor Books, 1955. (Ed. orig. The World Publishing Company.)

HD   Holmes, David C. *The Search for Life on Other Worlds.* Nova York: Bantam Books, 1966.

HDR   Heiney, Donald. *Recent American Literature.* Nova York: Barron's Educational Series, 1959.

HE   Hunter, Edward. *Brainwashing.* Nova York: Pyramid Books, 1958. (Ed. orig. Farrar, Straus and Cudahy.)

HEB   Hamilton, Edmond. *Beyond the Moon.* Nova York: Signet Books, 1950. (Ed. orig. Frederick Fell, Inc.)

HEM   Hemingway, Ernest. *A Moveable Feast.* Harmondsworth, Inglaterra: Penguin Books, 1966. (Ed. orig. Charles Scribner's Sons.)

HET   Haycox, Ernest. *The Earthbreakers.* Nova York: Pocket Books, Inc., 1953. (Ed. orig. Little, Brown and Company.)

HETB   Hoffer, Eric. *The True Believer.* Nova York: Mentor Books, 1958. (Ed. orig. Harper & Brother)

HEW   Hirsch, Edwin W. *Modern Sex Life.* Nova York: Signet Books, 1957.

HG   Howe, George. *Decision Before Dawn (Call It Treason).* Nova York: Pocket Books, Inc., 1951. (Ed. orig. The Viking Press.)

HGI   Heard, Gerald. *Is Another World Watching?* Nova York: Bantam Books, 1953. (Ed. orig. Harper and Brothers.)

HH   Hurwitz, Howard L. *An Encyclopedic Dictionary of American History.* Nova York: Washington Square Press, 1970.

HHO   Haber, Heinz. *The Walt Disney Story of Our Friend the Atom.* Nova York: Dell Publishing Company, Inc., 1956.

HJ   Hunter, John. *Badlands Buccaneer.* Nova York: Pocket Books, 1959.

HJC   Heller, Joseph. *Catch-22.* Nova York: Dell Publishing Company, 1968. (Ed. orig. Simon and Schuster, Inc.)

HJD   Hayes, Joseph. *The Desperate Hours.* Nova York: Perma Books, 1955. (Ed. orig. Random House, Inc.)

HJE   Hamner, Jr., Earl. *Spencer's Mountain.* Nova York: Dell Books, 1963. (Ed. orig. The Dial Press.)

HJH   Holt, John. *How Children Fail.* Nova York: Dell Publishing Company, Inc., 1970. (Ed. orig. Pitman Publishing Corporation.)

HJT Hersey, John. *The Wall*. Nova York: Pocket Books, Inc., 1954. (Ed. orig. Alfred A. Knopf.)

HL Hornstein, Lilian Herlands et al. *The Reader's Companion to World Literature*. Nova York: Mentor Books, 1956. (Ed. orig. The Dryden Press, Inc.)

HM Harris, Margaret e John Harris. *Arrow in the Moon*. Nova York: Pocket Books, Inc., 1955. (Ed. orig. William Morrow and Company.)

HMJ Herzberg, Max J. *The Reader's Encyclopedia of American Literature*. Londres: Methuen and Company Ltd., 1963. (Ed. orig. Thomas Y. Crowell.)

HMT Henry, Marilyn e Ron DeSourdis. *The Films of Alan Ladd*. Secaucus, Nova Jersey: Citadel Press, 1981.

HMTO Harrington, Michael. *The Other America*. Harmondsworth, Inglaterra: Penguin Books, 1963.

HO Hall, Oakley. *Warlock*. Nova York: Bantam Books, 1959. (Ed. orig. The Viking Press, Inc.)

HR Hall, Jr., Robert A. *Linguistics and Your Language*. Nova York: Anchor Books, 1960. (Ed. orig. Linguistica Press.)

HRA Heinlein, Robert A. *The Puppet Masters*. Nova York: Signet Books, 1952. (Ed. orig. World Editions, Inc.)

HRW Horton, Rod W. e Herbert W. Edwards. *Backgrounds of American Literary Thought*, 2. ed. Nova York: Appleton Century Crofts, 1967.

HS Hite, Shere. *The Hite Report*. Nova York: Dell Publishing Company, Inc., 1981. (Ed. orig. The Macmillan Publishing Company.)

HW Heuman, William. *Guns at Broken Bow*. Nova York: Gold Medal Books, 1950.

HWL Heath, W. L. *Violent Saturday*. Nova York: Bantam Books, 1956. (Ed. orig. Harper and Brothers.)

HWR Heuman, William. *Roll the Wagons*. Nova York: Gold Medal Books, 1951.

HWW Henry, Will. *Who Rides With Wyatt*. Nova York: Bantam Books, 1956. (Ed. orig. Random House, Inc.)

JE Jong, Erica. *Fear of Flying*. Nova York: Signet Books, 1974. (Ed. orig. Holt, Rinehart and Winston.)

JEP Jong, Erica. *Parachutes and Kisses*. Nova York: Signet Books, 1984.

JJ Jones, James. *Some Came Running*. Nova York: Signet Books, 1959. (Ed. orig. Charles Scribner's Sons.)

JJF Jones, James. *From Here to Eternity*. Nova York: Signet Books, 1954. (Ed. orig. Charles Scribner's Sons.)

JJS Jennings, John. *The Strange Brigade*. Nova York: Pocket Books, Inc., 1954. (Ed. orig. Little, Brown and Company.)

JM Jessup, M. K. *The Case for the Unidentified Flying Objects*. Nova York: Bantam Books, 1955. (Ed. orig. The Citadel Press.)

JR Jordan, René. *Clark Gable*. Nova York: Galahad Books, 1973.

JRE Johnson, Richard E. *In Quest of a New Psychology*. Nova York: Human Sciences Press, 1975.

JRR Jastrow, Robert. *Red Giants and White Dwarfs*. Nova York: Signet Books, 1969. (Ed. orig. Harper and Row, Publishers, Inc.)

JS Jourard, Sidney M. e Ted Landsman. *Healthy Personality*. 4. ed. Nova York: Macmillan Publishing Company, Inc., 1980.

JW Johnson, Wendell. *Living With Change*. Nova York: Harper and Row, Publishers, Inc., 1972.

KA Knight, Arthur. *The Liveliest Art*. Nova York: Mentor Books, 1959. (Ed. orig. The Macmillan Company.)

KAC Kinsey, Alfred C. et al. *Sexual Behavior in the Human Female*. Nova York: Pocket Books, Inc., 1965. (Ed. orig. W. B. Saunders Company.)

KD Keyhoe, Donald E. *Flying Saucers from Outer Space*. Nova York: Perma Books, 1954. (Ed. orig. Henry Holt and Company, Inc.)

KF Kavanaugh, Father James. *A Modern Priest Looks at his Outdated Church*. Nova York: Pocket Books, Inc., 1968. (Ed. orig. Trident Press.)

KJ Klaas, Joe. *Maybe I'm Dead*. Londres: Corgi Books, 1958.

KJS Knight, John. *The Story of My Psychoanalysis*. Nova York: Pocket Books, Inc. 1952. (Ed. orig. McGraw-Hill Book Company, Inc.)

KM Kantor, MacKinlay. *Andersonville*. Nova York: Signet Books, 1957. (Ed. orig. The World Publishing Company.)

KR Kübler-Ross, Elisabeth. *On Death and Dying*. Nova York: The Macmillan Company, 1970.

KRI Kent, Rockwell. *It's Me, O Lord*. Nova York: Dodd, Mead and Company, 1955.

KS Keene, Sam. *The Passionate Life: Stages of Loving*. Nova York: Harper and Row, Publishers, Inc., 1983.

LA Langguth, A. J. *Hidden Terrors*. Nova York: Pantheon Books, 1978.

LAK Lake, Alexander. *Killers in Africa*. Nova York: Perma Books, 1954. (Ed. orig. Doubleday and Company, Inc.)

LAS Lass, Abraham H. *A Student's Guide to 50 American Novels*. Nova York: Washington Square Press, 1966.

LB Lomax, Bliss. *The Fight for the Sweetwater*. Nova York: Pocket Books, 1951. (Ed. orig. Dodd, Mead and Company, Inc.)

LC Locke, Charles O. *The Hell Bent Kid*. Nova York: Popular Library, 1958. (Ed. orig. W. W. Norton and Company, Inc.)

LCT Laird, Charlton. *The Miracle of Language*. Nova York: Premier Books, 1957.

LD Linford, Dee. *Man Without a Star*. Nova York: Bantam Books, 1955. (Ed. orig. William Morrow and Company, Inc.)

LI Levin, Ira. *A Kiss Before Dying*. Nova York: Signet Books, 1954. (Ed. orig. Simon and Schuster, Inc.)

LJ Leonard, Jonathan Norton. *Flight Into Space*. Nova York: Signet Books, 1954. (Ed. orig. Random House, Inc.)

LJS Lauritzen, Jonreed. *Suzanne, Savage Vixen*. Nova York: Avon Books, 1955. (Ed. orig. Doubleday and Company, Inc.)

LL L'Amour, Louis. *Hondo*. Nova York: Gold Medal Books, 1953.

LLN Lawson, Larry. *Naked Spurs*. Nova York: Pyramid Books, 1958.

LM LeMay, Alan. *The Searchers*. Nova York: Popular Library, 1956. (Ed. orig. Harper and Brothers.)

LMC Levin, Meyer. *Compulsion*. Nova York: Pocket Books, Inc., 1959. (Ed. orig. Simon and Schuster, Inc.)

LMO Leinster, Murray. *Operation Outer Space*. Nova York: Signet Books, 1957. (Ed. orig. Fantasy Press.)

LMT Lott, Milton. *The Last Hunt*. Nova York: Pocket Books, Inc., 1956. (Ed. orig. Houghton Mifflin Company.)

LN Loomis, Noel. *The Buscadero*. Nova York: Bantam Books, 1956. (Ed. orig. The Macmillan Company.)

LNW Lewis, Norman. *Word Power Made Easy*. Nova York: Permabooks, 1955. (Ed. orig. Doubleday and Company, Inc.)

LR   Lindner, Robert. *The Fifty-Minute Hour*. Nova York: Bantam Books, 1958. (Ed. orig. Rinehart and Company, Inc.)

LRT   Lund, Robert. *The Alaskan*. Nova York: Bantam Books, 1955. (Ed. orig. The John Day Company.)

LRW   Langley, Roger e Richard C. Levy. *Wife Beating: The Silent Crisis*. Nova York: E. P. Dutton, 1977.

LW   Lederer, William J. *A Nation of Sheep*. Nova York: Crest Books, 1962. (Ed. orig. W. W. Norton and Company, Inc.)

MA Maslow, Abraham. *The Farther Reaches of Human Nature*. Harmondsworth, Inglaterra: Penguin Books, 1973. (Ed. orig. The Viking Press.)

MAT   Murphy, Audie. *To Hell and Back*. Nova York: Permabooks, 1951. (Ed. orig. Henry Holt and Company.)

MC   Morgan, Clifford T. *Introduction to Psychology*. Nova York: McGraw-Hill Book Company, Inc., 1956.

MD   Mankiewicz, Don M. *Trial*. Nova York: Dell Books, 1955. (Ed. orig. Harper and Brothers.)

MET   Marshall, Edison. *The Viking*. Nova York: Dell Books, 1958. (Ed. orig. Farrar, Straus and Cudahy, Inc.)

MF   Manfred, Frederick F. *Lord Grizzly*. Nova York: Pocket Books, Inc., 1955. (Ed. orig. McGraw-Hill Book Company, Inc.)

MG   Metalious, Grace. *Peyton Place*. Nova York: Dell Publishing Company, Inc., 1958. (Ed. orig. Julian Messner, Inc.)

MH   Miller, Henry. *A Devil in Paradise*. Nova York: Signet Books, 1956. (Ed. orig. New Directions.)

MHH   Marx, Harpo e Rowland Barber. *Harpo Speaks*. Londres: Coronet Books, 1978. (Ed. orig. Freeway Press, Inc.)

MHJ   Muller, H. J. *The Uses of the Past*. Nova York: Mentor Books, 1954. (Ed. orig. Oxford University Press, Inc.)

MJ   Miller, Joseph. *Arizona, The Grand Canyon State*. Nova York: Hastings House, 1956.

MJA   Michener, James A. *Hawaii*. Nova York: Bantam Books, 1961. (Ed. orig. Random House, Inc.)

MJL   Malmstrom, Jean. *Language in Society*. Nova York: Hayden Book Company, 1965.

MJM McCabe, John. *Mr. Laurel and Mr. Hardy*. Nova York: Signet Books, 1968. (Ed. orig. Doubleday and Company, Inc.)

MJV McConnell, James V. *Understanding Human Behavior*. Nova York: Holt, Rinehart and Winston, Inc., 1974.

ML Maltin, Leonard, et al., orgs. *TV Movies*. ed. rev. Nova York: Signet Books, 1974.

MM Mead, Margaret. *Male and Female*. Nova York: Mentor Books, 1955. (Ed. orig. William Morrow and Company, Inc.)

MMA McKernan, Maureen. *The Amazing Crime and Trial of Leopold and Loeb*. Nova York: Signet Books, 1957.

MMU McLuhan, Marshall. *Understanding Media*. Nova York: Signet Books, 1964. (Ed. orig. McGraw-Hill Book Company.)

MN Mailer, Norman. *The Deer Park*. Nova York: Signet Books, 1957. (Ed. orig. G. P. Putnam's Sons.)

MNH Mager, N. H. e S. K. Mager. *The Complete Letter Writer*. Nova York: Perma Books, 1957.

MR Meredith, Robert C. e John D. Fitzgerald. *Structuring Your Novel*. Nova York: Everyday Handbooks, Barnes and Noble Books, 1972.

MRI Matheson, Richard. *I Am Legend*. Greenwich: Gold Medal Books 1957.

MRM May, Rollo. *Man's Search for Himself*. Nova York: Signet Books, 1967. (Ed. orig. W. W. Norton and Company, Inc.)

MRMT McIver, Robert Morrison. *The Challenge of the Passing Years – My Encounter With Time*. Nova York: Pocket Books, Inc., 1963. (Ed. orig. Trident Press.)

MW, Manchester, William. *Death of a President*. Londres: Pan Books, 1968.

MWL Motley, Willard. *Let No Man Write my Epitaph*. Nova York: Signet Books, 1959. (Ed. orig. Random House, Inc.)

NB Nelson, Benjamin, org. *Freud and the Twentieth Century*. Nova York: Meridian Books, 1957.

NE Nathanson, E. M. *The Dirty Dozen*. Nova York: Dell Books, 1966. (Ed. orig. Random House, Inc.)

NEW Nowell, Elizabeth. *Thomas Wolfe* – A Biography. Londres: Heinemann, 1961. (Ed. orig. Doubleday and Company.)

NJ Needleman, Jacob. *The Indestructible Question*. Harmondsworth, Inglaterra: Penguin Books, 1994. (Ed. orig. Crossroad.)

NM Nurnberg, Maxwell e Morris Rosenblum. *How to Build a Better Vocabulary*. Nova York: Popular Library, 1961. (Ed. orig. Prentice-Hall, Inc.)

OC Oliver, Chad. *The Winds of Time*. Nova York: Pocket Books, Inc., 1959. (Ed. orig. Doubleday and Company, Inc.)

OE O'Connor, Edwin. *The Edge of Sadness*. Nova York: Bantam Books, 1962. (Ed. orig. Little, Brown and Company.)

OF O'Connor, Flannery. *Wise Blood*. Nova York: Signet Books, 1953. (Ed. orig. Harcourt, Brace and Company.)

OFW O'Rourke, Frank. *Warbonnet Law*. Nova York: Bantam Books, 1952. (Ed. orig. Random House.)

OH Overstreet, Harry e Bonaro Overstreet. *What We Must Know About Communism*. Nova York: Pocket Books, Inc., 1960. (Ed. orig. W. W. Norton and Company, Inc.)

OJ O'Hara, John. *Ourselves to Know*. Nova York: Bantam Books, 1961. (Ed. orig. Random House, Inc.)

OJT O'Hara, John. *Ten North Frederick*. Bantam Books, 1957. (Ed. orig. Random House, Inc.)

PC Parkhurst, Charles Chandler. *Business Communication for Better Human Relations*. Englewood Cliffs, Nova Jersey: Prentice-Hall, Inc., 1961.

PF Pohl, Frederick e C. M. Kornbluth. *Search the Sky*. Nova York: Ballantine Books, 1954.

PJ Pearce, Joseph Chilton. *The Crack in the Cosmic Egg*. Nova York: Pocket Books, Inc., 1975. (Ed. orig. Julian Press, Inc.)

PJW Prescott, John. *Wagon Train*. Nova York: Bantam Books, 1957. (Ed. orig. Random House, Inc.)

PL Payne, Lucille V. *The Lively Art of Writing*. Nova York: Mentor Books, 1969. (Ed. orig. Follet Publishing Company.)

PM Pei, Mario. *Swords for Charlemagne*. Hasbrouck Heights, Nova Jersey: Graphic Publishing Company, Inc., 1955. (Ed. orig. The John Day Company.)

PN Postman, Neil e Charles Weingartner. *Teaching as a Subversive Activity*. Harmondsworth, Inglaterra: Penguin Books, 1971. (Ed. orig. Delacorte Press.)

PR Pearl, Richard M. *How to Know the Minerals and Rocks*. Nova York: Signet Key Books, 1957. (Ed. orig. McGraw-Hill Book Company, Inc.)

PRT Payne, Robert. *The Chieftain*. Nova York: Pocket Books, Inc., 1954. (Ed. orig. Prentice-Hall, Inc.)

PV Packard, Vance. *The Naked Society*. Nova York: Pocket Books, Inc., 1965. (Ed. orig. David McKay.)

PVH Packard, Vance. *The Hidden Persuaders*. Nova York: Pocket Books, Inc., 1958. (Ed. orig. David McKay Company, Inc.)

QE Queen, Ellery. *Q. B. I. (Queen's Bureau of Investigation)*. Nova York: Pocket Books, Inc., 1956. (Ed. orig. Little, Brown.)

RC *The Report of the Commission on Obscenity and Pornography*. Nova York: Bantam Books, 1970.

RCT Ryan, Cornelius. *The Longest Day*. Nova York; Crest Books, 1960. (Ed. orig. Simon and Schuster, Inc.)

RD Ragan, David. *Movie Stars of the '40s*. Englewood Cliffs, Nova Jersey: Prentice-Hall, Inc., 1985.

RE Ruppelt, Edward J. *The Report on Unidentified Flying Objects*. Londres: Victor Gollancz Ltd., 1956.

RJ Roosevelt, James e Sidney Shalett. *Affectionately, F.D.R.* Nova York: Avon Books, 1959. (Ed. orig. Harcourt, Brace and Company.)

RK Roberts, Kenneth. *Boon Island*. Nova York: Doubleday and Company, Inc., 1956.

RL Rosten, Leo. *Captain Newman, M.D.* Nova York: Crest Books, 1963. (Ed. orig. Harper and Row, Publishers, Inc.)

RLI Roth, Lillian. *I'll Cry Tomorrow*. Londres: Four Square Books, 1959.

RN Ross, Nancy Wilson. *Three Ways of Asian Wisdom*. Nova York: Simon and Schuster, 1966.

RP Roth, Philip. *Portnoy's Complaint*. Nova York: Bantam Books, 1970. (Ed. orig. Random House, Inc.)

RQ Reynolds, Quentin. *70,000 to 1*. Nova York: Pyramid Books, 1958. (Ed. orig. Random House, Inc.)

RR Riegel, Robert E. e Robert G. Athearn. *America Moves West*. Nova York: Holt, Rinehart and Winston, 1964.

SB Schulberg, Budd. *Waterfront*. Nova York: Bantam Books, 1956. (Ed. orig. Random House, Inc.)

SBW Spicer, Bart. *The Wild Ohio*. Nova York: Bantam Books, 1954. (Ed. orig. Dodd, Mead and Company.)

SC Sagan, Carl. *Broca's Brain*. Nova York: Ballantine Books, 1980. (Ed. orig. Random House, Inc.)

SCD Simak, Clifford D. *City*. Nova York: Perma Books, 1954. (Ed. orig. Gnome Press, Inc.)

SE Shorter, Edward. *A History of Women's Bodies*. Harmondsworth, Inglaterra: Allen Lane, 1983. (Ed. orig. Basic Books, Inc.)

SEB Schiddel, Edmund. *Break-up*. Nova York: Avon Publications, Inc., 1954.

SEE Sproul, Edith E. *The Science Book of the Human Body*. Nova York: Pocket Books, 1955. (Ed. orig. Franklin Watts.)

SF Scarpetta, Frank. *Death to the Mafia*. Nova York: Belmont Towers Books, 1983.

SG Shirrefs, Gordon D. *Shadow Valley*. Nova York: Popular Library, 1958.

SGF Scheer, George F. e Hugh F. Rankin. *Rebels and Redcoats*. Nova York: Mentor Books, 1959. (Ed. orig. The World Publishing Company.)

SGT Swarthout, Glendon. *They Came to Cordura*. Nova York: Signet Books, 1959. (Ed. orig. Random House, Inc.)

SH Sell, Henry Blackman e Victor Weybright. *Buffalo Bill and the Wild West*. Nova York: Signet Books, 1959. (Ed. orig. Oxford University Press.)

SHE Stover, Herbert. *Powder Mission*. Nova York: Avon Books, 1951. (Ed. orig. Dodd, Mead and Company.)

SHO Shapley, Harlow. *Of Stars and Men*. Nova York: Washington Square Press, 1959. (Ed. orig. Beacon Press.)

SHR Smith, Huston. *The Religions of Man*. Nova York: Mentor Books, 1959. (Ed. orig. Harper and Brothers.)

SHS Shefter, Harry. *Shefter's Guide to Better Compositions*. Nova York: Washington Square Press, 1960.

SJ Schlesinger, Jr., A. M. *A Thousand Days*. Londres: Mayflower Books, 1967.

SJD Salinger, J. D. *Nine Stories*. Nova York: Bantam Books, 1966. (Ed. orig. Little, Brown and Company, Inc.)

SJE Steinbeck, John. *East of Eden*. Nova York: Bantam Books, 1967. (Ed. orig. The Viking Press, Inc.)

SJG Swerling, Jo e Abe Burrows. Guys and Dolls – A Musical Fable of Broadway – Based on a story and characters by Damon Runyon, in *From the American Drama*, org. por Eric Bentley. Nova York: Doubleday Anchor Books, 1956.

SJH Schaar, John H. *Escape from Authority*. Nova York: Basic Books, Inc., 1961.

SJJ Schifferes, Justus J. *Schifferes' Family Medical Encyclopedia*. Nova York: Permabooks, 1959. (Ed. orig. Little, Brown and Company.)

SJS Schaefer, Jack. *Shane*. Nova York: Bantam Books, 1950. (Ed. orig. Houghton Mifflin Company.)

SJSN Stearns, Jess. *Sisters of the Night*. Nova York: Popular Library, 1957. (Ed. orig. Julian Messner, Inc.)

SJST Steinbeck, John. *Sweet Thursday*. Nova York: Bantam Books, 1956. (Ed. orig. The Viking Press, Inc.)

SJV Southworth, John Van Duyn. *The Story of the World*. Nova York: Pocket Books, 1954. (Ed. orig. Iroquois Publishing Company, Inc.)

SK Schmidt, Karl P. e Robert F. Inger. *Living Reptiles of the World*. Londres: Hamish Hamilton, 1957. (Ed. orig. Chanticleer Press, Inc.)

SL Short, Luke. *Ambush*. Nova York: Bantam Books, 1951. (Ed. orig. Houghton Mifflin Company.)

SLE Stern, Lee Edward. *The Movie Musical*. Nova York: Pyramid Books, 1975.

SLS Shapiro, Lionel. *The Sixth of June*. Nova York: Bantam Books, 1956. (Ed. orig. Doubleday and Company, Inc.)

SLT Scott, Les. *Twilight Women*. Nova York: Beacon Books, 1952.

SM Savage, Mildred. *Parrish*. Nova York: Pocket Books, 1959. (Ed. orig. Simon and Schuster, Inc.)

SMS Stearns, Marshall. *The Story of Jazz*. Nova York: Mentor Books, 1958. (Ed. orig. Oxford University Press.)

SN Sigband, Norman B. *Effective Report Writing*. Nova York: Harper and Brothers, Publishers, 1960.)

SR Stirton, R. A. *Time, Life, and Man*. John Wiley and Sons, Inc., 1963.

SRE Spiller, Robert E. *The Cycle of American Literature*. Nova York: Mentor Books, 1957. (Ed. orig. The Macmillan Company.)

SRS Serling, Rod. *Stories from the Twilight Zone.* Nova York: Bantam Books, 1960.

SRU Sheckley, Robert. *Untouched by Human Hands.* Nova York: Ballantine Books, 1954.

SS Siegel, Scott e Barbara Siegel. *The Encyclopedia of Hollywood.* Nova York: Avon Books, 1991. (Ed. orig. Facts on File.)

SSG Stewart, Sidney. *Give Us This Day.* Nova York: Popular Library, 1958. (Ed. orig. W. W. Norton and Company, Inc.)

SSH Scheuer, Steven H., org. *Movies on TV and Videocassette 1991-1992.* Nova York: Bantam Books, 1990.

ST Sturgeon, Theodore. *More Than Human.* Nova York: Ballantine Books, 1953. (In association with Farrar, Straus and Young.)

SV Starrett, Vincent. *Best Loved Books of the Twentieth Century.* Nova York: Bantam Books, 1955.

SW Shiras, Wilmar H. *Children of the Atom.* Nova York: Avon Books, 1953. (Ed. orig. Gnome Press, Inc.)

SWJ Stuart, J. *Forbidden Planet.* Nova York: Bantam Books, 1956. (Ed. orig. Farrar, Straus and Cudahy, Inc.)

SWL Shumaker, Wayne. *Literature and the Irrational.* Nova York: Washington Square Press, 1966. (Ed. orig. Prentice-Hall, Inc.)

SWLM Shirer, William L. *Midcentury Journey.* Nova York: Signet Books, 1961. (Ed. orig. Farrar, Straus and Cudahy, Inc.)

SWLR Shirer, William L. *The Rise and Fall of the Third Reich.* Nova York: Crest Books, 1962. (Ed. orig. Simon and Schuster, Inc.)

SWM Schramm, Wilbur. *Men, Messages and Media.* Nova York: Harper and Row, Publishers, 1973.

SWS Saroyan, William. *A Secret Story.* Nova York: Popular Library, 1959. (Ed. orig. Doubleday and Company, Inc.)

T *TIME Magazine.*

TA Toffler, Alvin. *Future Shock.* Londres: Pan Books, 1971.

TB Turkus, Burton B. e Sid Feder. *Murder, Inc.* Londres: Four Square Books, 1958.

TD Tracy, Don. *Cherokee.* Nova York: Pocket Books, 1958. (Ed. orig. The Dial Press, Inc.)

TH Thompson, Howard. *James Stewart*. Nova York: Pyramid Books, 1974.

TJ Tolland, John. *The Rising Sun*. Nova York: Bantam Books, 1971. (Ed. orig. Random House, Inc.)

TM Thompson, Morton. *Not as a Stranger*. Nova York: Signet Books, 1956. (Ed. orig. Charles Scribner's Sons.)

TR Traver, Robert. *Anatomy of a Murder*. Nova York: Dell Books, 1959. (Ed. orig. St. Martin's Press.)

TRL Taylor, Robert Lewis. *The Travels of Jaimie McPheeters*. Nova York: Pocket Books, 1960. (Ed. orig. Doubleday and Company, Inc.)

TRW Turner, Robert. *Wagonmaster*. Nova York: Pocket Books, 1958.

TW Tucker, Wilson. *Man From Tomorrow*. Nova York: Bantam Books, 1955. (Ed. orig. Rinehart and Company, Inc.)

UJ Ullman, James Ramsey. *River of the Sun*. Nova York: Pocket Books, 1951. (Ed. orig. J. B. Lippincott Company.)

UL Uris, Leon M. *Battle Cry*. Nova York: Bantam Books, 1954. (Ed. orig. G. P. Putnam's Sons.)

UM Upton, Monroe. *Electronics for Everyone*. Nova York: Signet Key Books, 1957. (Ed. orig. The Devin Adair Company.)

VA Verrill, A. Hyatt. *The Strange Story of our Earth*. Nova York: Premier Books, 1956. (Ed. orig. L. C. Page and Company, Inc.)

VC Vivian, Charles H. e Bernetta M. Jackson. *English Composition*. Nova York: Barnes & Noble, Inc., 1966.)

VE Van Every, Dale. *The Final Challenge*. Nova York: Mentor Books, 1965. (Ed. orig. William Morrow and Company, Inc.)

VR Vernon, Roger L. *The Space Frontiers*. Nova York: Signet Books, 1955.

WA Watts, Alan W. *Man, Nature and Woman*. Nova York: Vintage Books, 1970. (Ed. orig. Pantheon Books, Inc.)

WAW Watts, Alan W. *The Way of Zen*. Nova York: Mentor Books, 1959. (Ed. orig. Pantheon Books, Inc.)

WC Wagley, Charles. *An Introduction to Brazil*. ed. rev. Nova York: Columbia University Press, 1971.

WCB Worth, C. Brooke e Robert K. Enders. *The Nature of Living Things*. Nova York: Signet Key Books, 1955.

WCG Wells, Carol G. *Right-Brain Sex* – Using Creative Visualization to

Enhance Sexual Pleasure. Nova York: Prentice-Hall Press, 1989.

WCN　Willingham, Calder. *Natural Child.* Nova York: Signet Books, 1953. (Ed. orig. The Dial Press, Inc.)

WD　Whitehead, Don. *The FBI Story.* Nova York: Pocket Books, Inc., 1958. (Ed. orig. Random House, Inc.)

WF　Wittels, Fritz. *Sex Habits of American Women.* Nova York: Avon Publications, 1953.

WH　Wouk, Herman. *Marjorie Morningstar.* Nova York: Signet Books, 1957. (Ed. orig. Doubleday and Company, Inc.)

WI　Wallace, Irving. *The R Document.* Londres: Corgi Books, 1977.

WJ　Watterson, Joseph. *Architecture* – Five Thousand Years of Building. Nova York: W. W. Norton and Company, Inc., 1950.

WJT　Wambaugh, Joseph. *The New Centurions.* Nova York: Dell Books, 1972. (Ed. orig. Little, Brown and Company.)

WL　White, Leslie Turner. *The Winged Sword.* Nova York: Pocket Books, 1957. (Ed. orig. William Morrow and Company, Inc., 1955.)

WM　Wolfenstein, Martha e Nathan Leites. *Movies: A Psychological Study.* Glencoe, Illinois: The Free Press, 1950.

WN　Wiener, Norbert. *The Human Use of Human Beings.* Nova York: Anchor Books, 1954. (Ed. orig. Houghton Mifflin Company.)

WP　Wheelwright, Philip. *The Burning Fountain.* Bloomington, Indiana: Indiana University Press, 1954.

WPI　Wellman, Paul I. *The Comancheros.* Nova York: Permabooks, 1954. (Ed. orig. Doubleday and Company, Inc.)

WPT　Wylie, Philip. *The Innocent Ambassadors*. Nova York: Pocket Books, Inc., 1958. (Ed. orig. Rinehart & Company, Inc.)

WR　Wright, Richard. *The Outsider*. Nova York: Signet Books, 1954. (Ed. orig. Harper and Brothers.)

WS　Whitfield, S. E. e Gene Roddenberry. *The Making of Star Trek.* Nova York: Ballantine Books, 1968.

WSM　Wilson, Sloane. *The Man in the Gray Flannel Suit.* Nova York: Pocket Books, Inc., 1956. (Ed. orig. Simon and Schuster, Inc.)

WW　Weathers, Winston e Otis Winchester. *The New Strategy of Style.* Nova York: McGraw-Hill Book Company, 1978.

YF Yerby, Frank. *The Saracen Blade.* Nova York: Pocket Books, Inc., 1953. (Ed. orig. The Dial Press.)

Bibliografia de Referências
Obras consultadas na seleção e definição dos verbetes

BERREY, Lester V. e Melvin Van Den Bark. *The American Thesaurus of Slang*, 2. ed. Nova York: Thomas Y. Crowell Co., 1956.

BOATNER, Maxine Tull e Gates, John Edward; edição revista e organizada por Adam Makkai. *A Dictionary of American Idioms*. Woodbury, Nova York: Barron's Educational Series, Inc., 1975.

COLLINS, Donald E. e Luiz L. Gomes *Dicionário de Gíria Americana Contemporânea*. São Paulo: Livraria Pioneira Editora, 1972.

COVE, Philip Babcock, org. e outros. *Webster's Third New International Dictionary*. Springfield, Massachusetts: G. & C. Merriam Co., 1971.

COWIE, A. P. e R. Mackin. *Oxford Dictionary of Current Idiomatic English*, volume 1: Phrasal Verbs. Oxford: Oxford University Press, 1990.

COWIE, A. P., R. Mackin e I. R. McCaig. *Oxford Dictionary of Current Idiomatic English*, volume 2: English Idioms. Oxford: Oxford University Press, 1990.

English Language Services. *Figurative Expressions* (The Key to English Series). Nova York: Collier-Macmillan International, 1967.

English Language Services. *Two-Word Verbs* (The Key to English Series). Nova York: Collier-Macmillan International, 1967.

GARRISON, Webb B. *Why You Say It*. Nova York: Abingdon Press, 1955.

GOMES, Luiz L. e Donald E. COLLINS. *Dicionário de Expressões Idiomáticas Americanas*. São Paulo: Livraria Pioneira Editora, 1964.

GURALNIK, David B., org. *Webster's New World Dictionary of the American Language,* Second College Edition. Cleveland, Nova York: William Collins e World Publishing Co., Inc., 1974.

HORNBY, A. S., A. P. COWIE, org. e outros. *Oxford Advanced Learner's Dictionary of Current English*, 4. ed. Oxford: Oxford University Press, 1993.

HOUAISS, Antônio, editor e outros. *Webster's English-Portuguese Dictionary*. Rio de Janeiro: Distribuidora Record de Serviços de Imprensa S.A., 1982.

KELLERMAN, Dana F., org. e outros. *A Dictionary of Contemporary and Colloquial Usage*, com prefácio de Roy H. Copperud. Chicago: Consolidated Book Publishers, 1971.

LANDY, Eugene E. *The Underground Dictionary*. Nova York: Simon and Schuster, 1971.

MARCH, Francis Andrew e Francis A. MARCH, Jr. *March's Thesaurus-Dictionary* – New Supplement by R. A. Goodwin. Garden City: Hanover House, 1958.

MISH, Frederick C., org. e outros. *Merriam-Webster's Collegiate Dictionary*, 10. ed. Springfield: Merriam-Webster, Incorporated, 1993.

NEILSON, William Allan, Thomas A. KNOTT e Paul W. CARHART, orgs. *Webster's New International Dictionary of the English Language*, 2. ed. unabridged. Springfield: G. & C. Merriam Company, 1957.

QUIRK, Randolph e Della SUMMERS, orgs. e outros. *Longman Dictionary of Contemporary English*, 3. ed. Harlow: Longman Group Ltd., 1995.

SANTOS, Agenor Soares dos. *Guia Prático de Tradução Inglesa*. 1. ed. São Paulo: Cultrix, 1986.

SERPA, Oswaldo. *Dicionário de Expressões Idiomáticas Inglês-Português/Português-Inglês*, 4. ed. Rio de Janeiro: Fename – MEC, 1982.

URDANG, Laurence e Stuart Berg FLEXNER, orgs. *The Random House College Dictionary*. Nova York: Random House, Inc., 1973.

VALLANDRO, Leonel e Lino VALLANDRO. *Dicionário Inglês-Português*, 2. ed. Porto Alegre: Editora Globo, 1956.

WENTWORTH, Harold e Stuart Berg FLEXNER, orgs. *Dictionary of American Slang*, supplemented edition. Nova York: Thomas Y. Crowell Company, 1967.

WHITFORD, Harold C. e Robert J. DIXSON. *Handbook of American Idioms and Idiomatic Usage*, new ed. Nova York: Regents Publishing Company, Inc., 1973.

WIENER, Solomon. *A Handy Book of Commonly-Used American Idioms*. Nova York: Handy Book Press, Inc., 1958.

WOOD, Frederick T. *English Verbal Idioms* (American edition). Nova York: Washington Square Press, Inc., 1967. (Ed. orig. St. Martin's Press.)